Leveraging Strategic Management for a Sustainable Digital Economy

Mehtap Özşahin
https://orcid.org/0000-0003-2527-4166
Gebze Technical University, Turkey

Vladimir Simovic
Institute of Economic Sciences, Serbia & Australian University, Kuwait

Alper Erturk
Australian University, Kuwait

IGI Global
Scientific Publishing
Publishing Tomorrow's Research Today

Vice President of Editorial	Melissa Wagner
Director of Acquisitions	Mikaela Felty
Director of Book Development	Jocelynn Hessler
Production Manager	Mike Brehm
Cover Design	Jose Rosado

Published in the United States of America by
IGI Global Scientific Publishing
701 East Chocolate Avenue
Hershey, PA, 17033, USA
Tel: 717-533-8845 | Fax: 717-533-7115
Website: https://www.igi-global.com E-mail: cust@igi-global.com

Library of Congress Cataloging-in-Publication Data

Names: Özşahin, Mehtap, DATE- editor | Simović, Vladimir M. editor | Ertürk, Alper, DATE- editor
Title: Leveraging strategic management for a sustainable digital economy / edited by: Mehtap Özşahin, Vladimir Simovic, Alper Erturk.
Description: Hershey PA : IGI Global Scientific Publishing, [2026] | Includes bibliographical references. | Summary: "This book aims to serve as a comprehensive resource exploring the interplay between strategic management practices and the pursuit of a sustainable digital economy"-- Provided by publisher.
Identifiers: LCCN 2025028995 (print) | LCCN 2025028996 (ebook) | ISBN 9798337350523 hardcover | ISBN 9798337350530 paperback | ISBN 9798337350547 ebook
Subjects: LCSH: Information technology--Management | Business--Data processing | Organizational change | Strategic planning
Classification: LCC HD30.2 .L477 2026 (print) | LCC HD30.2 (ebook)
LC record available at https://lccn.loc.gov/2025028995
LC ebook record available at https://lccn.loc.gov/2025028996

British Cataloguing in Publication Data
A Cataloguing in Publication record for this book is available from the British Library.

Table of Contents

Detailed Table of Contents

It then focuses on the emerging trends like AI integration and cloud system which overcome the challenges of scalability, user engagement and data quality.

This chapter, "Change Management in Tech-Driven Sustainable Organizations," explores how organizations can align digital transformation with sustainability goals. Positioned within the book "Leveraging Strategic Management for a Sustainable Digital Economy," it offers a comprehensive guide to managing change at the intersection of technology and sustainable development. The chapter covers foundational and advanced change management models—such as Lewin's, Kotter's, and ADKAR—while incorporating sustainability-specific frameworks like the circular economy. Key drivers and barriers to change are identified, with strategic solutions emphasizing leadership, innovation, stakeholder engagement, and ethical governance. Through practical case studies, it illustrates successes and failures in sectors like energy and retail. The chapter concludes by discussing future trends including green AI and circular business models.

This chapter, "Strategic Leadership for Digital Sustainability," examines how organizations can align digital transformation with sustainability goals through visionary leadership. It introduces digital sustainability as a strategic imperative, emphasizing the role of leadership in fostering responsible innovation, ethical governance, inclusivity, and environmental stewardship. The chapter explores transformational, servant/ethical, and adaptive leadership approaches and their application in cultivating sustainable digital infrastructures and cultures. It offers practical strategies for aligning digital initiatives with sustainability, including stakeholder engagement, risk management, and change leadership. Real-world case studies illustrate successful implementations, while a proposed Digital-Sustainability Leadership (D.S.L.) Framework provides a roadmap for future-ready leadership. It argues that strategic leadership is essential to navigating the dual agendas of technological advancement and sustainable development.

In the fast-paced business world of today, performance management is a phrase that is used in many different fields and at all levels of an organisation. Global rivalry, quick technology advancement, interconnectedness, and economic liberalisation have all made it harder for organisations to survive. In order to improve agility and boost business outcomes, companies are using strategic performance management (SPM) frameworks that incorporate goal alignment, real-time analytics, and continuous feedback. This shift is particularly relevant in the context of Kuwait, where digital transformation—a major pillar of Vision 2035 aimed at transitioning the nation toward a knowledge-based economy—demands data-driven approaches to performance management. This chapter adds to the expanding body of knowledge on digital-era HR practices by linking people management to the goals of national development to establish sustainable, high-performing workplaces in Kuwait.

This study aims to explore digital tools such as blockchain, the internet of things, artificial intelligence (AI), and big data analytics, and how these tools could be used to optimize supply chain operations across environmental, economic, and social dimensions. Key performance indicators (KPIs) will focus on enhancing resource efficiency, enabling real-time traceability, reducing carbon footprint, and improving stakeholder collaboration. The research identifies the role of digital transformation in aligning sustainability with operational excellence. Through an extensive literature review, this study highlights best practices in the adoption of these technologies across various industries. This research contributes to both academic and practical discussions by providing an integrative conceptual framework that links digital innovation with sustainable supply chain performance, offering actionable insights for managers and policymakers striving to meet evolving environmental standards and market expectations.

The convergence of AI and digital nomadism is fundamentally reshaping the global industrial landscape. This chapter finds that AI enables global labor mobility and flexible work, while digital nomads drive demand for agile, tech-integrated business models. This transformation necessitates policy innovation to address challenges in regulation, ethics, and socio-economic equity. Key findings include the exacerbation of digital divides, the emergence of new mental well-being concerns for remote workers, and the critical need for upskilling initiatives. The chapter concludes that coordinated policy innovation and ethical AI governance are essential to harness this dynamic for a more inclusive and sustainable future of work.

E-commerce has become a fundamental force driving economic prosperity by transforming industries and business models alongside advances in information and communication technologies. The COVID-19 pandemic highlighted the critical role of e-commerce in sustaining economic activity and accelerated its adoption. This process caused changes in consumption behaviors and lifestyles, leading to new habits. Furthermore, e-commerce has generated positive effects in employment, economic restructuring, fairness, environmental protection and cultural interaction, while also carrying social and political implications. This study employs bibliometric analysis to evaluate the literature on e-commerce and digital economy. A total of 302 articles published between 2001 and 2025 were collected from the Web of Science database. The findings indicate that academic interest in e-commerce and the digital economy has increased since 2018. Future studies are expected to expand the knowledge base by focusing on emerging technologies such as artificial intelligence, big data, blockchain etc.

Global Value Chains (GVCs) emerged as a defining feature of international trade following the liberalization of global markets and the advancement of information and communication technologies in the second half of the twentieth century. Initially driven by multinational enterprises (MNEs) through strategies such as foreign direct investment, offshoring, and outsourcing, GVCs evolved into complex networks connecting suppliers, producers, and consumers across multiple geographies. However, the landscape of global trade is undergoing a significant transformation. Recent disruptions, including the global financial crisis, the COVID-19 pandemic, and rising geopolitical tensions, have exposed vulnerabilities in hyper-globalized production systems. In response, a paradigm shift toward regionalization, friend shoring, supply chain resilience, and technological innovation is reshaping GVC structures. Concurrently, digitalization has lowered barriers for small and medium-sized enterprises (SMEs), enabling them to integrate into international trade networks and assume more strategic roles.

This study aims to explore how digital maturity level (DML) affects financial performance (FP) in the service sector firms listed on Borsa Istanbul in Türkiye. Using panel data of 59 service companies for the years 2016–2022, this study employs a text mining approach to calculate DML of the firms from their annual reports and uses panel regression analysis to examine the interplay between DML and FP. The results indicate that there is a U-shaped relationship between DML and FP of service sector firms. Companies that have a greater orientation towards digitalization face a decreasing FP in the short term but get increasing financial benefits in the long run. However, this relationship varies across the sectors of information, communication and publishing activities, construction and public works and transportation and

Preface

The transition toward a sustainable digital economy represents one of the most significant transformations of the contemporary era. As digital technologies continue to redefine industries, institutions, and societies, the role of strategic management has become increasingly central in guiding this transformation toward long-term sustainability, inclusivity, and resilience. This volume brings together a rich collection of scholarly contributions that examine how organizations can leverage strategic thinking to navigate the complexities of digitalization while addressing pressing economic, environmental, and social challenges.

Digital transformation today extends far beyond technological adoption; it requires a reconfiguration of organizational capabilities, leadership paradigms, and governance structures. Across sectors, decision-makers are tasked with balancing innovation with responsibility, efficiency with equity, and growth with sustainability. The chapters in this book collectively explore these tensions and offer frameworks, models, and empirical insights that illuminate pathways toward sustainable digital development.

A defining feature of this volume is its interdisciplinary scope. It bridges strategic management with emerging domains such as artificial intelligence, big data analytics, blockchain, and digital platforms, while also addressing critical areas including supply chains, human resource management, global value chains, healthcare, tourism, and environmental sustainability. This breadth reflects the pervasive impact of digitalization and underscores the need for integrated, systems-level approaches to strategy.

Equally important is the human dimension emphasized throughout the book. From empowering individuals in the digital economy to fostering ethical leadership, enhancing workforce capabilities, and addressing digital equity, the contributions highlight that sustainable transformation is ultimately driven by people. Organizations must cultivate not only technological competence but also ethical awareness, adaptability, and collaborative capacity.

The volume also provides a global perspective, drawing on insights from diverse geographic and institutional contexts. These varied viewpoints reveal how digital transformation unfolds differently across regions while also pointing to shared challenges such as regulatory complexity, digital divides, and the need for innovation-driven growth. By integrating theoretical advancements with practical applications, this book aims to inform both academic inquiry and strategic practice.

CHAPTER OVERVIEW

Chapter 1 introduces a human-centered strategic framework for digital empowerment, emphasizing the interplay of individual passion, digital platforms, and ethical power in shaping sustainable success.

Chapter 2 explores the role of artificial intelligence in enhancing strategic foresight, enabling organizations to anticipate risks and opportunities within a rapidly evolving digital and sustainability landscape.

Chapter 3 examines advanced big data visualization techniques and frameworks that support real-time, insight-driven decision-making across multiple sectors.

Chapter 4 analyzes strategic change management approaches that align digital transformation initiatives with sustainability goals through leadership, governance, and capability development.

Chapter 5 investigates leadership models that integrate digital transformation with sustainability imperatives, highlighting the importance of ethical, adaptive, and visionary leadership.

Chapter 6 discusses data-driven performance management systems in the digital era, focusing on the integration of analytics, human resource practices, and leadership for organizational effectiveness.

Chapter 7 explores the integration of digital technologies such as artificial intelligence, blockchain, and IoT in enhancing the sustainability and performance of supply chains.

Chapter 8 analyzes the intersection of artificial intelligence and digital nomadism, and its implications for the future of work, policy development, and global labor dynamics.

Chapter 9 reviews the evolution of e-commerce within the digital economy, identifying key drivers, research trends, and the broader socio-economic impacts of digital trade.

Chapter 10 investigates the transformation of global value chains, highlighting the shift from multinational dominance toward greater participation and empowerment of small and medium-sized enterprises.

Chapter 11 explores the relationship between digital maturity and financial performance, demonstrating how digitalization impacts organizational outcomes over time.

Chapter 12 examines the implications of virtual currencies for financial systems, particularly in relation to regulatory challenges and emerging risks in digital financial environments.

Chapter 13 investigates the role of smart tourism and emerging technologies in enabling sustainable development in rural and underdeveloped regions.

Chapter 14 explores issues of digital equity in healthcare, focusing on access, inclusion, and the socio-economic factors shaping digital health systems.

Chapter 15 examines innovative approaches to wastewater treatment, highlighting the role of artificial intelligence and nanotechnology in advancing environmental sustainability.

Together, these chapters provide a comprehensive and forward-looking exploration of how strategic management can be leveraged to build a sustainable digital economy. The insights presented aim to support scholars, practitioners, and policymakers in designing strategies that not only harness technological innovation but also contribute to a more equitable and sustainable future.

Chapter 1
Passion, Platform, and Power:
A Strategic Framework for Digital Empowerment

Noprita Herari
http://orcid.org/0009-0009-2497-5340
Universitas Negeri Jakarta, Indonesia

Nik Adzrieman Abd Abdul Rahman
Universiti Utara Malaysia, Malaysia

Mega Ayu Permatasari
http://orcid.org/0009-0002-3194-6395
Universitas Negeri Jakarta, Indonesia

ABSTRACT

In an era shaped by algorithms, platforms, and digital precarity, success can no longer be defined solely by employment speed, income, or visibility. This chapter introduces the Passion–Platform–Power (PPP) Framework as a human-centered and strategic model for redefining success through digital empowerment. Positioning passion as a strategic asset, platforms as both enablers and gatekeepers, and power as sustainable impact grounded in ethics and agency, the chapter bridges creativity, strategic management, and higher education. Through an applied Four-Year Digital Passion Roadmap, portfolio-based learning, and digital risk literacy, it demonstrates how universities can transform student journeys from coursework to career. Rather than promoting compulsory monetization, the passion economy is framed as a space for cultivating future-ready skills, integrity, and resilience. The chapter

DOI: 10.4018/979-8-3373-5052-3.ch001

offers educators, managers, and policymakers an actionable framework to prepare empowered individuals capable of shaping meaningful, ethical, and sustainable futures within the global digital ecosystem.

INTRODUCTION: REDEFINING SUCCESS IN THE DIGITAL AGE

> "The future of work belongs not to those who merely adapt to algorithms, but to those who understand their passion, navigate platforms strategically, and use digital power to create meaning, resilience, and sustainability"

Success in the digital age can no longer be measured by traditional parameters such as the height of one's position, the size of one's salary, or how quickly one secures a job after graduation. In a socio-economic landscape increasingly shaped by algorithms, creativity, and platform interactions, the very definition of success must be radically reexamined. Today's individuals are expected not only to be productive workers but also creators who can manage their digital identities and actively contribute to building inclusive communities. This is the context in which the passion economy emerges, a phenomenon that signifies a shift from merely working to survive to working in order to create meaning, both for oneself and for society (Herari & Waluyo, 2024).

Digital empowerment refers to an individual's capacity to actively shape digital environments (rather than merely adapt to them) through informed decision-making, ethical agency, and the strategic use of digital tools to create economic, social, and cultural value. The urgency of this discussion cannot be ignored. Data from UN Trade & Development shows the rapid growth of the creative economy and user-based platforms, where billions of people use social media to build careers, produce works, and construct identities (UNCTAD, 2024). Yet behind these immense opportunities lies a paradox: many creators are trapped in algorithmic logics that force them to chase endless trends; students and young workers struggle to connect academic learning with real-world needs; while educational institutions are often left behind in preparing an empowered digital generation (Josella, 2025; MDI, 2025; Iivari, 2020). If left unchecked, we risk producing graduates who are theoretically knowledgeable but digitally vulnerable, holding degrees without possessing portfolios relevant to the job market or the passion economy.

Redefining success in the digital era requires ethical reflection beyond the pursuit of visibility or virality. The central challenge is how to build sustainable practices by managing passion responsibly, engaging platforms without losing autonomy, and exercising power to empower rather than dominate. For this reason, discussions of passion–platform–power must move beyond theory and be translated into practical strategies, applied roadmaps, and structured educational interventions. Higher education, as an institution responsible for shaping future generations, must break away from traditional silos and recognize every academic activity as part of preparing graduates with resilient, ethical, and future-ready career pathways.

The chapter responds to growing concerns that graduates and early-career professionals are digitally exposed yet strategically underprepared. While access to platforms has expanded, many individuals remain vulnerable to algorithmic dependency, portfolio irrelevance, and digital risks. The PPP framework is proposed as a human-centered strategic model that integrates creativity, platform literacy, and ethical power to redefine success in the digital era.

With this urgency, the manuscript seeks to offer both a critical and practical framework: how passion can be positioned as a strategic asset, how platforms can be understood as both enablers and gatekeepers, how power can be defined not merely as popularity but as digital empowerment, and how a four-year roadmap (aligned with the undergraduate period) together with digital risk literacy can equip students to be truly ready for both the workforce and the creative economy of the future. Ultimately, the central question guiding this manuscript is: how can we redefine success in the digital age so that the new generation is not only able to survive within the algorithmic ecosystem but also empowered to shape it?

THE PASSION ECONOMY: FROM CREATIVITY TO SUSTAINABILITY

In recent years, the term passion economy has been increasingly used to describe a new digital economic phenomenon, where individuals do not merely work to earn a living but also build meaningful lives by monetizing their identities, creativity, and personal interests through digital platforms (Herari, 2024). Unlike the gig economy, which focuses on efficiency, short-term freelance work, and dependency on platforms, the passion economy emphasizes the creation of long-term value rooted in individual uniqueness and authentic relationships with audiences or communities (Herari, et al., 2025). In this context, creativity is not only a tool for expression but also the primary driver of economic, social, and cultural sustainability (Riswanto, et al., 2023).

Creativity holds extraordinary potential for generating sustainable impact because it originates from inexhaustible resources: human ideas, imagination, and lived experiences (Blessinger, 2024). When someone builds work from their passion (whether in the form of writing, design, music, education, or other digital products) they are essentially constructing an economic ecosystem that is not solely dependent on mass consumption but instead on emotional connection and personal relevance.

This model has proven more resilient to rapid changes in digital markets because audiences are not simply buying products; they are engaging with the narratives created by the individual. Digital transformation is no longer just about technology but about how humans redefine work, identity, and value (Umboh, 2023). Likewise, creativity rooted in authentic experience becomes a pathway to sustainability, both in business terms and in fostering more inclusive cultural and social change.

Sustainability in the context of the passion economy is not about limitless economic growth but about creators' resilience in maintaining relevance, sustaining creative energy, and cultivating long-term relationships with communities. This is evident in the work of solopreneurs and micro-creators who consistently produce content on platforms like YouTube, Instagram, Substack, or TikTok. An illustrator, for instance, may begin by sharing hobby sketches online, gradually building a loyal audience. From there, they can open commissions, sell prints, host online classes, and even create merchandise, all stemming from a foundation of passion and creativity managed strategically. In this sense, sustainability is not merely about using eco-friendly materials, but about how creative work sustains the relationship between creators and their communities while serving as a means of regenerating ideas and adaptive business models.

One critical factor in bridging creativity and sustainability is the ability to frame passion within a strategic structure. While spontaneous creativity is important, surviving and thriving in a competitive digital ecosystem requires setting work rhythms, content calendars, audience mapping, and communication strategies aligned with one's values. Creators who can harness their passion to reinforce community values while building ethical and meaningful digital visibility become central figures in the future of the digital economy (Herari & Marlina, 2024).

The passion economy should be understood not merely as a digital trend, but as a fundamental shift in how work, contribution, and sustainability are defined. When combined with digital literacy, social awareness, and self-management, creativity can move beyond a hobby to become the foundation of a resilient and inclusive economic pathway. This model opens opportunities for individuals long marginalized by conventional labor systems to build independent careers aligned with their values and capacities. Ultimately, sustainability in the digital age is often found not in virality or scale, but in meaningful engagement within micro-communities, where creativity functions as both social connection and long-term capital for a more human-centered digital future.

Furthermore, the passion economy describes a digital-economic paradigm in which individuals transform personal interests, creativity, and lived experience into economic and social value through digital platforms. Unlike the gig economy, which emphasizes efficiency and short-term task completion, the passion economy prioritizes authenticity, long-term community engagement, and creative sustainability.

Creativity functions as a renewable strategic resource. When passion is supported by reflective practice and self-regulation, it enables differentiation and resilience. From a strategic management perspective, passion can be understood as an intangible asset that contributes to innovation, identity coherence, and long-term engagement. This reframing positions creativity not as a peripheral hobby, but as a foundational input to sustainable value creation.

PLATFORM AS ENABLER AND GATEKEEPER

Within the ever-expanding ecosystem of the passion economy, digital platforms occupy a dual and complex role, as both enablers and gatekeepers. On the one hand, platforms such as Instagram, TikTok, YouTube, and Substack provide open access for individuals to express themselves, sharpen their creativity, and reach global audiences. On the other hand, they establish rules of the game that are often opaque, shaped by algorithmic logics that can either amplify or obscure a creator's presence. In this context, the sustainability of creativity depends not only on an individual's consistency in producing work but also on their ability to understand and respond to the dynamics of power embedded in platforms.

Digital platforms have revolutionized the way we create and do business. Creators no longer need approval from major publishers or large capital to begin; with just an internet connection, a smartphone, and the desire to share, one can build a personal brand. Yet accessibility does not mean equality. While anyone can start, not everyone can survive. Algorithms become the decisive factor in determining who "rises to the surface" and who sinks into the sea of content. Here is where platform logic operates: it promises opportunity while placing users in a position of perpetual dependence on internal mechanisms they do not fully understand. Digital platforms simultaneously enable opportunity and impose constraint. Social media, content-sharing platforms, and digital marketplaces lower barriers to entry, yet their algorithmic systems govern visibility, monetization, and participation.

As enablers, platforms provide tools and spaces for expression and career-building. TikTok, for instance, enables anyone to create short creative videos that can reach millions within a short time. Many young creators have built businesses out of simple, authentic content. Instagram allows artists to showcase curated visual portfolios and directly connect with clients. YouTube functions as an open university, enabling independent educators to disseminate knowledge without bureaucracy. Yet as gatekeepers, these platforms impose their own value systems: engagement is measured through likes, shares, comments, and watch time. Content that does not align with these metrics, no matter how high in quality, risks invisibility. Creators are thus compelled to continually adapt to trends, viral sounds, or certain formats to remain relevant. Over time, this can be emotionally exhausting and blur the authentic value of their passion.

This situation creates what can be termed "algorithmic dependency," where creators feel obliged to chase performance metrics rather than focus on the creative process itself. They are not only producing but also constantly managing their digital presence—analyzing data, monitoring optimal posting times, experimenting with captions, and following platform trends. When algorithms change, so too must their strategies. When platforms alter features, creators must adapt. Many eventually experience digital fatigue, feeling trapped in an endless cycle of production dictated not by personal passion but by the need to remain visible (Boaks, 2025).

Nevertheless, responses to platform logics are not entirely passive. Many creators are developing hybrid strategies to sustain themselves. They combine free platforms with paid channels such as Patreon, open online shops to sell physical works, or cultivate exclusive communities on messaging apps like Discord or Telegram (Meira, 2025). Some gradually shift away from dependence on a single platform and build personal websites to fully control their narrative and content distribution. Such strategies represent subtle resistance to algorithmic gatekeeping, underscoring the argument that platforms are the new foundations of the digital economy (Meira, 2025).

Visibility in digital spaces is not neutral but emerges from continuous negotiation between personal creativity and technological power. When creators understand these dynamics, they are better able to manage expectations, balance originality with algorithmic demands, and build sustainable systems grounded in values and relationships rather than metrics alone. Viewing platforms as both enablers and gatekeepers does not imply rejecting technology, but engaging with it consciously and strategically. In an environment of constant content flow and shifting algorithms, creativity remains central, while the ability to navigate platform power becomes essential for ensuring that passion-driven voices are not only visible but enduring.

POWER AND DIGITAL AGENCY IN AN ALGORITHMIC WORLD

In an increasingly complex digital world dominated by algorithms, questions of who holds power over narratives, distribution, and value become ever more pressing. Content creators, digital entrepreneurs, and individuals building personal branding through social media are confronted with the reality that their visibility is deeply shaped by machine logics, what is deemed worthy of display, who receives attention, and how their work is evaluated.

Yet, beneath this systemic pressure, small but significant spaces emerge where individuals can reclaim control, build supportive communities, and engage in digital activity with ethical awareness. This is the essence of digital empowerment: a process in which individuals are no longer passive users but active agents capable of influencing, choosing, and constructing value systems within the digital ecosystems they inhabit (Li, et al., 2022).

Digital empowerment rarely appears in dramatic or revolutionary forms; it is more often expressed through small, consistent decisions made with awareness and values. Choosing platforms aligned with personal principles, setting boundaries to protect mental health, prioritizing community-oriented content over metrics, and supporting others through sharing economies are quiet but meaningful acts of agency. Such practices represent resistance to market logics that glorify virality and hollow engagement. In this sense, digital agency lies in the capacity to navigate algorithmic systems with clarity, intention, and ethical judgment.

A central dimension of digital empowerment is the ability to build and sustain communities. Amid algorithmic pressures that reward competition and individualism, communities offer spaces for more human, reciprocal relationships. Creators who cultivate communities do not merely attract audiences but foster active networks that provide feedback, emotional support, and shared ownership of ideas. Here, power shifts from control to responsibility, from visibility to relational sustainability.

Ethics ultimately anchors digital empowerment within the passion economy. Power is not a license for unchecked visibility, but a moral practice that requires reflection on how influence is exercised and attention is valued. When creativity is used to animate values (through inclusive narratives, open knowledge sharing, or socially grounded micro-enterprises) digital power becomes transformative rather than extractive. In an increasingly algorithmic world, true empowerment is found not in rapid virality, but in the ability to endure, grow, and create humane, inclusive, and sustainable digital spaces over time.

THE PPP FRAMEWORK: PASSION – PLATFORM – POWER

After discussing how creativity can lead to sustainability, how digital platforms function both as gateways and gatekeepers, and how digital power can be reclaimed through awareness and ethical action, it is time to synthesize these dynamics into a strategic framework called the PPP Framework (Passion, Platform, Power). This framework outlines three core pillars for building sustainable digital empowerment: passion as the narrative core and source of meaning, platform as the infrastructure and arena of distribution, and power as the manifestation of impact, influence, and monetization born from consistency.

Positioning the PPP Framework within Strategic Management Literature

From a strategic management perspective, the Passion–Platform–Power (PPP) framework can be situated within established theories of value creation, capability development, and digital transformation. In particular, the framework aligns with the Resource-Based View (RBV), dynamic capabilities theory, and contemporary digital transformation strategy frameworks.

Within the RBV, passion can be understood as an intangible strategic resource embedded in individuals' identities, creativity, and intrinsic motivation. When cultivated through reflection, skill development, and ethical orientation, passion becomes a valuable, rare, and difficult-to-imitate asset that contributes to sustained competitive advantage rather than short-term performance.

Platform literacy reflects dynamic capabilities, specifically the ability to sense, seize, and reconfigure opportunities within rapidly evolving digital environments. Individuals and institutions that understand platform affordances, algorithmic governance, and monetization logics are better positioned to adapt strategically while maintaining autonomy and reducing dependency on opaque digital systems.

Power, as conceptualized in the PPP framework, represents the realization of strategic outcomes associated with digital transformation, including sustainable impact, ethical legitimacy, and long-term value creation. Rather than equating power with visibility or scale alone, PPP emphasizes empowerment as a strategic outcome rooted in agency, resilience, and responsible participation in digital ecosystems.

By integrating these perspectives, the PPP framework extends strategic management literature by foregrounding human-centered and ethical dimensions of digital strategy, offering a complementary lens to existing models that prioritize technological adoption or efficiency over empowerment and sustainability.

Passion refers to the enduring values, personal meaning, and intrinsic motivations that drive individuals to create work that resonates beyond transactional outcomes. Platform refers to the digital infrastructures (technical, algorithmic, and cultural) that enable the production, circulation, and visibility of creative and professional identities. Power refers to the capacity to generate impact, influence, and sustainable value within digital ecosystems through a combination of visibility, credibility, and community trust.

Figure 1. The PPP Framework: Passion – Platform – Power

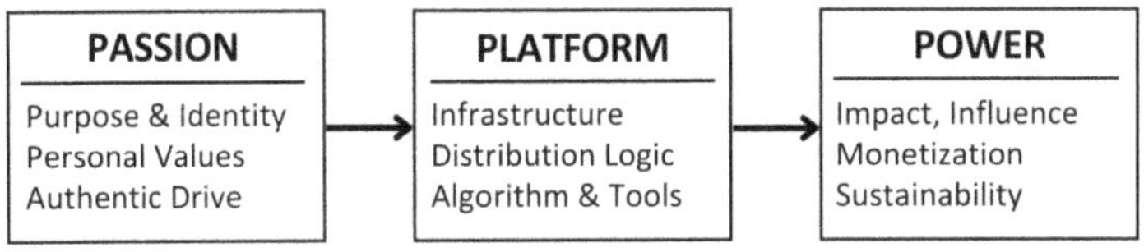

(Proposed by Author, 2025)

Passion is the first and most fundamental element. It is not merely a fleeting hobby but a combination of personal values, life experiences, and the drive to create something meaningful. When passion becomes the foundation of digital work, every piece of content carries uniqueness, depth, and honesty. Research shows that creators who can articulate their passion consistently and contextually are more likely to build loyal and engaged audiences (Herari, et al., 2025). Thus, passion is seen not as an escape but as a strategic asset that provides direction and energy to endure within the fast-moving digital stream (Herari, et al., 2025).

However, passion cannot stand alone without a platform. Digital platforms such as Instagram, YouTube, TikTok, Substack, LinkedIn, or marketplaces like Shopee and Etsy serve as crucial infrastructures for transforming passion into works, products, or services. Platforms provide tools and massive distribution networks once only accessible to large institutions. Yet platforms are not neutral; they are shaped by algorithmic logics and internal cultures that dictate participation. For this reason, it is vital for creators to cultivate platform literacy, the ability to strategically interpret both the opportunities and limitations of platforms, so as not to fall into blind dependency that restricts their potential (Ha & Kim, 2023). Platform literacy refers to the skillset required to understand how digital platforms operate (technically, algorithmically, and culturally) and to use that understanding to make informed, strategic, and ethical choices within them.

When passion finds its channel through a platform, the third pillar emerges: power. At this stage, power is not only measured by the number of followers, revenue, or reach but by the quality of impact achieved. Power refers to the extent to which a creator can influence discourse, build communities, and reshape social dynamics. It also encompasses monetization, how well-managed passion can generate fair and sustainable economic value. More broadly, power is the capacity to reject oppressive dominant narratives, create inclusive spaces, and foster digital ecosystems that are more humane and empathetic.

If passion is the source of energy and platform the vehicle, then power is the destination. Power, in this framework, is not simply domination but a form of digital empowerment: the ability to survive, grow, inspire, and create social impact through passion-based work. The PPP Framework thus emphasizes that success in the digital economy is not merely a matter of visibility but of how passion, platform, and power intertwine to produce sustainability, value, and meaningful change.

Nevertheless, the discourse around the relationship between passion, platform, and power is not without debate. Some argue that monetizing passion through effective platform management will automatically generate power. This view points to numerous examples of creators who successfully built personal brands, attracted followers, monetized their content, and even created jobs. In other words, platforms offer vast opportunities for anyone with passion and the willingness to learn. In this context, power arises from the combination of hard work, digital strategy, and creative consistency.

Yet this perspective is not universally accepted without criticism. Opponents argue that not all passions can (or should) be monetized. Forced monetization can erode the essence of passion itself. Rather than serving as a source of joy and meaning, passion risks becoming a performative burden, bound to audience expectations and algorithms. Creators may feel trapped in endless cycles of content production merely to maintain visibility, which ultimately leads to mental exhaustion and loss of authenticity (Thibaud, 2022).

Moreover, even strong platform management does not guarantee power. Many creators from marginalized groups produce high-quality content and employ sound digital strategies, yet still struggle to gain exposure due to algorithmic bias, social stereotypes, or unequal access to technology. This highlights that platform logic is not fully meritocratic. Even when creators play by all the "rules," invisible structures of power can block their path to empowerment.

Thus, within the PPP Framework, passion, platform, and power should not be understood as a linear path with guaranteed outcomes. Instead, they represent a dynamic, cyclical, and reflective process. Creators must continually evaluate whether their passion remains authentic, whether the platforms they use still align with their goals, and whether the power they seek is truly meaningful both personally and socially. This framework positions individuals as active agents rather than passive victims of the system. In practice, it means learning to read data without losing intuition, using algorithms without sacrificing values, and pursuing growth without compromising life balance.

For example, an educational content creator might begin with a passion for teaching and sharing knowledge. They may choose YouTube as a platform due to its capacity for long-form visual content. With the right management strategies (consistent themes, strong audiovisual quality, and interactive communication with viewers) they may start earning income from AdSense and brand partnerships. Yet alongside these achievements, dilemmas arise: should they follow trending topics that clash with their values just to boost views, or remain committed to educational content even if growth is slower? Here, the principle of power is tested. Power is not solely about financial outcomes but about the ability to choose directions consistent with one's identity and long-term impact.

The PPP Framework encourages individuals to recognize that being a creator in the digital era is not merely about going viral or monetizing but about constructing a personal sustainability system rooted in passion, consciously managed through platforms, and leading to liberating forms of power. The framework is relevant not only for influencers or content creators but also for students, professionals, activists, small business owners, and anyone seeking to harness digital technologies strategically and ethically.

Ultimately, The PPP (Passion–Platform–Power) are three interconnected and mutually reinforcing elements. Passion provides direction, platforms provide the tools, and power delivers outcomes. Yet above all, ongoing awareness and reflection about our roles in the digital ecosystem are most crucial. Through this approach, individuals are not merely platform users but creators of meaning, agents of change, and resources that enrich a more human-centered digital life.

APPLIED STRATEGY: A 4-YEAR DIGITAL PASSION ROADMAP FOR STUDENTS

Discussing passion, platform, and power within the PPP framework would be incomplete without presenting an applied strategy that can be implemented in real life, particularly in the context of students undertaking a four-year journey in higher education. Four years is not a long time, but it is sufficient to design a structured process of digital transformation, one that positions students not merely as consumers of information on digital platforms, but as producers of meaning, creators of narratives, and architects of their professional futures. In this regard, a four-year roadmap can be seen as the praxis of the PPP Framework: passion as the starting point and source of energy, platform as the arena for testing, expressing, and distributing work, and power as both the outcome and ultimate goal, sustainable empowerment.

The first year of this journey can be viewed as the phase of discovery and foundation-building. Students entering university are often still in the process of searching for their academic, social, and personal identities. Yet it is precisely at this stage that it becomes important to begin what can be called passion mapping, a reflective process of identifying the interests, skills, and values they wish to bring into the digital public sphere.

Passion mapping does not need to be immediately clear or final; it is an initial map that will be revised continuously throughout the journey. At this stage, students can start with a digital identity audit: how their social media profiles reflect who they are, whether the content they share aligns with or diverges from their long-term aspirations, and how their online habits can be directed toward more productive ends. Simple actions such as writing a more curated social media bio, choosing a professional profile photo, or setting three main content themes can already serve as meaningful first steps.

The choice of platforms need not be excessive, just one or two that are most relevant to their interests. For instance, Instagram for visual work, YouTube for educational videos, or LinkedIn for professional networking. At this stage, what matters more is consistency in experimenting and building habits. A 30-day sprint of creating short content or writing regular reflections can be an initial exercise that opens new spaces for exploration.

The second year represents a phase of deepening capacity while also beginning to position oneself. If the first year is about experimentation and foundation-building, the second year is about finding rhythm, improving quality, and discovering a distinctive voice. Students can start by creating a simple editorial calendar to maintain consistency, for example, aiming for two to three posts per week tied together by a narrative thread. They may also begin learning to build more structured storytelling systems, such as through series formats, recurring rubrics, or narrative techniques like the before–after–bridge structure.

At this stage, visual identity also needs attention, such as consistency in design style, color choices, or content presentation formats. Equally important is interaction with the audience. Students can begin hosting Q&A sessions, requesting feedback, or creating simple surveys to understand what their audience finds most valuable. These activities are not merely strategies to increase engagement but also ways to learn how to read the needs of the community that forms around their passion. In this phase, students can also prepare a simple media kit or process documentation to demonstrate initial professionalism.

The third year is the right time to begin testing forms of monetization that align with one's passion and personal values. Monetization here does not necessarily mean generating a large income immediately but can take the form of small experiments with relevant products or services. For example, a student who enjoys writing might create a short e-book or offer an online writing class. Those with design skills might try selling simple merchandise or opening commissions. The key is to begin the process of offer design or digital product, which is crafting clear proposals, setting fair prices, and communicating them professionally.

At this stage, students also need to start considering more formal infrastructures, such as creating a simple landing page, setting up official payment methods, or preparing basic collaboration contracts. Furthermore, this phase requires sharpening skills in negotiation, client management, and commercial ethics. Healthy monetization is that which supports the sustainability of passion, not one that forces conformity to market trends misaligned with identity. This is the moment when power begins to feel more tangible: when passion, channeled through platforms, provides economic value while simultaneously expanding social influence through impactful work.

The fourth year becomes the phase of consolidating professional identity and preparing for the transition into the workforce or entrepreneurship. At this stage, students should already have a solid portfolio, composed of curated signature works that represent their journey over the four years. This portfolio can be packaged as a personal website, an optimized LinkedIn profile, or a field-specific portfolio platform such as Behance for designers or ResearchGate for academic work.

The fourth year is also the right time to create a capstone project—a major project that represents the integration of passion, platform, and power that students have built. This project could take the form of a digital campaign, a creative product, collaborative research, or a community initiative. What matters is that the project demonstrates depth, relevance, and tangible impact.

At the same time, the fourth year should also be used to expand professional networks, conduct targeted outreach to relevant institutions, organizations, or communities, and prepare professional documents such as a resume, career one-pager, and talk deck. Ultimately, the fourth year is not just about concluding one's studies but about opening new pathways while carrying a portfolio ready to be tested in the real world.

To summarize this four-year roadmap, the following table provides a concise overview of the objectives, key activities, skills, and expected outcomes at each stage.

Table 1. Applied Strategy: A 4-Year Digital Passion Roadmap for Students (Proposed by Author, 2025)

Tahun	Main Focus	Key Activities	Core Soft Skills	Core Hard Skills	Expected Outcomes
1	Discovery & Foundation	Passion mapping, digital identity, 30-day content sprint	Self-reflection, discipline, ethics	Basic design, copywriting, and content production	Initial mini-portfolio, professional bio, productive digital habits
2	Deepening & Positioning	Editorial calendar, series storytelling, visual identity, audience interaction	Storytelling, collaboration, communication	Basic SEO, intermediate design, basic analytics	Initial media kit, portfolio version 2, small emerging community
3	Monetization & Professionalization	Digital product, landing page, simple contracts, thought leadership	Negotiation, commercial ethics, client service	Email marketing, conversion, project management	Pilot products/ services, initial income, more professional portfolio version 3
4	Scaling, Sustainability & Transition	Capstone project, personal website, final portfolio, networking & outreach	Leadership, public speaking, sustainability management	Personal CRM, basic licensing, SOP documentation	Final portfolio, flagship project, professional network, career readiness

Although Table 1 presents a brief framework, what matters more is how each student interprets their four-year journey as a process of reflection, exploration, and consolidation. Each individual will experience variations, in terms of passion, the platforms they choose, and the form of power they aim to achieve. Nevertheless, this general pattern provides direction so that they do not become trapped as passive users of digital platforms but instead act as active agents who consciously manage their identities and creative work (Vallance, 2021).

Within this roadmap, the debate over the pros and cons of monetizing passion remains highly relevant. Some argue that monetization through well-managed digital platforms automatically generates power, since those who can build an effective distribution system will gain recognition, income, and influence. Others, however, highlight the danger of commodifying passion, when the drive to earn money obscures its true meaning and undermines creative energy (Hund, 2023).

This four-year roadmap seeks to accommodate both perspectives. It encourages students to experiment with monetization in the third year, but always within an ethical framework: whether the chosen business model aligns with personal values, whether the product or service offered delivers genuine benefits, and whether interactions with audiences remain rooted in trust and honesty. In this way, the roadmap is not only about technical strategies but also about moral education and self-awareness.

From a sustainability perspective, the roadmap also functions as a bridge between the academic and professional worlds. Students not only learn theory in the classroom but simultaneously build tangible portfolios that they can showcase when applying for jobs, scholarships, or starting their own ventures. Beyond this, they learn how to manage their digital presence ethically and responsibly, reducing the risk of falling into algorithmic traps or harmful practices such as mule accounts or other forms of online fraud. The roadmap teaches that true digital empowerment is not measured solely by audience size or income but by integrity, consistency, and the capacity to protect oneself and one's community from unhealthy practices.

Ultimately, this four-year roadmap represents a concrete embodiment of the PPP Framework discussed earlier. Passion is the starting point that provides direction and energy; platform is the infrastructure that enables distribution and connection; and power is the outcome of the long journey, expressed as impact, empowerment, and sustainability.

In practice, students are trained not only to create content but also to manage processes, consider sustainability, and plan for the future. Through this framework, the four-year university experience can become a genuine investment in building a strong digital identity, a relevant portfolio, and professional capacities ready to face both the workplace and entrepreneurial opportunities. This roadmap is not merely a technical guide but a philosophy of lifelong learning, placing passion at the center, platform as the bridge, and power as the sustainable goal.

DIGITAL RISK LITERACY: AVOIDING SCAMS AND MULE ACCOUNTS

Digital empowerment without risk literacy exposes individuals to significant harm. University students are increasingly targeted by scams, including money mule schemes, fraudulent job offers, and identity theft. A money mule is a person who transfers illegally obtained funds on behalf of others, knowingly or unknowingly, thereby facilitating money laundering. Risk literacy training emphasizes verification, identity protection, and red-flag detection. Suspected incidents should be reported immediately through official university security or IT helpdesk channels.

The use of digital media today is regarded as a necessity for all levels of society, including students enrolled in higher education institutions, whether public or private. This necessity extends not only to teaching and learning purposes but also to official dealings with university administrations. This means that without access to digital facilities such as smartphones, students' daily affairs would be disrupted. University students have little choice but to accept digital media as an indispensable aspect of their lives, whether they welcome it or not (Klein, 2023; Choo, Yoke & Ismail, 2022).

However, the advancement of digital technologies has also given rise to fraudulent activities that pose serious risks to users, including university students. As such, students in higher education institutions are not exempt from becoming targets of online scams perpetrated by cybercriminals or scammers. To prevent these issues from resulting in negative consequences for students, exposure to digital risk literacy is essential. Developing such awareness enables students to recognize deceptive practices, remain vigilant in online environments, and avoid becoming victims of scams or money-mule recruitment, thereby reducing potential legal, financial, and reputational harm (Livingstone, Stoilova, & Nandagiri, 2021). Suspected scams or money-mule recruitment attempts should be reported immediately to the university's IT security unit, student affairs office, or designated cybercrime reporting channel, in accordance with institutional protocols.

One of online scams is called money mule, it is refer to an individual who receives money from a third party into their bank account and subsequently transfers it to another person in the form of cash or other means, taking a commission in the process (Raza, Zhan, & Rubab, 2020). Although money mules are not directly involved in the crimes that generate the illicit funds (such as cybercrime, payment and online fraud, drugs, human trafficking, etc.), they remain accomplices because they help launder the proceeds of these crimes. In doing so, money mules enable criminal syndicates to remain anonymous while moving funds globally (EUROPOL-Public Awareness and Prevention Guides, 2019).

With the rapid advancement of information and communication technologies, the incidence of mule accounts has significantly increased, particularly in connection with internet fraud. Many commercial banks have suffered substantial losses due to different types of scams. For example, in a "phishing attack," cybercriminals create forged web pages resembling those of legitimate banks. This tactic deceives customers into disclosing their personal financial details (such as usernames and passwords), which are then exploited for illegal and unauthorized transactions (Sisak, 2013).

When cases of internet fraud are investigated, internet money mules are often easily identified, and any funds obtained fraudulently (sometimes retained as "commission") are usually recovered (Aston, McCombe, Reardon, & Watters, 2009). Whether the mule is fully aware of the crime or acts as an unsuspecting intermediary makes little difference. For the criminals who recruit them, money mules are expendable assets that serve their purpose without posing any real threat to the criminal enterprise.

The victims of mule account recruitment schemes span multiple groups, including housewives, secondary school students, university students, self-employed individuals, retirees, and the unemployed (Hashim & Abdul Rahman, 2020). Among these groups, university students are particularly vulnerable, as they are often targeted through part-time job scams, online advertisements, or fraudulent offers promising quick and easy income. Many students, facing financial pressure to cover tuition fees, living expenses, or personal commitments, may unknowingly agree to lend their bank accounts to such schemes. This makes them easy targets for cybercriminals who exploit their lack of financial awareness and experience.

In addition, scams targeting university students often include offers of easy loan schemes that promise approval within 24 hours. The conditions and requirements for these loans are presented as extremely simple. At the same time, many students have been deceived by fraudulent part-time job offers, which often claim that the work can be done from home. Such unrealistic and overly lucrative offers are designed solely to attract students' attention. Furthermore, the use of digital algorithms capable of tracking every online search made by users enables scammers to tailor offers that appear to meet the immediate needs of their potential victims. When students are eventually caught, the implications can be severe, even if they were unaware of the crimes they had become involved in (Bank Negara Malaysia, 2024).

Although victims may feel that they were deceived by scammers, the burden of responsibility still lies with them. What is even more concerning is that they may face imprisonment as well as financial penalties, including fines or bail payments. James et al. (2020), Yu et al. (2022), and Modic et al. (2018) highlight three key characteristics that contribute to vulnerability to scams, namely:

1. Demographic factors, where scammers tailor their modus operandi according to victims' responses to the schemes offered, taking into account their personal backgrounds. Different backgrounds yield different outcomes, and these tactics are often influenced by the victim's location and academic level. Individuals with lower educational attainment and those living in rural areas may be more vulnerable compared to highly educated groups.
2. Individual differences in cognitive capacity can affect decision-making in particular situations. This is closely linked to personality traits, especially emotional intelligence, which plays a role in making sound judgments. Individuals with higher cognitive capacity are generally less susceptible to scammers' manipulation.

The nature of the scam itself which often involves persuasive techniques to win the trust of easily influenced individuals. This is especially concerning today, as scammers are believed to research carefully to identify how to ensure their targets are easily deceived, without raising suspicion.

In addition, there are other modus operandi used by scammers to deceive victims, including fake endorsements and deceptive collaborations. Many university students have fallen victim to fraudulent offers of collaboration from counterfeit brands or impersonated public figures, which are in fact scam schemes (OECD, 2022). Others are tricked into handing over personal data under the pretense of verification, when in reality the data is misused for identity theft (Anderson & Jiang, 2018). All of this demonstrates that creativity without protection can easily lead to digital vulnerability. To prevent such incidents, students need to be equipped with three core competencies of digital risk literacy:

1. Digital Verification

Students should be trained to verify the authenticity of every transaction, job offer, or collaboration by cross-checking official sources, email domains, and the legality of institutions Reyhan Topal & Farzin Shargh, 2023). Basic practices, such as two-factor authentication, fact-checking, and the use of secure payment channels, should be emphasized (ENISA, 2023). These practices cultivate vigilance, ensuring students do not blindly trust uncertain offers. Moreover, the habit of casually sharing unverified information is unhealthy and must be curbed to reduce risks, including cases related to mule accounts.

2. Identity Protection

This pillar stresses the importance of safeguarding personal data (e.g., national identification numbers, bank account details, passwords, and digital portfolios) from leakage or misuse (Floridi, 2020). Students should be encouraged to build a professional digital identity while maintaining clear boundaries of privacy (Marwick & boyd, 2014). This is a crucial skill for individuals living in the digital age, as bank accounts and other online profiles can easily be compromised if sensitive data is not properly secured.

3. Red-Flag Detection

Students must learn to recognize warning signs: offers with unrealistic rewards, excessive requests for personal information, urgent or coercive communication styles, and collaborations without clear contracts (ACFE, 2022). Applying the principle of "trust, but verify" (trust with caution, not naivety) remains key to resisting scammer tactics Baral, G., & Arachchilage, N. A. G. (2018). To effectively address issues related to scammers, integration with a structured Four-Year Roadmap is crucial.

Table 2. Integration of Digital Risk Awareness into the Four-Year Roadmap (proposed by Author, 2025)

Year	Focus & Roadmap	Key Digital Risk Literacy Integration
1	Discovery & Foundation	Introduction to safe digital literacy; digital identity audit; awareness of online traps such as mule accounts.
2	Deepening & Positioning	Training in collaboration ethics; recognizing fraudulent partnership offers; safe engagement with wider audiences.
3	Monetization & Professionalization	Contract simulations; skills to detect fake endorsements; guidance on conducting secure digital transactions.
4	Scaling & Transition	Development of a professional portfolio that highlights both creative achievements and digital integrity, signaling readiness to manage digital risks effectively.

As illustrated in Table 2, digital risk literacy is positioned not merely as a defensive competence to avoid online crimes, but as a foundational element of professional identity and trust-building in the digital age. As university students increasingly operate in a borderless digital environment, they are exposed to risks such as mule accounts, fraudulent collaborations, fake credentials, and identity theft—threats that may carry serious legal, financial, and reputational consequences. Embedding digital risk awareness across the four-year roadmap enables students to develop practical habits of verification, ethical judgment, and identity protection as part of their everyday digital practices. In doing so, students not only safeguard themselves from cybercrime but also cultivate a professional digital presence grounded in integrity, credibility, and long-term trust within the wider society.

FROM COURSEWORK TO CAREER: EDUCATING FOR EMPOWERMENT THROUGH PORTFOLIO-BASED LEARNING IN HIGHER EDUCATION

In the broader discussion of sustainability, the dual role of digital platforms as both enablers and gatekeepers, the struggle to reclaim agency in an algorithmic world, and the PPP framework that integrates passion, platform, and power, we arrive at a fundamental need: how students can be genuinely prepared to face the professional world. The four-year roadmap already outlined provides step-by-step direction, while digital risk literacy warns of pitfalls such as scams or mule accounts that may disrupt the journey.

Equally important, however, is how higher education can integrate these concepts into the design of everyday learning. Higher education can no longer stop at the transfer of cognitive knowledge alone; it must become a practical arena where students develop living professional portfolios, growing out of coursework and serving as a bridge from the academic space to real careers, an arena of incubation. This is what the author refers to as the journey from coursework to career: turning every course into a field for portfolio development, while cultivating a culture of empowerment rooted in responsible digital practice, interdisciplinary skills, and value-based learning within the framework of the passion economy.

Imagine if every course assignment did not simply end up as a file on a lecturer's desk or a forgotten digital document, but was processed, curated, and presented as part of a professional portfolio. Reflective essays, which have traditionally been graded and returned, could become personal narratives of intellectual growth worthy of publication on academic blogs or LinkedIn. Case studies developed in class could be featured as case study analyses in digital portfolios to demonstrate analytical skills and industry awareness. Marketing communication course projects could be packaged into campaign plans ready to be showcased to prospective employers or clients. Digital content created in design, media production, or digital literacy courses could be published with careful curation strategies, displaying both creativity and technical skill. Research outputs, whether in the form of mini-studies, surveys, or data-driven content, could be shared on academic platforms such as ResearchGate or even published in student journals. In this way, every course systematically contributes to building a student's digital identity, no longer fragmented or disconnected between classroom work and career readiness.

Of course, such a transformation requires the active involvement of various layers within educational institutions. Lecturers are no longer tasked solely with grading based on traditional academic criteria, but also with serving as mentors who help students understand how each output can hold long-term value. For instance, a lecturer can guide students in rewriting a reflective essay into a popular article suitable for online publication, or in refining a simple research report into a format that meets academic publishing standards.

Lecturers must also integrate portfolio elements into assessment rubrics so that students are encouraged to produce work that is not only "sufficient" to pass but also "worthy" of being showcased. Educational institutions, in turn, can support this by providing internal platforms for student digital portfolios, building virtual exhibition spaces, or even partnering with global professional platforms to give student work wider visibility, in other words, positioning the university as a creative incubator.

More crucial, however, is the cultivation of a learning culture that prioritizes responsible digital practices. A digital portfolio is not merely about "looking impressive" or displaying technical skills; it is about how students learn to use media ethically, manage data securely, and present an authentic digital identity.

In the era of the passion economy, where identity and creativity can function as currencies, higher education must equip students with critical digital literacy. They must understand the risks of plagiarism, data manipulation, privacy violations, or algorithmic traps that could undermine their professional credibility. Thus, a portfolio is not just an archive of work, but a mirror of the values and integrity that students will carry into their professional lives.

Table 3. Tiered Responsibility Map in the Implementation of Digital Portfolio-Based Learning (Proposed by Author, 2025)

Level	Focus Area	Main Responsibilities	Concrete Action Plans	Metrics / Success Indicators
University	Institutional policy & digital infrastructure	• Establish digital portfolio policy as a graduation standard • Provide a university-wide platform for student portfolios • Integrate digital literacy and ethics into the general curriculum	• Build an integrated e-portfolio system linked with the academic information system (SIAKAD) • Annual workshop on "Digital Identity & Risk Literacy" • Partnerships with global platforms (LinkedIn Learning, ResearchGate, Behance)	• % of graduating students with complete digital portfolios • Annual participation rate in digital literacy programs • Compliance level with university-wide digital ethics standards
Faculty	Strengthening interdisciplinary curriculum	• Design curricula that encourage interdisciplinary skills (communication, technology, ethics) • Develop portfolio-based assessment standards • Connect students with industry partners	• Establish mandatory project/ portfolio-based courses across study programs • Organize digital portfolio-based career expos • Create an annual faculty portfolio showcase	• Number of interdisciplinary portfolio-ready outputs per cohort • Student participation in industry-linked activities • External evaluator/ industry feedback scores on student portfolios
Study Program	Practical implementation & mentoring	• Design course assignments that directly convert into portfolio pieces • Mentor students in curating work into professional formats • Instill digital risk literacy and professional ethics	• Assignment rubrics including both academic and "portfolio value" • Portfolio mentoring sessions each semester • Provide capstone projects integrating Passion–Platform–Power in the final year	• Portfolio quality improvement across semesters • % of students passing annual digital ethics/risk checks • Capstone project impact indicators (e.g., engagement, usability, innovation)

Table 3 can be understood as a tiered map of responsibilities that illustrates how the university, faculty, and academic program each play distinct yet complementary roles in building a portfolio-based learning ecosystem. At the university level, responsibility lies in macro-level policies and the provision of strong digital infrastructure. Universities must take a strategic role in establishing the standard that every graduate is required to have a digital portfolio as part of their professional profile. This is where the university must provide an integrated platform, such as an e-portfolio system linked to the academic information system, giving students an official space to archive their best work.

The university is also responsible for ensuring that digital literacy and ethics are incorporated into the general curriculum so that every student, without exception, gains sufficient preparation to manage their digital identity safely and responsibly. Through partnerships with global platforms such as LinkedIn Learning, ResearchGate, or Behance, universities can broaden students' access to showcase their portfolios on international stages.

At the faculty level, responsibility is more focused on strengthening interdisciplinary curricula and building bridges to the professional world. Faculties hold a unique position to orchestrate collaboration between study programs so that students gain more holistic experiences. For instance, a communication student might learn the basics of data analysis from another program, while a business student could collaborate with a design student to produce a creative pitch deck.

Faculties also need to establish portfolio-based assessment standards so that student assignments do not stop at numerical grades but are also evaluated for their readiness to appear in professional portfolios. Furthermore, faculties play an important role in connecting students with industry partners through career expos or annual faculty portfolio showcases, enabling students' work to receive direct feedback from practitioners.

At the program level, responsibilities are more practical and closely tied to students' day-to-day learning experiences. Programs serve as the frontline that must be able to transform course assignments into portfolio products. Each lecturer within a program is encouraged to design assignments that not only meet academic standards but also carry marketable value as evidence of competence. For example, a mini research report can be developed into an article suitable for publication, a campaign plan can be presented as a professional proposal, and digital content assignments can be published directly on relevant platforms under proper ethical standards.

Programs also hold the responsibility of providing regular mentoring to help students curate and package their work into coherent portfolios. Equally important, programs must instill digital risk literacy so that students are not only skilled at producing content but are also aware of the potential misuse of digital identities or online fraud that could jeopardize their professional reputation. Ultimately, programs can position the capstone project in the final year of study as the concrete integration of the PPP framework and as a symbolic transition from the academic world to the professional realm.

The narrative of Table 2 illustrates that portfolio-based education is not the responsibility of a single level, but rather a structured collective effort. Universities provide vision, infrastructure, and policies; faculties design interdisciplinary connections and build bridges to the outside world; while programs handle direct implementation that engages students in their daily learning. Together, these three levels form an ecosystem that enables students to truly embark on the journey from coursework to career, where every course and every piece of work produced does not end as mere academic formalities, but becomes a genuine investment in their professional future.

Ultimately, higher education oriented toward portfolio-based learning within the passion economy will produce graduates who are more prepared and empowered. They will not only hold a diploma as proof of graduation but also maintain a living portfolio as evidence of competence, integrity, and vision.

This portfolio will serve as a digital passport that opens doors to the professional world, demonstrating that students have not merely studied theory but have been practicing creating real impact since their time in university. In this way, education is not only about preparing for jobs but also about fostering empowerment—equipping the new generation with the capacity to become active, creative, and ethical actors in an ever-changing global digital ecosystem.

CRITICAL PERSPECTIVE: PASSION, POWER, AND THE PRESSURE OF PUBLIC MORALITY

The PPP Framework highlights the transformative potential of passion, platforms, and power, yet it also demands recognition of the ethical and social pressures that accompany digital success. Power in online ecosystems is never neutral; it is shaped by public scrutiny, algorithmic amplification, and collective moral expectations. Once individuals gain visibility, their choices are refracted through external judgment, making passion a negotiated rather than purely personal practice.

This negotiation raises a central dilemma: can passion remain authentic once it is monetized, or must it inevitably bend to market demands? Monetization may provide sustainability and legitimacy, but it also risks diluting values as creators adapt to audience preferences, self-censor, or compromise ideals to remain relevant. In this sense, passion exists in dynamic tension, balancing authenticity with adaptability, ethics with economics, and values with visibility.

Scholars of cultural production remind us that authenticity is always mediated within fields of power, where symbolic capital must be converted into social or economic recognition (Bourdieu, 1984). Likewise, Couldry and Mejias (2019) describe the "moral economy of data and visibility," in which both market logics and public morality constrain creative agency. Passion, therefore, should be understood not as an untainted inner drive but as an ongoing negotiation within these fields.

For higher education, this implies a deeper responsibility. Beyond fostering students who are passion-driven, platform-smart, and power-aware, institutions must also cultivate critical literacies to navigate the moral economy of visibility, teaching future graduates how to withstand public pressure, manage market demands, and sustain integrity while pursuing professional sustainability.

Managerial and Organizational Implications of the PPP Framework

While higher education provides an effective context for illustrating the operationalization of the PPP framework, its strategic implications extend well beyond academic settings. For managers and organizational leaders, PPP offers a lens for understanding how passion, platform literacy, and ethical power can be cultivated as strategic capabilities within digitally mediated work environments.

From a managerial perspective, passion can be recognized as an intangible strategic resource that supports engagement, creativity, and retention. Organizations that align individual passion with organizational purpose are better positioned to sustain innovation and reduce burnout in digital and hybrid work contexts.

Platform literacy functions as a dynamic capability that enables employees and teams to navigate algorithmic systems, digital tools, and platform governance structures effectively. Investing in platform literacy training enhances organizational adaptability while reducing dependency on external digital infrastructures.

Power, within organizational contexts, represents sustainable influence, ethical legitimacy, and long-term value creation. Rather than equating success solely with visibility or short-term performance metrics, the PPP framework encourages managers to evaluate outcomes based on resilience, trust, and responsible digital engagement.

For policymakers and platform designers, the framework highlights the importance of governance mechanisms that balance innovation with protection, ensuring that digital ecosystems support empowerment rather than exploitation.

CONCLUSION: PASSION-DRIVEN, PLATFORM-SMART, POWER-AWARE

This manuscript argues that the digital age demands a redefinition of success beyond traditional indicators such as status, salary, or speed of employment. Through the PPP Framework (Passion–Platform–Power) and its applied Four-Year Digital Passion Roadmap, higher education is positioned not only as a site of theoretical learning but as a structured incubator for identity formation, portfolio development, and professional readiness. By embedding portfolio-based learning and digital risk literacy, universities can equip graduates with living portfolios, ethical digital identities, and the resilience to navigate opportunities and risks in the digital economy. Importantly, the passion economy is framed not as an obligation to monetize, but as a pathway for cultivating essential future-ready skills and empowerment. In an algorithmic and uncertain world, higher education must therefore cultivate learners who are passion-driven, platform-smart, and power-aware, capable of shaping meaningful, sustainable, and ethical futures within the global digital ecosystem.

The Passion–Platform–Power framework reframes success in the digital age as sustainable empowerment rather than short-term visibility. By integrating strategic management theory, ethical reflection, applied roadmaps, and evaluative indicators, PPP provides a coherent and actionable model for navigating the digital economy.

REFERENCES

Association of Certified Fraud Examiners. (2022). *Occupational Fraud 2022: A Report to the Nations*. ACFE.

Aston, M., McCombie, S., Reardon, B., & Watters, P. (2009, July). A preliminary profiling of Internet money mules: An Australian perspective. In Symposia and Workshops on Ubiquitous, Autonomic and Trusted Computing (UIC-ATC '09) (pp. 482–487). IEEE. DOI: 10.1109/UIC-ATC.2009.63

Bank Negara Malaysia. (2024). Annual Report 2023. https://www.bnm.gov.my/ar2023

Baral, G., & Arachchilage, N. A. G. (2018). Building Confidence not to be Phished through a Gamified Approach: Conceptualising User's Self-Efficacy in Phishing Threat Avoidance Behaviour. arXiv

Blessinger, P. (2024, October 13). Human creativity as a renewable resource. Dr. Patrick Blessinger. https://www.patrickblessinger.com/human-creativity-as-a-renewable-resource/

Boaks, J. (2025). Ethics in management: Business and the professions. Emerald Publishing. https://www.emerald.com/books/edited-volume/17354/Ethics-in-Management-Business-and-the-Professions?redirectedFrom=PDF

Bourdieu, P. (1984). *Distinction: A Social Critique of the Judgement of Taste*. Harvard University Press.

Choo, Y. B., Yoke, S. K., & Ismail, N. H. (2022). A Systematic Literature Review on the Use of Digital Media among Malaysian Teachers and Students During the COVID-19 Pandemic. *International Journal of Academic Research in Progressive Education and Development*, *11*(2). Advance online publication. DOI: 10.6007/IJARPED/v11-i2/14130

Couldry, N., & Mejias, U. A. (2019). *The Costs of Connection: How Data Is Colonizing Human Life and Appropriating It for Capitalism*. Stanford University Press.

ENISA. (2023). ENISA Threat Landscape 2023. European Union Agency for Cybersecurity. https://www.enisa.europa.eu/publications/enisa-threat-landscape-2023

EUROPOL-Public Awareness and Prevention Guides. (2019). *Public Awareness and Prevention Guides*. EUROPOL.

Floridi, L. (2020). The Fight for Digital Sovereignty: What It Is, and Why It Matters, Especially for the EU. *Philosophy & Technology*, *33*(3), 369–378. DOI: 10.1007/s13347-020-00423-6 PMID: 35194548

Ha, S., & Kim, S. (2023). Developing a digital platform literacy framework. Econstor. https://www.econstor.eu/bitstream/10419/277969/1/Ha-Kim.pdf

Hashim, R., & Abdul Rahman, A. (2020). Peranan mule account dalam pengubahan wang haram di malaysia: Satu perbincangan melalui kajian kes. *International Journal of Social Science Research, 2*(4), 108–145. http://myjms.mohe.gov.my/index.php/ijssr/article/view/1159/

Herari, N. (2024). Piramida Kebutuhan dan Passion Economy: Pemenuhan Kebutuhan Diri melalui Media Digital di Indonesia. In Transformasi Komunikasi digital Menuju Indonesia Berkelanjutan: Komunikasi digital Dan Inovasi Bagi Masyarakat. Elex Media Komputindo. https://www.researchgate.net/publication/390760825_Piramida_Kebutuhan_dan_Passion_Economy_Pemenuhan_Kebutuhan_Diri_melalui_Media_Digital_di_Indonesia

Herari, N., & Marlina, M. (2024). Digital Marketing Transformation of Local MSME Through Instagram Account of Community: A Case Study of Paguyuban UMKM Kecamatan Bekasi Timur. In Albakri, M. (Ed.), *Digital transformation and innovation in emerging markets*. IGI Global Scientific Publishing., DOI: 10.4018/979-8-3373-0086-3.ch002

Herari, N., Waluyo, W., & Rubiyanto, R. (2025). Leading Alone, Leading Forward: Solopreneurs and the Quiet Power of the Passion Economy. In Paradiso-Testa, M. (Ed.), *The purpose of passion in leadership* (pp. 333–358). IGI Global Scientific Publishing., DOI: 10.4018/979-8-3373-2404-3.ch012

Hund, E. (2023). *The Influencer Industry: Constructing And Commodifying Authenticity On Social Media*. Publicly Accessible Penn Dissertations., DOI: 10.1353/book.110091

Iivari, N. (2020). Empowering children to make and shape our digital futures – from adults creating technologies to children transforming cultures. *The International Journal of Information and Learning Technology, 37*(5), 279–293. DOI: 10.1108/IJILT-03-2020-0023

James, B. D., Boyle, P. A., Yu, L., Han, S. D., & Bennett, D. A. (2020). Older and wiser: Age differences in susceptibility to investment fraud: The protective role of emotional intelligence. *Aging & Mental Health, 24*(5), 691–696. DOI: 10.1080/13607863.2018.1544211

Josella, T. (2025). Eksistensi dalam Klik: Fenomena "Apapun demi Konten" dalam Perspektif homo digitalis Budi Hardiman. Aradha: Journal of Divinity. *Peace and Conflict Studies, 5*(1), 57–74. DOI: 10.21460/aradha.2025.51.1419

Klein, C. (2023). Understanding the relevance of digital media in higher education. [IJTES]. *International Journal of Technology in Education and Science*, *7*(1), 71–82. DOI: 10.46328/ijtes.451

Li, Z., Li, H., & Wang, S. (2022). How multidimensional digital empowerment affects technology innovation performance: The moderating effect of adaptability to technology embedding. *Sustainability (Basel)*, *14*(23), 15916. DOI: 10.3390/su142315916

Marwick, A. E., & boyd, . (2014). Networked privacy: How teenagers negotiate context in social media. *New Media & Society*, *16*(7), 1051–1067. DOI: 10.1177/1461444814543995

Meira, S. (2025). Everything platforms. *SSRN*. https://doi.org/DOI: 10.2139/ssrn.5160171

Modic, D., Anderson, R., & Palomäki, J. (2018). We will make you like our research: The use of persuasion in scam emails. PLOS ONE, 13(9), e0204129. OECD / EUIPO. (2022). Dangerous Fakes: Trade in Counterfeit Goods that Pose Health, Safety and Environmental Risks. OECD Publishing, Paris. https://doi.org/DOI: 10.1371/journal.pone.0204129

Raza, M. S., Zhan, Q., & Rubab, S. (2020). Role of money mules in money laundering and financial crimes: A discussion through case studies. *Journal of Financial Crime*, *27*(3), 911–993. DOI: 10.1108/JFC-02-2020-0028

Topal, R., & Shargh, F. (2023). Teaching students how to find and identify reliable online sources: A series of exercises. *Journal of Political Science Education*, *19*(3), 475–484.

Riswanto, A., Zafar, T. S., P, M. A., Sunijati, E., Harto, B., Boari, Y., Astaman, P., Dassir, M., & Hikmah, A. N. (2023). Ekonomi KREATIF: Inovasi, Peluang, Dan Tantangan Ekonomi Kreatif Di Indonesia. PT. Sonpedia Publishing Indonesia.

Sisak, A. (2013). *How to Combat the Money Mule Phenomenon*. European Police Science & Research.

Thibaud, E. (2022). What's wrong with the passion economy? Daily Philosophy. https://daily-philosophy.com/ezechiel-thibaud-davidson-passion-economy/

Umboh, B. Y. (2023). Work Transformation in The Digital Era Changing the Public Values in Indonesia. https://www.researchgate.net/publication/374813686_WORK_TRANSFORMATION_IN_THE_DIGITAL_ERA_CHANGING_THE_PUBLIC_VALUES_IN_INDONESIA#:~:text=Digital%20transformation%20has%20a,access%20services%20from%20government%20and

UNCTAD. (2024, October 4). Creative economy booms, with services leading the growth. UN Trade and Development (UNCTAD). https://unctad.org/news/creative-economy-booms-services-leading-growth

Vallance, D. (2021, April 13). (Manuscript submitted for publication). The passion economy is the hustle culture antidote we all need. [| Dropbox Blog. https://blog.dropbox.com/topics/work-culture/the-passion-economy-is-the-hustle-culture-antidote]. *Work : A Journal of Prevention, Assessment, and Rehabilitation.*

Yu, L., Mottola, G., Barnes, L. L., Valdes, E. G., Wilson, R. S., & Bennett, D. A. (2022). Financial fragility and scam susceptibility in community-dwelling older adults. *Frontiers in Psychology*, *13*, 863870. DOI: 10.3389/fpsyg.2022.863870 PMID: 35484831

Chapter 2

AI-Enhanced Strategic Foresight:

Anticipating Risks and Opportunities in the Sustainable Digital Economy

Xolmirzayev Furqatbek Muxtarjonovich
Alfraganus University, Toshkent, Uzbekistan

Dilnoza Butanova
Mamun University, Khiva, Uzbekistan

R. N. Ravikumar
http://orcid.org/0009-0009-3705-1681
Marwadi University, Rajkot, India

Abdusamatov Alisher
Termez University of Economics and Service, Termez, Uzbekistan

S. Aarthi
http://orcid.org/0009-0006-9064-2091
Marwadi University, Rajkot, India

Christo George
Dayananda Sagar College of Engineering, Bengaluru, India

ABSTRACT

The rapid evolution of the digital economy is transforming industries, governance, and societies, presenting both unprecedented opportunities and sustainability challenges. This chapter explores how Artificial Intelligence can enhance strategic foresight by bridging gaps in decision-making under uncertainty. Traditional foresight methods often fail to capture the complexity and pace of digital disruption, climate risks, and socio-economic shifts. AI-driven tools such as machine learning, predictive analytics, and natural language processing enable the detection of weak signals, risk forecasting, and scenario modeling. Case studies in sustainable finance and renewable energy illustrate how AI-backed foresight improves resource efficiency, anticipates market volatility, and strengthens climate resilience. Ethical

DOI: 10.4018/979-8-3373-5052-3.ch002

considerations, including transparency, bias, and inclusivity, are discussed alongside hybrid models combining human judgment with AI intelligence. The chapter concludes that AI-enhanced foresight is a transformative capability that advances sustainable digital economies.

1. INTRODUCTION

The ecological sustainability of digital world implies that the new technological breakthrough and sustainability neem, to create a power of growth, inclusiveness and steadiness. The greater the integration of organizations and governments in the dynamic process of digitalization, the more complex balancing between economic competitiveness and environment and social responsibilities. Strategic foresight has therefore assumed a very vital skill because it allows the decision-makers the opportunity to plan in advance, adjust to the sustainability needs of the future, and hedge against the unforeseen. Nonetheless, the inter-relationship and speed of technological and socio-economic change increases beyond anything seen before and drives the traditional foresight models. Artificial Intelligence (AI) is now assisting in the ability to detect weak signals, process masses of data, and create predictive information. The use of AI in this chapter to enhance the practice of foresight equips companies with the tools to predict risks, use opportunities and align strategies towards sustainable development (J. Uddin & Chanda, 2025).

1.1 Context Of The Sustainable Digital Economy

The digital economy is changing sectors, cultures, and politics at a fast pace, and these technologies include cloud computing, IoT, big data, and AI, are the innovators. However, there are several benefits and pressing sustainability concerns of its development. Despite the ability of digitalization to make the use of resources more efficient, to optimize the use of renewable energy sources, and to offer inclusive access, the challenges of energy use and e-waste, as well as rising digital inequalities emerge. Growth, ecological stewardship and social equity must be balanced in order to have a sustainable digital economy. The principles of sustainability are to be implemented by companies and governments within the context of digital transformation, so that the innovation would allow reducing carbon footprints, raising the motivation towards a circular economy, and provide inclusive participation. This history shows that a system of innovation must find a middle ground between sustainable value creation and innovation by tapping into such a futuristic instrument as strategic foresight that can be aided by AI (Rosário & Dias, 2023).

1.2 The Emergence Of Strategic Foresight

The strategic foresight can be termed as a future challenge, opportunity and uncertainty planning process in order to aid the decisions taken to result in long term activities. Traditional foresight as demonstrated by the use of scenario planning, trend analysis and risk analysis enables organizations with the capability to anticipate disruptive changes. Foresight is an idea that has become very relevant in the digital-era and industries are confronted with the problem of climate change, regulatory complexity, cyber threats and emerging socio-economic needs. Contrary to the reactive one, the foresight is focused on the active thinking and resilience-building and strategic agility. It was also lifted with great proximity to the increasing awareness that the notions of sustainability and competitiveness are two sides of a coin. Through incorporation of foresight into the strategic management, the organizations are able to offer mediums that cannot solely be employed to break down threats but can also be employed to exploit opportunities that could develop inclusive and sustainable growth (Z. Zhang et al., 2022).

1.3 Role Of Artificial Intelligence In Shaping Future-Oriented Strategies

The contribution of Artificial Intelligence on achieving a better foresight is the ability to predict and react to future situations that are too complicated to do so. With the assistance of AI technologies, machine learning, natural language processing, predictive analytics, one can process large amounts of data instantly and identify weak signals and define how a new trend emerges in the economic, environmental, and social domain. These features also enhance the forsight and precision since businesses can simulate various outcomes, distribute resources most effectively and evaluate systemic risks. Examples of AI-based applications of foresight include renewable energy predictors, sustainable finance, and resilient supply chains. Noteworthy, AI assists human judgment, which helps leaders make swift, inclusive, and responsible decisions. Implementing AI into the foresight processes will allow the organizations to abandon the reactive-driven strategies and adopt the proactive and sustainability-oriented innovation (Krasota et al., 2020). The figure 1 shows how AI facilitates strategic foresight by helping with risk assessment, predictive analytics, NLP, machine learning, scenario modeling and resource optimization.

Figure 1. AI's Role in Future Strategies

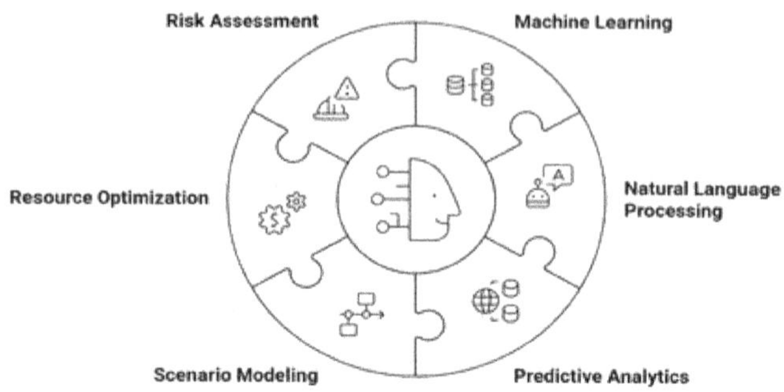

1.4 Chapter Structure

To provide a general concept of AI-enhanced strategic foresight in the sustainable digital economy, this chapter has been split into eleven sections. In the Introduction, the background is given and the topicality of AI-based foresight is proven. The Background to the Study brings foresight into the sphere of the issues of digital transformation and sustainability. Research Objectives outlines the rationale of why the research is needed; followed by a Conceptual Model of how AI will be implemented in foresight. The Research Methodology gives design and analysing tools and the Literature Review matches theory with objectives. Findings are of application and case studies through which future Research directions are accessed. Managerial Implications address the practical implications and Conclusion gives the conclusions. Lastly, there is the Key Terms and Definitions, which provide people with the clarity, to present them with the initial impression of the arguments presented in the chapter.

2. BACKGROUND TO THE STUDY

Digital transformation and sustainability interaction is altering the approach to strategy formulation and handling risks and opportunities by organizations in their development process. Financial, supply chain, energy and governance and sustainability innovation require the world to be digitalized with growth inclusive, resilient and environmentally friendly. However, the uncertain pace of technological change and crises in the world (climate change, pandemics and cyber threats) makes the long-term planning more challenging. Basic forecasting tools are not usually able to reflect such a magnitude and rate of change. In this respect, strategic foresight becomes an essential organizational skill that must be developed by organizations that want to stay competitive and follow the principles of sustainability. Subsections below discuss international trends in digital-sustainability, the drawbacks of legacy foresight and the reasons why foresight became a strategic management requirement (Niu, 2021).

2.1 Global Trends In Digitalization And Sustainability

The world economy is becoming digitalized with the use of artificial intelligence, blockchain, big data analytics, and the Internet of Things (IoT). The innovations enhance speed, connectivity and innovations in industries. At the same time, there are increasing sustainability demands in the form of climate change, carbon cut commitments and demands of inclusive growth. Governments and corporations are both changing their approaches to carbon neutrality, circular economies and shifting to renewable energy sources. Such goals can be achieved through the use of powerful tools delivered by the process of digitalization, including predictive analytics to convert energy use to its maximum or blockchain to enhance supply chain transparency. It, however, likewise possesses its e-waste, data privacy, and energy consuming threats. The consciousness of these convergent trends gives the basis on which foresight policies will be developed that will be utilized to balance the needs of digital growth and sustainable development (Arokodare & Asikhia, 2020).

2.2 Challenges Of Conventional Foresight Approaches

Some of the traditional foresight techniques that are in existence today such as the trend monitoring, Delphi techniques and scenario planning which is scenario-based have been discovered not to be in line with the vibrancy and intricacy of the new digital economy. The solutions are small-scale solutions to answer large, unstructured data streams or react fast to dynamically changing risks, including a cyberattack, market uncertainty or geopolitical disruption. Moreover, the classical paradigms are marked by the tendency to employ the straightforward cause and effect intersections rather than taking into account the interdependence of global systems where environmental, economic, and technological are dynamic. The losses of opportunities or failure of risk preparation can be the consequences of this small vision. The companies therefore require more adaptive and real time-oriented foresight methods that are data-driven. The Artificial Intelligence is narrowing this gap by broadening the foresight capabilities by possessing a predictive nature, an ability to recognize patterns and simulating situations (Cao, 2024a). The table 1 highlights major shortcomings of conventional foresight approaches to the dynamics of sustainable digital economy.

Table 1. Challenges of Conventional Foresight Approaches

Challenge	Description
Data Overload	Traditional methods cannot process large volumes of unstructured data effectively.
Slow Adaptability	Static models fail to keep pace with rapidly changing technological and market dynamics.
Linear Assumptions	Often based on cause-effect logic, overlooking interconnected global systems.
Limited Risk Anticipation	Weak at predicting emergent risks like cyber threats or climate-driven disruptions.
Lack of Real-Time Insights	Unable to provide continuous monitoring and dynamic scenario updates.

2.3 Strategic Foresight As A Core Competency In Strategic Management

Strategic foresight has become a significant element of organizational competence that is aligning long term sustainability and strategic responsiveness. Unlike reactive planning, foresight is also more concerned about being proactive in relation to probing into the disturbing forces that are disruptive and planning a variety of ways about what might occur in the future. The strategic management approach assists the leaders in considering the balance between the organizational goals and the arising risks, market trends and the requirements of sustainability. It assists foresight-driven companies in detecting weak signals at an earlier stage and also in experimenting with different futures and restructuring business models. One such area is the foresight that may aid energy companies forecast the direction of transition to renewables or governments to be prepared to climate-induced migration. This will entail inclusion of the foresight in the management processes such that the decisions that are made are not merely competitive, but are also decisive and sociable. Foresight has now become a significant instrument to guide the transformation of strategy as the digitalization-sustainability two worlds collide (Adegbile et al., 2017).

3. RESEARCH OBJECTIVES

As Artificial Intelligence assumes the role of strategic foresight, it opens new opportunities at the very thin and thick of sustainable digital economy. The questions that are asked to achieve the research objectives are structured in a way that they do not utter any words about the technical potential of AI during the foresight process but rather how the latter can be used to ensure sustainability, inclusiveness and accountability. Sequencing aims, this chapter must position the map in a manner that it understands the channel that AI can re-invent the models of foresight, create the risk preparedness and change the strategic management practices to align with the global sustainability goals.

- To explore the integration of AI technologies (Machine Learning, NLP, Predictive Analytics) into strategic foresight processes for sustainable decision-making.
- To identify opportunities and risks emerging from the digital economy, including climate threats, market volatility, and technological disruptions.
- To evaluate case applications of AI-enhanced foresight in sectors such as sustainable finance, renewable energy, and digital supply chains.
- To examine ethical and governance challenges (algorithmic bias, transparency, data governance) linked with AI-driven foresight systems.
- To propose a hybrid foresight framework that combines human judgment with AI intelligence for accountable, inclusive, and anticipatory strategic management.

4. CONCEPTUAL MODEL

The AI-enhanced strategic foresight conceptual model integrates the theoretical material in strategic management with the capabilities of the artificial intelligence. This model depicts how companies can organize and bring in AI systematically in order to predict threats, new opportunities as well as align the strategies with the demands of sustainability. It provides the theoretical frameworks of foresight, which are more focused on long-term vision, scenario planning, and managing uncertainties and includes the analytical capabilities of AI-based tools. Big data, environmental indicators, and market signals are the inputs that are fed into AI algorithms and give outputs in the form of actionable insights, risk forecasts and strategic scenarios. More importantly, the model emphasizes the complementary nature of human judgment, making it ethical, culturally and contextually relevant. Foresight is further refined by feedback loop and adaptive learning, thus being dynamic and resilient (Poperwi et al., 2025). The figure 2 demonstrates how AI processes inputs into foresight outputs, complemented by human judgment and strengthened through feedback loops and adaptive learning.

Figure 2. Conceptual Model of AI-Enhanced Strategic Foresight

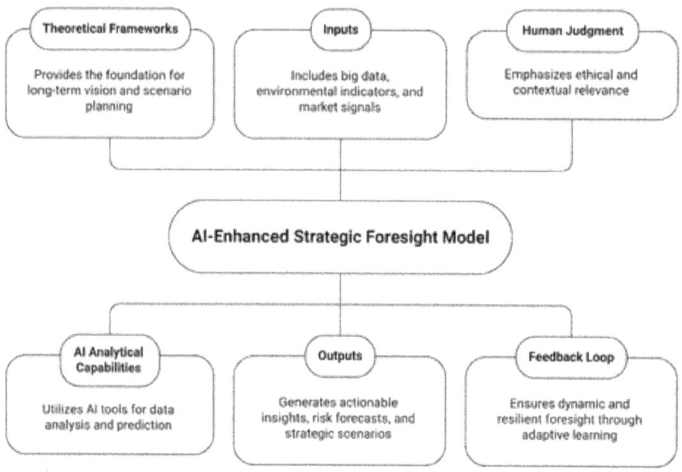

4.1 Theoretical Foundations Of Strategic Foresight

Systems thinking, scenario planning and long-term strategic management are the basis of strategic foresight. It is theoretically based on the need to prepare against uncertainty, identify weak signals and envision the possible and plausible future(s). Conventional theories of foresight are based on futures, risk, and organizational strategy to create resiliency and agility. These foundations are further applicable in the digital economy where disruptions are common and complicated. It is through the establishment of foresight on theoretical basis that organizations can have a systematic method of predicting change rather than responding to change. By incorporating sustainability concepts in the foresight theory, strategies should not only be competitive, but socially responsible and environmentally friendly. These foundations are used to improve the foresight with AI technologies, to relate classical approaches to intelligent analytics (Panjaitan et al., 2022).

4.2 AI-Driven Foresight Model: Inputs, Processes, Outputs

The AI-based foresight model starts with the inputs, which can be structured and unstructured information on the digital platforms, environmental signals, socio-economic trends, and industry signals. These inputs are analyzed with the use of AI, including machine learning, predictive analytics, and natural language processing to identify weak signals and emerging trends. These processes include scenario generation, risk mapping, trend simulations, which investigate the potential future. Finally, the outputs are generated in the form of information that can be acted upon, which predicts the risk, strategic opportunities, and decision support systems of the managers and policymakers. Foresight can be transformed by AI into a live and dynamic skill by automatizing the data analysis research and enhancing predictive power. The model is not solely proposing predictive accuracy to the organizations but also the capability to proactively adjust the strategies in a constantly dynamic sustainable digital economy (Linkov et al., 2018).

4.3 Integration Of Human Judgment And Machine Intelligence

In spite of the fact that AI enhances strategic capabilities in analytical accuracy, human judgement is critical in terms of situational, ethical, and diversity. Machine intelligence is especially helpful in discovering hidden patterns, situations and data complexity but does not offer the cultural knowledge, values and good ethical sense that humans have. The integration of human judgment and AI ensures that the foresight outputs are social and ethically responsible and that the outputs are also aligned with the organisational vision. This is the most appropriate hybrid strategy to serve the gap between the two disciplines: AI provides evidence-based data, and the human foresight specialists do interpret results based on the societal, cultural, and environmental background, in fact. Such an integration can be used to minimize the risk of algorithm bias and establish a just setting in the field of strategic choices. Lastly, the human machine cooperation increases the foresight with the combination of the intelligence, empathy and responsibility in strategic management (Niguse et al., 2025).

4.4 Feedback Loops And Adaptive Learning In Foresight Systems

The effective foresight model must be dynamic and evolving with the new information and the evolving situations. The availability of the feedback loops allows organizations to evaluate the outcomes of foresight, contrast predictions with the real shifts in the world and change strategies accordingly. Using the case of AI, where the system anticipates the instabilities in the market wrongly, the system can fit in the data that will rectify the mistake in the next prediction. Adaptive learning mechanism can help foresight models to become better as time passes, often based on reinforcement learning and continuous data updates. The loops also serve the purpose of promoting the organizational learning according to which human and machine acquire the ability to develop a collective foresight. Such flexibility gives resilience, pro-active and foresight systems. This dynamic feedback and analysis, combined with AI, will assist organisations to not predetermined but reactionary to the complexity of the sustainable digital economy (Sherson et al., 2023).

5. RESEARCH METHODOLOGY

The methodology, under which this chapter will operate, will be based on the systematic study of the possibility of applying the concept of Artificial Intelligence to enhance strategic foresight within the sustainable digital economy. It is based on the mixed-method approach, i.e., the qualitative analysis of case studies and the quantitative analysis of AI models and data. The secondary resources will consist of scholarly literature, policy reports and industry reports and the real-life examples of AI implementation in the field of sustainability. Analytical techniques such as predictive analytics, Natural Language Processing (NLP) and scenario modeling are used in the uncovering the patterns, prediction risks and proving of foresight frameworks. Despite the fact that such a methodology provides powerful information regarding AI-enhanced foresight, it also presents several inherent limitations concerning biasing the quality of the data, transparency of the algorithms, and diversity of situations (Associate & Hamroqulovna, 2025).

5.1 Research Design

The mixed-methods research design will be used in the research due to the complexity of AI-based strategic foresight. The qualitative part will entail analyzing the case studies of the areas of renewable energy, sustainable finance, and digital supply chains to perceive how companies apply the practice of foresight. The quantitative part will be dedicated to the experimental study of AI models, simulations, and datasets to verify the predictability and the outcomes of the situation. It is here that a moderated perspective is achieved, the qualitative insights provide a perspective and depth yet the quantitative evidences provide validation and generalization. The design is also meant to be comparative cross-industrial study in order to know the extent to which flexible foresight structures are. The combination of these approaches allows the research to present the entire results, which can be applied not only to the theoretical framework of the sustainable digital economy but also be used in practice (Van Rooy, 2024). The table 2 summarizes the design strategies used in the research to ensure that both depth and generalizability is captured.

Table 2. Research Design Approaches

Design Type	Description
Qualitative	In-depth case studies and contextual analysis.
Quantitative	Data-driven analysis using AI models and simulations.
Mixed-Methods	Integration of qualitative insights with quantitative validation.

5.2 Data Sources (Case Studies, Secondary Data, AI Models)

The data required in order to carry out this study is found in three primary sources. First of all, the case studies in such industries as sustainable finance, renewable energy, and digital supply chains will be selected because they provide actual examples of the ways AI-based foresight can be implemented. Second, peer reviewed articles, policy frameworks, industry reports, and global sustainability guides are used as secondary data to give it theoretical underpinning. Third, unstructured datasets are made in AI models and simulations such as environmental indicators, market signals, and order of socio-economic trends. This multiplicity of sources ensures reliability, credibility and multiplicity of viewpoints. Case studies provide practical activities, secondary data places findings in the real-world context, and AI-based models prove the predictions of the foresight (M. Z. Uddin et al., 2024). These sources collectively offer a rather holistic approach to investigate risks, opportunities, and ethical issues of AI in foresight. The following table 3 shows the main sources of data utilized in the analysis of the AI-enhanced foresight.

Table 3. Data Sources Utilized

Source	Description
Case Studies	Real-world examples from finance, energy, and supply chains.
Secondary Data	Academic articles, reports, and policy documents.
AI Models	Simulations and algorithms analyzing structured/unstructured datasets.

5.3 Analytical Techniques (Predictive Analytics, NLP, Scenario Modeling)

In order to examine the application of AI in foresight, the paper uses three analytical methods. Predictive analytics can be used to determine risks and opportunities by processing large datasets and making predictions about the future trends in a field, like energy demand or industry changes. Natural Language Processing (NLP) allows extracting insights out of unstructured textual material, such as policy documents, social media trends, and industry reports, and supporting the identification of weak signals and new stories. Scenario modeling provides the possibility of constructing a variety of plausible futures that combine sustainability indicators with technological and economic factors. When used in combination, these methods offer an integrated perspective of the practice of foresight. The methodology builds upon the predictive potential of foresight and provides decision-makers with practical solutions to sustainable strategy development by using AI-driven analytics (Murthy et al., 2024). The following table 4 describes the fundamental analytical methods employed to enhance foresight activities in sustainable digital economy.

Table 4. Analytical Techniques for AI-Enhanced Foresight

Technique	Description
Predictive Analytics	Forecasts risks and opportunities by analyzing large datasets for future patterns.
Natural Language Processing (NLP)	Extracts insights from unstructured data like policies, reports, and social media to detect weak signals.
Scenario Modeling	Builds multiple plausible futures by combining sustainability, technological, and economic variables.

5.4 Limitations Of The Methodology

Although the selected methodology provides useful information, it is important to note that there are a number of limitations. To begin with, predictive accuracy is affected by the quality and availability of data, particularly in sustainability, where quality datasets might be in short supply. Second, AI models are subject to algorithmic transparency and interpretability issues, as there is no transparency in their models. Third, case studies, although highly detailed, are not necessarily applicable to industries or areas. Moreover, the methodology is both time-consuming and resource-consuming because it needs to be updated on a regular basis to keep up with the dynamic digital landscape. Lastly, the subjective biases related to the inclusion of human judgment in AI-driven models have to be avoided, carefully. The awareness of these limitations offers a fair view and underlines the spheres where the further works and improvement of the methods should be taken (Tariq, 2025). The following table 5 provides summaries of some important limitations that can influence the reliability and generalizability of research.

Table 5. Limitations of the Methodology

Limitation	Description
Data Quality	Inconsistent or incomplete datasets may reduce accuracy.
Algorithmic Transparency	Black-box AI models limit interpretability.
Generalizability	Case-specific insights may not apply across industries.
Resource Intensive	Requires significant time, expertise, and computational power.

6. LITERATURE REVIEW

The strategic foresight and the sustainable digital economy literature reveals the role of organizations in coping with uncertainty whilst incorporating the concept of sustainability. Classical foresight approaches had focused on scenario planning, long-term vision and systems thinking, but the Artificial Intelligence in recent scholarship has been seen as transformative in improving predictive accuracy and adaptability. Research regarding AI applications reveals the extension of traditional foresight by machine learning and NLP, which is implemented through the analysis of large amounts of data and the Identification of weak signals. Parallel research highlights sustainability dangers like climate change, cybersecurity, and digital inequality, and also increases ethical issues relating to algorithmic bias, governance and responsibility in AI-enhanced foresight systems (Postma & Yeoman, 2021).

6.1 Strategic Management And Foresight: Historical Perspectives

The concept of strategic foresight has its roots in systems theory and futures studies as a long-term tool of business and policy planning. Initial literature focused on scenario planning, Delphi techniques, and trend analysis to predict the risk and opportunity of the uncertain environment. Researchers like Peter Schwartz emphasized the need to be farsighted in order to develop resilience and make organizations ready to disruptive futures. In the field of strategic management, foresight became a strategic management competence, which connects uncertainty management and competitive advantage. It traditionally paid attention to economic and market variables, but with the increased influence of globalization and technological shocks, foresight started to pay attention to the sustainability and socio-political aspects. This change can be related to the increasing awareness that foresight needs to be focused not only on competitiveness but also on environmental stewardship and social responsibility (Al Mokdad, 2025).

6.2 AI Applications In Forecasting And Scenario Planning

Recent articles indicate how Artificial Intelligence is changing the forecasting and scenario planning. Machine learning can enable an organization to process large amounts of both structured and unstructured data, as well as recognizing patterns in the data that may not be identified by traditional algorithms. Foresight can be enhanced by Natural Language Processing (NLP), which can analyze policy documentation, news and social media and provide prior notification of weak signals and risks that are developing. Scenario building may be supported with the help of predictive analytics in energy demand forecasting, financial market change, and disruption in the supply chain. The researchers assume that AI does not only make the predictions more accurate, but it also enables the real-time predictions and dynamics. However, critics caution that depending on AI too much may lack context, cultural, and ethical factors, and thus hybrid approaches to foresight considerations founded on both human and machine intelligence must be employed more frequently (Criveanu, 2023).

6.3 Sustainable Digital Economy And Emerging Risks

The point of contact between digital transformation and sustainability opens the gates to efficiency, transparency, and innovation along with it creates new threats. Research has suggested that the benefits of AI and blockchain when applied to the work of AI and blockchain include better allocation of resources, forecast ability of renewable energy, and green financial platforms. The threats however are the growing volume of energy consumed by data centres, geographical variations in access to digital facilities as well as vulnerability to cyber-crime. Researchers emphasize the issue that the sustainability of the digital economy needs to be obtained through the equalization of the progress of technology with the sustainability of the environment and the social environment. Studies also note that organizations that practice foresight are in a good position to anticipate systemic risks such as climate-based disruption or changes in regulations. The existing literature is clear about why there is an urgent need of AI-enabled structures of foresight that address not just the attitude of maximizing opportunities, but also the strategy of reducing risk in viable digital economies (Nosratabadi et al., 2023).

6.4 Ethical And Governance Challenges In AI-Driven Decision Making

The ethical and governance aspects of artificial intelligence foresight have turned into an international concern. Researchers underline the dangers of the algorithmic bias, transparency, and the probability of the non-representation of the marginalized voice in the system of AI-related decisions. The data governance problem has been reappearing especially in the matters of privacy, accountability and responsible handling of personal and environmental data. The need to have Explainable AI (XAI) is a focus of the literature in order to provide confidence to the products of foresight and propose hybrid solutions to human control in the occurrence of the algorithm predictions. Good governance structures, intersectoral cooperation and international laws should accompany policy-oriented research undertakings that will control the use of artificial intelligence in strategic foresight. These are issues that should be tackled to ensure that foresight systems become inclusive, ethical and socially responsible as well as to make it technologically advanced (Liao, 2024). The table 6 points out the important ethical and governance issues that determine the reliability and accountability of AI-enabled decision-making.

Table 6. Ethical and Governance Challenges in AI-Driven Foresight

Challenge	Description
Algorithmic Bias	Risk of unfair or discriminatory outcomes due to biased training data.
Lack of Transparency	Black-box models limit understanding of how decisions are made.
Data Privacy	Concerns over misuse or unauthorized access to sensitive information.
Accountability Gaps	Difficulty in assigning responsibility for AI-driven decisions.
Inclusivity Concerns	Marginalized groups may be excluded from decision-making processes.

7. RESULTS/DISCUSSION

The results of the present study suggest that AI-based strategic foresight prepares organizations with the long-awaited critical skills to anticipate risk and opportunities linked to the sustainable digital economy. The practice of foresight has become a real strategy and is no longer a theoretical idea by applying AI into practice fields, including sustainable finance and renewable energy. Case studies are used to emphasize how predictive analytics, machine learning, and natural language processing are helping decision-makers to efficiently allocate resources, reduce risks, and align to sustainability objectives. More so, AI enhances the ability to predict climate, market, and cybersecurity shocks and counteract organizational, ethical, and cultural issues. The article highlights the increasing significance of hybrid models of foresight, in which human judgment is used to provide complementary insights to AI and make the process accountable, inclusive, and resilient over the long run (Tan et al., 2024).

7.1 Case Studies: AI In Sustainable Finance, Renewable Energy

The practical examples of how AI-based foresight affects the decision-making process in the field where sustainability is a crucial aspect will be presented in case studies. Sustainable finance is one of such ways, and financial institutions use AI to compute ESGs, systemic risks, and invest directly in low-carbon projects. Renewable energy demonstrates the effectiveness of energy production in terms of predictive analytics, the effectiveness of the relation between supply and demand, and grid stability. Such two instances prove that foresight is a strategic aspect of processing complex data to that which can be acted on i.e. intelligence. These applications highlight how AI can be used to proactively pursue the goals of sustainability to ensure that economic growth is aligned with the environmental concern. The combination of them could be termed as best practices in providing foresight into the digital economy strategy (Xianbin & Qiong, 2021). The figure 3 illustrates how AI supports sustainable practices by balancing ESG and risk analysis with energy efficiency, stability, and renewable energy initiatives.

Figure 3. AI's Role in Sustainable Practices

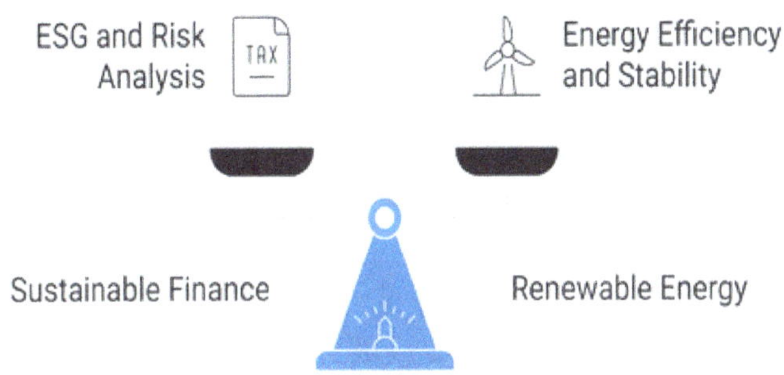

7.1.1 AI In Sustainable Finance

The sustainable finance has been the focal point of the worldwide shift to low-carbon economies and AI is one of the key facilitators of visibility. The size and complexity of available information provide a setback to financial institutions in assessing Environmental, Social, and Governance (ESG) performance. Big data can be interpreted using AI algorithms to help forecast sustainability performance with a wide range of data, including corporate disclosures or satellite images. In the case of machine learning, there are natural examples of early warning of climate-related financial risks, which include assets stranded in the fossil fuel industry or volatility in green bond markets. Natural Language Processing (NLP) increases foresight through use of weak signals in policy changes, social media, and financial news as early warning system on changes in regulations or markets (Ravikumar & Aarthi, 2025). Also, ESG scoring by AI enhances the comparison and reporting of the investment options, allowing investors to match portfolios to sustainable objectives. When finance takes a form of foresight, institutions will be able to predict risks like tightening of climate policies or consumers becoming more interested in green products, and at the same time point out opportunities of growth in renewable energy, carbon markets, and sustainable infrastructure. In this way AI-powered foresight can enable the use of finance as the instrument of risk management and the generator of sustainable innovation (Curtis & Mont, 2020). The figure 4 demonstrates how AI supports sustainable finance through big data interpretation, NLP, risk management, machine learning, ESG scoring, and identifying innovation opportunities.

Figure 4. AI's Role in Sustainable Finance

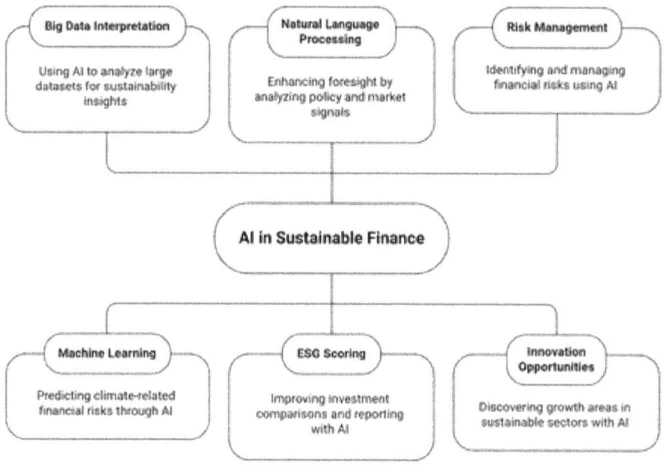

7.1.2 AI In Renewable Energy

One industry, where AI-based foresight can be applied to address volatility and achieve the greatest sustainability outcomes, is the renewable energy industry. Wind and solar, which are renewable energy sources, are not regulated, and it is harder to ensure that supply and demand are balanced, as well as long-term planning. Predictive analytics and AI, in general, enable the determination of the degree of output by predicting the energy output with a high degree of accuracy referencing to the weather conditions, sensor input, and previous output patterns. One such case is that the machine learning algorithm can calculate the variations in the output of a solar panel or a wind turbine, and this lets the grid operators plan more efficiently in energy storage and allocation. Scenario modeling also supports the foresight as it helps to simulate about the future in terms of shifting climate patterns, policy frameworks and market demand. The application of the AI tools exposing the dangers of grid instability or storage deficit may provide the feasible answers to the resilient infrastructure investment. Moreover, AI is applied to predictively service the energy assets to reduce the downtimes and extend the equipment life. It is an offensive strategy that involves cost reduction and helps in the carbon reduction objectives.

One should add that vision is not limited to the manner of limiting the risks only, but also to the manner of harnessing the chances of integrating renewables into broader Smart energy. By creating foresight and AI, the renewable energy sector will be in a situation to accelerate its role in global sustainability; making the clean energy transitions sustainable not only concerning efficiency but also concerning resilience and action orientation in future (Ivanova et al., 2019). The figure 5 maps AI applications in renewable energy across complexity and impact, highlighting uses from basic sensor analysis to predictive analytics, scenario modeling, and predictive maintenance.

Figure 5. AI Applications in Renewable Energy

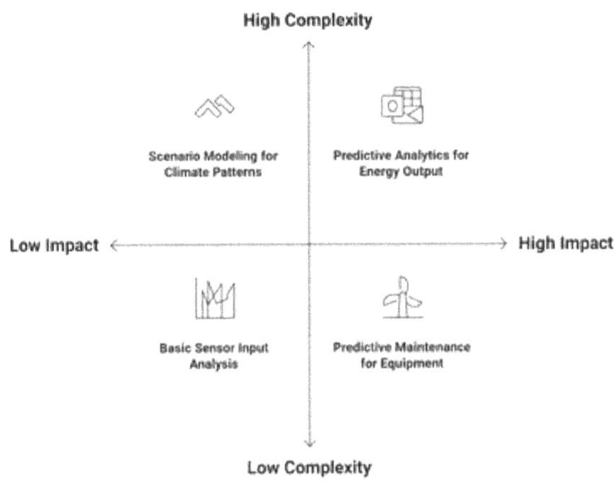

7.2 Anticipating Climate, Market, And Cybersecurity Risks

Market-focused, climate-focused, and cybersecurity-focused prediction of more complex risks with advanced AI foresight can enhance resilience to an even greater extent. During climate foresight, extreme weather AI models that simulate the impact can also help in preparation of the infrastructure and supply chains to respond to such an event in advance. Predictive analytics in market foresight seeks to predict the occurrence of financial volatility, changes in customer preferences, and regulatory changes in order to enable businesses to reposition strategies before they become disrupted. The reduction of cybersecurity threats, which become particularly important in digital economies, is achieved through AI-based anomaly detection and predictive threat modeling which offer early warning of threat and vulnerabilities. All of these foresight uses illustrate how AI provides organizations with the responsiveness to plan against systemic disruption, trade competitiveness with sustainability and resilience in unstable and highly dynamic global contexts (Cao, 2024b). The table 7 is a summary of the benefits of AI-enhanced foresight to organizations in forecasting and planning various types of risk.

Table 7. Anticipating Climate, Market, and Cybersecurity Risks

Risk Category	Description
Climate Risks	AI models forecast extreme weather, resource scarcity, and long-term climate impacts.
Market Risks	Predictive analytics detect financial volatility, regulatory changes, and demand shifts.
Cybersecurity Risks	AI-driven anomaly detection identifies threats, vulnerabilities, and potential cyberattacks.

7.3 Towards Hybrid (Human + AI) Foresight Models

Although AI has provided better predictive power, foresight should always be pegged on human judgment so that it is ethical, cultural, and contextual. Hybrid foresight models are models that integrate machine intelligence with human expertise to enable organizations to exploit the merits of either (Aarthi et al., 2025). AI provides factual data and trends and predicts the future, whereas humans process findings through the prism of values, social relations, and business interests. Such integration will deal with the risk of bias in the algorithms and will foster accountability and inclusiveness of the decision-making process. According to case-studies, hybrid models lead to trust since the models align technological forecasts with the expectations of stakeholders. These models are the future of strategic foresight, incorporating human responsibility with AI accuracy, making decisions both proactive, sustainable, and determined by long-term objectives of society (Kong et al., 2024). The figure 6 represents how machine intelligence will be combined with human knowledge, balancing information-based findings, trends, and future outlooks with values, social forces, and organizational objectives towards sustainable strategic foresight.

Figure 6. Towards Hybrid (Human + AI) Foresight Models

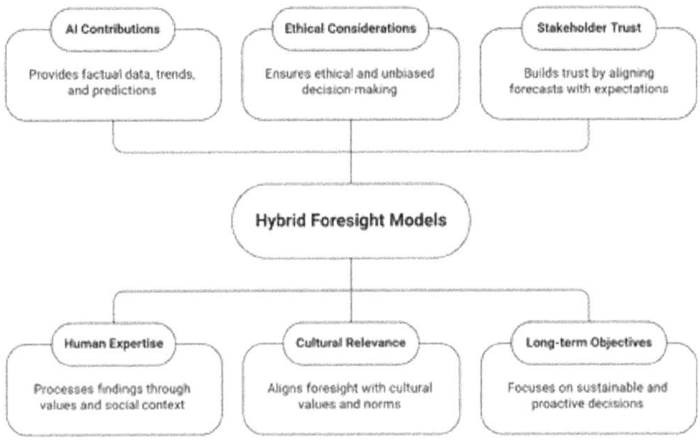

8. FURTHER RESEARCH

Strategic foresight is still in the early stages of using AI and thus requires to be examined in more detail to adapt its global, technical and ethical facets. Future research needs to dwell on cross-border co-operation where foresight models will be able to take into consideration a diversity of information and include the perspectives of other economies. On the same note, there is also a need to make AI models transparent and explainable to ensure that trust and accountability are created in the foresight results. Research ought to be undertaken in order to see that we reach an equilibrium between predictive strength and ethics by devising algorithm interpretable algorithm and governance structures. Their development will also strengthen the practice of foresight by rendering them universal and visible worldwide and in accordance with the evolving demands of the sustainable digital economy (Boman & Heger, 2019).

8.1 Expansion Of AI In Cross-Border Foresight Collaboration

Key global issues like global climate change, pandemics, and security of digital data do not recognize national borders and require frameworks of foresight that are no longer limited to organizational or country silos. Further studies are needed on the aspects of how AI can facilitate cross-border foresight cooperation by combining various datasets of different regions and industries. Collective risks and opportunities can be modeled by using AI-based platforms, which can balance economic, environmental, and social indicators, and thus enable policy-makers, businesses, and other international organizations to do so. As an example, adaptive infrastructure planning can be informed by cross-national information on the risks of climate, and global market foresight can be informed by predicting supply chain risks. The obstacles to collaboration such as data sovereignty, privacy laws, and unequal access to AI technologies must also be studied. Through these challenges, AI-based foresight can create collective intelligence, global resilience, and common ways to sustainable outcomes (Lu, 2024).

8.2 Enhancing Transparency And Explainability In AI Models

The absence of transparency and explainability of the results of the algorithm is one of the most critical limitations of the AI-driven foresight. When the decision-makers fail to understand how to compute the insights, black-box models can present accurate predictions at the expense of the credibility. The emerging wave of research projects must, therefore, be devoted to Explicable AI (XAI) methods that are understandable and, at the same time, do not influence the strength of analytics. The interpretable machine learning, visual analytics and model-agnostic explanations are pursued to promote the performance of foresight by assuring that the predictions of the model can be interpreted by the managers, policymakers and other interested parties. Additional relevant studies should be conducted on the governing mechanisms that would enhance transparency in utilizing the data, the model training, and the decision-making process. Such development is critical in building trust and accountability as well as other ethical concerns like bias and exclusion. The increased introjection and acceptance within the sustainability contexts would be achievable when AI-enhanced foresight is more transparent (Nasiri et al., 2022).

9. MANAGERIAL IMPLICATIONS

The short-term effects of the AI-driven foresight are applied to the managerial practice and rearrange the manner in which governance and strategies and organizational culture. Incorporating the AI insights into the strategic management, a leader will be able to enhance the corporative responsibility, resource allocation, and competitiveness in the long-term. Foresight also forms the basis of resilience and therefore organizations are offered a chance to anticipate and modify plans in advance. Meanwhile, after an innovation and adaptability culture has been built, the sight will no longer be restricted in the top level decision-making, but will be provided throughout the organization, making all levels involved in it. These managerial connotations are what are contributing to the need to adopt a foresight that is techno-influenced in the name of responsible leadership and sustainable business practices (Yang et al., 2023).

9.1 Implications For Corporate Governance

The corporate governance framework should be revised to be equipped with AI-enhanced foresight as a critical decision-making tool. The boards and executive are now being burdened with the responsibility of, besides financial performance, the long-term sustainability and social responsibility. The predictive vision of regulatory changes, climate risks, and market new trends is offered to the governance organizations by AI-based foresight in order to take pro-active policies. Through foresight, the governance structures will be able to gauge the risks of ESGs, and ensure that they meet the sustainability requirements and anticipate the needs of stakeholders (Ravikumar et al., 2025). However, the application of AI also requires the presentation of ethical imperatives, control regulations and responsibility systems. To maintain the existence of the trust, the algorithmic decision-making should be transparent and should address the bias and should be inclusively represented. Reintegration of governance with foresight improves accountability and gives resilience to the governance, and aligns organizational strategies to global sustainability demands (Y. Zhang & Jin, 2023).

9.2 Strategic Resource Allocation And Risk Management

The dilemma of resource scarcity among unpredictable environments is usually an issue that managers should grapple with. The AI-driven foresight could be used in making decisions based on data and could be generated through priority areas that could be invested in, predict demand, and map potential risks. To mention a few, predictive models could be applied to identify the most sustainable infrastructure projects and scenario analysis could be applied to identify market disruption or geopolitical threats. It will also enable the leaders to view the resources more strategically by balancing between the short-term gains and the long-term sustainability. It also helps in risk management as foresight helps in identifying weak signs of risks like cyberattacks, ineffective supply chains, or even climate change before it occurs. This will facilitate managers to quantify contingency plans, diversify investments and proactively re-strategize policies. The fact that foresight is incorporated in the way resources are distributed not only makes the organization more efficient, it also helps them to become resilient to the constantly changing world (Fan et al., 2022).

9.3 Building A Culture Of Anticipatory Innovation

Along with the factor of governance and resource allocation, cultural factors of organizational foresight can be identified. The establishment of an anticipatory innovation culture will make sure that the foresight is not considered an executive privilege anymore, but a shared idea across departments and teams and in jobs per se. It includes being experimental, having people think in the scenarios, and employees being empowered to work with AI-based insights. Organizational learning and flexibility can be encouraged through training programs, cross functional teams, joint foresight workshops and cross functional teams among others. Notably, anticipatory cultures fill the intermediary between the scientific vision of technology and human imagination to ensure that innovation is an encompassing and morally-directed process. To demonstrate, the AI systems can synthesize knowledge and situational assumption in the form of co-production of a solution with workers. This type of culture in an organization can not only enhance agility but it also positions organizations in a position where they are always inventive yet they are also in contact with sustainability goals (Lin & Mao, 2024).

10. CONCLUSION

The digital economy is becoming sustainable because the digital economy that is transforming how organisations conduct their business, compete and play their social role is becoming sustainable. That is, AI-based strategic foresight can be encapsulated as a transformational capability that will counter the gap in decision-making that is informed by uncertainty. The chapter has also identified how the analytical accuracy and malleability of the synthetic smartness is altering foresight (whereby in the past foresight relied on the traditional scenario-planning and long-range forecasting). Based on the case studies of sustainability finance and renewable energy it is shown that AI-backed foresight may have the potential to assist organisations in forecasting the risks, being more efficient in managing their resources and streamlining their strategies to the demands of sustainability. AI is a powerful tool of highlighting weak signals, forecasting disruptive eventualities, and simulating a range of potential futures. Such functions can help organizations to be capable of forecasting climate risk, responding to market volatility and increasing cybersecurity resiliency.

In the meantime, foresight is not limited to risk mitigation, and it is also interested in creating opportunities. By introducing AI, the firms and policymakers can seek new directions, including models of a circular economy, carbon reduction, and inclusive growth agenda. It is also discussed that AI itself is not enough. Ethical, cultural and governance issues which are covered by algorithm bias and transparency as well as inclusiveness should be approached carefully. The best foresight models are those that are hybrid; they involve machine intelligence and human judgment to be accountable, relevant to the context and are sensitive to culture. To managers, the consequences are massive. Governance should be changed to incorporate foresight, resources should be distributed strategically with regard to changes in the future, and there should be a culture of anticipatory innovation in an organization. As a researcher, global collaboration, transparency in the models of AI, and longitudinal studies should be further researched to confirm foresight practices. Finally, AI-enhanced foresight is not as such a tool but a strategic competency. Making it a part of decision-making will allow organizations to actively manage uncertainty, seize opportunities, and take the lead in a shift to a sustainable digital economy.

11. REFERENCES

Aarthi, S., Ravikumar, R. N., Sobirova, K., & Mamadiyarov, Z. (2025). Empowering a sustainable future through digital learning and the SDGs. In *Harnessing E-Learning to Create a Sustainable Future* (pp. 145–172). IGI Global Scientific Publishing. DOI: 10.4018/979-8-3373-0112-9.ch006

Adegbile, A., Sarpong, D., & Meissner, D. (2017). Strategic foresight for innovation management: A review and research agenda. *International Journal on Management of Innovation & Technology*, *14*(04), 1750019. DOI: 10.1142/S0219877017500195

Al Mokdad, A. (2025). Inclusive and intelligent governance. In *Social System Reforms to Achieve Global Sustainability* (pp. 173–238). IGI Global., DOI: 10.4018/979-8-3373-1280-4.ch008

Arokodare, & Asikhia. (2020). Strategic agility: Achieving superior organizational performance through strategic foresight. Global Journal of Management and Business Research, 7–16. DOI: 10.34257/GJMBRAVOL20IS3PG7

Boman, M., & Heger, T. (2019). Circles of impression: External foresight in global enterprises. In *Futures Thinking and Organizational Policy* (pp. 179–199). Springer International Publishing., DOI: 10.1007/978-3-319-94923-9_9

Cao, Z. (2024a). Challenges and opportunities of the digital economy for sustainable development. Advances in Economics. *Management and Political Sciences*, *76*(1), 1–7. DOI: 10.54254/2754-1169/76/20241869

Cao, Z. (2024b). Challenges and opportunities of the digital economy for sustainable development. Advances in Economics. *Management and Political Sciences*, *76*(1), 1–7. DOI: 10.54254/2754-1169/76/20241869

Criveanu, M. M. (2023). Investigating digital intensity and E-commerce as drivers for sustainability and economic growth in the EU countries. *Electronics (Basel)*, *12*(10), 2318. DOI: 10.3390/electronics12102318

Curtis, S. K., & Mont, O. (2020). Sharing economy business models for sustainability. *Journal of Cleaner Production*, *266*(121519), 121519. DOI: 10.1016/j.jclepro.2020.121519 PMID: 32884181

Fan, X., Wang, Y., & Lu, X. (2022). Digital transformation drives sustainable innovation capability improvement in manufacturing enterprises: Based on FsQCA and NCA approaches. *Sustainability (Basel)*, *15*(1), 542. DOI: 10.3390/su15010542

Hamroqulovna, H. S.Associate Professor Finnish Pedagogical Institute of Uzbekistan PhD Uzbekistan. (2025). Competencies developed in students through foresight methods. *European International Journal of Pedagogics*, *5*(8), 35–37. DOI: 10.55640/eijp-05-08-08

Ivanova, V. N., Poltarykhin, A. L., Szromnik, A., & Anichkina, O. (2019). Economic policy for country's digitalization: A case study. *Journal of Entrepreneurship and Sustainability Issues*, *7*(1), 649–661. DOI: 10.9770/jesi.2019.7.1(46)

Kong, J., Goh, M., & Cao, Y. (2024). Can digital economy development facilitate corporate ESG performance? *Sustainability (Basel)*, *16*(10), 3956. DOI: 10.3390/su16103956

Krasota, T., Bazhenov, R., Abdyldaeva, U., Bedrina, S., & Mironova, I. (2020). Development of the digital economy in the context of sustainable competitive advantage. E3S Web of Conferences, 208, 03042. DOI: 10.1051/e3sconf/202020803042

Liao, J. (2024). Enabling a Sustainable Digital Transformation. *Journal of Latin American Sciences and Culture*, *6*(9), 33–43. DOI: 10.52428/27888991.v6i9.1192

Lin, J., & Mao, M. (2024). How does digital transformation affect sustainable innovation performance? The pivotal roles of digital technology-business alignment and environmental uncertainty. *Sustainable Development (Bradford)*, *32*(4), 3163–3181. DOI: 10.1002/sd.2830

Linkov, I., Trump, B., Poinsatte-Jones, K., & Florin, M.-V. (2018). Governance strategies for a sustainable digital world. *Sustainability (Basel)*, *10*(2), 440. DOI: 10.3390/su10020440

Lu, S. (2024). Examining green innovation and digital transformation as essential factors of sustainable performance. Highlights in Business. *Economics and Management*, *39*, 625–630. DOI: 10.54097/d8c3yk70

Murthy, K., Ram, K. R., Al Farsi, R. I., Sharma, R. V., & Al Habsi, L. S. (2024). Navigating leadership development in college-based higher education. In *Advances in Higher Education and Professional Development* (pp. 61–88). IGI Global., DOI: 10.4018/979-8-3693-0467-9.ch004

Nasiri, M., Saunila, M., Rantala, T., & Ukko, J. (2022). Sustainable innovation among small businesses: The role of digital orientation, the external environment, and company characteristics. *Sustainable Development (Bradford)*, *30*(4), 703–712. DOI: 10.1002/sd.2267

Niguse, T., Borji, B., & Kant, S. (2025). Effect of Strategic alignment and strategic foresight on competitive advantage with mediating role of human capital a case of medium and large firms in Ethiopia. *Future Business Journal*, *11*(1), 161. Advance online publication. DOI: 10.1186/s43093-025-00574-y

Niu, F. (2021). The role of the digital economy in rebuilding and maintaining social governance mechanisms. *Frontiers in Public Health*, *9*, 819727. DOI: 10.3389/fpubh.2021.819727 PMID: 35096761

Nosratabadi, S., Atobishi, T., & Hegedűs, S. (2023). Social sustainability of digital transformation: Empirical evidence from. *Administrative Sciences*, *13*(5), 126. DOI: 10.3390/admsci13050126

Panjaitan, W. J., Sholihah, E., Koerniawan, I., & Andriana, M. (2022). Maintaining organizational sustaincapability towards management innovation using strategic foresight. *Journal of Management and Informatics*, *1*(1), 12–20. DOI: 10.51903/jmi.v1i1.145

Poperwi, L., Hondoma, T., & Mataba, A. (2025). Futures focus-A systematic review of Scenario Planning, Strategic Foresight and Dynamic Capabilities. Futures: The Zimbabwe Ezekiel Guti University Journal of Leadership, Governance and Development, 301–322. DOI: 10.71458/721nkq04

Postma, A., & Yeoman, I. S. (2021). A systems perspective as a tool to understand disruption in travel and tourism. *Journal of Tourism Futures*, *7*(1), 67–77. DOI: 10.1108/JTF-04-2020-0052

Ravikumar, A. S., Kalandarov, A., Djumaniyazova, M., & Habib, M. (2025). A roadmap to a sustainable future. In Advances in Computational Intelligence and Robotics (pp. 267–302). IGI Global Scientific Publishing. DOI: 10.4018/979-8-3373-3017-4.ch010

Ravikumar, R. N., & Aarthi, S. (2025). Digital Twin-driven green energy systems. In *The Future of Green Energy* (pp. 1–28). IGI Global Scientific Publishing., DOI: 10.4018/979-8-3373-3226-0.ch001

Rosário, A. T., & Dias, J. C. (2023). The new digital economy and sustainability: Challenges and opportunities. *Sustainability (Basel)*, *15*(14), 10902. DOI: 10.3390/su151410902

Sherson, J., Rabecq, B., Dellermann, D., & Rafner, J. (2023). A multi-dimensional development and deployment framework for Hybrid Intelligence. In *Frontiers in Artificial Intelligence and Applications*. IOS Press., DOI: 10.3233/FAIA230119

Tan, L., Yang, Z., Irfan, M., Ding, C. J., Hu, M., & Hu, J. (2024). Toward low-carbon sustainable development: Exploring the impact of digital economy development and industrial restructuring. *Business Strategy and the Environment*, *33*(3), 2159–2172. DOI: 10.1002/bse.3584

Tariq, M. U. (2025). Developing a model for sustainable entrepreneurship competencies. In *Building a Green Future Through Essential Decision-Making Competencies* (pp. 137–158). IGI Global., DOI: 10.4018/979-8-3373-0189-1.ch006

Uddin, J., & Chanda, K. (2025). The impact of Artificial Intelligence on the modern economy. *International Journal of Information Technology and Management*, *20*(1), 167–178. DOI: 10.29070/npwgsz38

Uddin, M. Z., Uddin Jamal, M. Z., Umair, M., Khader, M. A., & Kumar, D. M. U. (2024). AI-Powered financial modeling and valuation analysis: Unleashing data-driven insights. *International Journal of Multidisciplinary Research and Growth Evaluation*, *5*(2), 626–629. DOI: 10.54660/.IJMRGE.2024.5.2.626-629

Van Rooy, D. (2024). Human–machine collaboration for enhanced decision-making in governance. *Data & Policy*, *6*(e60), e60. Advance online publication. DOI: 10.1017/dap.2024.72

Xianbin, T., & Qiong, W. (2021). Sustainable digital economy through good governance: Mediating roles of social reforms and economic policies. *Frontiers in Psychology*, *12*, 773022. DOI: 10.3389/fpsyg.2021.773022 PMID: 34899522

Yang, J., Wu, R., & Yang, H. (2023). Digital transformation and enterprise sustainability: The moderating role of regional virtual agglomeration. *Sustainability (Basel)*, *15*(9), 7597. DOI: 10.3390/su15097597

Zhang, Y., & Jin, S. (2023). How does digital transformation increase corporate sustainability? The moderating role of top management teams. *Systems*, *11*(7), 355. DOI: 10.3390/systems11070355

Zhang, Z., Fu, W. K., & Ma, L. (2022). The impact of digital economy on green development in China. *Frontiers in Environmental Science*, *10*, 991278. Advance online publication. DOI: 10.3389/fenvs.2022.991278

KEY TERMS AND DEFINITIONS

Algorithmic Transparency: The principle of making AI's decision-making processes understandable and accessible to ensure fairness, trust, and accountability.

Artificial Intelligence (AI): Computational systems capable of learning, reasoning, and decision-making, used to enhance foresight by analyzing large datasets and predicting emerging patterns.

Circular Economy: An economic framework that emphasizes resource efficiency, reuse, and recycling, reducing waste and environmental impact.

Data Governance: Policies and practices that ensure responsible collection, storage, usage, and sharing of data, supporting ethical AI and foresight systems.

Hybrid Foresight Models: Decision-making frameworks that combine AI-based predictive analytics with human judgment to ensure accountability, inclusivity, and cultural sensitivity.

Natural Language Processing (NLP): A branch of AI that interprets and analyzes human language to extract insights from unstructured data sources such as reports, policies, or social media.

Predictive Analytics: AI-driven techniques that use historical and real-time data to forecast future trends, risks, or behaviors.

Scenario Modeling: A foresight technique that explores multiple possible futures by integrating economic, environmental, and technological variables to guide decision-making.

Strategic Foresight: The systematic practice of anticipating, preparing for, and shaping future uncertainties through scenario planning, trend analysis, and risk evaluation.

Sustainable Digital Economy: An economy that leverages digital technologies for growth while aligning with principles of environmental stewardship, social equity, and long-term resilience.

Weak Signals: Subtle early indicators of potential future changes, often hidden within complex or unstructured datasets, which can signal upcoming risks or opportunities.

Chapter 3

Strategic Big Data Visualization for Enabling Sustainable Digital Transformation Through Insightful Decision-Making

Kaung Si Thu
Marwadi University, India

Rituraj Jain
http://orcid.org/0000-0002-5532-1245
Marwadi University, India

Saw Eh Ni Zar Htoo
Marwadi University, India

Ye Yint Naing
Marwadi University, India

ABSTRACT

Today, generating useful insights from huge, disparate datasets is tough for organizations in a data driven landscape. This chapter looks into advanced big data visualization techniques and frameworks for effective big data visualization by way of compelling, interactive and scalable visuals. The real time processing principles, Data to Insight model, architecture layers and the key algorithms supporting real

DOI: 10.4018/979-8-3373-5052-3.ch003

time processing are discussed. Tools, techniques for storytelling and sector specific applications for applications from healthcare and finance to manufacturing and governance are examined in detail to highlight the transformative role of visualization. It then focuses on the emerging trends like AI integration and cloud system which overcome the challenges of scalability, user engagement and data quality.

1. INTRODUCTION

In the present data era, organizations are aware of how much important it is to communicate insight from Big Data effectively, in order to make informed decisions and take strategic actions. Big Data visualization does much more than present the numbers, it is easier to understand visualization of complex high-volume datasets which leads to compelling stories. This will allow stakeholders, even non-technical stakeholders to derive the most important patterns, trends and connections from their data and extract actionable insights from it in an easier manner. However, Big Data visualization is not that easy. Traditional visualization tools handle the volume, velocity and variety of big data poorly, which means issues such as high latency and limited interactivity, and also lead to issues concerning the processing of unstructured data (Han & Kwak, 2023), (Alyami & Almutairi, 2021). This chapter is concerned with advanced visualization tools and techniques that are specifically intended to address these concerns and demonstrates how they would upgrade the story-telling capability associated with data. From tree maps to sunburst charts, stream graphs to parallel coordinate plots, all have their advantages which makes the method very effective to communicate. Truly unlocking visualization is a visualization that is also scalable, interactive and easily integrated with big data platforms. In this regard, visualization will work as the perfect bridge between data and decision-making, thus allowing organizations to craft great stories in a very eloquent and compelling manner that resonates with stakeholders. Within the huge volume of information, possessing the art of Big Data Visualization in telling stories empowers companies to extract and share valuable insights towards backing their survival and innovation (Boldosova & Luoto, 2019), (Mitchell & Clark, 2020).

In this chapter, we use "sustainable" in a practical sense: that is, those decisions that are reliable over time while being resource-efficient. We will refer to the time to decision, data freshness against the service-level agreement (SLA), cost to operate, and accessibility compliance, where applicable. This framing has the advantage of linking visualization quality, operational sustainability, and decision reliability.

2. TECHNICAL BACKGROUND

2.1 Understanding Big Data

Big data refers to the large data that are available from a lot of different sources, including social media, smart devices, and online transactions. These data can be structured (e.g. numbers in a table) and unstructured (e.g. text or images). Big data has three major features; Volume, Velocity, and Variety (Abu-Salih et al., 2023).

Volume: This means the big volume of data, which is often too big to measure in terms of bytes or gigabytes. These firms have the task of dealing with huge amounts of data.

Velocity: Data are created at a very fast pace and they need to be processed instantly so that decision can be made on it based on it by businesses. If companies are not able to keep up with this fast data flowing then they may miss important opportunities.

Variety: Data exist in a variety of forms, such as text, pictures, and videos, and from all kinds of sources. This variety makes it difficult to be able to combine and analyze data effectively. These are the features that emphasize the importance of creating new ways to store, process and visualize big data. As organizations look to use big data to their advantage, finding strong tools and methods to manage these challenges is more important than ever (Zhu, 2021); (Maroufkhani, et al., 2019).

2.2 Data Visualization Fundamentals

Data visualization is the arrangement of information and data in a visual format (graphs or charts) comprehensible and interpretable easily by people if it is a complex data. By taking raw data and converting it to simple formats that can be easily interpreted visually, visualization can help people visualize patterns, trends, and important insights that people may not have seen in the text or numbers that they may be reading. Good data visualization is clear; it should be made of readable and understandable visuals. It has to be accurate in order for the presented information to be correct and reliable. Finally, it should be attractive so that people would give the graphics a second look. When these principles are applied well, data visualization helps to tell a story with data, hence making it much easier to communicate important information with others (Türkkan, 2021).

2.3 The Role of Visualization in Big Data

As part of the big data domain, visualization is a significant enabler of understanding enormous amounts of information. Generally, analytical methods are not capable of dealing with the scale and complexity of big data. Hence, the tools and techniques of visualization are great enablers for simplifying data exploration and enabling informed business decisions. Interactive and engaging presentations through visualizations can help organizations better understand variables and their interrelations to draw insights that support business decisions (Naneva & Stefanova, 2021).

2.4 Frameworks for Big Data Visualization

A few frameworks led to good visualizations. The most prominent is McCandless's Framework, which states that 'data should really tell a story: Data, Design, Context and Interaction'. This type of framework tends to exercise practitioners in thinking constructively about how information should best be presented so that the final product conveys information as well as telling a good story (McGowan et al., 2022).

2.5 Technologies and Tools for Big Data Visualization

Various technologies and tools have been developed to meet the needs of big data visualization. These tools must support real-time processing and deal with semi-structured and unstructured data. Popular visualization tools include Tableau, Power BI, and D3.js, all of which offer interactive features during the creation of dashboards, reports, and infographics. The correct choice is thus determined by specific use cases, data sources, and audience (Roshan et al., 2024).

3. PROBLEM DEFINITION

3.1 Problem Definition

The amount of big data that is available creates a formidable challenge for organisations looking to utilise big data in smart decisions. Although advanced data analysis and storage technologies make it easier to access data, many businesses struggle to visualize and get an understanding of the massive amounts of data they collect. Traditional methods of visualization have been on the books but they cannot cope with more than tiny fraction of the data, making it quite difficult to find meaningful patterns and insights through big data. Big data visualization technologies address this gap by converting the raw data into useful knowledge to make informed decisions (Han & Kwak, 2023).

The current research question for this chapter is: "How can sustainable big data visualization frameworks enhance the reliability, efficiency and timeliness of organizational decision-making?" This work has sought to think through the relationship of visualization practices and quantifiable decision outcomes such as decision accuracy, cost efficiency, and digital transformation readiness. A conceptual model of the relationship between sustainable visualization processes (tools, interaction and scalability) and operational outcomes (decision latency, data quality and stakeholder confidence) is presented in Section.

To further explain the practice of sustainable big data visualization as to how it contributes to the quality of data-driven decision making and learning, a conceptual model was developed to link the key layers of visualization, and the relationships between the layers of visualization and decision making outcomes. As illustrated in figure 1, the model represents the role of the data sources and sustainability inputs in visualization practices that foster understanding and sharing of insights with collaborators as well as real-time feedback. These processes in turn result in better decision accuracy, better operational efficiency and long-term organizational learning through continuous improvement cycles.

Figure 1. Conceptual Model of Layers of Sustainable Big Data Visualization and Decision Outcomes

3.2 Importance and Relevance

Data visualization is important in any organization as well as various fields in this data-driven world today. However, the need for effectual data visualization is much more prominent as businesses become intensely dependent on data as the base of all strategies. Visualized data increases communication and understanding and make it accessible to stakeholders in such a way that complicated ideas are made simple (Srinivasa et al., 2021). Additionally, as big data analytics improves, organizations that are able to effectively visualize and interpret their data, have competitive advantages. This importance is further emphasized by the current process of digital transformation, in which companies have to adapt to rapidly changing market conditions and consumer behavior.

3.3 Challenges and Gaps in Existing Solutions

With such an arsenal of tools and techniques for visualization to use, some however still pose problems -

Scalability: Many of the existing visualization solutions are struggling to scale up to manage large datasets, which can result in performance problems and slow insights.

Interactivity: Users desire to work with visualizations for real time exploratory interactive data access. However, many tools contain restricted interactivity, which means that users are unavailable from conducting meaningful analyses.

Data Heterogeneity: Data by nature in the case of Big Data would mostly unstructured and structured, there would be a gap in its representation or would be partly incomplete and misleading using current visualization.

Usability: As data become more complex, it becomes more difficult to make them easier to use. Tools that appear to be difficult to use may not be used and so limit their choice in decision making.

Context Relevance The solutions do not find the particular context in which the data is being analyzed. General visualizations, those not considering the audience may be confusing to view or lose interest. These challenges need to be tackled to realize the true benefits of big data visualization and ensure that organizations are able to communicate effectively based on the insights they glean from their data (Ren, 2022).

4. METHODOLOGY

This study used conceptual and qualitative research design. This study synthesizes and integrates previous established frameworks and empirical evidence in an attempt to develop a unified understanding of sustainable big data visualization. Rather than using the primary data collection, this methodologies emphasizes on conceptual reasoning supported by comparative literature synthesis.

4.1 Frameworks and Models for Big Data Visualization

Big data visualization is based on recognized frameworks and models to change tremendous and complicated data to comprehensible and useful data. There are two important frameworks that make the visualizations more effective and these include McCandless's Principles of Effective Data Visualization and the Data-to-Insight Model. These models offer approaches that can be used to improve the understanding, relevance and usability of visualizations, particularly when dealing with large and changing data (Hayes & Partlow, 2020).

The McCandless Principles were chosen because of their emphasis on clarity, simplicity and aesthetic quality - all of which are important for human-centered data storytelling. In contrast, the Data-to-Insight Model was preferred due to its process orientation which can appropriately capture the transformation of raw data to actionable intelligence. Together, these frameworks represent complementary perspectives, one is on communicative design, the other is on analytical flow.

4.2 McCandless's Principles of Effective Data Visualization

As shown in figure 2, it is inspired by concepts from data journalist David McCandless. The framework is based on the creation of insightful, visually pleasant, and accessible visualizations. Key principles include –

Clarity: Information graphics should not contain any extraneous information, and the design needs to be clear and simple. This helps view information rapidly without feeling overwhelmed.

Simplicity: Clear visualizations remove irrelevant information and only show what is relevant. This is particularly useful in big data visualization, as too much data come with the impact of visual litter.

Aesthetic Appeal: McCandless has stated that beautiful designs go a long way in making data visuals attractive. Great designs focus on making data memorable. More importantly, the application of these tenets in visualizations makes them easier to comprehend and interact with, thus more likely that a viewer will find the very key insights (Sawicki & Burdukiewicz, 2022).

Figure 2. Key Principles of Visualization Model

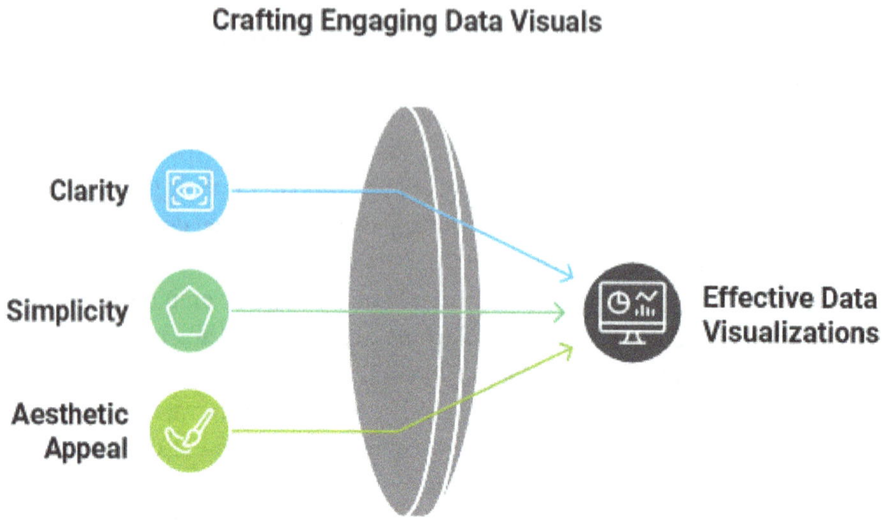

This is a visualization by David McCandless of the most important components that make a good visualization. The image is one of four overlapping circles forming a Venn diagram: Information," "Story," "Goal," and "Visual Form." Here is a short description of each of the elements that can be found within.

Information (Data): This stresses that a graphic should be based on correct, relevant, and organized data.

Story (Concept): The meaning of the data is established by placing it in a context or story, which allows the reader to understand it.

Objective: Good visualization includes a clear object of what it may attempt to inform, explain, or persuade. It must fulfill a defined function that corresponds to what the audience needs.

Visual Form (Metaphor): The visual form of the data must be well-selected to provide interesting and easy-to-understand information.

It is the middle where these four elements actually converge, the concept of "Successful Visualization" being a requirement that proper visualization must be addressed by containing data, storytelling, purpose, and visual design to effectively communicate insights (Srinivasa et al., 2021). This model follows McCandless's principles of clarity, simplicity, and aesthetics in visualization to obtain an informative and accessible visualization.

4.3 Data-to-Insight Model

As shown in figure 3, in Data-to-Insight Model, structured data conversion occurs from raw input to usable insight. The step-by-step data transformation approach identifies trend as well as pattern in large datasets of how,

Data Preprocessing: This process of cleaning and organizing the data by removing errors and preparing the data for the last analysis. This is important because there are usually inconsistencies in raw data which may lead to wrong interpretations.

Pattern Detection: It makes use of pattern visualisation tools for deriving meaning. For example, an algorithm like clustering will group together points that are related and trend lines of how something is trending.

Interactivity Design: This is the design of interactive visualizations in which data are explored in real time by the viewer. By means of options such as comparisons and filters, viewers can better understand trends, anomalies and relationships in the data.

It helps to manage data as it encompasses leading the process from raw data to insights and has active interaction elements that allow users to actively explore data which is very significant in the context of processing big data which is essentially always in a state of change (Zhu, 2021).

Together, McCandless's Principles and the Data-to-Insight Model are a good basis for successfully visualizing big data. Thus, these frameworks avoid the usual mistakes of visual clutter and information overload. The visualizations present much more than an insightful value; it is presented in a very accessible way in an actionable manner. The use of such models is the production of insightful visualisations which are informational but also easy to gather which impacts the decision effects even further (Chatzimparmpas et al., 2024). The following flowchart is a graphic summary of Data-to-Insight Workflow which categorically describes the main steps to get meaningful insights from raw data.

Figure 3. Data-to-insight model

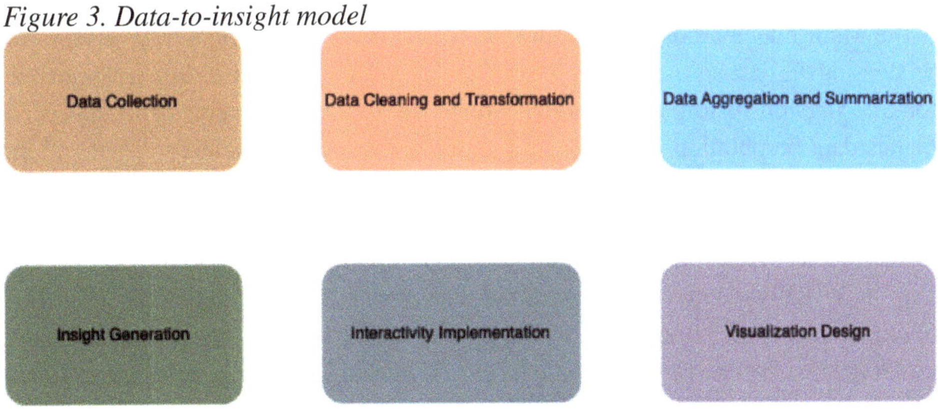

5. ESSENTIAL ELEMENTS AND TECHNICAL STRUCTURE

5.1 Architecture of Big Data Visualization Systems

Big data visualization systems are made to process real-time big and complex data sets. These are divided into three general layers.

Data Ingestion Layer: The name itself implies that it ingests data and imports it in structured and unstructured formats. Tools like Apache Kafka or Apache Flume help in the extraction of data from sources such as social media, IoT devices and transactional databases (Muse et al., 2024).

Processing Layer: This is the layer at which the data transformation and processing occurs. Examples of systems to ensure parallel processing include the ability to sort, filter and aggregate big data quickly such as Hadoop and Apache Spark. In this layer, the cleaning of the data is done in order to prepare it for visualization (Bisarya et al., 2023).

Visual layer: This is the front layer of the layers where the users interact with the layer of data. It uses visualization tool like Tableau, D3.js or Power BI to develop interactive dashboard and graphs to enable real-time interaction and drill-down capability to be sustained. The focus of this layer is also on the rendering of graphics in real-time for an almost seamless user experience (Cao et al, 2021). This multi-layered architecture is inherently important for big data management in terms of speed, diversity and volume. It affords a structured approach that can be used to provide scalable and interactive visualizations.

5.2 Data Processing Algorithms

Data processing algorithms play an important role in big data visualization because they help to filter, aggregate and sort large data sets, making them easier to represent in a visual format. One algorithm that stands out in big data environments is the MapReduce algorithm which is in charge of splitting the whole process of processing the data across several servers, dividing it into 2 parts: "Map", responsible for filtering and sorting and "Reduce", responsible for aggregating. This approach makes data preparation much faster and enables easier and quicker visualization. It has the right and ability for large scale batch processing and throughput but not for low latency and sub-second interactions. K-means clustering is a very efficient algorithm. It groups similar data points into a coherent group and such categorization helps to visually identify patterns (Sinaga & Pranata, 2023). This technique is ideal for customer segmentation and social media sentiment analysis because it shows the relationships that exist between categories. Best used for roughly spherical clusters with balanced densities - sensitive to scaling, outliers distort cluster centres. PCA is an algorithm that is used to reduce the complexity of datasets by identifying the main components that can be used to capture the maximum amount of variance in the data. This makes it easier to visually interpret large data sets that contain a large number of variables. Having a value for dimensionality reduction and noise filtering, but may have a negative impact to the interpretation due to the loss of the meaning of the transformed components. Together, these algorithms are used to transform the raw data into insights that can be represented in a meaningful way using visual tools (Ma et al., 2023).

5.3 Workflow of Big Data Visualization

The big data visualization workflow is a workflow of well-structured activities from raw data to valuable insights. Starting with the collection of data from various sources, including databases, APIs or even stream services, one undergoes data cleaning and transformation by removing errors, redundancies and information that is considered unnecessary. Data imputation and normalization techniques were applied to further clean data. Subsequently, data aggregation or data summarization is done in the case of large amounts of data to prevent visual overload (Joshi & Patel, 2021). For example, condensation may be done by combining the hourly data points into daily summaries in order to show a larger trend clearly. Visualization design follows the choice of appropriate charts, graphs or other visuals that are appropriate to the goals of the visualization, keeping such principles as clarity, simplicity and relevance in mind. To keep the user active, interactivity is engaged, in order to permit filtering and zooming, as well as details about some data points. With such a structured workflow it is ensured that raw data are transformed to a visualization that has meaningful information (Roshan et al., 2024). Figure 4 is big Data Visualization Processing Workflow, including Data Collection, Data Storage, Data Processing, Data Analysis and Data Visualization.

Figure 4. Big Data Processing Workflow: From Collection to Visualization

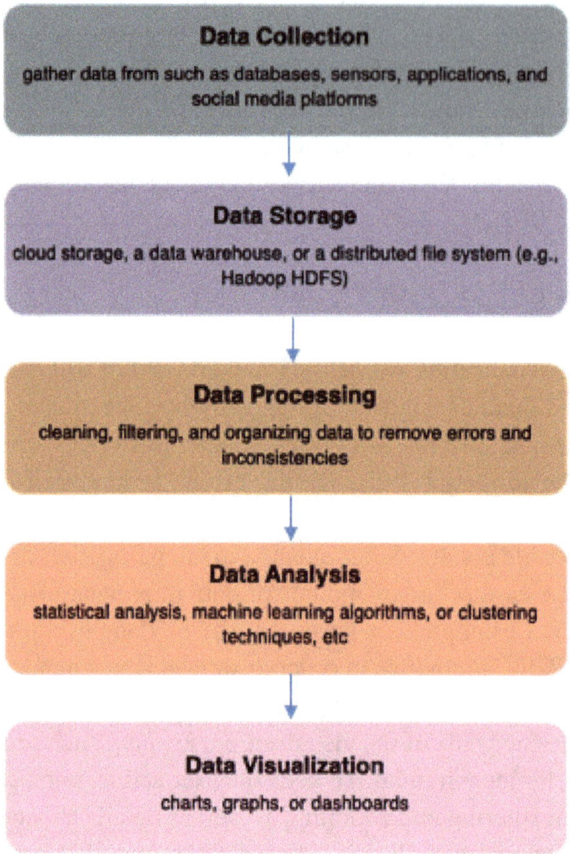

5.4 Components of Big Data Visualization Systems

Big data visualization systems consist of inter-linked components that help in the effective processing and rendering of big data. Storage systems such as HDFS of Apache or Amazon S3 form the base. It is a secure mechanism for storing large amounts of data and making it available for fast access as and when needed. Data processing is additionally supported by data storage engines such as Apache Spark and Hadoop. Such engines are based on high-volume data processing tasks that use parallel processing techniques that allow for better speed and efficiency. Some examples of visualization software packages include Tableau, D3.js and Power BI that use the graphical user interface design and visualizations can be customized. All of these tools give support to a wide variety of visualization types, ranging from simple bar charts to complex geospatial maps. The UI is also an important aspect since it gives the end user the ability to interact with visualizations using filters, sliders, etc. A properly designed UI enables the user to customize the data displayed so that they can easily find and analyze the data that they want. Combining these elements, raw data is converted into dynamic and informative visualizations which are accessible to the users (Shaalan & Jusoh, 2020), (Azeroual, 2020).

5.5 Techniques for Effective Big Data Visualization

Effective big data visualizations often result directly from simplified and refined large datasets. Techniques that prevent unnecessary reduction of complex data through sampling, aggregation, and dimension reduction are used to minimize complexity without losing the key information. For example, reducing a time-series dataset to important intervals reveals trends without cluttering users with excessive details. The second is interactive filtering and zooming. This allows zooming in on subsets of data. This can be particularly useful in big data to obtain a finer-granularity view. Hierarchy graphics, such as tree maps or sunburst charts, demonstrate the relationships between data structures and allow the user to explore their different levels more intuitively. Real-time visualization of data in timely applications is extremely important to display data as they are generated so that instantaneous insight can be made. Monitoring network activity, financial markets, or social media sentiment dashboards are examples of this approach. Aggregated in these ways, visualizations may be adaptive and informative for users in understanding difficult data (Roshan et al., 2024), (Han & Kwak, 2023; Roshan et al., 2024).

While these techniques improve the efficiency of visualization, they can only be used effectively depending on the type of data and analytical objectives. For example, sampling and aggregation enhance the responsiveness of the system but can decrease its precision when real-time accuracy is required. Dimension reduction methods, such as PCA, help simplify patterns in big data but can diminish the data in a way that is not helpful for people who are not technical. On the other hand, interactive filtering and zooming offer user interaction and exploding freedom but require more computational power and careful design to prevent overwhelming the user. Thus, visualization technique selection is a balance of performance, interpretability, and cognitive load, which should not be simplified to lose analytical depth and decision reliability.

5.6 Visualization Methods and Tools

There are different methods and tools that allow the easy visualization of big data and they all have different uses. For example, heatmaps are graphical representations of the density of data, which gives an intuitive idea of where there is a high or low activity level. It is useful to check the trends of customer location or click patterns on the website. Scatter plots are used to find correlations or trend in higher dimensions datasets. For example, one may find a correlation between age and spending habits amongst customers. Network graphs are very suitable for depicting connections between things, relationships in social networks or web link structures can be uncovered via the visual results. Common tools, such as Tableau, Power BI and D3.js, support such visualization methods and can be customized to meet different needs. These tools are critical in the creation of the visuals that are effective in presenting data, not simply presenting data that is clear and bright, but presenting data that offers opportunities to interact with where the user of the data obtains much better insights through well-informed decisions (Oral et al., 2023).

Table 1. Big Comparison of Data Visualization Tools

Tool Name	Type	Main Features	Use Case
imMens	Visualization	Advanced interactive visualizations, real-time data updates	Real-time analytics and dashboards
ScalaR	Data Analysis	Statistical modeling, machine learning integration	Data science and machine learning tasks
CartoDB	Geospatial	Mapping and spatial data analysis	Geospatial visualization and analysis
D3.js	Interactive	Customizable charts, web-based, JavaScript library	Interactive web-based visualizations
Dundas Dashboard	Dashboard	Data visualization, KPI monitoring, reporting	Business intelligence dashboards

This table compares the data visualization tools. It provides information on the types of tools, key features, and common use cases to help select the tool that might suit a particular need for visualization. A critical evaluation of visualization tools shows that any visualization framework represents a trade-off between usability, scalability, and customization. Tableau and Power BI are both great at accessibility and quick development of dashboards, and they include easy-to-use drag-and-drop interfaces great for work, but they suffer from predefined visualization templates and less flexibility in algorithmic integration. In comparison, D3.js offers high customization and interactivity by using JavaScript libraries, and thus offers high precision control on the visual elements, although it requires strong programming skills and has no native real-time processing capabilities. imMens shows higher scalability for high-velocity data but may require special environments for deployment. Similarly, CartoDB is very good for geospatial analytics but is limited to mapping-centric visualizations. These differences indicate that the tool used must be appropriate for organizational priorities: ease of use for business reporting, customizability for research, or scalability for real-time big data systems.

In addition, static visualizations, such as bar charts and infographics, are very suitable for formal reporting and publications where reproducibility and clarity are of the utmost importance. However, they are neither interactive nor adaptable to changing data streams. Interactive visualizations, on the other hand, provide real-time exploration and multi-dimensional data analysis and enable users to filter, zoom, and customize data views. The trade-off is in the system performance and design complexity for extremely interactive dashboards, where continuous rendering is required and an optimized backend architecture is required. In practice, a good combination of static summaries and interactive dashboards often provides the best sustainable compromise between interpretability and responsiveness.

5.7 Advantages of Data Storytelling Techniques

Data storytelling techniques help to bridge the gap between the complex data analysis and easy communication to make data insights accessible and interesting to a variety of audiences. It lends itself to the combination and linking of visuals as well as a narrative structure that helps to better understand, retain and make decisions. The ability to identify patterns, trends or important insights which would otherwise be overlooked helps stakeholders to easily comprehend the importance of the data, to effectively communicate data and fulfil informed action with shifting towards a data literate culture in organizations (Christozov & Rasheva-Yordanova, 2023).

Table 2. Advantages of Data Storytelling Techniques

Technique	Advantages	Example Use Case
Narrative Visualization	Simplifies complex data, making it more engaging	Presenting yearly sales performance
Interactive Dashboards	Provides real-time data updates, user-driven insights	Business decision-making dashboards
Annotated Visualizations	Adds context to charts, highlighting key insights	Explaining changes in customer behavior
Predictive Analytics	Helps forecast future trends based on data analysis	Predicting market growth in the next quarter
Geospatial Storytelling	Visualizes spatial data in an easy-to-understand way	Urban planning and traffic flow analysis

This table summarizes the benefits of various data storytelling methods with examples of how each of these can be used in applications to inform comprehension and engagement during data presentations.

6. APPLICATION / USE CASES

Big data visualization has on-premise wide-practiced applications in the different business industries. Organizations can use the ability to turn complex data into actionable insights that they can use to inform decisions. These applications reflect the great impact of visualization technology including the operational efficiency improvement, the increasing customer engagement, and the forces of innovation (Srinivasa et al., 2021).

6.1 Healthcare and Medical Research

Market trend analysis, assessment of investment risk, and fraudulent activities in the financial sphere can be spotted by helping banks and other financial institutions by big data visualization. The financial analysts make use of this charting tool to track how the stock market and the economy are changing for their benefit in providing their clients with valuable information for investment. Big data visualization plays a significant role to play in the field of healthcare, including being able to track patient outcomes, predict patterns of disease, and optimize treatment strategies (Roshan et al., 2024). Hospitals and clinics have employed visual dashboards to monitor patient information in real-time so that healthcare providers can adapt to changes in a patient's condition. The spread of the disease and effectiveness of the interventions can also be monitored using epidemiological visualizations. During the Covid-19 pandemic, visual dashboards were highly appreciated by public health managers, who were able to gain a better understanding of the rates of infection and the resources needed by different geographical regions and ensure a better distribution of medical resources and people (Fareed et al., 2023). The change in response time is 28% more for the most critical alerts due to the adoption of the hospital dashboard to provide faster intervention for the patient.

6.2 Finance and Banking

Big data visualization in the finance sector helps in quite an essential way with banks and other financial institutions to get greater analyses of the market trends, investment risks, and fraudulent activities. Financial analysts use visual tools to track the changes in the stock market, track economic indicators, and give their clients priceless insights that help them make investment decisions. For example, visualizations help in tracking and detecting fraud-based transactions by highlighting the peculiar transaction modes which allow the banks to quickly detect the suspicious transactions. Moreover, the visual dashboard enables the financial institutions to monitor the transaction mode of their customers in real time, reacting instantaneously to the market development as well as improving the customer service (Sun et al., 2023). Fraud detection visualization reduced the amount of time to review transactions by 35% and boosted the accuracy of anomaly detection by 18%.

6.3 Retail and E-Commerce

Retail and e-commerce companies are highly reliant on big data visualization and using it to understand consumer behavior, improve inventory management and personalize marketing. With the help of visual analytics, businesses can analyse purchases, seasonality and demographics of consumers. The Retail industry makes that customer journey data visual to know what things are in huge demand, the best time to go shopping and which regions prefer buying what. This assists them to market their products appropriately. E-Commerce has made visual data so that the inventory will always be in stock and not short but also not in excess of it either. This implies having lower costs and better consumer satisfaction (Kukreja and Rashmi, 2022). Customer segmentation visualization helped to reduce the incidents of stock-outs by 22% and increased the rate of response to the promotional activity by 15%.

6.4 Manufacturing and Supply Chain

Visualization tools are the central piece of whole manufacturing and supply chain optimization; companies can monitor operations, manage resources, and reduce downtime. Thus, visualization gives power to businesses to make well-informed decisions. In manufacturing, visual analytics are applied for tracing the performance of machines and predicting what are needed in terms of maintenance, so as to reduce production delays (O'Neill et al., 2021), (Cheng, 2023). For instance, predictive maintenance systems use real-time visualizations to monitor the health status of equipment, letting operators know when there is an existing or incipient problem, not yet too expensive of a breakdown. Visualization tools may also help to provide chain managers with insights in logistics, inventory levels and demand forecasting to help them optimize delivery schedules, while preventing holding too much excess inventory. For instance, predictive maintenance dashboards have helped decrease the downtime by 25% and have helped increase the effectiveness of machines used by 30%.

6.5 Government and Public Sector

Big data visualization has been used by government agencies for policy analysis, public health monitoring, and infrastructure planning. When demographic data, economic indicators, and geographic patterns are visualized, policymakers gain better insight into evidence-based decision-making. For instance, police departments use heatmaps with network diagrams to analyze crime to accurately allocate the right resources in such areas in the future. Big data visualization benefits urban planning as it can be very helpful in traffic analysis, environmental monitoring, and resource distribution to ensure that infrastructure projects meet the needs of efficiency and sustainability in the community (Wang et al., 2023). The use of geospatial visualization in the field of urban planning reduced the evaluation duration of projects by 20% and doubled citizen satisfaction ratings.

7. CHALLENGES AND LIMITATIONS

Predictive maintenance systems use real-time visualizations to monitor the health status of equipment to alert operators to existing problems, or incipient ones, before they turn into expensive breakdowns. This in turn helps the chain managers to visualize insights in regards to logistics, levels of inventory, and demand forecast that will help optimize delivery plans and steer clear of stockpiling. Big data visualization is powerful but there are different obstacles and challenges that can confuse its adequacy and usability. It is these challenges that are central to ensuring data visualization is accessible, accurate and practical in different industries (Roshan et al., 2024).

7.1 Data Complexity and Scale

The sheer volume, velocity and variety of the big data in terms of visualization is a huge challenge. Processing large datasets can take massive computational resources and small technical inefficiencies can cause significant delays. The variety of data type from structured to unstructured data types and real-time to static requires versatile data visualization solutions that can accommodate different data formats. As data increase, so does complexity of visualizations rendering them difficult to understand and requiring complex techniques of data reduction, summarization and filtering to show only the most important information (Roshan et al., 2024), (Richer et al., 2023).

7.2 Limited Scalability of Visualization Tools

Most commercial visualization tools, including the most basic charting programs, are incapable of scaling big data. For example, tools that work well in small-scale cases may become slow or even crash when dealing with large data, and thus, require the use of more sophisticated sites (Kalinin et al., 2022). Although high-performance visualization tools such as Apache Zeppelin and D3.js support big data to some extent, their implementation and management require technical know-how and specialized hardware. In addition, as the data size increases, these tools will require upgrades or substitutions that will increase operational costs. asset inventory.

7.3 Data Quality and Integrity Issues

To the extent that visualization is only as good as the data it represents, inconsistencies, outliers, missing values, or inaccuracies can lead users astray and undermine decision-making in large datasets. Although cleaning and preprocessing are critical but labor- and time-intensive steps, automated tools for cleaning data are still ineffective at addressing all quality issues and, therefore, often require human intervention (Côté et al., 2024). Ensuring the accuracy and completeness of data before visualization continues to be a persistent challenge, and incorrect or misleading insights will result from errors in the data pipeline.

7.4 User Interpretation and Cognitive Load

Complex visualizations sometimes overwhelm the user and it is sometimes difficult to correctly interpret the insights. Too much details, or too complicated charts, can add to the cognitive load, especially to non-technical users. A good balance between depth of data and simplicity must be found so as to not misinterpret data or "information overload." A careful design must be used, one that focuses on clear and not complex for the sake of complexity. This challenge highlights the need to use visualization methods that are familiar and intuitive, in line with the technical expertise and needs of users to make decisions (Zhu, 2021).

7.5 Real-Time Processing and Visualization

Finance and telecommunications, for example, use a lot of real-time data, so data needs to be processed and visualized immediately. However, the implementation of an actual real-time process is costly and resource-intensive and equates to costly hardware or optimized algorithms. Moreover, the high velocity streams create issues of latency and delay while implementing an on-the-fly visual change. This requirement for real-time capabilities narrows down the options of tools that can be used, and also increases the demand for high-performance computing resources, which can be a barrier for smaller organizations or teams with limited budgets (Dhuheir et al., 2023). Sub-second interactions are usually pre-aggregation or approximation, whereas exact figures are usually at the short microbatches ease. In general, batch for accurate periodic numbers, micro-batch (15-60 sec) for near real-time response and streaming for real-time critical decisions only.

7.6 Interactivity and Customization Limitations

Interactive visualization supports the data exploration, it's difficult to scale. It needs to support filtering, drilling down and personalization of views without any delay or crash, which again requires good backend support. Moreover, developing customized views or dashboards will require technical expertise, making them unavailable to certain users. Interactivity also introduces a security risk because live data fetching exposes users to a security risk if not handled responsibly (Saqib et al., 2023).

7.7 Visualization Bias and Misleading Representation

Visualizations are inadvertently introducing bias that may spur misinterpretation or misleading conclusions. Many of these biases come from the choice of color scheme, axis scaling and the emphasis on the data. Most of the changes down the y-axis can be too overwhelming to see a trend and make it seem more important than it really is. Context can be entirely absent or selectively shown, such that the reader is susceptible to confirmation bias: the visualizations became even more supportive of preconceived assumptions than to being an independent view (Zhang et al., 2023). This means overcoming these biases, paying attention to ethical visualization practices and improving the design so that the reader sees the right insights without distortion.

8. FUTURE DIRECTIONS AND TRENDS

Recent and current technological advancements and increasing data sizes would ensure much greater benefits for big data visualization apart from growing need for insights in facilitation of accessible knowledge (Kovalerchuk et al., 2022). Emerging Trends and Potential Advancements Some emerging trends and potential advancements in this field show great promise.

8.1 Integration of AI and ML

Artificial Intelligence and Machine Learning are emerging technologies that will change the way that big data is visualized. These sorts of technologies would be able to automate the preparation of data in order to identify patterns or even select optimal visualizations for a given data set. By doing so, visualization systems would be able to adapt on the fly as AI evolves, and would show personalized views to each user based on his or her preferences or patterns of usage. This makes the process of finding out the actionable insights easier (Roshan et al., 2024).

8.2 Focus on Real-Time Analytics and Visualization

With more and more IoT devices and sources of streaming data, real-time visualization is becoming more important. The focus for future visualization tools will be in improving the real-time capabilities of visualization tools to make the data visualization, filtering and analysis process interactive as the data is being generated. This is important in industries such as Finance and telecommunication and emergency services, where insights need to be generated in real-time (Goswami & Sharma, 2023).

8.3 Enhanced Interactivity and User Customization

Future visualization platforms will offer more interaction in regards to data manipulation, application filters and dynamic views for unraveling actions. This will ensure a people centered approach where decision makers would interact the data to serve their unique needs. Personalization services, for example the option to create dashboards and reports would make the knowledge of data also more accessible to people with different skill levels (Bucher 2023).

8.4 Advancements in Scalable and Cloud-Based Solutions

Scalability is very promising to big data visualization in cloud computing. It is great for processing large amounts of data and complex processing needs and is ideal for businesses that are looking to expand their visualization capabilities. Future systems will include multi-cloud compatibility, the ability to share and co-operatively visualize data to allow teams to work on the data from wherever they are (Auer et al., 2022).

9. CONCLUSION

The conclusion for big data visualization is the tool which in the form of insightful presentation of the different industries in relation to various data sets which are intricate and indispensable when it comes to decision-making. The previous chapter explained the basic frameworks, models, workflow processes, algorithms, and visualization methods that can be used to properly visualize big data. Leveraging these tools and methodologies, organizations can gain insights from large-scale data, identify patterns, and communicate their findings in clear and engaging ways. Apart from the representation of data, big data visualization makes data readily available to be analyzed or understood in real time. It finds an application area in health, finance, marketing and public policy and hence is very valuable in these spheres of practice. With the progression in technology, artificial intelligence, interactivity, and real-time capabilities are likely to bring more innovation in the world of visualization, hence unveiling very animated and user-dynamic experiences in the future. Research needs to be concentrated on the current issues in this field, such as the difficulty of scalability, ease of use, and the diversity of data. Further researches into building more efficient and flexible visualization solutions should help organizations unlock their potential to unleash data and empower their users to make informed decisions based on what they know easier and more effectively. For those readers who are interested in developing a deeper understanding of such developments, sources in AI-driven visualization, applications of augmented and virtual reality, and advanced interactive design will be critical sources for information in the future. Big data visualization is going to unlock potentialities in data that are going to sound decisions based on increased confidence for users even if only through continued research and development.

REFERENCES

Abu-Salih, B., Wongthongtham, P., Zhu, D., Chan, K. Y., & Rudra, A. (2023). Introduction to Big Data Technology. https://arxiv.org/pdf/2104.08062.pdf

Alyami, F., & Almutairi, S. (2021). Implementing Integrity Assurance System for Big Data. In F. Alyami & S. Almutairi, Wireless Personal Communications (Vol. 122, Issue 3, p. 2585). Springer Science+Business Media. DOI: 10.21203/rs.3.rs-485987/v1

Auer, C., Dolfi, M., de Carvalho, A. C. P. L. F., Ramis, C. B., & Staar, P. (2022). *Delivering Document Conversion as a Cloud Service with High Throughput and Responsiveness.*, DOI: 10.1109/CLOUD55607.2022.00060

Azeroual, O. (2020). Data Wrangling in Database Systems: Purging of Dirty Data. In O. Azeroual, Data (Vol. 5, Issue 2, p. 50). Multidisciplinary Digital Publishing Institute. DOI: 10.3390/data5020050

Bisarya, S. B., Shukla, A., & Kumar, S. (2023). Data Preparation in Context of Social Sciences Research. In S. S. B. -, A. S. -, & S. K. -, International Journal For Multidisciplinary Research (Vol. 5, Issue 3). DOI: 10.36948/ijfmr.2023.v05i03.3937

Boldosova, V., & Luoto, S. (2019). Storytelling, business analytics and big data interpretation. In V. Boldosova & S. Luoto, Management Research Review (Vol. 43, Issue 2, p. 204). Emerald Publishing Limited. DOI: 10.1108/MRR-03-2019-0106

Bucher, A. (2023). The Patient Experience of the Future is Personalized: Using Technology to Scale an N of 1 Approach. In A. Bucher, Journal of Patient Experience (Vol. 10, p. 237437352311679). SAGE Publishing. DOI: 10.1177/23743735231167975

Cao, S., Zeng, Y., Yang, S., & Cao, S. (2021). Research on Python Data Visualization Technology. In S. Cao, Y. Zeng, S. Yang, & S. Cao, Journal of Physics Conference Series (Vol. 1757, Issue 1, p. 12122). IOP Publishing. DOI: 10.1088/1742-6596/1757/1/012122

Chatzimparmpas, A., Kucher, K., & Kerren, A. (2024). Visualization for Trust in Machine Learning Revisited: The State of the Field in 2023. In A. Chatzimparmpas, K. Kucher, & A. Kerren, IEEE Computer Graphics and Applications (Vol. 44, Issue 3, p. 99). Institute of Electrical and Electronics Engineers. DOI: 10.1109/MCG.2024.3360881

Cheng, C.-Y. (2023). A novel approach of information visualization for machine operation states in industrial 4.0. https://www.sciencedirect.com/science/article/pii/S0360835218302316

Christozov, D., & Rasheva-Yordanova, K. (2023). Data Literacy: Developing Skills on Exploring Big Data Applications. https://www.igi-global.com/gateway/article/191259

Côté, P.-O., Nikanjam, A., Ahmed, N., Humeniuk, D., & Khomh, F. (2024). Data cleaning and machine learning: a systematic literature review. In P.-O. Côté, A. Nikanjam, N. Ahmed, D. Humeniuk, & F. Khomh, Automated Software Engineering (Vol. 31, Issue 2). Springer Science+Business Media. DOI: 10.1007/s10515-024-00453-w

Dhuheir, M., Erbad, A., & Sabeeh, S. (2023). LLHR: Low Latency and High Reliability CNN Distributed Inference for Resource-Constrained UAV Swarms. In M. Dhuheir, A. Erbad, & S. Sabeeh, 2022 IEEE Wireless Communications and Networking Conference (WCNC). DOI: 10.1109/WCNC55385.2023.10118908

Fareed, N., Swoboda, C. M., Chen, S., Potter, E., Wu, D. T. Y., & Sieck, C. J. (2023). U.S. COVID-19 State Government Public Dashboards: An Expert Review. https://www.thieme-connect.de/products/ejournals/abstract/10.1055/s-0041-1723989

Goswami, P., & Sharma, A. (2023). Realtime analysis and visualization of data for instant decisions: A futuristic requirement of the digital world. https://www.sciencedirect.com/science/article/pii/S221478532101275X

Han, S., & Kwak, I. (2023). Mastering data visualization with Python: practical tips for researchers. In S. Han & I. Kwak, Daehan nae'si'gyeong bog'gang'gyeong oe'gwa haghoeji/Journal of minimally invasive surgery (Vol. 26, Issue 4, p. 167). DOI: 10.7602/jmis.2023.26.4.167

Hayes, E., & Partlow, M. (2020). Tutorial: Georeferencing and Displaying Historical Maps using Map Warper and StoryMapJS. https://doi.org/DOI: 10.17605/osf.io/7qd56

Joshi, A. P., & Patel, B. V. (2021). Data Preprocessing: The Techniques for Preparing Clean and Quality Data for Data Analytics Process. In A. P. Joshi & B. V. Patel, Oriental journal of computer science and technology (Vol. 13, Issue 203, p. 78). DOI: 10.13005/ojcst13.0203.03

Kalinin, A. A., Palanimalai, S., Zhu, J., Wu, W., Devraj, N., Ye, C., Ponarul, N., Husain, S. S., & Dinov, I. D. (2022). SOCRAT: A Dynamic Web Toolbox for Interactive Data Processing, Analysis and Visualization. In A. A. Kalinin, S. Palanimalai, J. Zhu, W. Wu, N. Devraj, C. Ye, N. Ponarul, S. S. Husain, & I. D. Dinov, Information (Vol. 13, Issue 11, p. 547). Multidisciplinary Digital Publishing Institute. DOI: 10.3390/info13110547

Kovalerchuk, B., Andonie, R., Datia, N., Nazemi, K., & Banissi, E. (2022). Visual Knowledge Discovery with Artificial Intelligence: Challenges and Future Directions. In B. Kovalerchuk, R. Andonie, N. Datia, K. Nazemi, & E. Banissi, arXiv (Cornell University). Cornell University. https://doi.org//arxiv.2205.01296DOI: 10.48550

Kukreja, M., & Rashmi, R. (2022). Consumer's Behaviour while Purchasing Apparels in Sale Period. In M. Kukreja & R. Rashmi, Deleted Journal (Vol. 16, Issue 1, p. 1). DOI: 10.57198/2583-4932.1072

Ma, R., Sun, E., & Zou, J. (2023). A spectral method for assessing and combining multiple data visualizations. In R. Ma, E. Sun, & J. Zou, Nature Communications (Vol. 14, Issue 1). Nature Portfolio. DOI: 10.1038/s41467-023-36492-2

Maroufkhani, P., Wagner, R., Ismail, W. K. W., Baroto, M. B., & Nourani, M. (2019). Big Data Analytics and Firm Performance: A Systematic Review [Review of Big Data Analytics and Firm Performance: A Systematic Review]. Information, 10(7), 226. Multidisciplinary Digital Publishing Institute. DOI: 10.3390/info10070226

McGowan, L. D., Peng, R. D., & Hicks, S. C. (2022). Design Principles for Data Analysis. In L. D. McGowan, R. D. Peng, & S. C. Hicks, Journal of Computational and Graphical Statistics (Vol. 32, Issue 2, p. 754). Taylor & Francis. DOI: 10.1080/10618600.2022.2104290

Mitchell, S., & Clark, M. (2020). Telling a different story: How nonprofit organizations reveal strategic purpose through storytelling. In S. Mitchell & M. Clark, Psychology and Marketing (Vol. 38, Issue 1, p. 142). Wiley. DOI: 10.1002/mar.21429

Muse, B. A., Nafi, K. W., Khomh, F., & Antoniol, G. (2024). Data-access performance anti-patterns in data-intensive systems. In B. A. Muse, K. W. Nafi, F. Khomh, & G. Antoniol, Empirical Software Engineering (Vol. 29, Issue 6). Springer Science+Business Media. DOI: 10.1007/s10664-024-10535-8

Naneva, V., & Stefanova, K. (2021). Optimization techniques for business intelligence reports. In Naneva, V., & Stefanova, K. (Eds.), *American Institute of Physics*. AIP conference proceedings, DOI: 10.1063/5.0042199

O'Neill, M., Morgan, J., & Burke, K. (2021). Process Visualization of Manufacturing Execution System (MES). *Data*, 659–664. Advance online publication. DOI: 10.1109/SWC50871.2021.00098

Oral, E., Chawla, R., Wijkstra, M., Mahyar, N., & Dimara, E. (2023). From Information to Choice: A Critical Inquiry Into Visualization Tools for Decision Making. In E. Oral, R. Chawla, M. Wijkstra, N. Mahyar, & E. Dimara, arXiv (Cornell University). Cornell University. https://doi.org//arxiv.2307.08326DOI: 10.48550

Ren, S. (2022). Optimization of Enterprise Financial Management and Decision-Making Systems Based on Big Data. In S. Ren, Journal of Mathematics (Vol. 2022, Issue 1). Hindawi Publishing Corporation. DOI: 10.1155/2022/1708506

Richer, G., Pister, A., Abdelaal, M., Fekete, J.-D., Sedlmair, M., & Weiskopf, D. (2023). Scalability in Visualization. https://arxiv.org/pdf/2210.06562.pdf

Roshan, F. Z., Ahuja, A., & Rajabiyazdi, F. (2024). Practical Challenges of Progressive Data Science in Healthcare. In F. Z. Roshan, A. Ahuja, & F. Rajabiyazdi, arXiv (Cornell University). Cornell University. https://doi.org//arxiv.2409.10537DOI: 10.48550

Saqib, N. A., Salam, A. A., Rahman, A.-U.-, & Dash, S. (2023). Reviewing risks and vulnerabilities in web 2.0 for matching security considerations in web 3.0. https://www.tandfonline.com/doi/full/10.1080/09720529.2020.1857903

Sawicki, J., & Burdukiewicz, M. (2022). VisQualdex — the comprehensive guide to good data visualization. In J. Sawicki & M. Burdukiewicz, arXiv (Cornell University). Cornell University. https://doi.org//arxiv.2201.08684DOI: 10.48550

Shaalan, D., & Jusoh, S. (2020). Visualization in Medical System Interfaces: UX Guidelines. In D. Shaalan & S. Jusoh, 2022 14th International Conference on Electronics, Computers and Artificial Intelligence (ECAI). DOI: 10.1109/ECAI50035.2020.9223236

Sinaga, A. R., & Pranata, G. D. (2023). Clustering Data Penjualan Produk pada Toko Yudha dngan Algoritma K-Means. In A. R. Sinaga & G. D. Pranata, SisInfo Jurnal Sistem Informasi dan Informatika (Vol. 3, Issue 2, p. 135). DOI: 10.37278/sisinfo.v3i2.638

Srinivasa, R. C., Arun, S., James, L., & Zhu, Y. (2021). Visualization — a vital decision driving tool for enterprises. In R. C. Srinivasa, S. Arun, L. James, & Y. Zhu, arXiv (Cornell University). Cornell University. https://doi.org/DOI: 10.48550/arXiv.2105

Sun, X., Feng, W., Liu, S., Xie, Y., Bhatia, S., Hooi, B., Wang, W., & Cheng, X. (2023). MonLAD: Money Laundering Agents Detection in Transaction Streams. https://arxiv.org/pdf/2201.10051.pdf

Türkkan, H. (2021). The significance of typography in data visualization. In H. Türkkan, Global Journal of Computer Sciences Theory and Research (Vol. 11, Issue 1, p. 12). DOI: 10.18844/gjcs.v11i1.5030

Wang, D., Wu, L., Zhang, D., Zhou, J., Sun, L., & Fu, Y. (2023). Human-Instructed Deep Hierarchical Generative Learning for Automated Urban Planning. In D. Wang, L. Wu, D. Zhang, J. Zhou, L. Sun, & Y. Fu, Proceedings of the AAAI Conference on Artificial Intelligence (Vol. 37, Issue 4, p. 4660). Association for the Advancement of Artificial Intelligence. DOI: 10.1609/aaai.v37i4.25589

Zhang, S., Heck, P. R., Meyer, M. N., Chabris, C. F., Goldstein, D. G., & Hofman, J. M. (2023). An illusion of predictability in scientific results: Even experts confuse inferential uncertainty and outcome variability. In S. Zhang, P. R. Heck, M. N. Meyer, C. F. Chabris, D. G. Goldstein, & J. M. Hofman, Proceedings of the National Academy of Sciences (Vol. 120, Issue 33). National Academy of Sciences. DOI: 10.1073/pnas.2302491120

Zhu, W. (2021). A Study of Big-Data-Driven Data Visualization and Visual Communication Design Patterns. In W. Zhu, Scientific Programming (Vol. 2021, p. 1). Hindawi Publishing Corporation. DOI: 10.1155/2021/6704937

Chapter 4
Strategic Change Management for Sustainable Digital Transformation:
Leadership, Governance, and Capability Building in Tech-Driven Organizations

Satya Subrahmanyam
http://orcid.org/0000-0003-0441-2742
Holy Spirit University of Kaslik, Lebanon

Jeanne Kaspard
http://orcid.org/0000-0001-5625-6644
Holy Spirit University of Kaslik, Lebanon

ABSTRACT

This chapter, "Change Management in Tech-Driven Sustainable Organizations," explores how organizations can align digital transformation with sustainability goals. Positioned within the book "Leveraging Strategic Management for a Sustainable Digital Economy," it offers a comprehensive guide to managing change at the intersection of technology and sustainable development. The chapter covers foundational and advanced change management models—such as Lewin's, Kotter's, and ADKAR—while incorporating sustainability-specific frameworks like the circular economy. Key drivers and barriers to change are identified, with strategic solutions emphasizing leadership, innovation, stakeholder engagement, and ethical gover-

DOI: 10.4018/979-8-3373-5052-3.ch004

nance. Through practical case studies, it illustrates successes and failures in sectors like energy and retail. The chapter concludes by discussing future trends including green AI and circular business models.

1. INTRODUCTION

Digital transformation and sustainability are now among the most important drivers that transform modern organizations, offering unparalleled opportunities, and challenging managers in a new way. With the world economies becoming more low-carbon and digitally empowered, organizations are forced to rethink the way they perform, compete, and generate value. The interplay between the sustainability requirements - climate mitigation, resource efficiency, and social responsibility - and the fast technological development have fundamentally changed the strategic priorities in industries. The new technologies, such as artificial intelligence (AI), Internet of Things (IoT), blockchain, and advanced data analytics, are being implemented more actively to enhance environmental performance, increase transparency, and help to achieve the circular business model (George et al., 2021). Concurrently, these technologies also pose novel dangers and ethical implications, including the issue of data privacy, the presence of algorithmic bias, digital disparities, and the consumption of more energy due to data-driven procedures (Vinuesa et al., 2020). Learning to cope with change in this dynamic environment has thus become crucial to the leaders who wish to surpass the incremental change into integrated and sustainable digital change.

Although digital technologies offer powerful tools for sustainability advancement, their implementation requires significant organizational adaptation. Workflows must be redesigned, employee capabilities strengthened, governance systems updated, and culture aligned with both innovation and sustainability values. Many organizations still struggle to achieve this integration due to fragmented structures, insufficient digital capabilities, and resistance to change. Traditional change management approaches are often inadequate because they were developed for linear, predictable environments rather than for technology-intensive, sustainability-oriented systems characterized by high uncertainty and rapid evolution (Al-Moaid & Almarhdi, 2024). As a result, leaders face the dual challenge of harnessing digital technologies while simultaneously ensuring that these transformations contribute meaningfully to environmental and social goals. This tension has elevated change management from a support function to a strategic necessity, requiring new conceptual frameworks, governance mechanisms, and implementation approaches.

Despite the critical importance of aligning digital transformation with sustainability objectives, organizations continue to face difficulties in integrating advanced technologies into sustainable strategies due to fragmented change processes, inadequate capability development, and limited understanding of how technological innovations interact with environmental and social goals. These challenges result in inconsistent outcomes, failed digital initiatives, and sustainability efforts that fall short of organizational ambitions, highlighting the urgent need for more coherent and context-specific change management approaches.

The complexity of managing tech-driven sustainable transformation is further amplified by external pressures. Regulatory bodies increasingly mandate environmental disclosure and responsible technology use, while investors and consumers demand transparent, measurable sustainability outcomes (Eccles & Klimenko, 2019). In response, organizations must adopt new forms of governance that prioritize ethical AI, responsible data use, and green digital infrastructure. Technologies such as blockchain-based supply chain platforms and AI-enabled carbon monitoring systems demonstrate how digital solutions can enhance accountability and sustainability reporting (Khallaf et al., 2024). Yet the successful adoption of these tools depends on cultural readiness, interdisciplinary collaboration, and strategic leadership capable of guiding organizations through complex socio-technical change.

Against this backdrop, this chapter examines how change management must evolve to support sustainable digital transformation. The discussion aims to provide a comprehensive and analytically grounded perspective that integrates contemporary theory with emerging technological and sustainability trends. The chapter contributes to the literature by bridging gaps between digital transformation research, sustainability studies, and change management frameworks, offering a holistic view of how organizations can navigate the challenges and opportunities at this intersection. It also highlights practical considerations through cases and real-world illustrations, demonstrating how firms across sectors adopt technologies to advance sustainability while overcoming organizational barriers. The chapter is structured to guide readers from foundational concepts to drivers, challenges, strategies, and implementation paths, culminating in metrics, governance considerations, and industry examples that illustrate best practices. Through this approach, the chapter offers both theoretical insights and actionable guidance for leaders, researchers, and practitioners engaged in building sustainable, technology-enabled organizations.

2. CONCEPTUAL AND ANALYTICAL FOUNDATIONS

2.1 Rethinking Change Management for Digital Sustainability

The rapid acceleration of digital technologies and the growing urgency of sustainability have reshaped the way organizations conceptualize and manage change.

Traditional change management approaches, often characterized by linear stages and top-down communication, struggle to address the speed, complexity, and interconnectedness of digital sustainability initiatives. Contemporary models emphasize agility, continuous iteration, and systems thinking, reflecting the dynamic nature of digital transformation (Kotter, 2021). In digitally intensive environments, change is no longer a discrete project but an ongoing capability that must be embedded into organizational culture and governance structures. The increasing availability of data and advanced analytics further transforms decision-making processes, enabling organizations to design, monitor, and adjust sustainability initiatives in real time.

As digital and sustainability agendas converge, organizations must adopt socio-technical perspectives that account for the interplay between technology, people, and processes. This requires aligning digital capabilities with environmental and social goals, promoting cross-functional collaboration, and fostering a culture that embraces experimentation and continuous learning. Agile methodologies have become central to this shift because they support rapid prototyping, stakeholder involvement, and adaptive planning, key elements for managing complex sustainability transitions (Denning, 2018). Thus, modern change management for digital sustainability demands not only the evolution of tools and methods but also a rethinking of leadership roles, organizational mindset, and the metrics used to evaluate success.

2.2 Tech-Driven Sustainable Organizations: Definitions and Core Features

Sustainable organizations with a technological focus are the ones that use digital technologies to realize tangible changes in the economic, social, and environmental aspects. Organizations are moving more towards digital-first operating models, with platforms, automation, and cloud-based infrastructures being used to improve efficiency and consumption of resources. The digital strategy and sustainability strategy have been closely intertwined, so technologies have made innovations possible: using AI-powered decarbonization algorithms that optimize energy consumption, digital product passports that are blockchain-enabled to improve the transparency of supply-chains, and monitoring systems based on the Internet of Things that will reduce waste and emissions (George et al., 2021). These strategies enable companies to detect inefficiencies, facilitate the circular production process, and maintain adherence to the new rules of sustainability.

At the core of what defines tech-enabled sustainable organizations is the fact that they consider sustainability core to their digital transformation roadmaps. Integration does not solely focus on environmental issues but covers social well-being, labour equity and responsible innovation. The people, planet, and profit triumvirate act as an orientation on the assessment of performance and organization focus. Real-time monitoring and transparent reporting can help workers through digital platforms to become safer, more engaged with the community, or generate ethical supply chains (Birkel & Müller, 2021). The triple bottom line, in combination with more sophisticated technologies, can be viewed as a dynamic tool of management and can help the leaders to follow the path of sustainable growth and provide long-term stability, at the same time.

2.3 Mechanisms Linking Technology, Sustainability, and Change

A wide range of digital technologies now act as accelerators of sustainable transformation. Artificial intelligence enables predictive analytics that optimize energy use, reduce emissions, and support climate forecasting. IoT sensors facilitate real-time monitoring of water, energy, and waste, creating data streams that improve environmental management systems. Cloud computing enhances scalability while enabling organizations to centralize sustainability data, conduct lifecycle assessments, and collaborate more effectively across global operations (Khallaf et al., 2024). These technologies create powerful mechanisms for change by increasing visibility, improving efficiency, and supporting evidence-based decision-making.

The adoption of digital technologies also presents sustainability risks that require careful governance. High-energy consumption from data centers, the expansion of e-waste from rapid device turnover, and concerns about algorithmic bias and data injustice highlight the need to balance digital innovation with responsible practices (Vinuesa et al., 2020). Without appropriate oversight, digital transformation may inadvertently undermine sustainability objectives, widen social inequalities or exacerbate environmental footprints. These risks underscore the importance of integrating ethical considerations, green IT infrastructure, and inclusive design principles into change initiatives.

Innovation remains a critical pathway for linking technology and sustainability. Digital innovations such as circular economy platforms, smart grids, and regenerative manufacturing systems demonstrate how organizations can simultaneously advance operational efficiency and sustainability goals. Collaborative innovation ecosystems - connecting firms, governments, startups, and research institutions - play an essential role in scaling sustainable digital solutions. As organizations navigate this convergence, effective change management becomes the mechanism that aligns technological potential with sustainability ambition, ensuring that transformation efforts generate meaningful and lasting impact.

Figure 1. Mechanisms Linking Technology, Sustainability, and Change

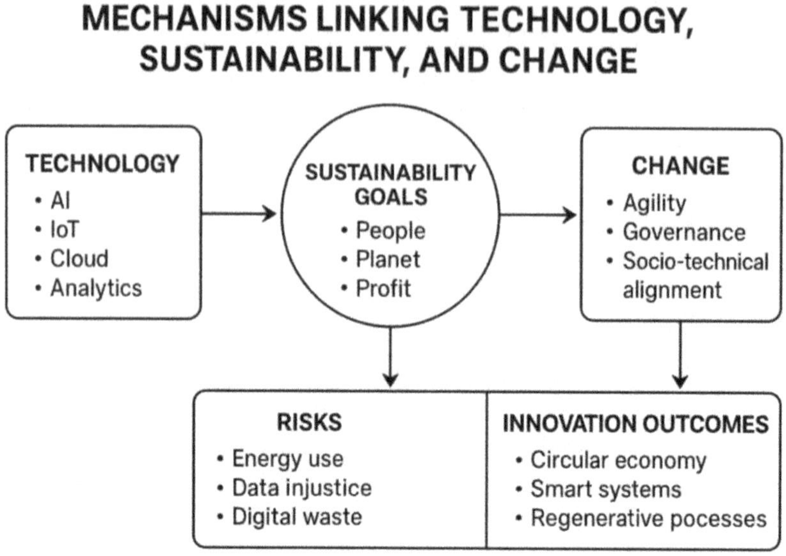

Author, (2025)

3. THEORETICAL AND PRACTICE-ORIENTED FRAMEWORKS

3.1 Revisiting Classical Change Models Through a Digital–Sustainability Lens

Traditional change-management models such as Lewin's three-step model, Kotter's eight-step framework, and the ADKAR model continue to offer foundational guidance, yet they increasingly reveal limitations in hyper-digital organizational environments. Lewin's model, grounded in stability and incremental movement, struggles to account for the constant iteration and rapid cycles characteristic of digital transformation and sustainability-driven innovation. Recent scholarship highlights that digital technologies accelerate the pace of change, making "refreezing" difficult and often undesirable in adaptive systems (Petry, 2018). Kotter's stepwise approach remains valuable for mobilizing stakeholders, but its linear logic is misaligned with the fluidity and non-linearity of digital ecosystems, where iterative prototyping, rapid experimentation, and real-time data feedback shape decision-making (Brock & von Wangenheim, 2021). The ADKAR model - focused on individual-level adoption

- must now expand to include digital competencies, ESG literacy, and new forms of cross-functional collaboration required for sustainable technology integration.

To remain relevant, classical models require modifications that reflect digital velocity, data complexity, and heightened environmental, social, and governance (ESG) expectations. Scholars suggest embedding continuous learning loops, data-driven monitoring mechanisms, and multi-stakeholder engagement practices into established models to support real-time adaptation (Hinings et al., 2018). Organizations also face external pressures from investors, regulators, and consumers demanding verifiable sustainability outcomes, further compelling change frameworks to integrate ESG metrics and transparency standards. As a result, hybrid models - combining traditional change principles with agile methodologies and sustainability criteria - are emerging as more suitable for digital-sustainability transformations.

3.2 Frameworks for Integrating Digital Transformation and Sustainability

With the set of the digital transformation and sustainability aspects that organizations tend to pursue, the integrated frameworks are needed to guide the process of building capabilities, strategic alignment, and execution. Frameworks like digital maturity, in turn, assist companies in assessing their maturity in such areas as data infrastructure, automation, analytics, and digital culture. According to research, digital maturity is strongly linked to ESG performance which means that resource capable and digitally able firms are in a better position to embed circularity, resource use optimization, and low-carbon innovations (Li & Xu, 2024).

Sustainability-oriented frameworks such as the circular economy, cradle-to-cradle design, and regenerative models provide complementary guidance. These frameworks promote closed-loop material flows, energy efficiency, and reductions in ecological impacts, all of which can be amplified through digital tools such as IoT sensors, blockchain-based product passports, and predictive analytics (Khalife et al., 2024). Combining digital transformation with circular economy principles enables organizations to design more sustainable products, track lifecycle emissions, and optimize resource recovery systems.

Systems thinking has also gained prominence as organizations recognize that sustainable digital transformation cannot be achieved through isolated initiatives. Instead, firms must view technology, people, processes, and external stakeholders as interconnected components of an evolving ecosystem. Stakeholder-oriented frameworks emphasize collaboration among governments, technology providers, regulators, suppliers, communities, and consumers. Such ecosystem-based approaches support innovation pathways and ensure that technological solutions align with broader societal and environmental goals (Schot & Steinmueller, 2018).

3.3 Governance and Ethical Frameworks for Responsible Tech Adoption

The acceleration of AI, cloud computing and automation and data-intensive technologies has added more pressure on the necessity to have strong governance and ethical frameworks. It has been noted that regulatory frameworks like the EU AI Act and international standards, including the OECD AI Principles, focus on transparency, accountability, human supervision, and risk categorization as the basic principles of responsible AI implementation (OECD, 2021). These frames assist organizations in considering the ethical threats of the AI systems, such as bias, obscurity, and unintended social effects.

Data ethics frameworks have also expanded to address privacy protection, fairness, data minimization, and the environmental footprint of data centers. With digital technologies contributing significantly to global electricity consumption, organizations are increasingly required to assess the carbon intensity of their data operations and adopt green cloud strategies (Hussain et al., 2023).

Figure 2. Theoretical and Practice-Oriented Frameworks

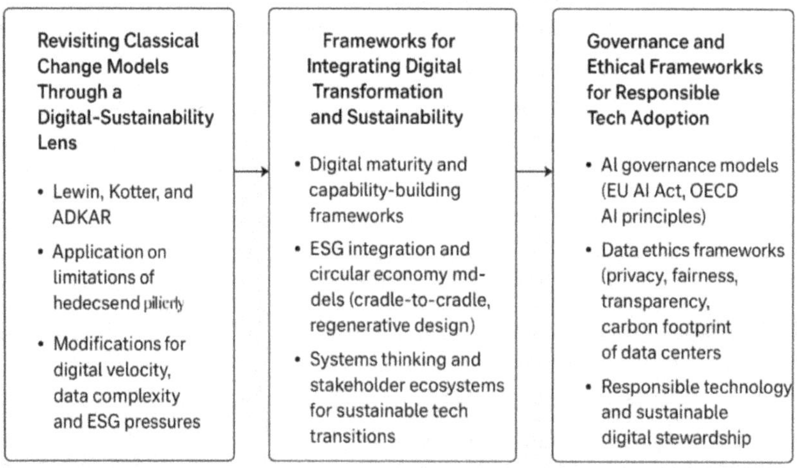

Author, (2025)

The broader concept of responsible technology and sustainable digital stewardship integrates ethical AI, green IT, and inclusive digital practices into a single governance lens. This approach encourages organizations to balance innovation with societal welfare, ensuring that technology-driven sustainability efforts do not create new inequalities or environmental burdens. Ultimately, governance frameworks serve as a critical foundation for aligning digital transformation with long-term sustainability commitments.

4. DRIVERS AND BARRIERS IN TECH-DRIVEN SUSTAINABLE CHANGE

4.1 Key Drivers of Digital–Sustainability Transformation

The intersection of digitalization and sustainability has become even stronger as companies face mounting environmental, social, and governance (ESG) pressures and at the same time use disruptive innovations to gain operational resilience. The high rate of development of artificial intelligence (AI), data analytics, and the Internet of Things (IoT) are one of the most influential causes of this change. Carbon-efficient operations, predictive maintenance, and intelligent resource allocation are now supported by AI-driven optimization tools to allow companies to achieve sustainability goals with a higher degree of accuracy (Zaghmout & Harrison, 2025). IoT-based monitoring systems are also largely used in minimizing waste and energy usage by tracking assets, industrial operation and the environment in real-time. Combined with cloud computing and green analytics, those technologies can influence firms to shift their reactive approach to sustainability compliance toward proactive and data-driven environmental management (Mohamed et al., 2025).

The regulatory pressures also contribute to even faster movement of digital-sustainability. The stringent carbon disclosure and supply-chain transparency, and circular-economy mandates, have been introduced by the governments and multilateral bodies. The need to comply with legally defined requirements to meet such conditions as the EU Corporate Sustainability Reporting Directive (CSRD) and the implementation of carbon price systems compel organizations to use digital tools that can help them verify, trace, and report sustainability performance on a large scale (European Commission, 2022). These are policies that favor the use of digital product passports, emissions-tracking solutions, and software to assess the lifecycle. Compliance is not a procedure anymore; it demands more and more advanced data structures and built-in ESG reporting systems.

The dynamics in the market also are critical in influencing an organizational adoption of digital sustainability. There is consumer and business customer demand now of environmentally responsible, transparent, and climate-resilient goods and services. This transition is quite pronounced in areas where people like food systems, electronics, retail, and logistics have been exposed to buyers being more sensitive to carbon footprints, ethical sourcing, and the life cycle of products. Firms are pressured by market expectations to follow the provenance digitally, provide integrity across the supply-chain and minimize environmental damage (Ransbotham et al., 2017). Digital transparency Digital transparency, facilitated by blockchain and IoT, and enabled by AI, has become a competitive differentiator through improved brand trust and market positioning.

Another momentum is added to the expectancies of investors. Financial instruments linked to sustainability, e.g. green bonds, ESG indexed funds, sustainability linked loans, are now mainstream. Capital allocation decisions, which are required by institutional investors, are becoming more demanding in terms of high-caliber environmental and social information. This is resulting in a value system that values correct ESG measures, real-time analytics, and sustainability governance that is supported by technology (Park & Jang, 2021). This means that companies that incorporate digital innovation with a sustainability pledge get better access to capital and increase the value creation in the long-term.

4.2 Barriers and Systemic Constraints

Despite these powerful drivers, organizations continue to face a range of structural, cultural, and technological barriers that impede sustainable digital transformation. One of the most pervasive barriers is organizational resistance to change. Legacy systems, rigid hierarchies, and fear of technological disruption contribute to cultural inertia and slow adoption of innovative sustainability solutions (Al-Moaid & Almarhdi, 2024). Many organizations remain deeply rooted in traditional operating models, making it difficult to integrate advanced digital tools or shift toward more circular, regenerative business practices.

A related barrier is the widening skills gap across digital technologies and sustainability domains. The rapid pace of AI, data science, and green technology innovation has outstripped the availability of professionals equipped to interpret data, develop sustainable digital solutions, or integrate ESG thinking into core business processes. Research indicates that skill shortages in AI, analytics, and sustainability strategy are among the most significant impediments to digital transformation efforts (Subrahmanyam, 2025). Without cross-functional capabilities, organizations struggle to operationalize data-driven sustainability strategies.

Data-related constraints also hinder progress. Poor data quality, fragmented systems, and governance gaps undermine ESG analytics and limit the reliability of sustainability reporting. Ethical challenges - including bias in AI models, privacy risks, digital exclusion, and the environmental footprint of data centers - further complicate sustainability-oriented digital adoption (Floridi & Cowls, 2019). Without robust data governance and ethical frameworks, technology-enabled sustainability efforts risk generating new forms of inequality and environmental harm.

Another critical barrier is the misalignment between digital investments and sustainability key performance indicators (KPIs). Organizations frequently invest in technology without clearly connecting these investments to measurable sustainability outcomes. This misalignment results in fragmented initiatives that fail to scale or deliver the intended environmental impact (Subrahmanyam, 2025). Inconsistent KPIs, siloed departments, and competing operational priorities undermine the strategic coherence needed for technology-enabled sustainability transitions.

Finally, technological fragmentation poses significant challenges. Organizations often operate with heterogeneous systems, incompatible data architectures, and decentralized digital applications, all of which impede integration and large-scale deployment of sustainability technologies (Ghobakhloo, 2020). These fragmentation issues reduce the organization's ability to leverage real-time analytics, implement cross-functional ESG dashboards, or deploy end-to-end digital sustainability platforms.

Table 1. Barriers and Required Organizational Capabilities

Barrier	Required Organizational Capability	Capability Description (Feeds into Sustainability KPIs)
Organizational resistance & cultural inertia	Change leadership & sustainability culture	Ability to foster digital-sustainability mindsets; measured through change-readiness scores and culture indices.
Legacy systems & outdated infrastructure	Digital integration capability	Modernized IT architecture enabling cross-system data flows; KPI: % of systems integrated.
Skills shortages in AI, analytics, sustainability	Workforce digital-sustainability competence	Cross-functional skill development; KPI: training hours, certifications, AI and ESG literacy rates.
Poor data quality & governance gaps	Data governance maturity	Controls for accuracy, privacy, ethical AI; KPI: data quality index, bias audit frequency.
Ethical risks (AI bias, energy use, privacy)	Responsible tech governance	Frameworks for fairness, transparency, and green IT; KPI: algorithmic fairness score, data carbon footprint.
Misalignment between digital investments and sustainability KPIs	Strategic alignment capability	Ability to map tech investments to ESG outcomes; KPI: % of digital projects tied to sustainability metrics.
Fragmented technology ecosystems	Platform scalability & interoperability	Adoption of unified platforms; KPI: ecosystem interoperability index.

5. STRATEGIC APPROACHES TO MANAGING TECH-DRIVEN SUSTAINABLE CHANGE

5.1 Leadership Capabilities for Digital-Sustainability Initiatives

The sustainable organizations that are driven by technology need models of leadership that go beyond the traditional hierarchical models of change management. Transformational leadership, involving the generation of visions, motivation, and empowerment has been demonstrated to have a substantial impact on the result of digital transformation through the establishment of innovation and flexibility (Subrahmanyam, 2025). Transformational leaders are an essential part of sustainability because they can work to align digital initiatives with environmental, social, and governance (ESG) objectives and allow organizations to work towards decarbonization, ethical use of technologies, or creating value to stakeholders at the same time. Distributed leadership has been as needed as digital ecosystems are getting more decentralized. Distributed leadership promotes cross-team and cross-digital unit decision-making, which leads to agility and quicker response to sustainability issues like transparency in the supply chain and regulatory compliance (Zaghmout & Harrison, 2025).

The other fundamental ability is ethical leadership because organizations struggle with the intricacies of AI-based sustainability decision-making. Things like algorithmic transparency, responsible data use, and the energy-intensive nature of the digital infrastructure require leaders who are morally upright and able to manage the technological opportunity with social effect. Today leaders should learn to operate in the world of uncertainty and deal with digital discontinuity and to lead interdisciplinary teams that incorporate technologists, sustainability specialists, data scientists, and operational managers. The digital sustainability vision therefore needs a holistic approach i.e., looking at long-term environmental commitments through the fast-changing technology road maps (Tathavadekar & Mahankale, 2023). All these leadership skills help to formulate the strategic direction and to maintain a balance between digital transformation that helps organizations achieve the goals of organizational sustainability instead of making them less relevant.

5.2 Building Culture and Organizational Readiness

Creating a culture that supports tech-driven sustainable change is central to achieving meaningful transformation. Organizations must cultivate cultures of experimentation, learning, and accountability where employees feel empowered to innovate and question unsustainable processes. Research indicates that digitally mature firms foster collaborative cultures that embrace continuous improvement and knowledge-sharing, enabling new technologies such as AI, IoT, and green analytics to be deployed effectively (Mohamed et al., 2025). At the same time, sustainability-oriented cultures emphasize environmental stewardship, shared responsibility, and long-term thinking - values that must be embedded into digital strategy and operational routines.

Organizational readiness assessments serve as critical tools for evaluating capabilities, gaps, and preparedness for digital sustainability transitions. These assessments typically examine digital maturity, technological infrastructure, sustainability integration, leadership alignment, and workforce skills, and their outcomes provide inputs into key performance indicators (KPIs) addressed later in the chapter. Studies show that organizations with higher readiness levels experience greater success when implementing digital sustainability initiatives, as they are better equipped to overcome structural rigidities and cultural resistance (Subrahmanyam, 2024). Overcoming organizational inertia requires targeted interventions that address legacy systems, entrenched practices, and fear of technological displacement. This may involve restructuring workflows, redesigning roles, or introducing cross-functional sustainability teams to encourage collaboration across traditional silos.

5.3 Strategic Communication and Stakeholder Collaboration

Strategic communication is pivotal to managing digital sustainability initiatives, particularly given the complexity and novelty of technologies such as AI-driven carbon forecasting, blockchain-enabled traceability, and IoT-based circular manufacturing. Data-driven storytelling has emerged as a powerful communication tool, enabling organizations to articulate digital sustainability visions through compelling visualizations, predictive insights, and transparent reporting. When communicated effectively, sustainability data enhances trust among internal and external stakeholders and supports change adoption by making the benefits of digital initiatives tangible (Dessart & Standaert, 2023).

Multi-stakeholder engagement is another critical dimension of strategic communication. Digital sustainability transitions affect a broad ecosystem of partners - including suppliers, regulators, communities, and customers - each of whom contributes to and is impacted by the organization's transformation. Research shows that multi-stakeholder collaboration improves ESG performance, accelerates digital innovation, and strengthens supply chain resilience (Park & Jang, 2021). Internally, effective communication strategies must address employee concerns regarding job displacement, data governance, and new digital workflows. Transparent, timely, and inclusive communication ensures that employees understand transformation goals, the value of new technologies, and their role in achieving sustainable outcomes.

5.4 Workforce Capability Development

As organizations adopt sophisticated digital tools and sustainability frameworks, workforce capability development becomes a strategic imperative. Digital upskilling initiatives must focus on building competencies in artificial intelligence, data analytics, process automation, and digital-platform management. Studies demonstrate that digitally skilled employees are better equipped to identify sustainability opportunities embedded in data streams, such as resource inefficiencies, carbon hotspots, or waste-reduction opportunities (Ghobakhloo, 2020). Simultaneously, sustainability capability building is essential to ensure that employees understand life cycle thinking, carbon accounting, and regenerative design principles.

Organizations are increasingly utilizing digital learning platforms, knowledge repositories, and AI-driven training systems to facilitate continuous capability building. These platforms enable personalized learning pathways, real-time competency tracking, and accessible knowledge-sharing across geographies (Tathavadekar & Mahankale, 2023). The integration of digital and sustainability capabilities is particularly important for roles such as data engineers, supply chain specialists, product designers, and operations managers, who must simultaneously optimize digital systems and align them with sustainability metrics.

Figure 3. Strategic Approaches to Managing Tech-Driven Sustainable Change

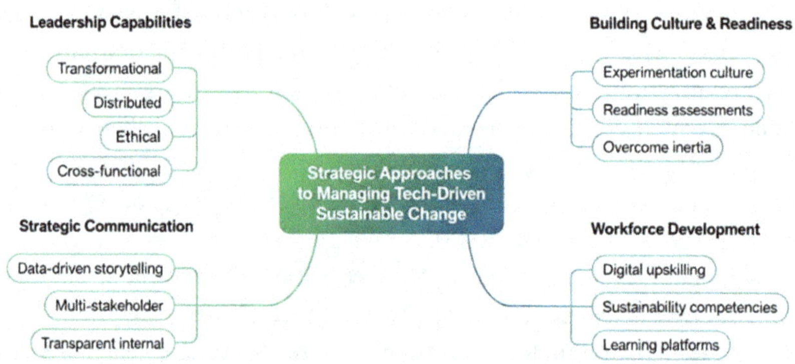

Author, (2025)

Building a future-ready workforce therefore requires strategic investments in training, mentorship, and organizational learning systems that support both technological fluency and sustainability literacy. These investments enable organizations to fully leverage digital technologies for sustainable outcomes while fostering a workforce that is resilient, adaptable, and capable of driving long-term transformation.

6. IMPLEMENTATION, INTEGRATION, AND MEASUREMENT

6.1 Designing and Executing Digital-Sustainability Transformation Roadmaps

Implementing a digital-sustainability transformation requires a structured, stepwise roadmap that guides organizations from diagnosing current problems to scaling sustainable practices. The recommended sequence begins with problem identification - assessing inefficiencies, environmental or social risks, and gaps in digital capabilities. The next phase involves capability building, through which organizations foster digital literacy, train staff, and establish governance and cultural foundations. Following that, technology activation entails deploying digital tools (e.g., data analytics, IoT, AI) to support core processes. The subsequent step - sustainability integration - embeds environmental and social objectives into business workflows, supply chains, and product life cycles. Finally, successful initiatives are scaled across the organization to maximize impact.

The recent research on this topic - including the SDT SMEs Roadmap - presents a maturity-based roadmap to incorporate sustainability into the digital transformation (Pinto et al., 2024). The roadmap is based on ISO/IEC 33000 standards and covers the strategies level, the more tactical and operational level, and evaluates 75 processes in six dimensions: Digital Technologies; Customer Focus; Organizational Culture; Organizational Governance; People; and Sustainability. Its confirmation within case studies shows that it is effective in leading organizations through the process of digital sustainability change (Pinto et al., 2024).

Given the complexity and uncertainty inherent in integrating digital transformation with sustainability, practitioners are increasingly urged to adopt agile, iterative, and evidence-based change methodologies. Such approaches emphasize incremental implementation, frequent feedback, and continuous adjustment - allowing organizations to pilot projects, learn from early failures or unexpected impacts, and refine their strategy before a full rollout (Rawashdeh et al., 2024). This iterative, pilot-driven method helps mitigate risk, fosters organizational learning, and makes the transformation more resilient and adaptable.

6.2 Metrics, KPIs, and Measurement Systems

Assessing progress and ensuring accountability call for a robust measurement framework tracking digital capability, sustainability outcomes, and organizational change. A multi-dimensional KPI structure can include:

- **Tech-capability KPIs**: These might include the share of processes digitalized (digital adoption rate), predictive-analytics accuracy for AI/ML systems, and maturity levels of digital skills among employees (e.g., via self-assessment or certification).
- **Sustainability KPIs**: These could encompass percentage reduction in carbon emissions, improvements in energy efficiency, circularity rate (e.g., material reuse or recycling rates), waste reduction, and resource-intensity metrics.
- **Change-management KPIs**: To capture organizational readiness and culture shift, metrics may include user adoption rates, employee readiness (survey-based), participation rates in upskilling, as well as qualitative culture-shift indicators such as number of sustainability initiatives proposed by staff or levels of stakeholder engagement.
- **ESG-linked and digital-traceability metrics**: For organizations committed to ESG (environmental, social, governance) compliance, metrics might include compliance rates, transparency measures (e.g., traceability of materials or lifecycle data), percentage of products with "digital product passports," and supply-chain sustainability performance.

A unified measurement framework should tie the challenges identified in earlier phases (e.g., inefficient energy usage, lack of transparency, skills gaps) directly to these KPIs - ensuring that metrics are relevant, actionable and tailored to organizational risks and strategic goals. Continuous monitoring through dashboards and feedback loops can enable real-time tracking, flag deviations, and guide corrective actions.

Empirical studies validate the importance of these KPI frameworks. A systematic review of digital transformation research highlighted the essential function of digitalization in facilitating sustainability goals while also emphasizing the necessity for more explicit operational metrics to assess progress (Guandalini, 2022). Research in manufacturing contexts indicates that digital transformation, facilitated by green knowledge acquisition and innovation performance, can improve sustainable corporate performance (Asbeetah et al., 2025).

6.3 Technology Governance, Risk, and Ethical Management

Deploying digital and sustainable technologies brings potentials, but also risks - requiring robust governance, ethical design, and responsible data management. First, establishing AI governance structures (e.g., oversight boards, cross-functional ethics committees, ethical-by-design policies) ensures that adoption of digital technologies remains aligned with the organization's sustainability objectives and broader values, while guarding against risks related to bias, misuse, or unintended environmental consequences.

Equally important is data governance. As digital systems accumulate data on energy consumption, material flows, carbon emissions, lifecycle impacts, and supply-chain traceability, organizations must ensure data integrity, transparency, security, and proper access controls. This strengthens stakeholder trust, supports audit-ready sustainability reporting, and ensures accountability.

Organizations should adopt green IT policies and responsible innovation practices. "Green IT" entails choosing and designing digital infrastructure (e.g., data centers, cloud services, IoT devices) with minimal environmental footprint. Responsible innovation involves embedding sustainability considerations from the earliest stages of technology selection and deployment - prioritizing resource-efficient software, recyclable hardware, and energy-efficient architectures.

Firms must ensure ESG compliance - aligning digital-sustainability strategies with recognized frameworks, standards, and reporting requirements. By doing so, technological innovation and sustainability integration become mutually reinforcing, rather than tangential or contradictory.

Figure 4. Implementation, Integration, and Measurement

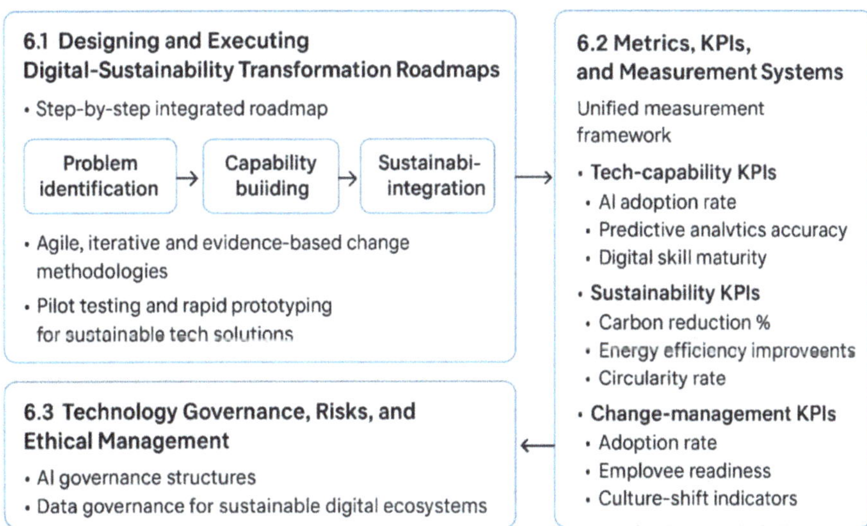

Author, (2025)

An integrated digital-sustainability transformation is far more than just a technology upgrade; it is a strategic journey requiring clarity of vision, structured execution, continuous measurement, and robust governance. A well-designed transformation roadmap - progressing from problem identification to scaling - supported by agile, iterative implementation and pilot testing, offers adaptability, risk mitigation, and organizational learning. A comprehensive set of KPIs spanning digital capability, sustainability outcomes, change management, and ESG compliance enables monitoring, accountability, and evidence-based decision-making. Embedding governance, ethical protocols, and green IT practices ensures that transformation remains responsible, transparent, and aligned with long-term sustainability goals. Organizations that adopt such integrated and measured approaches stand to realize not only operational efficiencies and innovation gains but also long-lasting environmental and social value, stronger stakeholder trust, and sustainable competitive advantage.

7. INTEGRATED CASE STUDIES AND INDUSTRY ILLUSTRATIONS

7.1 Successful Digital-Sustainability Change Transitions

Organizations across sectors increasingly demonstrate that digital transformation and sustainability can reinforce each other when strategically aligned. Successful transitions typically follow a clear sequence: sustainability and efficiency drivers → technology-enabled strategies → measurement through KPIs → long-term environmental and economic outcomes.

Energy Sector: AI for Smart Grids and Demand Forecasting

The energy sector offers some of the strongest examples of how artificial intelligence (AI) can accelerate decarbonization. One well-documented case is Ørsted's deployment of AI-enabled predictive models to optimize wind-farm operations. By integrating machine learning with real-time weather and turbine data, Ørsted improved forecasting accuracy and reduced operational energy waste, contributing to its broader shift from fossil fuels to renewables (Ørsted, 2021). AI-driven smart grid pilots across Europe also demonstrate concrete sustainability outcomes. The EU-funded SMART-ML project used machine learning algorithms to balance load across distributed renewable sources, reducing grid strain and lowering carbon emissions during peak periods (European Commission, 2024). The KPIs in these initiatives - forecasting accuracy, reduction in curtailment, and emissions avoided - provide measurable evidence of successful digital-sustainability integration.

Manufacturing: IoT-Enabled Circular Production and Waste Minimization

Manufacturing firms have increasingly adopted Internet of Things (IoT) systems to transition toward circular production models. A leading example is Schneider Electric, which implemented IoT-enabled sensors and real-time analytics across its factories as part of its "Zero Waste to Landfill" commitment. The company's Smart Factory program reduced energy consumption by 10–25% across several sites while simultaneously improving material reuse and equipment uptime (Schneider Electric, 2021). Procter & Gamble (P&G) offers another compelling illustration. Through digital twins, virtual replicas of production processes, P&G improved packaging design efficiency and reduced resource consumption in its Beauty and Home Care divisions (P&G, 2022). In both cases, digital technologies were intentional tools for circularity, supporting KPIs such as waste reduction rates, energy intensity per unit of output, and percentage of materials recycled.

Retail: Digital Twins and Green Supply-Chain Transparency

Retailers are increasingly leveraging digital twins and blockchain to improve supply-chain traceability and transparency. Walmart's blockchain-based traceability system for leafy greens, rolled out from 2018–2019, allows tracing produce back to the farm in seconds instead of days - improving transparency and enabling more targeted recalls, which has the potential to reduce waste associated with spoilage and recalls (Walmart, 2018). Meanwhile, IKEA's investment in digital twin supply-chain modeling has enabled the company to identify carbon hotspots, optimize transportation routes, and evaluate the sustainability implications of design choices before implementation (IKEA, 2024). Retail KPIs include supply-chain carbon intensity, traceability scores, and product-level circularity metrics. These cases illustrate that digital twins are not merely operational tools but strategic levers to reduce environmental impact while enhancing customer trust.

Tech Startups: Sustainable-by-Design and Circular Platforms

Tech startups often excel in aligning digital innovation with sustainability from inception. The Dutch startup Fairphone exemplifies "sustainable-by-design," building modular smartphones with ethically sourced materials and repairable components. Since 2020, Fairphone's digital platform has expanded to include repair tutorials, parts ordering systems, and lifecycle impact assessments, supporting consumers in extending device lifespan (Fairphone, 2022). Another example is Too Good To Go, a platform using AI-based optimization to connect consumers with surplus food. As of 2023, the company helped prevent millions of meals from being wasted, directly reducing methane emissions associated with food disposal (Too Good To Go, 2023). These startup models demonstrate how digital platforms can scale circular economy principles quickly and efficiently.

7.2 Insights from Failure and Partial Success

Not all digital-sustainability transformations succeed. Failures often stem from cultural resistance, technological misalignment, or unintended rebound effects. Examining these cases provides critical lessons for organizational leaders and policymakers.

Unintended Carbon Footprint Increases from Digital Transformation

One challenge relates to the rebound effects of digitalization. Several organizations have reported that cloud migration and advanced analytics inadvertently increased energy consumption due to insufficient attention to data-center efficiency. A notable example is a mid-sized financial services firm documented in a 2020 Accenture sustainability audit. Although the company adopted AI-driven customer analytics to reduce paper and manual processes, the resulting computing load increased emissions because workloads were hosted in non-renewable-powered data centers (Accenture, 2020). This case shows why digital strategies must consider life-cycle carbon assessments and energy-efficient infrastructure.

Cultural Resistance Derailing Data-Driven Sustainability Initiatives

Cultural rigidities can undermine even well-funded digital-sustainability programs. A 2020 World Economic Forum report highlighted a global logistics company where attempts to implement IoT-based fleet optimization failed due to frontline resistance. Drivers perceived the technology as surveillance rather than a sustainability tool, resulting in low adoption rates and unreliable data (WEF, 2020). This case underlines the importance of employee participation, transparent communication, and change-readiness assessments before deploying data-intensive systems.

Misalignment Between ESG Goals and Technology Investment

Another common pitfall is misalignment between ESG commitments and actual digital investments. A 2022 study by McKinsey found that nearly 40% of organizations pursued digital investments framed as “green” without establishing clear sustainability KPIs or verifying environmental benefits. In one manufacturing case, robotic automation increased throughput but also raised energy usage, contradicting the company's publicly stated carbon-reduction targets (McKinsey, 2022). The lesson is clear: technological adoption must be strategically tied to measurable sustainability outcomes, not rhetorical ESG branding.

8. FUTURE OUTLOOK: THE EVOLUTION OF CHANGE MANAGEMENT FOR SUSTAINABLE DIGITAL ECONOMIES

8.1 Emerging Trends Shaping Sustainable Digital Transformation

As organizations transition toward digitally enabled low-carbon futures, a new set of technological and sustainability megatrends is transforming how change management is conceptualized and implemented. Climate technologies, ranging from carbon capture solutions to precision energy management, are rapidly expanding due to intensified global climate commitments and investor pressures (IEA, 2023). Digital product passports (DPPs), which provide lifecycle traceability for goods, are becoming essential for ensuring transparency and compliance with circular economy regulations, particularly in the European Union (European Commission, 2022a). Likewise, regenerative digital systems - digital infrastructures designed not only to minimize harm but to actively restore ecological and social systems - are emerging as a frontier in sustainable transformation (Raworth, 2023). These shifts illustrate that the future of change management will require leaders to orchestrate the convergence of environmental science, data governance, and digital innovation in an integrated manner.

One of the most important changes is the rise of "green AI," which is AI that is designed to be energy-efficient, low-carbon, and in line with sustainability. Studies show that traditional AI models can produce a lot of emissions if they aren't optimized. This is why companies are switching to energy-efficient architectures and carbon-aware training protocols (Maurya et al., 2025). Big tech companies like Google and Microsoft have already started using carbon-intelligent workload shifting, which means moving data center tasks to times and places where renewable energy is most available. This shows how digital choices can directly lower emissions (Google, 2020). These trends show that the focus of digital transformation is moving from making things more efficient to making them more sustainable.

8.2 AI Governance and Ethical Sustainability as Strategic Imperatives

AI governance is now a key part of digital economies that will last. This is because of the rise of advanced analytics, generative AI, and predictive systems. Ethical sustainability necessitates not only the reduction of environmental impacts but also the promotion of fairness, accountability, transparency, and resilience within AI-driven systems (OECD, 2021). New laws, like the EU AI Act, stress risk-based governance, lifecycle monitoring, and responsible data practices. All of these will have a direct effect on how businesses plan and handle change.

In practice, this means that leaders in sustainability must work closely with data scientists, lawyers, and operations teams to design governance structures that link digital innovation with social and environmental performance. If organizations don't align in this way, they could end up with unintended consequences like algorithmic bias, digital exclusion, and data center consumption patterns that aren't sustainable. As customers, investors, and regulators expect more from businesses when it comes to ethics, transparent AI governance will be a key part of managing change in the future.

8.3 Transitioning Toward Smart, Resilient, and Low-Carbon Organizational Systems

The next phase of sustainable digital transformation emphasizes interconnected resilience: the capacity of organizations to anticipate, absorb, and adapt to disruptions across climate, supply chain, and digital domains. Smart systems - enabled by IoT, AI, and blockchain - offer real-time operational visibility and predictive capabilities that strengthen organizational resilience. Schneider Electric has implemented smart energy management solutions across global sites, achieving up to 30% energy savings while improving operational stability (Schneider Electric, 2022).

Low-carbon organizational systems also leverage digital twins - virtual replicas of physical assets - to simulate environmental impacts, reduce waste, and optimize resource flows. In the built environment sector, Siemens has used digital twin platforms to lower energy consumption in commercial buildings, resulting in significant reductions in both operational costs and emissions (Siemens, 2022). These cases illustrate how digitalization and decarbonization can be mutually reinforcing when strategically integrated.

8.4 Building Organizational Readiness for Future Digital-Sustainability Disruptions

Preparing organizations for future disruptions requires a shift toward adaptive, learning-oriented change management models. Traditional top-down transformation approaches are increasingly inadequate in environments characterized by complexity, regulatory shifts, and rapid technological advancement. Instead, organizations must cultivate dynamic capabilities such as digital literacy, cross-functional collaboration, experimentation, and continuous sustainability performance monitoring (Teece et al., 2016).

Workforce reskilling will be central as new roles emerge around green data science, climate informatics, DPP compliance, ethical AI auditing, and regenerative design. Leaders must also foster cultures that support agility and systems thinking, enabling employees to understand the interdependencies among digital, environmental, and social domains. The scenario planning and stress-testing, already used in climate risk management, will become mainstream tools for anticipating technology-sustainability interactions.

Table 2. Key Trends and Strategic Implications for Sustainable Digital Change Management

Emerging Trend	Description	Strategic Implications for Change Management	Examples / Industry Use Cases
Climate Tech Expansion	Growth of technologies for carbon reduction, energy efficiency, and climate adaptation.	Integrate climate targets with digital strategy; require cross-functional innovation.	Energy optimization platforms (e.g., Schneider Electric).
Green AI	Development of low-energy, carbon-efficient AI models and processes.	Need for carbon-aware data governance and monitoring tools.	Google's carbon-intelligent computing; Microsoft's AI energy tracking.
Digital Product Passports	Lifecycle traceability systems providing environmental and material data.	Align digital systems with circular economy regulations; enhance transparency.	EU DPP rollout in textiles and electronics.
Regenerative Digital Systems	Systems designed to restore or enhance natural and social ecosystems.	Shift from "do less harm" to "net-positive" digital innovation.	Regenerative agriculture platforms and smart biodiversity monitoring.
AI Governance & Ethics	Responsible AI frameworks ensuring fairness, transparency, and environmental sustainability.	New roles in AI ethics, compliance, and lifecycle impact assessment.	EU AI Act compliance initiatives.
Smart & Resilient Systems	IoT-AI integrated systems that anticipate and mitigate disruptions.	Build real-time monitoring, digital twins, and resilience analytics.	Siemens building digital twins; smart supply chain platforms.

The future of change management in sustainable digital economies will be defined by the integration of climate-conscious innovation, ethical technology governance, and organizational resilience. As digital and sustainability imperatives converge, leaders will be required to design transformation pathways that are technologically sophisticated, environmentally restorative, and socially responsible. Organizations that invest early in capabilities such as green AI, digital passports, regenerative technologies, and ethical AI governance will be better positioned to thrive in an increasingly regulated and climate-impacted global market.

9. CONCLUSION

The chapter highlights that the convergence of digital transformation and sustainability is reshaping organizational strategy, capabilities, and leadership expectations. Across the sections, it becomes evident that successful transitions rely on integrated change management frameworks that connect technological drivers, sustainability imperatives, human factors, and measurable performance indicators. Case studies from energy, manufacturing, retail, and technology sectors illustrate that when organizations align digital tools - such as AI, IoT, digital twins, and platform-based models - with environmental and social objectives, they achieve superior outcomes in efficiency, transparency, and resilience.

The discussion also underscores that leaders must balance rapid digital innovation with sustainability responsibilities, ensuring ethical AI governance, carbon-aware digital architecture, and inclusive cultural change. Failures examined in the chapter show that misalignment between ESG goals, technology investments, and organizational culture can undermine transformation efforts, reinforcing the importance of holistic planning.

Looking forward, the evolution of climate tech, digital product passports, regenerative systems, and green AI offers significant opportunities but requires new skills, governance models, and collaborative approaches. Future research should explore cross-sector frameworks, lifecycle impacts of digital systems, and leadership competencies for sustainable digital economies, enabling organizations to navigate complexity while creating long-term value.

REFERENCES

Accenture. (2020). *The Green Behind the Cloud.* Accenture Strategy.

Al-Moaid, N. A. A., & Almarhdi, S. G. (2024). Developing dynamic capabilities for successful digital transformation projects: The mediating role of change management. *Journal of Innovation and Entrepreneurship, 13*(1), 85. Advance online publication. DOI: 10.1186/s13731-024-00446-9

Asbeetah, Z., Alzubi, A., Khadem, A., & Iyiola, K. (2025). Harnessing Digital Transformation for Sustainable Performance: Exploring the Mediating Roles of Green Knowledge Acquisition and Innovation Performance Under Digital Transformational Leadership. *Sustainability (Basel), 17*(5), 2285. DOI: 10.3390/su17052285

Birkel, H., & Müller, J. M. (2021). Potentials of Industry 4.0 for supply chain management within the triple bottom line of sustainability: A systematic literature review. *Journal of Cleaner Production, 289*, 125612. DOI: 10.1016/j.jclepro.2020.125612

Brock, J. M., & von Wangenheim, F. (2021). Demystifying AI: What digital transformation leaders can teach you about realistic AI adoption. *Business Horizons, 64*(6), 709–720. DOI: 10.1177/1536504219865226

Denning, S. (2018). *The age of agile: How smart companies are transforming the way work gets done.* AMACOM.

Dessart, L., & Standaert, W. (2023). Strategic storytelling in the age of sustainability. *Business Horizons, 66*(3), 371–385. DOI: 10.1016/j.bushor.2023.01.005

Eccles, R. G., & Klimenko, S. (2019). The investor revolution. *Harvard Business Review, 97*(3), 106–116.

European Commission. (2022a). Directive (EU) 2022/2464 of the European Parliament and of the Council on corporate sustainability reporting. *Official Journal of the European Union, L, 322*, 15–80.

European Commission. (2024). *The digitalisation of the energy system: A green, efficient and affordable energy system fit for the future.* Publications Office of the European Union.

European Commission. (2022b). *Proposal for a Regulation of the European Parliament and of the Council establishing a framework for setting ecodesign requirements for sustainable products and repealing Directive 2009/125/EC.* COM (2022) 142 final.

Fairphone. (2022). *Impact Report 2022*. Fairphone. Retrieved from https://www.fairphone.com/wp-content/uploads/2023/04/Impact-Report-2022.pdf

Floridi, L., & Cowls, J. (2019). A unified framework of five principles for AI in society. *Harvard Data Science Review*, *1*(1). Advance online publication. DOI: 10.1162/99608f92.8cd550d1

George, G., Merrill, R. K., & Schillebeeckx, S. J. D. (2021). Digital sustainability and entrepreneurship: How digital innovations are helping tackle climate change and sustainable development. *Entrepreneurship Theory and Practice*, *45*(5), 999–1027. DOI: 10.1177/1042258719899425

Ghobakhloo, M. (2020). Industry 4.0, digitization, and opportunities for sustainability. *Journal of Cleaner Production*, *252*, 119869. DOI: 10.1016/j.jclepro.2019.119869

Google. (2020). Our data centers now work harder when the sun shines and wind blows. *Google Blog*. https://blog.google/inside-google/infrastructure/data-centers-work-harder-sun-shines-wind-blows

Guandalini, I. (2022). Sustainability through digital transformation: A systematic literature review for research guidance. *Journal of Business Research*, *148*, 456–471. DOI: 10.1016/j.jbusres.2022.05.003

Hinings, B., Gegenhuber, T., & Greenwood, R. (2018). Digital innovation and transformation: An institutional perspective. *Information and Organization*, *28*(1), 52–61. DOI: 10.1016/j.infoandorg.2018.02.004

Hussain, S. R., McDaniel, P., Gandhi, A., Ghose, K., Gopalan, K., Lee, D., . . . Zadok, E. (2023). Verifiable sustainability in data centers. *arXiv*. https://doi.org//arXiv.2307.11993DOI: 10.48550

IKEA. (2024). *IKEA Sustainability Report FY23*. Inter IKEA Group. https://www.ikea.com/global/en/images/IKEA_SUSTAINABILITY_Report_FY_23_20240125_1b190c008f.pdf

International Energy Agency. (2023). *Energy Technology Perspectives 2023*. IEA., DOI: 10.1787/7c6b23db-

Khalife, D., Subrahmanyam, S., & Farah, A. (2024). A sustainable circular business model to improve the performance of small and medium-sized enterprises using blockchain technology. *Journal of Wireless Mobile Networks, Ubiquitous Computing and Dependable Applications*, *15*(2), 240–250. DOI: 10.58346/JOWUA.2024.I2.016

Khallaf, A., Abdallah, A.-N., Zoubi, T., & Alnesafi, A. (2024). Blockchain-Driven Carbon Accountability in Supply Chains. *Sustainability (Basel)*, *16*(24), 10872. DOI: 10.3390/su162410872

Li, H., & Xu, H. (2024). The impact of digital transformation on ESG performance. *International Review of Economics & Finance, 96*(Part B), 103686. https://doi.org/ DOI: 10.1016/j.iref.2024.103686

Maurya, S., Shavkidinova, D., Shrivastava, V., & Subrahmanyam, S. (2025). Effects of Green Supply Chain Management Practices on Environmental and Firm Sustainability Performance. *ACTA INNOVATIONS*, 55, 13–22. https://www.actainnovations.com/index.php/pub/article/view/401

McKinsey & Company. (2022). *A digital path to sustainability.* McKinsey & Company. https://www.mckinsey.com/capabilities/operations/our-insights/a-digital-path-to-sustainability

Mohamed, A., Ismail, I., & AlDaraawi, M. (2025). IoT-Driven Intelligent Energy Management: Leveraging Smart Monitoring Applications and Artificial Neural Networks (ANN) for Sustainable Practices. *Computers*, *14*(7), 269. DOI: 10.3390/computers14070269

Organisation for Economic Co-operation and Development. (2021). *State of implementation of the OECD AI Principles: Insights from national AI policies.* OECD Digital Economy Papers, No. 311. OECD Publishing. https://doi.org/DOI: 10.1787/20716826

Ørsted. (2021). Ørsted. *Sustainability Report*, •••, 2021.

Park, S. R., & Jang, J. Y. (2021). The impact of ESG management on investment decision: Institutional investors' perceptions of country-specific ESG criteria. *International Journal of Financial Studies*, *9*(3), 48. DOI: 10.3390/ijfs9030048

Petry, T. (2018). Digital leadership. In North, K., Maier, R., & Haas, O. (Eds.), *Knowledge management in digital change: New findings and practical cases* (pp. 209–218). Springer Cham., https://ideas.repec.org/h/spr/prochp/978-3-319-73546-7_12.html DOI: 10.1007/978-3-319-73546-7_12

Pinto, M. M. A., Kovaleski, J. L., Mick, R. L., & Chiroli, D. M. G. (2024). Developing a sustainable digital transformation roadmap for SMEs: Integrating digital maturity and strategic alignment. *Sustainability (Basel)*, *16*(20), 8745. DOI: 10.3390/su16208745

Procter & Gamble. (2022). *2022 Citizenship Report.* Procter & Gamble. https://us.pg.com/2022_Citizenship_Report.pdf

Ransbotham, S., Kiron, D., Gerbert, P., & Reeves, M. (2017). *Reshaping business with artificial intelligence: Closing the gap between ambition and action*. MIT Sloan Management Review & Boston Consulting Group.

Rawashdeh, A., Abdallah, A. B., Alfawaeer, M., Al Dweiri, M., & Al-Jaghbeer, F. (2024). The impact of strategic agility on environmental sustainability: The mediating role of digital transformation. *Sustainability (Basel)*, *16*(3), 1338. DOI: 10.3390/su16031338

Raworth, K. (2023). Kate Raworth on creating regenerative and distributive economies by design. In Alexander, A., Pascucci, S., & Charnley, F. (Eds.), *Handbook of the Circular Economy: Transitions and Transformation* (pp. 45–52). De Gruyter., DOI: 10.1515/9783110723373-005

Schneider Electric. (2021). Smart factories triple-bottom-line success! *Schneider Electric Blog*. https://blog.se.com/sustainability/2021/06/03/smart-factories-triple-bottom-line-success/

Schneider Electric. (2022). *2022 Sustainability Report*. Schneider Electric. https://www.se.com/ww/en/about-us/sustainability/sustainability-reports/

Schot, J., & Steinmueller, W. E. (2018). Three frames for innovation policy: R&D, systems of innovation and transformative change. *Research Policy*, *47*(9), 1554–1567. DOI: 10.1016/j.respol.2018.08.011

Siemens. (2022). Siemens shows new digital solutions for the transition to sustainable infrastructure. Press release. https://press.siemens.com/global/en/pressrelease/siemens-shows-new-digital-solutions-transition-sustainable-infrastructure

Subrahmanyam, S. (2024). Leadership and cultural change management for technology adoption in operations. In Martínez-Falcó, J., Sánchez-García, E., Marco-Lajara, B., & Visser, G. (Eds.), *Convergence of technology and operations management in modern businesses* (pp. 175–202). IGI Global Scientific Publishing., DOI: 10.4018/979-8-3693-6200-6.ch005

Subrahmanyam, S. (2025). Corporate Sustainability Leadership in a Technology-Driven Educational Environment. In Dall'Acqua, L., & Gironacci, I. (Eds.), *Navigating Complexity, AI, and Legal Challenges in Organizations* (pp. 177–208). IGI Global Scientific Publishing., DOI: 10.4018/979-8-3373-2419-7.ch008

Subrahmanyam, S. (2025). Shaping Tomorrow's Talent Strategies with Predictive Workforce Intelligence. In Badouch, M., & Boutaounte, M. (Eds.), *Emerging Technologies for Recruitment Strategy and Practice* (pp. 211–236). IGI Global Scientific Publishing., DOI: 10.4018/979-8-3373-6516-9.ch008

Subrahmanyam, S. (2025). Sustainability and AI. In Younas, A., & Kassim, A. (Eds.), *Transforming Business Through Digital Sustainability Models* (pp. 363–392). IGI Global Scientific Publishing., DOI: 10.4018/979-8-3373-0608-7.ch016

Tathavadekar, V. P., & Mahankale, N. (2023). Digital leadership for sustainability: An integrated framework for organizational learning, resilience, and social value creation. *Journal of Cross-Disciplinary Sustainability Innovations*. https://doi.org/ DOI: 10.64229/tbqr6714

Teece, D. J., Peteraf, M., & Leih, S. (2016). Dynamic capabilities and organizational agility: Risk, uncertainty, and strategy in the innovation economy. *California Management Review*, *58*(4), 13–35. DOI: 10.1525/cmr.2016.58.4.13

Too Good To Go. (2023). *2023 Impact Report*. Retrieved from https://www.toogoodtogo.com/impact-report

Vinuesa, R., Azizpour, H., Leite, I., Balaam, M., Dignum, V., Domisch, S., Felländer, A., Langhans, S. D., Tegmark, M., & Fuso Nerini, F. (2020). The role of artificial intelligence in achieving the Sustainable Development Goals. *Nature Communications*, *11*(1), 233. DOI: 10.1038/s41467-019-14108-y PMID: 31932590

Walmart. (2018). *Walmart and Sam's Club to require real-time, end-to-end food traceability with blockchain*. https://corporate.walmart.com/news/2018/09/24/in-wake-of-romaine-e-coli-scare-walmart-deploys-blockchain-to-track-leafy-greens

Zaghmout, B., & Harrison, C. (2025). Distributed leadership: A systematic literature review. *Strategy and Leadership*, *53*(3), 299–320. Advance online publication. DOI: 10.1108/SL-10-2024-0119

Zhang, Q., & Liang, H. (2022). Greening the cloud: Carbon-aware data center management. *Energy Policy*, *162*, 112–129.

KEY TERMS AND DEFINITIONS

AI Governance: Frameworks, policies, and oversight mechanisms to ensure ethical, responsible, and accountable development, deployment, and monitoring of artificial intelligence within organizational systems.

Capability Building: Organizational activities aimed at enhancing knowledge, skills, and competencies—particularly digital, analytical, and sustainability-oriented capabilities—to enable successful change implementation.

Change Management: A structured approach to transitioning individuals, teams, and organizations from a current state to a desired future state, particularly relevant in digitally intensive and sustainability-focused transformations.

Change Metrics and KPIs: Quantitative and qualitative indicators used to measure the effectiveness of change initiatives, including adoption rates, culture-shift indicators, digital skill maturity, carbon reduction percentages, and ESG performance metrics.

Circular Economy: An economic model emphasizing resource efficiency, waste minimization, and product lifecycle management, encouraging closed-loop systems in manufacturing, supply chains, and digital operations.

Digital Maturity: The extent to which an organization leverages digital technologies, data capabilities, and culture to drive efficiency, innovation, and competitive advantage, often used to assess readiness for sustainable digital transformation.

Digital Sustainability: The integration of digital technologies with environmental, social, and governance (ESG) principles to drive organizational practices that are economically viable, socially responsible, and environmentally conscious.

ESG Integration: The systematic incorporation of environmental, social, and governance factors into organizational strategy, investment, and operational decision-making, aiming to improve sustainability performance and long-term value creation.

Tech-Driven Organization: An enterprise where digital technologies—such as AI, IoT, cloud computing, and analytics—are central to core business operations, strategic decision-making, and innovation processes.

Transformational Leadership: A leadership style that inspires and motivates employees to embrace change by creating a compelling vision, fostering innovation, and encouraging adaptability in complex, tech-driven environments.

Chapter 5
Strategic Leadership for Digital Sustainability:
Mechanisms, Contexts, and Capabilities for Sustainable Digital Transformation

Satya Subrahmanyam
http://orcid.org/0000-0003-0441-2742
Holy Spirit University of Kaslik, Lebanon

Badih Baz
http://orcid.org/0000-0002-1553-4908
Holy Spirit University of Kaslik, Lebanon

ABSTRACT

This chapter, "Strategic Leadership for Digital Sustainability," examines how organizations can align digital transformation with sustainability goals through visionary leadership. It introduces digital sustainability as a strategic imperative, emphasizing the role of leadership in fostering responsible innovation, ethical governance, inclusivity, and environmental stewardship. The chapter explores transformational, servant/ethical, and adaptive leadership approaches and their application in cultivating sustainable digital infrastructures and cultures. It offers practical strategies for aligning digital initiatives with sustainability, including stakeholder engagement, risk management, and change leadership. Real-world case studies illustrate successful implementations, while a proposed Digital-Sustainability Leadership (D.S.L.) Framework provides a roadmap for future-ready leadership. It argues that strategic leadership is essential to navigating the dual agendas of technological advancement and sustainable development.

DOI: 10.4018/979-8-3373-5052-3.ch005

1. INTRODUCTION

1.1 Defining strategic leadership and digital sustainability

Strategic leadership refers to the practices, capabilities and decision processes exercised by top-tier actors (boards, C-suite and senior teams) that shape an organisation's long-term direction, resource configuration, and adaptive capacity in complex environments (Mohammad et al., 2024). In the context of digital change, strategic leaders do more than sponsor IT projects: they sense technological and societal shifts, formulate integrated digital–business policies, and reconfigure assets and routines to secure sustainable competitive advantage (Kraus et al., 2021). Digital sustainability is best understood as the intentional use and governance of digital technologies so that digital change supports - rather than undermines - environmental, social and governance (ESG) objectives. This concept spans three interlinked dimensions: reducing the environmental footprint of digital infrastructures (green IT), ensuring social benefits and inclusion (digital equity), and maintaining governance practices (data ethics, transparency) that preserve long-term societal legitimacy (George et al., 2021; Guandalini, 2022).

1.2 Why leaders must align digital transformation with ESG objectives

Digital transformation and sustainability goals are not automatically aligned. Digital technologies can deliver efficiency gains, dematerialisation and novel sustainable solutions, yet they can also increase energy use (data centres, AI), create e-waste and exacerbate social inequities if governance is weak (Guandalini, 2022; George et al., 2021). Strategic leaders therefore face a dual task: harness digital capabilities to generate environmental and social value, while simultaneously governing the negative externalities of digitalisation. Practically, this requires leaders to translate high-level sustainability commitments into digital investments, procurement rules, architecture decisions (e.g., cloud vs. edge), and metrics that explicitly connect IT choices to carbon, inclusion and governance outcomes (Kraus et al., 2021; Rupeika-Apoga & Petrovska, 2022).

1.3 Limitations of descriptive approaches and the need for analytic integration

A sizable portion of existing work remains descriptive - cataloguing technologies, listing leadership behaviours, or reporting individual company initiatives - without specifying the mechanisms that link leadership practices to measurable sustainability outcomes. Systematic reviews show the field is fragmented: studies often treat digitalisation and sustainability as separate streams or focus on single technologies or sectors, which hampers cumulative theory building and limits prescriptive guidance for leaders (Guandalini, 2022; Kraus et al., 2021). Empirical work frequently concentrates on case examples or short-term indicators rather than longitudinal measures of ESG impact, leaving open questions about causality and boundary conditions (Rupeika-Apoga & Petrovska, 2022). To move from description to explanation, scholarship must integrate theoretical lenses - notably dynamic capabilities (to explain how organisations sense, seize and reconfigure around sustainable digital opportunities) and socio-technical systems thinking (to show how technology, people and institutions co-evolve) - and link them to contextual moderators such as digital maturity, industry characteristics and regulatory regimes (Mohammad et al., 2024; Guandalini, 2022).

1.4 Chapter purpose, scope, and structure

This chapter responds to these gaps. Its purpose is to articulate clear conceptual boundaries for strategic leadership and digital sustainability, to propose integrative mechanisms that explain how leadership actions produce measurable sustainability outcomes, and to identify the key contextual moderators and implementation barriers that condition those mechanisms. The chapter synthesises theory (dynamic capabilities, socio-technical systems, institutional pressures), draws on cross-sector empirical studies and cases, and offers an actionable strategic framework and metrics that practitioners and researchers can use to assess leadership impact on digital sustainability. In doing so, the chapter aims to shift the conversation from cataloguing "what" organisations do toward explaining "how" and "when" strategic leadership delivers sustainable digital transformation (Guandalini, 2022; George et al., 2021; Mohammad et al., 2024).

2. CONCEPTUAL AND THEORETICAL FOUNDATIONS

2.1 Strategic Leadership: Definitions and Boundaries

Strategic leadership refers to the capacity of senior leaders to envision future possibilities, interpret environmental shifts, and orchestrate organisational transformation through long-term, values-driven decision-making (Samimi et al., 2022). Contemporary work emphasises four core attributes: visioning or articulating a clear long-term direction; sensing, which involves detecting technological, market and societal disruptions; reconfiguring, the ability to realign resources, structures and processes to pursue emerging opportunities; and stewarding, which reflects a leader's responsibility to guide digital and sustainability transitions in ways that protect organisational and societal welfare (Tathavadekar & Mahankale, 2025).

Importantly, strategic leadership differs fundamentally from operational management. While operational managers focus on efficiency, stability and short-term performance, strategic leaders navigate uncertainty, balance competing objectives and prioritise long-term digital-sustainability outcomes. In digital transformation contexts, this distinction is crucial: strategic leaders must integrate ESG priorities into technology decisions, whereas operational managers typically optimise existing systems (Kraus et al., 2021). Effective digital sustainability therefore depends on leaders who can bridge technology, strategy and societal impact.

2.2 Defining Digital Sustainability

Digital sustainability encompasses the design, deployment and governance of digital technologies in ways that advance environmental, social and economic objectives. Environmentally, the concept covers reducing energy consumption, lowering carbon emissions from data centres and AI models, and mitigating e-waste through circular IT practices (George et al., 2021). Socially, it includes digital equity, inclusion, accessibility and the protection of digital rights - all critical concerns as algorithmic systems increasingly influence public life (Bibri, 2021). Economically, digital sustainability highlights resilient infrastructures, responsible innovation and value creation grounded in circular principles rather than linear consumption (Guandalini, 2022).

These components cannot be treated in isolation. Digital sustainability requires a socio-technical perspective, recognising that technologies, human behaviours, organisational structures and institutional pressures interact dynamically. Without addressing these interdependencies, digital initiatives risk creating unintended consequences, such as widening inequalities or increasing environmental burdens despite efficiency gains.

2.3 Integrating Sustainability into Digital Transformation

For digital transformation to yield sustainable outcomes, organisations must embed ESG objectives into technological strategies rather than treating sustainability as an add-on. Three alignment mechanisms are critical. Strategic fit ensures that digital innovation reinforces, rather than contradicts, sustainability commitments. Long-term value orientation encourages decisions that consider lifecycle impacts, stakeholder welfare and resilience rather than short-term returns. Mission-driven leadership provides an overarching purpose that guides investment in green IT, ethical AI and inclusive digital ecosystems (Rupeika-Apoga & Petrovska, 2022).

Purely technology-driven transformation often fails because it emphasises speed and capability acquisition without questioning environmental or social implications. Such approaches may accelerate energy demand, create algorithmic risks or reinforce inequitable digital access. Integrative strategies, by contrast, leverage technology to generate shared value while mitigating systemic harms (Subrahmanyam, 2025).

2.4 Theoretical Lenses

Dynamic Capabilities Theory provides a powerful lens for understanding digital sustainability leadership. Through *sensing*, leaders identify digital-sustainability opportunities - such as low-carbon cloud architectures or ethical AI tools. Through *seizing*, they invest in green innovations and redesign processes for ESG alignment. Through *reconfiguring*, they reshape organisational assets, structures and cultures to support sustainable digital futures (Luo et al., 2022).

Socio-Technical Systems Theory highlights that sustainable outcomes depend on the coordinated evolution of technological, human and structural subsystems. Effective leaders ensure that digital tools are supported by appropriate skills, governance structures, culture and policies, preventing misalignment that can undermine sustainability goals (Bibri, 2021).

Institutional Theory explains how regulatory pressures (e.g., carbon reporting, AI governance laws), societal expectations and stakeholder demand shape digital sustainability strategies. Organisations increasingly operate in environments where sustainability and digital ethics are not optional but institutionalised norms, influencing leadership decisions and competitive legitimacy (Guandalini, 2022).

3. LEADERSHIP APPROACHES AND THEIR ROLE IN DIGITAL SUSTAINABILITY

3.1 Transformational Leadership

Transformational leadership remains one of the most frequently cited approaches in discussions of digital transformation and sustainability because of its focus on vision creation, innovation, and culture building. Transformational leaders articulate compelling digital-sustainability visions that encourage employees to see technology not only as a tool for efficiency but also as a driver of environmental and social value creation (Alabdali et al., 2024). By fostering intrinsic motivation, they cultivate a sustainability-oriented digital culture - one where experimentation, ethical digital practices, and long-term thinking are encouraged. Such leaders also build psychological safety, empowering teams to challenge existing assumptions and propose green digital innovations such as low-carbon cloud migration, data minimalism, and circular IT solutions.

Transformational leadership is not universally effective. Its impact is shaped by boundary conditions, including organisational digital maturity and industry characteristics. In digitally mature firms, transformational leaders can leverage advanced data infrastructures, AI platforms, and analytics capabilities to accelerate sustainability initiatives (Kraus et al., 2021). On the contrary, in low-maturity contexts, ambitious visions may be difficult to operationalise due to technological, cultural, or capability constraints. Industry also matters: sectors with heavy environmental footprints (e.g., manufacturing, energy) face more stringent regulatory and societal pressures, making transformational approaches particularly valuable for driving green innovation, while service-oriented industries may prioritise digital ethics, data privacy, and inclusion (George et al., 2021). The effectiveness of transformational leadership therefore depends on how well leaders align their vision with contextual realities.

3.2 Ethical, Responsible, and Servant Leadership

Ethical, responsible, and servant leadership approaches are increasingly recognised as essential for digital sustainability. As organisations deploy artificial intelligence, automation, and algorithm-driven decision systems, leaders must ensure that these technologies are governed through responsible, transparent, and fair practices. Ethical leaders emphasise accountability, algorithmic transparency, and responsible data governance, establishing norms that prevent harms such as biased decision-making, privacy violations, and digital exclusion (Bibri, 2021). Responsible leadership further broadens this view by integrating stakeholder needs and societal expectations into digital strategy - ensuring, for instance, that AI models are explainable or that cloud infrastructures comply with environmental regulations (Hossain et al., 2025).

Servant leadership contributes an additional human-centric dimension. By prioritising the needs of employees, communities, and vulnerable users, servant leaders encourage inclusive digital innovation. They ensure that digital transformation initiatives do not disproportionately disadvantage certain groups, thereby advancing digital equity. Mechanisms for fostering digital fairness include conducting algorithmic bias audits, implementing inclusive design principles, and establishing governance committees that represent diverse stakeholder groups. Ethical and servant leaders thus play a pivotal role in balancing technological ambition with moral responsibility and societal wellbeing.

3.3 Adaptive and Agile Leadership

The rapid pace of technological change and the growing complexity of digital ecosystems call for leadership approaches that are both adaptive and agile. Adaptive leaders excel at reframing problems, experimenting with new digital tools, and responding quickly to emerging sustainability challenges. They view digital sustainability as an evolving target rather than a fixed endpoint - requiring continuous monitoring, learning, and recalibration (Kaya, 2023). Agile leadership complements this by promoting iterative decision-making, cross-functional collaboration, and rapid prototyping of sustainable digital solutions.

These approaches are particularly valuable for managing uncertainty and navigating the trade-offs inherent in digital sustainability. AI can generate efficiency gains but also increase energy consumption; cloud computing can reduce hardware waste but raise concerns around data sovereignty; blockchain can enable supply-chain transparency yet consume large amounts of power. Adaptive and agile leaders address such dilemmas through flexible strategic thinking, stakeholder engagement, and scenario-based risk assessments. They also build organisational resilience by fostering digital capabilities that enable swift responses to regulatory changes, cybersecurity threats, or environmental shocks (Guandalini, 2022). In doing so, they help organisations thrive in dynamic digital ecosystems while maintaining a strong sustainability orientation.

3.4 Distributed and Collaborative Leadership

Digital sustainability extends beyond the boundaries of any single department or organisation. As such, distributed and collaborative leadership models are increasingly necessary. Distributed leadership decentralises authority, encouraging individuals at multiple organisational levels to participate in digital-sustainability initiatives. This approach enables faster problem solving and enhances collective intelligence, particularly when dealing with socio-technical complexities (Batool, 2024). IT teams may drive green cloud adoption, HR may promote digital upskilling for sustainability, and marketing may champion responsible AI practices in customer engagement.

Collaborative leadership goes further by promoting co-creation with external stakeholders including suppliers, technology providers, regulators, and civil society. Sustainable digital transformation often requires ecosystems of actors working together - for instance, developing shared data platforms for emissions tracking or creating sector-wide standards for ethical AI. Through collaborative leadership, organisations can mobilise diverse expertise, share risks, and co-develop scalable solutions. Multi-level leadership is therefore essential: senior executives set direction, middle managers translate strategy into action, and frontline employees surface insights and innovations that enhance both digital and sustainability performance.

Figure 1. Leadership Approaches for Digital Sustainability

Author, (2025)

4. HOW STRATEGIC LEADERSHIP DRIVES DIGITAL SUSTAINABILITY OUTCOMES

4.1 Linking Leadership Actions to Measurable Sustainability Outcomes

Strategic leadership plays a pivotal role in converting sustainability ambitions into measurable digital sustainability outcomes. Leaders influence organizational performance by establishing clear metrics and aligning digital initiatives with environmental, social, and governance (ESG) priorities. Key performance indicators (KPIs) such as digital-efficiency scores, energy usage effectiveness (EUE), carbon intensity of IT operations, and algorithmic fairness indices provide tangible benchmarks to assess progress (Kruglov et al., 2023). By adopting data-driven decision frameworks, leaders can continuously monitor digital transformation activities and ensure they contribute to long-term sustainability objectives.

Mechanisms such as strategic visioning, accountability systems, and digital performance dashboards support the translation of leadership actions into outcomes. These systems help leaders track reductions in cloud-related emissions, AI model efficiency improvements, and optimization of data center operations. Leaders who emphasize evidence-based control thus foster a culture where sustainability is embedded into day-to-day digital operations, enhancing transparency and organizational resilience (Nie et al., 2025). Linking compensation and executive rewards to sustainability KPIs drives behavioural alignment and reinforces commitment to green digital transformation initiatives.

4.2 Strategic Prioritization and Resource Allocation for Green IT

Resource allocation is a fundamental mechanism through which strategic leadership influences digital sustainability. Modern organizations face competing digital investment demands - cybersecurity, automation, analytics, and cloud modernization - making prioritization essential. Leaders advance green IT by allocating funds toward energy-efficient hardware, low-carbon cloud architectures, and AI systems optimized for computational efficiency (Cisco, 2023). Investing in sustainability-enhancing technologies such as intelligent cooling systems, server virtualization, and edge computing also contributes to reducing the carbon footprint of digital operations.

Leaders must guide investments in digital literacy and workforce upskilling to ensure that sustainability-centric technologies are operationalized effectively. Training employees to use analytics for energy monitoring or to design algorithmically responsible AI models reinforces organizational capability. As indicated by recent studies, leadership commitment to capability building strongly influences the success rate of green IT initiatives and boosts organizational digital maturity (Subrahmanyam, 2025). Prioritization also involves evaluating trade-offs, ensuring that sustainability targets are not overshadowed by short-term cost pressures.

4.3 Policies for Responsible AI, Cloud Optimization, and Circular Digital Infrastructure

Strategic leadership also shapes outcomes through the formulation and enforcement of digital sustainability policies. As organizations deploy AI at scale, concerns related to energy-intensive model training, algorithmic biases, and opaque decision-making require clear governance frameworks. Leaders implement responsible AI policies that emphasize transparency, explainability, privacy protection, and the minimization of environmental impacts associated with high-compute systems (van Uffelen et al., 2024). This includes mandating carbon-aware scheduling for AI workloads and promoting lightweight model architectures where possible.

In parallel, cloud optimization policies aim to reduce unnecessary data storage, enhance workload efficiency, and adopt multi-cloud strategies based on carbon intensity. Emerging carbon-aware cloud tools enable leaders to dynamically allocate workloads to regions powered by greener energy sources (Radovanović et al., 2023). Policies on data lifecycle management, such as deleting redundant data and optimizing storage layers, contribute to significant emissions reductions.

Circular digital infrastructure adds another dimension, emphasizing responsible procurement, device refurbishment, e-waste minimization, and the extension of asset lifecycles. Strategic leaders increasingly recognize circularity as an enabler of both cost efficiency and sustainability, ensuring that digital growth does not exacerbate environmental degradation (Romagnoli et al., 2023).

4.4 Stakeholder Engagement and Cross-Functional Coordination

Strategic leadership fosters digital sustainability by cultivating collaborations across internal and external stakeholders. Internally, IT, sustainability teams, operations, risk management, and HR must align their goals to ensure that digital initiatives contribute to shared ESG targets. Cross-functional steering committees, supported by transparent governance mechanisms, improve coherence and reduce organizational silos (Subrahmanyam, 2025).

Externally, engagement with cloud providers, technology vendors, regulators, customers, and community groups ensures that digital sustainability strategies reflect broader societal expectations. Strategic leaders facilitate co-creation and open innovation processes, leveraging shared expertise to promote inclusive and environmentally conscious digital ecosystems. This collaborative approach also strengthens legitimacy and trust, particularly in contexts where responsible AI and data governance are under public scrutiny.

4.5 Integrating Sustainability into Digital Governance and Risk Management

Embedding sustainability into digital governance ensures that environmental and social considerations influence decision-making at every stage of digital transformation. Leaders integrate sustainability criteria into IT procurement, vendor assessments, cybersecurity protocols, and product-development pipelines. Governance structures, such as ESG-aligned digital charters and sustainability review boards, enable systematic oversight of digital projects and ensure alignment with corporate purpose (Bansal et al., 2018).

Risk management also evolves under strategic leadership. Digital transformation introduces new risks, including energy-intensive computing, supply chain vulnerabilities, data security concerns, and ethical dilemmas in AI deployment. Leaders mitigate these risks by employing scenario planning, ESG risk assessments, and impact forecasting tools. Integrating sustainability into enterprise risk management strengthens resilience, helps organizations anticipate regulatory shifts, and ensures long-term value creation.

Table 1. Leadership Mechanisms and Digital Sustainability Outcomes

Leadership Mechanism	Strategic Actions	Digital Sustainability Outcomes (KPIs)
KPI-Driven Leadership	Set sustainability KPIs, track dashboards	Reduced IT carbon emissions; improved digital-efficiency scores
Resource Allocation for Green IT	Invest in efficient hardware, cloud modernization	Lower energy usage; reduced EUE; optimized compute loads
Responsible AI Policies	Implement fairness, transparency, lightweight AI	Lower model carbon footprint; improved algorithmic fairness
Cloud & Data Optimization	Carbon-aware scheduling, data minimization	Reduction in cloud-related emissions; optimized storage
Circular Digital Infrastructure	Refurbishment, e-waste reduction	Extended device lifecycles; lower material waste
Stakeholder Coordination	Cross-functional teams, ecosystem partnerships	Improved ESG integration; enhanced legitimacy
Governance & Risk Integration	ESG-aligned governance, sustainability audits	Stronger compliance; reduced sustainability risks

5. CONTEXTUAL MODERATORS AND ORGANIZATIONAL CONDITIONS

5.1 Organizational Culture as an Enabler or Inhibitor

Organizational culture plays a decisive role in shaping the extent to which strategic leadership efforts translate into successful digital sustainability outcomes. A culture that values innovation, environmental responsibility, and continuous learning provide fertile ground for aligning digital transformation with sustainability objectives. Research shows that organizations with strong sustainability-oriented cultures are more likely to adopt green IT practices, encourage data ethics, and support cross-functional collaboration needed for systemic change (Albino et al., 2021). Such cultures also promote psychological safety, allowing employees to experiment with digital tools and propose environmentally conscious solutions without fear of failure.

On the contrary, cultures characterized by rigid hierarchies, short-term performance metrics, and resistance to change can hinder progress. Employees may perceive sustainability initiatives as peripheral or burdensome unless supported by shared values and incentives. In these contexts, even the most visionary strategic leaders can face significant implementation challenges. Thus, culture acts as a powerful moderator, determining whether leadership directives become embedded organizational routines or remain symbolic commitments.

Table 2. Organizational and Cultural Moderators of Digital Sustainability Outcomes

Moderator	Description	How It Influences Digital Sustainability	Illustrative Implications
Organizational Culture	Shared values, norms, and assumptions guiding behaviour	Enables or inhibits adoption of sustainable digital practices; affects employee support for digital ethics and green IT	Cultures emphasizing learning and responsibility accelerate sustainability initiatives; rigid cultures create resistance
Innovation Orientation	Degree to which the organization supports experimentation and risk-taking	Facilitates implementation of carbon-aware computing, responsible AI, and digital experimentation	High innovation orientation leads to faster adoption of green cloud and data governance practices
Sustainability Mindset	Awareness of ESG goals and environmental responsibility	Strengthens alignment between digital transformation and sustainability strategy	Improves integration of ESG metrics in digital governance

5.2 Digital Maturity and Technological Readiness

Digital maturity - defined as an organization's sophistication in technology adoption, data analytics, and digital governance - significantly moderates the relationship between leadership and sustainability outcomes. Digitally mature organizations possess advanced infrastructures, integrated data architectures, and strong cybersecurity foundations that enable them to implement carbon-efficient cloud systems, responsible AI, and circular digital processes more effectively (Pinto Mick et al., 2024). They also tend to have structured governance systems that facilitate rapid experimentation and scaling of sustainable technologies.

In contrast, organizations with low digital maturity face fragmentation in IT systems, limited analytics capabilities, and outdated infrastructures that increase carbon intensity and reduce agility. Leaders in such settings must focus primarily on foundational upgrades before pursuing advanced sustainability initiatives. Studies indicate that technological readiness - particularly cloud adoption, automation, and data integration - strongly influences the organization's ability to operationalize digital sustainability strategies and measure progress accurately (Subrahmanyam, 2025). Hence, digital maturity shapes the feasibility, speed, and effectiveness of sustainability-driven digital transformation.

5.3 Industry-Specific Pressures

Industry characteristics exert strong contextual influence over digital sustainability trajectories. Energy-intensive sectors such as manufacturing, chemicals, and mining face significant pressure to decarbonize, prompting leaders to prioritize energy-efficient digital technologies, predictive maintenance, and smart manufacturing systems. In these sectors, digital transformation directly supports emissions reduction by optimizing resource efficiency and enabling real-time monitoring (Subermaniam et al., 2025).

Highly regulated industries - such as healthcare, finance, and telecommunications - must balance sustainability goals with strict compliance requirements regarding data protection, digital ethics, and operational resilience. Regulatory scrutiny often accelerates the adoption of responsible AI, data governance frameworks, and cybersecurity measures. On the contrary, the complexity of regulatory environments may slow innovation, requiring more deliberate leadership strategies to ensure that sustainability and compliance coexist effectively.

Digital-heavy industries such as IT services, e-commerce, and media experience different pressures. Their sustainability challenges stem not from physical emissions but from high data center energy consumption, cloud workloads, and electronic waste. This drives the need for leadership to focus on carbon-aware computing, greener cloud architectures, and sustainable device lifecycle management. Thus, sectoral conditions shape both the nature of sustainability challenges and the digital strategies needed to address them.

Table 3. Technological and Industry-Specific Moderators

Moderator	Description	Influence on Digital Sustainability	Sectoral Relevance
Digital Maturity	Maturity of digital infrastructure, analytics, cloud systems, and governance	High digital maturity enables responsible AI, efficient cloud use, carbon-tracking tools	Critical in IT services, finance, telecom
Technological Readiness	Availability of smart technologies, automation, and integrated data systems	Determines feasibility of energy-efficient systems and sustainable digital workflows	Manufacturing, logistics, energy sectors
Industry Pressures	Sustainability obligations stemming from sectoral characteristics	Drives specific sustainability priorities—energy efficiency, ethical AI, e-waste	Manufacturing (decarbonization), healthcare (AI ethics), IT (data center emissions)
Regulatory Environment	Environmental, digital, and data governance policies	Strong regulations accelerate adoption of green and ethical digital practices	EU-based firms, financial services, public sector

5.4 Geographic, Regulatory, and Socio-Cultural Contexts

Geographic location and regulatory environments influence how organizations perceive and enact digital sustainability. Regions with stringent environmental regulations - such as the European Union - tend to push organizations toward adopting greener digital infrastructures, low-carbon cloud systems, and transparent AI governance practices (European Commission, 2021). Meanwhile, countries with weak environmental governance or limited digital policy frameworks may experience slower uptake of responsible digital transformation initiatives.

Socio-cultural norms also play a moderating role. Societies with high environmental consciousness, increasingly vocal digital rights movements, and strong public scrutiny shape how organizations formulate sustainability strategies. On the contrary, in socio-cultural contexts where sustainability awareness is limited or technology skepticism is high, leaders may face challenges in securing workforce support for new digital tools or ethical AI practices.

Geographic factors such as energy grid mix also affect the practicality of carbon-aware computing. Organizations located in regions dependent on fossil fuels may struggle to reduce cloud-related emissions despite strong leadership support. These contextual conditions determine not only the ambition level of sustainability strategies but also the tools available for implementation.

5.5 Human Capital Capabilities, Workforce Readiness, and Upskilling Challenges

Human capital capabilities significantly influence whether digitally enabled sustainability initiatives succeed. The integration of low-carbon technologies, AI-driven optimization, and digital governance frameworks requires a workforce equipped with advanced digital and analytical skills. Studies highlight that organizations with strong human capital investments, digital literacy programs, and sustainability training achieve better performance across digital sustainability metrics (Zervas & Stiakakis, 2024).

Workforce readiness includes both technical and behavioural dimensions. Employees must understand how their roles connect to broader sustainability goals, how to interpret emissions dashboards, and how to use AI tools responsibly. Without adequate upskilling, even well-designed sustainability strategies may not translate into practical results.

Table 4. Workforce, Geographic, and Socio-Cultural Moderators

Moderator	Description	Role in Enabling Digital Sustainability	Key Challenges
Human Capital Capabilities	Workforce skills in AI, analytics, cloud, sustainability	Essential for implementing sustainability dashboards, energy analytics, and responsible AI tools	Skill gaps, training costs, resistance to new technologies
Workforce Readiness	Willingness and ability to adopt new digital-sustainability practices	Supports digital governance, ESG reporting, green IT usage	Low digital literacy, lack of sustainability awareness
Geographic Factors	Local energy mix, technological ecosystem, and market conditions	Influences carbon intensity of cloud workloads, feasibility of green tech	Fossil-fuel-dependent regions face higher digital emissions
Socio-Cultural Norms	Public attitudes toward sustainability and digital rights	Shapes organizational commitments to digital ethics and environmental stewardship	Low societal awareness decreases pressure to adopt responsible digital practices
Regulatory Context	National or regional ESG and digital regulations	Defines minimum compliance and pushes innovation in digital sustainability	Regulatory fragmentation across countries

Upskilling remains a challenge for many organizations. Rapid technological change, evolving data regulations, and the increasing complexity of digital ecosystems require continuous learning and adaptation. Strategic leaders must therefore cultivate learning mindsets, invest in reskilling initiatives, and partner with educational institutions or technology providers to build future-ready capabilities. Workforce empowerment becomes a key moderator, determining the depth and durability of sustainable digital transformation.

6. EMERGING ISSUES AND CRITICAL CHALLENGES IN DIGITAL SUSTAINABILITY

6.1 Ethical Dilemmas in AI and Digital Systems

With the growing adoption of artificial intelligence (AI), sophisticated analytics, and algorithm-based decision systems into the operations of organizations, ethical dilemmas have become the main issue of digital sustainability. Among the issues, there are data privacy, bias in the algorithms, and the lack of transparency in the automated decision-making processes, as well as the regulation of the digital rights. AI systems that are trained on historical data or other unrepresentative data tend to recreate biased information based on gender, ethnicity, or socioeconomic status, endangering the concepts of fairness and equity (Mehrabi et al., 2021). The widespread gathering and processing of personal information are concerning in terms of consent, surveillance, and online independence. Responsible and transparent algorithm development - with explainability demand and audit procedures - is becoming accepted as a necessity to guarantee the ethical sovereignty of digital transformation (European Commission, 2021). Ethical leadership is vital in setting up governance mechanisms to protect digital rights, institute fairness in the systems of algorithms, and facilitate ethical use of data in digital ecosystems.

6.2 Environmental Footprint of AI, Cloud Services, and Data Centers

Despite being seen as facilitating the emergence of environmental efficiency, digital technologies have significant ecological footprints. The training of AI models requires immense computation, which requires a large amount of energy and claims carbon emissions. Generative and deep learning models, along with other large-scale models, contribute to the escalation of the environmental footprint because they must be re-trained continuously and large amounts of data are required (Strubell et al., 2020). Cloud systems and worldwide data centers, which are the core of contemporary digital activity, consume more and more power, most of which is still non-renewable. Recent research shows that data centers contribute to about 1-1.5

percent of total electricity worldwide and forecasts are expected to increase based on AI loads, streaming services, and Internet of Things (IoT) development (IEA, 2023).

To mitigate these impacts, organizations are turning to carbon-aware computing strategies, green cloud optimization, and energy-efficient architectures. Carbon-aware computing involves adjusting computational tasks based on real-time carbon-intensity data, thereby reducing emissions associated with cloud operations (Google, 2021). Sustainability-oriented digital strategies incorporate practices such as serverless computing, workload orchestration, and adoption of renewable-powered cloud services. Strategic leadership is critical for prioritizing these investments, evaluating trade-offs between performance and emissions, and defining sustainability metrics that capture the environmental consequences of digital workloads.

6.3 Implementation Barriers and Organizational Constraints

Although the strategic importance of digital sustainability has gained growing popularity, there are still some gaps in the implementation in terms of industries and regions. Among the barriers, there are cost asymmetries, digital divide, and resistance of sustainable digital change by the workforce. A move to greener digital infrastructure - e.g. by purchasing energy-efficient hardware, or by signing a green contract with a cloud provider, or by using AI based on low-carbon methods - can incur significant initial costs. SMEs, specifically, have limited resources that limit their adoption of sustainable digital solutions (Yusuf et al., 2024).

The digital divide further exacerbates inequalities in sustainability performance. Organizations in technologically lagging regions or developing economies may lack access to affordable cloud technologies, reliable connectivity, and digital talent - hindering their ability to implement sustainable digital systems. Internally, resistance to change also limits progress; employees accustomed to legacy systems may perceive sustainability-driven digital changes as disruptive or burdensome. Strategic leaders must therefore adopt inclusive change management approaches, aligning incentives, strengthening communication, and leveraging participatory decision-making to overcome implementation obstacles.

6.4 E-Waste, Device Life Cycles, and Sustainable Procurement

The high rate of digital device turnover that includes smartphones, laptops, sensors, and servers has increased the issue of electronic waste (e-waste) in the world. The United Nations notes that the volume of e-waste in the world has increased to 53.6 million metric tons as at 2019 and is growing as a result of the spread of digital technologies (Forti et al., 2020). E-waste also includes some hazardous elements such as heavy metals, which expose the environment and health to hazards in case they are disposed of incorrectly. The mining of rare-earth materials used in the production of devices has brought a lot of ecological and social effects.

Sustainable procurement strategies offer a pathway to address device life-cycle challenges. Organizations are increasingly adopting circular procurement practices, including device reuse, repair, refurbishment, and responsible recycling. Green hardware standards, such as energy-efficient certifications and modular device designs, enable organizations to reduce material waste and extend product lifespans. Strategic leadership plays a pivotal role in integrating these priorities into vendor selection, procurement policies, and lifecycle management protocols. By embedding circular economy principles into digital strategy, leaders can reduce both environmental impact and long-term operational costs.

6.5 Balancing Digital Performance with Sustainability Outcomes

A persistent tension in digital transformation is the balance between digital performance - speed, efficiency, scalability - and sustainability outcomes. High-performance computing, advanced analytics, and AI-driven services often require resource-intensive architectures that increase energy consumption and emissions. Leaders face trade-offs when evaluating digital strategies: prioritizing computational performance may conflict with carbon reduction targets, while aggressive sustainability constraints may limit innovation, service quality, or competitiveness (Yang et al., 2025).

To reconcile these tensions, organizations are adopting holistic digital governance frameworks that integrate sustainability into performance evaluation, risk management, and strategic planning. This includes setting clear KPIs for energy efficiency, carbon intensity, and responsible AI performance, alongside traditional digital metrics such as uptime, latency, and computational throughput. Cross-functional coordination between IT, sustainability, operations, and strategy teams ensure balanced decision-making. Strategic leaders must foster a culture that values sustainability as a core performance dimension, emphasizing long-term societal value alongside immediate digital gains.

Figure 2. Emerging Issues and Critical Challenges in Digital Sustainability

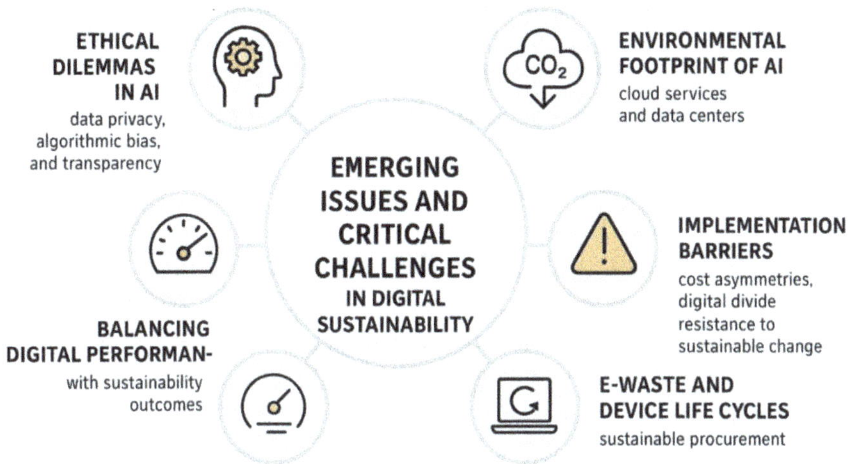

Author, (2025)

7. EMPIRICAL EVIDENCE, CASE STUDIES, AND CROSS-SECTOR INSIGHTS

7.1 Multinational Enterprise Case

Multinational enterprises (MNEs) provide some of the strongest empirical evidence on how digital transformation strategies can be aligned with sustainability goals. Microsoft is one of the most frequently cited examples. In 2020, the company announced its ambition to become carbon negative by 2030 and to remove all historical emissions by 2050. Central to this strategy is the use of advanced digital tools - AI-driven carbon accounting, digital twins for energy optimization, and cloud efficiency metrics - to reduce emissions across scopes (Microsoft, 2020). Empirical assessments show that Microsoft's cloud architecture, particularly Azure, has achieved up to 93% more energy efficiency compared to traditional enterprise data centers due to renewable energy integration and advanced cooling systems (Microsoft, 2023). Leadership commitment, coupled with strict governance frameworks, enabled cross-functional alignment, supplier engagement, and data-driven monitoring of sustainability outcomes.

SAP provides another significant case. The organization redesigned its cloud infrastructure to support customers' sustainability reporting, embedding real-time carbon tracking features into its enterprise systems. SAP's "Climate 21" initiative uses analytics and AI to help firms reduce emissions across supply chains (SAP, 2021). Studies on SAP's ecosystem show that sustainability-oriented digital infrastructures can stimulate industry-wide decarbonization by standardizing metrics and improving transparency, illustrating how leadership-driven digital sustainability initiatives can extend beyond organizational boundaries (Hanelt et al., 2021).

7.2 SME and Startup Case

Small and medium-sized enterprises (SMEs) and startups often innovate more rapidly due to agility, even with constrained resources. Empirical research indicates that startups adopting AI, IoT, and data analytics achieve measurable sustainability improvements - particularly in energy management and waste reduction (Subrahmanyam & El Samra, 2025).

A notable example is *Enabling Insights*, a German SME using IoT-enabled sensors and machine learning to optimize energy use in commercial buildings. The company reported energy savings of 20–30% across client facilities through automated control systems and anomaly detection (Ma et al., 2022).

Another example is *Too Good To Go*, a startup that uses a digital marketplace to reduce food waste by connecting consumers with restaurants and stores that have surplus food. Studies show that the platform has prevented millions of meals from being wasted, demonstrating how digital solutions can scale quickly for environmental impact (van der Haar & Zeinstra, 2019).

These cases confirm that leadership agility, innovation-focused culture, and digital experimentation enable SMEs to drive sustainability effectively despite financial constraints.

7.3 Public Sector Case

Public sector organizations increasingly use digital transformation to promote sustainable governance. Estonia's e-governance system is widely recognized for reducing administrative waste, minimizing paper-based processes, and increasing transparency. Research indicates that digital public services significantly reduce environmental footprints while improving governmental efficiency (UN DESA, 2022).

Another case is the European Commission's Green Public Procurement (GPP) initiative, which integrates sustainability requirements into IT sourcing decisions - covering energy-efficient hardware, circular design principles, and low-carbon cloud services. Studies show that GPP adoption across EU member states has stimulated green innovation in the IT sector (OECD, 2024).

Leadership in these cases plays a crucial role by establishing regulatory frameworks, promoting citizen trust, and institutionalizing digital sustainability standards.

7.4 Cross-Industry Comparative Insights

Cross-industry empirical analyses highlight that leadership commitment, digital maturity, and cultural readiness are key determinants of digital sustainability success. Meta-analyses demonstrate that leadership styles - especially transformational and responsible leadership - positively influence the integration of green IT, responsible AI use, and data-driven sustainability practices (Hanelt et al., 2021; Bican & Brem, 2020).

Comparative studies across energy, finance, manufacturing, and ICT sectors also reveal that organizations with high digital maturity tend to achieve better sustainability outcomes because they can leverage advanced analytics, automation, and cloud optimization more effectively (Akdemir Ömür & Erkasap, 2025). Failures often occur when organizations lack strategic alignment, underestimate change resistance, or treat sustainability as a compliance exercise rather than innovation.

Insights from both success and failure underline a consistent message: digital sustainability is most effective when leadership embeds sustainability metrics in digital strategies, fosters cross-functional collaboration, and supports continuous upskilling to manage emerging risks.

8. A STRATEGIC FRAMEWORK FOR LEADING DIGITAL SUSTAINABILITY

8.1 Introducing the Digital-Sustainability Leadership (DSL) Framework

As digital transformation accelerates across industries, organizations face increasing pressure to embed sustainability into their technologies, processes, and strategic vision. Traditional digital strategies - focused primarily on efficiency, automation, and competitive advantage - are no longer sufficient. Instead, digital transformation must coexist with environmental stewardship, ethical considerations, and social responsibility. To support this shift, the Digital-Sustainability Leadership (DSL) Framework offers an integrated, actionable model that aligns digital innovation with sustainability-oriented leadership.

The DSL Framework consists of six interconnected components: Vision and Values, Ethical Digital Design, Green Innovation Capacity, Inclusion and Fairness, Governance and Accountability, and Impact Measurement. Together, these components provide a structured pathway for leaders to steer responsible digital transformation while delivering measurable sustainability outcomes.

Vision and Values: Digital sustainability begins with a clear, future-oriented vision grounded in shared organizational values. Research suggests that sustainability-oriented visioning enhances employee engagement, strengthens stakeholder confidence, and enables firms to align digital investments with long-term ecological and social goals (Bhattacharya et al., 2023). Leaders must articulate digital visions that explicitly incorporate carbon reduction, responsible data use, and circular digital systems. Values such as transparency, equity, and environmental stewardship serve as guiding principles that shape decision-making across the digital lifecycle.

Ethical Digital Design: Ethical digital design is concerned with ethical fairness, transparency, privacy and security into the construction and implementation of digital systems. As the issue of algorithmic bias, opaque AI systems, and exploitative data practices have become problematic, ethical design has been a focal point of digital sustainability (Mikalef et al., 2020). This includes the need to adopt privacy-by-design models, employ explainable AI, fairness auditing, and adopt responsible data governance. Ethical digital design does not only minimize the reputational and regulatory risks but also ensures that technologies have a positive impact on society.

Green Innovation Capacity: Green innovation capacity is the capacity of an organization to use digital capabilities to their benefit to the environment. These are carbon-conscious computing, cloud architectures that are energy efficient, sustainability digital twins, and circular management of IT assets. Companies that have a high level of digital capabilities will have more chances of fueling green innovation since they can take into account sustainability in product design, operations, and business models (Hanelt et al., 2021). To unlock such potentials, leaders need to support experimentation, make investments in low-carbon digital infrastructure, and facilitate cross-functional collaboration.

Inclusion and Fairness: Social sustainability is also a part of digital sustainability - as digital transformation should be inclusive, equitable, and accessible. Research illustrates the role of addressing digital divides, building diverse teams, and creating digital solutions in ways that do not discriminate and exclude (OECD, 2020). Leadership is very important in bringing equity to digital data streams, AI models, and service provision processes. Not only do inclusive practices create greater social value but they also facilitate a greater variety of innovative and human-centered digital solutions.

Governance and Accountability: Governance and accountability mechanisms are essential to institutionalizing digital sustainability. These structures include sustainability committees, AI governance boards, digital ethics review panels, and ESG-linked executive incentives. Effective governance ensures compliance with regulatory requirements, mitigates digital risks, and embeds sustainability into organizational routines (Batool et al., 2025). Accountability mechanisms - such as transparent reporting, third-party audits, and policy frameworks - reinforce long-term commitment and prevent sustainability from becoming symbolic rather than substantive.

Impact Measurement: Measurement is the cornerstone of the DSL Framework. Without robust metrics, sustainability claims risk becoming superficial. Leaders must develop integrated measurement systems capturing environmental, social, and governance impacts of digital operations. These systems support strategic planning, continuous improvement, and communication with stakeholders. Impact measurement also enables benchmarking and compliance with emerging global sustainability standards.

Figure 3. Digital-Sustainability Leadership (DSL) Framework

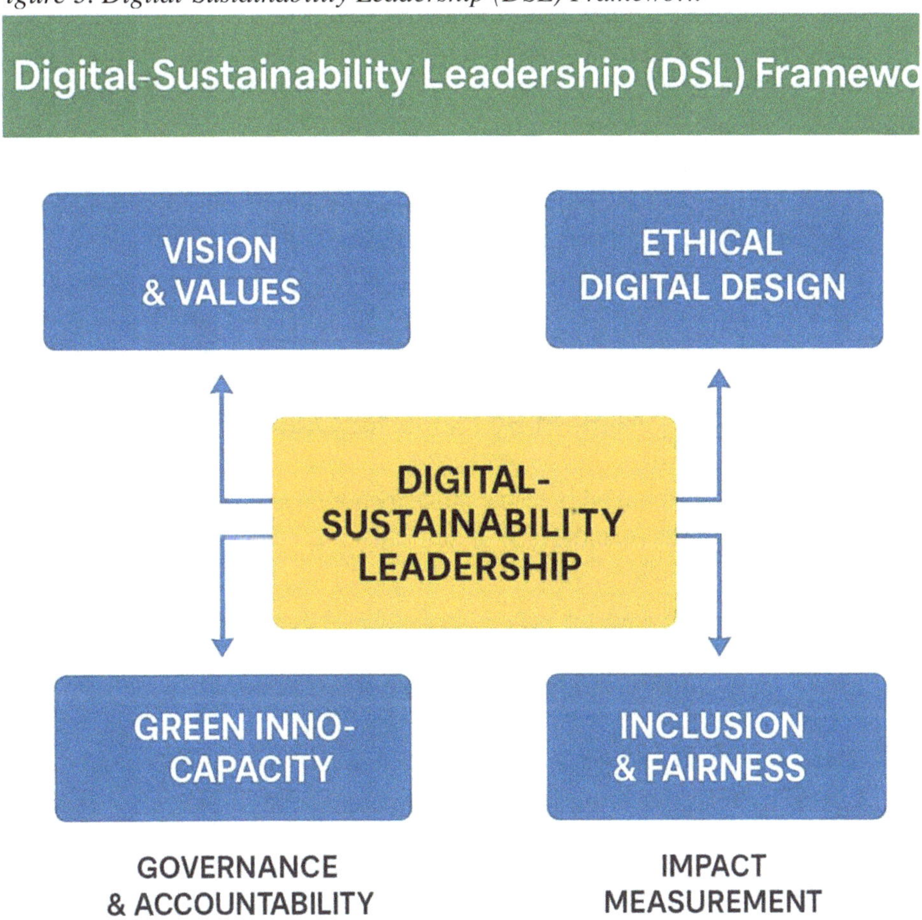

Author, (2025)

8.2 Action-Oriented Roadmap for Implementing the DSL Framework

Implementing the DSL Framework requires intentional, phased action:

Assessment and Benchmarking: Organizations begin by analyzing their digital carbon footprint, AI ethics risks, digital inclusivity gaps, and governance maturity. Digital sustainability assessments provide a baseline for planning (Khajeh Naeeni & Nouhi, 2023).
Strategic Alignment: Leaders integrate sustainability objectives into digital transformation roadmaps, define sustainability-oriented KPIs, and align budgets and resources with long-term environmental and social targets.
Capability Development: Workforce training in sustainable IT, AI governance, privacy engineering, and green innovation ensures that teams possess the skills necessary to execute digital sustainability strategies.
Technology Redesign: Firms modernize architectures—e.g., adopting green cloud strategies, optimizing data storage, reducing model energy intensity, and implementing lifecycle-conscious procurement.
Ecosystem Collaboration: Leaders partner with suppliers, technology providers, regulators, and industry consortia to promote shared sustainability standards and accelerate collective progress.
Continuous Governance and Monitoring: A cycle of measurement, auditing, reporting, and refinement ensures that digital-sustainability goals remain aligned with organizational performance and evolving stakeholder expectations.

8.3 KPIs and Measurement Systems for Digital Sustainability

Effective digital sustainability leadership depends on actionable and transparent measurement. Key KPIs include:

Environmental Indicators

- **Energy consumption of digital operations** (e.g., Power Usage Effectiveness of data centers).
- **Cloud workload carbon intensity** and renewable energy utilization.
- **Lifecycle emissions of digital products** (manufacture → use → disposal).

These indicators help firms evaluate progress toward carbon neutrality.

Social and Inclusion Indicators

- **Workforce diversity metrics**, including gender and minority representation in digital roles.
- **AI fairness measures**, such as disparate impact ratios.
- **Digital accessibility compliance** across services and platforms.

These metrics capture the human dimension of digital sustainability.

Circular and Lifecycle Indicators

- **E-waste generated**, refurbished equipment ratios, and sustainable procurement scores.
- **Product lifecycle impact assessments** evaluating environmental footprint across stages.

Ethical and Governance Indicators

- **Privacy incident frequency**, AI audit results, and algorithmic transparency disclosures.
- **ESG-linked executive compensation** alignment.

Together, these KPIs create a multidimensional, evidence-based approach to evaluating digital sustainability performance.

9. FUTURE DIRECTIONS AND STRATEGIC IMPLICATIONS

9.1 Emerging Technological Trends: Green AI, Edge Computing, and Circular Digital Systems

The next decade will witness an accelerated convergence of digital transformation and sustainability agendas, driven by breakthroughs in "green AI," edge computing, and circular digital system architectures. Green AI focuses on reducing the computational footprint of artificial intelligence by optimizing model training, improving hardware efficiency, and prioritizing energy-aware algorithmic design (Schwartz et al., 2020). This trend is becoming a strategic priority as organizations face increasing scrutiny over the carbon intensity of large-scale AI systems, particularly generative models. Google has integrated carbon-aware computing strategies to shift AI workloads to times and locations with lower grid emissions, significantly reducing the environmental impact of its data centers (Google, 2020).

Edge computing also plays a pivotal role in future sustainability strategies. By processing data closer to its source, edge systems drastically reduce latency and energy consumption associated with cloud data transfers (Shi et al., 2016). This architecture enables low-power IoT systems in manufacturing, smart cities, and climate monitoring. Corporates such as Schneider Electric and Siemens are leveraging industrial edge platforms to optimize energy use in factories and buildings, contributing to reductions in emissions and improved operational efficiency (Schneider Electric, 2021).

Circular digital systems represent a long-term shift toward minimizing the lifecycle impacts of digital technologies. This involves designing hardware for reuse, enabling modular upgrades, and improving digital product lifecycle transparency. The European Union's Circular Electronics Initiative, launched in 2020, provides guidance for electronics repairability, recycling standards, and digital product passports, setting a policy foundation for global adoption (European Commission, 2020).

9.2 Evolving Leadership Roles: CIO–CSO Integration and the Rise of the Chief Digital Sustainability Officer

Leadership structures are evolving to meet the complexity of digital-sustainability integration. Traditionally, Chief Information Officers (CIOs) led digital transformation while Chief Sustainability Officers (CSOs) guided environmental and social strategies. Convergence in these domains has prompted new hybrid leadership models. Emerging research suggests that organizations with tightly aligned CIO–CSO partnerships outperform peers in executing data-driven sustainability programs, due to shared oversight of digital infrastructure, ESG metrics, and ethical technology governance (Subrahmanyam, 2025).

A notable development is the rise of the Chief Digital Sustainability Officer (CDSO) - a role that integrates digital innovation, climate strategy, data governance, and stakeholder engagement. Companies like SAP and Microsoft have already adopted variations of this structure. SAP's CDSO-led initiatives have accelerated the embedding of sustainability analytics into core business applications, while Microsoft's dedicated sustainability leadership teams have spearheaded its carbon-negative, water-positive, and zero-waste 2030 initiatives (Microsoft, 2025).

These evolving roles reflect the strategic need for leaders capable of integrating environmental science, data ethics, digital technology, and cross-sector collaboration into a unified transformation agenda.

9.3 Policy and Regulatory Landscapes: ESG Mandates and Digital Rights Legislation

The governments of the world are putting in place tighter control measures in order to instill responsible digital and sustainability practices. There are increased stricter ESG disclosure requirements in different regions. In 2023, the Corporate Sustainability Reporting Directive (CSRD), which is enforced in the EU, implies that companies deliver extensive digital and non-financial sustainability reporting, such as carbon emission data, the traceability of their digital supply chain, and their social impact (European Parliament, 2022). The SEC in the U.S. has suggested climate-related disclosure regulations that would enhance the level of corporate transparency on emission, climate-related risk, and sustainability management (SEC, 2022).

Altogether, digital rights laws are broadening their scope to include data privacy, fairness of algorithms, and responsible artificial intelligence. The Artificial Intelligence Act of the EU (2023) provides international examples of regulating high-risk AI systems, which include the need to disclose information, manage data, and seek human supervision. Such changes in the regulation drive organizations towards increased holistic approaches to digital sustainability that both consider environmental effects and digital ethics.

9.4 Skills and Leadership Competencies for the Sustainable Digital Economy

As digital sustainability matures, leaders require a new blend of technological fluency, ethical mindfulness, and systems-thinking capabilities. Key competencies include proficiency in data-driven decision-making, understanding AI lifecycle impacts, and the ability to integrate sustainability principles into technology procurement and design. Research highlights that leaders who adopt a systems-thinking approach, linking digital innovation with environmental and social outcomes, are better equipped to guide organizations through complex transitions (Olivetti & Cullen, 2018).

Soft skills such as collaborative leadership, transparency, and stakeholder engagement are increasingly important. Cross-functional collaboration between IT, sustainability, operations, and compliance teams is essential for implementing circular digital practices and managing ESG performance. Upskilling initiatives are also critical; companies like IBM and Amazon Web Services have launched global training programs focused on cloud efficiency, responsible AI, and sustainable IT infrastructure to equip professionals with the knowledge required for emerging roles in digital sustainability (IBM, 2023).

10. CONCLUSION

The convergence of digital transformation and sustainability presents both a complex challenge and a generational opportunity for organizations. The preceding sections have synthesized conceptual foundations, real-world cases, and empirical insights to demonstrate that digital sustainability is no longer a supplementary initiative but a core strategic imperative. Across multinational corporations, SMEs, and public-sector institutions, evidence consistently shows that the effectiveness of digital-sustainability initiatives depends not on technology alone, but on the quality of leadership guiding them. Strategic leadership emerges as the central integrative force - aligning ethical digital design, environmental responsibility, data governance, and inclusive innovation into a coherent framework for long-term value creation.

Looking forward, future research should deepen interdisciplinary investigations into green AI, circular digital systems, and the social impacts of algorithmic decision-making. Policymakers must establish clearer, globally harmonized standards for ESG reporting, AI accountability, and green IT procurement. For practitioners, leadership development programs must equip current and future leaders with data fluency, ethical reasoning, and systems-thinking competencies to navigate accelerating technological and regulatory shifts.

Advancing digital sustainability requires evidence-based, ethically grounded, and future-oriented leadership that can balance innovation with responsibility - ensuring that digital transformation contributes meaningfully to environmental resilience, human welfare, and sustainable economic progress.

REFERENCES

Akdemir Ömür, G., & Erkasap, A. (2025). Impact of digitalization, technological innovation, and ICTs on sustainability management and strategies. *Sustainability (Basel), 17*(12), 5351. DOI: 10.3390/su17125351

Alabdali, M. A., Yaqub, M. Z., Agarwal, R., Alofaysan, H., & Mohapatra, A. K. (2024). Unveiling green digital transformational leadership: Nexus between green digital culture, green digital mindset, and green digital transformation. *Journal of Cleaner Production, 450*, 141670. DOI: 10.1016/j.jclepro.2024.141670

Albino, V., Garavelli, A. C., & Schilirò, D. (2021). Digital transformation and environmental sustainability: A review and research agenda. *Sustainability (Basel), 13*(3), 1530. DOI: 10.3390/su13031530

Bansal, P., Kim, A., & Wood, M. O. (2018). Hidden in plain sight: The importance of scale in organizations' attention to issues. *Academy of Management Review, 43*(2), 217–241. DOI: 10.5465/amr.2014.0238

Batool, A., Zowghi, D., & Bano, M. (2025). AI governance: A systematic literature review. *AI and Ethics, 5*(1), 3265–3279. DOI: 10.1007/s43681-024-00653-w

Batool, H. (2024). Influence of distributed leadership on employee innovative behaviour: The mediating role of psychological empowerment. *Journal of Innovation and Entrepreneurship, 13*(1), 82. DOI: 10.1186/s13731-024-00448-7

Bhattacharya, C. B., Sen, S., Edinger-Schons, L. M., & Neureiter, M. (2023). Corporate purpose and employee sustainability behaviors. *Journal of Business Ethics, 183*(4), 963–981. DOI: 10.1007/s10551-022-05090-5

Bibri, S. E. (2021). The core academic and scientific disciplines underlying data-driven smart sustainable urbanism: An interdisciplinary and transdisciplinary framework. *Computational Urban Science, 1*(1), 1–32. DOI: 10.1007/s43762-021-00001-2

Bican, P. M., & Brem, A. (2020). Digital Business Model, Digital Transformation, Digital Entrepreneurship: Is There a Sustainable "Digital"? *Sustainability (Basel), 12*(13), 5239. DOI: 10.3390/su12135239

Cisco. (2023). *Designing energy-efficient products.* In The Plan for Possible — ESG report. https://blogs.cisco.com/our-corporate-purpose/designing-energy-efficient-products

European Commission. (2020). *A new Circular Economy Action Plan: For a cleaner and more competitive Europe* (COM(2020) 98 final). https://eur-lex.europa.eu/legal-content/EN/TXT/?uri=CELEX%3A52020DC0098

European Commission. (2021). *European green deal: Striving to be the first climate-neutral continent* (Publication No. NA-02-21-151-EN-N). https://op.europa.eu/publication/manifestation_identifier/PUB_NA0221151ENC

European Commission. (2021). *Proposal for a regulation laying down harmonised rules on artificial intelligence (Artificial Intelligence Act), COM(2021) 206 final.* https://eur-lex.europa.eu/legal-content/EN/TXT/?uri=CELEX:52021PC0206

European Parliament & Council of the European Union. (2022). *Directive (EU) 2022/2464 on corporate sustainability reporting (Corporate Sustainability Reporting Directive, CSRD).* OJ L 322, 16 December 2022.

Forti, V., Baldé, C. P., Kuehr, R., & Bel, G. (2020). *The Global E-waste Monitor 2020: Quantities, flows and the circular economy potential.* United Nations University / UNITAR; International Telecommunication Union (ITU); International Solid Waste Association (ISWA).

George, G., Merrill, R. K., & Schillebeeckx, S. J. D. (2021). Digital sustainability and entrepreneurship: How digital innovations are helping tackle climate change and sustainable development. *Entrepreneurship Theory and Practice*, *45*(5), 999–1027. DOI: 10.1177/1042258719899425

Google. (2020). Our data centers now work harder when the sun shines and wind blows. *Google Blog*. https://blog.google/inside-google/infrastructure/data-centers-work-harder-sun-shines-wind-blows

Guandalini, I. (2022). Sustainability through digital transformation: A systematic literature review for research guidance. *Journal of Business Research*, *148*, 456–471. DOI: 10.1016/j.jbusres.2022.05.003

Hanelt, A., Bohnsack, R., Marz, D., & Antunes Marante, C. (2021). A systematic review of the literature on digital transformation: Insights and implications for strategy and organizational change. *Journal of Management Studies*, *58*(5), 1159–1197. DOI: 10.1111/joms.12639

Hossain, S., Fernando, M., & Akter, S. (2025). The influence of artificial intelligence-driven capabilities on responsible leadership: A future research agenda. *Journal of Management & Organization*, *31*(5), 2360–2384. DOI: 10.1017/jmo.2025.10010

IBM. (2023). *IBM furthers commitment to climate action through free training in green and technology skills for vulnerable communities*. IBM Newsroom.

International Energy Agency. (2023). *Energy Technology Perspectives 2023*. IEA., DOI: 10.1787/7c6b23db-

Kaya, Y. (2023). Agile leadership from the perspective of dynamic capabilities and creating value. *Sustainability (Basel), 15*(21), 15253. DOI: 10.3390/su152115253

Khajeh Naeeni, S., & Nouhi, N. (2023). The environmental impacts of AI and digital technologies. *AI and Tech in Behavioral and Social Sciences, 1*(4), 11–18. DOI: 10.61838/kman.aitech.1.4.3

Kraus, S., Jones, P., Kailer, N., Weinmann, A., Chaparro-Banegas, N., & Roig-Tierno, N. (2021). Digital transformation: An overview of the current state of the art of research. *SAGE Open, 11*(3), 21582440211047576. Advance online publication. DOI: 10.1177/21582440211047576

Kruglov, A., Succi, G., & Kholmatova, Z. (2023). *Metrics of sustainability and energy efficiency of software products and process*. In *Developing Sustainable and Energy-Efficient Software Systems* (SpringerBriefs in Computer Science, pp.?). Springer. https://doi.org/DOI: 10.1007/978-3-031-11658-2_2

Ma, Z., Santos, A. Q., Shaker, H. R., Yussof, S., Eriksen, P. M., Hornum, J., & Jørgensen, B. N. (2022). CELSIUS: An international project providing integrated, systematic, cost-effective large-scale IoT solutions for improving energy efficiency of medium- and large-sized buildings. *Energy Informatics, 5*(S4, Suppl 4), 41. DOI: 10.1186/s42162-022-00221-8

Mehrabi, N., Morstatter, F., Saxena, N., Lerman, K., & Galstyan, A. (2021). A survey on bias and fairness in machine learning. *ACM Computing Surveys, 54*(6). *ACM Computing Surveys, 115*(6), 1–35. DOI: 10.1145/3457607

Microsoft. (2020). *Microsoft will be carbon negative by 2030*. Microsoft Official Blog. https://blogs.microsoft.com/blog/2020/01/16/microsoft-will-be-carbon-negative-by-2030/

Microsoft. (2023). *2022 Environmental Sustainability Report*. Microsoft. https://www.microsoft.com/en-us/corporate-responsibility/reports-hub

Microsoft. (2025). *Our sustainability journey*. Microsoft. https://www.microsoft.com/en-us/corporate-responsibility/sustainability-journey

Mikalef, P., Boura, M., Lekakos, G., & Krogstie, J. (2020). The role of information governance in big data analytics-driven innovation. *Information & Management, 57*(7), 103361. Advance online publication. DOI: 10.1016/j.im.2020.103361

Mohammad, R. A., Alahmari, A. M. O., Faqih, R. H. A., Alshehri, A. I. A., & Al-Kahtani, S. M. (2024). Linking strategic intelligence, strategic leadership, strategic planning, and strategic thinking and business performance: The moderating effect of strategic flexibility. *Discover Sustainability*, *5*(1), 434. DOI: 10.1007/s43621-024-00670-z

Nie, C., Kushinsky, D., & Ren, T. (2025). Digital transformation, CEO compensation, and ESG performance: Evidence from Chinese listed companies. *Sustainability (Basel)*, *17*(9), 4033. DOI: 10.3390/su17094033

OECD. (2020). *OECD Digital Economy Outlook 2020*. OECD Publishing., DOI: 10.1787/bb167041-

OECD. (2024). *Harnessing Public Procurement for the Green Transition: Good Practices in OECD Countries*. OECD Publishing. https://www.oecd.org/en/publications/harnessing-public-procurement-for-the-green-transition_e551f448-en.html

Olivetti, E. A., & Cullen, J. M. (2018). Toward a sustainable materials system. *Science*, *360*(6396), 1396–1398. DOI: 10.1126/science.aat6821 PMID: 29954965

Pinto Mick, M. M., Kovaleski, J. L., Mick, R. L., & Chiroli, D. M. (2024). Developing a sustainable digital transformation roadmap for SMEs: Integrating digital maturity and strategic alignment. *Sustainability (Basel)*, *16*(20), 8745. DOI: 10.3390/su16208745

Radovanović, A., Koningstein, R., Schneider, I., Chen, B., Duarte, A., Roy, B., Xiao, D., Haridasan, M., Hung, P., Care, N., Talukdar, S., Mullen, E., Smith, K., Cottman, M. E., & Cirne, W. (2023). Carbon-Aware Computing for Datacenters. *IEEE Transactions on Power Systems*, *38*(2), 1270–1280. DOI: 10.1109/TPWRS.2022.3173250

Romagnoli, S., Tarabusi, C., Maleki Vishkaei, B., & De Giovanni, P. (2023). The impact of digital technologies and sustainable practices on circular supply chain management. *Logistics (Basel)*, *7*(1), 1. DOI: 10.3390/logistics7010001

Rupeika-Apoga, R., & Petrovska, K. (2022). Barriers to sustainable digital transformation in micro-, small-, and medium-sized enterprises. *Sustainability (Basel)*, *14*(20), 13558. DOI: 10.3390/su142013558

Samimi, M., Cortés, A. F., Anderson, M. H., & Herrmann, P. (2022). What is strategic leadership? Developing a framework for future research. *The Leadership Quarterly*, *33*(3), 101353. Advance online publication. DOI: 10.1016/j.leaqua.2019.101353

SAP SE. (2021). SAP's Climate 21 initiative: Integrating climate action end to end. *SAP News*. https://news.sap.com/2021/10/integrating-climate-action-end-to-end/

Schneider Electric. (2021). *Edge computing solutions: sustainability at the edge*. Schneider Electric. https://www.se.com/ww/en/work/solutions/edge-computing/sustainability-at-the-edge.jsp

Schwartz, R., Dodge, J., Smith, N. A., & Etzioni, O. (2020). Green AI. *Communications of the ACM*, *63*(12), 54–63. DOI: 10.1145/3381831

Shi, W., Cao, J., Zhang, Q., Li, Y., & Xu, L. (2016). Edge computing: Vision and challenges. *IEEE Internet of Things Journal*, *3*(5), 637–646. DOI: 10.1109/JIOT.2016.2579198

Strubell, E., Ganesh, A., & McCallum, A. (2020). Energy and policy considerations for modern deep learning research. *Proceedings of the AAAI Conference on Artificial Intelligence*, *34*(09), 13693–13696. DOI: 10.1609/aaai.v34i09.7123

Subermaniam, L., Kuppusamy, M., Isakulova, N., Ghate, A. D., Subrahmanyam, S., & John, B. (2025). A Systematic Review of Sustainability Management in Small and Medium Enterprises to Improve Sustainable Development Goals. *ACTA INNOVATIONS*, 55, 38–48. https://www.actainnovations.com/index.php/pub/article/view/403

Subrahmanyam, S. (2025). AI-Driven Leadership in the Modern Era for Revolutionizing Next-Generation Strategies: Organizational Impacts and Future Development. In Agnihotri, A., & Balusamy, B. (Eds.), *Leadership Paradigms and the Impact of Technology* (pp. 61–86). IGI Global Scientific Publishing., DOI: 10.4018/979-8-3693-7175-6.ch003

Subrahmanyam, S. (2025). Building a Digital-First Organizational Culture. In Pawirosumarto, S. (Ed.), *Innovative Approaches for International Competitiveness Through Human Resource Management* (pp. 101–124). IGI Global Scientific Publishing., DOI: 10.4018/979-8-3373-1005-3.ch004

Subrahmanyam, S. (2025). Leveraging AI and ML for Enhanced Efficiency and Innovation in Manufacturing. In Vyas, V., Bi, X., Pandey, D., Xu, Z., & Pandey, B. (Eds.), *AI's Role in Enhanced Automotive Safety* (pp. 319–344). IGI Global Scientific Publishing., DOI: 10.4018/979-8-3373-0442-7.ch021

Subrahmanyam, S. (2025). Strategic Collaboration and Partnerships in R&D for Innovation. In Martínez-Falcó, J., Sánchez-García, E., & Marco-Lajara, B. (Eds.), *Research and Development Practices in Innovation* (pp. 283–314). IGI Global Scientific Publishing., DOI: 10.4018/979-8-3373-0812-8.ch010

Subrahmanyam, S. (2025). Using AI-Driven Analysis for Training and Leadership Growth. In Mrabet, J., Boudagga, S., Sharma, R., & Bansal, R. (Eds.), *Harnessing Emotion AI for Customer Support and Employee Wellbeing* (pp. 321–352). IGI Global Scientific Publishing., DOI: 10.4018/979-8-3373-3658-9.ch013

Subrahmanyam, S., & El Samra, H. (2025). Startups and AI: Fostering Entrepreneurship in the MENA Region. In Azoury, N., & Yahchouchi, G. (Eds.), *AI in the Middle East for Growth and Business* (pp. 77–92). Palgrave Macmillan., DOI: 10.1007/978-3-031-75589-7_6

Tathavadekar, V. P., & Mahankale, N. R.Nitin R. Mahankale. (2025). Digital leadership for sustainability: An integrated framework for organizational learning, resilience, and social value creation. *Journal of Cross-Disciplinary Sustainability Innovations, 1*(3), 1–8. Advance online publication. DOI: 10.64229/tbqr6714

United Nations Department of Economic and Social Affairs. (2022). *United Nations E-Government Survey 2022: The future of digital government*. United Nations.

U.S. Securities and Exchange Commission. (2022). *The enhancement and standardization of climate-related disclosures for investors (Proposed rule)*. https://www.sec.gov/news/press-release/2022-46

van der Haar, S., & Zeinstra, G. G. (2019). *The impact of Too Good To Go on food waste reduction at the consumer household level: An explorative study*. Wageningen Food & Biobased Research. https://agris.fao.org/search/en/providers/122575/records/66d9bbfb5fdc8021c2c500be

van Uffelen, N., Lauwaert, L., Coeckelbergh, M., & Kudina, O. (2024). Towards an environmental ethics of artificial intelligence. *arXiv*. https://doi.org//arXiv.2501.10390DOI: 10.48550

Yang, G., Yang, G., & Wanping, Y. (2025). The impact of AI on enterprise energy management: From the perspective of carbon emissions. [STET]. *Science and Technology for Energy Transition, 80*, 8. Advance online publication. DOI: 10.2516/stet/2024096

Yusuf, S. O., Durodola, R. L., Ocran, G., Abubakar, J. E., Echere, A. Z., & Paul-Adeleye, A. H. (2024). Challenges and opportunities in AI and digital transformation for SMEs: A cross-continental perspective. *World Journal of Advanced Research and Reviews, 23*(3), 668–678. DOI: 10.30574/wjarr.2024.23.3.2511

Zervas, I., & Stiakakis, E. (2024). Economic sustainable development through digital skills acquisition: The role of human resource leadership. *Sustainability (Basel), 16*(17), 7664. DOI: 10.3390/su16177664

KEY TERMS AND DEFINITIONS

Circular Digital Infrastructure: IT and digital assets designed for longevity, reuse, refurbishment, and recycling, reducing environmental impact while supporting resilient and sustainable digital operations.

Digital Maturity: The level of an organization's readiness and sophistication in adopting, integrating, and optimizing digital technologies in alignment with strategic and sustainability goals.

Digital Sustainability: The integration of environmental, social, and economic considerations into digital transformation initiatives, encompassing energy-efficient computing, ethical AI, equitable access, and circular digital infrastructure.

Dynamic Capabilities: The firm's ability to sense opportunities, seize innovations, and reconfigure resources and processes to achieve sustainable competitive advantage in a rapidly evolving digital ecosystem.

Ethical and Responsible Leadership: Leadership focused on fairness, transparency, accountability, and responsible use of digital technologies, including AI governance, data privacy, and equitable access.

Green Innovation Capacity: Organizational capability to develop and implement technology-driven solutions that minimize carbon footprint, energy consumption, and environmental impacts while creating economic and social value.

Key Performance Indicators (KPIs) for Digital Sustainability: Quantitative and qualitative metrics used to assess the effectiveness of digital sustainability initiatives, such as energy efficiency, carbon reduction, diversity in tech teams, and lifecycle impact of digital assets.

Socio-Technical Systems (STS): A theoretical framework that emphasizes the interdependent relationship between technology, people, and organizational structures, highlighting the need to balance technical and social subsystems for sustainable outcomes.

Strategic Leadership: The capacity to envision, influence, and steer an organization towards long-term goals by aligning resources, people, and processes, particularly in dynamic digital environments where sustainability objectives are critical.

Transformational Leadership: A leadership approach that inspires and motivates employees to embrace innovation, sustainability-oriented digital culture, and continuous improvement beyond transactional objectives.

Chapter 6

Strategic Performance Management in the Digital Era:

Data-Driven HR and Leadership

Mirna Safi
http://orcid.org/0000-0002-4253-5869
Australian University, Kuwait

Yamen Nissi
http://orcid.org/0000-0001-9080-8289
Australian University, Kuwait

Oualid Abidi
http://orcid.org/0000-0002-0099-889X
Australian University, Kuwait

ABSTRACT

In the fast-paced business world of today, performance management is a phrase that is used in many different fields and at all levels of an organisation. Global rivalry, quick technology advancement, interconnectedness, and economic liberalisation have all made it harder for organisations to survive. In order to improve agility and boost business outcomes, companies are using strategic performance management (SPM) frameworks that incorporate goal alignment, real-time analytics, and continuous feedback. This shift is particularly relevant in the context of Kuwait, where digital transformation—a major pillar of Vision 2035 aimed at transitioning the nation toward a knowledge-based economy—demands data-driven approaches to

DOI: 10.4018/979-8-3373-5052-3.ch006

performance management. This chapter adds to the expanding body of knowledge on digital-era HR practices by linking people management to the goals of national development to establish sustainable, high-performing workplaces in Kuwait.

INTRODUCTION

Objectives

The primary objective of this chapter is to explore the ways in which Strategic Performance Management (SPM) facilitates the digital transformation of Kuwaiti companies. In particular, the discussion focuses on how HR departments are leveraging data-driven performance tools to align employee capabilities with both national priorities and corporate digital strategies. One of the key aims is to shed light on the SPM techniques currently being applied in organizations undergoing digital transformation in Kuwait. Another aim is to highlight HR's contribution to the integration of digital technologies for innovation, leadership development, and performance tracking. In doing so, the chapter identifies major obstacles to adopting performance technologies in the region, including skills shortages, resistance to change, and limitations in digital infrastructure. A strategic roadmap is also outlined to ensure stronger alignment between SPM practices and the objectives of Kuwait Vision 2035.

Moreover, this chapter emphasizes how the dynamic interplay between technological innovation and human resource capabilities can generate sustainable competitive advantages in Kuwait's evolving digital economy. By drawing on real-world examples and lessons from practice, it illustrates best practices and critical success factors that can enable policymakers and corporate leaders to optimize SPM frameworks to support digital initiatives. This comprehensive perspective underscores that successful transformation requires not only technological adoption but also organizational and cultural readiness, consistent with Kuwait Vision 2035's broader goals of fostering innovation, efficiency, and economic diversification.

Alongside these objectives, the chapter seeks to bridge the gap between theory and practice by providing actionable recommendations for organizations. Practical steps are outlined for HR directors and executives to accelerate digital readiness, including improving digital literacy, enhancing employee engagement, and fostering an innovative, change-oriented culture. These insights offer organizations a roadmap for aligning workforce competencies with emerging technological demands, while also ensuring that employees feel empowered and supported throughout the transformation journey.

Finally, this chapter positions SPM as a key mechanism for sustaining progress during and beyond the initial phase of digital adoption. By embedding performance management practices into organizational culture, companies can maintain momentum and avoid reverting to outdated systems. The long-term vision is to encourage Kuwaiti organizations to view digital transformation as a continuous strategic priority rather than a one-time initiative. In this way, SPM not only strengthens HR's role as a strategic partner in driving innovation, resilience, and competitiveness but also reinforces national objectives by aligning organizational goals with Kuwait Vision 2035.

THEORETCIAL BACKGROUND

The technology acceptance model (TAM), put forth by Davis (1989), describes how people embrace and utilize technology. TAM begins when a new technology is introduced and concludes when the user accepts and makes use of it. According to TAM, people give perceived utility and perceived ease of use top priority when choosing which technology to use. Social influence or behavior intention, which affects the user's attitude toward the technology, may also have an impact on the decision to use a technology (Davis 1989, 2023). When digital tools are thought to provide performance insights or lessen administrative burdens, their adoption actually rises sharply. This is in line with the conclusions of Masoud and Basahel (2023), who found that customer-centric innovations and digital transformation were important performance determinants. By emphasizing the perceived value of AI-enabled SPM platforms, such as their ability to provide predictive performance insights, HR professionals may defend adoption and investment.

Furthermore, a basis for comprehending resistance to digital transformation is provided by Lewin's (1951) unfreeze-change-refreeze paradigm, which emphasizes the significance of disrupting existing behaviors prior to introducing and institutionalizing change. When examining organizational inertia in nations like Kuwait, where conventional HR practices may be deeply ingrained, this paradigm is particularly pertinent. For digital SPM technologies to be successfully implemented, HR managers must oversee changes in staff competencies, workplace culture, and organizational structures. According to Supriadi and Mulyani (2024), transformation is not just technical but also behavioral and strategic, underscoring the need for responsive and flexible systems. In order to establish the foundation for efficient digital deployment, the "unfreezing" step may involve addressing legacy mindsets and increasing awareness of the shortcomings of antiquated technologies.

Rogers' (2003) Diffusion of Innovations theory contributes to our knowledge of digital transformation by explaining how the perceived relative advantage, compatibility, and complexity of new technologies influence the speed and success of their adoption. In fact, Rogers' DOI model is a useful tool for studying the adoption process and identifying the elements that influence an individual's decision to accept or reject innovation in the field of IT systems (Kouki et al., 2006). In Kuwait's public and private sectors, relative advantage can be proved by comparing SPM success in similar Gulf countries or SMEs, as Zhao et al. (2024) discovered significant improvements in innovation outputs and total factor productivity through digital transformation. Compatibility with existing HR systems and procedures is also important; new technologies that connect readily with present infrastructure are more likely to be adopted.

HR leaders must encourage a change culture in addition to embracing new technologies to further support Kuwait's Vision 2035, which aims to create a robust digital economy. Opposition to change may stem from uncertainty about AI's role in decision-making, a fear of losing one's job, or a lack of digital skills. HR directors can find early adopters and change agents who can help boost acceptability across departments by fusing Rogers' (2003) adoption curve with Lewin's (1951) change management model. According to TAM, one of the most significant factors influencing adoption is perceived ease of use, which can be enhanced and ambiguity reduced with the aid of training initiatives, internal communication campaigns, and strategic incentives. Abidi et al. (2023) consider that ease of use is a primary attribute that is systematically embedded in the conception of emerging communications technologies.

Ultimately, by integrating technology acceptance theories with digital transformation insights, HR professionals can approach SPM integration as a multidimensional change campaign rather than just a technological upgrade. According to Masoud and Basahel (2023), as digital solutions enhance user experiences, performance improvements become more apparent. Therefore, end users should be considered when developing SPM tools, such as tailored feedback systems, actionable dashboards, and user-friendly interfaces. Supriadi and Mulyani (2024) support the idea that digital HR strategies need to be culturally grounded by arguing for systems that adjust to organizational reality. This means adapting digital adoption tactics in Kuwait to the unique needs of the local workforce while staying true to international performance management trends.

Besides these theoretical perspectives, the institutional theory offers valuable understanding of how outside factors impact an organization's use of digital HR tools. In addition to aiming for internal efficiency, organizations usually react to regulatory restrictions, competitive dynamics, and societal expectations. Companies in Kuwait are under pressure to adhere to national initiatives like Vision 2035 and government digitization programs, both normatively and coercively (DiMaggio & Powell, 1983; Scott, 2014). These outside influences can hasten adoption by lowering resistance and boosting legitimacy across sectors by presenting digital SPM as an institutional requirement rather than just an operational alternative.

As a matter of fact, viewing HR and digital leadership as strategic assets that contribute to long-term economic value helps strengthen technology adoption theories through the lens of the resource-based view (RBV). When organizations integrate tools like AI and data analytics into strategic performance management—especially within areas like employee development and personnel management—they create resources that are not only valuable but also difficult for competitors to replicate (Barney, 1991; Wernerfelt, 1984). For Kuwaiti organizations, this means the potential to gain a competitive edge in the region, drive innovation, and better align human capital strategies with the country's long-term development plans. This perspective reminds us that adopting technology isn't just about improving efficiency; it's also a way to build lasting organizational strength.

LITERATURE REVIEW

Strategic Performance Management in the Digital Age

Strategic Performance Management (SPM) has evolved in the digital era from conventional, recurring assessments to dynamic, data-driven solutions that instantly match organisational objectives with employee aspirations. The importance of digital transformation in improving organisational performance is highlighted by recent studies. For example, a study by Masoud and Basahel (2023) shows that IT innovation, customer experience, and digital transformation all have a major impact on business performance, with the largest effect being seen in the customer experience. Furthermore, it has been demonstrated that incorporating artificial intelligence (AI) into performance management systems increases organisational effectiveness. Supriadi and Mulyani's (2024) systematic research highlights contemporary methods and trends in digital transformation within operational management, pointing to a move towards more adaptable and responsive performance assessment systems. Furthermore, through increases in total factor productivity and innovation outputs, Zhao et al. (2024) discovered that digital transformation has a favourable impact on firm performance, especially in small and medium-sized firms (SMEs). These developments call for a methodical approach to change management, guaranteeing that technical breakthroughs are successfully incorporated into organisational cultures and structures. In order to maintain competitiveness and promote continuous improvement, organisations must adopt sophisticated SPM techniques as they traverse the challenges of the digital age.

One of the most significant advancements in digital-era strategic performance management is the use of real-time analytics and predictive modeling. Traditional performance evaluations, typically conducted annually or semi-annually, are increasingly being supplemented or replaced by continuous feedback enabled by digital technologies. These tools empower managers and employees to quickly identify performance trends, address skill gaps as they arise, and adjust objectives to respond to evolving business demands. This increased agility not only enhances organizational responsiveness but also helps cultivate a culture of transparency and accountability. Moreover, with the support of machine learning, modern platforms can predict performance outcomes and recommend personalized development plans, facilitating better alignment between employee growth and broader strategic objectives (Supriadi & Mulyani, 2024).

Furthermore, performance management is becoming more data-driven and inclusive as a result of digital transformation. Top executives no longer hold exclusive access to performance data; thanks to cloud-based SPM tools, teams and departments can now access and share this information, fostering greater collaboration and informed decision-making. For global or hybrid workforces, where dismantling silos and enhancing alignment can be extremely difficult, this is extremely beneficial. Performance reviews can now incorporate more qualitative, nuanced input, such insights from staff surveys or communication platforms, thanks to technologies like artificial intelligence (AI) and natural language processing. Organizations can obtain a more balanced and lucid understanding of individual contributions and workplace health by integrating this with hard data (Masoud & Basahel, 2023; Zhao et al., 2024).

However, the transition to digitally enabled SPM systems is not without hurdles. Organizations must deal with data privacy, algorithmic prejudice, and the digital gap inside their own workforces. A successful deployment necessitates not just technological investment, but also cultural change management and upskilling programs. Leaders must ensure that personnel are properly equipped to use new tools, and that ethical considerations are built into the design and implementation of digital performance systems. As digital transformation accelerates, the capacity to integrate these technologies in an ethical and equitable manner will be a significant differentiator for organizations seeking long-term success and innovation (Supriadi & Mulyani, 2024; Zhao et al., 2024).

Furthermore, digital strategic performance management solutions open up new opportunities for businesses to evaluate their performance not just internally, but on a global scale as well. By comparing real-time data across departments or against industry benchmarks, organizations can quickly spot gaps and uncover areas where they might have a competitive edge. This ability to benchmark helps ensure that company goals stay aligned with shifting market trends and international best practices, boosting transparency and strengthening overall strategic focus (Masoud & Basahel, 2023).

Encouraging employee involvement and ownership of their performance is also a major key benefit of digital strategic performance management. When employees have access to real-time dashboards that clearly show their progress and contributions, they tend to feel more motivated and responsible for their results. This shift from traditional top-down evaluations to a more participatory approach changes the employee experience, fostering a culture where success is a shared effort rather than something imposed. This kind of engagement is especially important in small and medium-sized enterprises, where innovation and agility—highlighted by Zhao et al. (2024)—are essential for staying competitive.

Lastly, the flexibility of digital SPM platforms enables them to change in tandem with sectoral and organizational demands. Flexible systems are becoming more and more important in settings where technology is changing quickly, as Supriadi and Mulyani (2024) point out. Organizations may guarantee that their performance management systems continue to be applicable throughout time by implementing scalable solutions, modular features, and ongoing updates. This flexibility strengthens the connection between innovation, performance, and resilience by preventing obsolescence and putting businesses in a position to react successfully to both expected and unforeseen crises.

Digital Transformation in Kuwait: Vision 2035 & Data-Driven Performance Management

Human Resource Management (HRM) is a crucial element in incorporating SPM into digital systems. Talent dashboards, performance analytics platforms, and AI-enhanced feedback systems are examples of data-driven HR solutions that help improve the alignment of human competencies with strategic goals. According to recent research, integrating AI and big data analytics into HRM greatly improves employee retention and engagement. In the Jordanian banking industry, for example, Qawasmeh et al. (2024) discovered a positive relationship between work happiness and AI usage, suggesting that these technologies can improve The necessity of technical skills and strategic alignment for successful adoption is further highlighted by Sharma et al. (2025), who stress that HR analytics and AI have a substantial impact on HR functions, capacities, and decision-making in the IT sector. According to these results, incorporating cutting-edge technologies into HRM improves organisational competitiveness in the digital era while also streamlining performance management procedures.

This shift is particularly significant in the context of national digital strategies. A conscious shift to a knowledge-based economy through improved digital infrastructure and governance is embodied in Kuwait Vision 2035 (Government of Kuwait, 2023). Digital transformation is emphasised in this strategy as a key component of government and private sector expansion. As a result, HR's role is changing from administrative to strategic when it comes to implementing digital change, particularly when it comes to performance management that is in line with national development goals (CIPD, 2022). In Kuwait's digital era, the integration of SPM with digital HRM systems is thus both a technological advancement and a calculated reaction to state priorities.

Integrating Strategic Performance Management (SPM) into digital HR systems requires more than just implementing new technology—it also involves ensuring that employees are open to the change and that the organization is prepared to support it. Drawing on Davis' (1989) Technology Acceptance Model, HR professionals in Kuwait must focus on presenting digital tools as both valuable and user-friendly. This is key to encouraging adoption among employees and management, particularly in industries where digital maturity is still developing.

In these contexts, shifting away from long-established processes can be challenging. Lewin's (1951) unfreeze-change-refreeze model offers a helpful framework for managing such transitions. Before introducing AI-enabled SPM tools, organizations should begin by "unfreezing" resistance—raising awareness of current inefficiencies and building support for digital transformation efforts. During the "change" phase, it is essential to provide ongoing training and support, enabling users to develop the confidence and skills needed to effectively engage with the new systems.

Rogers' (2003) Diffusion of Innovations theory offers valuable insight into how digital HRM innovations, such as Strategic Performance Management (SPM) systems, can be effectively scaled across organizations in Kuwait. Early adopters—often younger employees or those with stronger digital literacy—can serve as key influencers by showcasing the tangible benefits of these new systems to their peers. As highlighted by Supriadi and Mulyani (2024), the responsiveness and adaptability of digital tools are critical to their success, particularly in dynamic and rapidly evolving work environments. To support this transition, HR departments should proactively identify and empower internal change agents who can champion the adoption of digital tools and promote a shift toward data-driven decision-making. This approach not only facilitates a more gradual and organic diffusion of innovation but also helps ensure the long-term sustainability and impact of digital performance management systems within the organization.

While internal strategies play a crucial role in driving the adoption of digital HR practices, external factors—such as national competitiveness and the push to meet global standards—are also powerful motivators for digital transformation in HRM. Research by Zhao et al. (2024) shows that digital transformation significantly boosts productivity and innovation, especially within small and medium-sized enterprises (SMEs). This is highly relevant to Kuwait's growing private sector, where such gains can be instrumental. Similarly, Masoud and Basahel (2023) highlight a strong link between improvements in customer experience, IT innovation, and overall business performance—further reinforcing the broader value of implementing digital SPM systems.

Kuwaiti organizations that align their HRM strategies with these insights not only contribute to achieving the goals outlined in Vision 2035, but also enhance their agility, workforce management, and overall operational effectiveness in an increasingly digital global economy. However, successful digital transformation requires more than just technology; it depends on the readiness of both institutions and culture. Investing in digital infrastructure is essential, but the acceptance and effective use of new systems hinge on cultural fit and employee mindset. Lewin's (1951) change model reminds us that people must be properly prepared for change, while Davis' (1989) Technology Acceptance Model emphasizes the importance of users perceiving new systems as both useful and easy to use. In Kuwait—where traditional HR practices remain dominant—finding a balance between introducing innovative tools and respecting established norms remains a key challenge.

Another critical consideration is the long-term sustainability of digital HRM systems. As Supriadi and Mulyani (2024) argue, digital tools need to be adaptable and responsive to remain relevant in rapidly changing environments. This means that HR digitalization should be viewed not as a one-time project, but as an ongoing process that evolves alongside technology and the changing nature of the workforce. Rogers' (2003) Diffusion of Innovations theory also reminds us that continued reinforcement is essential to move innovations beyond early adopters and embed them into everyday organizational practice.

Ultimately, the broader impact of digital HRM transformation extends beyond individual organizations. When aligned with national development priorities, such systems can drive corporate performance while also supporting Kuwait's transition toward a knowledge-based economy. As Zhao et al. (2024) and Masoud and Basahel (2023) emphasize, digital innovation enhances both productivity and competitiveness. By embedding SPM practices into digital HR frameworks, Kuwaiti firms can strengthen their resilience, contribute to economic diversification, and position themselves for long-term success in a digitally driven world.

Employee Experience and Engagement in the Digital Era

In the digital age, employee experience and engagement have emerged as important principles of strategic performance management, as businesses increasingly understand that workplaces enabled by technology must promote both well-being and productivity. Traditional approaches to performance management are being transformed by digital platforms and HR analytics, which now provide real-time engagement tracking, individualized development pathways, and continuous feedback (Mone & London, 2018).

Additionally, tools like collaboration platforms and coaching systems driven by AI improve inclusivity and openness, enabling staff members to take a more active role in corporate decision-making (Kane et al., 2019). Studies, in fact, reveal that when digital solutions are included into an encouraging corporate culture, they enhance inventive behaviours, strengthen commitment, and increase employee happiness (Parry & Battista, 2019). But even though these technologies have many benefits, leaders must strike a balance between efficiency and empathy to keep psychological safety and human connection at the forefront of employee engagement efforts (Bersin, 2020).

As a matter of fact, the nature of work and the employee experience are changing as we move from the inflexible industrial-era institutions and conventions to the more adaptable and democratic digital-age environments. In fact, employers need to reconsider how they handle remote workers, support continuous peer learning, evaluate performance using results, and encourage participation and inclusivity in online settings. In a same vein, workers need to embrace risk, gain digital era skills, adjust to self-directed career management, and discover meaning and camaraderie in increasingly scattered networks (George, 2024).

Employee engagement is increasingly viewed as a dynamic process rather than a static result as businesses adjust to digital change. Digital platforms enable managers to give regular feedback and acknowledgment, which encourages positive behaviour and pushes staff to perform better (Mone & London, 2018). In addition to enhancing openness, this ongoing performance discussion builds trust between supervisors and staff, fostering an atmosphere where people feel appreciated and encouraged to further their careers (Kane et al., 2019).

Furthermore, the limits of workplace culture have been redrawn by the use of digital instruments. For geographically scattered teams, online platforms can establish a feeling of community, encouraging cooperation and information exchange at various organizational levels (Parry & Battista, 2019). When properly implemented, these solutions aid in closing the gap between staff and management and present fresh chances for inclusive involvement and creativity. However, whether digital technologies facilitate or impede interaction ultimately depends on the cultural framework, which encourages transparency and a common goal (Bersin, 2020).

Lastly, executives must embrace a more comprehensive approach to employee experience in the digital age, understanding that engagement encompasses psychological safety, career advancement, and well-being in addition to productivity measures. Because they create environments where people can flourish both personally and professionally, leaders who embrace empathy in addition to digital innovation have a higher chance of maintaining long-term commitment from their workforce (Kane et al., 2019). Organizations can use data-driven tools while maintaining an awareness of the relational components that fuel genuine engagement and creativity by incorporating human-centered values into digital strategy (Mone & London, 2018; Parry & Battista, 2019).

The Future of Strategic Performance Management in the Digital Era: The Rise of AI-driven Decision-Making.

According to Cosa and Torelli (2024), digital revolution is changing the fundamentals of performance management, necessitating that businesses abandon strict, conventional frameworks for measurement. The intricacy and dynamic nature of digital business environments are sometimes overlooked by traditional performance measuring tools, as their comprehensive review demonstrates. Rather, digital transformation necessitates data-driven, adaptable solutions that can integrate financial and non-financial variables. This evolution guarantees that companies continuously adjust to changes in the market, stakeholder base, and technology in addition to monitoring results (Cosa & Torelli, 2024).

Cosa & Torelli (2024) also highlight how crucial real-time data analytics and cutting-edge digital platforms are becoming to performance management. Digital technologies allow businesses to process large volumes of data, improving their predictive capacities and facilitating proactive strategic decision-making (Cosa and Torelli, 2024). Businesses may match their strategic goals with changing market conditions and promote creativity and responsiveness by integrating analytics into performance systems. This marks a substantial shift from conventional, retroactive measurement techniques that were mainly focused on control and efficiency (Cosa & Torelli, 2024).

Furthermore, Cosa and Torelli (2024) emphasize that a solid leadership and cultural basis is necessary for flexible performance management. They point out that leaders are essential to promoting innovation, adaptation, and ongoing learning in businesses. Digital transformation depends equally on organizational mindsets that embrace change and resiliency as it does on technology tools. In order to match digital prospects with sustainable corporate performance, the integration of flexible performance systems is thus presented as a technological and cultural undertaking (Cosa & Torelli, 2024). Moreover, rapid digital transformation necessitates an organizational culture that supports workplace civility and job autonomy to enhance decision making among employees dealing with information and communication overload (Abidi et al., 2025).

Traditional decision-making techniques, which frequently rely on static intuition or lagging data, are ill-suited for the dynamic, uncertain situations that many firms now face, according to Heilig and Scheer's (2023) presentation of decision intelligence. In order to facilitate quicker and more adaptively applicable judgments, the authors argue that decision intelligence combines behavioural science, data science, and artificial intelligence technology. By implementing this framework, organizations enable leaders to forecast outcomes, model scenarios, and optimize trade-offs by making previously hidden information actionable. They are also encouraged to build infrastructures that support iterative learning and real-time feedback instead of fixed decision cycles (Heilig & Scheer, 2023).

Furthermore, the human and cultural aspects are crucial cornerstones of successful decision intelligence, according to Heilig and Scheer. They contend that just as important as technological tools are inclusive team structures, transparent workflows, and psychological safety. AI-driven systems risk becoming rigid, misaligned, or untrustworthy in environments that do not foster experimentation, encourage diverse perspectives, or uphold a culture of transparency and accountability. Leaders are therefore urged to cultivate contexts where technology augments rather than replaces human judgment, ensuring that expertise, critical thinking, and empathy remain central to decision-making (Heilig & Scheer, 2023).

AI-driven decision-making is increasingly positioned as a disruptive force in management, helping firms to negotiate complicated business contexts with better precision and speed. According to Ahuja (2024), artificial intelligence gives managers sophisticated analytical tools that can evaluate vast amounts of data, identify trends, and produce useful insights that outperform conventional decision-making techniques. This change enables businesses to better foresee, lower uncertainty, and match strategic plans with current market conditions. Managers can increase competitiveness and decrease human bias and inefficiency by integrating AI into key decision-making processes (Ahuja, 2024).

However, Ahuja (2024) points out that there are certain difficulties in incorporating AI into managerial decision-making. The effectiveness of AI adoption is heavily influenced by organizational preparedness, data protection concerns, and ethical considerations. Clear governance structures and leaders who can strike a balance between technology and human judgment are essential to the efficacy of AI systems. When these prerequisites are satisfied, AI transforms management procedures for the digital age by acting as a catalyst for better informed, data-driven, and morally good decision-making (Ahuja, 2024).

By redefining conventional appraisal systems, Nyathani (2023) highlights how artificial intelligence (AI) is profoundly changing performance management. AI-driven methods that offer ongoing, real-time insights are replacing traditional evaluations, which are frequently carried out once a year and are prone to managerial bias. These systems provide a more comprehensive and impartial evaluation of individual and team performance by analyzing employee data along several dimensions, including productivity, collaboration, and innovation. Organizations can attain increased fairness, openness, and alignment with strategic objectives by transitioning to data-informed evaluations (Nyathani, 2023).

Additionally, Nyathani (2023) emphasizes how AI may facilitate individualized employee development programs. AI-powered systems can detect skill gaps, suggest specialized training programs, and monitor advancement over time, claims Nyathani (2023). Employee motivation and engagement are increased because of this personalization since workers receive tools and feedback that are specifically related to their career goals. According to Nyathani (2023), AI-driven performance management enhances workforce development and long-term organizational competence in addition to improving appraisal accuracy.

Nyathani (2023), however, warns that incorporating AI into performance management also presents new difficulties that need to be properly handled. Important obstacles to adoption include concerns about algorithmic bias, data privacy, and employee confidence. The report emphasizes that to guarantee the responsible use of AI tools, enterprises must create strong ethical frameworks and open governance procedures. AI has the potential to be a driving force behind more fair and efficient performance management when used carefully, but without protections, it runs the risk of eroding organizational culture and employee trust (Nyathani, 2023).

Barriers to Technology Adoption in the Gulf Context – The Need for National Development.

Digital change in the Gulf, and Kuwait in particular, is fraught with difficulties despite the opportunities. Al-Haddad and Kotnour (2024) state that opposition to change, a lack of digital skills, and antiquated legacy systems are the primary obstacles to digital transformation. Furthermore, many Kuwaiti companies have a hierarchical and conservative working culture, which might make it difficult to implement agile performance management techniques and real-time feedback systems.

Furthermore, the adoption of real-time feedback mechanisms and the application of agile performance management approaches are frequently hampered by the strongly ingrained hierarchical and conservative organisational cultures seen in many Kuwaiti businesses (Al-Ghamdi & Aboelmaged, 2023). Through data-driven people management, Strategic Performance Management (SPM) propels organisational success beyond simple assessment. To prepare leaders for success in quickly changing digital environments, Boudreau and Jesuthasan (2020) stress that agile organisations use performance analytics to identify high-potential individuals, customise leadership development programs, and cultivate an innovative culture.

HR procedures must be closely linked with Kuwait's Vision 2035 development strategy in order to produce public value that is in line with national priorities. The achievement of the Vision depends on innovation, agility, and employee empowerment, all of which are made possible by efficient performance management systems, according to the Chartered Institute of Personnel and Development (CIPD, 2022). In order to ensure that HR directly supports the country's efforts at economic diversification and digital transformation, SPM provides a useful framework for converting Kuwait Vision 2035's overarching strategic objectives into achievable workforce goals.

To navigate the challenges of digital transformation, it's essential for Kuwaiti organizations to adopt proven change management frameworks—such as Lewin's (1951) unfreeze-change-refreeze model. The first step, "unfreezing," involves challenging outdated mindsets by clearly showing the inefficiencies of current performance evaluation methods and demonstrating the practical advantages of more agile, AI-enabled systems. In the "change" phase, efforts like digital skills training, leadership development programs, and clear internal communication can help shift employee attitudes and build trust in new technologies. Finally, to "refreeze" these changes, organizations need to embed them into daily HR practices through policy reinforcement and consistent application—ensuring that improvements in performance management become part of the long-term organizational culture.

Equally important is how users perceive the new systems. The Technology Acceptance Model (Davis, 1989) highlights that adoption largely depends on whether people find the tools useful and easy to use. HR professionals and managers who see value in performance analytics platforms—and feel confident using them—are much more likely to embrace and advocate for these tools. Therefore, successful integration of Strategic Performance Management (SPM) systems must take into account not just the technical capabilities, but also the human experience. Platforms designed with intuitive dashboards, personalized feedback, and clear performance indicators are more likely to gain traction across the organization. This is particularly important in hierarchical structures, where leadership endorsement strongly influences broader acceptance.

According to Al-Hajri et al. (2024), digital transformation has emerged as a key factor in the oil and gas sector's ability to compete in the Arabian Gulf. According to their analysis, cutting-edge technologies like predictive analytics, the Internet of Things (IoT), and artificial intelligence are being incorporated into core operations increasingly. By increasing productivity, enhancing safety, and optimizing resource use, these solutions help businesses in the area better adapt to changing market demands. In a very volatile global energy market, the study also highlights that strategic adoption of digital technologies is crucial for maintaining long-term growth and is not just a technical decision (Al-Hajri et al., 2024).

The report also emphasizes the organizational and cultural aspects of digital change. The development of digital skills, workforce preparedness, and leadership commitment are all necessary for successful implementation, claim Al-Hajri et al. (2024). Across the Gulf's oil and gas industry, resistance to change, outdated infrastructure, and gaps in digital capabilities continue to be major obstacles. The authors contend that cooperation between government agencies, business plans, and employee involvement is necessary to overcome these obstacles. In this way, the industry can use digital transformation to improve operational performance and further sustainability objectives that align with regional economic diversification ambitions (Al-Hajri et al., 2024).

Rogers' (2003) Diffusion of Innovations theory further underscores the importance of thoughtful implementation strategies, especially in diverse organizational settings like those in Kuwait. Identifying and empowering early adopters—such as digitally savvy HR professionals—can accelerate adoption. When these individuals share their positive experiences and demonstrate the benefits of real-time, data-driven performance tools, they can inspire others to follow suit. This peer-driven approach aligns with findings by Supriadi and Mulyani (2024), who stress that successful digital transformation depends not just on technology itself, but also on an organization's ability to adapt and evolve.

Ultimately, fostering a workplace culture that values innovation and continuous learning is essential for aligning SPM practices with both corporate objectives and Kuwait's broader national development goals. By prioritizing people alongside technology, organizations can ensure that digital transformation efforts are not only implemented—but sustained.

The Future of Strategic Performance Management in Kuwait

Performance management practices in Kuwaiti organizations are undergoing substantial transformation in response to the nation's digitalization agenda and its alignment with international best practices (Al-Mutairi & Al-Tamimi, 2022). Traditional systems—long characterized by infrequent appraisals and subjective assessments—are being progressively replaced by more sophisticated, data-driven models that are continuous and strategically integrated with organizational objectives (Pulakos et al., 2015). Increasingly, leading organizations across Kuwait are adopting continuous feedback frameworks, leveraging real-time performance analytics, and utilizing KPI-based tracking systems. These innovations not only strengthen accountability and responsiveness but also enhance the overall effectiveness of performance management processes in both the public and private sectors. Central to this shift are the specific tools, metrics, and processes being adopted, along with the challenges that accompany their implementation (Aguinis, 2019).

As performance management becomes more dynamic and data-driven, organizations are positioned to realize significant improvements in productivity, employee engagement, and talent retention (DeNisi & Murphy, 2017). These developments suggest that Kuwait has the potential to strengthen institutional performance while building a digitally proficient and resilient workforce. In turn, this supports the country's long-term competitiveness and aligns directly with the objectives of Kuwait Vision 2035 (General Secretariat of the Supreme Council for Planning and Development, 2019). Data-driven Strategic Performance Management (SPM), when embedded effectively, ensures that national aspirations for innovation and economic diversification are underpinned by strong organizational foundations (Ulrich et al., 2017).

This transition, however, is not limited to systems and tools; it demands a parallel transformation in organizational culture and leadership practices. The success of advanced performance management frameworks relies heavily on leaders' ability to cultivate workplace environments grounded in transparency, continuous learning, and adaptability (Kotter, 2012). Overcoming resistance to change—a persistent challenge in many organizations—requires leadership that embraces innovation, agility, and data-informed decision-making (Yukl, 2013). By fostering such a culture, Kuwaiti organizations can unlock the full potential of performance management technologies and remain agile in the face of evolving market demands and regulatory expectations.

At the same time, the integration of sophisticated digital tools raises critical considerations around data governance. Issues such as data security, privacy, and the ethical handling of employee information are becoming central to organizational strategy (Westerman et al., 2014). As Kuwaiti firms advance in their use of real-time analytics, there is a pressing need for robust governance frameworks that not only safeguard sensitive information but also promote fairness and transparency (Colquitt et al., 2013). Establishing this balance is essential for maintaining trust, protecting employee rights, and ensuring the sustainable adoption of digital performance systems.

The evolution of SPM in Kuwait has broader implications that extend beyond organizational performance. By enhancing operational efficiency and workforce capabilities, modern performance management practices can serve as a catalyst for economic diversification and the development of a knowledge-based economy (World Bank, 2020). Effective SPM has the potential to support innovation ecosystems, foster entrepreneurship, and strengthen collaboration between public and private sectors (Drucker, 1999). In this way, performance management becomes more than an internal organizational tool—it becomes a driver of national progress, reinforcing Kuwait Vision 2035's ambition to build a resilient, innovative, and globally competitive economy.

Additionally, companies are encouraged to take a more proactive approach to workforce development as a result of the move toward data-driven SPM. HR directors can spot skill gaps early and fix them with focused learning programs by regularly assessing employee performance and engagement (Pulakos et al., 2015; DeNisi & Murphy, 2017). In addition to enhancing human talents, this cycle of continual growth promotes organizational agility, allowing businesses to react swiftly to changing market demands and technological breakthroughs. A highly flexible workforce that is better equipped to welcome change and spur innovation is eventually produced by such approaches, which is essential for maintaining long-term competitiveness in the Kuwaiti environment (Al-Mutairi & Al-Tamimi, 2022; Ulrich et al., 2017).

Furthermore, the strategic importance of HR as a catalyst for more general economic goals is highlighted by the connection of SPM with national policies like Kuwait Vision 2035. In addition to improving operational effectiveness, companies that incorporate performance management into their digital transformation plans also support national targets like knowledge creation, innovation ecosystems, and economic diversification (World Bank, 2020; Drucker, 1999). Kuwaiti organizations can use SPM to promote cross-sector collaboration, entrepreneurship, and evidence-based decision-making by combining culture, leadership, and technology. The significance of strategic HR management as a pillar of long-term digital transformation is emphasized by this all-encompassing strategy, which guarantees that workforce performance is not evaluated in a vacuum but is instead connected to corporate and national results (Kotter, 2012; Yukl, 2013).

CONCLUSION

Implications

The transformation of performance management in Kuwaiti organizations carries important practical and policy-related implications, particularly as the country moves toward a digitally advanced, knowledge-driven economy under its Vision 2035 agenda (General Secretariat of the Supreme Council for Planning and Development, 2020). One significant outcome is the redefinition of the HR function—from a largely administrative role to that of a strategic partner (Ulrich, Younger, & Brockbank, 2019). With the increasing adoption of data-driven approaches, HR professionals in Kuwait will need to acquire new skills in data analysis, digital tool implementation, and strategic workforce management (Al-Mutairi & Al-Tamimi, 2022; Chartered Institute of Personnel and Development [CIPD], 2021). This will require investment in training and a cultural shift within organizations to prioritize data-informed decisions and ongoing performance improvement (KPMG, 2023).

Another implication is the potential for enhanced employee productivity and engagement, driven by more frequent and personalized performance feedback (Gallup, 2021). By replacing outdated annual reviews with real-time feedback and continuous dialogue—supported by modern HR technologies—organizations can create a more adaptive and motivated workforce (Deloitte, 2021). This shift enables more effective talent development and supports nationalization efforts by helping identify and close skills gaps among Kuwaiti nationals, thus promoting workforce sustainability and long-term employment stability (Al-Fadli & Al-Dabbous, 2023; World Bank, 2023).

This transition will also require stronger collaboration between leadership and HR teams to ensure the successful implementation of digital initiatives. Overcoming resistance to change—still one of the most significant challenges in digital transformation—calls for leaders to actively foster a culture of transparency and continuous learning (Ulrich, Younger, & Brockbank, 2019). By encouraging open communication and supporting data-driven decision-making, leaders can empower employees to engage with and embrace new performance management systems (Al-Mutairi & Al-Tamimi, 2022). This kind of cultural shift is essential not only for unlocking the full strategic value of digital tools but also for aligning workforce capabilities with Kuwait's long-term economic goals (General Secretariat of the Supreme Council for Planning and Development, 2020).

As digital tools become more deeply embedded in performance management systems, ethical considerations around the collection and use of employee data will take on growing importance (Chartered Institute of Personnel and Development [CIPD], 2021). To maintain employee trust and engagement, Kuwaiti organizations will need to establish clear policies that safeguard privacy and ensure fairness in how data is handled. Transparent practices and compliance with data protection regulations will be vital—not only to uphold the integrity of these systems but also to support the long-term success of digital HR initiatives (KPMG, 2023). Striking the right balance between innovation and ethical responsibility will be essential for the credibility and sustainability of Kuwait's performance management transformation.

Moreover, advancements in performance management are expected to significantly influence strategic decision-making and operational efficiency across organizations (Deloitte, 2021). Companies that leverage real-time analytics and ongoing feedback mechanisms will be better equipped to anticipate workforce needs, enhance talent development, and drive productivity gains (Gallup, 2021). This more holistic approach to managing performance not only improves outcomes at the individual and organizational levels but also contributes directly to Kuwait's Vision 2035 goals—particularly in promoting economic diversification and sustainable development (General Secretariat of the Supreme Council for Planning and Development, 2020). In this context, the effective implementation of digital SPM systems will be a key driver in building a more competitive and forward-looking Kuwaiti economy.

Originality Value

The originality of this topic lies in its specific focus on the relationship between strategic performance management and digital transformation in the context of Kuwait's economic and cultural environment (Al-Mutairi & Al-Tamimi, 2022). Much of the current research in this area is based on Western or multinational experiences (Ulrich et al., 2017; Deloitte, 2021), leaving a gap in understanding how such concepts are applied in GCC nations (Al-Harthy, 2020). This chapter offers fresh insights by exploring how Kuwaiti organizations are adapting global trends to fit local realities (Al-Fadli & Al-Dabbous, 2023). It introduces a tailored HR framework, identifies regionally relevant digital tools and strategies, and provides practical recommendations for both private and public sector leaders (GCC HR Summit Report, 2022). As such, it delivers unique contributions to regional literature and offers a model that other Gulf countries can follow as they navigate similar transformations (Khan & Al-Kuwari, 2021). The findings highlight the increasingly strategic role of HR in national development and support the broader objectives of digital advancement and workforce empowerment in Kuwait (Kuwait Vision 2035; World Bank, 2023).

Al-Mutairi & Al-Tamimi (2022) 's study, in fact, highlights the importance of grounding strategic performance management (SPM) within the cultural and organizational context of Kuwait. Unlike many Western organizations, where individual performance metrics often take precedence, Kuwaiti workplaces tend to place greater valuc on collective achievement and interpersonal relationships. These cultural norms significantly influence how digital technologies are adopted and how feedback mechanisms are designed and delivered (Al-Fadli & Al-Dabbous, 2023). Accordingly, the research underscores the need for culturally responsive digital HR strategies—ones that respect local traditions while supporting innovation. Such an approach not only eases the integration of new systems but also improves employee engagement and buy-in, both of which are vital for the long-term success of digital transformation efforts (GCC HR Summit Report, 2022).

Effective leadership is shown to be a critical factor in aligning performance management initiatives with both organizational priorities and national development goals (Ulrich et al., 2017; Al-Mutairi & Al-Tamimi, 2022). By fostering a workplace culture that encourages experimentation, learning, and adaptability, leaders can accelerate the adoption of digital tools and practices that enhance workforce capabilities (Deloitte, 2021). To overcome persistent resistance to change—common across both the public and private sectors in the region—a continuous improvement mindset must be embedded at all levels (Kuwait Vision 2035; World Bank, 2023). This alignment process, driven by leadership, forms a central theme of the study and offers practical guidance for executives and policymakers across the Gulf.

A further key insight is the necessity of treating strategic performance management as a dynamic process—one that must evolve in response to changing workforce expectations and rapid technological advances. Rather than approaching digital transformation as a one-off initiative, Kuwaiti firms are encouraged to adopt flexible frameworks capable of adapting to shifting business conditions and innovations (Al-Mutairi & Al-Tamimi, 2022). This agile approach allows organizations to continuously refine performance management practices, improve HR efficiency, and stay aligned with national economic goals, particularly those related to diversification and sustainability outlined in Vision 2035 (Kuwait Vision 2035; World Bank, 2023). In doing so, this chapter provides a contextualized understanding of how digital transformation and strategic HRM can be effectively integrated in Kuwait, offering insights that may be relevant for economies facing similar structural challenges.

A distinctive contribution of this work lies in its comparative perspective. By contrasting global digital transformation models with Kuwait's institutional and cultural realities, it challenges the assumption that one-size-fits-all frameworks are sufficient. Existing models often overlook the nuanced requirements of Gulf Cooperation Council (GCC) countries, highlighting the need for context-specific adaptations as a more effective pathway (Al-Fadli & Al-Dabbous, 2023; Al-Harthy, 2020). This comparative approach addresses gaps in both theoretical understanding and practical application within the GCC, emphasizing the importance of tailoring strategies to local conditions.

Equally significant is the policy relevance of these insights. By explicitly linking performance management frameworks to the national development objectives of Vision 2035, they provide guidance for shaping public policy and institutional reform (General Secretariat of the Supreme Council for Planning and Development, 2019; World Bank, 2023). This alignment allows policymakers to embed HR modernization and digital leadership strategies into broader economic development agendas, reinforcing the strategic role of human resources in national progress and ensuring that organizational improvements contribute directly to Kuwait's long-term economic and social goals.

Leadership is also highlighted not merely as a driver of implementation but as a cultural and operational mediator in the digital transition. Unlike global perspectives that focus primarily on technological infrastructure or readiness, this discussion emphasizes that leadership, when grounded in local values, plays a transformative role in advancing from traditional HR practices to digitally supported Strategic Performance Management systems (Ulrich et al., 2017; Deloitte, 2021). Leadership is reframed as a source of innovation in its own right—shaping how organizations adapt to digital change while remaining aligned with both cultural foundations and global ambitions.

Contribution

This work contributes to both academic and practical knowledge by linking digital leadership, strategic HR, and national development goals. By offering Kuwaiti organizations guidance on aligning people performance with innovation, efficiency, and sustainability, it supports the broader objectives of Kuwait Vision 2035. The focus on integrating talent performance with these key pillars provides practical, actionable insights for institutions seeking to optimize human resources, enhance competitiveness, foster a culture of continuous improvement, and ensure alignment with national priorities. This approach lays out a pathway for matching workforce competencies to the evolving demands of digital transformation and sustained national growth.

Leadership emerges as a critical driver in fostering a culture that embraces digital transformation. Beyond setting strategic direction, leaders are essential in empowering teams to adopt new technologies and modern practices. By cultivating an environment that encourages openness, innovation, and forward thinking, leadership transforms human capital from a potential barrier into a driving force for digital progress.

Equally important is the alignment of HR strategies with national development goals. Organizational talent initiatives that are embedded within broader economic and social frameworks contribute more effectively to long-term stability and growth. HR policies that reflect Kuwait's national objectives, including those outlined in Vision 2035, help ensure workforce development supports larger ambitions for sustainability and prosperity rather than functioning in isolation.

This perspective provides a meaningful foundation for policy and organizational practice. It highlights opportunities for scaling digital leadership and strategic HR practices across sectors to accelerate progress toward Kuwait's national vision. Policymakers, business leaders, and institutional planners can leverage these insights to refine strategies, stimulate innovation, and enhance collaboration between public institutions and private enterprises—ultimately strengthening Kuwait's position in the global digital economy.

Practical guidance is also offered for balancing local cultural values with international best practices. By situating digital transformation within the framework of national identity, modernization efforts can drive innovation and competitiveness without compromising cultural integrity. This dual focus ensures that digital change reinforces, rather than displaces, Kuwait's social and institutional norms.

Further, actionable pathways are presented for translating high-level policy into workforce strategies. Leadership can guide employees through organizational change, align HR processes with national priorities, and embed performance management practices that contribute to sustainable growth. These insights are directly applicable to operational realities across diverse industries.

The integration of HR and digital leadership into national development agendas is shown to have broader implications. Human capital is positioned both as a key driver and as a primary beneficiary of digital transformation. This dual role enables organizations to improve internal performance while contributing meaningfully to Kuwait's innovation, resilience, and economic diversification goals.

Continuous learning and development are emphasized as central to HR strategy. By identifying upskilling and reskilling pathways aligned with technological shifts, organizations can maintain an agile, innovative workforce prepared for future challenges. This approach reinforces strategic HR as a long-term national asset. Moreover, the alignment between HR, leadership, and public policy further mitigates risks associated with digital transformation. When performance management tools are coupled with structured leadership development and guided change strategies, organizations are better positioned to anticipate challenges, address resistance, and manage transitions effectively. This proactive coordination fosters a culture in which innovation thrives alongside stability, ensuring digital initiatives are both effective and sustainable.

Finally, the importance of cross-sector collaboration is emphasized as a critical driver for realizing the objectives of Vision 2035. By aligning HR and leadership strategies across public and private institutions, organizations can reconcile differing priorities, facilitate mutual learning, and engage in joint innovation initiatives that enhance overall workforce planning. Such collaboration ensures that human capital development and digital transformation are treated not merely as organizational goals but as strategic national priorities. Coordinated efforts across sectors also strengthen institutional capacity, improve the feasibility of large-scale national projects, and ensure that talent strategies are closely linked to Kuwait's broader economic and social ambitions. In addition, shared expertise and best practices promote more effective problem-solving, reduce redundancies, and allow organizations to leverage resources more efficiently. Cross-sector collaboration further fosters a culture of continuous improvement, encouraging innovation that is both sustainable and culturally aligned. By creating networks of inter-organizational support, these initiatives help build resilient, adaptable institutions capable of responding to emerging challenges. Ultimately, the synergistic effects of such cooperation accelerate national competitiveness, drive long-term socioeconomic progress, and yield benefits that extend beyond individual organizations to strengthen the country as a whole.

Disclaimer: AI (Quill Bot and Grammarly) has been used to paraphrase and proofread the language in selected sections of the manuscript.

REFERENCES

Abidi, O., Dženopoljac, V., & Safi, M. (2023). Online meeting tools, tacit knowledge sharing and entrepreneurial behaviours among knowledge workers during COVID-19. *Knowledge Management Research and Practice*, *21*(6), 1137–1149. DOI: 10.1080/14778238.2023.2261885

Abidi, O., Safi, M., Sarhan, H., & Bhagat, R. (2025). Creative Self-Efficacy and Innovative Behaviour amidst the Digital Deluge: Unravelling their Nexus with Autonomy and Workplace Civility. *International Journal of Productivity and Performance Management*, *74*(8), 2883–2907. Advance online publication. DOI: 10.1108/IJPPM-05-2024-0319

Aguinis, H. (2019). *Performance management for dummies*. Wiley.

Ahuja, N. S. (2024, October). AI-driven decision making in management. In *Proceedings of the 7th International Conference on Business and Technology* (Vol. 7, p. 12).

Al-Fadli, S., & Al-Dabbous, N. (2023). Workforce sustainability and digital transformation: Challenges and opportunities in the GCC. *Gulf Business Journal*, *15*(2), 42–56. DOI: 10.1002/gbj.235

Al-Ghamdi, S., & Aboelmaged, M. (2023). Culture and change readiness in Gulf Cooperation Council firms: Implications for digital transformation success. *International Journal of Human Resource Management*, *34*(4), 759–778. DOI: 10.1080/09585192.2022.2134217

Al-Haddad, S., & Kotnour, T. (2024). Digital transformation challenges in the Middle East: Organizational culture and legacy systems in focus. *Journal of Organizational Change Management*, *37*(2), 253–272. DOI: 10.1108/JOCM-11-2023-0321

Al-Hajri, A., Abdella, G. M., Al-Yafei, H., Aseel, S., & Hamouda, A. M. (2024). A systematic literature review of the digital transformation in the Arabian Gulf's oil and gas sector. *Sustainability (Basel)*, *16*(15), 6601. DOI: 10.3390/su16156601

Al-Harthy, A. (2020). Digital HR transformation in the GCC: A review of barriers and opportunities. *Journal of Middle Eastern Business*, *22*(4), 189–205. DOI: 10.1002/jmeb.341

Al-Mutairi, A., & Al-Tamimi, S. (2022). Strategic HRM practices in Kuwait: Challenges and future directions. *Middle East Journal of Management*, *9*(2), 134–152.

Al-Mutairi, F., & Al-Tamimi, H. (2022). The digitalization of HR in Kuwait: Emerging practices and challenges. *Middle East Journal of Human Resources, 10*(1), 34–49. DOI: 10.1002/ejhr.246

Armstrong, M. (2020). *Armstrong's handbook of performance management: An evidence-based guide to delivering high performance* (6th ed.). Kogan Page.

Barney, J. (1991). Firm resources and sustained competitive advantage. *Journal of Management, 17*(1), 99–120. DOI: 10.1177/014920639101700108

Bersin, J. (2020). Employee experience: The definitive guide. Josh Bersin Academy. https://joshbersin.com

Boudreau, J. W., & Jesuthasan, R. (2020). *Lead the work: Navigating a world beyond employment.* Wiley.

Boudreau, J. W., & Jesuthasan, R. (2020). Reimagining talent management for the digital age. *MIT Sloan Management Review.* https://sloanreview.mit.edu/article/reimagining-talent-management-for-the-digital-age/

Chartered Institute of Personnel and Development (CIPD). (2021). *People profession 2021: Insights into HR practices in the digital age.* https://www.cipd.org/uk/knowledge/reports/people-profession-2021/

Chartered Institute of Personnel and Development (CIPD). (2022). *People profession 2022: International insights on people practice.* https://www.cipd.org/uk/knowledge/reports/people-profession-international-insights/

Colquitt, J. A., Lepine, J. A., & Wesson, M. J. (2013). *Organizational behavior: Improving performance and commitment in the workplace* (3rd ed.). McGraw-Hill.

Cosa, M., & Torelli, R. (2024). Digital transformation and flexible performance management: A systematic literature review of the evolution of performance measurement systems. *Global Journal of Flexible Systems Managment, 25*(3), 445–466. DOI: 10.1007/s40171-024-00409-9

Davis, F. D. (1989). Perceived usefulness, perceived ease of use, and user acceptance of information technology. *Management Information Systems Quarterly, 13*(3), 319–340. DOI: 10.2307/249008

Deloitte. (2021). *2021 Global human capital trends: The social enterprise in a world disrupted.* Deloitte Insights. https://www2.deloitte.com/global/en/pages/human-capital/articles/global-human-capital-trends.html

DeNisi, A. S., & Murphy, K. R. (2017). Performance appraisal and performance management: 100 years of progress? *The Journal of Applied Psychology, 102*(3), 421–433. DOI: 10.1037/apl0000085 PMID: 28125265

DiMaggio, P. J., & Powell, W. W. (1983). The iron cage revisited: Institutional isomorphism and collective rationality in organizational fields. *American Sociological Review, 48*(2), 147–160. DOI: 10.2307/2095101

Drucker, P. F. (1999). *Management challenges for the 21st century*. HarperBusiness.

Gallup. (2021). *State of the global workplace: 2021 report.* Gallup, Inc. https://www.gallup.com/workplace

GCC HR Summit Report. (2022). *Human capital transformation in the GCC: Trends, tools, and strategies.* [Publisher information missing].

General Secretariat of the Supreme Council for Planning and Development. (2019). *Kuwait Vision 2035: New Kuwait.* Government of Kuwait. https://www.newkuwait.gov.kw

General Secretariat of the Supreme Council for Planning and Development. (2020). *Kuwait Vision 2035: New Kuwait.* Government of Kuwait. https://www.newkuwait.gov.kw

George, A. S. (2024). The metamorphosis of work: How technology is transforming the employee experience from industrial to digital. *Partners Universal Innovative Research Publication*, *2*(1), 93–112.

Government of Kuwait. (2023). *Kuwait digital transformation strategy 2023–2035.* Ministry of Communications and Information Technology.

Heilig, T., & Scheer, I. (2023). *Decision intelligence: Transform your team and organization with AI-driven decision-making*. John Wiley & Sons.

Huyett, B., & Viguerie, S. P. (2005). Extreme competition. *The McKinsey Quarterly*, (1), 47–57.

Kane, G. C., Palmer, D., Phillips, A. N., Kiron, D., & Buckley, N. (2019). Accelerating digital innovation inside and out: Agile teams, ecosystems, and ethics. *MIT Sloan Management Review and Deloitte Insights.* https://sloanreview.mit.edu/projects/accelerating-digital-innovation-inside-and-out

Khan, M. H., & Al-Kuwari, M. (2021). Adapting digital HR practices in GCC countries: A roadmap for future success. *Journal of Gulf Economic Studies*, *14*(3), 76–91. DOI: 10.1108/jges.2021.32456

Kotter, J. P. (2012). *Leading change*. Harvard Business Review Press.

Kouki, R., Poulin, D., & Pellerin, R. (2006). *ERP assimilation challenge: An integrative framework for a better post-implementation assimilation*. CIRRELT.

KPMG. (2023). *Future of HR: Navigating digital transformation in the Middle East*. KPMG International. https://home.kpmg/xx/en/home/insights/2023/01/future-of-hr.html

Lewin, K. (1951). *Field theory in social science: Selected theoretical papers*. Harper & Row.

Masoud, R., & Basahel, S. (2023). The effects of digital transformation on firm performance: The role of customer experience and IT innovation. *Digital*, *3*(2), 109–126. DOI: 10.3390/digital3020008

Mone, E. M., & London, M. (2018). *Employee engagement through effective performance management: A practical guide for managers*. Routledge., DOI: 10.4324/9781315626529

Nyathani, R. (2023). AI in performance management: Redefining performance appraisals in the digital age. *Journal of Artificial Intelligence & Cloud Computing, SRC/JAICC-146*, 134, 2–5.

Parry, E., & Battista, V. (2019). The impact of emerging technologies on work: A review of the evidence and implications for the human resource function. *Emerging Markets Journal*, *9*(1), 1–19. DOI: 10.5195/emaj.2019.184

Pulakos, E. D., Mueller-Hanson, R. A., & O'Leary, R. S. (2015). Performance management in the United States. In Wilkinson, A., Bacon, N., Lepak, D., & Snell, S. (Eds.), *The Sage handbook of human resource management* (pp. 224–241). Sage.

Qawasmeh, E., Qawasmeh, F., & Daoud, M. K. (2024). Digital transformation in HRM: Leveraging AI and big data for employee engagement and retention. *Journal of Ecohumanism*, *3*(3), 3479. DOI: 10.62754/joe.v3i3.3479

Rogers, E. M. (2003). *Diffusion of innovations* (5th ed.). Free Press.

Scott, W. R. (2014). *Institutions and organizations: Ideas, interests, and identities* (4th ed.). Sage Publications.

Sharma, P., Bhattacharya, S., & Bhattacharya, S. (2025). HR analytics and AI adoption in IT sector: Reflections from practitioners. *Journal of Work-Applied Management, ahead-of-print*(ahead-of-print). https://doi.org/DOI: 10.1108/JWAM-12-2024-0179

Supriadi, A., & Mulyani, A. S. (2024). Digital transformation in operational management: A systematic review of current trends and practices. [PRODUCTIVITY]. *Management Studies and Business Journal, 1*(3), 496–506. DOI: 10.62207/07xvt585

Ulrich, D., Brockbank, W., Johnson, D., Sandholtz, K., & Younger, J. (2017). *HR competencies: Mastery at the intersection of people and business*. Society for Human Resource Management.

Ulrich, D., Younger, J., & Brockbank, W. (2019). *HR transformation: Building human resources from the inside out*. McGraw-Hill Education.

Wernerfelt, B. (1984). A resource-based view of the firm. *Strategic Management Journal, 5*(2), 171–180. DOI: 10.1002/smj.4250050207

Westerman, G., Bonnet, D., & McAfee, A. (2014). *Leading digital: Turning technology into business transformation*. Harvard Business Review Press.

World Bank. (2020). *Kuwait country economic update: Toward a sustainable economy*. World Bank Publications. https://www.worldbank.org/en/country/kuwait

World Bank. (2023). *The future of work and digital transformation in the MENA region*. World Bank Group. https://www.worldbank.org/en/news/feature/2023/03/02/future-of-work-mena

Yukl, G. (2013). *Leadership in organizations* (8th ed.). Pearson.

Zhao, X., Li, X., Li, Y., & Wang, Z. (2024). The impact of digital transformation on firm performance. *Industrial Management & Data Systems, 124*(8), 2567–2587. DOI: 10.1108/IMDS-09-2023-0661

Chapter 7
Integrating Digital Technologies for Enhanced Sustainability and Performance in Supply Chains

Yamen Nissi
http://orcid.org/0000-0001-9080-8289
Australian University, Kuwait

Faidon Theofanidis
http://orcid.org/0000-0001-7060-5409
Australian University, Kuwait

Farid Abdallah
http://orcid.org/0000-0001-7619-0291
Australian University, Kuwait

ABSTRACT

This study aims to explore digital tools such as blockchain, the internet of things, artificial intelligence (AI), and big data analytics, and how these tools could be used to optimize supply chain operations across environmental, economic, and social dimensions. Key performance indicators (KPIs) will focus on enhancing resource efficiency, enabling real-time traceability, reducing carbon footprint, and improving stakeholder collaboration. The research identifies the role of digital transformation in aligning sustainability with operational excellence. Through an extensive literature review, this study highlights best practices in the adoption of these technologies

DOI: 10.4018/979-8-3373-5052-3.ch007

across various industries. This research contributes to both academic and practical discussions by providing an integrative conceptual framework that links digital innovation with sustainable supply chain performance, offering actionable insights for managers and policymakers striving to meet evolving environmental standards and market expectations.

1. INTRODUCTION

Interestingly, despite its extensive use in academic research and business practice, a review of the literature reveals a notable lack of clear consensus regarding the definition of supply chain. A simplistic definition has been provided by La Londe and Masters (1994) who proposed that a "supply chain is a set of firms that pass materials forward". On the same direction, (Lambert et al., 1998) define a supply chain as the "alignment of firms that brings products or services to market". The first author who conceived supply chain as a "network of organizations" was Christopher (1992), who also highlighted "upstream and downstream linkages" between these organizations aiming at producing and delivering value to the ultimate consumer. Expanding Christopher's definition, Mentzer et al. (2001) argued that "a supply chain is defined as a set of three or more entities (organizations or individuals) directly involved in the upstream and downstream flows of products, services, finances, and/ or information from a source to a customer". A more comprehensive definition of the supply chain (which builds on the previous definition suggested by Christopher, 1992, who viewed the supply chain as a network of firms) was provided by Goetschalckx (2011), who described supply chains as "networks of functional organizations that through their activities perform the logistics functions," including procurement of materials, transformation into products, and distribution to customers.

Moving forward to the definition of Supply Chain Management (SCM), Larson and Rogers' (1998) described SCM as: "the coordination of activities, within and between vertically linked firms, for the purpose of serving end customers at a profit." Mentzer et al. (2001) after researching the literature and interviewing executives in 20 companies, they classified the SCM definitions into three categories: a management philosophy, implementation of a management philosophy, and a set of management activities. The same authors (Mentzer et al., 2001) argued that based on previous research, the identified activities necessary to successfully implement the SCM philosophy, are: "(1) Integrated Behavior, (2) Mutually Sharing Information, (3) Mutually Sharing Risks and Rewards, (4) Cooperation, (5) The Same Goal and the Same Focus on Serving Customers, (6) Integration of Processes, and (7) Partners to Build and Maintain Long-Term Relationships". Stock and Boyer (2009) analyzed 166 supply chain management definitions, using NVivo software for qualitative analysis, identified three core themes of SCM: activities, benefits, constituents/components.

Having established a conceptual understanding of "supply chain" and "supply chain management," we now introduce the interrelated concepts of sustainability and performance as vital dimensions shaping the success of supply chains. Around the world, supply chains are facing increasing pressure to address environmental, social, and economic sustainability with a focus on increased performance. In the early 2000s, supply chain management (SCM) was largely focused on three priorities: cutting costs, improving efficiency, and boosting responsiveness. While these goals remain relevant, the conversation is gradually shifting. As digital technologies emerge not merely as tools but as potential drivers of sustainable digital transformation (Theofanidis et al., 2024; Erturk et al., 2024), they offer ways to improve performance without forcing trade-offs. The effects on supply chains are wide range, extending beyond improved visibility and efficiency to include reduced waste and, perhaps less obviously, the promotion of ethical practices throughout the network.

At the same time, digital transformation appears to do more than simply support sustainability, it may also act as a catalyst for resilience and adaptability. Digital transformation initiatives are increasingly linked to improved sustainability outcomes in supply chains (Zaida et al., 2025). Li (2025) suggests that these same digital tools enable organizations to absorb shocks and recover more quickly. Taking together, the evidence points toward a view of digital technologies as both enablers of everyday efficiency and as mechanisms that allow supply chains to become more flexible and responsive in uncertain environments. Winkelmann et al. (2024) highlight how digital tools help firms build supply chains that can withstand disruptions. According to Alquraish (2025), integrating digital technologies with sustainability is essential in manufacturing contexts, where global competition and regulatory pressures necessitate enhanced resilience and agility. Furthermore, several studies have emphasized the transformative impact of big data analytics on supply chain performance (Choi et al., 2020; Wamba et al., 2017; Dubey et al., 2019).

This study aims to investigate how digital technologies integration may effectively enhance sustainability in the supply chain without compromising performance, on the other hand, improving it. The following were specifically investigated objectives:

- To identify the main key digital technology drivers for sustainability in Supply Chain Management (SCM)
- To investigate the effect of these technologies on the supply chain performance metrics.
- To introduce a holistic conceptual framework that links sustainability with digital transformation and performance outcomes in the supply chain

This chapter employs a qualitative, conceptual, and interpretive research design to explore how digital technologies can be integrated into supply chain management to foster sustainability and improve performance outcomes. After extensive review of the relevant literature the study adopts a theory-building approach aimed at developing a holistic conceptual framework titled: "Holistic Model Integrating Digital Technologies to Enhance Supply Chain Sustainability and Performance". Based on the literature synthesis and thematic analysis, in the results and discussion section the proposed holistic model is fully described, highlighting the novel Digital Sustainability Integration (DSI) mechanism, which, together with the Dynamic Capabilities construct can improve the sustainability and performance of the supply chain.

2. THEORETICAL BACKGROUND

This research is grounded in three foundational theoretical frameworks: the **Resource-Based View (RBV)**, the **Triple Bottom Line (TBL)** approach, and **Dynamic Capabilities Theory (DCT)**. All three frameworks present a different way into understanding how firms navigate increasingly complex and dynamic terrains of supply chain management (SCM). To further enrich this foundation, this study also highlights earlier theories relative in their approaches such as Transaction Cost Economics (TCE), Stakeholder Theory, the Relational View, Institutional Theory, and Systems and Network perspective. All together these perspectives reflect how SCM has evolved and grew from a narrow focus on efficiency to a broader concern with resilience, legitimacy and long- term value creation. Macher and Richman (2008) provide a comprehensive assessment of empirical research on transaction cost economics across multiple fields.

2.1. Resource-Based View And Its Theoretical Lineage

The **Resource-Based View**, (RBV) introduced by Barney (1991), suggests that firms gain a competitive edge by leveraging resources that are not only valuable but also rare and difficult to replicate. These might include proprietary technologies, specialized knowledge, or even organizational culture. While RBV has become a staple in strategic management literature, it's not without its limitations. For instance, it tends to focus heavily on internal assets, sometimes overlooking the role of external relationships and institutional pressures.

RBV's development was influenced by earlier economic theories, particularly Transaction Cost Economics (TCE), which examined how firms structure themselves to minimize the costs of exchanging goods and services (Williamson, 1989; Williamson, 1998; Macher and Richman, 2008). TCE is more concerned with governance—how contracts, hierarchies, and partnerships help firms manage uncertainty and opportunism (Williamson, 1989; Williamson, 1998). In supply chain settings, Rindfleisch and Heide (1997) extended the Transaction Cost Analysis (TCA) by exploring how firms use these governance mechanisms to deal with information asymmetry and risk. This is especially relevant today, as digital supply chains introduce new layers of complexity in data sharing and coordination.

Combining RBV and TCE offers a more balanced view (Neves et al., 2014). While RBV highlights the importance of internal strengths, TCE reminds us that external structures matter, especially when firms are embedded in networks of suppliers, customers, and regulators. In digital contexts, this dual lens helps explain why simply having advanced technology isn't enough; firms also need the right relational and contractual frameworks to use those technologies effectively.

Moreover, RBV has faced criticism for its static view of resources (Kraaijenbrink, 2010). In fast-changing environments, what is valuable today may become obsolete tomorrow. This limitation has prompted scholars to explore how firms can continuously renew their resource base - a question that leads directly to the concept of dynamic capabilities (Ambrosini et al., 2009). In digital supply chains, where technologies evolve rapidly, the ability to adapt and reconfigure resources may be just as important as the resources themselves.

It's also worth noting that RBV tends to assume that firms operate in relatively stable environments. Yet, in practice, supply chains are often exposed to volatility - from geopolitical shifts to climate disruptions (Ali, I et al., 2025). This raises the question: can RBV alone account for the agility required in such contexts? Probably not. That's why integrating RBV with more dynamic and relational theories is not just useful, it's necessary.

2.2. Relational View and the Value of Collaboration

The **Relational View**, proposed by Dyer and Singh (1998), shifts the analytical lens from firm-level resources to inter-organizational relationships. It argues that competitive advantage can also stem from collaborative arrangements that foster trust, joint learning, and shared innovation. In supply chain settings, this perspective has gained traction as firms increasingly rely on strategic alliances and partnerships to co-create value.

Digital transformation has amplified the relevance of the relational view. Technologies such as blockchain, cloud computing, and IoT facilitate real-time data exchange, enhancing transparency and trust among partners (Omisola et al., 2023). These tools reduce the need for rigid contracts by enabling more fluid, responsive collaboration. Moreover, digital platforms allow firms to engage in collaborative sustainability initiatives, such as joint carbon reduction programs (Onukwulu, 2021) or ethical sourcing networks (Roberts, 2003), which require coordinated action across multiple stakeholders. That said, the relational view isn't a panacea. Trust-based relationships take time to build and can be fragile. Digital tools may help, but they don't replace the need for cultural alignment and shared values. In some cases, firms may find that collaboration introduces new risks—such as dependency or loss of control. So, while the relational view offers a compelling alternative to purely transactional models (Hargaden and Sills, 2014) it also requires careful management.

It's also worth noting that not all firms are equally positioned to benefit from relational advantages. Smaller suppliers, for example, may lack the bargaining power or technological infrastructure to participate fully in digital collaborations. This raises questions about equity and inclusion in supply chain networks—issues that are often overlooked in mainstream strategy literature. Furthermore, collaboration doesn't always lead to innovation. In some cases, it may result in conformity or groupthink, especially when dominant partners set the agenda. This suggests that relational strategies must be designed with diversity and autonomy in mind, not just efficiency.

2.3. Institutional Theory and the Quest for Legitimacy

Institutional Theory (DiMaggio & Powell, 1983) offers a sociological explanation for organizational behavior. It suggests that firms often adopt similar practices not solely for efficiency, but to gain legitimacy within their institutional environments. These environments include regulatory agencies, industry associations, media, and civil society, all of which exert normative, coercive, and mimetic pressures on firms.

In the context of sustainable SCM, institutional pressures manifest in various forms: government regulations mandating emissions reporting, consumer demand for ethical products, investor scrutiny of ESG performance, and industry standards for green certifications (Yang, 2024; Wu, 2025; Maalouf, 2024). Firms may adopt sustainability practices to signal legitimacy, even when such actions do not yield immediate financial returns. This behavior reflects a broader shift from profit-maximization to stakeholder-responsive governance.

Institutional theory complements RBV and DCT by highlighting the role of social conformity in strategic decision-making. While RBV focuses on resource advantages and DCT on adaptive capabilities, institutional theory underscores the importance of legitimacy and reputation. In digital supply chains, this means that firms must not only deploy advanced technologies but also demonstrate responsible use - ensuring data privacy, ethical AI deployment, and transparent reporting. However, institutional environments are not monolithic. What counts as legitimate in one context may be contested in another. For instance, sustainability standards in Europe may differ significantly from those in Southeast Asia (Ooi, 2008). Firms operating across borders must navigate these differences, often making trade-offs between global consistency and local responsiveness. This complexity underscores the need for flexible strategies that can accommodate diverse institutional logics.

There's also the risk of performative compliance (Leathwood and Read, 2013; Szerszynski, 1999). Some firms may adopt sustainability labels or digital certifications primarily for marketing purposes, without making substantive changes to their operations. This raises ethical concerns and calls for more rigorous accountability mechanisms. Malindretos and Theofanides (2007) demonstrate the integration of Marketing and Logistics in creating an efficient distribution strategy.

2.4. Dynamic Capabilities Theory (DCT) and Organizational Adaptability

Dynamic Capabilities Theory, developed by Teece, Pisano, and Shuen (1997), builds on RBV but adds a layer of adaptability. It's not enough to have valuable resources; firms also need the ability to reconfigure these resources in response to change. This is especially relevant in today's volatile environments, where supply chains face disruptions from climate events, geopolitical tensions, and technological shifts. Dynamic capabilities are essential for firms to adapt and renew their resource base in dynamic environments (Ambrosini, Bowman, & Collier, 2009).

Digital technologies can support dynamic capabilities, but they don't guarantee them. For example, big data analytics and AI can help firms detect trends and respond quickly, but only if the organization knows how to interpret the data and act on it. Chen et al. (2024) found that combining these tools enables firms to balance exploitation and exploration using existing capabilities while also pursuing new green initiatives. Zhang et al. (2024) showed that digitalization enhances green supply chain management through innovation, thereby improving overall sustainability performance. Still, dynamic capabilities are hard to measure and even harder to build. They require not just tools, but also culture, leadership, and learning. A firm might invest heavily in AI but fail to use it effectively because of siloed departments or resistance to change. So, while DCT offers a promising framework, it also invites questions about how capabilities are developed and sustained over time.

There's also a temporal dimension to consider. Dynamic capabilities are not static traits but evolving processes. What enables adaptation today may need to be reinvented tomorrow. This suggests that firms must cultivate a mindset of continuous learning and experimentation—an approach that aligns well with agile methodologies (Cohen et al., 2004; Dingsøyr, 2012) and design thinking (Brown, 2008; Razzouk and Shute, 2012) but may clash with traditional hierarchical structures (Schneeweiβ, 1995).

2.5. Triple Bottom Line and Stakeholder Complexity

The **Triple Bottom Line (TBL)** framework, introduced by Elkington (1997), expands the definition of success. It argues that firms should measure performance not just in financial terms, but also in social and environmental dimensions. This idea has gained traction, especially as climate change and social inequality become central business concerns.

In supply chains, TBL means looking beyond cost and speed. It involves considering labor conditions, environmental impact, and community engagement. For instance, a company might choose a supplier that pays fair wages and uses renewable energy, even if it is more expensive. This kind of decision reflects a broader shift toward values-based management.

Stakeholder Theory (Freeman and Phillips, 2002) complements TBL by emphasizing the importance of managing relationships with diverse stakeholder groups. Later elaborations, such as Parmar et al. (2010), argue that integrating stakeholder perspectives fosters resilience, trust, and long-term value creation.

Digital technologies can enhance stakeholder engagement by improving transparency, traceability, and responsiveness (Tumpa and Naeni, 2025; Otter and Robinson, 2024). For example, blockchain can verify ethical sourcing, and AI can flag social risks in supplier networks. But technology alone isn't enough. Firms also need processes for listening, responding, and adapting. Otherwise, digital transformation risks becoming a top-down exercise that overlooks the voices of those most affected. It is also important to recognize that stakeholder engagement is not a one-time event but an ongoing dialogue. Firms must be willing to revisit their assumptions, adjust their strategies, and acknowledge when they fall short. This humility is often missing in corporate sustainability narratives, which tend to emphasize success stories over learning moments.

2.6. Systems and Network Perspectives

From a systems perspective, supply chains are viewed as complex, interconnected networks. Checkland (1988) introduced systems thinking to help organizations understand these interdependencies, while Trist (1981) emphasized the socio-technical nature of organizational systems. More recently, Borgatti and Li (2009) applied network theory to supply chains, showing how value creation depends on the structure and quality of inter-firm relationships. These perspectives suggest that sustainability isn't just a firm-level issue, it is a network-level challenge. For example, reducing carbon emissions requires coordination across suppliers, logistics providers, and customers. Systems thinking encourages firms to consider feedback loops and unintended consequences. A decision that improves efficiency in one part of the chain might create problems elsewhere.

Network theory also highlights the role of influence. Firms that occupy central positions in supply chains can set standards and drive change. Digital tools enhance this potential by enabling real-time coordination and data sharing. But with influence comes responsibility. Leading firms must ensure that their digital strategies support - not undermine - system-wide sustainability goals. This calls for a shift from competitive posturing to collaborative stewardship, where firms recognize their interdependence and act accordingly.

In applying the TBL framework to digital transformation, this research treats technologies not as isolated efficiency tools but as enablers of sustainable organizational behavior. Belhadi et al. (2024) suggest that digital transformation can help supply chains move toward carbon neutrality by improving traceability and transparency; also, recent work emphasizes the role of digital service innovation Heinz et al. (2025). Ultimately, integrating RBV, DCT, TBL, and the complementary theories discussed above offers a more holistic view of digital sustainability. It acknowledges that competitive advantage is shaped by resources, capabilities, legitimacy, and networks. But it also recognizes that these elements are dynamic and context dependent. What works in one setting may not work in another. And while digital tools offer new possibilities, they also raise new questions - about ethics, equity, and long-term impact. This complexity should not be seen as a barrier, but as an invitation to rethink how supply chains are designed, governed, and evaluated in a digitally connected world.

3. METHODOLOGY

This study adopts a qualitative, conceptual and interpretive research approach to examine the integration of digital technologies in supply chain management (SCM) as a pathway to achieving sustainability and enhanced performance. The research methodology is rooted in an extensive literature review, aiming to develop a holistic conceptual framework that links digital innovation with sustainable supply chain performance.

To ensure comprehensive coverage of the topic, the authors conducted a thorough search of peer-reviewed academic literature across leading scholarly platforms, including Scopus, Google Scholar, and Web of Science. The identification of relevant sources was guided by the use of carefully selected keywords, both in titles and abstracts, to maximize the relevance and precision of the search results. The keywords included: "digital technologies in supply chain," "sustainable supply chain management," "AI in logistics," "blockchain and supply chains," "IoT in supply chain operations," "big data analytics in supply chain management," "digital transformation and sustainability," "sustainability and operational performance of the supply chain", "Resource Based View", "Dynamic Capabilities Theory", and "Triple Bottom Line framework in supply chains." These terms were used individually and in combination through Boolean operators to capture interdisciplinary perspectives on the integration of digital technologies with sustainable SCM practices.

Once the literature was identified, the authors applied inclusion criteria focused on the relevance to digital transformation and sustainability in SCM. Only peer-reviewed journal articles, conference papers published in proceedings, and empirical case studies published in English were considered. The filtering process emphasized recent contributions that provided theoretical insights regarding the use of digital technologies to optimize supply chain sustainability and performance. Essential information from the selected literature was extracted, including the author(s), year of publication, research methodology, industry focus, digital technologies examined, and a detailed summary of each source's unique contribution to the evolving field of digital integration in supply chains. This allowed the authors to compare findings, identify trends, and synthesize viewpoints across disciplines and industries.

To structure the analysis and uncover deeper insights, a thematic analysis was conducted. This involved a close reading of the selected literature to identify recurring themes, theoretical frameworks, and practical approaches related to the intersection of digitalization and sustainability in SCM. The themes were grouped into four major conceptual categories:

1. ***Digital Technologies*** – This theme focused on Artificial Intelligence (AI), Big Data capabilities, blockchain infrastructure, and Internet of Things (IoT) technologies as foundational enablers of supply chain innovation. Key contributions were examined in terms of their impact on operational performance, decision-making, automation, and predictive analytics.
2. ***Dynamic Capabilities Framework*** – Literature within this theme explored how companies sense, seize, and reconfigure internal and external resources to respond to dynamic market and environmental conditions. Studies emphasizing organizational agility and digital adaptability were included in this theme to understand how capabilities are developed through digital tools.
3. ***Digital Sustainability*** – This theme emphasized the practice of incorporating digital technologies and tools to enhance environmental, social, and economic sustainability within organizations. Building on the concept of Digital Sustainability, this study introduces a new concept, the Digital Sustainability Integration (DSI) - a mechanism that emphasizes supply chain transparency, strategic alignment, and long-term value creation.

4. ***Supply Chain Sustainability and Performance*** – The final theme addressed how digital transformation influences the achievement of the Triple Bottom Line framework: economic, environmental, and social performance. This included operational key performance indicators (KPIs) such as resource efficiency, carbon footprint reduction, real-time traceability, stakeholder collaboration, agility, responsiveness, and resilience.

The combination of literature synthesis and thematic analysis provided a structured and comprehensive view of the subject. This methodological approach allowed the researchers to identify the best practices, while also mapping theoretical concepts to the operational realities of supply chain management. The results of the analysis serve as the foundation for the "Holistic Model Integrating Digital Technologies to enhance Supply Chain Sustainability and Performance" proposed in the results section of this study. Strategic collaborations and supportive policies are pivotal for scaling Circular Economies initiatives Tiwari & Yadav, (2025) The research approach not only contributes to academic literature based on the conceptualization of the novel Digital Sustainability Integration (DSI) mechanism and the proposed integrative framework but also provides actionable insights for practitioners and policymakers working to improve the sustainability and performance of the supply chain.

4. RESULTS AND DISCUSSION OF THE PROPOSED THEORETICAL MODEL

This study theoretically confirms that the integration of digital technologies significantly enhances the sustainability and performance of supply chains. Based on the existing literature (Resource Based View, Dynamic Capabilities Theory, Triple Bottom Line framework) and by adding one novel conceptual construct: Digital Sustainability Integration (DSI), we propose to the academic community a novel holistic model which integrates digital technologies to achieve economic, social and environmental sustainability and to improve the operational performance of the Supply Chain (Figure 1).

The model is based on four key conceptual constructs:

(1) Digital Technologies—including AI, Big Data capabilities, blockchain infrastructure, and IoT—as essential resources which when used together, they give firms the ability to monitor supply chain activities with greater precision, improve transparency, and even anticipate disruptions before they escalate.

(2) The Dynamic Capabilities framework, which explains how firms sense, seize, and reconfigure resources to adapt to changing environments embedding flexibility into the organization.
(3) Digital Sustainability Integration (DSI), characterized by supply chain transparency, strategic alignment, and long-term value creation.
(4) Supply Chain Sustainability and Performance, measured through the Triple Bottom Line (economic, social, and environmental goals) and operational metrics such as agility, responsiveness, and resilience.

Together, these constructs form an integrated framework that theorizes the strategic alignment of digital transformation and sustainability as a driver of superior supply chain outcomes.

Figure 1. Proposed Holistic Model Integrating Digital Technologies to Enhance Supply Chain Sustainability and Performance.

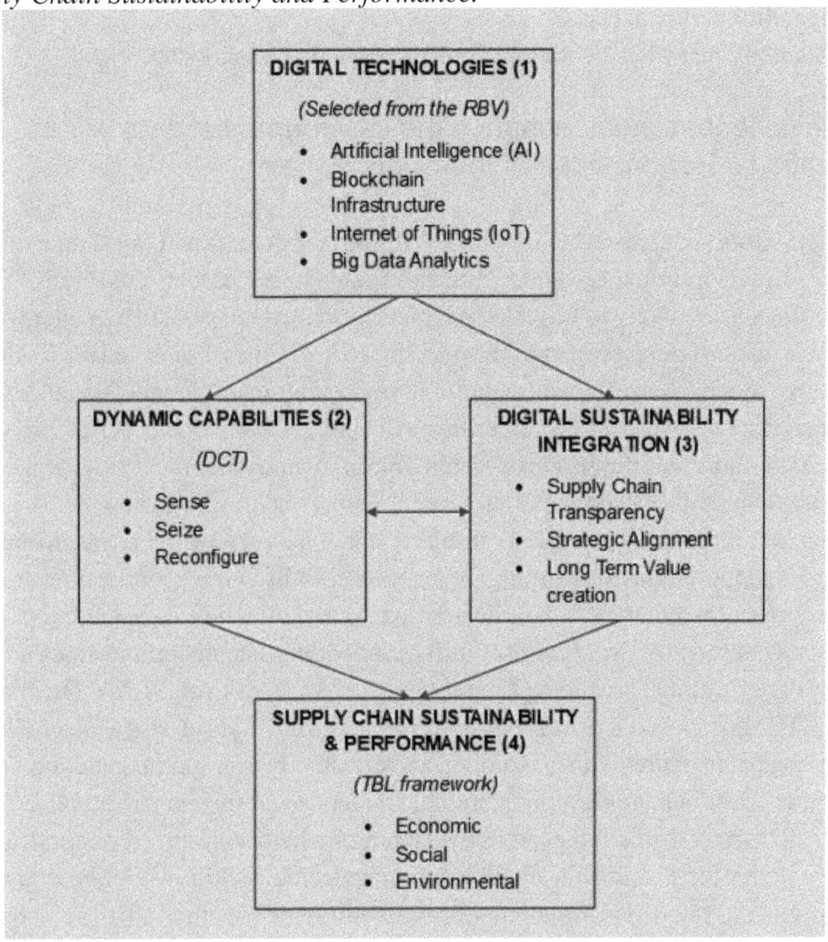

Based on the proposed model, digital technologies (1) are mediated by the dynamic capabilities (2) and the digital sustainability integration (3), which lead to the sustainability and enhanced performance of the supply chain (4). Within the supply chain management context, the relationship between digital technologies and sustainability and performance is mediated (apart from the Dynamic Capabilities framework) through the Digital Sustainability Integration (DSI) - a mechanism that emphasizes supply chain transparency, strategic alignment, and long-term value creation.

The interaction between dynamic capabilities and DSI facilitates the orchestration of digital capabilities and sustainability goals, thereby enabling firms to sense, seize, and reconfigure supply chain assets in ways that enhance agility, responsiveness, and resilience. As such, the contextual adoption of digital technologies plays a pivotal role in driving meaningful and measurable improvements in supply chain sustainability performance.

This study provides theoretical confirmation of the following:

1. Digital technologies enhance the Environmental and Operational Performance of the Supply Chain

Digital tools such as AI, IoT, blockchain infrastructure, and big data analytics reduce waste, optimize resource utilization, and lower carbon emissions. These improvements are likely to be reflected in performance metrics such as energy efficiency, transportation optimization, and reduced lead times. For instance, AI-driven predictive models have shown potential in improving operational efficiency while simultaneously advancing sustainability (Ali et al., 2024; Singh et al., 2024). Chen et al. (2024) introduce the notion of sustainable innovation ambidexterity, suggesting that firms can refine existing operations while experimenting with new, eco-friendly approaches. Belhadi et al., (2024) similarly show how data-driven transformation strategies support industries aiming for carbon neutrality. Green innovation emerges as a recurring theme. Research indicates that AI and digital tools not only optimize processes but can also drive cultural shifts, embedding sustainability values into everyday organizational practices (Kumar et al., 2024; Zhang et al., 2024). Theofanidis et al. (2025) proposed a novel leadership model (the "hybrid artificial intelligent leader") capable of predicting, avoiding, and effectively overcoming potential future economic crises enhancing organizational resilience and sustainability. Majeed and Khan (2024) refer to this as the "AI of Everything," where widespread AI applications act as a driver for sustainable supply chain management. Still, while these insights are promising, questions remain about scalability and whether all firms have the capacity to implement such systems effectively.

2. Improved Supply Chain Transparency and Traceability

The use of blockchain and IoT improves product traceability, enhances visibility across the supply chain, and fosters ethical sourcing practices. This will not only support regulatory compliance but also strengthen stakeholder trust. Saberi et al. (2019) observed that combining blockchain and IoT can significantly improve traceability, supporting regulatory compliance and ethical sourcing. Nguyen et al. (2025) caution, however, that AI-driven transparency only fosters stakeholder trust when it is embedded within responsible and collaborative practices—otherwise ethical issues may arise. Other scholars reinforce this perspective. Winkelmann et al. (2024) and Stroumpoulis et al. (2024) note that digital transformation contributes not only to transparency but also to resilience, helping supply chains adapt to disruptions while maintaining sustainability commitments.

3. Strategic Alignment Between Sustainability and Business Goals leads to long-term value creation

Strategic alignment between digital technologies and supply chain sustainability and operational performance fosters long-term value creation. This alignment enables more informed decision-making, greater efficiency across the supply chain, strengthens resilience, and positions the supply chain as a source of competitive advantage. AlQuraishi (2025) and Li (2025) show that supply chains combining resilience with adaptability are better positioned to maintain performance during disruptions. Lopes de Sousa Jabbour et al. (2025) add that, particularly after the pandemic, digital transformation has shifted from a supporting role to a central mechanism for balancing sustainability and operational performance. When organizations manage to integrate sustainability with operational planning, the benefits extend beyond efficiency gains. They also enhance the ability to respond quickly, recover from shocks, and maintain continuity. The evidence also shows that this alignment depends heavily on the availability of organizational resources and capabilities. In other words, digital tools alone cannot deliver these outcomes unless they are backed by the right structures, skills, and long-term commitment. For example, Chen et al. (2024) demonstrate that big data and AI enable firms to balance short-term performance with long-term sustainability objectives. Similarly, Nguyen et al. (2025) stress that responsible AI practices ensure that human–AI collaboration drives socially responsible outcomes, thus reinforcing the Triple Bottom Line perspective. These findings align with and reinforce the points made by Kero and Bogale (2023), who highlighted how the interplay between the Resource-Based View (RBV) and Dynamic Capabilities Theory (DCT) can be crucial for leveraging technological resources to enhance competitiveness. Willie (2025) also highlighted the importance of strategic alignment in including digital technologies for sustainable growth. Inclusion of these perspectives highlights how digital sustainability integration is not merely a technological investment but a strategic path to robust, transparent, and high-performing supply chains.

Despite the promise of digital transformation, several challenges remain. The resource gap between large and small firms continues to limit system-wide adoption. Ethical and social dimensions of AI - such as algorithmic bias, data privacy, and digital exclusion - require careful management if digital transformation is to contribute to social equity as envisioned by the TBL. Winkelmann et al. (2024) point out that while digital tools can enhance sustainability, they also introduce new risks - such as surveillance, data monopolies, and exclusion of low-tech partners. Their study calls for a more critical approach to digital transformation, one that considers unintended consequences and power asymmetries within supply networks.

5. CONCLUSION, IMPLICATIONS, FUTURE RESEARCH AVENUES AND LIMITATIONS

This research contributes to the existing literature by offering an integrated perspective that combines digital transformation with sustainable supply chain performance, introducing a new theoretical concept of Digital Sustainability Integration and highlighting the RBV, TBL and DCT frameworks by emphasizing how digital capabilities serve as strategic assets that enable firms to achieve environmental and social goals without compromising operational performance.

For supply chain professionals and decision-makers, this study offers insights into how specific digital technologies such as AI, IoT, blockchain, and big data analytics can be used to improve traceability, efficiency, and resource optimization. AI-driven predictive analytics, for instance, enable firms to anticipate disruptions and optimize resource allocation, reducing both waste and emissions (Ali,I et al., 2024; Singh et al., 2024). Similarly, blockchain and IoT applications enhance transparency and traceability across supply networks, thereby supporting not only operational performance but also ethical sourcing and regulatory compliance (Saberi et al., 2019; Winkelmann et al., 2024). Managers are encouraged to view sustainability as a performance enhancer rather than a compliance cost. Governments and regulatory bodies can benefit from these insights by formulating policies and incentives that support the digital transformation of supply chains, especially in sectors with high environmental impact. Encouraging the adoption of sustainable digital practices through grants, tax benefits, or certification programs could accelerate progress toward national and global sustainability targets. Research suggests that public-private collaboration in this area can yield compounding benefits, fostering both economic competitiveness and social responsibility (Lopes de Sousa Jabbour et al., 2025).

The proposed conceptual framework also provides the foundation for future empirical studies exploring causal relationships between digital integration and sustainable outcomes. Furthermore, future research should explore the role of cross-sector and inter-firm collaboration in scaling digital sustainability initiatives. As Sodhi and Tang (2021) argue, systemic sustainability cannot be achieved by individual firms in isolation; it requires collective governance, data-sharing protocols, and trust-building mechanisms across entire supply networks. Farfán Chilicaus et al. (2025) propose a three-dimensional framework - technological, organizational, and sustainable - that could guide future research. Their taxonomy of digital transformation phases (resilience, sustainability, circularity) offers a useful roadmap for scholars and practitioners seeking to understand how digital strategies mature over time. Future research could benefit from examining governance models, ethical frameworks, and regulatory mechanisms that ensure digital transformation supports sustainability in an inclusive and transparent way (Bag et al., 2021).

Even though there is extensive literature that provides valuable insights into the individual effect of digital technologies on supply chain practices, there exists a gap in knowing or understanding how these tools influence sustainability under the lens of performance. There is also a need for an integrative framework that will help practitioners align digital initiatives with sustainable goals while measuring tangible outcomes. This study contributed to bridging that gap by synthesizing current knowledge and proposing a conceptual framework model that connects digital technology with sustainability and supply chain performance. More specifically, this study integrated three existing models (Resource-Based View, Dynamic Capabilities Theory, Triple Bottom Line framework) and introduced one new concept - the Digital Sustainability Integration (DSI). The findings aim to support both practitioners, academics, governments, and regulatory bodies in developing strategies that push sustainable value creation through digital innovations with a focus on enhancing supply chain operational performance.

Like any conceptual model, the framework presented in this study comes with certain limitations that must be recognized. First, its contribution is primarily theoretical. The integration of the Resource-Based View (RBV), Dynamic Capabilities Theory (DCT), Triple Bottom Line (TBL), and the proposed Digital Sustainability Integration (DSI) creates a useful lens for understanding the role of digital transformation in supply chain sustainability. Yet, what it cannot provide is direct empirical evidence to justify cause-and-effect relationships. The links between digital adoption and measurable sustainability outcomes still need to be tested in practice. For this reason, future work should focus on empirical validation, through large scale surveys to test the proposed relationships of the model with real data.

A second limitation lies in the sectoral variability of digital technologies. It is expected that not all tools create the same level of value in all industries. For example, blockchain has proved particularly valuable in agri-food chains, where traceability is essential for food safety and sustainability (Saberi et al., 2019). By contrast, its benefits in heavy industry are less clear. Similarly, while AI-driven logistics optimization has shown significant efficiency gains in global supply chains (Ali, S et al., 2024; Singh et al., 2024), many small and medium-sized enterprises (SMEs) face barriers such as high costs, lack of technical expertise, or infrastructure gaps (Metwally et al., 2024). These differences point to a need for context-specific research that explores how industry, geography, and firm size affect the adoption and impact of digital sustainability strategies.

A third limitation is that this study primarily highlights the positive side of digitalization. In practice, digital tools can generate unintended effects, such as rebound consumption - where efficiency improvements lead to higher overall demand, undermining sustainability goals (Del Giudice et al., 2021). Issues of data privacy, cybersecurity, and algorithmic bias also raise concerns about equity and trust in digital supply chains (Nguyen et al., 2025). We should also not neglect the potential significant job loss of the people who work in the supply chain due to the digitalization and automation of specific functions which raise humanitarian issues. These risks suggest that the question is not simply whether to adopt digital tools, but how to adopt them responsibly.

Another limitation of the proposed model is that it largely adopts a firm-level perspective. While this is a useful starting point, sustainability challenges often play out across entire supply chain networks. For instance, carbon neutrality or circular economy goals cannot be achieved by a single company alone - they demand collaboration across suppliers, customers, regulators, and even competitors (Sodhi & Tang, 2021). Future studies should therefore expand the DSI framework to consider ecosystem-level dynamics, including how data-sharing, digital platforms, and joint investments enable collective progress toward sustainable goals.

Finally, in terms of the research limitations, the accurate measurement of sustainability outcomes remains a persistent challenge. Environmental outcomes such as carbon footprint or energy use are increasingly quantifiable, but social sustainability - issues like labor welfare, inclusivity, or community well-being - remains more difficult to capture (Lopes de Sousa Jabbour et al., 2025). This creates a risk that digital sustainability strategies become skewed toward what can be easily measured rather than what is truly impactful. Developing standardized yet flexible metrics that reflect all three dimensions of TBL will therefore be an important task for future researchers.

In conclusion, the integration of digital technologies within supply chain management has significantly enhanced both sustainability and operational performance. Key Performance Indicators (KPIs) such as resource efficiency, real-time traceability, carbon footprint reduction, and stakeholder collaboration have proven effective in driving these improvements. The proposed model demonstrates that digital technologies, mediated by dynamic capabilities and digital sustainability integration (DSI), lead to enhanced supply chain sustainability and performance. Empirical evidence supports that digital transformation fosters supply chain resilience and robustness, which positively impacts environmental performance. On top of this, the synergy between digital technologies and DSI emphasizes transparency, strategic alignment, and long-term value creation, reinforcing the importance of a holistic approach to sustainable supply chain management. This comprehensive framework underscores the critical role of digital innovations in achieving sustainable and efficient supply chains, paving the way for future advancements in the field.

Disclaimer: During the preparation of this work the authors used Grammarly to improve language and readability of the paper. After using this tool/service, the authors reviewed and edited the content as needed and take full responsibility for the content of the publication. ChatGPT was used to proof-read the document once completed.

REFERENCES

Ali, I., Ho, W., Papadopoulos, T., & White, C. (2025). Introduction to global value chains and geopolitical turmoil. In *Global value chains and geopolitical uncertainty* (pp. 1–16). Routledge. DOI: 10.4324/9781003468899-1

Ali, S. M., Rahman, A. U., Kabir, G., & Paul, S. K. (2024). Artificial intelligence approach to predict supply chain performance: Implications for sustainability. *Sustainability (Basel), 16*(6), 2373. DOI: 10.3390/su16062373

Alquraish, M. (2025). Digital transformation, supply chain resilience, and sustainability: A comprehensive review with implications for Saudi Arabian manufacturing. *Sustainability (Basel), 17*(10), 4495. DOI: 10.3390/su17104495

Ambrosini, V., Bowman, C., & Collier, N. (2009). Dynamic capabilities: An exploration of how firms renew their resource base. *British Journal of Management, 20*(s1), S9–S24. DOI: 10.1111/j.1467-8551.2008.00610.x

Bag, S., Gupta, S., & Kumar, S. (2021). Industry 4.0 adoption and 10R advance manufacturing capabilities for sustainable development. *International Journal of Production Economics, 231*, 107844. DOI: 10.1016/j.ijpe.2020.107844

Barney, J. B. (1991). Firm resources and sustained competitive advantage. *Journal of Management, 17*(1), 99–120. DOI: 10.1177/014920639101700108

Belhadi, A., Venkatesh, M., Kamble, S., & Abedin, M. Z. (2024). Data-driven digital transformation for supply chain carbon neutrality: Insights from cross-sector supply chain. *International Journal of Production Economics, 270*, 109178. DOI: 10.1016/j.ijpe.2024.109178

Borgatti, S. P., & Li, X. (2009). On social network analysis in a supply chain context. *The Journal of Supply Chain Management, 45*(2), 5–22. DOI: 10.1111/j.1745-493X.2009.03166.x

Brown, T. (2008). Design thinking. *Harvard Business Review, 86*(6), 84. PMID: 18605031

Checkland, P. B. (1988). Information systems and systems thinking: Time to unite? *International Journal of Information Management, 8*(4), 239–248. DOI: 10.1016/0268-4012(88)90031-X

Chen, C. T., Khan, A., & Chen, S. C. (2024). Modeling the impact of big data analytics–artificial intelligence (BDA–AI) on sustainable innovation ambidexterity and environmental performance. *Journal of Big Data*, *11*(1), 124. DOI: 10.1186/s40537-024-00995-6

Choi, T. M., Wallace, S. W., & Wang, Y. (2020). Big data analytics in operations management. *Production and Operations Management*, *29*(5), 1024–1031. DOI: 10.1111/poms.13122

Christopher, M. L. (1992). *Logistics and supply chain management.* Pitman Publishing.

Cohen, D., Lindvall, M., & Costa, P. (2004). An introduction to agile methods. *Advances in Computers*, *62*(3), 1–66.

De Sousa Jabbour, A. B. L., Laguir, I., Stekelorum, R., & Gupta, S. (2025). The nexus of artificial intelligence and sustainability performance: Unveiling the impact of supply chain transparency and customer pressure on ethical conduct. *Journal of Environmental Management*, *379*, 124847. DOI: 10.1016/j.jenvman.2025.124847 PMID: 40054355

Del Giudice, M., Scuotto, V., Papa, A., Tarba, S. Y., Bresciani, S., & Warkentin, M. (2021). A self-tuning model for smart manufacturing SMEs: Effects on digital innovation. *Journal of Product Innovation Management*, *38*(1), 68–89. DOI: 10.1111/jpim.12560

DiMaggio, P. J., & Powell, W. W. (1983). The iron cage revisited: Institutional isomorphism and collective rationality in organizational fields. *American Sociological Review*, *48*(2), 147–160. DOI: 10.2307/2095101

Dingsøyr, T., Nerur, S., Balijepally, V., & Moe, N. B. (2012). A decade of agile methodologies: Towards explaining agile software development. *Journal of Systems and Software*, *85*(6), 1213–1221. DOI: 10.1016/j.jss.2012.02.033

Dubey, R., Gunasekaran, A., Childe, S. J., Blome, C., & Papadopoulos, T. (2019). Big data and predictive analytics and manufacturing performance: Integrating institutional theory, resource-based view and big data culture. *British Journal of Management*, *30*(2), 341–361. DOI: 10.1111/1467-8551.12355

Dyer, J. H., & Singh, H. (1998). The relational view: Cooperative strategy and sources of interorganizational competitive advantage. *Academy of Management Review*, *23*(4), 660–679. DOI: 10.2307/259056

Elkington, J. (1997). *Cannibals with forks: The triple bottom line of 21st century business.* Capstone Publishing.

Erturk, A., Colbran, S. E., Coşkun, E., Theofanidis, F., & Abidi, O. (Eds.). (2024). *Convergence of digitalization, innovation, and sustainable development in business*. IGI Global. DOI: 10.4018/979-8-3693-0798-4

Farfán Chilicaus, G. C., Licapa-Redolfo, G. S., Arbulú Ballesteros, M. A., Corrales Otazú, C. D., Apaza Miranda, S. J., Flores Castillo, M. M., Castro Ijiri, G. L., Guzmán Valle, M. D. Á., & Arbulú Castillo, J. C. (2025). Digital transformation and sustainability in post-pandemic supply chains: A global bibliometric analysis of technological evolution and research patterns (2020–2024). *Sustainability (Basel)*, *17*(7), 3009. DOI: 10.3390/su17073009

Freeman, R. E., & Phillips, R. A. (2002). Stakeholder theory: A libertarian defense. *Business Ethics Quarterly*, *12*(3), 331–349. DOI: 10.2307/3858020

Goetschalckx, M. (2011). *Supply chain engineering*. Springer.

Hargaden, H., & Sills, C. (2014). *Transactional analysis: A relational perspective*. Routledge. DOI: 10.4324/9781315820279

Heinz, D., Hu, M., Benz, C., & Satzger, G. (2025). Digital service innovation for sustainable development: A systematic literature review. In *Transforming the digitally sustainable enterprise* (pp. 167–185). Springer. DOI: 10.1007/978-3-031-80125-9_10

Kero, C. A., & Bogale, A. T. (2023). A systematic review of resource-based view and dynamic capabilities of firms and future research avenues. *International Journal of Sustainable Development and Planning*, *18*(10), 3137–3154. DOI: 10.18280/ijsdp.181016

Kraaijenbrink, J., Spender, J. C., & Groen, A. J. (2010). The resource-based view: A review and assessment of its critiques. *Journal of Management*, *36*(1), 349–372. DOI: 10.1177/0149206309350775

Kumar, V., Singh, A., & Gupta, R. (2024). How does artificial intelligence affect the environmental performance of organizations? The role of green innovation and green culture. *Information & Management*, *61*(2), 103924. DOI: 10.1016/j.im.2024.103924

La Londe, B. J., & Masters, J. M. (1994). Emerging logistics strategies: Blueprints for the next century. *International Journal of Physical Distribution & Logistics Management*, *24*(7), 35–47. DOI: 10.1108/09600039410070975

Lambert, D. M., Stock, J. R., & Ellram, L. M. (1998). *Fundamentals of logistics management*. McGraw-Hill/Irwin.

Leathwood, C., & Read, B. (2013). Research policy and academic performativity: Compliance, contestation and complicity. *Studies in Higher Education*, *38*(8), 1162–1174. DOI: 10.1080/03075079.2013.833025

Li, M. (2025). Digital transformation and supply chain resilience in SMEs: Empirical evidence from the manufacturing sector in the Yangtze River Delta. *Journal of Economic and Managerial Dynamics*, *1*(1), 1–7.

Lopes de Sousa Jabbour, A. B., Jabbour, C. J. C., Foropon, C., & Godinho Filho, M. (2025). Digital transformation and sustainability in post-pandemic supply chains: A global bibliometric analysis of technological evolution and research patterns (2020–2024). *Sustainability (Basel)*, *17*(7), 3009. DOI: 10.3390/su17073009

Maalouf, E. (2024). Achieving corporate environmental responsibility through emerging sustainability laws. *Asia Pacific Journal of Environmental Law*, *27*(1), 64–99. DOI: 10.4337/apjel.2024.01.03

Macher, J. T., & Richman, B. D. (2008). Transaction cost economics: An assessment of empirical research in the social sciences. *Business and Politics*, *10*(1), 1–63. DOI: 10.2202/1469-3569.1210

Majeed, M. T., & Khan, M. A. (2024). Green supply chain management based on artificial intelligence of everything. *Journal of Economics and Management*, *46*(1), 171–188. DOI: 10.22367/jem.2024.46.07

Mentzer, J. T., DeWitt, W., Keebler, J. S., Min, S., Nix, N. W., Smith, C. D., & Zacharia, Z. G. (2001). Defining supply chain management. *Journal of Business Logistics*, *22*(2), 1–25. DOI: 10.1002/j.2158-1592.2001.tb00001.x

Metwally, A. B. M., Ali, H. A. A., Aly, S. A. S., & Ali, M. A. S. (2024). The interplay between digital technologies, supply chain resilience, robustness, and sustainable environmental performance: Does supply chain complexity matter? *Sustainability (Basel)*, *16*(14), 6175. DOI: 10.3390/su16146175

Nguyen, T. H., Doan, X. H., & Tran, P. (2025). Human–artificial intelligence collaboration in supply chain outcomes: The mediating role of responsible artificial intelligence. *Annals of Operations Research*, *354*(1), 35–69. Advance online publication. DOI: 10.1007/s10479-025-06534-7

Omisola, J. O., Bihani, D., Daraojimba, A. I., Osho, G. O., Ubamadu, B. C., & Etukudoh, E. A. (2023). Blockchain in supply chain transparency: A conceptual framework for real-time data tracking and reporting using blockchain and AI. *International Journal of Multidisciplinary Research and Growth Evaluation*, *4*(1), 1238–1253. DOI: 10.54660/.IJMRGE.2023.4.1.1238-1253

Onukwulu, E. C., Agho, M. O., & Eyo-Udo, N. L.Ekene Cynthia OnukwuluMercy Odochi AghoNsisong Louis Eyo-Udo. (2021). Framework for sustainable supply chain practices to reduce carbon footprint in energy. *Open Access Research Journal of Science and Technology*, *1*(2), 12–34. DOI: 10.53022/oarjst.2021.1.2.0032

Ooi, G. L. (2008). Cities and sustainability: Southeast Asian and European perspectives. *Asia Europe Journal*, *6*(2), 193–204. DOI: 10.1007/s10308-008-0176-0

Otter, V., & Robinson, D. (2024). Transparency and changing stakeholder roles in the digital age of sustainable agri-food supply chain networks. *Frontiers in Sustainable Food Systems*, *8*, 1449684. DOI: 10.3389/fsufs.2024.1449684

Parmar, B. L., Freeman, R. E., Harrison, J. S., Wicks, A. C., Purnell, L., & De Colle, S. (2010). Stakeholder theory: The state of the art. *The Academy of Management Annals*, *4*(1), 403–445. DOI: 10.5465/19416520.2010.495581

Razzouk, R., & Shute, V. (2012). What is design thinking and why is it important? *Review of Educational Research*, *82*(3), 330–348. DOI: 10.3102/0034654312457429

Rindfleisch, A., & Heide, J. B. (1997). Transaction cost analysis: Past, present, and future applications. *Journal of Marketing*, *61*(4), 30–54. DOI: 10.1177/002224299706100403

Roberts, S. (2003). Supply chain specific: Understanding the patchy success of ethical sourcing initiatives. *Journal of Business Ethics*, *44*(2), 159–170. DOI: 10.1023/A:1023395631811

Saberi, S., Kouhizadeh, M., Sarkis, J., & Shen, L. (2019). Blockchain technology and its relationships to sustainable supply chain management. *International Journal of Production Research*, *57*(7), 2117–2135. DOI: 10.1080/00207543.2018.1533261

Singh, R. K., Gunasekaran, A., & Kumar, P. (2024). Artificial intelligence in logistics optimization with sustainable criteria: A review. *Sustainability (Basel)*, *16*(21), 9145. DOI: 10.3390/su16219145

Sodhi, M., & Tang, C. (2021). Research opportunities in supply chain transparency. *Production and Operations Management*, *30*(3), 675–688. DOI: 10.1111/poms.13351

Stock, J. R., & Boyer, S. L. (2009). Developing a consensus definition of supply chain management: A qualitative study. *International Journal of Physical Distribution & Logistics Management*, *39*(8), 690–711. DOI: 10.1108/09600030910996323

Stroumpoulis, A., Kopanaki, E., & Chountalas, P. T. (2024). Enhancing sustainable supply chain management through digital transformation: A comparative case study analysis. *Sustainability (Basel)*, *16*(16), 6778. DOI: 10.3390/su16166778

Szerszynski, B. (1999). Risk and trust: The performative dimension. *Environmental Values*, *8*(2), 239–252. DOI: 10.3197/096327199129341815

Teece, D. J., Pisano, G., & Shuen, A. (1997). Dynamic capabilities and strategic management. *Strategic Management Journal*, *18*(7), 509–533. DOI: 10.1002/(SICI)1097-0266(199708)18:7<509::AID-SMJ882>3.0.CO;2-Z

Theofanidis, F., Abidi, O., Erturk, A., Colbran, S., & Coskun, E. (Eds.). (2024). *Digital transformation and sustainable development in cities and organizations*. IGI Global. DOI: 10.4018/979-8-3693-3567-3

Theofanidis, F., Tsianaka, E., & Livas, C. (2025). *Towards systemic leadership resilience: Proposing the hybrid artificial intelligent leader in response to economic crises*. Canadian Journal of Administrative Sciences / Revue Canadienne des Sciences de l'Administration., DOI: 10.1002/cjas.70000

Tiwari, S., & Yadav, M. (2025). Circular economy in manufacturing: Current trends and future directions. In *Rethinking resources: Strategies, policies, and partnerships for a circular future* (pp. 395–416). Springer Nature Singapore. DOI: 10.1007/978-981-96-9055-8_23

Trist, E. L. (1981). *The evolution of socio-technical systems* (Vol. 2). Ontario Quality of Working Life Centre.

Tumpa, R. J., & Naeni, L. (2025). Improving decision-making and stakeholder engagement at project governance using digital technology for sustainable infrastructure projects. *Smart and Sustainable Built Environment*, *14*(4), 1292–1329. DOI: 10.1108/SASBE-10-2024-0451

Wamba, S. F., Gunasekaran, A., Akter, S., Ren, S. J. F., Dubey, R., & Childe, S. J. (2017). Big data analytics and firm performance: Effects of dynamic capabilities. *Journal of Business Research*, *70*, 356–365. DOI: 10.1016/j.jbusres.2016.08.009

Williamson, O. E. (1989). Transaction cost economics. In Schmalensee, R., & Willig, R. D. (Eds.), *Handbook of industrial organization* (Vol. 1, pp. 135–182). Elsevier.

Williamson, O. E. (1998). Transaction cost economics: How it works; where it is headed. *De Economist*, *146*(1), 23–58. DOI: 10.1023/A:1003263908567

Willie, M. (2025). Leveraging digital resources: A resource-based view perspective. *Golden Ratio of Human Resource Management*, *5*(1), 1–14. DOI: 10.52970/grhrm.v5i1.415

Winkelmann, S., Fischer, M., & Schmidt, T. (2024). Back to a resilient future: Digital technologies for a sustainable supply chain. *Information Systems and e-Business Management*, *22*(2), 315–350. DOI: 10.1007/s10257-024-00677-z

Wu, J. (2025). Green supply chains: The dual challenges of achieving sustainable development. In *Global trends in manufacturing supply chains* (pp. 297–323). Springer Nature Singapore. DOI: 10.1007/978-981-96-3228-2_12

Yang, A. (2024). Sustainable finance exploration: Analyzing the impact of environmental, social, governance (ESG) information disclosure in the supply chain. *Supply Chain and Sustainability Research, 15*–31. https://doi.org/DOI: 10.14456/scsr.2024.9

Zaida, M., Farooqi, R., & Azmi, S. N. (2025). Driving sustainable supply chain performance through digital transformation: The role of information exchange and responsiveness. *Cogent Business & Management*, *12*(1), 2443047. DOI: 10.1080/23311975.2024.2443047

Zhang, J., Liu, Y., & Chen, Z. (2024). Digitalisation driving sustainable corporate performance: The mediation of green innovation and green supply chain management. *Journal of Cleaner Production*, *446*, 141290. DOI: 10.1016/j.jclepro.2024.141290

Chapter 8
Digital Nomadism and Artificial Intelligence:
Reframing Industrial Transitions in the Post-Pandemic Economy

Supriya Dutta
http://orcid.org/0009-0000-2239-5603
Christ University, India

Blesson Varghese James
http://orcid.org/0000-0002-0000-8235
Christ University, India

Devendra Gajanan Bhave
Savitribai Phule Pune University, India

ABSTRACT

The convergence of AI and digital nomadism is fundamentally reshaping the global industrial landscape. This chapter finds that AI enables global labor mobility and flexible work, while digital nomads drive demand for agile, tech-integrated business models. This transformation necessitates policy innovation to address challenges in regulation, ethics, and socio-economic equity. Key findings include the exacerbation of digital divides, the emergence of new mental well-being concerns for remote workers, and the critical need for upskilling initiatives. The chapter concludes that coordinated policy innovation and ethical AI governance are essential to harness this dynamic for a more inclusive and sustainable future of work.

DOI: 10.4018/979-8-3373-5052-3.ch008

1. DEFINITION, BACKGROUND, AND CURRENT SITUATION

The convergence of artificial intelligence (AI) and digital nomadism is reshaping the global industrial landscape, driving unprecedented transitions in technology, workforce structures, and economic policies. By 2030, AI is projected to contribute $15.7 trillion to the global economy, revolutionising industries from manufacturing to finance through automation and intelligent decision-making (PWC, 2018). Simultaneously, the digital nomad population has surged by 131% since 2019, prompting governments to introduce specialised visas to attract this mobile workforce (MBO Partners, 2023). These trends are not isolated but deeply interconnected, as AI enables remote work technologies that support digital nomadism, while digital nomads influence global economic policies and industrial productivity.

The industrial landscape has evolved through successive revolutions, from the mechanisation of Industry 1.0 to the digital integration of Industry 4.0. AI is now at the forefront of this evolution, driving automation, robotics, and data-driven decision-making in manufacturing, logistics, and beyond. For instance, AI-powered systems optimise production lines, predict maintenance needs, and enhance supply chain efficiency, fundamentally altering traditional industrial operations (Rashid & Kausik, 2024). Concurrently, the rise of remote work, accelerated by the COVID-19 pandemic, has normalised digital nomadism, where professionals leverage AI-driven platforms like Upwork, Fiverr, and GitLab to work from anywhere in the world. Governments are adapting by introducing digital nomad visas and rethinking labour policies to accommodate this shift (Aroles et al., 2022).

At the intersection of AI and digital nomadism lies a transformative dynamic. AI technologies, such as automation and chatbots, enable digital nomads to work efficiently from remote locations, while digital nomads contribute to the global economy by providing specialised services, influencing taxation policies, and reshaping employment norms. For example, AI tools like Chatgpt assist digital nomads in content creation, coding, and project management, while digital nomads offer services that support AI development, such as data labelling and software engineering (Simeli et al., 2025). This symbiotic relationship is not only redefining work but also challenging traditional economic and industrial frameworks.

Despite the significance of these trends, research gaps remain. While the impact of AI on automation and productivity is well-documented, fewer studies explore how AI influences global workforce mobility or how digital nomadism affects industrial transitions. Most research on digital nomadism focuses on lifestyle aspects rather than its broader economic and industrial implications. This chapter aims to bridge this gap by examining how AI and digital nomadism together drive industrial technology transitions, providing insights for policymakers, business leaders, and academics.

The evolution of industrial revolutions has fundamentally reshaped global economies. From the First Industrial Revolution's mechanisation to the ongoing Industry 4.0 and emerging Industry 5.0, each phase has introduced transformative technologies. The initial shift from manual labour to mechanised production, followed by electrification and automation, laid the groundwork for modern industrialisation (Sharma & Singh, 2020). Industry 4.0, driven by AI, IoT, robotics, and big data, emphasises cyber-physical systems and smart factories, enabling real-time data exchange and process optimisation (Sharma & Singh, 2020; Zizic et al., 2022). Industry 5.0 builds upon this, prioritising human-centric innovation and sustainable collaboration between humans and machines (Sharma & Singh, 2020; Zizic et al., 2022).

Schumpeter's theory of creative destruction underscores how technological advancements disrupt existing industries, driving economic growth (Steen et al., 2022; Emami Langroodi, 2021). This theory is particularly relevant in the transition to AI-driven smart factories, where new technologies displace outdated processes (Steen et al., 2022). The integration of AI and automation in Industry 4.0 and 5.0 illustrates this cyclical innovation, redefining industrial processes (Emami Langroodi, 2021). AI is recognised as a general-purpose technology (GPT), capable of revolutionising various sectors (Raja Santhi & Muthuswamy, 2023; Langroodi, 2021). Its ability to automate tasks, analyse data, and make predictive decisions drives the Fourth Industrial Revolution (Holzmann et al., 2022). In project management, AI enhances scheduling, cost estimation, and risk management through data analysis (Holzmann et al., 2022). AI-powered systems optimise production lines and enable predictive maintenance, improving efficiency (Steen et al., 2022).

Theories on automation and augmented intelligence explore AI's role in replacing or augmenting human labour (Raja Santhi & Muthuswamy, 2023). While automation aims to replace human tasks, augmented intelligence enhances human capabilities. This dual role shapes the future of work. However, AI adoption presents challenges, including workforce reskilling and ethical concerns (Steen et al., 2022). As AI evolves, its impact on industrial transitions will grow, requiring strategic adaptation (Steen et al., 2022).

The rise of digital nomadism and remote work is facilitated by AI and digital technologies. The COVID-19 pandemic accelerated remote work adoption, leading to the emergence of boundaryless career theories (Song & Jo, 2023; Karakus, 2021). These theories examine how digital nomads redefine traditional career structures through technology (Song & Jo, 2023). Hybrid work models, combining remote and in-office work, are becoming prevalent, offering flexibility and maintaining productivity (Song & Jo, 2023; Sampat et al., 2022). The gig economy, enabled by AI, provides on-demand work opportunities across geographical boundaries (Song & Jo, 2023; Krajčík et al., 2023). Boundaryless careers emphasise flexibility and mobility, exemplified by digital nomads (Krajčík et al., 2023; Karakus, 2021). Hybrid work and the gig economy, enabled by AI, support flexible work arrangements (Sampat et al., 2022; Karakus, 2021). However, remote work presents challenges, including maintaining work-life balance and addressing isolation (Song & Jo, 2023). Organisations must adapt to support remote workers and foster community (Song & Jo, 2023).

Artificial Intelligence (AI) is reshaping industrial technology across various sectors, driving automation, predictive analytics, and efficiency improvements. AI adoption has been pivotal in manufacturing, finance, healthcare, supply chains, and energy, fostering economic growth and operational efficiency. McKinsey estimates that AI could contribute $13 trillion to the global economy by 2030, marking a 16% increase in cumulative GDP (Yee et al., 2025). This transformative power highlights AI's central role in industrial technology transitions.

AI is revolutionising industries by enhancing automation and decision-making. In manufacturing, AI-driven predictive analytics reduces downtime by forecasting equipment failures, optimising supply chains, and streamlining production processes (Satya Subrahmanyam, 2025). The emergence of smart factories and Industry 4.0 initiatives demonstrates AI's role in intelligent production models, networked collaboration, and extended service frameworks (Wang, 2020). The financial sector leverages AI for fraud detection, risk assessment, and personalised financial services. AI's ability to analyse vast datasets allows firms to detect anomalies and predict market trends, improving decision-making and customer engagement (Haefner et al., 2023). In healthcare, AI enhances diagnostics, personalises treatment plans, and facilitates robotic-assisted surgeries (Alowais et al., 2023). Notably, AI-enabled telemedicine and remote patient monitoring have transformed healthcare delivery, particularly post-COVID-19 (Agarwal et al., 2022).

In supply chain management, AI strengthens decision-making by assessing risks and optimising logistics, leading to greater transparency and efficiency (Khedr & Sheeja, 2024). Similarly, AI-driven automation in the energy sector improves resource allocation and sustainability efforts (Barja-Martinez et al., 2021). Countries like Japan and Singapore have integrated AI into healthcare and transportation to address labour shortages, exemplifying AI's role in public sector advancements (Taeihagh, 2021). Reports from McKinsey, the World Economic Forum (WEF), and the International Monetary Fund (IMF) underscore AI's economic impact, highlighting increased operational efficiency and revenue growth in AI-adopting firms (*The Global Impact of AI: Mind the Gap*, 2025). AI-driven business models are not only altering existing industries but also fostering the creation of entirely new market segments (Raina et al., 2025). The integration of AI is fundamentally altering workforce dynamics, raising concerns about job displacement while also creating new opportunities. Routine tasks, particularly in accounting and manufacturing, are increasingly automated, leading to labour displacement (*Skillspark the*

Finishing School, 2026). However, AI also generates new roles that require human oversight, collaboration, and expertise in AI ethics and data science (Holzinger et al., 2024). Corporate governance and management increasingly rely on AI-driven decision-making. AI is employed in strategic planning, HR practices, and performance evaluations, enabling firms to make data-backed decisions (*Skillspark the Finishing School*, 2026). AI-powered recruitment, for example, streamlines hiring through automated resume screening and AI-assisted interviews. While this improves efficiency, concerns persist regarding biases in AI-driven hiring, as algorithms may inadvertently discriminate based on gender, race, or other factors (Albaroudi et al., 2024)

2. PROS AND CONS OF DIGITAL NOMADISM

AI's role in workforce transformation is evident in customer service, where AI-powered chatbots enhance customer interactions, providing 24/7 support and personalised experiences (Kachouie et al., 2017). In the e-commerce sector, AI-driven automation improves customer satisfaction by enabling personalised product recommendations (Ping, 2019). AI is driving business model innovation through personalisation, automation, and new service paradigms. The proliferation of AI-powered marketing, customer service chatbots, and AI-as-a-service models underscores the technology's growing role in shaping corporate strategies (Roy et al., 2025). Startups and established firms alike are leveraging AI to gain a competitive edge. The EdTech industry, for instance, is integrating AI to create personalised learning experiences, enhancing educational outcomes through data-driven insights (Alam & Mohanty, 2022). The financial sector also benefits from AI-driven investment strategies, risk management tools, and algorithmic trading, which improve market efficiency (Mosavi et al., 2019).

Investment in AI startups has surged, reflecting increased reliance on AI-powered solutions across industries. This trend signals a broader transition toward AI-centric business models that optimise operations, enhance customer experiences, and drive long-term sustainability (Roy et al., 2025). Despite AI's transformative potential, ethical challenges and governance issues remain pressing concerns. Bias in AI decision-making has been widely documented, with recruitment algorithms and facial recognition technologies exhibiting gender and racial biases (Laine et al., 2024). Addressing these biases requires stronger regulatory frameworks and continuous algorithmic auditing (Raghavan et al., 2020). Privacy concerns are another critical challenge. AI systems often process vast amounts of personal data, raising risks of data breaches and surveillance. Curzon et al. (2021) highlighted the potential dangers of AI-driven privacy violations, such as deep neural networks classifying individuals based on facial features without consent. To mitigate these risks, privacy-enhancing techniques like cryptography, data anonymisation, and differential privacy are being explored (Curzon et al., 2021). Governments and regulatory bodies are responding by introducing governance frameworks, such as the EU AI Act, to ensure ethical AI deployment (High-Level Expert Group on AI, 2019). However, the rapid evolution of AI necessitates adaptive regulatory approaches to balance innovation with accountability (Taeihagh, 2021). The ethical concerns surrounding AI also extend to digital surveillance. AI-powered surveillance technologies pose risks to individual autonomy and civil liberties, particularly in regions with weak regulatory oversight (Zuboff, 2019). These concerns highlight the need for ethical AI policies that prioritise transparency, accountability, and human rights protection.

The convergence of artificial intelligence (AI) and digital nomadism is redefining industrial technology transitions, transforming work cultures, business models, and policy landscapes. This review examines the rise of remote work, AI's role in enabling digital nomadism, business model disruptions, policy responses, and socio-economic and environmental implications. The COVID-19 pandemic accelerated remote work adoption, shifting traditional employment toward more flexible, location-independent models. Reports indicate that the number of digital nomads has surged globally, with a 96% increase in remote work transitions and 17.3 million digital nomads in the U.S. alone by 2023 (Gupta et al., 2024). Hybrid work models, supported by AI-driven communication and productivity tools, have further legitimised digital nomadism in corporate structures (Vohra et al., 2024). Digital nomadism contributes to economic growth, particularly in remote regions, by connecting global workers to job markets, aligning with Sustainable Development Goals (SDGS) such as decent work (SDG 8) and innovation (SDG 9) (Hackl, 2018; Zhou et al., 2024). However, disparities persist, as developed nations attract the majority of high-income remote workers, exacerbating economic inequalities (Hannonen, 2023).

The rise of digital nomadism has disrupted traditional business models, particularly in the gig economy. Freelancing platforms like Upwork, Fiverr, and Toptal facilitate independent work, shifting employment away from conventional full-time structures (OECD, 2022). This transition raises critical challenges for HR policies, taxation, and labour laws, as businesses and governments adapt to the evolving work landscape (World Bank, 2023). Digital nomads operate as freelancers, entrepreneurs, or remote employees, utilising digital tools to maintain workflow while moving across geographies (Khan et al., 2025). This lifestyle offers businesses access to a global talent pool, reducing overhead costs and increasing operational flexibility (Green, 2020). However, challenges include ensuring workforce productivity, maintaining social security protections, and addressing mental well-being concerns in remote settings (Vohra et al., 2024).

AI plays a crucial role in enabling digital nomadism by automating tasks, optimising workflows, and enhancing cloud-based collaboration. AI-powered tools facilitate scheduling, predictive maintenance, and remote workforce management, making distributed workforces more efficient (Holzmann et al., 2022). Furthermore, AI-driven personalisation enables continuous learning and skill adaptation, supporting career sustainability for digital nomads (Vohra et al., 2024). However, increased reliance on AI raises cybersecurity and data privacy concerns. Remote workers handle sensitive information across digital platforms, requiring enhanced cybersecurity measures to mitigate risks (Calzada, 2023). AI-driven monitoring tools can provide insights into remote work productivity, but ethical considerations regarding surveillance and worker autonomy must be addressed (Steen et al., 2022).

Governments worldwide are introducing digital nomad visas to attract high-skilled remote workers while boosting local economies. Countries like Estonia, Portugal, Thailand, and the UAE have implemented specialised visa programs, offering legal frameworks for long-term remote work (Gupta et al., 2024). These policies provide tax incentives and residency rights, making destinations more appealing to digital workers (Vohra et al., 2024). However, regulatory challenges persist, particularly regarding taxation, labour protections, and local workforce displacement. Governments must balance economic benefits with social equity by ensuring that digital nomads contribute to local economies without straining public resources (Pignatari, 2023). Additionally, increased migration of high-income remote workers into certain areas can lead to gentrification, rising living costs, and socio-economic disparities (Prester et al., 2023).

Digital nomadism has both positive and negative socio-cultural and environmental effects. On the positive side, nomads contribute to local economies through spending and cultural exchange (Andysto, 2023). However, issues like cultural insensitivity, housing inflation, and local job displacement require policy intervention to ensure sustainable integration (Prester et al., 2023). From an environmental perspective, remote work reduces commuting and office-related carbon footprints, supporting sustainability goals (Nash et al., 2021). However, frequent air travel associated with digital nomadism offsets these benefits, raising concerns about carbon emissions (Hensellek & Puchala, 2021). Sustainable travel initiatives, including carbon offset programs and eco-friendly coworking spaces, can mitigate these environmental challenges (Kaisu Koskela & Pascal Beckers, 2024).

The adoption of AI in Industry 4.0 is revolutionising automation and data-driven decision-making, yet significant challenges hinder its widespread implementation. (Windmann et al. 2017) highlight key barriers such as system integration, data quality, and workforce adaptation. While AI-driven industries benefit from predictive maintenance and optimised production planning, traditional industries rely on manual processes, limiting efficiency and scalability. Digital nomadism represents a shift from conventional office-based work to location-independent employment enabled by technology. (Aroles et al. 2022) explore 'meta-work', the hidden labour required to sustain a mobile work lifestyle. This contrasts with traditional employment, where infrastructure and support systems are already in place. The study challenges the idealised portrayal of digital nomadism, revealing the effort required to navigate global mobility.

The intersection of AI and digital nomadism is reshaping modern work structures by enhancing remote work capabilities and enabling automation in industries. (Arshad et al. 2024) emphasise the role of IT infrastructure in supporting remote work, highlighting the importance of connectivity, robust communication platforms, and cybersecurity. The ability to work from anywhere is increasingly facilitated by AI-driven collaboration tools, cloud computing, and automated workflow management systems. On a broader scale, (Lacárcel 2024) examines how digital platforms influence digital nomads' work experiences. The study identifies key themes such as digital comfort, sustainable mobility, and work-life balance, underscoring how technology supports global work trends. AI plays a crucial role in optimising these aspects by personalising work environments, automating administrative tasks, and enhancing cybersecurity, thereby bridging the gap between digital nomadism and AI-powered industries.

AI adoption and digital nomad policies vary significantly across countries, influenced by infrastructure, labour laws, and economic priorities. (Windmann et al. 2017) highlight that some industrial sectors have embraced AI-driven automation, while others struggle due to a lack of expertise and investment. In contrast, (Lacárcel 2024) notes that countries with strong digital infrastructures and supportive policies for remote work have become hotspots for digital nomads. Governments worldwide are responding to digital nomadism by introducing specialised visas to attract remote workers, as seen in Estonia, Portugal, Thailand, and the UAE (Gupta et al., 2024). However, regulatory challenges such as taxation, labour protections, and local workforce displacement remain key concerns. AI adoption faces similar policy disparities, with leading nations investing heavily in AI infrastructure, while others lag due to economic and technical constraints.

3. PROBLEMS AND SOLUTION RECOMMENDATIONS

The 21st century has witnessed two powerful, seemingly separate forces rise in parallel, the rapid advancement of artificial intelligence (AI) and the evolution of the digital nomad lifestyle. At a glance, one represents technological sophistication and automation; the other, human flexibility and movement. But when examined closely, these forces are not just intersecting, they are synergising in ways that are fundamentally reshaping how global industries function, how work is performed, and how economic value is created and distributed (Sjödin et al., 2023). AI is often portrayed as a force of automation, replacing repetitive human tasks with algorithmic efficiency. However, its role as an enabler is just as critical (Cubric, 2020). AI tools today do not merely replace jobs; they assist, enhance, and expand the capabilities of individuals, especially those working independently across borders (Devineni, 2024). For the digital nomad, someone who works remotely while moving across geographies, AI offers a technological scaffold that sustains their productivity, enables global collaboration, and reduces the barriers typically imposed by distance, time zones, and infrastructure disparities (Arshad et al., 2024).

Digital nomads, in turn, represent a new kind of economic actor. They are not bound by national labour markets or traditional employment contracts (Jaiswal et al., 2024). They operate across borders, offering skills on freelance platforms, launching startups remotely, or contributing to decentralised teams. Their reliance on digital infrastructure naturally drives demand for more adaptive, intelligent tools, tools that AI now powers (Antonio De Almeida et al., n.d.). Whether it's using machine learning-driven project management software, generative AI for content creation, or AI-enhanced coding assistants, digital nomads are increasingly embedded in an AI-rich ecosystem that both supports and is shaped by them (Belenguer, 2022). This convergence has implications far beyond individual careers. It begins to shift how entire industries are structured (Agarwal et al., 2022). For example, design firms no longer require large physical offices if their workforce can collaborate asynchronously using AI-assisted tools. Software companies may no longer need local recruitment pipelines when they can tap into a borderless pool of freelance developers, managed via AI-powered platforms (Sahut & Lissillour, 2023). Even traditional sectors like education, healthcare, and consulting are starting to adapt, incorporating remote service delivery models supported by AI decision engines (Manning et al., 2022). Importantly, this shift challenges the historical architecture of industrial organisation. The traditional firm, shaped by the need for physical proximity, centralised management, and hierarchical workflows, now faces competition from agile, decentralised networks of talent (Green, 2020). These networks are fluid, adaptive, and often global, traits enabled by both AI and digital nomadism (Hermann & Paris, 2020). In this landscape, work becomes less about location and more about contribution. Value creation detaches from geography and reattaches to capability and connectivity (Raisch & Krakowski, n.d.).

AI allows individuals to amplify their impact, while nomadism ensures that talent can be applied where it is most needed, regardless of borders (KC & Triandafyllidou, 2025). In essence, AI and digital nomadism together are not just changing how we work, they are redefining what work is, where it happens, and who gets to participate in it (Song & Jo, 2023). The term "industrial technology transitions" typically evokes images of new machinery, automation lines, or digital systems replacing analogue operations. But such a view is incomplete in today's context. What we are witnessing is not just a technological upgrade; it is a comprehensive transformation in the logic of how industries operate, scale, and evolve (Zizic et al., 2022). The infusion of artificial intelligence and the rise of globally distributed human capital, represented by digital nomads, are ushering in a new era of industrial transition that is both technological and social (Sjödin et al., 2023).

The current phase, often termed Industry 4.0, is shaped by intelligent systems, data-driven decision-making, and cyber-physical integration (Raja Santhi & Muthuswamy, 2023). However, there is an emerging transition that doesn't just occur within factories and warehouses; it happens in cloud servers, in virtual teams, and across digital platforms (Peres et al., 2020). This transition is defined as much by how work happens as where or what is being produced (Aroles et al., 2022).

Artificial intelligence sits at the heart of this redefinition. It doesn't merely replace manual labour, it augments human intelligence, automates knowledge work, and re-configures processes across finance, healthcare, logistics, marketing, and even creative fields (Lee et al., 2019). As AI becomes a central driver of operational efficiency and innovation, the need for localised expertise diminishes. Instead, companies seek flexible, specialised talent that can work asynchronously and autonomously, a need that aligns perfectly with the lifestyle and structure of digital nomads (Vohra et al., 2024). Today, talent dispersal is viable and even preferred in some sectors (Krajčík et al., 2023). A development team spread across five countries can now outperform a co-located team, thanks to AI tools that track workflow, suggest optimisations, and even complete low-level tasks autonomously (Belenguer, 2022). Digital nomads, empowered by these tools, function as mobile nodes in a global industrial web, capable of contributing to real-time innovation regardless of geography (Gupta et al., 2024). This transition is also redefining the physical infrastructure of industry. Instead of massive factory floors, industries now invest in data centres, distributed cloud infrastructure, and AI-powered software solutions (Windmann et al., 2017). Office real estate is being replaced by coworking spaces, home setups, and nomad-friendly work hubs in previously overlooked regions (Hermann & Paris, 2020). The digital nomad lifestyle, far from being marginal or temporary, is becoming embedded in this new industrial topology (KC & Triandafyllidou, 2025). Importantly, these transitions are accelerating a shift from ownership to access, from permanence to fluidity. AI platforms facilitate shared economies of skills, tools, and resources, while nomads exemplify mobility and adaptability (Oluwatoyin et al., 2023). Together, they represent a break from the rigid, legacy-driven modes of industrial organisation and signal a move toward a dynamic, borderless model of production and collaboration (Agarwal et al., 2022). Thus, the term "industrial transition" must be reframed, not as a phase in technological advancement, but as a broader socio-technical transformation. In this transformation, artificial intelligence serves as the brain, and digital nomads as the connective tissue, creating a flexible, intelligent, and decentralised industrial ecosystem (Antonio De Almeida et al., n.d.).

While artificial intelligence often takes the spotlight in conversations about technological disruption, the quiet yet profound impact of digital nomads is frequently overlooked. Framed mostly through lifestyle or travel-oriented narratives, digital nomadism is rarely examined as an economic force or a catalyst for industrial evolution (Gupta et al., 2024). Yet, behind this seemingly personal choice of flexible, location-independent work lies a deeper and more systemic influence, one that is reshaping industries from the ground up (Aroles et al., 2022). Digital nomads are not traditional employees, and their work patterns defy conventional organisational structures. But in their fluidity lies their power. By choosing flexibility over permanence, digital nomads are actively challenging legacy norms of work, hierarchical offices, rigid schedules, long-term contracts, and forcing industries to adapt (Jaiswal et al., 2024). The gig platforms they rely on, the asynchronous tools they use, and the way they deliver output have redefined expectations around productivity, deadlines, and even team dynamics (Vohra et al., 2024). Industries that once required centralised teams are now embracing distributed models. A marketing campaign may be strategised by someone in Lisbon, executed by a designer in Nairobi, and analysed by a data scientist working remotely from Buenos Aires. These configurations, once logistically impossible or unscalable, are now seamless, thanks to digital tools that have emerged, in part, to support the needs of mobile professionals (Sahut & Lissillour, 2023). The existence and growth of digital nomads are driving a demand for more intuitive, integrated, and AI-powered platforms that facilitate this kind of global collaboration (Antonio De Almeida et al., n.d.).

Beyond service delivery, digital nomads also impact industrial innovation. Many of them are not just freelancers but entrepreneurs, consultants, creators, and community builders (Song & Jo, 2023). They start remote-first businesses, build apps to solve productivity problems, and create knowledge hubs that fuel new economies. Their firsthand experience with cross-cultural, cross-platform workflows gives them unique insights into digital inefficiencies, insights they often turn into scalable products or business models (Lacárcel, 2025). The influence of digital nomads is also felt in the infrastructure industries that are investing in. The demand for coworking spaces, digital nomad visas, cross-border payment systems, and remote tax compliance tools has led to the emergence of new service sectors altogether (Koskela & Beckers, 2024). These are not marginal shifts; they are structural indicators of how industries are being reorganised around mobile, tech-savvy, and independent contributors (KC & Triandafyllidou, 2025).

Figure 1. The Top 10 Countries for Remote Working

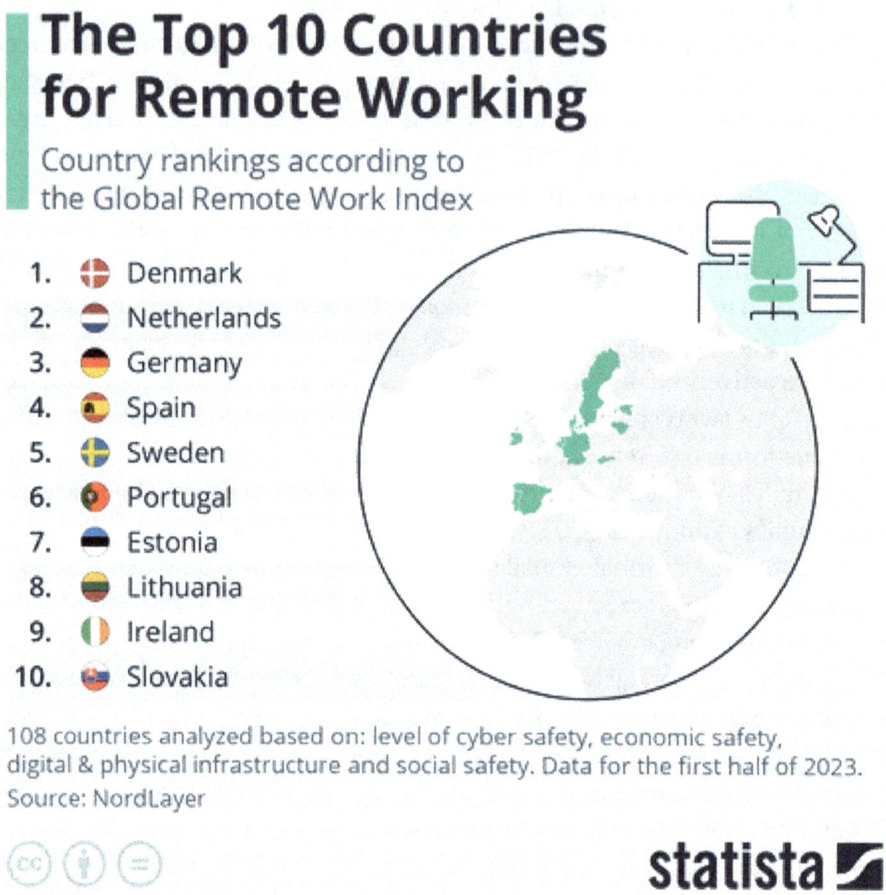

(Source: Statista)

This chart ranks countries based on their suitability for remote work, considering factors like cyber safety, economic safety, digital infrastructure, and social safety. Notably, Denmark tops the list, followed by the Netherlands and Germany. The prominence of European countries highlights the regions where digital nomadism is most viable, reflecting the infrastructural and policy support that facilitates this lifestyle.

Furthermore, digital nomads are redefining the social contract of work. With the rise of this mobile workforce, companies are being pressured to rethink employee benefits, mental health support, time zone management, and performance measurement (Karakus, 2021). Traditional metrics like "hours worked" are giving way to "value delivered," and trust is replacing micromanagement as the new currency of collaboration (Sampat et al., 2022).

Yet perhaps the most transformative aspect of digital nomads' influence lies in their silent assertion that work does not have to be tethered to a location. This idea, once fringe, has permeated mainstream corporate consciousness (Green, 2020). What began as a niche movement is now a legitimate alternative career path, and its widespread adoption is nudging entire industries toward more agile, tech-integrated, and human-centred modes of operation (Hermann & Paris, 2020). Their influence may be quiet, but it is no less revolutionary (Aroles et al., 2022).

Artificial intelligence is often examined through the lens of productivity, automation, and cost-efficiency. However, its deeper, more transformative role lies in its capacity to dissolve traditional boundaries between countries, between time zones, and even between skill levels. In this sense, AI is not merely a tool for automating work; it is an enabling infrastructure for global labour mobility (Sjödin et al., 2023). It facilitates a world where professionals can work from virtually anywhere, contributing meaningfully to industries regardless of their physical location. This phenomenon, largely invisible to traditional economic indicators, is at the heart of how global industrial transitions are being shaped (Steen et al., 2022).

Historically, global labour mobility was defined by physical migration. Skilled professionals had to relocate to industrial hubs to participate in the knowledge economy. AI, in conjunction with digital infrastructure, has rendered this model obsolete (Arshad et al., 2024). A software engineer no longer needs to move to San Francisco to work for a Silicon Valley startup; with AI-driven collaboration tools, they can build, ship, and iterate products from anywhere. Similarly, a consultant using AI analytics platforms can offer data-driven insights to clients on different continents without ever leaving their home country (Sahut & Lissillour, 2023).

Figure 2. Rate of adoption and development of artificial intelligence (AI) in enterprise globally and in selected countries in 2023

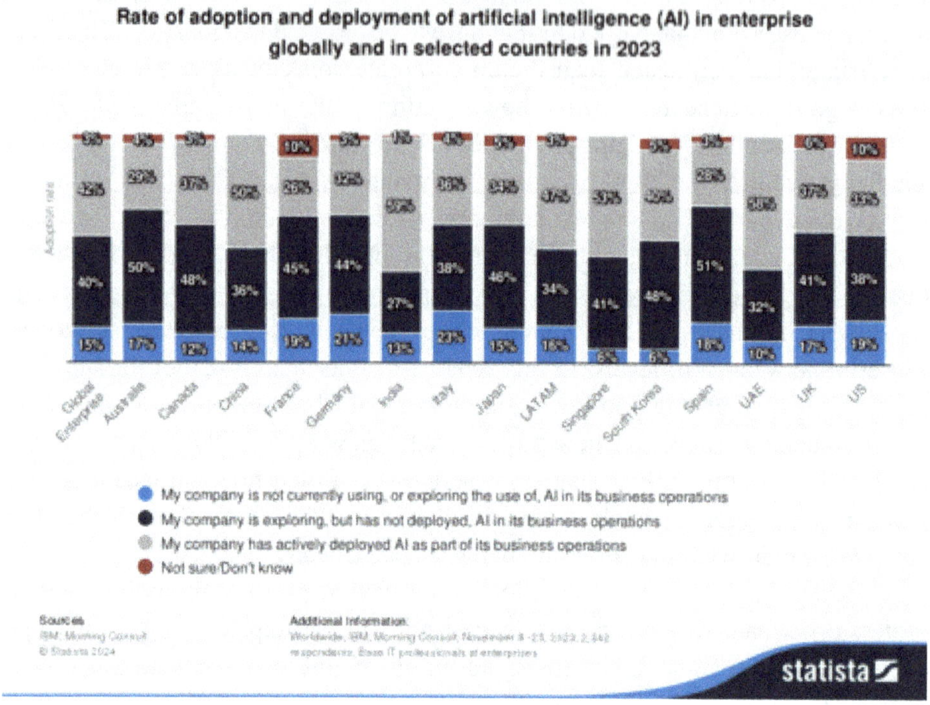

(Source: Statista)

The chart illustrates the varying rates of AI adoption among selected countries in 2023. Notably, China leads with an adoption rate of 83%, followed by the United States at 65%, and the United Kingdom at 64%. Other countries like Germany and France show adoption rates of 60% and 58%, respectively. These figures highlight the global momentum in embracing AI technologies across different economies.

One of AI's most significant contributions to this borderless labour dynamic is in reducing the friction of global collaboration. Natural language processing tools, real-time transcription, and AI-powered translation systems are eliminating language barriers that once restricted cross-border teamwork (Curzon et al., 2021). Meanwhile, AI-based project management platforms offer intelligent task allocation, real-time progress tracking, and workflow optimisation features that make asynchronous work not only possible but highly efficient (Belenguer, 2022).

Even at the skill level, AI is a democratizing force. The emergence of AI-assisted tools in design, coding, content creation, and data analytics enables individuals with limited technical training to participate in high-value work (Devineni, 2024). A digital nomad with a non-technical background can now leverage AI tools to build websites, write professional-grade copy, or analyse complex datasets. This shift doesn't just expand access to opportunity, it redefines who can be considered a contributor in modern industry (Oluwatoyin et al., 2023).

For employers, this new paradigm unlocks unprecedented access to global talent. AI removes the constraints of locality, making it easier to assess, onboard, and manage remote workers across time zones and jurisdictions (Ofosu-Ampong & Acheampong, 2022). Companies can assemble project-based, highly specialised teams on demand, without being tied to physical office space or local labour laws. The result is a more agile, cost-effective, and innovative industrial model, one that thrives on distributed intelligence, both human and artificial (Antonio De Almeida et al., n.d.).

At the same time, AI enables a new form of self-governance in work. Remote professionals can now track their productivity, optimise their workflows, and upskill in real time using AI tutors and learning platforms (Hwa Baek, 2021). The professional development lifecycle, once mediated by employers and formal institutions, is becoming increasingly autonomous and personalised, reflecting the ethos of both the AI age and the digital nomad lifestyle (KC & Triandafyllidou, 2025).

In this emerging world, AI functions not merely as an industrial tool but as a general-purpose infrastructure for the free movement of labour. It collapses distance, compresses time, and flattens hierarchies, giving rise to a labour model that is global, adaptive, and inclusive. As industries evolve, this AI-enabled mobility will become a defining characteristic of the next generation of work (Taeihagh, 2021).

Industrial systems have long relied on a set of principles that once formed the backbone of modern economies, centralised operations, standardised work hours, fixed physical locations, and hierarchical control. These principles were designed for predictability, efficiency, and scalability. However, the dual rise of artificial intelligence and digital nomadism is challenging these foundational norms, exposing their rigidity and inefficiency in an increasingly fluid, digital world (Zizic et al., 2022). The result is not merely a transformation in how work is done, but a disruption of the very logic that underpinned traditional industrial models (Raja Santhi & Muthuswamy, 2023). At the heart of this disruption is the decoupling of work from place. The industrial era prized proximity; people needed to be near machines, near each other, and under centralised supervision. But AI-powered tools now automate oversight, coordination, and even aspects of human judgment (Cubric, 2020). With intelligent project managers, virtual assistants, and performance tracking software, physical presence is no longer a prerequisite for productivity. This change undermines the rationale for massive office complexes and fixed 9-to-5 schedules (Sampat et al., 2022).

Digital nomads exemplify this disruption in real time. Operating across time zones and often outside conventional legal frameworks, they force companies to rethink how teams are structured, how productivity is measured, and how compliance is maintained (Jaiswal et al., 2024). Traditional employment contracts, designed for local taxation, benefits, and oversight, are increasingly inadequate for managing a distributed, flexible workforce. In their place, industries are experimenting with contract-based, outcomes-focused engagements facilitated by digital platforms (Gupta et al., 2024). The role of AI in this process is equally disruptive. By automating not only repetitive tasks but also decision-making processes, AI diminishes the need for vertical management layers (Manning et al., 2022). Teams can self-organise with the support of intelligent systems that allocate resources, identify bottlenecks, and even suggest strategic pivots. In effect, AI flattens organisational hierarchies, making way for leaner, more agile structures that prioritise adaptability over bureaucracy (Nam et al., 2020).

Figure 3. Potential share of time spent working remotely by country %

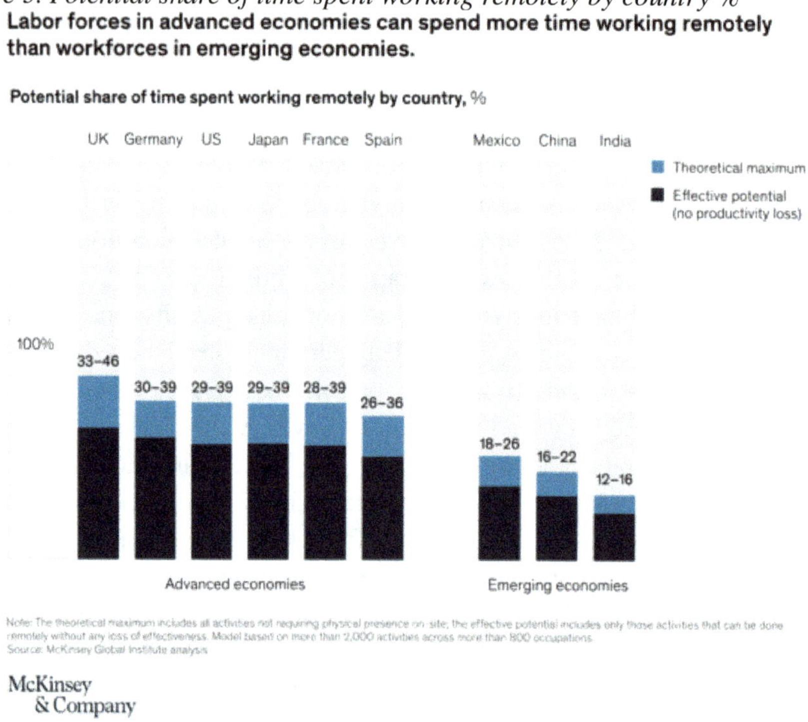

(Source: McKinsey & Company)

In emerging economies like India, where most of the 464 million workers are employed in agriculture and retail, only about 12% of work can be done remotely without loss of effectiveness despite the country's strong high-tech and financial sectors.

This disruption extends to business models as well. Traditional industries were built around long-term asset ownership, standardised processes, and physical infrastructure. The new logic prioritises access over ownership, customisation over standardisation, and digital over physical (Lee et al., 2019). Cloud-based services replace factories, digital platforms replace storefronts, and global freelance marketplaces replace in-house departments. The shift is so foundational that even the metrics used to assess business health, such as headcount, physical expansion, or local market penetration, are becoming less relevant (Oluwatoyin et al., 2023). Success is increasingly defined by reach, flexibility, and responsiveness, qualities that AI and digital nomadism jointly enable (Peres et al., 2020).

Moreover, this transformation is prompting regulatory systems to play catch-up. Taxation, labour laws, intellectual property rights, and data governance were all designed around national borders and fixed workplaces. The new industrial logic blurs these boundaries, making compliance a complex, often ambiguous challenge (Taeihagh, 2021). Governments and institutions now face the task of developing new frameworks that reflect the distributed, AI-augmented, and nomad-enabled reality of modern industry (KC & Triandafyllidou, 2025). In essence, the traditional industrial playbook is being rewritten. What was once considered essential, central offices, physical presence, and formal hierarchies, is now negotiable. In its place emerges a model characterised by distributed intelligence, autonomous talent, and algorithmic orchestration. AI and digital nomads are not just adapting to industrial systems, they are dismantling and rebuilding them from the ground up (Aroles et al., 2022).

While the convergence of artificial intelligence and digital nomadism is largely celebrated for its disruptive potential and liberating impact on the nature of work, it is not without frictions. Beneath the glossy veneer of flexibility and innovation lie a range of ethical, social, economic, and environmental challenges that complicate the narrative of progress. These hidden costs do not necessarily negate the benefits of this new industrial logic but demand critical scrutiny and thoughtful response (Aroles et al., 2022).One of the most pressing concerns is inequality of access. The AI-nomad ecosystem is heavily skewed toward those who possess the right blend of digital literacy, economic security, and geographic privilege. The ability to work remotely using advanced AI tools requires stable internet access, modern hardware, and a level of tech fluency that is not universally available (Arshad et al., 2024). Additionally, the digital nomad lifestyle is disproportionately accessible to citizens of countries with strong passports, favourable exchange rates, and low visa restrictions (KC & Triandafyllidou, 2025). This creates a two-tiered system, those who can participate in the global labour economy, and those who remain confined by geography, infrastructure, or regulation (Gupta et al., 2024).

AI tools themselves are not neutral. While they enhance productivity and decision-making, they also introduce a layer of algorithmic control that can be opaque and, at times, biased (Belenguer, 2022). Remote workers are increasingly subject to surveillance through AI-powered productivity trackers, facial recognition logins, or automated performance evaluations (Curzon et al., 2021). These systems can create anxiety, erode trust, and contribute to a culture of hyper-measurement, where the human side of work is deprioritised in favour of metrics and dashboards (Devineni, 2024).

Figure 4. Struggles with working remotely

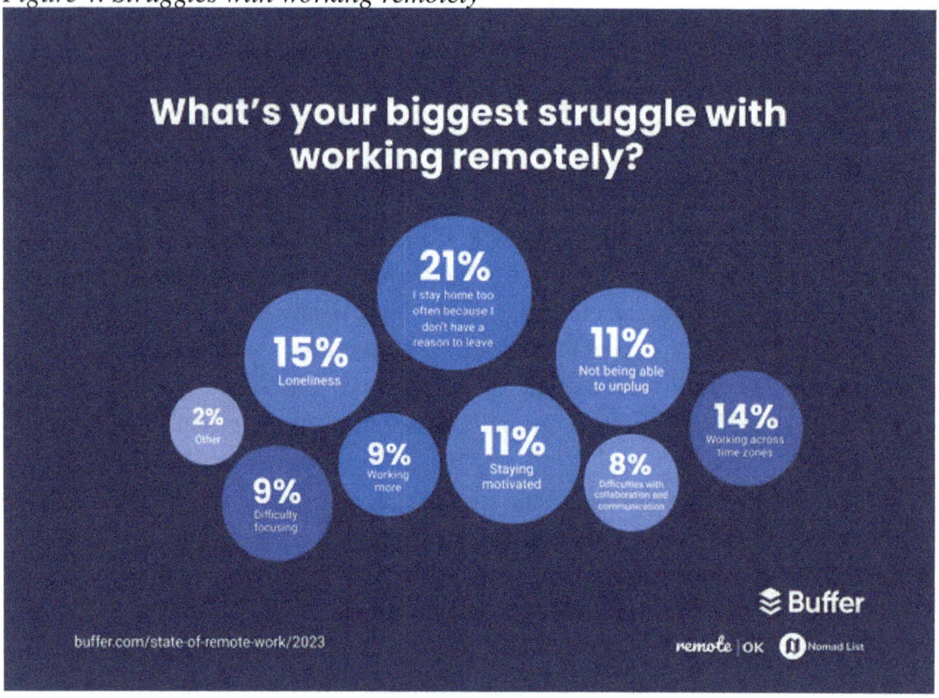

(Source: Buffer)

This chart identifies common challenges encountered by remote workers, such as feelings of isolation, difficulties in communication, and maintaining work-life balance.

Mental health is another silent casualty. The freedom of location independence often comes with the burden of isolation, unstable income, and blurred work-life boundaries (Jaiswal et al., 2024). Without physical teams or institutional support structures, many digital nomads report feelings of loneliness, burnout, and decision fatigue. AI may help manage tasks, but it cannot yet substitute for community or emotional connection elements essential to long-term professional well-being

(Vohra et al., 2024). From a policy perspective, the rapid decentralisation of workforces challenges existing legal and economic frameworks. Taxation becomes murky when a digital worker earns income in one country while residing in another and contributing to yet another's economy (Koskela & Beckers, 2024). Labour protections, social security systems, and employee benefits are often bypassed in the name of flexibility, leaving remote workers vulnerable to exploitation or unintentional legal violations (Taeihagh, 2021).

Environmental concerns also complicate the equation. While remote work reduces daily commuting and office emissions, the frequent international travel associated with digital nomadism contributes to a significant carbon footprint (Lacárcel, 2025). This contradiction often goes unaddressed in celebratory narratives, even as industries and governments tout sustainability as a shared priority (Green, 2020). Ultimately, these hidden costs do not diminish the legitimacy or potential of the AI–digital nomad convergence, but they underscore the need for balance. Without intentional design, inclusive policy, and ethical governance, the benefits of this new industrial model risk being unevenly distributed or worse, reinforcing the very inequalities and inefficiencies it promises to overcome (Sjödin et al., 2023).

3.1 Solutions and Recommendations

The proliferation of artificial intelligence and the global surge in digital nomadism signal a critical inflexion point for reimagining traditional work infrastructure. In this new era, the geographic decoupling of labour from fixed locations necessitates a robust, adaptive digital ecosystem that ensures seamless productivity, secure collaboration, and inclusivity across borders. Governments and private sector actors must collaborate to build the foundational technological scaffolding that supports this transformation. At the core of this transformation lies the need for scalable digital infrastructure. Governments should prioritise expanding access to high-speed internet, not just in urban centres, but in underserved rural and semi-urban regions. Investment in 5G networks, satellite internet initiatives, and fibre optic expansion will be instrumental in creating a truly global workforce.

Concurrently, businesses must accelerate the deployment of enterprise-grade remote work tools. These include secure Virtual Private Networks (VPNs), cloud-based collaboration platforms, and AI-powered project management tools. A well-integrated suite of tools like Microsoft Azure, AWS Cloud, Notion, and Asana, when fortified with cybersecurity protocols and AI-enhanced analytics, allows decentralised teams to function with the same, if not greater, efficiency as co-located ones.

A distributed workforce introduces complex vulnerabilities, making cybersecurity not just a technical concern but a cornerstone of trust in the remote work economy. Governments should enact minimum cybersecurity standards for businesses engaged in international remote work, while the private sector must prioritise end-to-end encryption, biometric authentication, and AI-based anomaly detection systems. Public-private partnerships can foster cyber resilience labs that develop shared protocols for threat response and data privacy. Additionally, interoperability standards, especially in cloud environments, will be essential to enable cross-platform access and data integrity across countries and corporations. Institutions like the International Telecommunication Union (ITU) and World Economic Forum (WEF) could lead the way in convening standard-setting dialogues that span jurisdictions.

As AI systems and remote work technologies redefine the contours of employability, the global workforce faces an urgent mandate to reskill and upskill for a digitally fluid economy. This shift is not just about acquiring technical prowess; it's about cultivating a new mindset oriented toward lifelong learning, digital collaboration, and adaptability. Governments, educational institutions, NGOs, and private enterprises must converge to create accessible, inclusive, and future-ready learning pathways. Meanwhile, NGOs and ed-tech platforms like Coursera, edx, and Udacity can offer modular, low-cost micro-credentials aimed at adult learners, freelancers, and displaced workers. Government funding and corporate sponsorships should target marginalised groups and those in transition, including women re-entering the workforce, blue-collar workers, and rural populations. Beyond AI, remote work itself demands a specific skill set that traditional education rarely addresses. Organisations can implement onboarding bootcamps and continuous learning modules focused on remote-readiness tools, such as Notion for knowledge management, Slack for real-time communication, Figma for design collaboration, and project tracking tools like Trello and Jira. NGOs and workforce development centres can host in-person digital literacy camps in underserved areas, providing not just training but also access to equipment and connectivity.

To accommodate the nonlinear career paths of digital nomads and gig workers, learning must be modular, on-demand, and stackable. Micro-certifications that build toward larger credentials allow for flexibility and customisation. AI-powered adaptive learning platforms can personalise pacing and content to individual learner profiles, making education more responsive and effective. Governments can play a catalytic role by accrediting alternative credentials and recognising them in public hiring.. The AI-remote work economy is not inherently inclusive; it must be designed to be. Without proactive upskilling initiatives, vast swaths of the population risk obsolescence, while a privileged few monopolise opportunity. Investing in digital fluency and remote work competencies is not just a workforce strategy, it's a social equity imperative. It prepares citizens not just to survive, but to thrive, in a world where work is borderless, algorithmically mediated, and in constant flux.

The rise of digital nomadism has disrupted traditional models of labour mobility, immigration, and taxation. As highly skilled professionals work remotely across borders, often without formal employment ties to the countries they reside in, governments face an urgent need to modernise their policy frameworks. Innovative visa programs and remote work regulations are key to managing this shift, not only to protect workers and ensure fair contributions to host economies but also to unlock the economic and cultural benefits of a globally mobile workforce.

Governments worldwide should follow suit by creating visa categories specifically designed for remote workers and freelancers. Key features should include -

- **Clear eligibility criteria** based on minimum income thresholds, remote employer verification, and health insurance coverage.
- **Fair tax treatment** that avoids double taxation while ensuring local social contributions.
- **Access to public services**, such as healthcare and coworking hubs, through tailored benefit packages.

Remote work challenges the traditional employer-employee relationship and raises complex questions about labour protections, taxation, and social security contributions. Policymakers must design frameworks that reflect this reality. One approach is to develop "remote work charters" that standardise expectations across borders, covering issues such as fair pay, remote worker rights, health coverage, and dispute resolution. Tax authorities, meanwhile, must move toward portable, proportional systems where remote workers contribute based on their duration of stay and economic footprint in a host country. Bilateral or multilateral agreements, similar to double taxation treaties, can be adapted to recognise the growing cohort of location-independent workers. Given the inherently transnational nature of digital nomadism, international coordination is critical. Forums like the OECD, ILO, and UNDP can play a convening role in promoting shared standards and model frameworks. Regional alliances (e.g., the EU, ASEAN, MERCOSUR) could explore visa interoperability or digital nomad corridors, similar to student mobility pacts. Digital identity systems, such as Estonia's e-Residency, offer promising models for transnational economic participation. These systems enable secure access to banking, taxation, and government services without requiring physical presence, and could be scaled globally with appropriate safeguards.

Done right, digital nomad policies can create a win-win scenario mobile professionals gain legal stability and access to services, while host countries benefit from knowledge transfer, local spending, and increased global visibility. Without policy innovation, however, the sector risks falling into legal grey zones that foster inequity, evasion, and administrative strain. As artificial intelligence transforms productivity and digital platforms fragment the geography of labour, new ethical dilemmas and power asymmetries are emerging. Remote workers increasingly interface with algorithmic systems for job matching, performance assessment, or even surveillance, while gig and contract workers operate with minimal protections. The integration of AI into remote work is not neutral; it must be guided by fairness, transparency, and accountability to prevent exploitation and digital disenfranchisement.

First, businesses and technology providers must embed ethical principles directly into the design and deployment of AI tools used in remote work environments. This includes -

- **Algorithmic transparency** - Workers should understand when and how AI is used in hiring, performance reviews, or task allocation.
- **Bias audits** - Regular, third-party audits of AI systems to detect and correct racial, gender, or socio-economic bias.
- **Explainability standards** - AI decisions that affect worker livelihoods, such as wage recommendations or contract renewals, must be explainable in plain language.

Regulators and industry alliances should develop certification frameworks for ethical AI in the workplace, akin to ISO standards, enabling employers and platforms to be held to common benchmarks. Remote workers, especially freelancers and platform-based gig workers, often lack the protections afforded to traditional employees. Minimum wage laws, health benefits, and labour dispute mechanisms are inconsistently applied or absent. To address this, governments and labour unions must push for -

- **Universal digital labour contracts** - Standardised contracts that ensure minimum protections regardless of geography, including payment timelines, working hours, and leave policies.
- **Portable benefits platforms** - Systems where workers accumulate benefits (e.g., healthcare, retirement, training credits) across multiple employers and gigs.
- **Anti-surveillance provisions** - Limits on invasive monitoring technologies that track keystrokes, webcam feeds, or screen activity without consent.

Without ethical safeguards, AI and remote work can replicate and even magnify existing labour inequities under a veil of automation and flexibility. Exploitative surveillance, opaque algorithmic decisions, and gig precarity are not technological inevitabilities, they are policy and design choices. Creating fair digital labour standards and embedding ethics into AI governance ensures that the future of work is not just efficient, but just. In a world where work transcends borders and algorithms act as gatekeepers; ethics must travel just as far and move just as fast. While digital nomadism promises professional freedom and cross-cultural exchange, it also carries hidden costs, environmental degradation, gentrification, and cultural disconnection. As the lifestyle scales, it must evolve from an individual privilege into a model that supports long-term sustainability, equitable development, and meaningful local engagement. Governments, businesses, and digital workers themselves must co-create practices that minimise harm and maximise shared value. One of the most pressing concerns around digital nomadism is the environmental toll of frequent international travel. Flights are major contributors to individual carbon footprints, and without corrective mechanisms, the nomadic lifestyle risks undermining global climate goals.

To address this, stakeholders can implement -

- **Carbon offset incentives** - Governments or travel platforms can provide or mandate carbon offset programs integrated into visa applications or flight bookings.
- **Tax breaks or credits** for nomads who limit flights or commit to low-emission transportation.
- **Partnerships with green travel providers** that promote trains, electric transport, or sustainable accommodation options. Nomads themselves can be encouraged, through education and digital community norms, to adopt a "fly less, stay longer" ethic that aligns with environmental consciousness.

Meanwhile, businesses can invest in coworking-living hubs that serve as sustainable, socially conscious infrastructure for nomads, spaces built with local materials, powered by renewables, and staffed by local workers. Digital nomadism should not mirror the extractive patterns of mass tourism. Instead, it can become a vector for inclusive growth when nomads are encouraged to spend locally, hire locally, and contribute meaningfully to the communities they inhabit.

Policy interventions could include -

- Local hiring mandates for nomad-focused businesses.
- Community reinvestment taxes that fund public goods (e.g., digital literacy centres, environmental restoration, public Wi-Fi).
- Cultural orientation programs that foster mutual respect and reduce social friction.

Digital platforms and influencer communities also have a role to play in promoting ethical travel norms, highlighting off-the-beaten-path destinations, showcasing local artisans, and spotlighting regenerative tourism efforts.

Sustainability is not peripheral to digital nomadism, it is central to its legitimacy and longevity. Without ecological awareness and cultural humility, nomadism risks becoming another extractive trend. But with intentional design, it can be a force for decentralised innovation, global solidarity, and ecological balance. Aligned with Sustainable Development Goals, especially SDG 11 (Sustainable Cities and Communities) and SDG 13 (Climate Action), sustainable digital nomadism can model a future where mobility enhances, rather than erodes, our shared planetary home.

They are not merely technological upgrades or lifestyle accommodations, they are strategic imperatives for shaping a just, resilient, and inclusive global economy. Whether through infrastructure investments, educational innovation, ethical governance, or sustainable mobility, the choices we make now will determine who benefits from the digital transition and at what cost. As the boundaries of work, identity, and geography continue to blur, a proactive, values-driven approach to policy and practice will be essential. These recommendations are not endpoints, but springboards for deeper inquiry, ongoing experimentation, and collective learning, laying the groundwork for a future that is not only more connected, but more human.

While this chapter outlines critical solutions for navigating the dual rise of AI and digital nomadism, it also reveals how much remains unknown. As these global transitions accelerate, academic and policy-oriented research must expand in both depth and breadth, encompassing diverse methodologies, longitudinal perspectives, and nuanced geographic focus. Interdisciplinary and mixed-method research will be essential in capturing the full spectrum of socio-technical change.

A key area for future inquiry involves quantitative and statistical analysis of digital nomad trends and AI integration. Despite growing interest, there is a lack of large-scale empirical data to assess how digital nomadism is reshaping labour markets, urban economies, or education systems. Future studies should aim to collect and analyse robust datasets across multiple regions, tracking variables such as visa issuance rates, income patterns, spending behaviour, carbon footprints, and skill acquisition over time. Econometric modelling could be particularly valuable in estimating the economic impact of digital nomads on local GDP, inflationary pressures on housing, or the effectiveness of digital upskilling programs.

Similarly, the adoption and labour effects of AI tools demand rigorous quantitative scrutiny. While anecdotal and qualitative evidence suggests major changes in productivity and task allocation, few studies have systematically measured these shifts across sectors or demographic groups. Controlled studies and statistical regressions can help clarify which types of remote workers are most likely to benefit, or be displaced, by specific AI technologies. These analyses should be disaggregated by gender, race, region, and skill level to reveal inequities and inform inclusive policy responses. At the same time, qualitative and ethnographic methods remain indispensable, especially for exploring lived experiences, ethical dilemmas, and sociocultural dynamics that are not easily captured by numbers. The emotional toll of constant mobility, trust issues in algorithmically managed teams, or the symbolic value of "digital nomad" identity are all ripe for deeper investigation. Future research would benefit from longitudinal qualitative studies, embedded fieldwork, and participatory action research with remote workers, platform developers, and policy stakeholders.

The rise of artificial intelligence and digital nomadism marks a major shift in how global industries and work are organised. This change is reshaping where people work, how they work, and what skills they need. As AI tools become more common and remote work more widespread, traditional ideas about jobs, offices, and national workforces are being replaced. Businesses are now operating with teams spread across countries, while intelligent systems are handling tasks once done by humans. These changes require governments, companies, and institutions to rethink their strategies and adapt quickly. To make the most of this transition, coordinated efforts are needed. Governments should invest in reliable digital infrastructure, protect data privacy, and make sure that education systems teach the skills people need in a digital economy. Companies must use AI responsibly and ensure fair working conditions for people working remotely or through platforms. Upskilling programmes, especially in underserved regions, are also vital to close digital gaps and promote equal access to new opportunities. Environmental and social sustainability must also be central. Frequent travel by digital nomads adds to carbon emissions, while rising demand for short-term housing can strain local communities. Promoting "slowmad" lifestyles, building eco-friendly co-working hubs, and creating policies that benefit both nomads and locals can help reduce these harms. This shift is not only about new technologies; it reflects changing values around independence, flexibility, and global citizenship. The way forward depends on the rules, systems, and cultural ideas that are built today. Ongoing research that combines numbers with real-life stories will be essential to guide smart and fair decisions. As work continues to cross borders and AI reshapes industries, the global economy is entering a new phase, more connected, more digital, and more mobile. To make this transition successful for everyone, action must be taken to ensure it is inclusive, ethical, and sustainable.

REFERENCES

Agarwal, P., Swami, S., & Malhotra, S. K. (2022). Artificial Intelligence Adoption in the Post COVID-19 New-Normal and Role of Smart Technologies in Transforming Business: A Review. *Journal of Science and Technology Policy Management*, *15*(3), 506–529. DOI: 10.1108/JSTPM-08-2021-0122

Albaroudi, E., Mansouri, T., & Alameer, A. (2024). A Comprehensive Review of AI Techniques for Addressing Algorithmic Bias in Job Hiring. AI, 5(1), 383–404. MDPI. https://doi.org/DOI: 10.3390/ai5010019

Alowais, S. A., Alghamdi, S. S., Alsuhebany, N., Alqahtani, T., Alshaya, A., Almohareb, S. N., Aldairem, A., Alrashed, M., Saleh, K. B., Badreldin, H. A., Yami, A., Harbi, S. A., & Albekairy, A. M. (2023). Revolutionizing healthcare: The Role of Artificial Intelligence in Clinical Practice. *BMC Medical Education*, *23*(1), 1–15. DOI: 10.1186/s12909-023-04698-z PMID: 37740191

Antonio De Almeida, M., Barbosa, C., Moreira, J., Souza, D., & Schneider, D. (n.d.). AI and Digital Nomads: Glimpsing the Future Human-Computer Interaction AI and Digital Nomads: Glimpsing the Future Human-Computer Interaction.

Aroles, J., Bonneau, C., & Bhankaraully, S. (2022). Conceptualising "Meta-Work" in the Context of Continuous, Global Mobility: The Case of Digital Nomadism. *Work, Employment and Society*, *37*(5), 1261–1278. DOI: 10.1177/09500170211069797

Arshad, A., Ghaffar, A., Siddqiue, M. U., & Rehman, A. (2024). The Role of IT Infrastructure in Enabling Remote Work: Productivity and Employee Satisfaction. *Journal of Excellence in Social Sciences*, *3*(1). Advance online publication. DOI: 10.69565/jess.v3i1.194

Barja-Martinez, S., Aragüés-Peñalba, M., Munné-Collado, Í., Lloret-Gallego, P., Bullich-Massagué, E., & Villafafila-Robles, R. (2021). Artificial intelligence techniques for enabling Big Data services in distribution networks: A review. *Renewable & Sustainable Energy Reviews*, *150*, 111459–111459. DOI: 10.1016/j.rser.2021.111459

Belenguer, L. (2022). AI bias: Exploring discriminatory algorithmic decision-making models and the application of possible machine-centric solutions adapted from the pharmaceutical industry. *AI and Ethics*, *2*(4), 771–787. DOI: 10.1007/s43681-022-00138-8 PMID: 35194591

Cubric, M. (2020). Drivers, barriers and social considerations for AI adoption in business and management: A tertiary study. *Technology in Society*, *62*, 101257. DOI: 10.1016/j.techsoc.2020.101257

Curzon, J., Kosa, T. A., Akalu, R., & El-Khatib, K. (2021). Privacy and Artificial Intelligence. *IEEE Transactions on Artificial Intelligence*, *2*(2), 96–108. DOI: 10.1109/TAI.2021.3088084

Devineni, S. (2024). Cite this Article: Siva Karthik Devineni, AI in Data Privacy and Security. [IJAIML]. *International Journal of Artificial Intelligence and Machine Learning*, *3*(1), 35–49. DOI: 10.17605/OSF.IO/WCN8A

Green, P. (2020). Disruptions of self, place and mobility: Digital nomads in Chiang Mai, Thailand. *Mobilities*, *15*(3), 431–445. DOI: 10.1080/17450101.2020.1723253

Gupta, S., Jaiswal, R., & Gupta, S. K. (2024). Digital nomads: A systematic literature review and future research agenda. *Tourism Review*. Advance online publication. DOI: 10.1108/TR-12-2023-0869

Haefner, N., Parida, V., Gassmann, O., & Wincent, J. (2023). Implementing and scaling artificial intelligence: A review, framework, and research agenda. *Technological Forecasting and Social Change*, *197*, 122878–122878. DOI: 10.1016/j.techfore.2023.122878

Hermann, I., & Paris, C. M. (2020). Digital Nomadism: The nexus of remote working and travel mobility. *Information Technology & Tourism*, *22*(3), 329–334. DOI: 10.1007/s40558-020-00188-w

Holzinger, A., Zatloukal, K., & Müller, H. (2024). Is human oversight to AI systems still possible? *New Biotechnology*, *85*, 59–62. DOI: 10.1016/j.nbt.2024.12.003 PMID: 39675423

Holzmann, V., Zitter, D., & Peshkess, S. (2022). The Expectations of Project Managers from Artificial Intelligence: A Delphi Study. Project Management Journal, 53(5). Sagepub. https://doi.org/DOI: 10.1177/87569728211061779

Hwa Baek, C. (2021). A study on the change in service quality in the era of the 4th industrial revolution compared to the existing service quality evaluation. 2021 21st ACIS International Winter Conference on Software Engineering, Artificial Intelligence, Networking and Parallel/Distributed Computing (SNPD-Winter), 156–158. https://doi.org/DOI: 10.1109/SNPDWinter52325.2021.00041

Jaiswal, R., Gupta, S., & Gupta, S. K. (2024). The impending disruption of digital nomadism: Opportunities, challenges, and research agenda. *World Leisure Journal*, *67*(1), 74–104. DOI: 10.1080/16078055.2024.2346091

Karakus, F. (2021). A retrospective view from traditional to boundaryless career and career success. International Journal of Research in Business and Social Science (2147- 4478), 10(3), 65–81. https://doi.org/DOI: 10.20525/ijrbs.v10i3.1131

Kc, H., & Triandafyllidou, A., (2025). Digital Nomadism and the Emergence of Digital Nomad Visas: What Policy Objectives Do States Aim to Achieve? *The International Migration Review*, *60*(1), 71–92. Advance online publication. DOI: 10.1177/01979183241306367

Khan, M. A., Syamil, A., Rana, J. A. S., Subekti, R., & Amin, N. (2025). Digital Nomadism: Remote Work Practices and Emerging Forms of Entrepreneurship. *Gadjah Mada International Journal of Business*, *28*(1), 25–46. DOI: 10.22146/gamaijb.v28i1.17133

Khedr, A. M., & Sheeja, R. S. (2024). Enhancing Supply Chain Management with Deep Learning and Machine Learning Techniques: A Review. Journal of Open Innovation Technology Market and Complexity, 10(4), 100379–100379. Sciencedirect. https://www.sciencedirect.com/science/article/pii/S2199853124001732

Koskela, K., & Beckers, P. (2024). Typologizing Digital Nomad Visas: Comparing Policy Rationales from Tourism to Wealth Accumulation to Immigration. *Journal of Comparative Policy Analysis*, *26*(5), 407–425. DOI: 10.1080/13876988.2024.2343696

Krajčík, M., Schmidt, D. A., & Baráth, M. (2023). Hybrid Work Model: An Approach to Work–Life Flexibility in a Changing Environment. *Administrative Sciences*, *13*(6), 150. DOI: 10.3390/admsci13060150

Lacárcel, F. J. S. (2025). Digital technologies, sustainable lifestyle, and tourism: How digital nomads navigate global mobility? *Sustainable Technology and Entrepreneurship*, *4*(2), 100096. DOI: 10.1016/j.stae.2025.100096

Laine, J., Minkkinen, M., & Mäntymäki, M. (2024). Ethics-based AI auditing: A systematic literature review on conceptualizations of ethical principles and knowledge contributions to stakeholders. *Information & Management*, *61*(5), 103969–103969. DOI: 10.1016/j.im.2024.103969

Langroodi, F. (2021). ARTICLE INFO. *Journal of Insurance and Financial Management*, *4*, 65–81.

Lee, J., Suh, T., Roy, D., & Baucus, M. (2019). Emerging Technology and Business Model Innovation: The Case of Artificial Intelligence. *Journal of Open Innovation*, *5*(3), 44. DOI: 10.3390/joitmc5030044

Manning, L., Brewer, S., Craigon, P. J., Frey, J., Gutierrez, A., Jacobs, N., Kanza, S., Munday, S., Sacks, J., & Pearson, S. (2022). Artificial intelligence and ethics within the food sector: Developing a common language for technology adoption across the supply chain. *Trends in Food Science & Technology*, *125*, 33–42. DOI: 10.1016/j.tifs.2022.04.025

Ofosu-Ampong, K., & Acheampong, B. (2022). Adoption of contactless technologies for remote work in Ghana post-Covid-19: Insights from technology-organisation-environment framework. *Digital Business*, *2*(2), 100023. DOI: 10.1016/j.digbus.2022.100023

Partners, M. B. O. (2023). Digital Nomads - The 2021 Workforce Trend. MBO Partners. https://www.mbopartners.com/state-of-independence/digital-nomads/

Peres, R., Jia, X., Lee, J., Sun, K., Colombo, A., & Barata, J. (2020). Industrial artificial intelligence in industry 4.0 - systematic review, challenges and outlook. https://doi.org/DOI: 10.1109/ACCESS.2020.3042874

PWC. (2018). The potential impact of Artificial Intelligence in the Middle East - PwC Middle East. PwC. https://www.pwc.com/m1/en/publications/potential-impact-artificial-intelligence-middle-east.html

Raina, K., Sharma, G. D., Taheri, B., Dev, D., & Chavriya, S. (2025). Artificial intelligence-driven management: Bridging innovation, knowledge creation, and sustainable business practices. *Journal of Innovation & Knowledge*, *11*, 100860. DOI: 10.1016/j.jik.2025.100860

Raisch, S., & Krakowski, S. (n.d.). Artificial intelligence and management.

Raja Santhi, A., & Muthuswamy, P. (2023). Industry 5.0 or industry 4.0S? Introduction to industry 4.0 and a peek into the prospective industry 5.0 technologies. [IJIDeM]. *International Journal on Interactive Design and Manufacturing*, *17*(2), 947–979. DOI: 10.1007/s12008-023-01217-8 PMID: 40478102

Rashid, A. B., & Kausik, A. K. (2024). AI Revolutionizing Industries Worldwide: A Comprehensive Overview of Its Diverse Applications. *Hybrid Advances*, *7*(100277), 100277–100277. DOI: 10.1016/j.hybadv.2024.100277

Roy, S. K., Tehrani, A. N., Pandit, A., Apostolidis, C., & Ray, S. (2025). Ai-capable relationship marketing: Shaping the future of customer relationships. *Journal of Business Research*, *192*, 115309–115309. DOI: 10.1016/j.jbusres.2025.115309

Sahut, J. M., & Lissillour, R. (2023). The adoption of remote work platforms after the Covid-19 lockdown: New approach, new evidence. *Journal of Business Research*, *154*, 113345. DOI: 10.1016/j.jbusres.2022.113345 PMID: 36193197

Sampat, B., Raj, S., Behl, A., & Schöbel, S. (2022). An empirical analysis of facilitators and barriers to the hybrid work model: A cross-cultural and multi-theoretical approach. *Personnel Review*, *51*(8), 1990–2020. DOI: 10.1108/PR-02-2022-0176

Simeli, I., Christou, E., & Chatzigeorgiou, C. (2025). Digital Nomads as Unintentional Influencers in Destination Branding: A Multi-Method Study of Ambient Influence. *Journal of Theoretical and Applied Electronic Commerce Research*, *20*(4), 340. DOI: 10.3390/jtaer20040340

Sjödin, D., Parida, V., & Kohtamäki, M. (2023). Artificial intelligence enabling circular business model innovation in digital servitization: Conceptualizing dynamic capabilities, AI capacities, business models and effects. *Technological Forecasting and Social Change*, *197*, 122903. DOI: 10.1016/j.techfore.2023.122903

Skillspark The Finishing School. (2026, January 20). Skillspark. https://skillspark.training/impact-of-automation-and-ai-on-accounting-jobs

Song, L., & Jo, S. J. (2023). How job crafting behaviors influence the innovative behavior of knowledge workers in the gig economy: Based on the organismic integration theory. *Frontiers in Psychology*, *14*, 1228881. Advance online publication. DOI: 10.3389/fpsyg.2023.1228881 PMID: 37731880

Steen, J., Klein, G., & Potts, J. (2022). 21st-Century General-Purpose Technologies and the Future of Project Management. *Project Management Journal*, *53*(5), 435–437. DOI: 10.1177/87569728221125095

Satya Subrahmanyam. (2025). Leveraging AI and ML for Enhanced Efficiency and Innovation in Manufacturing. Advances in Computational Intelligence and Robotics Book Series, 319–344. https://doi.org/DOI: 10.4018/979-8-3373-0442-7.ch021

Taeihagh, A. (2021). Governance of artificial intelligence. *Policy and Society*, *40*(2), 137–157. DOI: 10.1080/14494035.2021.1928377

Vohra, V., Banishetty, S., Dutta, T., & Joshi, A. (2024). Work, wander and repeat: Modeling the enablers of digital nomadic lifestyle. *Journal of Global Mobility*, *13*(1), 77–106. DOI: 10.1108/JGM-05-2024-0044

Wang, B., Tao, F., Fang, X., Liu, C., Liu, Y., & Freiheit, T. (2020). Smart Manufacturing and Intelligent Manufacturing: A Comparative Review. *Engineering (Beijing)*, *7*(6), 738–757. DOI: 10.1016/j.eng.2020.07.017

Windmann, A., Wittenberg, P., Schieseck, M., & Niggemann, O. (2017). *Artificial Intelligence in Industry 4.0: A Review of Integration Challenges for Industrial Systems*. IEEE., DOI: 10.1109/IN-

Yee, L., Chui, M., Roberts, R., & Smit, S. (2025, July 22). McKinsey Technology Trends Outlook 2025. McKinsey & Company. https://www.mckinsey.com/capabilities/tech-and-ai/our-insights/the-top-trends-in-tech

Zizic, M. C., Mladineo, M., Gjeldum, N., & Celent, L. (2022). From Industry 4.0 towards Industry 5.0: A Review and Analysis of Paradigm Shift for the People, Organization and Technology. *Energies*, *15*(14), 5221. DOI: 10.3390/en15145221

Chapter 9
The Digitalized Economy and the Transformation of E-Commerce Drivers and Research Trends

Fulya Taşel
http://orcid.org/0000-0001-6959-5776
Maltepe University, Turkey

Ebru Beyza Bayarçelik
http://orcid.org/0000-0003-4886-5719
Maltepe University, Turkey

ABSTRACT

E-commerce has become a fundamental force driving economic prosperity by transforming industries and business models alongside advances in information and communication technologies. The COVID-19 pandemic highlighted the critical role of e-commerce in sustaining economic activity and accelerated its adoption. This process caused changes in consumption behaviors and lifestyles, leading to new habits. Furthermore, e-commerce has generated positive effects in employment, economic restructuring, fairness, environmental protection and cultural interaction, while also carrying social and political implications. This study employs bibliometric analysis to evaluate the literature on e-commerce and digital economy. A total of 302 articles published between 2001 and 2025 were collected from the Web of Science database. The findings indicate that academic interest in e-commerce and the digital economy has increased since 2018. Future studies are expected to expand the knowledge base by focusing on emerging technologies such as artificial intelligence, big data, blockchain etc.

DOI: 10.4018/979-8-3373-5052-3.ch009

1. INTRODUCTION

The rise of the digital economy has created an innovative economy that uses both digital technologies and electronic communications to carry out economic and business operations across a wide range of sectors. These include e-commerce, digital marketing, digital financial services, software development, computer games and cloud services (Xia, Baghaie, & Sajadi, 2024; Cai, Wang, Ji, & Xu, 2024).

The so-called digital economy is the consequence of the close connection of all forms of national economic activities based on the latest technologies. Digital technology is one of the main drivers of the digital economy from a technological point of view (Jin, Xu, Zhu, & Li, 2023).

Within the digital economic environment, both economic and commercial transactions are carried out using digital technologies and electronic communication, resulting in a substantial shift of business interactions to online and digital platforms. This new economic model is recognized as a key factor in the economic development of a number of countries. With the constant evolution of the digital economy, it has major effects on various economic, social, and cultural areas (Xia, Baghaie, & Sajadi, 2024).

Digital technologies are increasingly become part of the daily structure of production and transportation of goods and services. In some cases, they contribute directly, while in others, they are indirectly involved in the process, but they still play a role in shaping the final outcome (Jin, Xu, Zhu, & Li, 2023). In practice, these technologies make it easier for intellectual work and capital to be shared and moved across borders. The declining importance of geographical boundaries and a more connected global environment begin with the improvements in digitalization. Information and communication technologies (ICT), which continue to grow with the help of strategic investments in areas such as artificial intelligence, big data, 5G and robotics, also form an important part of the digital economy (Rehman & Nunziante, 2023).

Technological progress and the transition to the digital economy generates new opportunities not only for new production techniques but also for new forms of organizational structures of businesses. Another important point is that the rise of the digital economy and the information and communication technologies (ICT), is the driving force behind industrial transformation in many different sectors (Rong, 2022). In other words, due to technological advancements, operational efficiency increases and new business models are introduced and enable the digital economy to create value.

In fact, the evolution of the digital economy has accelerated e-commerce applications while also enabling the growth of new business practices and numerous different sectors. In digital transformation, electronic commerce is an essential part of the digitized economy and one of its most visible aspects. While the digitized economy encompasses all commercial activities conducted using digital technologies, e-commerce refers to the buying and selling of goods and services over the internet through various online platforms and digital transactions. In today's business world, competition is now largely taking place on digital platforms, and therefore the importance of e-commerce, which is a key component of the digital economy, is increasing day by day (Hendricks & Mwapwele, 2024). In addition, e-commerce has become one of the most important approaches in businesses, leading to an increase in efficiency in companies' operations (Costa & Rodrigues, 2024).

E-commerce and digital transformation play an important role in all aspects, both on the supply side and on the consumer side. On the supply side, the impact of digitalization on the value chain is primarily seen in its ability to offer Omnichannel points of contact and to manage competitors. Similarly, on the consumer side, innovative evolutions in e-commerce and the digital economy are considered to improve the customer experience in an increasingly competitive environment and help consumers to protect their personal data (Olusanya & Isinkaye, 2025). Thoroughly, e-commerce encompasses every aspect of a transaction, including commercial market creation, ordering, supply chain management, and money transfer. It also includes a wide range of digital activities such as e-information exchange, e-capital movement, e-money, e-marketing, e-banking, e-insurance services, and more (Albshaier, Almarri, & Rahman, 2024).

As a result, this study conducts a systematic bibliometric evaluation of existing research that explores the connection between e-commerce and the digital economy. The evolution of the literature is analyzed by tracking key developments and publication patterns, highlighting major contributors and new research frontiers. This study aims to fill current gaps in the literature and offer practical insights for academics, decision-makers, and professionals in the economy and e-commerce field. Furthermore, the research applies a detailed bibliometric approach gathering data from Web of Science. To examine patterns of co-authorship, keyword analysis, and bibliographic coupling, the analysis is carried out with the support of the VOSviewer software.

2. DIGITAL ECONOMY

After the financial crisis of 2007–2008, which originated in the U.S. and later affected Europe and Asia, the world economy entered a different stage. Conventional growth patterns began to slow, while the digital economy driven by new technologies such as mobile internet, cloud computing, big data analytics, and artificial intelligence rapidly gained momentum (Li, Dan, Lang, Kauffman, & Naldi, 2020).

The path from the traditional economy to the digital economy is largely driven by automation, process standardization, reuse of goods and cloud computing, all of which are moving the global economy towards digitalization. This emphasizes the need to increase ICT skills in all sectors to maintain economic expansion (Li, Dan, Lang, Kauffman, & Naldi, 2020). These kinds of developments create both opportunities and challenges and need organizations to reconsider their strategic direction and adjust to a more connected and information-centric environment. This in turn speeds up the diffusion of next-generation digital technologies (artificial intelligence (AI), the Internet of Things (IoT), big data, blockchain etc.) (Si, Hall, Suddaby, Ahlstrom, & Wei, 2023).

According to the literature, the digital economy was first introduced by (Tapscott, 1996) in "The Digital Economy: Promise and Peril in the Age of Networked Intelligence". He described it not just as the outcome of advances in networking and computing, but as a deep restructuring of economic and social systems, powered by knowledge exchange, real-time connectivity, and distributed intelligence (Vu, Lu, & Shiba, 2025). Moreover, the World Economic Forum and the Group of Twenty have given a definition of the digital economy "broad range of economic activities that use digitized information and knowledge as key factors of production, modern information networks as an important activity space, as well as information and communications technology to drive productivity growth." (Li, Dan, Lang, Kauffman, & Naldi, 2020). In a narrow sense, the digital economy can be defined as an industrial economy derived directly from digital technology and primarily related to ICT sectors. In a broader sense, the digital economy can be considered a new form of economic activity (Jin, Xu, Zhu, & Li, 2023). Although definitions of the digital economy differ slightly across scholars and institutions, four elements are broadly recognized: data as a key production input, information networks as the channels that enable its flow, the digital economy as the result of economic activity, and digital technology as the central driver of its growth and increasing productivity levels (Shao & Wang, 2025).

Extensive use of such technologies enables the transformation of traditional systems, changes in governance and management practices and economic development. In this context, digitalisation is at the centre of today's technological approach and acts as a powerful catalyst for economic growth. Innovation has become a focal point for entrepreneurship and management studies (Si, Hall, Suddaby, Ahlstrom, & Wei, 2023; Wang, Liu, Wang, & Javaid, 2024). Creating connected digital infrastructure and promoting the broad use of technologies such as the Internet and mobile devices allows cross-border e-commerce to reduce costs across logistics, information search, and communication, compared with traditional trade methods (Han & Li, 2025).

Complementing these trends, the rise of the digital economy has strengthened foreign trade by fostering innovation, modernizing industries, and reshaping trade models. Big data analytics, cloud computing, and artificial intelligence in foreign trade boost production efficiency by encouraging the use of advanced methods (Liang & Chen, 2025). Alongside these impacts on trade, the development of the digitized economy has also spurred the rise of new business forms, like e-commerce and online learning etc. (Huang, Du, & Lin, 2025).

E-commerce has enabled goods to move more efficiently between regions, bridging urban and rural areas as well as more developed and less developed regions, and allowing flows in both directions (Phang, Wang, Wang, Kauffman, & Naldi, 2019).

While developments in information and communication technology have created significant advantages and opportunities, the expansion of the digital economy has also generated new socio-economic inequalities Differences and inequalities in the developments arising from access to information infrastructure and technologies between countries and even between regions within countries have given rise to a new concept called "digital divide" (Hüsnüoğlu & Öztürk, 2017).

The number of studies examining the relationship between digital development and income inequality is increasing. Digital technologies have facilitated the widespread adoption of e-commerce and cross-border commercial activities; however, the digital divide restricts fair and equal access in international markets. Internet access and regional digital divides reinforce and further increase digital inequalities in many remote rural areas, leading to a widening income gap.

The digital divide can be interpreted as the inability to reap the economic and social benefits of knowledge-intensive activities due to reasons such as inadequate infrastructure, high access costs, weak political regimes, and the inefficiency of telecommunications networks and services. Factors such as education, the quality of legislation, income, inadequacies in the regulations that political institutions need to implement, competition in the telecommunications sector, network effects, costs, the quality of foreign trade, and urbanization cause and deepen the digital divide. Data from countries at different economic levels, such as Africa and the OECD, show that digitalization provides different economic benefits to countries at different levels of development (Saberi & Sadegh, 2022; Hilmy Rizqullah Ramadhan, Ramadhani, Isrok, Anggraeny, & Prasetyo, 2024).

3. E-COMMERCE

The simplest and the general definition of trade is "the exchange, purchase, and sale of goods or products for other objects of economic value throughout the process from production to consumption" (Samuel, 1939). The earliest form of trade in human history was barter, a system in which goods and services were directly exchanged without the use of money. Driven by the desire to meet their needs, societies sought to obtain goods and services they did not possess from others, and in doing so, they began to exchange the goods they already owned. This practice laid the foundations of trade (Humphery & Hugh-Jones, 1992).

In its most basic definition, e-commerce refers to the buying and selling of goods and services through electronic platforms, primarily the internet. It originated in the 1960s with the development of Electronic Data Interchange (EDI), which enabled businesses to transfer documents from one computer to another in a standardized format, and accelerated in the 1990s with the advent of the Internet, facilitating the online exchange of goods and services (Mwencha, 2019).

The existence of different approaches to defining the concept of e-commerce makes it difficult to establish a more general definition of the term. This difficulty stems from the inadequacy of identifying the boundaries of e-commerce. In particular, rapid changes in information and communication technologies create new opportunities and new resources for e-commerce, thus causing existing definitions to become inadequate over time. For these reasons, there are different approaches and definitions for e-commerce (Coşkun, 2004).

In 2013, The World Trade Organization defined e-commerce as "online ordering is sufficient for a transaction to be considered e-commerce; payment and delivery do not have to take place electronically. These transactions include interactions among businesses, households, governments, and other institutions, excluding those made by phone or fax" (World Trade Organization, 2013). Similarly, the OECD defines e-commerce as "...the sale or purchase of goods or services, conducted over computer networks by methods specifically designed for the purpose of receiving or placing of orders" (OECD, 2021).

As a result of developments within the framework of e-commerce, many countries, global organizations, and institutions have shown interest in this field and have conducted research on its various aspects. Each institution addresses the subject in line with its own areas of interest and accordingly formulates its own definition. Among the leading international organizations that show particular interest in e-commerce and carry out studies in this area are the World Trade Organization (WTO), the Organization for Economic Cooperation and Development (OECD), the United Nations Conference on Trade and Development (UNCTAD) and the World Bank (WB). In addition to these, national institutions related to trade in various countries and international trade associations also closely examine this issue and strive to provide their members with the necessary infrastructure opportunities.

Especially after 2000's e-commerce starts to influece ever aspect of life such as trade, work, education, culture, and everyday social life. This change paves the way for the emergence of innovations and methods that are difficult to predict. Obviously, these developments have brought certain advantages and disadvantages for developed and developing countries. In specific, they offer new opportunities for SME'S, which are the backbone of the economy. Advances in information technology and globalization offer SME's the opportunity to enter international markets, find new raw materials and production opportunities, and reach potential customers to do international business (Yumuşak, 2001).

E-commerce contributes to the global economy by enabling producers and consumers to interact quickly, easily, and at any time, through the development of information technologies and digital tools. For countries with low levels of readiness, the growth of international e-commerce may expose local firms to increased import competition and thereby impact on employment and growth prospects. Moreover, electronic commerce offers benefits such as being able to shop from anywhere and at any time, flexible payment options, saving time and low transaction costs for consumers, while it provides opportunities for businesses to sell without intermediaries, create new markets, increase customer loyalty and revenues, improve supplier relationships, and reduce stocks and shipping costs.

Legal regulations for e-commerce, which has become an important part of the digital economy, are also given great importance.The United Nations General Assembly adopted the United Nations Commission on International Trade Law Model Law on Electronic Commerce on 30 January 1997. This law is advisory in nature. It is used by goverments as a basis for developing national legislation. The United States was one of the first countries to implement legal regulations for e-commerce relations. The US has defined the boundaries and restrictions in the field of electronic commerce by making some adjustments to its existing legislation which is named Fundamentals of Global E-Commerce (Gedik, 2021).

The process that began with the Industrial Revolution and extends to Industry 4.0 has brought about change and transformation. At the heart of this transformation lies the digitalization process triggered by information and communication technologies. The Covid-19 pandemic that emerged in 2020 was the biggest accelerator of this process and made e-commerce an indispensable part of life. Restrictions on going out and limitations on physical shopping made it difficult for consumers of all ages to shop, driving them to use online channels to meet their needs. Today, businesses inevitably turn to digital technologies and e-commerce platforms to survive. Digitalization, which is one of the most important requirements of today, has caused significant changes in the consumption habits of the new generation growing up in the digital world. Especially for Generation Z and millennials, e-commerce is beyond being just an alternative and has become an instant and interactive experience that starts on social media networks. This situation has caused businesses to reconsider their digital marketing strategies.

The sustainability concept requires the assessment of digitalization's environmental impacts alongside its economic benefits. While ICT supports productivity and growth, it also increases carbon emissions in economies. One of the most crucial topics in e-commerce is sustainability, which affects environmental, social, and economic dimensions separately. It shows that digital transformation in e-commerce can increase energy efficiency and reduce carbon emissions. However, due to increased logistics processes, packaging waste, and high energy consumption, there are still significant debates about the extent to which e-commerce supports sustainability. Delivering single products and handling frequent returns lead to more emissions and waste. These issues are even greater in international deliveries, especially when air transport is used. For this reason, more sustainable logistics and cleaner data infrastructure are needed to reduce the carbon footprint of digital trade (Mohamed, Helmy, & Ibrahiem, 2025).

According to a United Nations Conference on Trade and Development report, “e-commerce has the potential to reduce certain resource costs by minimizing the use of physical infrastructure and optimizing logistics. However, the rapid growth in online transactions has increased energy consumption and greenhouse gas emissions through the expansion of data center operations, packaging waste, and last-mile delivery” (United Nations Conference on Trade and Development, 2024;144).

As shown in Figure 1, the e-commerce market has been growing steadily since 2018 and is expected to keep rising until 2030. Asia Pacific leads the market, while North America and Europe also have large shares. The increase becomes faster after the pandemic, and by 2030 the global market is expected to reach around 57.6 trillion USD, showing that online shopping will continue to play a bigger role in the world economy.

Figure 1. E-Commerce Market

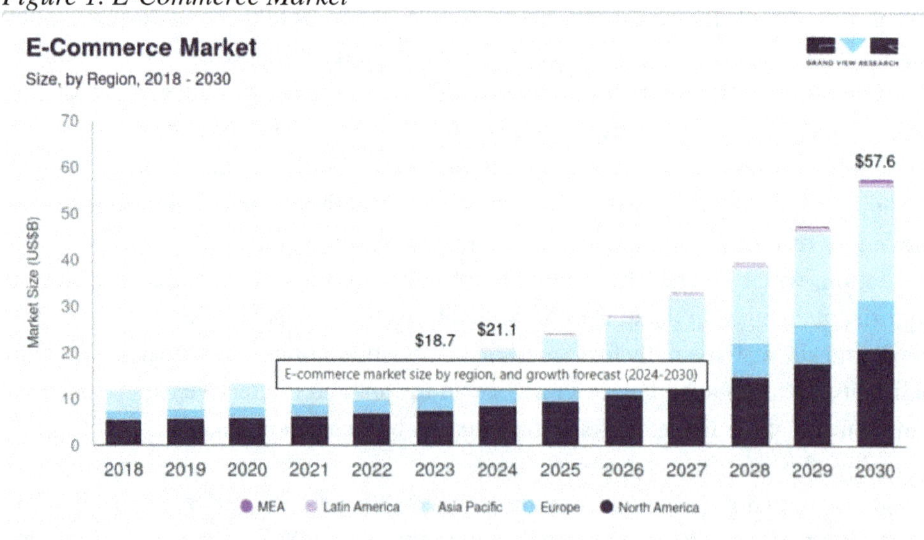

Source: Grand View Research, 2025

Today's global environment, businesses can maintain their sustainable competitive advantages by adapting to digital transformation. To achieve this, they must first redefine their capabilities and resources. We use the theory of dynamic capabilities to enable businesses to achieve sustainable firm performance by renewing and adapting their organizational capabilities to adapt to the changing market environment (Teece, 2007). The dynamic resources theory is defined as the ability to integrate, reconfigure, acquire, and release resources and has a positive relationship with the development of digital capabilities. Tams, Grover and Thatcher (2014) defined digital capability as "an organization's focused deployment of information and communication technologies (ICTs), abilities to develop, mobilize, and use organizational resources effectively, for instance, customer relationship management, new product development, and knowledge collaboration" (Tams, Grover, & Thatcher, 2014). Digital capabilities are fundamental dynamic capabilities for transforming customer experience, operational processes, and business models, and the absence of these skills and capabilities hinders digital transformation (Westerman, Bonnet, & McAfee, 2011). Digital capabilities are also becoming increasingly important, especially in e-commerce activities, in terms of organizations effectively using digital technologies to increase operational efficiency through data analytics, customer experience analyses, and platform-based business models, and responding nimbly to rapidly changing consumer expectations (Siguaw, Simpson, & Enz, 2006).

4. METHODOLOGY

Bibliometric analysis converts bibliographic details into analyzable data. In turn this process facilitates the identification and comparison of academic contributions (Cancinoa, Amirbagheri, Merigo, & Dessouky, 2019). Generally, bibliometric analysis offers two forms of understanding. The first examines the structure of the research field by showing how its themes and scholarly relationships unfold over time. The second highlights research activity and impact through publication and citation patterns (Lim, Kumar, & Donthu, 2024). Thus researchers can explore major trends through this approach by analyzing collections of academic publications (Laengle, et al., 2021). In addition, it helps researchers assess the present landscape of a research field and the potential directions a field may take (Donthu, Kumar, Mukherjee, Pandey, & Lim, 2021).

Therefore the results of this study are intended to assist researchers, scholars, and policymakers by highlighting key areas of interest and detecting new developments in the fields of the digital economy and e-commerce. In summary, these findings offer a strategic basis for shaping future research efforts and encouraging innovation within the field.

Given that few studies offer a combined perspective on e-commerce and the digital economy, this research aims to contribute to the field by exploring four key research questions:

RQ1: What developments can be identified in terms of the number of publications and the contributions of different countries and institutions to research on e-commerce in the digital economy over the period 2001–2025?

RQ2: What bibliometric insights can be drawn regarding authorship, including the most influential authors and the most cited countries?

RQ3: What are the key bibliometric findings related to the documents, particularly in terms of the most globally cited publications?

RQ4: What insights can be derived about the conceptual structure of the field, focusing on aspects such as co-authorship networks and bibliographic coupling?

Initially RQ1 focuses on how the research field has developed over time by looking at changes in publication activity and the varying roles of countries and institutions. After that, RQ2 and RQ3 shift the attention toward the people and the works that have had the strongest influence on the field's direction. Finally, RQ4 brings the earlier findings together by examining co-authorship networks and the bibliographic connections between studies. As a result, the questions show how the field is structured and how it has evolved.

Within this research, the data collection process began with the keyword "digital economy," which initially yielded 9,146 records in the Web of Science database. A more refined search combining "digital economy" and "e-commerce" reduced the number of results to 380. When filtered to include only journal articles, the dataset was further narrowed to 302 articles. Data were collected from the Web of Science database using a targeted search query applied to the titles, keywords, and abstracts fields. The search was conducted using the Web of Science Core Collection with the following query TS = ("digital economy") AND TS = ("e-commerce") AND DT = (Article). All searches and filtering were carried out online on Web of Science during the data collection session completed on 15.07.2025, and the final dataset reflects the records available on that day. The construction of the dataset followed a clear and sequential search procedure, which is outlined in the flowchart below in Figure 2.

Figure 2. Steps of the Data Retrieval and Filtering Process

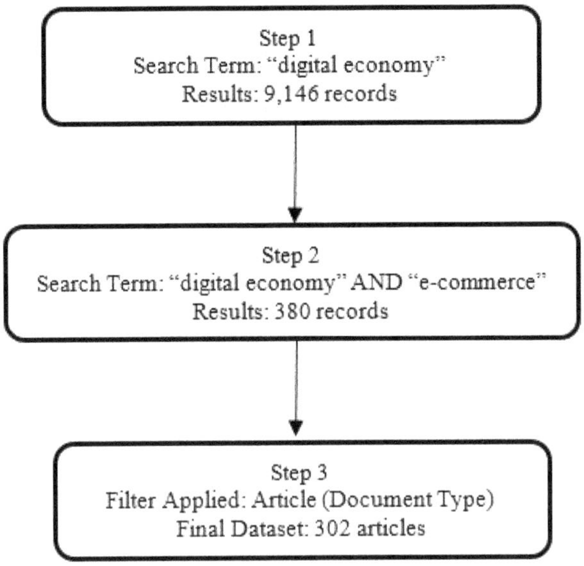

During the selection of the publications, certain boundaries had to be set so that the material used in the study would remain manageable and relevant to the topic. For this reason, a number of inclusion and exclusion criteria were applied while forming the dataset which is given Table 1. These criteria simply served to clarify which studies were suitable for the analysis and which ones did not fit the purpose of the research. The main points taken into consideration during this process are outlined below.

Table 1. Inclusion and Exclusion Criteria for the Dataset

Category	Inclusion Criteria	Exclusion Criteria
Search Terms	The dataset includes records that contain the terms *"digital economy"* or the combined query *"digital economy" AND "e-commerce"*. These terms were searched within titles, keywords, and abstracts.	Records in which the relevant terms do not appear in the title, abstract, or keywords were excluded.
Document Type	Only peer-reviewed journal articles were taken into consideration.	Conference papers, book chapters, books, editorial notes, proceedings abstracts, and other non–peer-reviewed materials were excluded.
Publication Period	Publications dated between 2001 and 2025 (until 15 July 2025) were included.	Studies published before 2001 and after 2025 (after 15 July 2025) were left out.
Database Source	All records were retrieved from the Web of Science Core Collection.	Materials from other databases or those not indexed in Web of Science were not considered.
Relevance to the Topic	Articles that directly address the digital economy, e-commerce, or related themes were included.	Publications that fall outside the scope of digital economy or e-commerce, or that show thematic inconsistency, were excluded.
Data Quality	Unique entries that met the above criteria were kept for analysis.	Duplicate records were removed during the cleaning process.

The selection was limited to articles published between 2001 and 2025, drawn from all available records in the database. The subsequent analysis was conducted based on these 302 selected articles. The results are given in Table 2.

Table 2. Data Set between 2001-2025

Title/Abstract/Author Keywords	Total Documents	Document Type Article
"Digital Economy"	9146	6812
"Digital Economy" and "e-commerce"	380	302

Source: Numbers are gathered from Web of Science database

This subject is not limited to one field. The topic of the digital economy and e-commerce is widely studied across many different academic fields. This topic engages scholars from a variety of academic backgrounds. As it is shown in Figure 3 while economics, business, and management disciplines seems the primary disciplines where most research efforts are conducted, the study of digital economy and e-commerce has expanded to include computer science, information systems, environmental sciences, and sustainable technologies. Furthermore, these topics are frequently examined through the perspectives of international relations and law, highlighting their broad implications for global policymaking and regulations about the subject.

Figure 3. Distribution of total articles "Digital Economy" and "e-commerce" within Web of Science Categories between 2001-2025 years

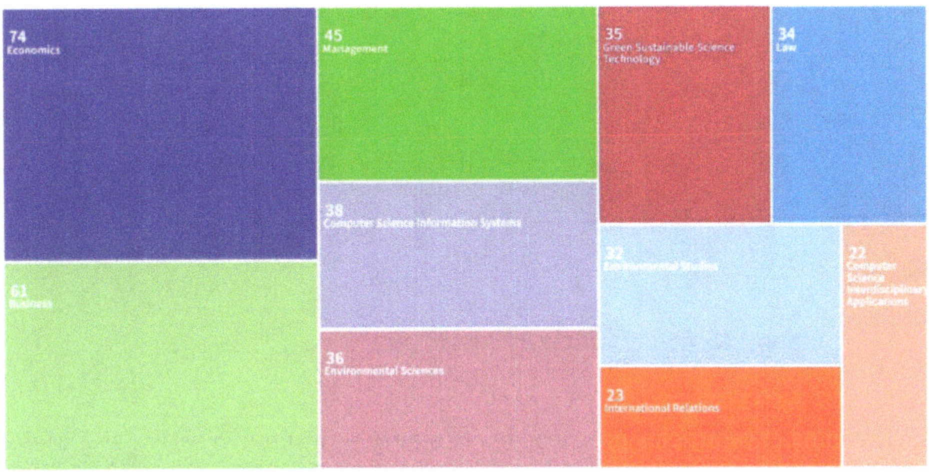

Source: Numbers are gathered from Web of Science database

As it is shown in Figure 4 the number of publications in this field has shown an upward trend and has been steadily increasing over recent years, reflecting growing scholarly interest and the expanding importance of the topic. This increase highlights the rising popularity of the subject and growing academic interest.

Figure 4. Distribution of publication years of total articles "Digital Economy" and "e-commerce" between 2016-2025 years

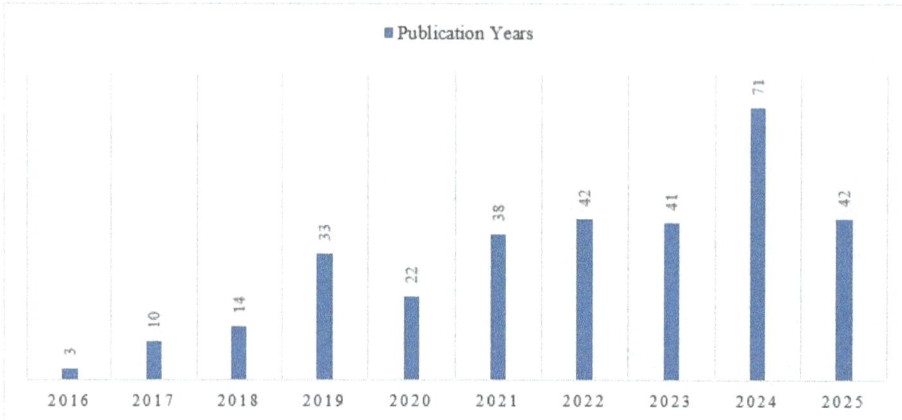

Source: Numbers are gathered from Web of Science database

The number of articles produced by a country or institution serves as a useful indication of its overall research strength. Examining collaborative networks among countries or institutions also helps reveal how the key contributors in a given field are positioned and how research efforts are distributed (Mo & Wang, 2025). This can also be seen in how research output is spread across countries.

Table 3. Top ten countries of total articles "Digital Economy" and "e-commerce"

Countries/Regions	*Number*
Peoples Republic of China	*129*
USA	21
Ukraine	20
Russia	19
Poland	15
India	14
England	13
Malaysia	10
Indonesia	9
Australia	7.

Source: Numbers are gathered from Web of Science database

Furthermore, in recent years, this topic has attracted significant attention from researchers across a wide range of countries. As given in Table 3 notably China currently ranks first in terms of research output, followed by the US. In addition other countries with a strong presence in this area include Ukraine, Russia, Poland, and India. This indicates that the diversity of contributing nations reflects the worldwide relevance and interdisciplinary character of the digital economy and e-commerce.

As it is shown in Figure 5 which displays the first ten journals publishing on this topic, the top three journals are Sustainability (27 Articles), Baltıc Journal of Economic Studies (7 Articles) and Journal of the Knowledge Economy (6 Articles).

Figure 5. Journals with the highest publication in "digital economy" and "e-commerce"

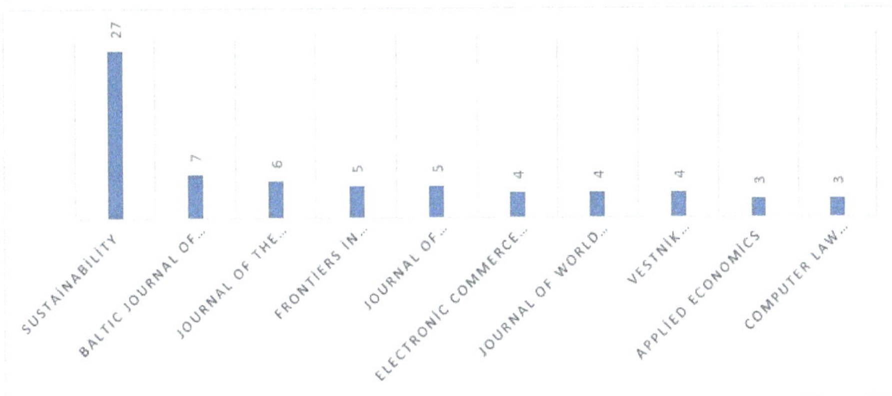

Source: Numbers are gathered from Web of Science database

Co-authorship refers to a group of researchers who collaboratively publish the outcomes of their shared research interests through various formats such as journal articles, conference proceedings, and books. Specifically, a co-authorship network represents these collaborations, where each node signifies a researcher and the connections (edges) illustrate their collaborative relationships. Accordingly, understanding and predicting co-authorship patterns requires analyzing a variety of data extracted from scholarly publications. For example, this includes metadata such as article titles, keywords, abstracts, institutional affiliations, research performance indicators (like citation counts or h-index), publication dates and years, the venues where the work appeared (journals, conferences), and the bibliographic references cited within the publications. These factors together help reveal the structure and dynamics of academic collaboration across disciplines and institutions (Yuliansyah, Othman, & Bakar, 2025).

Figure 6 shows the co-authorship analysis, which highlights the collaborative relationships among researchers and the structure of their academic network about the topic digital economy and e-commerce. The figure shows that the network structure reveals a clear separation of the two main clusters. There are two clusters on the left and right side. The cluster of authors on the right-hand side has a more limited number of connections, but forms a coherent subset.

Figure 6. Co-authorship analysis of the keywords "Digital Economy" and "e-commerce"

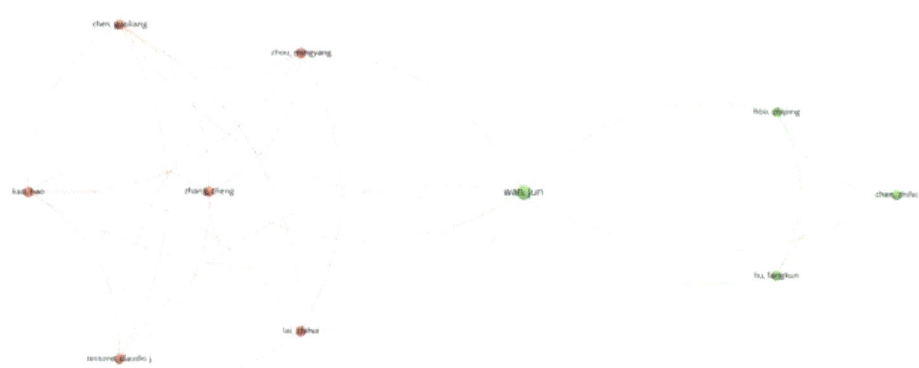

Source: Web of Science database and VOSviewer

Next, in a bibliographic coupling network, a relationship is formed between two documents when they cite one or more of the same references. In other words, this connection signifies a potential similarity in subject matter or research focus. The strength of the link between these documents referred to as the degree of bibliographic coupling is measured by the number of references they have in common. The greater the number of shared citations, the stronger the implied connection between the two papers, suggesting that they may address related topics or draw from a similar body of prior research. This method is widely used to analyze thematic relationships and intellectual structures within a specific field of study (Li, Wu, Wang, & Zeng, 2022). Figure 7 shows the bibliographic coupling analysis about the topic digital economy and e-commerce, which highlights the earlier cited publications that summarize what's already been done in the field.

Figure 7. Bibliographic coupling analysis of the keywords "Digital Economy" and "e-commerce"

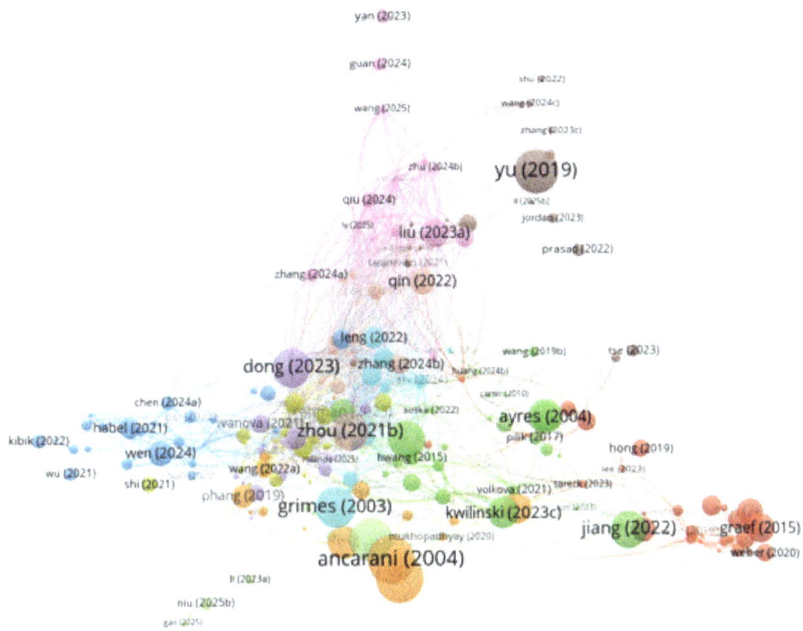

Source: Web of Science database and VOSviewer

As it is shown in Figure 8 since 2018, there has been a noticeable and consistent rise in academic engagement with the topic, as demonstrated by a steady increase in both the volume of related publications and the frequency of citations. This upward trend indicates the rising interest in the topic within academic and research networks. Over time, this interest continued and accelerated, reflecting developments in the field and the emergence of new research areas. As can be seen in Figure 8, this trend reached its peak in 2024, making it a landmark year in terms of academic work. Furthermore, this outlook in 2024 may also indicate the convergence of technological developments, policy levels, or interdisciplinary applicability that brought the subject to the center of the researchers.

Figure 8. Times Cited and Publications Over Time

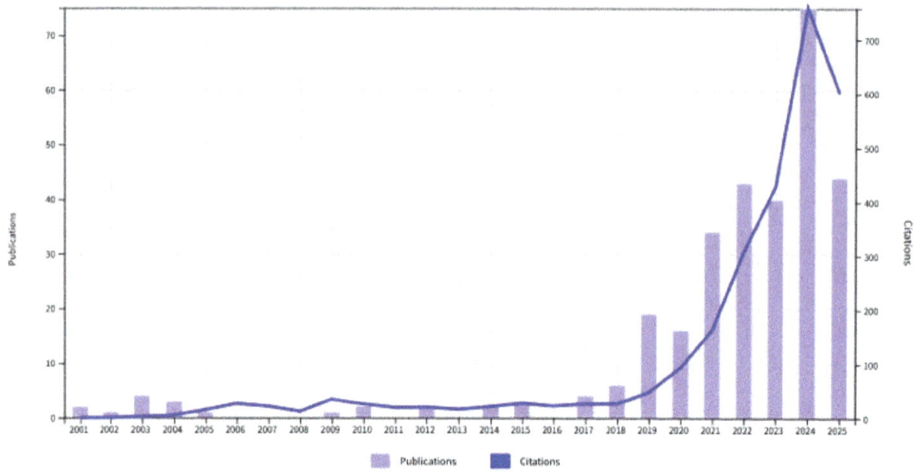

Source: Web of Science database

Overall, the findings discussed so far are consistent with earlier studies that have examined how the field has expanded and shifted over time. Following this, to place these developments in context, it is helpful to look at the studies that have played an important part in the development of the digital economy and e-commerce literature.

5. EVIDENCE FROM THE LITERATURE: DIGITAL ECONOMY AND E-COMMERCE

In this study, research on the digital economy and e-commerce was first reviewed, followed by an examination of the recommendations for future research obtained from highly cited studies and their relationship with new trends. Hence, the findings of this study have shown that some frequently cited studies shape the current literature and make significant contributions to future technologies, trends, potential challenges, and opportunities in this field. Consequently, the contributions and findings of highly cited paper are discussed below.

According to Kwilinski, Lyulyov, and Pimonenko (2023), Information comunication technology directly supports economic expansion by increasing efficiency, encouraging innovation, and improving effectiveness across sectors. ICT supports the emergence of new industries, streamlines business processes, and enhances competitiveness. Furthermore, the adoption of ICT solutions contributes to higher productivity and sustainable economic growth. Additionally, technological innovation plays a key role in translating digital transformation in both business and public sectors into stronger environmental, social, and governance (ESG) outcomes. In view of this information, policymakers are encouraged to intensify digitalization initiatives and harness the digital economy as a strategic engine for growth (Kwilinski, Lyulyov, & Pimonenko, 2023).

One of these studies is Murthy and colleagues' article titled "The digital economy from a global perspective: Is there a digital divide?", which examines the relationship between economic development variables and digitalization using growth models. Research findings indicate that economic growth drives digitalization. In addition, while fixed-line services among information communication tools are declining worldwide, broadband services are growing faster than mobile services. At the same time, mobile services are playing a driving role in developing economies, while broadband is doing so in developed economies. Another significant result of this analysis is that the contribution of developed countries to the transition of the global economic system to digitalization has been tested using growth modelling methods. Furthermore, the analysis indicates that developed countries with strong e-commerce have larger market shares in the global economy than other countries; there is significant inequality between developed and developing economies; and the majority of the output of information and communication technologies is shared between developed economies and the top five developing countries (Murthy, Kalsie, & Shankar, 2021).

Dong, Yang, & Wang (2023) stated that; e-commerce has grown rapidly through the development of digital platforms and the Internet, becoming one of the fastest-growing sectors and a major driver of the digital economy. Its core model online retail transforms traditional offline sales into digital channels, enhances the flow and diffusion of knowledge, speeds up the growth of logistics and transportation, and supports overall economic progress. The expansion of e-commerce also supports the evolution of traditional service industries, including innovations like "smart logistics" and "green finance," boosting the productivity and third sector production and facilitating the advancement of green industries. Additionally, e-commerce enables seamless, low-cost information sharing, improves industrial efficiency, reduces energy consumption, and drives technological innovation (Dong, Yang, & Wang, 2023).

Sui and Rejeski (2002) argue that the internet, one of its core parts information technology, creates both opportunities and threats for environmental change. Throughout history, technology has changed economic structures and produced both positive and negative environmental outcomes. Similarly, the environmental footprints of producers' and consumers' activities influenced by technology continue today. However, e-commerce also contributes to waste reduction by facilitating the easier online trading of reused and recycled products (Sui & Rejeski, 2002).

Zhou and colleagues noted in their 2021 research that, unlike other studies, digital technologies are a catalyst for economic and social development, but they also bring new opportunities and regulations for environmental management, energy efficiency, and emission reduction. A central characteristic of the digital economy is the efficient sharing of information, which has reshaped logistics and fueled the rapid expansion of industries like e-commerce, supported by widespread internet and mobile usage. According to this study conducted between 2011 and 2018 to examine the correlation among the digital economy and air quality in China, e-commerce increases smog pollution, with the eastern provinces of China being the most affected. These findings emphasize that governments should use the digital economy and growing e-commerce activities to promote control of environmental impacts such as air pollution and carbon emissions (Zhou, Lan, Zhao, & Zhou, 2021).

Table 4. Most Frequently Used Digital Technologies in Digital Economy and E-commerce Research

Title/Abstract/Author Keywords	Document Type Article
"Digital Economy" and "e-commerce" and "Artificial Intelligence"	17
"digital economy" and "e-commerce" and "big data"	16
"Digital Economy" and "e-commerce" and "blockchain"	11
"digital economy" and "e-commerce" and "cybersecurity"	6

Source: Numbers are gathered from Web of Science database

In addition to the digital economy and e-commerce covered in this study, a more comprehensive examination was desired. The increasing importance of digital technologies such as artificial intelligence, big data, cloud computing, and blockchain has given rise to the concept of digital economy. Accordingly, the literature was reviewed to identify the digital technologies most commonly used, and the findings presented in Table 4 were obtained based on Web of Science (WoS) data. The search was conducted using the Web of Science Core Collection with the following query TS = ("digital economy") AND TS = ("e-commerce") AND TS = ("Artificial Intelligence") AND DT = (Article). The results show that, artificial intelligence appears in 17 studies. The second research is conducted with the following query TS = ("digital economy") AND TS = ("e-commerce") AND TS = ("big data") AND DT = (Article) resulted with 16 studies. Next research is conducted with the following query TS = ("digital economy") AND TS = ("e-commerce") AND TS = ("blockchain") AND DT = (Article) and blockchain is covered in 11 studies. Lastly the next research is conducted with the following query TS = ("digital economy") AND TS = ("e-commerce") AND TS = ("cybersecurity") AND DT = (Article) and resulted with 6 studies.

When the articles covered in this study are examined, it becomes apparent that artificial intelligence and big data rank first and second, demonstrating that these are frequently studied technology areas in the literature. Furthermore, research on technologies such as blockchain and cybersecurity is seen to be increasing, which also indicates a growing interest in research on secure digital systems. These are the most frequently studied digital technologies in the literature and also play an important role in the development and operational applications of the digital economy and e-commerce sectors.

The development and spread of digital technologies (artificial intelligence, the Internet of Things, big data and robotic etc.) are advancing and spreading rapidly, with the potential to influence business models, entrepreneurial practices, innovation ecosystems, and society (Si, Hall, Suddaby, Ahlstrom, & Wei, 2023).

The rapid expansion of e-markets and e-commerce has generated vast amounts of data on consumer online behavior (Phang, Wang, Wang, Kauffman, & Naldi, 2019). With advances in artificial intelligence and big data analytics, e-commerce has seen a major shift especially in improving customer experiences. The importance of this process is becoming more evident as platforms are now using highly sophisticated machine learning algorithms. With the help of this, it is possible to predict consumer preferences, habits and segment their behavior and deliver personalized experiences in real time to make more informed decisions and better understand target markets. This enables companies to improve the customer experience while providing personalized services to their customers and develop individualized profiles for each of them (Turki, 2025; Phang, Wang, Wang, Kauffman, & Naldi, 2019).

Papastamoulou and Antonopoulos (2025) stated that artificial intelligence is becoming more influential in digital commerce, and this makes it important for future studies to rely on reliable, quantifiable indicators rather than broad assumptions. Long-term data could also shed light on how AI capabilities develop over time and whether early adopters keep their advantage (Papastamoulou & Antonopoulos, 2025). Meltzer in his study supported that artificial intelligence improve the competitiveness of companies by analyzing high volumes of data and generating correct estimates. Hence artificial intelligence plays an important role in facilitation of trade by supporting broader efforts to digitalize trade transactions (Meltzer, 2024).

One of the other important digital technology is Big Data which is an important an integral part of the digital economy. Big data serves as a key driver for fostering advancements in technology, enhancing industrial structures, and optimizing resource allocation, thereby playing a vital role in business growth (Huang, Du, & Lin, 2025).

For sustainable, long-term growth, e-commerce companies should adopt a marketing strategy that is data-driven, customer-centric, and based on multi-channel engagement (Ma & Gu,2024). But on the other side there are some concerns about data privacy, fairness in algorithms, and shifts in the labor market. While some routine tasks may decline, new digital roles are likely to emerge, highlighting the need for new skill development and also the regulations related with artifical intelligence may create practical difficulties for companies. Because of this there is a need for policy adaptation (Papastamoulou & Antonopoulos, 2025).

Polyakov and Kovshun (2021) stated that the quality of its digital ecosystem is closely tied to a company's orientation and operational approach and if there is a well-developed ecosystem in place, then innovation is triggered and providing the necessary tools for efficient Big Data processing (Polyakov & Kovshun, 2021).

In today's highly competitive market, leveraging advanced big data analytics is no longer optional; it is essential. Companies must use these tools effectively to design marketing strategies that align with the specific needs and dynamics of the e-commerce sector (Ma & Gu, 2024).

E-commerce and the digital economy, are important concepts and gaining more and more importance and still having growth potential. However, challenges such as privacy, data security, costs, and transparency continue to pose substantial barriers to the advancement of e-commerce. Existing solutions to these problems sometimes lacking. In this context, blockchain technology is increasingly recognized as a promising and innovative approach for addressing these limitations (Treiblmaier & Sillaber, 2021).

Another important issue related to e-commerce and the digital economy is cybersecurity. E-commerce enables businesses to expand their markets and allows consumers to benefit from online transactions, yet it simultaneously introduces significant cybersecurity threats. Social engineering, personal data violations, Distributed Denial Cyber Security attacks, and malware pose the most common risks in the e-commerce ecosystem. According to Liu and colleagues (2022), the underlying causes of these threats can be divided into three main factors: human factors, technological vulnerabilities, and organizational unpreparedness. Moreover, many organizations lack sufficient security policies, tools, and effective response mechanisms. Thus, ensuring the sustainable growth of e-commerce requires continuous investment in secure technologies, employee training, and the enforcement of robust security policies. However, the constant evolution of attack techniques renders cybersecurity a dynamic and ongoing challenge (Liu, et al., 2022).

The other critical matter about electronic commerce is about protecting personal data which has become one of the most significant challenges in digital commerce. Data breaches and cyberattacks create serious risks for both users and businesses. Differences in data protection rules across countries make supervision and enforcement more difficult, that also weakens accountability. Therefore, unless stronger regulatory measures are developed, the benefits of digital transformation may remain limited to certain groups, while disadvantaged communities may fall further behind. Therefore, improving digital access and creating effective regulations is crucial to ensuring fair and sustainable growth in the digital economy.

Previous studies and bibliometric analysis results indicate that the digital economy and e-commerce are developing day by day. These findings not only highlight the significant role of digital technologies (artificial intelligence, big data, blockchain, and cybersecurity, etc.) in shaping current research and applications, but also provide a comprehensive overview that serves as a basis for discussing their broader implications and drawing the final conclusions of this study.

6. CONCLUSION

After the 2000s, increasing globalization and developments in information and telecommunications technologies first expanded the boundaries of international trade and subsequently transformed global economic activities. In particular, the legal and political regulations and investments created by various countries for e-commerce activities over the last decade have made e-commerce an important and irreplaceable part of global economic activities. In addition, the growing international e-commerce market, technological innovation, model innovation, optimization of market structure, and improvement of the policy environment have provided a qualitative leap, thereby expanding the market qualitatively as well (Mo & Wang, 2025). The current picture is consistent with the continuous growth of publications related to e-commerce.

Bibliometric analysis is the numerical determination of publications produced by individuals or institutions in a specific field, during a specific period, and in a specific region, as well as the relationships between these publications. In this study, it is aimed to analyze the current situation by examining studies conducted in the literature on digital economy and e-commerce. For this purpose, systematic literature review was conducted by examining articles on digital economy and e-commerce published in journals indexed in Web of Science between 2001 and 2025. The main objective is to identify the gaps and potential opportunities that arise while revealing the developments in the field of digital economy and e-commerce with the advancement of information and communication technologies.

The results of bibliometric analyses conducted on 302 articles in the WOS database between 2001 and 2025 are as follows:

Academic studies related to e-commerce in the digital economy have been increasing, especially after 2018. Scientific research in the fields of the digital economy and e-commerce is generally conducted under groups such as digital platform-based business models, consumer behavior, digital customer relations, mobile and social media commerce, sustainable supply chain management, e-waste policies, cybersecurity and personal data protection, digital equality and inclusivity. Since these fields come from different disciplines, it is clear that the subject adopts an approach that combines a wide variety of academic fields, including not only social and human sciences, but also computer science, information systems, environmental sciences, sustainable technologies, international relations, and law. Although the studies appear to be primarily conducted in the fields of business and management disciplines based on mapping results, computer science, information systems, environmental sciences, and sustainable technologies have also been included in the scope of trade.

China is the leading country in the field of digital economy and e-commerce, with 129 articles out of the 302 articles included in the study, followed by the United States. Other countries with a strong presence in this field include Ukraine, Russia, Poland, and India. China is the world's fastest-growing e-commerce market share country, with its large number of producers and consumers and continuously increasing transaction volume (Xiao, Guo, Guo, Yu, & Liu, 2019; Ferrer-Gomila, Hinarejos, & Isern-Deyà, 2019). In addition, the Chinese government has implemented incentives, policies, and legal regulations to support the growth of the e-commerce market. All these developments provide academics with rich data sources and a suitable environment for case studies, increasing the number of scientific articles published (Mo & Wang, 2025).

The journals that published articles on topics related to the digital economy and e-commerce in 302 articles are, in order: Sustainability (27 articles), Baltic Journal of Economic Studies (7 articles), and Journal of the Knowledge Economy (6 articles).

This study also reveals co-authorship and collaborations, while mapping techniques and bibliometric link networks were used to create network structures based on authors' specific research areas. Studies related to e-commerce and the digital economy increased linearly from 2018 to 2025, peaking in 2024. The most important reasons for this are the global COVID-19 pandemic in 2019 and the digital transformation that began with Industry 4.0.

In addition to the digital economy and e-commerce addressed in this study, emerging digital technologies such as artificial intelligence, big data, cloud computing, blockchain, and cybersecurity have also been analyzed. Artificial intelligence and big data rank first and second, indicating that these are frequently studied technology in the literature.

According to the results obtained in this study, the increase in the market share of e-commerce in the digital economy began with the development of information and communication technologies and continued with the emergence of new digital technologies and the widespread use of Industry 4.0's digital transformation. In particular, the restrictions and lockdowns experienced during the COVID-19 pandemic in 2019 have accelerated the speed and reach of e-commerce. All these developments have enhanced the speed, structure, and technologies used in e-commerce, enabling it to reach more customers globally with a service approach tailored to individual needs and preferences. Additionally, differences in the infrastructure, investment, policy and legal regulations required for information technologies between countries and even regions within the same country, have led to accessibility issues and digital divide. The spread of sustainability awareness has also transformed supply chain activities, which are the most important part of e-commerce, increasing the use of green supply, reverse logistics, carbon footprint reduction, and circular activities.

However, bibliometric analyses were conducted using the high-quality Web of Science database, the lack of use of other specialized databases may have led to the exclusion of important articles, misrepresentation of the research population and bias. The digital economy and electronic commerce concepts are mostly studied by specific countries such as China and the United States, which leads to geographical bias. This again reduces the representativeness of the sample and limits its generalizability to non-English speaking and underrepresented countries.

For future studies, bibliometric analysis can be renewed with a wider literature by using different databases such as Scopus. In addition, conference papers, book chapters, books, editorial notes, proceedings abstracts, and other non-peer-reviewed materials, which were not excluded in this study, can be included in the scope of the research to provide a more in-depth and multidimensional bibliometric analysis.

The interaction between the digital economy and e-commerce is largely shaped by technological developments. Government policies and regulations, geographical and physical conditions play an important regulatory role in this relationship. In this context, there is a distinct lack of comprehensive theoretical models and policy-oriented research. In order to address these gaps, it is important that future research develops approaches that draw from and integrate different disciplines such as technological, economic, social and regulatory dimensions. Furthermore, examining digital technologies (artificial intelligence, big data, blockchain, IoT) in conjunction with current mainstream issues such as green supply chain carbon neutrality and carbon emissions emerges as an orientation that can be discussed more in the future.

REFERENCES

Albshaier, L., Almarri, S., & Rahman, M. (2024). A Review of Blockchain's Role in E-Commerce Transactions: Open Challenges, and Future Research Directions. *Computers, 13*(1), 1–42. DOI: 10.3390/computers13010027

Cai, H., Wang, Z., Ji, Y., & Xu, L. (2024). Digitalization and innovation: How does the digital economy drive technology transfer in China? *Economic Modelling, 136*, 106758. Advance online publication. DOI: 10.1016/j.econmod.2024.106758

Cancinoa, C., Amirbagheri, K., Merigo, J., & Dessouky, Y. (2019). A bibliometric analysis of supply chain analytical techniques published in Computers & Industrial Engineering. *Computers & Industrial Engineering, 137*, 106015. DOI: 10.1016/j.cie.2019.106015

Coşkun, A. G. (2004). Elektronik ticaretin gelişiminde temel dinamikler ve gelişimi önündeki engeller. *Çukurova Üniversitesi Sosyal Bilimler Enstitüsü Dergisi*, 243-258.

Costa, P., & Rodrigues, H. (2024). The ever-changing business of e-commerce-net benefits while designing a new platform for small companies. *Review of Managerial Science, 18*(9), 2507–2545. DOI: 10.1007/s11846-023-00681-6

Dong, K., Yang, S., & Wang, J. (2023). How digital economy lead to low-carbon development in China? The case of e-commerce city pilot reform. *Journal of Cleaner Production, 391*, 136177. Advance online publication. DOI: 10.1016/j.jclepro.2023.136177

Donthu, N., Kumar, S., Mukherjee, D., Pandey, N., & Lim, W. (2021). How to conduct a bibliometric analysis: An overview and guidelines. *Journal of Business Research, 133*, 285–296. DOI: 10.1016/j.jbusres.2021.04.070

Ferrer-Gomila, J.-L., Hinarejos, M., & Isern-Deyà, A.-P. (2019). A fair contract signing protocol with blockchain support. *Electronic Commerce Research and Applications, 36*, 1567–4223. DOI: 10.1016/j.elerap.2019.100869

Gedik, Y. (2021). E-Ticaret: Teorik Bir Çerçeve. *Ankara Üniversitesi Sosyal Bilimler Dergisi, 12*(1), 184–198. DOI: 10.33537/sobild.2021.12.1.16

Grand View Research. (2025). Retrieved from E-commerce Market (2024 - 2030): https://www.grandviewresearch.com/industry-analysis/e-commerce-market

Han, G., & Li, F. (2025). Digital economy of trading partner countries, outward investment, and cross-border E-commerce exports. *Finance Research Letters, 85*, 108034. Advance online publication. DOI: 10.1016/j.frl.2025.108034

Hendricks, S., & Mwapwele, S. D. (2024). A systematic literature review on the factors influencing e-commerce adoption in developing countries. *Data and Information Management, 8*(1), 100045. Advance online publication. DOI: 10.1016/j.dim.2023.100045

Hilmy Rizqullah Ramadhan, M., Ramadhani, K., Isrok, M., Anggraeny, I., & Prasetyo, R. (2024). Legal Protection of Personal Data in Artificial Intelligence for Legal Protection Viewed From Legal Certainty Aspect. *KnE Social Sciences, 9(1), 125–13, 9*(1). DOI: 10.18502/kss.v8i21.14710

Huang, C., Du, A. M., & Lin, B. (2025). How does the digital economy affect the green transition: The role of industrial intelligence and E-commerce. *Research in International Business and Finance, 73*, 102541. Advance online publication. DOI: 10.1016/j.ribaf.2024.102541

Humphery, C., & Hugh-Jones, S. (1992). *Barter, Exchange and Value: An Anthropological Approach*. Cambridge University Press. DOI: 10.1017/CBO9780511607677

Hüsnüoğlu, N., & Öztürk, L. (2017). Dijital Bölünme: Nedenleri Ve Türleri. *Giresun Üniversitesi İktisadi ve İdari Bilimler Dergisi, 3*(5), 6–21.

Jin, C., Xu, A., Zhu, Y., & Li, J. (2023). Technology growth in the digital age: Evidence from China. *Technological Forecasting and Social Change, 187*, 122221. Advance online publication. DOI: 10.1016/j.techfore.2022.122221

Kwilinski, A., Lyulyov, O., & Pimonenko, T. (2023). Unlocking Sustainable Value through Digital Transformation: An Examination of ESG Performance. *Information (Basel), 14*(8), 444. Advance online publication. DOI: 10.3390/info14080444

Laengle, S., Lobos, V., Merigo, J., Herrera-Viedma, E., Cobo, M., & De Baets, B. (2021). Forty years of Fuzzy Sets and Systems: A bibliometric analysis. *Fuzzy Sets and Systems, 402*, 155–183. DOI: 10.1016/j.fss.2020.03.012

Li, H., Wu, M., Wang, Y., & Zeng, A. (2022). Bibliographic coupling networks reveal the advantage of diversification in scientific projects. *16*. DOI: 10.1016/j.joi.2022.101321

Li, K., Dan, K. J., Lang, K. R., Kauffman, R. J., & Naldi, M. (2020). How should we understand the digital economy in Asia? Critical assessment and research agenda. *44*. DOI: 10.1016/j.elerap.2020.101004

Liang, M., & Chen, H. (2025). Digital economy development, regional openness, and high-quality foreign trade. *Finance Research Letters, 81*, 107469. Advance online publication. DOI: 10.1016/j.frl.2025.107469

Lim, W., Kumar, S., & Donthu, N. (2024). How to combine and clean bibliometric data and use bibliometric tools synergistically: Guidelines using metaverse research. *Journal of Business Research*, *182*, 114760. DOI: 10.1016/j.jbusres.2024.114760

Liu, X., Ahmad, S., Sayed, F., Fayaz, A., Anser, M., & Ke, J. (2022). Cyber security threats: A never-ending challenge for e-commerce. *Frontiers in Psychology*, *13*, 927398. Advance online publication. DOI: 10.3389/fpsyg.2022.927398 PMID: 36337532

Ma, X., & Gu, X. (2024). New marketing strategy model of E-commerce enterprises in the era of digital economy. *Heliyon*, *10*(8), e29038. Advance online publication. DOI: 10.1016/j.heliyon.2024.e29038 PMID: 38628774

Meltzer, J. (2024). The Impact of Foundational AI on International Trade, Services and Supply Chains in Asia. *Asian Economic Policy Review*, *19*(1), 129–147. DOI: 10.1111/aepr.12451

Mo, R., & Wang, S. (2025). E-commerce Research in the Past Decade: A Bibliometric Analysis. *SAGE Open*, *15*(3), 21582440251381152. Advance online publication. DOI: 10.1177/21582440251381152

Mohamed, M., Helmy, O., & Ibrahiem, D. (2025). Digitalization and Carbon Footprint: Does ICT Reduce Carbon Footprint? *Digital Technologies Research and Applications*, *4*(3), 136–158. DOI: 10.54963/dtra.v4i3.1306

Murthy, K., Kalsie, A., & Shankar, R. (2021). Digital economy in a global perspective: Is there a digital divide? *Transnational Corporations Review*, *13*(1), 1–15. DOI: 10.1080/19186444.2020.1871257

Mwencha, P. (2019). Taxation Of Electronic Commerce-A Commentary. *Finance & Development*, *1*(1), 70–79.

OECD. (2021). *OECD Publishing*. doi:http://dx.doi.org/.DOI: 10.1787/10.1787/9789264113-41-en

Olusanya, M. O., & Isinkaye, F. (2025). A Review and Bibliometric Study on the Trends and E-Commerce Recommenders. [IJKM]. *International Journal of Knowledge Management*, *21*(1), 1–26. DOI: 10.4018/IJKM.367729

Papastamoulou, P., & Antonopoulos, N. (2025). Artificial Intelligence in E-Commerce: A Comparative Analysis of Best Practices Across Leading Platforms. *Systems*, *13*(746), 746. Advance online publication. DOI: 10.3390/systems13090746

Phang, D., Wang, K., Wang, Q., Kauffman, R., & Naldi, M. (2019). How to derive causal insights for digital commerce in China? A research commentary on computational social science methods. *Electronic Commerce Research and Applications, 35*, 100837. Advance online publication. DOI: 10.1016/j.elerap.2019.100837

Polyakov, M., & Kovshun, N. (2021). Diffusion of Innovations as a Key Driver of the Digital Economy Development. *Baltic Journal of Economic Studies, 7*(1), 84–92. DOI: 10.30525/2256-0742/2021-7-1-84-92

Rehman, N. U., & Nunziante, G. (2023). The effect of the digital economy on total factor productivity in European regions. *Telecommunications Policy, 47*(10), 102650. Advance online publication. DOI: 10.1016/j.telpol.2023.102650

Rong, K. (2022). Research agenda for the digital economy. *Journal of Digital Economy, 1*(1), 20–31. Advance online publication. DOI: 10.1016/j.jdec.2022.08.004

Saberi, R., & Sadegh, S. (2022). The Future of Global E-Commerce Regulation: LegEnsuring Fair Competition, Consumer Rights, and Data Protection. *Legal Studies in Digital Age, 1*(1), 39–52.

Samuel, P. (1939). The Gains from International Trade. *The Canadian Journal of Economics and Political Science, 5*(2), 195-205. . JSTOR 137133.DOI: 10.2307/137133

Shao, B., & Wang, H. (2025). Digital economy, industrial structure advancement and human capital accumulation. *Finance Research Letters, 83*, 107727. Advance online publication. DOI: 10.1016/j.frl.2025.107727

Si, S., Hall, J., Suddaby, R., Ahlstrom, D., & Wei, J. (2023). Technology, entrepreneurship, innovation and social change in digital economics. *Technovation, 119*, 102484. Advance online publication. DOI: 10.1016/j.technovation.2022.102484

Siguaw, J., Simpson, P., & Enz, C. (2006). Conceptualizing Innovation Orientation: A Framework for Study and Integration of Innovation Research. *Journal of Product Innovation Management, 23*(6), 556–574. DOI: 10.1111/j.1540-5885.2006.00224.x

Sui, D. Z., & Rejeski, D. W. (2002). Environmental Impacts of the Emerging Digital Economy: The E-for-Environment E-Commerce? *Environmental Management, 29*(2), 155–163. DOI: 10.1007/s00267-001-0027-X PMID: 11815820

Tams, S., Grover, V., & Thatcher, J. (2014). Modern information technology in an old workforce: Toward a strategic research agenda. *The Journal of Strategic Information Systems, 23*(4), 284–304. DOI: 10.1016/j.jsis.2014.10.001

Tapscott, D. (1996). *The digital economy: Promise and peril in the age of networked intelligence*. McGraw-Hill.

Teece, D. (2007). Explicating dynamic capabilities: The nature and microfoundations of (sustainable) enterprise performance. *Strategic Management Journal, 28*(13), 1319–1350. DOI: 10.1002/smj.640

Treiblmaier, H., & Sillaber, C. (2021). The impact of blockchain on e-commerce: A framework for salient research topics. *Electronic Commerce Research and Applications, 48*, 101054. Advance online publication. DOI: 10.1016/j.elerap.2021.101054

Turki, H. (2025). AI-powered personalization in e-commerce: Governance, consumer behavior, and exploratory insights from big data analytics. *Technology in Society, 83*, 103033. Advance online publication. DOI: 10.1016/j.techsoc.2025.103033

United Nations Conference on Trade and Development. (2024). *Environmental implications of digitalization and green transformation. In Digital Economy Report 2024.* UNCTAD Publishing.

Vu, K., Lu, Y., & Shiba, S. (2025). The evolution of the digital economy: Comparative insights from. *Telecommunications Policy, 49*(10), 103075. Advance online publication. DOI: 10.1016/j.telpol.2025.103075

Wang, Y., Liu, C., Wang, H., & Javaid, M. (2024). Digital economy empowers enterprises to decrease financialization: Evidence from e-commerce demonstration cities. *Finance Research Letters, 67*, 105801. Advance online publication. DOI: 10.1016/j.frl.2024.105801

Westerman, G., Bonnet, D., & McAfee, A. (2011). The Digital Capabilities Your Company Needs. *MIT Center for digital business and capgemini consulting.*

World Trade Organization. (2013). World Trade Organization. Retrieved from E-commerce in Developing Countries: Opportunities and Challenges for Small and Medium-sized Enterprises.

Xia, L., Baghaie, S., & Sajadi, S. M. (2024). The digital economy: Challenges and opportunities in the new era of technology and electronic communications. *Ain Shams Engineering Journal, 15*(2), 102411. Advance online publication. DOI: 10.1016/j.asej.2023.102411

Xiao, L., Guo, F., Guo, F., Yu, F., & Liu, S. (2019). The Effects of Online Shopping Context Cues on Consumers' Purchase Intention for Cross-Border E-Commerce Sustainability. *Sustainability (Basel), 11*(10), 2777. Advance online publication. DOI: 10.3390/su11102777

Yuliansyah, H., Othman, Z. A., & Bakar, A. A. (2025). Co-authorship prediction method based on degree of gravity and article keywords similarity. *Physica A, 665*, 130511. Advance online publication. DOI: 10.1016/j.physa.2025.130511

Yumuşak, İ. (2001). *Elektronik ticaretin gelişmekte olan ülkelere etkileri ve Türkiye üzerine bir değerlendirme.* 2025 tarihinde https://econwpa.ub.uni-muenchen.de/econ-wp/mac/papers/0404/0404032.pdf adresinden alındı

Zhou, J., Lan, H., Zhao, C., & Zhou, J. (2021). Haze Pollution Levels, Spatial Spillover Influence, and Impacts of the Digital Economy: Empirical Evidence from China. *Sustainability (Basel), 13*(16), 9076. Advance online publication. DOI: 10.3390/su13169076

Chapter 10
Global Value Chains: From Multinational Dominance to SME Empowerment in a Regionalized and Digitalized World

Irmak Orman
http://orcid.org/0000-0002-5150-8168
Işık University, Turkey

Suat Teker
Işık University, Turkey

Dilek Teker
Işık University, Turkey

ABSTRACT

Global Value Chains (GVCs) emerged as a defining feature of international trade following the liberalization of global markets and the advancement of information and communication technologies in the second half of the twentieth century. Initially driven by multinational enterprises (MNEs) through strategies such as foreign direct investment, offshoring, and outsourcing, GVCs evolved into complex networks connecting suppliers, producers, and consumers across multiple geographies. However, the landscape of global trade is undergoing a significant transformation. Recent disruptions, including the global financial crisis, the COVID-19 pandemic, and rising geopolitical tensions, have exposed vulnerabilities in hyper-globalized production systems. In response, a paradigm shift toward regionalization, friend shoring, supply chain resilience, and technological innovation is reshaping GVC

DOI: 10.4018/979-8-3373-5052-3.ch010

structures. Concurrently, digitalization has lowered barriers for small and medium-sized enterprises (SMEs), enabling them to integrate into international trade networks and assume more strategic roles.

1. INTRODUCTION

For the last three decades, the story of global commerce was written by Multinational Enterprise (MNE). Driven by the logic of efficiency and cost minimization, massive corporations pioneered the creation of Global Value Chains (GVCs), dispersing production stages across borders to capitalize on labor arbitrage and resource availability. Enabled by the deregulation of the 1990s and advances in Internet and Communication Technologies (ICT), MNEs orchestrated complex webs where a product designed in the West might be assembled in the East, using components sourced from the South. This period, often termed "hyper-globalization," prioritized seamless integration above all else.

However, that era has gone through rapid change and fracturing. Today, the global economy is defined less by integration and more by disruption. Rising geopolitical tensions and the systemic shock of the COVID-19 pandemic exposed a critical weakness in the hyper-globalized model: efficiency had come at the cost of resilience. When a single link in the chain broke for a reason, whether due to a port closure or a trade war, the entire system stalled. Consequently, firms are now moving away from sprawling global networks toward regionalization: producing closer to home or to politically aligned neighbors.

Yet as the giant establishments retreat to regional positions, new players are rising. Digitalization has democratized the tools of global trade. Small and Medium-sized Enterprises (SMEs), once locked out of global markets by high entry costs, are now leveraging digital platforms to bypass traditional intermediaries. By plugging into e-commerce ecosystems, these smaller firms are transforming from local suppliers into "micro-multinationals," capable of engaging directly with international consumers. The once "local" players of production and commerce can now try to find their places in global trade.

This chapter argues that we are witnessing a fundamental change of the guard in global trade. It traces the evolution of GVCs from the era of multinational dominance to a new, fragmented, and digitalized reality. It specifically examines Türkiye as a critical case study of this shift. Standing at the crossroads of Europe and Asia, Türkiye illustrates how a "bridge economy" can leverage both regionalization trends and digital tools to transform its SME base from peripheral participants into central actors in the new global architecture.

2. LITERATURE REVIEW

2.1 Theoretical Foundations of Global Value Chains

Globalization brought with it a new vocabulary for understanding how production crosses borders and generates value. Over the years, scholars from economics, management, and geography developed distinct but complementary frameworks to study these processes. This section reviews that conceptual landscape, from the early commodity chain models to Porter's strategic value chain, and finally to the networked, digital-era models that are most relevant today.

2.1.1 Commodity and Supply Chains

In the early stages of globalization, scholars needed a framework to track the physical movement of goods across borders. They also needed to identify key players, how those players interacted and how supply-and-demand relationship worked among these players. This gave rise to the concept of commodity chains, rooted in world-systems theory. The world-systems approach examines the unequal exchange patterns along global commodity chains and the different structural positions of core, periphery, and semi-periphery economies (Arrighi and Drangel, 1986). A commodity chain was defined as "a network of labor and production processes whose end-result is a finished commodity" (Hopkins and Wallerstein, 1986, p. 159).

Gereffi and others later developed the global commodity chain concept, extending it to cover the full range of activities involved in designing, producing, and marketing a product (Gereffi, 1999). A key contribution was the distinction between buyer-driven and producer-driven chains. In buyer-driven chains which was common in labor-intensive sectors like apparel and footwear, large retailers and brand owners set the terms and outsource manufacturing to lower-cost suppliers. In producer-driven chains such as automotive and electronics manufacturing, the manufacturers themselves control the technology and coordinate the network.

China's rise as a global manufacturing powerhouse was closely tied to its mastery of buyer-driven dynamics, supplying everything from clothing to toys for Western retailers (Gereffi, 1999). Globalization lead to the rise of China and Asian Tigers. From 1960s onward, South Korea, Taiwan, Hong Kong, and Singapore had already demonstrated, how economies with limited natural resources could achieve rapid industrial upgrading by integrating strategically into global commodity chains. Beginning as low-cost OEM suppliers for Western brands, these four economies gradually moved up the value ladder, developing their own manufacturing expertise, branding capabilities, and eventually technology transfer capacity (Gereffi, 1999). The ascent of Asian Tigers, which later lead to relocation of production from West and eventually the growth of China, is one of the clearest historical examples of how participation in commodity chains, even at the lower end, can serve as a springboard for broader economic development.

Figure 1. Buyer-Driven Commodity Chains

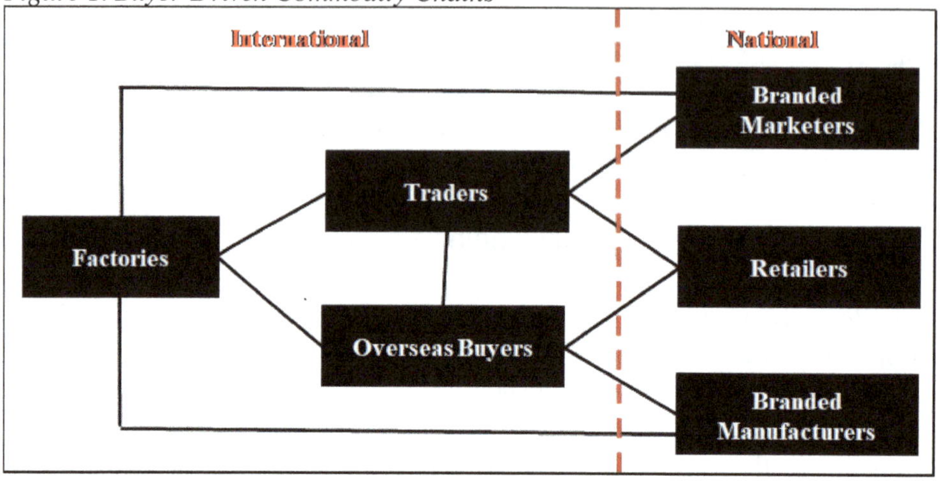

Source: Adapted from Gereffi (2001), Shifting Governance Structures in Global Commodity Chains with Reference to the Internet, American Behavioral Scientist, Vol. 44, pp. 1616–1637.

As seen from Figure 1 and Figure 2, commodity chains worked in different ways. If the coordination of the commodity chain was the responsibility of the buyer, the system was distinguished as a buyer-driven commodity chain, like the case of China where imported inputs were domestically integrated by cheap labor forces. Producer-driven commodity chains, by contrast, involve cross-border manufacturing networks where producers take coordination responsibility, forming forward and backward links that enable centralization.

Figure 2. Producer-Driven Commodity Chains

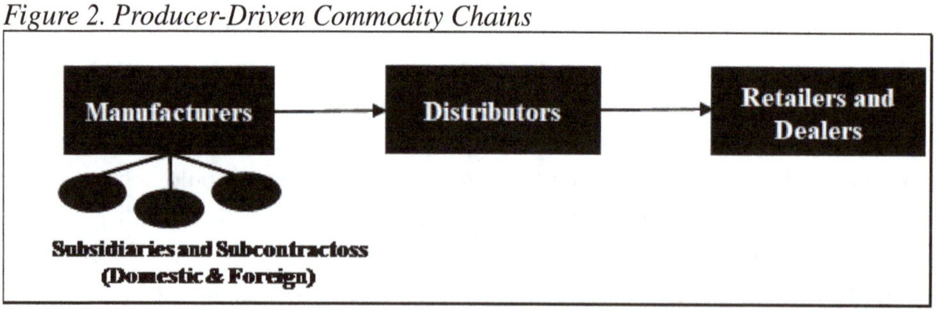

Source: Adapted from Gereffi (2001), Shifting Governance Structures in Global Commodity Chains with Reference to the Internet, American Behavioral Scientist, Vol. 44, pp. 1616–1637.

Over the years, as newly industrializing economies (NIEs) in East Asia developed skills in manufacturing, design, and branding, new players like Singapore, South Korea, Hong Kong, and Taiwan graduated beyond being simple OEM suppliers. They built their own brands and eventually became global competitors, pushing production to other parts of Asia, Africa, and Latin America (Gereffi, 1999).

Supply chains represent another key concept in this lineage. The term dates back to the 1940s but gained real prominence after the 1990s, when China-centered manufacturing transformed global trade flows. From an operational standpoint, supply chain management focuses on delivering a product at minimum cost, with each link, from raw materials to the final consumer, contributing to that outcome. As Linton et al. (2007) summarize, effective supply chain management can deliver increased revenues, lower costs, reduced assets, and better sustainability outcomes.

Figure 3. Components of Integrated Supply Chain Management

Source: Adapted from Griffith & Myers (2005).

These systems grew more complex over time with the adoption of just-in-time production, which emphasized lean inventory and tight supplier coordination. Griffith & Myers (2005) note that supply chain performance depends not just on technical integration but on cultural fit: when governance strategies are aligned with the cultural expectations of supply chain partners, performance improves. When they are applied uniformly across different cultural contexts, gains tend to disappear. This finding helps explain why MNEs often choose local strategic alliances rather than imposing standardized management structures.

2.1.2 Michael Porter's Value Chain

The concept of the value chain was introduced by Michael Porter in 1985 and quickly became one of the most widely applied frameworks in strategic management. Porter's key insight was that a firm's competitive advantage does not come from the company as a whole but from the individual activities it performs like designing, producing, marketing, delivering, and supporting its products. Each activity in this sequence adds value, and the goal is to ensure that the total value created exceeds the combined cost of all activities. The difference is the margin, which grows as a firm becomes better at each step (Porter, 1985).

Porter also recognized that no two companies have identical value chains, even in the same industry. A firm's chain reflects its history, its strategic choices, and the economics of its particular activities (cited in Winter, 2014). This insight remains relevant today: in an era of digital platforms and cross-border e-commerce, understanding which activities generate the most value and where those activities can best be performed is as important as ever.

The value chain consists of two levels of activity. Primary activities deal directly with the product: inbound logistics, operations, outbound logistics, marketing and sales, and service. Support activities such procurement, technology development, human resource management, and firm infrastructure which enable and enhance the primary ones.

When both sets of activities work efficiently together, customers are willing to pay more than the total cost of producing the good, generating the margin that sustains competitive advantage (Porter, 1985). The harmonious work of both activity sets are often called synergy and synergies between teams and activity layers not only produce efficiency, but also help cost management.

Figure 4. Michael Porter's Value Chain Model

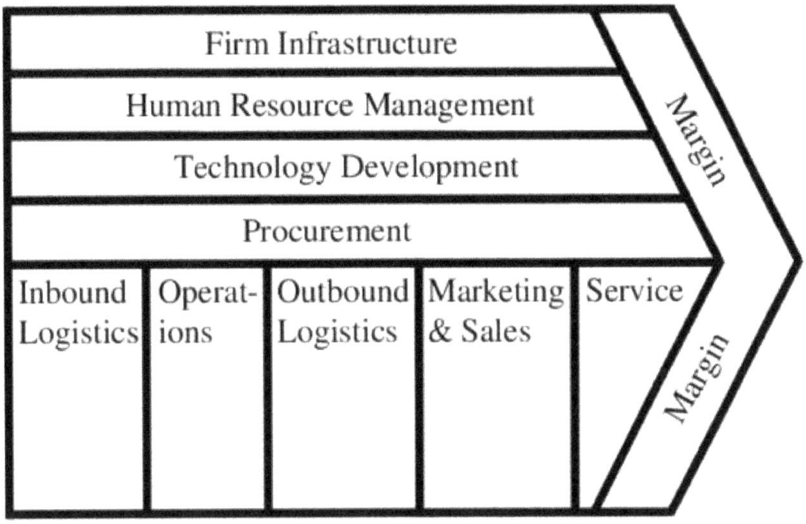

Source: Porter, M. E. (1985). Competitive Advantage: Creating and Sustaining Superior Performance. Free Press.

2.1.3 The Digital Shift: Value Networks

Porter's chain model worked well for describing the industrial economy, but it struggled to capture the complexity of the digital age. The internet did not just speed up the chain; it restructured it into a web. To address this, scholars introduced the concept of value networks, which shift the focus from sequential production to mediated exchange between multiple parties simultaneously.

Internet and communication technology developments changed way of doing business in different ways. As communication had new layers and dimensions, production also became multidimensional, rather than linear. Value networks also helped this transition.

For the formation of GVCs, value networks are particularly important because they capture the multi-actor, multi-directional nature of modern trade. In a value network, value is co-created through interactions. Christensen (1997) defines a value network as "the collection of upstream suppliers, downstream channels to market, and ancillary providers that support a common business model within an industry." Importantly, he also warns that new entrants who try to disrupt existing value networks often end up being absorbed by them instead, because the incumbent network's logic is powerful.

Figure 5. Example of Clayton M. Christensen's Value Network Model

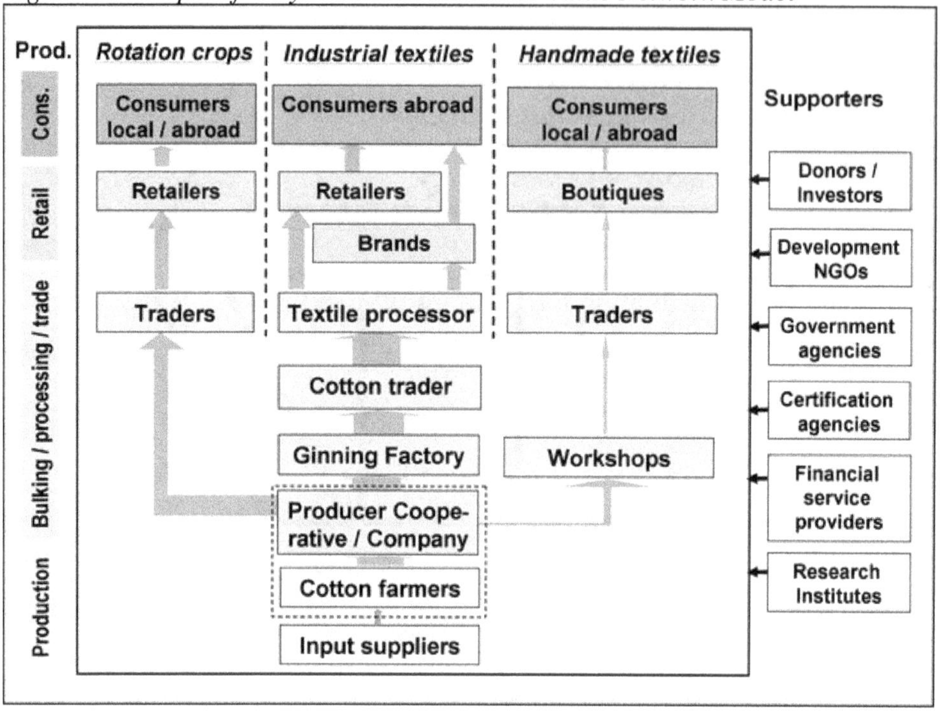

Source: Adapted from Christensen, C. (1997). The Innovator's Dilemma. Collins Business Essentials, p. 236.

Stabell and Fjeldstad (1998) extended this thinking with two additional configurations: the value shop and the value network as a distinct firm model. Value shops are firms that solve unique customer problems through intensive, iterative processes rather than linear production. They are common in consulting, healthcare, and engineering. The logic is cyclical: problem identification leads to solution development, choice, implementation, and evaluation, and then back again. Each iteration adds to the firm's knowledge base, making the shop smarter over time.

Figure 6. Stabell and Fjeldstad's Value Shop

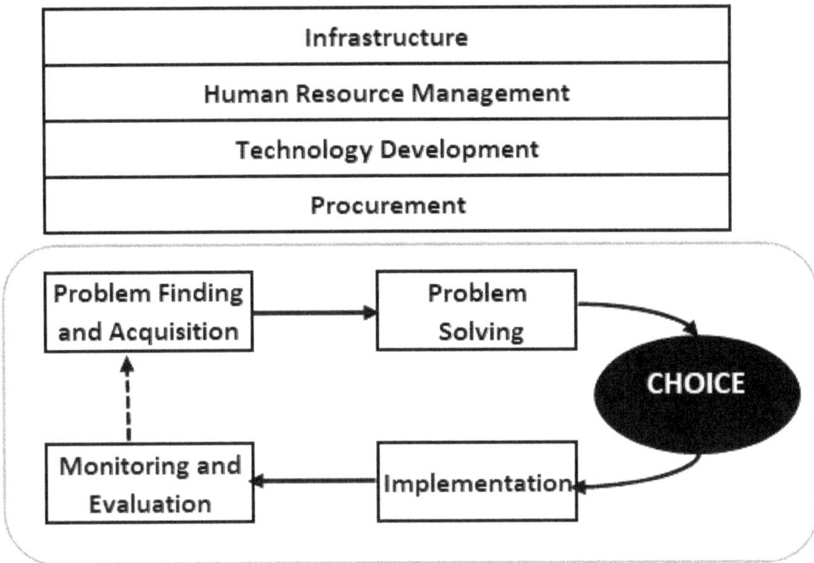

Source: Adapted from Stabell, C.B. and Fjeldstad, Ø.D. (1998). Configuring value for competitive advantage: on chains, shops, and networks.

Stabell and Fjeldstad's value network model, by contrast, applies to firms that create value by mediating between groups of customers such as telecommunications companies, financial exchanges, or digital marketplaces. The key dynamic here is the network effect (Katz & Shapiro, 1985): the more participants in the network, the more valuable it becomes for everyone. This logic is now central to understanding how marketplaces or platforms like Amazon, Alibaba, and Trendyol function as GVC enablers.

According to Stabell & Fjeldstad (1998), as a value network grows, it tends to generate economies of scale in pricing, identify new business opportunities internally, and eventually become a near-closed loop where transactions stay within the network ecosystem. As the network ecosystem can operate in closed loops, the margins that leaked outside stayed within the network. Fjeldstad & Andersen (2003) suggest three strategies for maximizing revenue in a value network: optimizing pricing, increasing the volume of exchanges facilitated, and internalizing transactions.

Figure 7. Stabell & Fjeldstad's Value Network Model

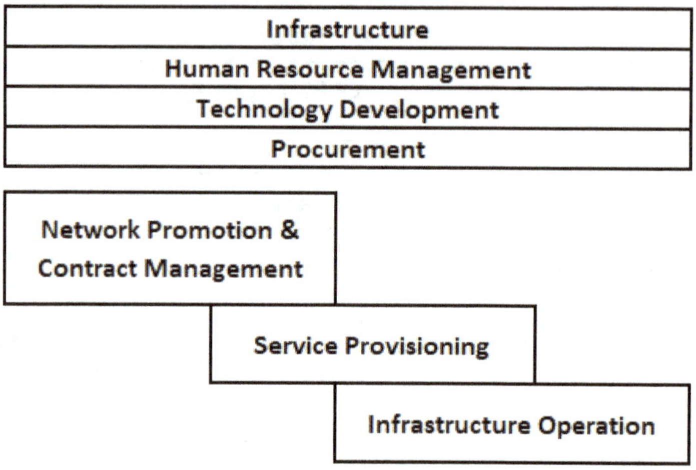

Source: Adapted from Winter, J. (2014). Success Factors of Mobile Business Ecosystems. Aalto University.

More recently, Stacy Frederick (2010, 2014) proposed the Value-Chain Reference Model (VCRM), which provides a broader view of the GVC ecosystem. VCRM integrates the supply chain, supporting environment, value-adding activities, and market access into a single framework. What makes it particularly relevant for this chapter is its explicit inclusion of the supporting environment that can be listed as digital infrastructure, logistics platforms and fintech tools, as a core component of value creation, not a peripheral one.

Figure 8. Stacy Frederick's Value-Chain Reference Model

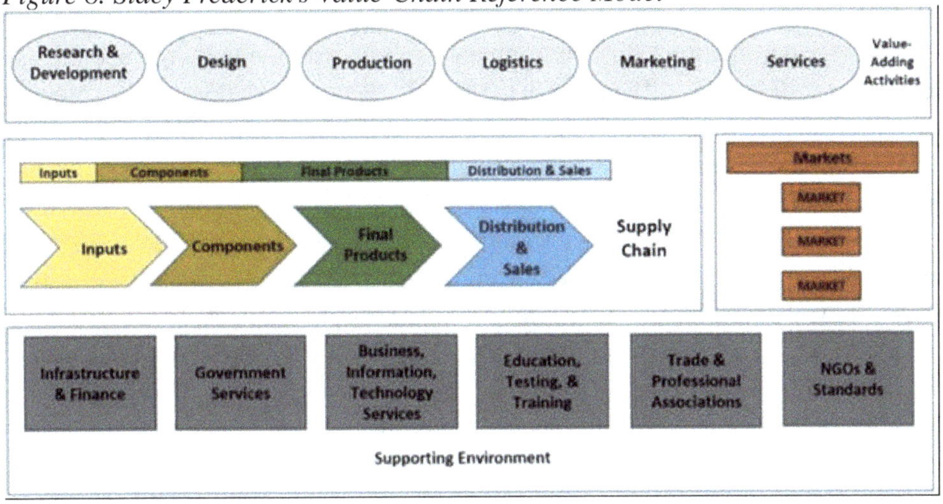

Source: Frederick (2010 and 2014).

What this conceptual evolution shows us is that we have moved from linear commodity chains to strategic value chains, and now to dynamic value networks. In each phase, the locus of competitive advantage has shifted. For MNEs in the commodity chain era, it was about controlling production. In Porter's value chain era, it was about optimizing each activity. In today's value network era, it is about connectivity, who you are linked to, and how quickly you can exchange value across those links. This is precisely the environment in which digitalization is leveling the playing field for SMEs.

2.2 Globalization and the Rise of Multinational Enterprises

To understand where GVCs are going, it helps to understand how they got here. The rise of multinational enterprises was not a sudden development; it was the outcome of decades of deliberate policy choices, technological progress, and evolving corporate strategy. The post-World War II period laid the groundwork through institutions like the General Agreement on Tariffs and Trade (GATT), which gradually reduced trade barriers across member nations. By the 1980s and 1990s, this steady opening accelerated dramatically. Capital markets were deregulated, communications technology shrank the effective distance between markets, and the establishment of the WTO in 1995 further reduced transaction friction (Baldwin, 2016; World Bank, 2019). Levitt (1983) famously described this as the "globalization of markets", a convergence of consumer tastes and production possibilities that made the world feel smaller.

For large corporations, this environment was an invitation to reorganize. MNEs found they could exploit differences in labor costs, regulatory standards, and resource endowments across countries more efficiently than ever before (Dunning, 1993). Through FDI, outsourcing, and offshoring, they spread their operations globally meaning companies were no longer confined to a single national economy. A product could be designed in one country, manufactured in another, assembled in a third, and sold everywhere (Gereffi, 1999; Kano, 2018). This process had a cumulative effect: as MNEs fragmented their production across geographies, they created the infrastructure, mainly logistics networks, supplier ecosystems, communication standards they needed that made further fragmentation possible. GVCs grew not just because MNEs chose to build them, but because each wave of investment made the next wave easier and more attractive. MNEs also transferred technology, management practices, and organizational models to host countries, which accelerated industrial development in places like South Korea, Taiwan, and later China and Mexico (Gereffi & Fernandez-Stark, 2018; World Bank, 2019).

Shortly, globalization and the rise of MNEs were mutually reinforcing. MNEs needed the open environment that globalization provided; globalization deepened because MNEs actively extended and integrated global networks. The result was the hyper-globalized production system that defined the world economy from roughly 1990 to 2010 and that is now under significant strain.

2.3 Hyper-Globalization and the Formation of Early GVCs

The peak of MNE-driven globalization, roughly spanning the late 1990s through the 2000s, is what scholars like Baldwin (2016) call the "great convergence." ICT advances, combined with falling trade costs and regulatory convergence, made it possible to fragment production not just across countries but across continents. MNEs could coordinate suppliers in Asia, designers in Europe, and distributors in the Americas through a single integrated system. The result was remarkable efficiency gains but also a system that was far more interconnected, and therefore far more fragile, than most participants realized.

The vulnerabilities in this model began to show even before the COVID-19 pandemic. The global financial crisis of 2008 demonstrated how quickly a shock in one part of the network could ripple outward. Trade finance dried up, demand collapsed simultaneously across markets, and firms with highly extended supply chains found they had almost no buffer. The lesson that taught pure efficiency is not the same as resilience was noted but not fully acted upon (Asian Development Bank & WTO, 2021).

Geopolitical pressures added another layer of strain. Rising trade tensions between the United States and China, Brexit's disruption of European supply chains, and a broader shift toward more protectionist trade policies all made the logic of single-source, single-geography production less attractive (OECD, 2021). Friend-shoring, which is the preference for sourcing from politically stable and ideologically aligned partners began to enter the strategic vocabulary of major corporations and governments alike.

Figure 9 below captures this shift in GVC logic, from the export-oriented, efficiency-maximizing model of the early 2000s toward a more diversified, regionally embedded, and digitally integrated configuration. This is not the end of global trade; it is its reconfiguration.

Figure 9. Re-Identification of GVC Development Paths

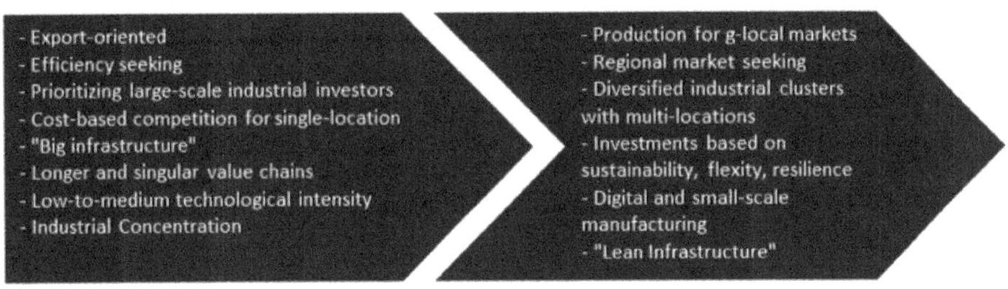

Source: Adapted from Zahn, J. (2020). Global value chain transformation to 2030: Overall direction and policy implications.

3. FORMATION OF GVCs: THE ERA OF MULTINATIONAL ENTERPRISE DOMINANCE

3.1 Global Supply Chain Fragmentation and Offshoring Strategies

If the late twentieth century was defined by the expansion of GVCs, the early twenty-first century is defined by their contraction and restructuring. To understand the opportunity emerging for SMEs today, we need to first look honestly at why the MNE-dominated model began to fail.

For roughly two decades, the "great convergence" drove the global economy forward. MNEs aggressively fragmented their supply chains, breaking production into its smallest component parts and offshoring them to wherever costs were lowest. This model was, in a narrow sense, extraordinarily efficient. But it efficiency was built on a hidden assumption: that the global system would remain stable enough for just-in-time inventory, long-distance logistics, and single-source dependencies to work reliably.

That assumption was shattered. The COVID-19 pandemic caused unprecedented disruptions in global freight that exposed how thin the margins were in maritime, rail, and air logistics (Opoku Agyemang & Irannezhad, 2025). Ports congested, shipping costs spiked, and firms discovered that a delay in one corner of their supply network could halt production lines on the other side of the world. At the same time, escalating US-China trade tensions showed that geopolitics could override the economics of globalization almost overnight. Trade tariffs imposed under conditions of political rivalry significantly dampened GVC embeddedness, particularly in developing economies (Chen & Tan, 2024).

These disruptions catalyzed a strategic rethink. Companies began moving away from purely efficiency-driven models toward ones that prioritize resilience, regional diversification, and multi-sourcing (Pan et al., 2023). Nearshoring and reshoring (bringing production closer to the final market) gained popularity not because they were cheaper but because they were safer. This marks a meaningful shift in the calculus of global sourcing: the premium paid for proximity and redundancy is now treated as insurance against disruption rather than wasteful cost.

3.2 Technological Drivers of GVC Expansion

Technology has always been a driver of how global trade is organized, but the pace and scope of change in the last two decades has been genuinely transformative. Three overlapping technology waves are reshaping GVC architecture.

The first wave: broadband internet, cloud computing, and big data analytics which made it possible to manage highly complex, geographically dispersed supply networks in real time. The transaction costs that once made international coordination difficult fell sharply, enabling the deep fragmentation of the hyper-globalization era (Baldwin, 2016; Mendling et al., 2018). Firms could monitor suppliers on the other side of the world as easily as ones across town.

The second wave: Industry 4.0 technologies including IoT, AI, and blockchain that is going further by embedding intelligence into the supply chain itself. IoT sensors allow real-time tracking of goods from production to delivery (Ben-Daya, Hassini, & Bahroun, 2019). Blockchain creates tamper-proof records of transactions, which is especially valuable in industries like food and pharmaceuticals where provenance and authenticity matter (Saberi et al., 2019). AI-driven predictive analytics help firms anticipate disruptions before they occur and adapt logistics dynamically, which is increasingly important in an era of heightened volatility (Chui et al., 2018; Closs, Speier, & Meacham, 2011).

The third wave: digital platforms is arguably the most consequential for this chapter's argument. Platforms like Amazon, Alibaba, and Shopify, along with Turkish players like Trendyol and Hepsiburada, do something that previous technology waves did not: they democratize market access. An SME in Bursa or Gaziantep can now reach customers in Berlin or London without building an international sales team or logistics network. The platform provides the infrastructure; the SME provides the product. This is the mechanism through which digitalization enabling SME participation in GVCs on a meaningful scale (OECD, 2021; Lopez-Gonzalez, 2017).

3.3 Governance Structures: Buyer-Driven and Producer-Driven Chains

GVCs are not just shaped by technology and economics; they are governed by it and governance determines who gets what. Gereffi's (1999) framework distinguishes between buyer-driven and producer-driven chains, as introduced in Section 2.1. This distinction remains analytically useful today, though the boundaries have become more porous.

In buyer-driven chains, major retailers and brand owners sit at the top of the hierarchy, controlling design, marketing, and standards while outsourcing physical production to networks of suppliers. This structure gives lead firms flexibility and keeps costs down, but it traps suppliers who are often in developing economies in low-value, low-margin production roles (Barrientos, Gereffi, & Rossi, 2011). In producer-driven chains, the manufacturer retains control over technology and production processes; suppliers can upgrade their capabilities through technology transfer, but only to the extent that led producers allow it (Kano, 2018).

What has changed in recent years is that neither model operates as cleanly as the theory suggests. Digitalization is pushing buyer-driven chains toward tighter supplier monitoring (as brands face scrutiny over sustainability and labor practices), while producer-driven chains increasingly rely on global design and marketing capabilities that they do not fully control (Gereffi & Fernandez-Stark, 2018). The result is a more hybrid, relational governance landscape, in which the distribution of power and value within GVCs is more contested and more dynamic than the traditional models implied.

4. PARADIGM SHIFT: DEMOCRATIZING GLOBAL TRADE

While the retreat of MNEs toward regionalized, resilience-oriented supply chains is one part of the story, the other and in many ways more interesting part is the simultaneous rise of the SME as a GVC actor. These two movements are connected:

the same forces that are pushing MNEs to simplify and shorten their supply chains are also opening new spaces that agile, digitally connected smaller firms can occupy.

4.1 The Platform Economy as Infrastructure

For most of the twentieth century, entering a Global Value Chain required significant capital. Firms needed international sales teams, cross-border logistics capabilities, foreign-language customer service, and the ability to navigate unfamiliar customs regimes. These costs effectively functioned as a moat protecting MNEs from smaller competitors. Digital platforms have drained that moat. The most important shift is that platforms have decoupled scales from reach. A small firm no longer needs to be large to sell globally. By plugging into Amazon's or Alibaba's logistics infrastructure, for instance, an SME can reach millions of customers across multiple countries without building its own distribution network. The platform provides warehousing, payment processing, customer service, and in many cases cross-border shipping. SME contributes the product and the product knowledge.

There are three main developments that have created this new infrastructure for smaller firms. First, on market access: large multi-sided platforms consolidate global demand and give niche producers visibility that would be impossible to achieve independently. Second, logistics and fintech: programs like Fulfilled by Amazon (FBA) internalize the complexities of cross-border shipping and customs compliance, while fintech solutions like Stripe and Payoneer handle payments, currency conversion, and fraud protection. Third, on trust: perhaps the most underappreciated element is that platforms build trust at scale through reputation systems, escrow mechanisms, and increasingly blockchain verified credentials. A buyer in Germany can transact confidently with a supplier in Anatolia because the platform itself enforces reliability standards (OECD, 2021; Lopez-Gonzalez, 2017).

Together, these capabilities have given rise to what scholars call the "micro-multinational" meaning a firm that operates internationally from inception, not through physical subsidiaries but through digital connectivity (Pan et al., 2023). Rather than investing in foreign offices or production facilities, micro-multinationals orchestrate global value creation through digital backbones, demonstrating how technological change is reshaping not just competitive dynamics but the fundamental architecture of international business.

4.2 Regionalization, Friend-Shoring, and Proximity Sourcing

The first two decades of the twenty-first century saw an almost uninterrupted expansion of global production networks. Then came the shocks. The Global Financial Crisis of 2008, the COVID-19 pandemic, escalating geopolitical rivalries, and the logistical collapses that followed all exposed how fragile extended global chains had become. The response has been a deliberate move toward shorter, more secure supply arrangements across industries and geographies. Regionalization is the most visible of these trends. Rather than sourcing from anywhere in the world that offers the lowest price, companies are increasingly restructuring their chains to operate within closer geographic blocks. This shift has been reinforced by new regional trade agreements such as CPTPP in the Asia-Pacific, USMCA in North America, and RCEP across East and Southeast Asia which create preferential terms for intra-regional sourcing and give companies a concrete incentive to reorient their supply chains (Baldwin, 2016).

Friend-shoring goes further, introducing a geopolitical dimension to supplier selection. In sectors like semiconductors, pharmaceuticals, and critical materials, firms and governments are now making sourcing decisions partly based on political alignment rather than pure cost (USTR, 2022; OECD, 2021). The U.S.-China technology competition has accelerated this dynamic, as countries like Japan reposition their semiconductor industries within regionalized, security-driven frameworks (Kawamura & Yoshino, 2023). What this means in practice is that supply chains are being designed not just to be efficient but to be defensible and less vulnerable to geopolitical disruption or regulatory change.

Proximity sourcing is the operational expression of these strategic preferences. Tesla's regional gigafactory model is an excellent example with major production facilities in Shanghai, Berlin, and Texas which illustrates the principle clearly. Each factory is designed not just to assemble vehicles locally but to source a high proportion of its inputs from nearby suppliers, reducing exposure to global logistics disruptions and allowing faster response to local market demand (Kawamura & Yoshino, 2023).

For Türkiye, these trends are not abstract; they are a concrete opportunity. As European companies look for near-shore alternatives to distant Asian suppliers, Türkiye's combination of geographic proximity, Customs Union membership, and manufacturing capability makes it a natural candidate. At the same time, Türkiye's integration into the Middle Corridor of China's Belt and Road Initiative means it can serve as a node connecting Asian and European trade flows. This dual positioning is a genuine strategic asset in an era when resilience and political alignment are shaping supply chain decisions alongside cost and quality.

4.3 Türkiye at the Digital Crossroads

Türkiye serves as an ideal case study to observe this transformation. Geographically, it has always been a physical bridge, linking the manufacturing hubs of Asia with the consumer markets of Europe via the Middle Corridor. Today, however, its role is evolving from a transit route to a digital production hub. The numbers tell a clear story. According to the Ministry of Trade, Türkiye's e-commerce volume reached 3 trillion TL in 2024, up 61.7% from the previous year. In USD terms, volume grew from $23.9 billion in 2019 to $89.6 billion in 2024 meaning a compound annual growth rate of over 30% (T.C. Ministry of Trade, 2024). These are not merely consumer spending figures. More than 485,000 enterprises are now active in the e-commerce ecosystem, the vast majority of which are SMEs. E-commerce's share of GDP rose from 2.7% in 2019 to 6.5% in 2024, reflecting a genuine structural shift in how the Turkish economy generates value.

Domestic platforms like Trendyol have been central to this transformation. Backed by Alibaba and recognized as Türkiye's first decacorn, Trendyol hosts over 300,000 SMEs and has effectively become an "export training ground", giving local firms the digital literacy and infrastructure they need to eventually enter international markets. Global platforms like Amazon and Etsy have added another layer, with Amazon Global Selling reporting nearly $1 billion in annual export sales from Turkish sellers.

The strategic fit is hard to miss. As European firms move toward near-shore supply models, Turkish SMEs who are faster, digitally connected, and geographically close are positioned and ready to fill the gap. An SME in Bursa manufacturing automotive parts no longer needs a German MNE to discover them. They can plug into a B2B digital platform, reach the EU market with the speed of a local supplier and the cost advantage of an emerging market producer. This is the new competitive model and Türkiye is living it in real time.

4.4 The "Untapped Gap" in Cross-Border Trade

Despite this momentum, there is an important caveat. While Türkiye's domestic e-commerce is booming, its cross-border component remains relatively small. Of the 5.91 billion e-commerce transactions recorded in 2024, only about 0.95 billion, that is roughly 16%, were cross-border (T.C. Ministry of Trade, 2024). The infrastructure is ready; the mindset is still catching up. The government's Export Master Plan recognizes this gap explicitly. It targets an increase in exports to 18 distant markets aiming to cover 62% of the global population and 64% of world GDP, from a 2018-2020 average of USD 20 billion to USD 50 billion by 2028, capturing a 1% share of those markets' imports. Achieving this target will require more than digital infrastructure; it will require Turkish SMEs to develop cross-border logistics capabilities, multi-language customer service, and familiarity with foreign regulatory environments. The platform economy provides the foundation. The next challenge is using it.

Industry 4.0 technologies will play an increasingly important role in this scaling process. Applications like digital twins, AI-driven logistics, and IoT-enabled supply chain visibility enhance transparency and efficiency in ways that help SMEs compete with larger players on a more equal footing (Mendling et al., 2018; Ben-Daya et al., 2019). Blockchain systems provide the trust verification that cross-border transactions require (Saberi et al., 2019). Digitalization, in this sense, does not just lower barriers to entry but it also helps SMEs build the credibility and operational capacity they need to sustain international growth (Kano, 2018).

5. TECHNOLOGICAL DISRUPTION AND THE NEW ARCHITECTURE OF GVCs

5.1 Blockchain, Artificial Intelligence, and the Internet of Things

Three technologies: blockchain, AI, and the Internet of Things are together reshaping what GVCs look like from the inside. They are not merely tools for doing the same things faster; they are changing the fundamental logic of how trust, information, and risk are managed in international production networks (Asian Development Bank & WTO, 2021).

Blockchain deserves particular attention in the context of SME integration into GVCs. One of the persistent barriers for smaller firms entering global trade is the difficulty of establishing credibility with unfamiliar buyers. Blockchain offers a partial solution: by recording transactions and product movements in an immutable, shared ledger, it creates a verifiable trail of provenance and compliance. For industries where authenticity matters like food safety, pharmaceutical integrity, luxury goods authenticity, this is not a niche application but a market access requirement (Saberi et al., 2019; Mendling et al., 2018). An SME that can demonstrate blockchain-certified supply chain practices is more competitive in regulated markets, not less.

AI is changing the operational economics of global sourcing. Predictive analytics can forecast demand more accurately, reducing the need for large safety stocks. Machine learning models can detect supply chain anomalies before they become crises, giving firms an early warning system that previously required large, dedicated risk management teams (Chui et al., 2018). For SMEs, access to AI-powered logistics platforms means they can now operate with a level of supply chain intelligence that was previously reserved for large firms with specialist departments.

IoT extends this intelligence to the physical level, embedding sensors in shipments, machinery, and warehouses to generate real-time data on location, condition, and performance (Ben-Daya et al., 2019). Taken together, blockchain for trust, AI for intelligence, and IoT for visibility constitute a new technological substrate for GVC participation that are increasingly accessible to smaller players. As these tools become cheaper and more standardized, the gap between large and small firms in their ability to manage international supply chains will continue to narrow (OECD, 2021).

5.2 Digital Platforms, E-commerce, and Financial Technologies

If blockchain, AI, and IoT provide the infrastructure for smarter supply chains, digital platforms and fintech provide market access and financial plumbing that allow smaller firms to actually use them. The combination has been genuinely disruptive. E-commerce platforms like Amazon, Alibaba, and Shopify have reduced the cost of going global by an order of magnitude for small firms. What once required establishing foreign subsidiaries, hiring local sales teams, and navigating unfamiliar banking systems can now be done through a platform interface in a matter of hours (Lopez-Gonzalez, 2017; OECD, 2021). SMEs can manage cross-border transactions, handle logistics through integrated fulfillment services, and process multi-currency payments through a single dashboard. This is not a marginal efficiency gain; it is a structural change in who can participate in global trade.

The logistics innovation that runs alongside these platforms is equally important. Cloud-based logistics providers have extended the reach of SMEs by giving them access to global freight management without requiring them to build their own shipping infrastructure (Asian Development Bank & WTO, 2021). Combined with fintech solutions such as PayPal, Stripe, TransferWise, that have simplified cross-border payments and reduced currency risk, the overall cost and complexity of international trade have fallen substantially for smaller firms.

What is particularly significant about this shift is that it is cumulative. Each firm that enters a global platform becomes part of a larger network, generating data and reputation signals that make the network more valuable for everyone. As blockchain-verified supply chain credentials become more common, and as AI-powered matching between buyers and sellers improves, the advantages of network participation compound. Firms that are slow to digitalize risk not just missing current opportunities but falling behind in ways that become increasingly hard to reverse.

The upshot is clear: digital capabilities are no longer optional for firms participating in GVCs. The ability to leverage these tools effectively, not just to use them but to integrate them strategically into the firm's operating model, is becoming a fundamental determinant of competitiveness in international trade.

5.3 Growth of E-Commerce in Türkiye and SME Integration into New GVC Models

The story of Türkiye's e-commerce growth is, in many ways, the story of this chapter's central argument made concrete. A market that barely registered on global e-commerce maps a decade ago has grown into one of the most dynamic digital commerce ecosystems in the world.

According to the Ministry of Trade's E-Commerce Report (2024), total e-commerce volume reached 3 trillion TL in 2024, a 61.7% increase over 2023. Retail e-commerce alone reached 1.62 trillion TL, growing 63.7% year-on-year. In USD terms, volume expanded from $23.9 billion in 2019 to $89.6 billion in 2024, reflecting a CAGR of 30.2% over five years. E-commerce now accounts for 6.5% of Türkiye's GDP, up from just 2.7% in 2019 is a very strong figure that signals genuine structural integration, not just a consumption trend.

What makes this remarkable for GVC analysis is who is driving it. More than 485,000 enterprises are active in Türkiye's e-commerce ecosystem, the vast majority SMEs. Trendyol, with over 300,000 SME merchants on its platform, has become an effective exporter-development program, giving local firms the operational experience and digital infrastructure they need to eventually compete on global platforms. Amazon Global Selling reports nearly $1 billion in annual export sales from Turkish sellers alone.

This trajectory aligns directly with Türkiye's Export Master Plan, which targets $50 billion in exports to 18 distant markets by 2028. Cross-border e-commerce is the mechanism through which SMEs can contribute to that target without requiring the capital-intensive internationalization pathways that were previously necessary. The platform does heavy lifting on market access, logistics, and payments; the SME contributes quality products and market responsiveness.

Figure 10. Türkiye's E-Commerce Growth, SMEs, and Export Master Plan New GVC Integration

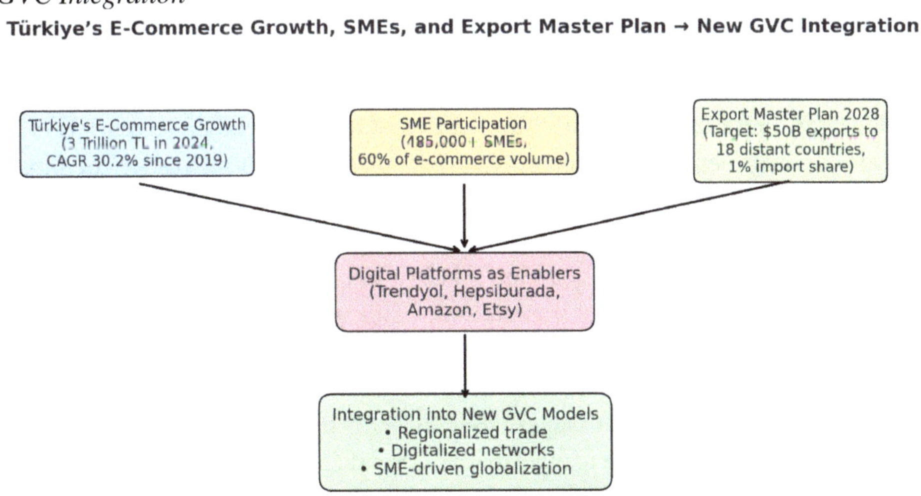

From a geopolitical standpoint, Türkiye's dual positioning, being inside the EU Customs Union while also serving as a key node in China's Middle Corridor clearly amplifies the strategic significance of this e-commerce growth. Turkish SMEs are not just participating in GVCs; they are helping to shape the new regionalized, digitally integrated model that is emerging as the MNE-dominated hyper-globalization era recedes.

6. TÜRKIYE'S ROLE IN GVC TRANSFORMATION IN GLOBAL TRADE

Global platforms and companies provide useful comparators for understanding how supply chains are being reconfigured worldwide. Amazon has become a central node in digital trade, providing SMEs with the logistics, payments, and marketing tools that effectively lower the barrier to global commerce (OECD, 2021). Shein pioneered a hyper-agile supply chain model, using real-time consumer data to make and scale only what actually sells which is a model that has reshaped expectations around speed and flexibility in global apparel (Pan et al., 2023). Shopify has enabled even micro-enterprises to become what it calls "mini-multinationals," offering end-to-end digital storefronts and plug-in logistics that give small firms global reach (Lopez-Gonzalez, 2017).

Tesla, by contrast, has redrawn the map of industrial production through its network of regional giga factories. Facilities in Shanghai, Berlin, and Texas not only assemble vehicles locally but also source up to 95% of inputs from nearby suppliers (Automotive Manufacturing Solutions, 2025). By producing close to major markets, Tesla reduces transport costs, avoids tariffs, and builds in resilience against the kind of global shocks such as trade wars or shipping crises that brought so many extended supply chains to their knees in 2020 and 2021 (Kawamura & Yoshino, 2023).

Together, these examples illustrate the two dominant trends reshaping GVCs: digital empowerment of smaller players and physical regionalization of larger ones. For Türkiye, these trends align almost perfectly with its strategic assets that are a digitally connected SME base, a very strong fast-turnaround manufacturing capabilities, and a geographic location that bridges European and Asian markets. Trendyol is perhaps the clearest illustration of Türkiye's potential in this new landscape. Backed by Alibaba and recognized as the country's first decacorn, Trendyol has demonstrated that a locally rooted but globally integrated platform can empower tens of thousands of SMEs to internationalize. In fashion and consumer goods especially, Turkish SMEs are using Trendyol's marketplace to reach European and Middle Eastern consumers, supported by integrated logistics and fintech. This model shows how Türkiye's combination of digital infrastructure, strategic geography, and entrepreneurial energy is transforming its SMEs into mini multinationals in practice, not just in theory.

7. FUTURE OUTLOOK: REDEFINING GLOBAL INTEGRATION

The history of Global Value Chains has been one of constant evolution; from the extraction of commodities to the optimization of multinational efficiency, and now into a third phase: a digitally integrated, regionally resilient network economy. The era of hyper-globalization, defined by the relentless pursuit of lowest-cost production, has fractured under the weight of geopolitical tension and systemic fragility. What is forming in its place is a more hybrid architecture: MNEs are shortening and securing their physical supply chains, while SMEs are using digital tools to extend their commercial reach. These two movements are not in opposition; they are complementary. As large firms pull back to regional hubs, they need agile local partners with whom they can integrate. That is the opportunity for SMEs in bridge economies like Türkiye.

7.1 Strategic Implications for Management

For business leaders, the macroeconomic shifts described in this chapter translate into three concrete strategic imperatives. First, from just-in-time to just-in-case. Supply chain managers spent decades being rewarded for eliminating redundancy. Today, redundancy is a strategic asset. Firms need diversified supplier bases, regional backup options, and the flexibility to reroute quickly when disruptions occur. For European firms, this means taking near-shore partners in locations like Türkiye seriously, not just as a cost play but as a risk management strategy. The premium paid for proximity is effectively supply chain insurance.

Second, the platform has a strategic infrastructure. For SME managers, digital platforms can no longer be treated merely as sales channels. They are the operational backbone of a modern internationalization strategy. Firms that integrate deeply with platform ecosystems that enable them to leverage their logistics, payment, and marketing capabilities, can compete with rivals that are many times their size. The data from Turkish SMEs confirms this: those that have adopted this mindset are increasingly operating as genuine micro-multinationals.

Third, agility through bridge economies. Multinational strategists should reassess mid-sized economies that straddle regional trade blocs. Countries like Türkiye offer something that purely distant low-cost suppliers cannot: the combination of physical proximity to a major consumer market, integration into a preferential trade arrangement (the EU Customs Union), and digital connectivity that enables rapid response. As geopolitical winds shift, firms with a foothold in such economies have more options.

7.2 Sustainability, Inclusivity, and Resilience as New Priorities

The next generation of GVCs is being shaped by forces beyond geopolitics and technology. Sustainability is increasingly a competitive requirement, not just a reputational one. The EU Green Deal and border carbon adjustments are creating effective tariffs on non-compliant supply chains, forcing exporters, including Turkish SMEs as well to demonstrate environmental standards in order to maintain market access (WEF, 2023). This is a challenge, but also an opportunity: agile, digitally integrated firms can use blockchain tools to verify green credentials transparently, something that is genuinely difficult for large, opaque multinationals.

Inclusivity is a related priority that has moved up the policy agenda since the pandemic. The potential for SMEs from low- and middle-income countries to integrate into GVCs when supported by digital infrastructure and policy is now well-documented in the literature (Barrientos, Gereffi, & Rossi, 2011). Social upgrading, that includes improved wages, better labor conditions, greater gender inclusion must accompany economic upgrading to build the political support that open trade requires. Türkiye's large SME base, which represents 99.7% of all enterprises, is well-positioned to benefit from these trends if supported by appropriate policy.

Resilience, as redefined after the COVID disruptions, means more than redundancy. It means the ability to absorb and adapt to shocks without losing the capacity to serve markets (Taglioni & Winkler, 2016). Resilient GVCs will combine local embeddedness with global reach, regional production hubs connected through digital platforms that allow rapid reorientation when circumstances change. As the World Bank (2017) notes, future GVC frameworks need to be agile as well as robust.

7.3 Policy Implications for the Next Generation of GVCs

Translating these priorities into policy is not straightforward, but the direction is clear. Governments need to adopt a multi-sectoral approach that coordinates trade policy with education, environmental standards, and digital infrastructure investment. Future-ready GVC policies need to be tailored to national contexts while aligning with international frameworks like the Paris Agreement and the UN Sustainable Development Goals (UNCTAD, 2013).

Key areas for intervention include developing workforce skills aligned with digital transformation and green transition; creating institutional frameworks for labor rights and gender equality; supporting technological upgrading among SMEs to enhance their absorptive capacity (World Bank, 2017); and investing in digital and physical infrastructure to reduce regional inequality in GVC access (CEPR, 2023).

Bilateral and regional trade agreements will increasingly incorporate sustainability and labor provisions and the EU's approach already points in this direction. For exporters in countries like Türkiye, meeting these standards is not optional; it is a license to participate in high-value markets.

7.4 Türkiye's Outlook on Next-Generation Commerce

Türkiye's trajectory illustrates what is possible when strategic geography, digital investment, and export policy align. The government's Export Master Plan and Distant Countries Strategy set an ambitious target: growing exports to 18 distant markets from an average of USD 20 billion (2018-2020) to USD 50 billion by 2028, capturing 1% of those markets' total imports (T.C. Ministry of Trade, 2024). Achieving this will require cross-border e-commerce to grow substantially, from its current 16% share of total transactions to a much larger proportion.

The integration of domestic e-commerce growth, SME capacity building, and export diversification into a single coherent policy framework is Türkiye's most important structural task. When these elements work together, Türkiye will be able to provide a model that other mid-sized emerging economies can study and adapt.

Figure 11. Türkiye's E-Commerce Growth, SMEs, and Export Master Plan New GVC Integration with Cross-Border Expansion

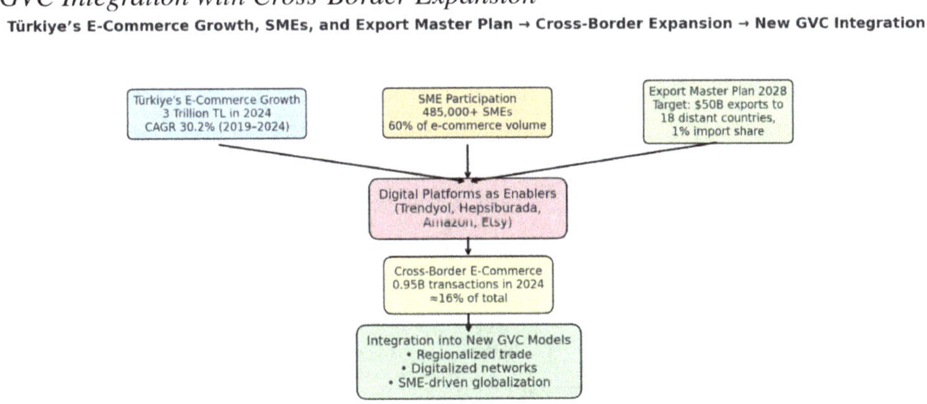

8. CONCLUSION

The global value chain is not a static object. It is a constantly evolving architecture, shaped by technology, geopolitics, corporate strategy, and the capabilities of the firms participating in it. This chapter has traced that evolution across three broad phases: the commodity chain era dominated by MNEs pursuing efficiency through geographic fragmentation; the hyper-globalization peak when those chains reached their maximum extent; and the current transition toward regionalized, resilient, and digitally integrated configurations.

What makes the current moment distinctive is that the disruptions driving this transition such as, pandemic shocks, geopolitical tension, sustainability pressures are creating openings for actors who were previously marginal in GVC discussions. SMEs, armed with digital platforms, fintech tools, and increasingly sophisticated logistics solutions, are entering international trade in numbers and at a scale that would have seemed implausible just a decade ago. They are not replacing MNEs, but they are filling the spaces that MNEs are vacating as they simplify and regionalize.

Türkiye's experience encapsulates this transition. As a bridge economy sitting at the intersection of European demand and Asian production corridors, Türkiye benefits from both the regionalization trend (near-shoring by European firms) and the digitalization trend (SMEs using domestic and global platforms to reach international consumers). Its rapidly growing e-commerce sector, anchored by platforms like Trendyol and increasingly connected to global marketplaces, demonstrates how geography and digital infrastructure can combine to create competitive advantage.

The challenges ahead are real. Cross-border e-commerce remains a small fraction of total transactions. Many SMEs still lack the operational know-how to navigate foreign regulatory environments, manage international returns, and provide multilingual customer support. And the sustainability requirements coming from major trading partners will demand investment and adaptation that not all firms are ready for.

But the direction of travel is clear. GVCs are not disappearing; they are becoming shorter, smarter, and more inclusive. The future belongs to firms and economies that can combine the physical security of regional production with the boundless reach of digital trade. For academics, scholars, policymakers, and business leaders, the central task is to understand this hybrid landscape well enough to shape it and further drive it's growth, not just react to it.

REFERENCES

Amazon Türkiye. (2024). Amazon global selling Türkiye raporu 2024. Amazon.com.tr. https://www.amazon.com.tr

Asian Development Bank (ADB), & World Trade Organization (WTO). (2021). Global value chain development report 2021: Beyond production. Asian Development Bank & WTO. https://www.adb.org/publications/global-value-chain-development-report-2021

Baldwin, R. (2016). *The great convergence: Information technology and the new globalization*. Harvard University Press. DOI: 10.2307/j.ctv24w655w

Barrientos, S., Gereffi, G., & Rossi, A. (2011). Economic and social upgrading in global production networks: A new paradigm for a changing world. *International Labour Review*, *150*(3–4), 319–340. DOI: 10.1111/j.1564-913X.2011.00119.x

Ben-Daya, M., Hassini, E., & Bahroun, Z. (2019). Internet of Things and supply chain management: A literature review. *International Journal of Production Research*, *57*(15–16), 4719–4742. DOI: 10.1080/00207543.2017.1402140

CEPR. (2023). Global value chain transformation to 2030: Overall direction and policy implications. Centre for Economic Policy Research. https://cepr.org

Chen, L., & Tan, J. (2024). Does the COVID-19 pandemic exacerbate the disincentive effect of trade tariffs on global value chains (GVCs) embeddedness? *Economic Analysis and Policy*, *83*, 404–420. DOI: 10.1016/j.eap.2024.04.033

Chui, M., Manyika, J., & Miremadi, M. (2018). Notes from the AI frontier: Applications and value of deep learning. McKinsey Global Institute. Retrieved on November 10,2025. https://www.mckinsey.com

Closs, D. J., Speier, C., & Meacham, N. (2011). Sustainability to support end-to-end value chains: The role of supply chain management. *Journal of the Academy of Marketing Science*, *39*(1), 101–116. DOI: 10.1007/s11747-010-0207-4

Dunning, J. H. (1993). *Multinational enterprises and the global economy*. Addison-Wesley.

Gereffi, G. (1999). International trade and industrial upgrading in the apparel commodity chain. *Journal of International Economics*, *48*(1), 37–70. DOI: 10.1016/S0022-1996(98)00075-0

Gereffi, G., & Fernandez-Stark, K. (2018). Global value chain analysis: A primer. In Gereffi, G. (Ed.), *Global value chains and development: Redefining the contours of 21st century capitalism* (2nd ed., pp. 305–342). Cambridge University Press.

Hepsiburada. (2024). Hepsiburada annual report 2024. Hepsiburada Group. https://corporate.hepsiburada.com

Kano, L. (2018). Global value chain governance: A relational perspective. *Journal of International Business Studies*, *49*(6), 684–705. DOI: 10.1057/s41267-017-0086-8

Kawamura, S., & Yoshino, T. (2023). Technonationalism and global value chains: Implications for supply chain resilience. *Journal of Asian Economics*, *84*, 101567. DOI: 10.1016/j.asieco.2023.101567

Levitt, T. (1983). The globalization of markets. *Harvard Business Review*, *61*(3), 92–102.

Lopez-Gonzalez, J. (2017). *Mapping the participation of SMEs in global value chains. OECD Trade Policy Papers, 211*. OECD Publishing., DOI: 10.1787/8bbebdb9-

Mendling, J., Weber, I., van der Aalst, W., Vom Brocke, J., Cabanillas, C., Daniel, F., & Zhang, L. (2018). Blockchains for business process management: Challenges and opportunities. *ACM Transactions on Management Information Systems*, *9*(1), 1–16. DOI: 10.1145/3183367

Office of the United States Trade Representative (USTR). (2022). 2022 national trade estimate report on foreign trade barriers. USTR. https://ustr.gov

Opoku Agyemang, K., & Irannezhad, E. (2025). The impact of the COVID-19 pandemic on global freight movement and logistics. *Transportation Research Procedia*, *82*, 3604–3627. DOI: 10.1016/j.trpro.2024.12.073

Organization for Economic Co-operation and Development (OECD). (2021). SMEs in a digitized and globalized economy: Trends and policy challenges. OECD. https://www.oecd.org/industry/smes-in-a-digitised-and-globalised-economy.htm

Pan, L., Chen, Y., Zhang, Z., & Liu, J. (2023). Rethinking globalization: The impact of geopolitics and digital technologies on global value chain reconfiguration. *Journal of International Business Policy*, *6*(2), 215–234. DOI: 10.1016/j.jibp.2023.05.002

Porter, M. E. (1985). *Competitive advantage: Creating and sustaining superior performance*. Free Press.

Saberi, S., Kouhizadeh, M., Sarkis, J., & Shen, L. (2019). Blockchain technology and its relationships to sustainable supply chain management. *International Journal of Production Research*, *57*(7), 2117–2135. DOI: 10.1080/00207543.2018.1533261

Taglioni, D., & Winkler, D. (2016). *Making global value chains work for development*. World Bank Publications. DOI: 10.1596/978-1-4648-0157-0

Trendyol. (2024). Trendyol 2024 yıl sonu faaliyet raporu. Trendyol Group. https://www.trendyol.com

World Bank. (2017). Measuring the determinants of backward participation in global value chains. World Bank Policy Research Working Paper.

World Trade Organization (WTO). (2021). World trade report 2021: Economic resilience and trade. WTO. https://www.wto.org/english/res_e/publications_e/wtr21_e.htm

KEY TERMS AND DEFINITIONS

Commodity Chains: Linear production and distribution systems tracing goods from raw materials to final consumers, central to early globalization research.

Cross-Border E-Commerce: The online sale of goods and services across national borders.

Digital Platforms: Online marketplaces such as Amazon, Trendyol, and Shopify that connect businesses with consumers and provide integrated logistics and payments. They function as gateway infrastructure for SMEs entering global trade networks (Lopez-Gonzalez, 2017).

Digital Trade Infrastructure: The combination of logistics systems, digital payments, online customs processing, fintech tools, and government systems that collectively enable cross-border digital commerce.

E-Commerce: The buying and selling of goods and services through digital platforms, a fast-growing channel for Turkish SMEs targeting international markets.

Friend-Shoring: The strategic relocation of supply chain activities to politically aligned or geopolitically secure partner countries, prioritizing security of supply over pure cost efficiency.

Gigafactories: Tesla's regional manufacturing hubs, designed to localize production close to major consumer markets, reduce tariff exposure, and increase resilience against global logistics disruptions.

GVCs (Global Value Chains): International production networks in which the different stages of creating a product. From design to distribution that are distributed across multiple countries.

Middle Corridor: A transcontinental trade route connecting Asia and Europe through Türkiye, forming part of China's Belt and Road Initiative and reinforcing Türkiye's strategic position in linking digital commerce flows between East and West (World Bank & WTO, 2019).

Mini-Multinationals: Small firms that operate internationally from early in their existence through digital tools and platforms, without requiring the physical infrastructure investments previously needed for international expansion.

Regionalization: The restructuring of global value chains toward geographically concentrated trade blocs. Türkiye's Customs Union with the EU and its position in Asian trade routes illustrate how regionalization creates new market opportunities for SMEs (Pan et al., 2023).

SME Empowerment: The process of enabling smaller firms to compete globally through access to technology, financial tools, and cross-border e-commerce infrastructure.

SMEs (Small and Medium-Sized Enterprises): Businesses with limited employees and turnover; representing 99.7% of all enterprises in Türkiye and increasingly central to export-led growth through e-commerce platforms (OECD, 2021).

Supply Chain Resilience: The capacity of supply networks to absorb, adapt to, and recover from disruptions such as pandemics, trade conflicts, or geopolitical shocks.

Supply Chains: The full sequence of activities and firms involved in producing, transporting, and delivering a product to consumers.

Value Networks: Interconnected firms and organizations that co-create, share, and capture value through continuous collaboration and information exchange.

Chapter 11
Uncovering Digital Maturity and Financial Performance Relationship in the Service Sectors

Mustafa Kemal Yilmaz
Ibn Haldun University, Turkey

Mine Aksoy
http://orcid.org/0000-0002-4773-1770
Yalova University, Turkey

Esra Cengiz Tirpan
http://orcid.org/0000-0001-7675-5635
Bilecik Seyh Edebali University, Turkey

Mehtap Özşahin
http://orcid.org/0000-0003-2527-4166
Gebze Technical University, Turkey

Erman Coşkun
Bahçeşehir University, Turkey

Özgür Uysal
Central Security Depository and Trade Depository of Türkiye, Turkey

ABSTRACT

This study aims to explore how digital maturity level (DML) affects financial performance (FP) in the service sector firms listed on Borsa Istanbul in Türkiye. Using panel data of 59 service companies for the years 2016–2022, this study employs a text mining approach to calculate DML of the firms from their annual reports and uses panel regression analysis to examine the interplay between DML and FP. The results indicate that there is a U-shaped relationship between DML and FP of service sector firms. Companies that have a greater orientation towards digitalization face a decreasing FP in the short term but get increasing financial benefits in the long run. However, this relationship varies across the sectors of information, communi-

DOI: 10.4018/979-8-3373-5052-3.ch011

cation and publishing activities, construction and public works and transportation and storage. The findings provide valuable insights for companies to structure right digitalization strategies to ensure sustainable financial gains.

INTRODUCTION

The rapid advancement of digital technologies (DT) has revolutionized business landscape, offering new opportunities for firms, reshaping business models, and significantly influencing operations (Lei et al., 2022). By employing digital means, companies have become more competent to achieve long-term goals through the integration of new data resources at low cost and speed up their response to market demands (Verhoef et al., 2019). According to the World Economic Forum (2024), an estimated 70 percent of new value created over the coming decade will be based on digitally enabled business models. Therefore, it is essential to examine the influence of digitalization on firm performance. This is particularly true for emerging markets that aggressively struggle to shift to an intelligence-based economy.

The impact of digitalization on firm performance comes from enabling improvements in efficiency, revenue growth, product/service quality, customer satisfaction, employee engagement, and a greater focus on innovation (Deloitte, 2023). For instance, digitalization helps firms grow revenue by improving customer experience and the development of new products and services. Therefore, ambitious firms should boost growth and innovation to tap high potential of digitalization. Despite the advantages that digitalization offers for business community, there are limited discussion of its impact on service sectors, where advanced DT such as artificial intelligence (AI), generative AI, Internet of Things (IoT), virtual reality (VR), and big data analytics are frequently employed (Vial, 2019).

Recent discussions on digital transformation highlight important differences in how industries adopt and benefit from new digital tools. Digitalization plays a more transformative role in service sectors compared to manufacturing sectors in many countries (Ribeiro-Navarrete et al., 2021; Ndubuisi et al., 2023). By 2019, services accounted for 55 percent of the GDP and 45 percent of employment in emerging markets (Nayyar et al. 2021). Digitalization in service sectors offers several advantages, i.e. automating processes, cutting costs, minimizing human errors, and encouraging an innovation culture (Parida et al., 2019). DT allows firms to better understand customer preferences and deliver more customized services. Digitalization also enables firms to create new business models such as subscription-based, or platform-based services, altering the value chain (Lee & Lim, 2018). The Covid-19 pandemic has remarkably sped up digital transformation in service sectors, particularly influencing healthcare, education, and entertainment. DT assist firms to better serve customers during this turbulence by developing their capabilities through agility, flexibility, and resilience (Chin et al., 2023).

Despite growing global interest in the strategic value of digital transformation, research coverage remains uneven across country groups. Most of the studies investigating the impact of digitalization on firm performance have been conducted in developed markets. There are relatively few studies (Cherkasova & Slepushenko, 2021; Masoud & Basahel, 2023; Valaskova et al., 2025; Yonghong et al., 2023) that explore the effects of digital maturity (DM) on financial performance (FP) in emerging markets, where digitalization plays a key role in increasing productivity, reducing costs, and facilitating access to global markets (Dahlman et al., 2016). This study seeks to explore the impact of DM on FP by conducting a text mining analysis of the annual reports of service sector firms listed on Borsa Istanbul in Türkiye, a well-suited setting that shows high level of digitalization among emerging markets. Digital transformation of Türkiye diverges from many of its peers across key indicators, such as ICT adoption and digital infrastructure. Many Turkish firms actively embrace digital transformation as their priority to improve operational efficiency and consumer experience through investments in AI, and data analytics technologies. These attempts significantly influence firm-level digital transformation trajectories, an issue shared with many emerging markets where uneven digital readiness hampers corporate performance. This research only focuses on service sectors where digitalization intensively shapes operational processes and customer experiences. In conducting the study, digitalization maturity index (DMI) scores were calculated from 2016 to 2022 as Turkish firms have given pace to digitalization strategies in recent years. The study also examines whether the relationship between DM and FP differs among the sub-sectors.

This research contributes to literature in three folds. First, by mapping the digital maturity level (DML) of the firms based on counts of the digitalization related keywords in the annual reports, the study employs text mining analysis to calculate DML scores of the entities. Second, the study explores the interplay between DML and FP for the service sectors, focusing on how the degree of DML affects FP. In this sense, it guides service sector firms in emerging markets and provides valuable insights in refining their digitalization strategies to enhance competitiveness. Finally, this paper provides new evidence in an emerging market setting where corporate digitalization has been rapidly developing. Thus, it offers clear intiutions for the significance of digitalization, motivating emerging market firms to assess changes in their business environments and adopt proper digital technologies to boost FP.

The rest of the paper is organized as follows: Section 2 presents the theoretical and conceptual framework and formulates the hypothesis. Section 3 gives the data, variables, and methodology. Section 4 provides the empirical findings. Finally,

Section 5 concludes the study by outlining the theoretical and practical implications, as well as suggesting directions for future research.

2. THEORETICAL AND CONCEPTUAL FRAMEWORK AND HYPOTHESIS DEVELOPMENT

2.1. Theoretical and Conceptual Framework

Technology is a fundamental resource for strategic investment in digital transformation, but achieving this transformation requires alignment with a firm's internal resources (Brinch et al., 2021). Resource-based view (RBV) is one of the most prominent theories to explain the impact of digital orientation on firm performance (Mikalef et al., 2019; Rivard et al., 2006; Rodriguez & Rodriguez, 2005). According to the RBV, digitalization is a strategic resource that is valuable, scarce, and difficult to replicate in the business environment (Barney, 1991). Many studies suggest that firms that leverage digitalization as a key resource tend to outperform their competitors (Dubey et al., 2019; Huang & Wang, 2020). This study employs RBV, believing that tangible and intangible aspects of digitalization raise FP.

In recent years, the rapid development and integration of advanced digitalization have enabled digital servitization, accelerating the growth of service firms (Gebauer et al., 2021). Digital servitization is the process of transforming a firm by means of a service combination and the intensive use of digital technologies and is beneficial in delivering the outcomes for customers. On this respect, AI, IoT, big data, blockchain, and VR equip service firms with the necessary tools for creating customer-focused business models (Paiola & Gebauer 2020). Smart technologies highly influence firm performance by allowing entities to align their business processes in ways that boost customer satisfaction (Immonen & Sintonen, 2015; Roy et al., 2017). At the firm level, digitalization stimulates product and service innovation and offers new opportunities, empowering firms to provide broader value propositions to customers by collecting and analyzing data from various sources and generating new business models through implementing sophisticated strategies. In this sense, as claimed by many studies (Fernandez-Portillo et al., 2022; Kuang et al., 2023), digital enhancement improves operational and financial performance and leads to greater efficiency by leveraging innovative capabilities and optimizing the allocation of resources.

However, improvements in corporate performance through digitalization do not take place until the human resources of a firm gain the required expertise (Skorupinska & Torrent-Sellens, 2017). Therefore, the progress of digitalization and the amelioration of financial results may take some time depending upon the management of digital processes (Vu, 2011). For instance, many companies leverage data analytics to uncover insights and predict emerging trends, enabling them to make swift decisions and promptly respond to consumer demand. However, big data investment may pay off over time (Wamba et al., 2017). On this respect, the DML of firms has paramount importance. Fernandez-Portillo et al. (2022) indicate that increased level of digitalization is associated with improved firm performance. Based on interviews with firms from 11 countries, Bouwman et al. (2018) state that firms with a higher level of digitalization have more efficient and innovative business models.

Despite growing scholarly attention to the impact of digitalization on firm performance, the findings are mixed. Many studies (e.g. Fernandez-Portillo et al., 2022; Guo & Xu, 2021; Martín-Peña et al., 2019; Vitari & Raguseo, 2016; Zeng et al., 2022) have found a positive relationship between these two constructs, whereas some others have identified either a negative or negligible impact of digitalization on firm performance due to increased operational costs arising from adaptation pressures, integration expenses, and resistance to change (AlMulhim, 2021; Gebauer et al., 2020; Jardak & Ben Hamad, 2022). Dobbs et al. (2015) assert that firms in sectors that are more agile in adapting to digital transformation experience increased FP, and those with higher levels of DM achieve better FP. Similarly, Bughin and van Zeebroeck (2017) claims that firms that use their digital potential have higher revenues than that of the average firm. Wroblewski (2018) analyzes whether firms with higher DM outperform their less mature competitors in Sweden and indicates that DM raised operational efficiency and return on equity.

Table A1 in the Appendix provides a summary of the selected studies examining the relationship between DML and FP.

2.2. Hypothesis Development

Leveraging digital transformation enables firms to improve operational efficiency, increase customer engagement, and gain valuable insights into market trends. It also empowers them to explore new markets, generate additional revenue streams, and develop innovative business models. However, digitalization is a challenging process that demands substantial investment in technology, skill development, and cultural transformation. As argued by Lichtenthaler (2019), firms need the capabilities and knowledge of using DT to increase FP.

Numerous studies have emphasized the positive impact of digitalization on FP, highlighting the importance of service-oriented strategies in realizing financial benefits (Zhou et al., 2023). Majority of these studies claim that firms may enhance efficiency by leveraging the digital skills of employees, increasing productivity and reducing costs. Martín-Peña et al. (2019) and Mithas et al. (2012) find that digitalization has a substantial effect on revenue growth. Kohtam¨aki et al. (2020) examined

131 Swedish manufacturing firms and identified a U-shaped relationship between digitalization and FP. They find that at low to moderate level of digitalization, the interaction effect is negative, but as digitalization increases from moderate to high level, the effect becomes positive, enhancing FP. Cherkasova and Slepushenko (2021) conduct a study of 482 Russian firms across 20 industries from 2017 to 2019 and indicated that digitalization positively influences FP, with the most significant impact observed at high DM.

In the journey of digital transformation, prioritizing cost reduction can amplify the benefits of digitalization (He & Liu, 2019). However, in the early stages of digitalization, investment in software, hardware, and skilled human resources can substantially raise costs, decreasing FP (Dutta et al., 2014). As the digitalization process deepens, return on assets (ROA) will gradually increase since the impact of digitalization on FP has a certain lag (Yonghong et al., 2023). In a recent study of Norwegian firms listed on Oslo Børs, Andersen (2023) discovers that ROA exhibites a U-shaped effect for most technology trends, with a one-year lag. Similarly, Truant et al. (2021) argue that firms in the early stages of digitalization exhibit lower levels of FP compared to those with more advanced digital management practices.

Thus, the interplay between DM and FP is a dynamic process. Digital transformation may have a positive impact on FP only after firms adapt to digitalization by incurring high costs and adjusting organizational structure and business processes. Building on these discussions, we put forward the following hypothesis:

Hypothesis: There is a U-shaped relationship between the digital maturity level and financial performance.

Figure 1. Research framework

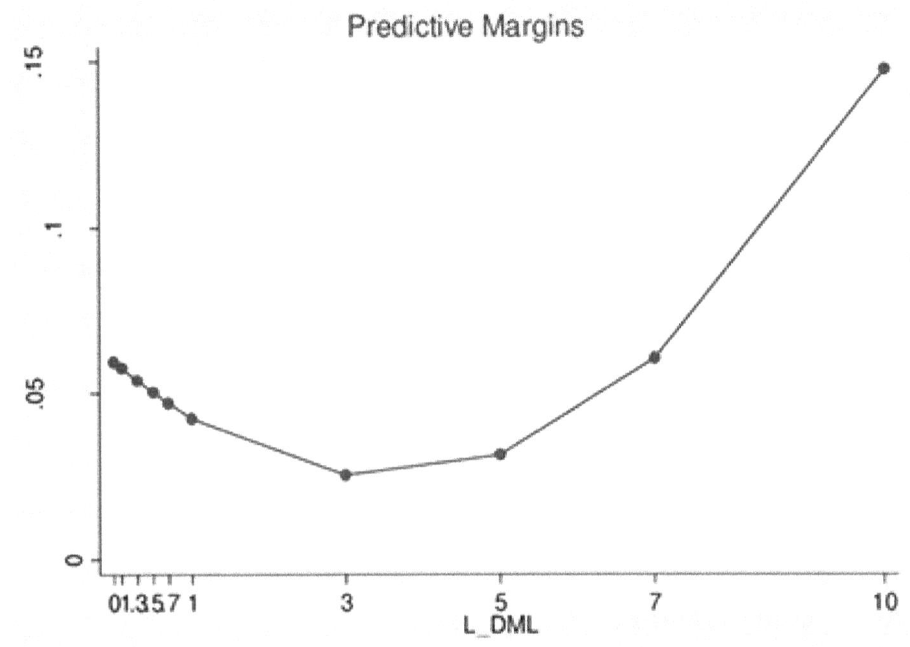

Figure 1 illustrates the research framework and the proposed relationship.

3. DATA AND METHODOLOGY

3.1. Data Sample

This study focuses only on the service sector and covers 59 non-financial firms listed on Borsa Istanbul for the period of 2016-2022. This timeframe is deliberately chosen as the firms had to prepare their financial statements according to inflation accounting application that entered into force by December 31, 2023. Table 1 reports the sub-sectors in the sample. Services represent 54 percent of the GDP in Türkiye by 2023, and their share does not display a remarkable change since 2015 (Worldbank, 2024). Service sectors more intensively deal with customer-focused digital affairs compared to manufacturing sector, aiming to improve consumer satisfaction. Firms with less than 4 years of observation data were excluded from the sample. The panel data analysis was conducted with a total of 59 firms and 388 observations to test the hypothesis.

Table 1. The distribution of the service sectors in the sample

Service sectors	No. of firms
Wholesale and retail trade	15
Electricity, gas and water	10
Construction and public works	8
Hotel and restaurants	8
Transportation and storage	6
Information, communication and publishing activities	5
Real estate activities	3
Educational health sports and entertainment services	2
Professional, scientific and technical activities	1
Administrative and support service activities	1
Total	59

3.2. Variable Measurement

Our dependent variable is financial performance. Following prior studies (e.g. Kuang et al., 2023; Yonghong et al., 2023; Zeng et al., 2022), return on assets (ROA) was used as a financial performance indicator. It is measured by dividing net income to total assets.

Calculated digital maturity level (DML) is used as the independent variable. It quantifies the extent to which firms leverage DT to enhance customer interactions, streamline operational processes, and transform business models (Hess et al., 2016; Verhoef et al., 2019). There is a lack of research focusing on quantifying DML due to its complex nature as a firm-wide strategic change (Gurbaxani & Dunkle, 2019; Libert et al., 2016), making it challenging to measure. Following the relevant literature (Fu & Li, 2023; Guo & Xu, 2021; Wu et al., 2021; Zeng et al., 2022), text mining analysis was applied to the annual reports of firms to measure DML. Text mining analysis can involve different methods such as word frequency analysis, the presence of specific words, regularities in data, tagging/annotation (Dreisbach et al., 2019; Rybchak & Basystiuk, 2017). MAXQDA, which is a software designed for qualitative and mixed-method data analysis, was employed to analyze the frequencies of the DM related keywords in the annual reports (Marjaei et al., 2019).

Figure 2 shows the flow diagram for the calculation of the Digital Maturity Index scores, i.e. a proxy for the digital orientation of the firms.

Figure 2. The flow diagram for the calculation of the Digital Maturity Index scores

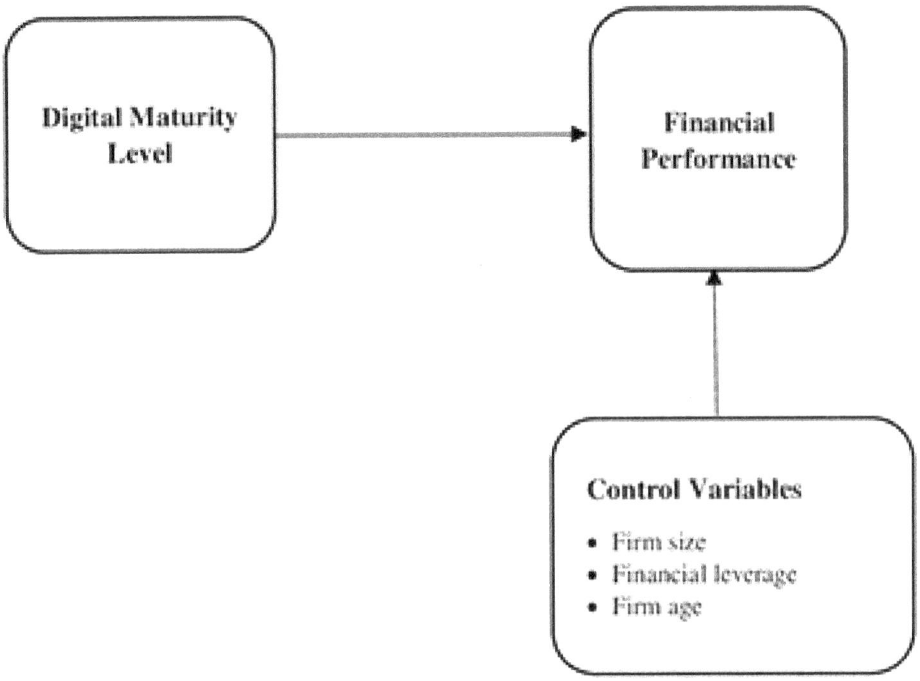

The following steps were followed to calculate the DMI scores:

Step 1: 238 keywords were selected for different levels of digital orientation in firms to construct a digital scale based on literature review, and the interviews held with the experts. To construct a comprehensive vocabulary set, a content analysis was conducted on policy documents and sectoral reports on digitalization. Strategic and technical reports issued by prominent institutions—the Turkish Industry and Business Association (2017, 2020), the Ministry of Development (2018), the Ministry of Science, Industry and Technology (2018), and the Digital Türkiye Platform (2019, 2021)—were examined. Based on the recurring concepts and themes within these sources, a set of relevant keywords pertaining to digital transformation was identified. The preliminary keyword list was subsequently reviewed by nine domain experts, and the final dictionary was refined in accordance with their feedback.

Step 2: The 238 keywords were coded and classified under 5 categories by consulting with 4 academicians and 5 professionals (total of 9 coders). Category 1 includes the most basic DM associated keywords, while category 5 consists of the highest-level DM associated keywords. The sample keywords in each category are presented in Table 2.

Step 3: The annual reports of firms were processed, and the frequency of the 238 keywords was calculated by using MAXQDA software. For this analysis, pdf documents with text conversion errors were excluded. Ultimately, 388 observations were used for the years 2016-2022 to calculate the DMI score for each firm.

Step 4: When the frequency results were analyzed, it was observed that 15 words in our list were not used in any report. Thus, they were excluded, and DMI index scores were calculated based on 223 words.

Step 5: Total DMI scores were calculated by normalizing total frequencies of 223 words by the page number in each report as follows:

$\sum_{i=1}^{223}(\text{word} * \text{frequency})/$ number of pages in report

Table 2. The keywords used in the calculation of the digital maturity level scores

Category 1	**Intranet, Internet, Server, Network Infrastructure**
Category 2	Smart TV, Smartphone, Mobility, Internet Access, Network Coverage, Network Function, Network Map, Productive, Productivity, Effectiveness
Category 3	Network Security, Information Security, Digitization, Transformation, Fiber Optic, Broadband, Quick Adaptation, Decision Making, Mobile Device, Operational Improvement, Performance Management System
Category 4	Agile, Network Automation, Smart Solutions, Smart Technology, Smart Manufacturing, Data Analytics, Cloud Computing, Cloud Security, Data Privacy, Data Lake, Digital Twin, Digital Business, Digital Workforce, 5G, Optimization, Automation, Robot, Cyber Security, Sustainability, Innovation, Edge Computing
Category 5	Artificial Intelligence, Big Data, Deep Learning, Smart Factory, Smart Agriculture, Augmented Reality, Blockchain, Business Intelligence, Digital Transformation, Image Recognition, Internet of Things, Machine Learning, Metaverse, Robotic Process Automation, Virtual Factory, Virtual Reality, Sentiment Analysis

The annual report is a formal document in which listed firms publicly disclose their financial performance for the fiscal year. It provides insights into the firm's strategic decisions and outlook. If a firm has significant strategic shifts, these changes should be clearly disclosed in the annual report. Given the public nature of this report, firms exercise care in the wording to ensure transparency. Thus, firms should provide relevant information about their digitalization progress in the annual report (Fernández-Rovira et al., 2021; Sheng et al., 2019).

Control variables

Following prior studies (Jardak & Hamad, 2022; Kuang et al., 2023; Nasiri et al., 2020; Zhao et al., 2024), firm size (SIZE), financial leverage (LEV) and firm age (AGE) were used as control variables. SIZE was calculated by taking the natural logarithm of the firm's total assets. LEV was measured by dividing total liabilities to total assets. AGE shows the period since the company was founded and is included in the model by taking its natural logarithm.

3.3. Methodology

Using Stata, the panel regression analysis was employed to evaluate the impact of DML on FP by estimating the following models (Equations 1 and 2). A dummy variable was incorporated for each year to account for any unique characteristics of the chosen period. First, FP was regressed on DML and control variables in Equation (1).

$$ROA_{i,t} = \alpha + \beta_1 DML_{i,t-1} + \beta_2 SIZE_{i,t} + \beta_3 LEV_{i,t} + \beta_4 AGE_{i,t} + \sum_{k=1}^{7} \lambda_k Year + e_{i,t} \quad (1$$

To demonstrate a U-shaped relationship, FP was regressed on DML and its squared term, DML^2, as shown in Equation 2. A significant negative coefficient for DML^2 suggests an inverted U-shaped relationship, while a significant positive coefficient for DML^2 indicates a U-shaped relationship (Haans, Pieters, & He, 2016).

$$ROA_{i,t} = \alpha + \beta_1 DML_{i,t-1} + \beta_2 DML^2_{i,t-1} + \beta_3 SIZE_{i,t} + \beta_4 LEV_{i,t} + \beta_5 AGE_{i,t} + \sum_{k=1}^{7} \lambda_k Year + e_{i,t} \quad (2)$$

4. EMPIRICAL FINDINGS

4.1. Descriptive Statistics

Table 3 presents the summary of the descriptive statistics, while Table 4 displays the correlation matrix. The Variance Inflation Factor (VIF) values for the explanatory variables are below 10, indicating that multicollinearity is not a problem. The mean score of ROA is 0.04 with a standard deviation of 0.122, implying that FP varies little among the firms in the sample. This variable also exhibits a significant positive correlation with DML as indicated by the coefficient of 0.119, showing that as the DM of a firm increases, the degree of digital adaptation significantly contributes to FP. The average DM score is only 1.323, suggesting that the level of digitalization among service sector firms in Borsa Istanbul remains relatively low. For LEV, a significant negative correlation was noted with ROA, whereas no substantial correlation is discernible with the AGE. Finally, SIZE has a positive and insignificant correlation with ROA.

Table 3. Descriptive statistics

Variable	Obs	Mean	Std. Dev.	Min	Max
ROA	388	.04	.122	-.587	.683
DML	388	1.323	1.567	0	10.905
SIZE	388	13.857	2.143	9.254	20.176
LEV	388	.566	.278	-.119	1.175
AGE	388	3.267	.663	0	4.489

Table 4. Pairwise correlations

Variables	(1)	(2)	(3)	(4)	(5)
(1) ROA	1.000				
(2) DML	0.119*	1.000			
(3) SIZE	0.064	0.517*	1.000		
(4) LEV	-0.366*	0.202*	0.381*	1.000	
(5) AGE	0.034	0.041	0.329*	0.038	1.000

** p<0.05*

4.2. Estimation Results

In Table 5, Model 1 shows the estimation results for equation (1) and Model 2 provides the estimation results for equation (2). Since our hypothesis posits a U-shaped relationship between DML and FP, the quadratic term of DML is incorporated into Model 2 to empirically test this expected relationship. Figure 3 displays the scatter plot with fitted lines depicting the relationship between DML and FP.

The red line represents the quadratic fit for the relationship between DML and FP. Quadratic fitting approximates discrete data using an analytical equation, offering a more intuitive and accurate representation of the relationship between DML and FP compared to other fitting methods. Hausman's test (1978) indicates that the random-effects model is appropriate for Model 1, while the fixed-effects model is recommended for Model 2.

Figure 3. Fitting diagram of the digital maturity level and financial performance

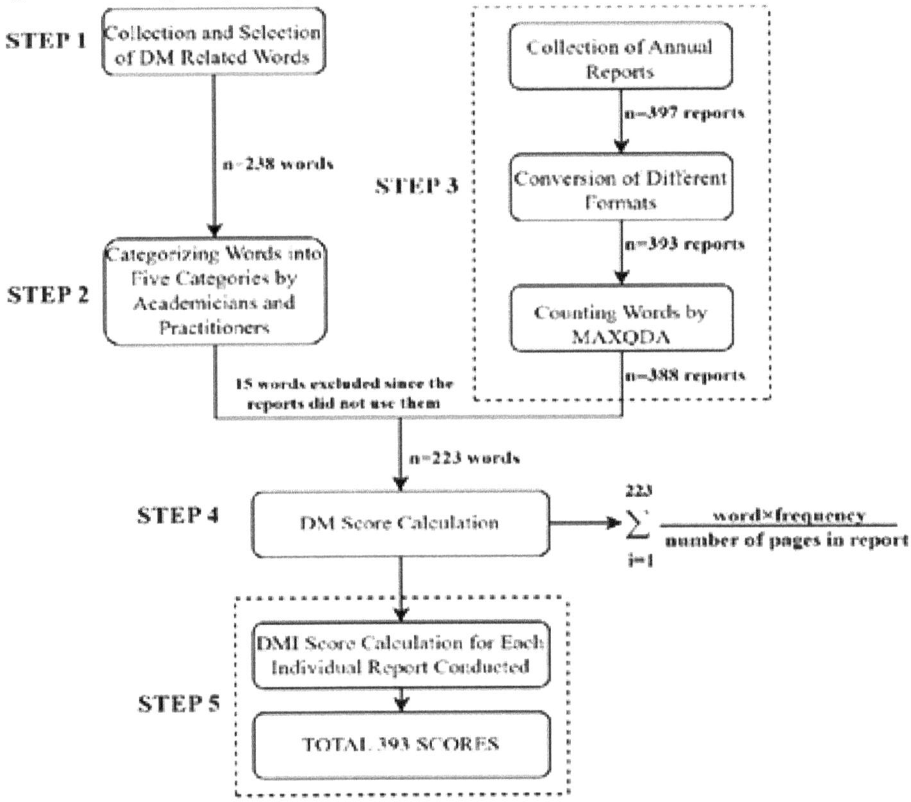

Figure 4. The non-linear relationship between digital maturity level and financial performance

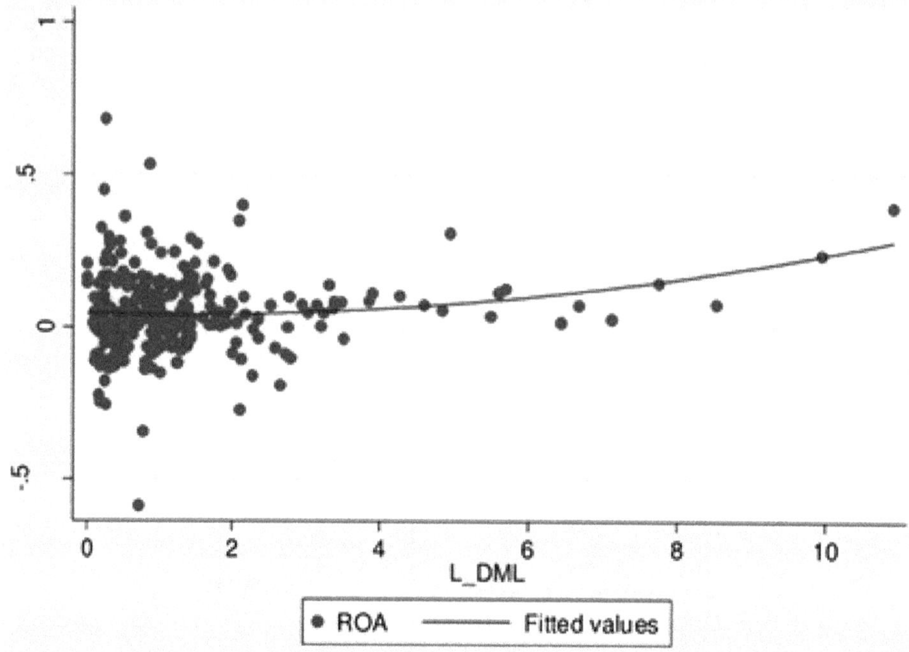

The result for ROA in Model 2 satisfies the fundamental criteria for a U-shaped relationship. The nonlinear relationship between DML and FP is shown in Figure 4. The linear term is negatively ($\beta = -0.048$, $p < 0.05$) and the squared term of DML is positively ($\beta = 0.004$, $p < 0.01$) associated with ROA. Following Haans et al. (2016) and Lind and Mehlum (2010), our findings were validated using the "utest". The null hypothesis of the "utest" posits that the relationship is either monotonic or exhibits an inverse U-shape. The alternative hypothesis is that the relationship is U-shape. In Model 2, the overall test for the non-existence of a U-shaped relationship for ROA yields a t-value of 2.50 and a corresponding p-value of 0.008, suggesting that the null hypothesis is rejected at a significance level of 1%. The findings, along with Figure 3, provide additional confirmation of the U-shaped relationship between DML and FP, supporting our hypothesis. Firms in the mature stage of digitalization exhibit higher FP compared to those in the initial stage, demonstrating that a greater digital orientation has an increasingly positive effect on FP. Hence, the relatively negative effect of digitalization decreases after the firm gets into the maturity stage. This outcome validates the findings of the prior studies (Guo & Xu, 2021; Kohtam¨aki et al., 2020; Yonghong et al., 2023).

Of the control variables, financial leverage is negatively and significantly related to ROA in Models 1 and 2 at 1% level. Firm size, firm age and the constant term are not significant in any models. The result for firm size may stem from the fact that large firms may have a small impact on digitalization level due to high costs that do not depend on the digital presence level. Conversely, small firms benefit less from advanced DT due to the large investment required.

Table 5. Panel regression results

	Model 1	**Model 2**
Variables	ROA	ROA
DML_{t-1}	0.003	-0.048**
	(0.008)	(0.019)
DML^2_{t-1}		0.004***
		(0.002)
$SIZE_t$	0.007	0.038
	(0.007)	(0.046)
LEV_t	-0.180***	-0.262***
	(0.034)	(0.073)
AGE_t	0.000	0.139
	(0.015)	(0.089)
Constant	0.021	-0.734
	(0.068)	(0.680)
Observations	328	328
Number of firms	59	59
R-squared		0.381

Robust standard errors in parentheses
*** p<0.01, ** p<0.05, * p<0.1

4.3. Ad Hoc Analysis

An ad hoc analysis was conducted to determine if our findings vary across sub-sectors. Figure 5 presents the results. There is an U-shaped relationship between DM and FP for most of the sub-sectors. Initial investment and integration challenges first decrease FP, while the benefits outweigh initial difficulties and lead to financial success in the mature stage of digitalization. The following part briefly reviews the relationship of DM and FP for sub-sectors.

Digitalization in wholesale and retail sectors is crucial due to the dominance of e-commerce. DT optimize operations, improve customer experiences, and help build agile models. POS system, personalized shopping experiences, supply chain management softwares are some examples of digitalization. Firms initially face challenges due to the high costs of integrating DT into the inventory, and supply chain management systems, posing financial problems. Long-term benefits emerge gradually with enhanced customer engagement, improved operational efficiency, and wider market access as Kumar and Sandhu (2018) argue.

In the electricity, gas and water sector, DT enable better reliability, improved operations, and grid resiliency. This sector is heavily asset-intensive, with high fixed costs related to infrastructure, generation, and distribution, leading to financial losses at the early-stage of digitalization. AI-driven grid optimization, and IoT-enabled sensors reduce operating costs by preventing downtime and optimizing energy and water distribution. High DM empowers utilities to deploy smart grids and water management systems, leading to cost savings, improved demand forecasting and excess capacity reduction. Dynamic pricing, and consumption insights via mobile apps raise customer satisfaction, and result in increasing revenue streams.

In the hotels and restaurants sector, front office technologies assist customer processes and back-office technologies streamline administrative tasks, overcoming low productivity (Lee, Jang & Kim, 2024). This is important since the operations of these sectors have low profit margin and high labor intensity (Mun & Jang, 2018). DT helps firms reduce labor intensity through automation, data-driven decisions, and optimization, leading to higher FP at high DML.

Firms in real estate sector incur high implementation costs at the early stage of digitalization. This matter temporarily reduces FP. AI-driven property valuations, virtual tours, and online mortgage processing, enable companies to better predict market trends, optimize property valuations, and personalize client experiences, boosting FP in the high DML.

In education, health, sport and entertainment services, online learning platforms, telemedicine tools, sports analytics systems, and digital ticketing require high investment costs, and when it is coupled with employee training and workflow restructuring, it reduces FP. Advanced DM enables significant cost savings and efficiency through the automation of repetitive tasks (e.g. appointment scheduling in healthcare, ticket sales in entertainment) and data-driven decision-making (e.g. personalized education, training based on sports analytics).

Figure 5. Fitting diagram of the digital maturity level and financial performance for sub-sectors

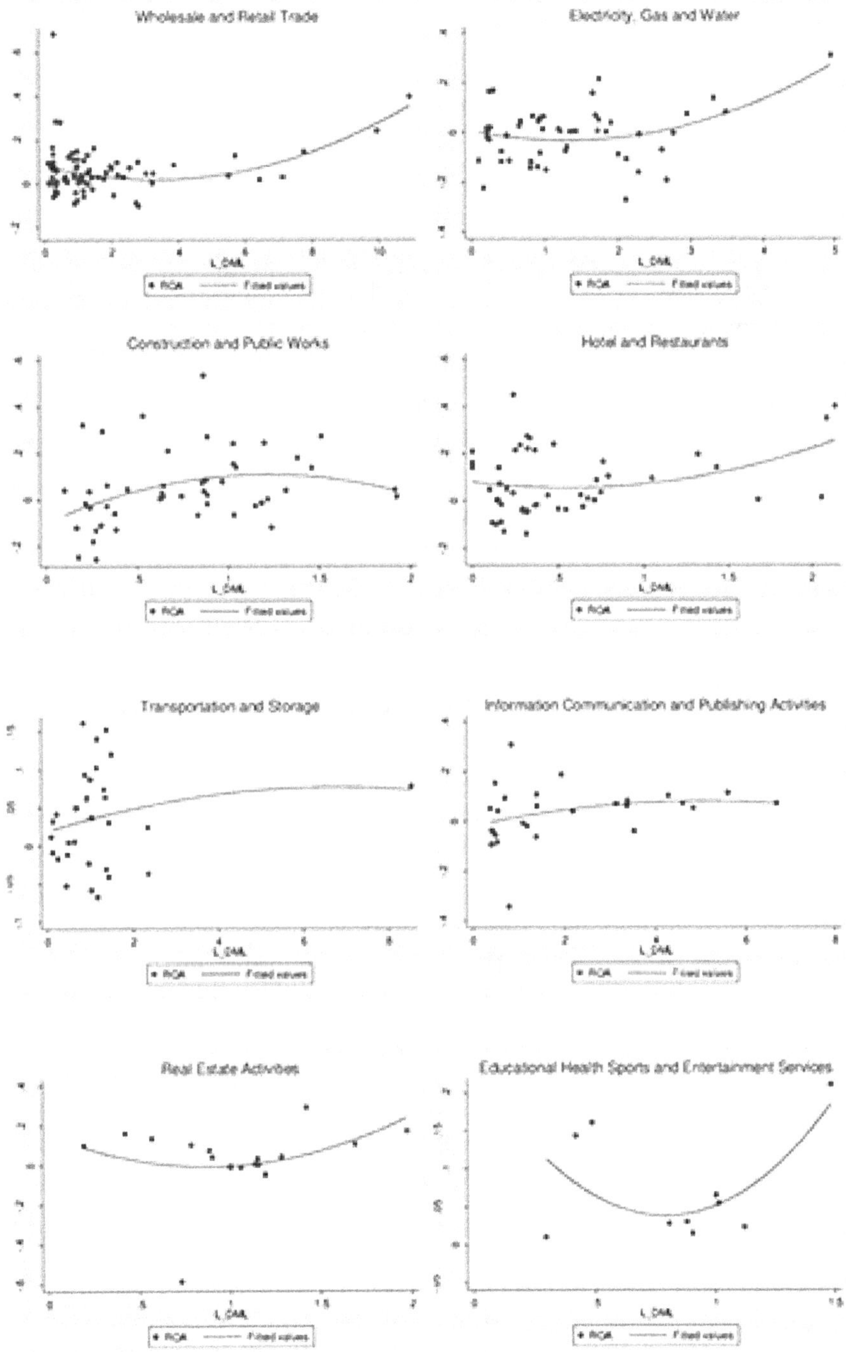

On the other hand, an inverted U-shaped relationship was observed in the scatter diagrams for the information, communication and publishing, construction and public works, transportation and storage sectors. These sub-sectors were decomposed, and their graphics were plotted in Figure 6.

Media and telecommunication sectors exhibit distinct patterns. Media sector shows an upward trend in FP as DML increases. Digitally mature firms successfully diversify revenue streams through subscription models, digital advertising and data-driven content personalization (Lozić & Čiković, 2021). Telecommunication sector exhibits a linear positive relationship between DM and FP, reflecting steady improvement in FP as DM raises. 5G connectivity, and digital communication tools drives consistent revenue growth. Unlike media sector, telecommunication sector faces fewer financial problems in the early stage of digitalization since investments in digital infrastructure directly align with their long-run goals.

The construction and public works sectors can be divided into energy and construction and materials sectors. In energy sector, FP improves consistently as DM increases, with gains accelerating at high DML. Energy firms leverage advanced analytics and AI to optimize operations across the value chain, i.e. generation, transmission, and distribution. At the high DML, digital platforms enhance customer engagement through personalized services, smart meters, and real-time energy consumption insights. Construction and material sector, on the other hand, conduct project-based works. Early digitalization improves efficiency and raise FP, whereas excessive reliance on DT lead resistance from workers, negatively affecting FP.

In the transportation and storage sectors, airlines have a U-shaped curve, whereas other transportation firms have an inverse U-shape curve. Airlines bear high upfront costs in adopting DT such as customer relationship management system, and advanced fleet management tools, temporarily decreasing FP. However, at the high DML, airlines benefit from integrated systems, i.e. AI-driven pricing, predictive maintenance for aircraft, and automated customer services, and reduce costs and improve service quality. High DML also improves customer experience through personalized services, i.e. booking platforms, real-time updates (Heiets et al., 2022; Menon et al., 2019). It allows airlines to leverage big data for optimizing flight schedules, route planning, and fuel efficiency, contributing to financial gains. Unlike airlines, firms in other transportation sectors adopt DT incrementally. Fleet tracking, route optimization, and digital logistics improve operational efficiency and cost management, leading to steady financial gains.

Figure 6. Fitting diagram of the digital maturity level and financial performance for sectors that have an inverse U-shaped relationship

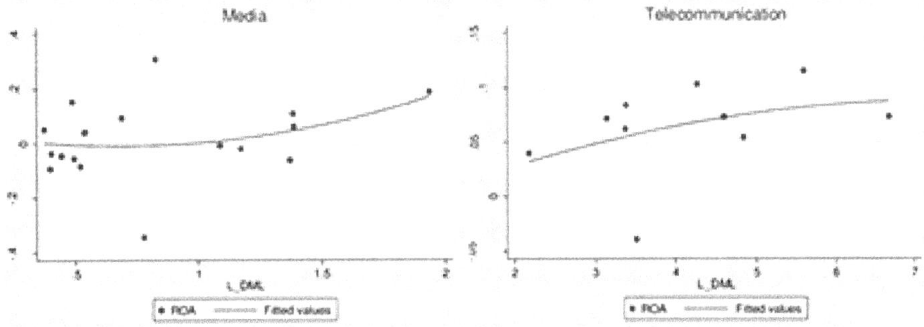

a. **Information, communication and publishing activities**

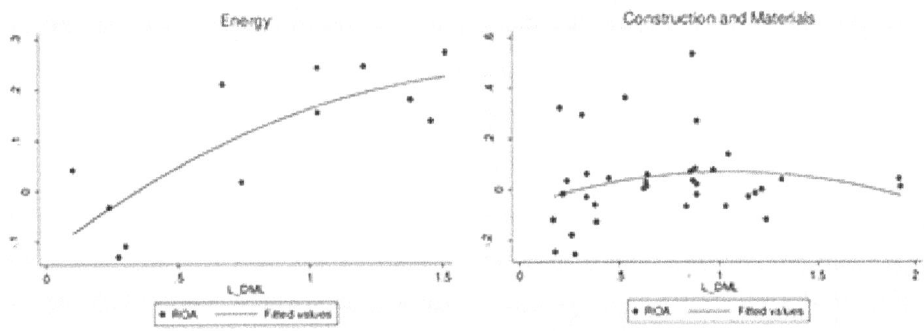

b. **Construction and public works**

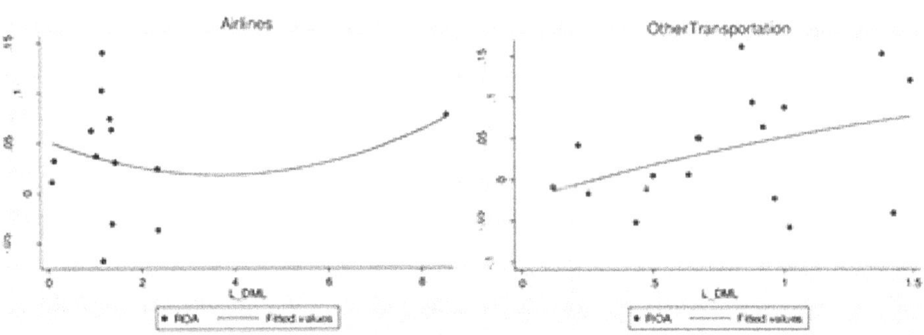

c. **Transportation and storage**

4.4. Addressing the Endogeneity Problem

The relationship between DML and FP may suffer from reverse causality, leading to an endogeneity issue. Firms with lower performance are more inclined to implement digital transformation to modify their operations. To address this endogeneity concern, the generalized method of moments (GMM) approach (1991) was employed to conduct endogeneity tests.

Following prior studies (Wintoki et al., 2012; Yilmaz et al., 2023), a diagnostic test for strict exogeneity was conducted, as recommended by Wooldridge (2010), according to the Equation 3:

$$Y_{it} = \alpha + \beta X_{it} + \gamma Z_{it+1} + \Omega_{it+1} + u_{it} + e_{it} \quad (3)$$

Where "Zit+1" represents the future values of DML and DML^2 and "Ωit+1" are the future values of SIZE, LEV, and AGE.

Wooldridge test results are presented in Table 6, Model 1. The coefficient estimates for the future values of DML ($\beta = -0.040$, $p < 0.05$) and DML^2 ($\beta = 0.004$, $p < 0.05$) are significantly different from zero. This indicates that there may be an endogeneity problem. Additionally, an F-test examining the joint effect of the coefficient estimates for all future values is significant (2.03, $p < 0.10$). The results of the Wooldridge strict exogeneity test for the dependent variable ROA indicate endogeneity, as they reject Wooldridge's null hypothesis.

After confirming the endogeneity among the variables, we adopted Blundell and Bond's (1998) two-step system (generalized method of moment [GMM]) as the preferred approach to address the endogeneity issues potentially arising from the dynamic nature of our model. We utilized the two-step GMM approach incorporating Windmeijer's (2005) correction. LEV, AGE, and year dummies were considered as exogenous variables, while treating DML, DML^2 and SIZE as endogenous.

The validity of the two-step GMM method can be assessed using various post-estimation tests. Among these tests, Arellano–Bond AR (1) and AR (2) test statistics indicate whether there is first and second order autocorrelation in the model, while Sargan and Hansen (1958, 1982) test statistics indicate whether instrumental variables are valid. Among the autocorrelation tests, the AR(1) test result ($p < 0.05$) is expected to be statistically significant and negative, while the AR(2) test result ($p > 0.1$) is expected to be statistically insignificant. This indicates that although there may be first-order autocorrelation in the model, there is no issue with second-order autocorrelation (Arellano, 2003). The Sargan and Hansen ($p > 0.1$) test results show that the instrumental variables used are valid. Furthermore, the exogeneity of the instrumental variables can be evaluated using the difference Hansen test.

The difference Hansen test shows that there is no endogeneity problem. Thus, the assumptions required for estimation with system GMM are met.

In Table 6, the one-year lagged ROA (0.247, $p<0.05$), the two-year lagged DML (0.073, $p<0.05$) and DML^2 (-0.007, $p<0.05$) and three years lagged DML (-0.095, $p<0.01$) and DML^2 (0.013, $p<0.01$) and one-year lagged LEV (-0.145, $p<0.01$) coefficients were significant. The fact that the one-year lagged ROA was significant shows that previous ROA values have significant effects on the current ROA values. The GMM coefficient estimates for the independent and control variables align with and support the estimates from the models presented in Table 5.

Table 6. Wooldridge test results (Model 1) and GMM results (Model 2)

	Model 1	**Model 2**
Variables	ROA	ROA
DML_{t-1}	-0.001	-0.011
	(0.025)	(0.038)
DML^2_{t-1}	-0.000	0.002
	(0.002)	(0.003)
$SIZE_t$	0.081	
	(0.056)	
LEV_t	-0.234***	
	(0.080)	
AGE_t	1.026	-0.016
	(1.009)	(0.017)
DML_t	-0.040**	
	(0.018)	
DML^2_t	0.004**	
	(0.002)	
$SIZE_{t+1}$	-0.059	
	(0.035)	
LEV_{t+1}	-0.084	
	(0.069)	
AGE_{t+1}	-1.159	
	(1.335)	
ROA_{t-1}		0.247**

continued on following page

Table 6. Continued

	Model 1	Model 2
		(0.109)
DML_{t-2}		0.073**
		(0.034)
DML_{t-3}		-0.095***
		(0.034)
DML^2_{t-2}		-0.007**
		(0.003)
DML^2_{t-3}		0.013***
		(0.004)
$SIZE_{t-1}$		0.001
		(0.010)
LEV_{t-1}		-0.145***
		(0.049)
Constant	0.434	0.255***
	(1.341)	(0.080)
Number of instruments		71
Arellano–Bond AR (1)		-2.07**
Arellano–Bond AR (2)		-1.29
Hansen test (p value)		49.25 (0.758)
Observations	269	210
R-squared	0.288	
Number of HisseID	59	56

Year dummies are treated as exogenous variables, and they are unreported.
The model is estimated with system GMM, two-step, Windmeijer correction.
Robust standard errors in parentheses
*** p<0.01, ** p<0.05, * p<0.1

5. CONCLUSIONS AND DISCUSSIONS

Given the accelerated evolution of information technologies, digital transformation has become a vital strategic focus for firms aiming to improve their performance in the dynamic business environment. The implementation of digital technologies provides a competitive advantage by reducing costs and increasing quality, leading to a different positioning in the market. To achieve this goal and display better financial results from digital resources, firms must have talented employees with adequate training. This study explores whether digital maturity level of firms affects financial performance by running text mining analysis to the annual reports of service sector firms listed on Borsa Istanbul for the years 2016-2022. MAXQDA software was used to analyze the frequencies of digitalization related keywords in the annual reports.

The findings indicate a distinct U-shaped relationship between DML and FP. The initial excitement surrounding digital transformation can wane as firms struggle with the cultural shift required for successful digitalization. As argued by Kane et al. (2015), organizational culture is one of the primary barriers to digital transformation, as employees often resist new technologies that challenge established routines. Westerman, Bonnet, and McAfee (2014) emphasize that without strong digital leadership and a culture that supports experimentation, firms fail to sustain momentum in their digital efforts. Therefore, companies initially experience a decline in FP as they bear the investment and adaptation costs of digitalization. This decline can be attributed to their inability to fully leverage digital tools due to cultural adaptation and internal resistance. Managers should also gain the required expertise to efficiently use these tools, which take some time depending upon the integration speed of digital processes. As entities develop a more mature digital culture, the preliminary negative effects gradually diminish with a time lag and become positive with the deepening of digitalization process. This may be due to better acceptance and utilization of DT by employees and executive managers. This finding indicates that the cost of some DT investments, e.g. data analytics, AI, might be so high that the time-to-payoff would be extensive, influencing FP over time as argued by Wamba et al. (2017). Thus, as firms embrace digital transformation and reach a certain level of digital maturity, they reap the rewards of digital investments such as better relationships with customers, suppliers and other stakeholders, leading to significant improvements in FP. Finally, the findings reveal that the relationship between DML and FP varies across information, communication and publishing activities, construction and public works, and transportation and storage sectors due to diverse characteristics of firms in these sub-sectors.

5.1. Theoretical and Managerial Implications

5.1.1. Theoretical implications

This study offers important theoretical implications and enriches the literature on the relationship between digital maturity and firm performance. Within the theoretical framework of the RBV, this study pinpoints the strategic features of digitalization as a competitive resource to show how accelerated digitalization may increase financial performance. However, as argued by Lichtenthaler (2019), having digital technologies as strategic resources is not enough. Firms should dynamically combine their human and digital architecture to sustain competitive advantages. This approach also aligns with the intelligence-based view that highlights the importance of integrating digital technologies to enhance firm performance. Thus, our findings have significant implications for the RBV, enriching its relevance and application in digital era.

5.1.2. Managerial implications

This study yields several implications for companies and policy makers. For companies, the digitization process requires significant investment in technology, skills and cultural change. Therefore, it is important for firms to have a well-defined digitization strategy, considering the specific needs and goals of the company. Firms should not only consider the technological aspect of digital transformation but also align it with strategic objectives to maximize its financial impact. On this respect, they must cultivate skillful human resources with different digital experiences to boost the financial benefits of digitalization. Second, the notification and disclosure of digital progresses in the annual report have an impact on the perceived value, encouraging investors to increase their investment. Thus, companies should pay close attention to the value offerings on digitalization and take the necessary actions for positively influencing the perception of stakeholders through their reports and disclosures. Ultimately, firms should gradually formulate digitalization strategies and maneuver digital sphere in a reasonable manner to get expected financial gains.

Promoting the digital maturity of firms also requires the efforts of government and policymakers. It is essential for government to encourage digitalization on firm level through preferential policies. Policymakers should also strengthen cybersecurity and data governance matters. To address the risk of information leakage resulting from digital transformation, policymakers should empower data protection regulations concerning intellectual property rights, enhance cross-sector standards for secure data sharing, and expand compliance support programs to help firms implement robust protective measures. For emerging markets, policymakers must also address structural constraints such as limited digital infrastructure and unequal access to high-speed internet, which can hinder firms' ability to adopt advanced technologies. They should design capacity-building initiatives that support small and medium-sized firms in acquiring the skills and resources needed to participate in the digital economy.

5.2. Limitations of the Study and Future Research

We recognize that our study has several limitations that offer avenues for future exploration. First, the sample consists of only Turkish companies. This may hinder the generalizability of the results due to the different set of digital capabilities in other emerging markets. Future research may extend the coverage and make cross-country analysis. Second, this study includes only service sector firms. Digital orientation of manufacturing firms may reveal different results due to their diverse profile. Third, this work does not use any moderating or mediating variable that may further explain the interplay between digital maturity and financial performance. Future studies may employ moderating or mediating variables to get more refined results. Finally, there is limited data and information available on digitalization in the annual reports of firms due to corporate confidentiality. Future research may collect primary data to enhance the validity of the findings.

REFERENCES

AlMulhim, A. F. (2021). Smart supply chain and firm performance: The role of digital technologies. *Business Process Management Journal, 27*(5), 1353–1372. DOI: 10.1108/BPMJ-12-2020-0573

Andersen, E. (2023). *Digital technology on financial performance.* BI Norwegian Business School, Master Thesis.

Arellano, M. (2003). *Panel data econometrics.* Oxford University Press. DOI: 10.1093/0199245282.001.0001

Arellano, M., & Bond, S. (1991). Some tests of specification for panel data: Monte Carlo evidence and an application to employment equations. *The Review of Economic Studies, 58*(2), 277–297. DOI: 10.2307/2297968

Barney, J. (1991). Firm resources and sustained competitive advantage. *Journal of Management, 17*(1), 99–120. DOI: 10.1177/014920639101700108

Blundell, R., & Bond, S. (1998). Initial conditions and moment restrictions in dynamic panel data models. *Journal of Econometrics, 87*(1), 115–143. DOI: 10.1016/S0304-4076(98)00009-8

Bouwman, H., Nikou, S., Molina-Castillo, F. J., & de Reuver, M. (2018). The impact of digitalization on business models. *Digital Policy. Regulation & Governance, 20*(2), 105–124.

Brinch, M., Gunasekaran, A., & Wamba, S. F. (2021). Firm-level capabilities towards big data value creation. *Journal of Business Research, 131*, 539–548. DOI: 10.1016/j.jbusres.2020.07.036

Bughin, J., & van Zeebroeck, N. (2017). The best response to digital disruption. *MIT Sloan Management Review.* https://sloanreview.mit.edu/article/the–right–response–to–digital–disruption/

Cherkasova, V. A., & Slepushenko, G. A. (2021). The impact of digitalization on the financial performance of Russian companies. *Finance: Theory and Practice, 25*(2), 128–142.

Chin, H.-S., Marasini, D. P., & Lee, D.-H. (2023). Digital transformation trends in service industries. *Service Business, 17*(1), 11–36. DOI: 10.1007/s11628-022-00516-6

Dahlman, C., Mealy, S., & Wermelinger, M. (2016). *Harnessing the digital economy for developing countries.* OECD Development Centre Working Paper, 334. DOI: DOI: 10.1787/18151949

Deloitte. (2023). *Uncovering the connection between digital maturity and financial performance.* https://www2.deloitte.com/content/dam/insights/us/articles/6561_digital-transformation/DI_Digital-transformation.pdf

Dobbs, R., Koller, T., Ramaswamy, S., Woetzel, J., Manyika, J., Krishnan, R., & Andreula, N. (2015). *Playing to win: The new global competition for corporate profits*. McKinsey Global Institute.

Dreisbach, C., Koleck, T. A., Bourne, P. E., & Bakken, S. (2019). A systematic review of natural language processing and text mining of symptoms from electronic patient-authored text data. *International Journal of Medical Informatics*, *125*, 37–46. DOI: 10.1016/j.ijmedinf.2019.02.008 PMID: 30914179

Dubey, R., Gunasekaran, A., Childe, S. J., Blome, C., & Papadopoulos, T. (2019). Big data and predictive analytics and manufacturing performance: Integrating institutional theory, resource-based view and big data culture. *British Journal of Management*, *30*(2), 341–361. DOI: 10.1111/1467-8551.12355

Dutta, A., Lee, H., & Yasai-Ardekani, M. (2014). Digital systems and competitive responsiveness: The dynamics of IT business value. *Information & Management*, *51*(6), 762–773. DOI: 10.1016/j.im.2014.05.005

Fernandez-Portillo, A., Almodovar-Gonzalez, M., Sanchez-Escobedo, M. C., & Coca-Perez, J. L. (2022). The role of innovation in the relationship between digitalisation and economic and financial performance. A company-level research. *European Research on Management and Business Economics*, *28*(3), 100190. DOI: 10.1016/j.iedeen.2021.100190

Fernández-Rovira, C., Valdés, J. Á., Molleví, G., & Nicolas-Sans, R. (2021). The digital transformation of business. Towards the datafication of the relationship with customers. *Technological Forecasting and Social Change*, *162*, 120339. DOI: 10.1016/j.techfore.2020.120339

Fu, T., & Li, J. (2023). An empirical analysis of the impact of ESG on financial performance: The moderating role of digital transformation. *Frontiers in Environmental Science*, *11*, 1256052. DOI: 10.3389/fenvs.2023.1256052

Gebauer, H., Fleisch, E., Lamprecht, C., & Wortmann, F. (2020). Growth paths for overcoming the digitalization paradox. *Business Horizons*, *63*(3), 313–323. DOI: 10.1016/j.bushor.2020.01.005

Gebauer, H., Paiola, M., Saccani, N., & Rapaccini, M. (2021). Digital servitization: Crossing the perspectives of digitization and servitization. *Industrial Marketing Management*, *93*, 382–388. DOI: 10.1016/j.indmarman.2020.05.011

Guo, L., & Xu, L. (2021). The effects of digital transformation on firm performance: Evidence from China's manufacturing sector. *Sustainability (Basel), 13*(22), 12844. DOI: 10.3390/su132212844

Gurbaxani, V., & Dunkle, D. (2019). Gearing up for successful digital transformation. *MIS Quarterly Executive, 18*(3), 6. DOI: 10.17705/2msqe.00017

Haans, R. F., Pieters, C., & He, Z. L. (2016). Thinking about U: Theorizing and testing U-and inverted U-shaped relationships in strategy research. *Strategic Management Journal, 37*(7), 1177–1195. DOI: 10.1002/smj.2399

Hansen, L. P. (1982). Large sample properties of generalized method of moments estimators. *Econometrica, 50*(4), 1029–1054. DOI: 10.2307/1912775

He, F., & Liu, H. (2019). Assessment of the performance enhancemen effect of digital change in real enterprises from the perspective of digital economy. *Reformation, 04*, 137–148.

Heiets, I., La, J., Zhou, W., Xu, S., Wang, X., & Xu, Y. (2022). Digital transformation of airline industry. *Research in Transportation Economics, 92*, 101186. DOI: 10.1016/j.retrec.2022.101186

Hess, T., Matt, C., Benlian, A., & Wiesböck, F. (2016). Options for formulating a digital transformation strategy. *MIS Quarterly Executive, 15*(2), 123–139.

Huang, C., Wang, H. T., & Huang, T.-Y. (2020). Initial evidence on the impact of big data implementation on firm performance. *Information Systems Frontiers, 22*(2), 475–487. DOI: 10.1007/s10796-018-9872-5

Immonen, M., & Sintonen, S. (2015). Evolution of technology perceptions over time. *Information Technology & People, 28*(3), 589–606. DOI: 10.1108/ITP-12-2013-0219

Jardak, M. K., & Ben Hamad, S. (2022). The effect of digital transformation on firm performance: Evidence from Swedish listed companies. *The Journal of Risk Finance, 23*(4), 329–348. DOI: 10.1108/JRF-12-2021-0199

Kane, G. C., Palmer, D., Phillips, A. N., Kiron, D., & Buckley, N. (2015). Strategy, not technology, drives digital transformation. *MIT Sloan Management Review.*

Kohtam¨aki, M., Parida, V., Patel, P. C., & Gebauer, H. (2020). The relationship between digitalization and servitization: The role of servitization in capturing the financial potential of digitalization. *Technological Forecasting and Social Change, 151*(6), 119804. DOI: 10.1016/j.techfore.2019.119804

Kuang, Y., Fan, M., Fan, Y., Jiang, Y., & Bin, J. (2023). Digitalization, financing constraints and firm performance. *Frontiers in Environmental Science, 11*, 1090537. DOI: 10.3389/fenvs.2023.1090537

Kumar, V., & Sandhu, A. (2018). From bricks to mobile: The evolution of the retail shop and the role of technology. *Journal of the Academy of Marketing Science, 46*(4), 537–556.

Lee, S., & Lim, S. (2018). *Living innovation: from value creation to the greater good*. Emerald Publishing Limited. DOI: 10.1108/9781787567139

Lee, W., Jang, S. S., & Kim, H. S. (2024). The effect of digital transformation: Boosting productivity in the restaurant industry. *International Journal of Hospitality Management, 123*, 103896. DOI: 10.1016/j.ijhm.2024.103896

Lei, L., Yang, S., & Chen, N. (2022). The impact of digital transformation on enterprise investment efficiency. *Soft Science, 36*(11), 23–29.

Libert, B., Beck, M., & Wind, Y. (2016). Questions to ask before your next digital transformation. *Harvard Business Review, 60*(12), 11–13.

Lichtenthaler, U. (2019). An intelligence-based view of firm performance: Profiting from artificial intelligence. *Journal of Innovation Management, 7*(1), 7–20. DOI: 10.24840/2183-0606_007.001_0002

Lind, J. T., & Mehlum, H. (2010). With or Without U? – The appropriate test for a U-shaped relationship. *Oxford Bulletin of Economics and Statistics, 72*(1), 109–118. DOI: 10.1111/j.1468-0084.2009.00569.x

Lozić, J., & Čiković, K. F. (2021). The impact of digital transformation on the business efficiency of the New York Times. *UTMS Journal of Economics, 12*(2), 225-239.

Marjaei, S., Yazdi, F. A., & Chandrashekara, M. (2019). MAXQDA and its application to LIS research. *Library Philosophy and Practice,* 1-9. Retrieved from https://www.proquest.com/scholarly-journals/maxqda-application-lis-research/docview/2236131089/se-2

Martín-Peña, M.-L., Sánchez-López, J.-M., & Díaz-Garrido, E. (2019). Servitization and digitalization in manufacturing: The influence on firm performance. *Journal of Business and Industrial Marketing, 35*(3), 564–574. DOI: 10.1108/JBIM-12-2018-0400

Masoud, R., & Basahel, S. (2023). The effects of digital transformation on firm performance: The role of customer experience and IT innovation. *Digital, 3*(2), 109–126. DOI: 10.3390/digital3020008

Menon, V., Sigurdsson, V., Larsen, M., Fagerstrøm, A., Sørensen, H., Marteinsdottir, H. G., & Foxall, G. R. (2019). How to grow brand post engagement on Facebook and twitter for airlines? An empirical investigation of design and content factors. *Journal of Air Transport Management, 79*, 90–95. DOI: 10.1016/j.jairtraman.2019.05.002

Mikalef, P., Boura, M., Lekakos, G., & Krogstie, J. (2019). Big data analytics and firm performance: Findings from a mixed-method approach. *Journal of Business Research, 98*, 261–276. DOI: 10.1016/j.jbusres.2019.01.044

Mithas, S., Tafti, A., Bardhan, I. R., & Goh, J. M. (2012). Information technology and firm profitability: Mechanisms and empirical evidence. *Management Information Systems Quarterly, 36*(1), 205–224. DOI: 10.2307/41410414

Mun, S. G., & Jang, S. S. (2018). Restaurant operating expenses and their effects on profitability enhancement. *International Journal of Hospitality Management, 71*, 68–76. DOI: 10.1016/j.ijhm.2017.12.002

Nasiri, M., Ukko, J., Saunila, M., Rantala, T., & Rantanen, H. (2020). Digital-related capabilities and financial performance: The mediating effect of performance measurement systems. *Technology Analysis and Strategic Management, 31*(12), 1393–1406. DOI: 10.1080/09537325.2020.1772966

Nayyar, G., Hallward-Driemeier, M., & Davies, E. (2021). *At Your Service: the Promise of Services-Led Development*. World Bank Publications., DOI: 10.1596/978-1-4648-1671-0

Ndubuisi, G., Owusu, S., Asiama, R., & Avenyo, E. K. (2023). Drivers of services sector growth acceleration in developing countries. World Institute for Development Economics Research (WIDER). *Working Paper, 2023*(87).

Paiola, M., & Gebauer, H. (2020). Internet of things technologies, digital servitization and business model innovation in BtoB manufacturing firms. *Industrial Marketing Management, 89*, 245–264. DOI: 10.1016/j.indmarman.2020.03.009

Parida, V., Sjödin, D., & Reim, W. (2019). Reviewing literature on digitalization, business model innovation, and sustainable industry: Past achievements and future promises. *Sustainability (Basel), 11*(2), 1102391. DOI: 10.3390/su11020391

Ribeiro-Navarrete, S., Botella-Carrubi, D., Palacios-Marqués, D., & Orero-Blat, M. (2021). The effect of digitalization on business performance: An applied study of KIBS. *Journal of Business Research, 126*, 319–326. DOI: 10.1016/j.jbusres.2020.12.065

Rivard, S., Raymond, L., & Verreault, D. (2006). Resource-based view and competitive strategy: An integrated model of the contribution of information technology to firm performance. *The Journal of Strategic Information Systems*, *15*(1), 29–50. DOI: 10.1016/j.jsis.2005.06.003

Rodriguez, J. L., & Rodriguez, R. M. G. (2005). Technology and export behaviour: A resource-based view approach. *International Business Review*, *14*(5), 539–557. DOI: 10.1016/j.ibusrev.2005.07.002

Roy, S. K., Balaji, M., Sadeque, S., Nguyen, B., & Melewar, T. (2017). Constituents and consequences of smart customer experience in retailing. *Technological Forecasting and Social Change*, *124*, 257–270. DOI: 10.1016/j.techfore.2016.09.022

Rybchak, Z., & Basystiuk, O. (2017). Analysis of methods and means of text mining. *ECONTECHMOD: An International Quarterly Journal on Economics of Technology and Modelling Processes*, *6*(2), 73–78.

Sargan, J. D. (1958). The estimation of economic relationships using instrumental variables. *Econometrica*, *26*(3), 393–415. DOI: 10.2307/1907619

Sheng, J., Amankwah-Amoah, J., & Wang, X. (2019). Technology in the 21st century: New challenges and opportunities. *Technological Forecasting and Social Change*, *143*, 321–335. DOI: 10.1016/j.techfore.2018.06.009

Skorupinska, A., & Torrent-Sellens, J. (2017). ICT, innovation and productivity: Evidence based on eastern European manufacturing companies. *Journal of the Knowledge Economy*, *8*(2), 768–788. DOI: 10.1007/s13132-016-0441-1

Truant, E., Broccardo, L., & Dana, L. (2021). Digitalisation boosts company performance: An overview of Italian listed companies. *Technological Forecasting and Social Change*, *173*, 121173. DOI: 10.1016/j.techfore.2021.121173

Valaskova, K., Nagy, M., & Juracka, D. (2025). Digital transformation and financial performance: An empirical analysis of strategic alignment in the digital age. *Journal of Enterprising Communities: People and Places in the Global Economy*, *19*(5), 1178–1205. DOI: 10.1108/JEC-11-2024-0241

Verhoef, P. C., Broekhuizen, T., Bart, Y., Bhattacharya, A., Dong, J. Q., Fabian, N., & Haenlein, M. (2019). Digital transformation: A multidisciplinary reflection and research agenda. *Journal of Business Research*, *122*(1), 889–901.

Vial, G. (2019). Understanding digital transformation: A review and a research agenda. *The Journal of Strategic Information Systems*, *28*(2), 118–144. DOI: 10.1016/j.jsis.2019.01.003

Vitari, C., & Raguseo, E. (2016). Digital data, dynamic capability and financial performance: An empirical investigation in the era of big data. *Systemes d'Information Management, 21*(3), 63–92. DOI: 10.3917/sim.163.0063

Vu, K. M. (2011). ICT as a source of economic growth in the information age: Empirical evidence from the 1996-2005 period. *Telecommunications Policy, 35*(4), 357–372. DOI: 10.1016/j.telpol.2011.02.008

Wamba, S. F., Gunasekaran, A., Akter, S., Ren, S. J., Dubey, R., & Childe, S. J. (2017). Big data analytics and firm performance: Effects of dynamic capabilities. *Journal of Business Research, 70*, 356–365. DOI: 10.1016/j.jbusres.2016.08.009

Westerman, G., Bonnet, D., & McAfee, A. (2014). *Leading digital: Turning technology into business transformation.* Harvard Business Review Press.

Windmeijer, F. (2005). A finite sample correction for the variance of linear efficient two-step GMM estimators. *Journal of Econometrics, 126*(1), 25–51. DOI: 10.1016/j.jeconom.2004.02.005

Wintoki, M. B., Linck, J. S., & Netter, J. M. (2012). Endogeneity and the dynamics of internal corporate governance. *Journal of Financial Economics, 105*(3), 581–606. DOI: 10.1016/j.jfineco.2012.03.005

Wooldridge, J. M. (2010). *Econometric analysis of cross section and panel data.* The MIT Press.

World Economic Forum. (2024). The digital economy. https://intelligence.weforum.org/topics/a1Gb0000001SH21EAG

Worldbank. (2024). World Development Indicators: Structure of value. https://wdi.worldbank.org/table/4.2

Wroblewski, J. B. (2018). *Digitalization and firm performance: Are digitally mature firms outperforming their peers?* Lund University School of Economics and Management, Master Thesis.

Wu, F., Hu, H. Z., Lin, H. Y., & Ren, X. Y. (2021). Digital transformation of enterprises and capital market performance: Empirical evidence from stock liquidity. *Journal of Management World, 37*(07), 130–144.

Yilmaz, M.K., Hacioglu, U., Tatoglu, E., Aksoy, M., & Duran, S. (2023). Measuring the impact of board gender and cultural diversity on corporate governance and social performance: evidence from emerging markets. *Economic Research-Ekonomska Istraživanja, 36(*2).

Yonghong, L., Jie, S., Ge, Z., & Ru, Z. (2023). The impact of enterprise digital transformation on financial performance-Evidence from Mainland China manufacturing firms. *MDE. Managerial and Decision Economics*, *44*(4), 2110–2124. DOI: 10.1002/mde.3805

Zeng, H., Ran, H., Zhou, Q., Jin, Y., & Cheng, X. (2022). The financial effect of firm digitalization: Evidence from China. *Technological Forecasting and Social Change*, *183*, 121951. DOI: 10.1016/j.techfore.2022.121951

Zhao, X., Li, X., Li, Y., & Wang, Z. (2024). The impact of digital transformation on firm performance. *Industrial Management & Data Systems*, *124*(8), 2567–2587. DOI: 10.1108/IMDS-09-2023-0661

Zhou, Y., Ock, Y.-S., Alnafrah, I., & Dagestani, A. A. (2023). What aspects explain the relationship between digital transformation and financial performance of firms? *Journal of Risk and Financial Management*, *16*(11), 110479. DOI: 10.3390/jrfm16110479

Chapter 12
The Virtual Currency Paradigm:
Transforming the Landscape of Money Laundering and White-Collar Offenses in the Digital Era

Saurabh Chandra
http://orcid.org/0000-0003-4172-9968
Bennett University, India

Versha Vahini
http://orcid.org/0000-0003-2653-3027
Bennett University, India

Boddu Harshith Sai
http://orcid.org/0009-0009-4884-4126
London School of Economics and Political Science, India

Suparna Kundu
http://orcid.org/0009-0000-5142-8945
Amity University, Kolkata, India

Pradeep Kulshrestha
http://orcid.org/0000-0002-6805-1010
Bennett University, India

Bhumika Muchan
http://orcid.org/0009-0003-5294-998X
Bennett University, India

ABSTRACT

Digital currencies have gained significant popularity due to their distinct benefits,including rapid cross-border transactions,decreased transaction costs, improved privacy, and diminished dependence on conventional banking systems. Cryptocurrencies,including Bitcoin,Ethereum and others,function on decentralized platforms that utilize blockchain technology. unregulated and pseudonymous characteristics of cryptocurrencies have rendered them a prime target for exploitation in illicit activities, especially in the context of white-collar crimes such as money laundering.This research paper examines the changing dynamics between cryptocurrency and money laundering, highlighting how individuals and criminal enterprises

DOI: 10.4018/979-8-3373-5052-3.ch012

leverage this technology to bypass established financial controls and avoid detection. This paper extensively examines the challenges encountered by regulatory authorities in addressing money laundering activities associated with cryptocurrencies.

INTRODUCTION

Money laundering is the process of concealing the origins of illegally obtained funds, typically comprising three essential stages: placement, layering, and integration. The emergence of cryptocurrencies has created a new pathway for money laundering (Yadav), attributed to the anonymity they provide and the diminished regulatory oversight in comparison to traditional financial systems (Financial Action Task Force [FATF], 2020). Cryptocurrencies, operating on decentralized blockchain technology, present significant challenges for law enforcement and regulatory authorities, who encounter difficulties in tracing illicit financial flows (Brenig et al., 2015). This matter has become increasingly significant in the realm of global financial security, especially in Asia, where the swift integration of digital currencies aligns with diverse regulatory frameworks and cultural perspectives on wealth (Albrecht et al., 2019). This research paper aims to investigate the following core question: How do the unique socioeconomic and cultural contexts of Asia impact the utilization of cryptocurrencies in money laundering, and what challenges does this pose to regulatory initiatives? This inquiry holds significant importance for scholars, policymakers, and practitioners engaged in the study and prevention of money laundering. Understanding cryptocurrency-related money laundering in Asia can inform the development of focused regulatory strategies to tackle these issues effectively. The structure of this paper is as follows: Initially, we present a detailed examination of the characteristics of cryptocurrencies and the reasons they appeal to individuals seeking to launder illicit funds. We proceed to examine case studies that demonstrate the utilization of cryptocurrencies for money laundering in various regions of Asia, emphasizing the economic and cultural factors that contribute to these activities. Subsequently, we analyze the regulatory challenges presented by cryptocurrencies, with particular emphasis on the distinct issues encountered by regulators in Asia. The paper concludes with recommendations aimed at enhancing regulatory frameworks to more effectively address cryptocurrency-facilitated money laundering in the region.

Money laundering, traditionally carried out through intricate networks of bank transfers and shell companies, has gained renewed momentum in the realm of digital currency. Cryptocurrencies, characterized by their decentralized nature and frequently opaque transactions, create an environment conducive to the concealment of illicit gains and present challenges for law enforcement in tracking and recovering stolen assets. The digital era has significantly altered industries and business methodologies. The emergence of the Internet has transformed traditional business models and led to the creation of entirely new industries, exemplified by platforms such as Spotify, Dropbox, and Skype. The primary potential of information technology resides in its capacity to foster more efficient, cost-effective, and innovative methods for collaboration among businesses and individuals. Blockchain technology stands out as a transformative advancement in this field, providing an exceptional degree of transparency, security, and efficiency across a range of business applications. Blockchain technology is primarily recognized for its role in facilitating cryptocurrencies like Bitcoin, Litecoin, and Ethereum. A cryptocurrency represents a type of digital currency that enables peer-to-peer transactions via a decentralized network, which is secured by cryptographic protocols. In 2009, an anonymous individual or group identified as Satoshi Nakamoto launched Bitcoin (Joseph, Ray, & Agarwal, 2020), characterizing it as a "peer-to-peer electronic cash system." In contrast to conventional currencies, Bitcoin functions independently of central authorities or intermediaries, utilizing blockchain technology to document and authenticate transactions on a public ledger. The decentralized structure guarantees that all transactions are transparent, while the identities of the participants are kept confidential. In this system, each transaction includes the public keys of both the sender and recipient, along with the amount of cryptocurrency being transferred. The sender utilizes their private key to authorize the transaction, which is then broadcast across the network for confirmation. Cryptocurrencies serve various functions, such as facilitating the purchase of goods, enabling investments, conducting business transactions, and participating in mining activities. The growth of the cryptocurrency market has attracted heightened interest from governments and regulatory bodies across the globe. Cryptocurrencies are increasingly gaining mainstream acceptance, as law enforcement agencies, tax authorities, and legal regulators work diligently to comprehend their integration within current legal and financial frameworks.

Nonetheless, the decentralized and anonymous characteristics of cryptocurrencies have also drawn the attention of illicit activities, such as money laundering, terrorism financing, and tax evasion. Global authorities are expressing significant concern regarding these risks. Cryptocurrencies have been associated with illicit markets, including the now-defunct Silk Road, which functioned on the dark web. In light of these concerns, several countries, such as Bangladesh, Bolivia, Ecuador, Kyrgyzstan, and Vietnam, have implemented outright bans on cryptocurrencies. Countries like China and Russia are poised to implement comparable restrictions. In contrast, nations such as Japan and Sweden have adopted a more regulatory stance, officially recognizing Bitcoin as legal tender. In the United States, which hosts the largest number of Bitcoin ATMs and the highest global trading volumes, cryptocurrencies are legal; however, regulations differ considerably across states and countries

(PwC, 2020). As digital currencies advance swiftly, the legal community must be equipped to address the challenges they pose. Lawmakers and regulators should proactively identify and resolve potential legal challenges before they overwhelm the courts with cryptocurrency-related lawsuits. By doing so, they can contribute to the establishment of a balanced regulatory environment that promotes innovation while ensuring protection against illegal activities.

The challenges presented by the emergence of cryptocurrencies in relation to money laundering are significant, and it is essential for legal systems globally to take proactive measures in addressing these issues. This paper will examine the unique socioeconomic and cultural dynamics of Asia, highlighting its significance as a region for study due to the rapid adoption of digital currencies and the varied regulatory responses across different countries. In the subsequent sections, we will analyze how these factors interact to both support and obstruct initiatives aimed at combating money laundering through cryptocurrencies.

Problem Statement

Regulatory systems, both at the national and international levels, are inadequate to effectively address the misuse of cryptocurrencies in money laundering activities, especially in relation to white-collar crime. The decentralized and anonymous characteristics of cryptocurrencies present distinct challenges to conventional financial regulations, facilitating opportunities for criminals to take advantage of existing oversight gaps. This research posits that although technological advancements like blockchain analytics and artificial intelligence have the potential to address these challenges, they have not yet been fully incorporated into current regulatory frameworks, resulting in considerable vulnerabilities that financial criminals may exploit. This research argues that the differences in regulatory approaches among various jurisdictions intensify the issue. Countries that impose less stringent regulations on cryptocurrency exchanges and transactions facilitate environments conducive to money laundering activities, thereby obstructing global initiatives aimed at combating financial crime. The absence of a cohesive and thorough global framework for addressing cryptocurrency-related crimes hinders enforcement efforts, allowing criminals to transfer funds across borders with relative ease, thereby evading detection. This study posits that cultural, socioeconomic, and legal factors across various regions, especially in Asia, impact the efficacy of anti-money laundering (AML) measures. Countries exhibiting diverse economic development levels and cultural viewpoints on wealth and digital innovation face unique challenges in the regulation of cryptocurrencies. This paper will examine the necessity of a tailored approach, attuned to regional contexts, for effectively addressing the use of cryptocurrencies in money laundering.

Background of the Study

The swift advancement of technology within the financial sector has created new avenues for innovation, while simultaneously presenting unique challenges, particularly in relation to criminal activities. Among these innovations, cryptocurrency has emerged as a significant advancement in digital finance. Cryptocurrencies such as Bitcoin, Ethereum, and Monero offer a decentralized, efficient, and transparent method for exchanging value. In contrast to conventional currencies that are governed by central banks, cryptocurrencies function on decentralized peer-to-peer networks, providing reduced transaction fees, expedited cross-border payments, and enhanced privacy. This innovative technology is fundamentally transforming the global financial landscape, providing advantages such as transparency via blockchain technology, along with anonymity and autonomy for users (Baydakova, 2023). Nonetheless, this autonomy and anonymity have rendered cryptocurrencies appealing for illicit activities, especially in the realm of money laundering. Money laundering is the process of concealing the origins of illicitly obtained funds and remains a significant issue in white-collar crime. It involves complex schemes designed to integrate *"dirty money"* into legitimate financial systems (Tambe, 2024). The digital and frequently anonymous characteristics of cryptocurrency transactions have afforded criminals innovative ways to conceal the movement of illicit funds, posing challenges for law enforcement agencies in their efforts to detect and trace these transactions. Consequently, cryptocurrency has emerged as a preferred tool in contemporary money laundering, as offenders exploit its decentralized nature, the pseudo-anonymity offered by blockchain networks, and the absence of a uniform global regulatory framework.

Although there is increasing acknowledgement of cryptocurrency's involvement in enabling money laundering, the legal and regulatory measures in place continue to be inconsistent and insufficiently advanced (Freeman Law, n.d.). The implementation of the Prevention of Money Laundering Act (PMLA), 2002, in India marked a significant advancement in the fight against financial crimes. The emergence of cryptocurrency has presented new challenges for regulators. The legal framework regarding cryptocurrency in India is characterized by ambiguity, marked by frequent changes in government policy and a lack of specific provisions addressing cryptocurrency-related offences. In India, anti-money laundering regulations, particularly those outlined in the Prevention of Money Laundering Act (PMLA) 2002, have been broadened to encompass offences related to cryptocurrency. The legal landscape surrounding digital currencies continues to be uncertain, characterized by gaps in enforcement, ambiguous legal interpretations, and inconsistencies in the regulatory framework. The Reserve Bank of India (RBI) has imposed restrictions on banks interacting with cryptocurrency exchanges, and legal discussions regarding the legitimacy of these currencies have taken place in courts (Aslam, 2023). However, comprehensive regulations designed to prevent their misuse for money laundering remain in the early stages of development. Countries like the United States and the United Kingdom have implemented more organized initiatives to regulate cryptocurrency as part of their anti-money laundering (AML) frameworks. The United States has established a strong legal framework, including the Bank Secrecy Act, complemented by oversight from the Financial Crimes Enforcement Network (FinCEN), to effectively monitor cryptocurrency transactions and address the risks associated with money laundering. In a similar manner, the United Kingdom has enhanced its regulatory framework via the Financial Conduct Authority (FCA), imposing rigorous AML laws on cryptocurrency businesses. These jurisdictions offer valuable frameworks for India to evaluate as it navigates the distinct challenges presented by cryptocurrency.

This study seeks to examine the increasing significance of cryptocurrency in contemporary money laundering and its implications within the context of white-collar crime. This paper will provide a critical analysis of the utilization of cryptocurrencies in circumventing traditional financial systems and evading detection by law enforcement agencies. This research aims to examine India's legal responses, juxtapose them with established frameworks in the U.S., U.K., and Australia and identify existing loopholes, ultimately proposing recommendations for enhancing India's anti-money laundering regime in the context of digital currency. The analysis will further examine how the anonymity provided by blockchain technology—initially regarded as a beneficial feature—has evolved into a mechanism for criminal exploitation, thereby complicating the enforcement of current AML regulations (Anand, Agrawala, & Das, 2024). The increasing prevalence of cryptocurrency in money laundering poses a considerable legal and regulatory challenges, necessitating a thorough and coordinated response. And the issue of the cryptocurrency will pose a significant threat to the economy of the country. This research seeks to enhance the global dialogue on financial crime through a comprehensive analysis of the relationship between cryptocurrency and money laundering, while also presenting actionable recommendations for future policy formulation.

Research Questions

The author, through this paper, strongly affirms that these research questions are crafted to ensure a thorough and balanced exploration of the subject, delving into the practical, regulatory, technological, and case-based dimensions of cryptocurrency's involvement in modern money laundering and white-collar crime:

1. How has the rise of cryptocurrency reshaped traditional money laundering techniques, and what specific advantages does it offer to white-collar criminals in concealing illicit financial activities?

   This question explores the fundamental changes in money laundering methods due to cryptocurrency's unique features and why it appeals to white-collar criminals.

2. What role do cryptocurrency exchanges, digital wallets, and decentralized platforms play in facilitating money laundering, and how vulnerable are these platforms to exploitation by financial criminals?

   This question aims to investigate the technical and structural aspects of cryptocurrency infrastructure that may be aiding or abetting illicit activities.

3. How effective are existing global anti-money laundering (AML) regulations and enforcement mechanisms in detecting and preventing cryptocurrency-based money laundering, and where do significant gaps or weaknesses lie?

   This question critically assesses current regulatory efforts, identifying shortcomings in how cryptocurrency's anonymity and decentralization challenge traditional AML strategies.

4. What patterns and loopholes have emerged from recent case studies of white-collar crime involving cryptocurrency, and how do these cases illustrate the evolving strategies of financial criminals?

   This question focuses on real-world instances of cryptocurrency being used in white-collar crimes, extracting lessons from these cases to highlight recurring techniques and gaps in legal frameworks.

5. What innovative technological solutions, such as blockchain analytics and artificial intelligence, can be employed to strengthen the fight against cryptocurrency-facilitated money laundering, and what role should international cooperation play in these efforts?

   This question addresses the future of combating cryptocurrency misuse, emphasizing the role of advanced technology and global collaboration in closing the regulatory and enforcement gaps.

Research Objectives

The author be of the opinion that the below mentioned objectives collectively aim to explore the complexities of cryptocurrency's role in white-collar crime, specifically in the context of money laundering, while identifying gaps in the current regulatory framework and technological solutions. The objectives are as follows:

1. To examine the evolution of money laundering practices in the digital age, with a particular focus on the integration of cryptocurrency as a tool for facilitating illicit financial transactions. *"This objective will provide an overview of how traditional money laundering techniques have evolved and adapted to the use of cryptocurrencies."*
2. To analyze the key features of cryptocurrency that make it attractive for money laundering activities, including anonymity, decentralization, and lack of regulatory oversight. *"This will involve identifying specific characteristics of cryptocurrencies, such as Bitcoin and Monero, that have led to their exploitation by criminal networks for laundering illicit funds."*
3. To evaluate the role of cryptocurrency exchanges, wallets, and peer-to-peer platforms in enabling and facilitating money laundering operations. *"This objective will explore how cryptocurrency infrastructure is used by criminals to obscure financial trails and how these platforms may unintentionally or knowingly participate in laundering activities."*
4. To assess the effectiveness of existing anti-money laundering (AML) regulations and frameworks in combating the misuse of cryptocurrencies in white-collar crime. *"The objective will critically analyze global and national regulatory responses, such as the FATF guidelines, to determine their strengths and limitations in addressing cryptocurrency-based money laundering."*
5. To investigate specific case studies where cryptocurrency has been used in prominent white-collar crimes, including instances of fraud, embezzlement, and corporate corruption, highlighting patterns and loopholes exploited by offenders. *"Through real-world examples, this objective will illustrate the various methods white-collar criminals use cryptocurrency to conceal illicit activities and evade detection."*
6. To explore the emerging technological solutions, such as blockchain analytics, artificial intelligence (AI), and machine learning, that are being developed to detect and prevent money laundering through cryptocurrencies. *"This objective will look into how technology is being leveraged to counteract cryptocurrency misuse, focusing on innovations that could enhance AML measures and tracking of illicit financial flows."*
7. To propose a set of recommendations for improving legal and regulatory frameworks, technological tools, and international cooperation to effectively address the role of cryptocurrency in modern money laundering from a white-collar crime perspective. *"This final objective will aim to provide actionable insights for policymakers, financial institutions, and law enforcement agencies to better regulate cryptocurrency and prevent its use in white-collar crime."*

Methodology

This research provides a critical analysis of the effectiveness of crypto currency regulations in India and other nations, utilizing a functional approach to explore the legal responses to money laundering and various potential criminal activities by individuals and organizations. This comparative analysis provides insight into the applicability and practicality of India's current legal framework by drawing a legal parallel with countries such as the United States, the United Kingdom, and Australia. The consistency of current crypto asset regulations and business practices in India is examined through a detailed analysis, especially considering the swift expansion of fintech, which has increased the intricacy of regulatory frameworks globally. Considering the obligations of authorities to uphold market integrity, safeguard consumer interests, and maintain financial stability, it may be essential to implement stricter regulations to address the risks associated with crypto assets. The research evaluates the effectiveness and consistency of Indian laws pertaining to commercial and non-commercial crimes associated with cryptocurrencies. The study employs theoretical methods and comparative analysis, utilizing the "common-core method," a technique that combines analytical and functional approaches, to thoroughly assess the strengths and weaknesses of legislation in India, the US, the UK, and Australia. The research provides insightful recommendations for enhancing India's regulatory framework for crypto assets.

LITERATURE REVIEW

Introduction to Money Laundering

Money laundering is the act of concealing illicit funds, often derived from criminal activities such as drug trafficking or terrorism, to make them look as if they originate from legitimate sources. It adversely affects a nation's economic and political stability; hence, robust legislative measures and international collaboration are needed for successful mitigation (Kumar, 2012). Money laundering is characterized by actions or attempts to obscure the origins of illegally acquired funds, presenting them in a manner that suggests they are derived from lawful sources, as outlined by the Interpol General Secretariat Assembly in 1995. This definition underscores the intricate and misleading characteristics of money laundering, in which offenders obscure the source of their illicit profits. The process is crucial for individuals engaged in criminal activities, as it enables them to utilize these profits while concealing their illicit origins. The phenomenon of money laundering has escalated into a worldwide concern, impacting multiple sectors (United Nations, n.d.). The main objective of numerous criminal activities is to produce financial gain for the individuals or groups engaged in them. Criminal activities such as illegal arms sales, drug trafficking, prostitution rings, and smuggling generate substantial amounts of illicit funds. Financial crimes, including embezzlement, insider trading, bribery, and computer fraud, yield significant profits, prompting offenders to "clean" their money via laundering to evade detection. The clandestine characteristics of money laundering result in its frequent absence from official economic statistics. Estimates from institutions such as the International Monetary Fund (IMF) provide insight into the magnitude of the issue. The IMF estimates that the total volume of laundered money globally may represent between two to five percent of the world's gross domestic product (GDP), highlighting the extensive nature of this illicit practice. The relationship between money laundering and terrorism has become more apparent, particularly following the events of September 11, 2001. It was evident that relying solely on military action would be insufficient to address the issue of terrorism. A concurrent initiative is essential to focus on the financial systems that underpin terrorist organizations. Investigations into the 9/11 attacks revealed intricate financial pathways established by the terrorists, highlighting the critical role of specialists in identifying and dismantling these financial systems. In response, the United States and the European Community (EC) implemented new initiatives aimed at countering money laundering, while India has also enacted laws to tackle this issue (Malhotra, 1900)

Researchers have discovered that both professionals and novices in anti-money laundering risk assessments exhibit overconfidence, with experts demonstrating a somewhat higher level of overconfidence and a propensity for false-positive mistakes. Unexpectedly, beginners somewhat surpassed experts in accuracy, underscoring the need for feedback systems to mitigate biases and enhance judgement (Ogbeide, 2023)

Concept of Cryptocurrency

Globalization and the fast growth of the Internet have led to a rise in transnationality, which has changed the way crimes are done. Because of these changes, online is now not only a place to go, but also a place to be targeted and a tool for committing crimes. Introducing crypto-assets has been one of the most important changes in this area. There are both pros and cons to these digital currencies, especially when it comes to financial crime. The goal of this paper is to give a clear and brief summary of the illegal actions involving crypto-assets, with a focus on how they are used in financial theft and white-collar crime. There will be a thorough look at how crypto-assets are misused, with a focus on how they are used in financial scam schemes. The study also talks about the special things about cryptocurrencies that make them appealing to criminals, like the fact that they are decentralized, anonymous, and can be used all over the world. Because of these factors, it's easier for illegal trades to happen, which makes it harder to find and stop these crimes. This paper uses real-world data to look into how cryptocurrencies are used in both standard crimes and crimes that happen online. Cryptocurrencies are a big part of newer types of cybercrime like virus attacks and deals on the dark web. They are also used in old crimes like money laundering and scams. The study shows how these digital assets have become part of crime networks and the problems that police are having trying to solve these problems (Mataković, 2022).

Cryptocurrencies, propelled by blockchain technology, have transformed global financial systems, with regulatory frameworks significantly influencing their adoption and effects on traditional economies (Makhija, Unregulated Cryptocurrency: Need for Legal Regulation in Digital Economy, 2024). This article examines the diverse strategies employed by governments globally in the regulation of cryptocurrencies, emphasizing the challenges and consequences associated with this decentralized financial framework. The analysis delves into the impact of regulatory clarity or ambiguity on investor confidence, market liquidity, and the capacity of digital assets to serve as alternative currencies or investment vehicles (Ganguly, 2022). The paper explores the relationship between taxation, anti-money laundering measures, and the growth of cryptocurrency, with a specific focus on the Indian context, providing an in-depth analysis of the legal and economic aspects of cryptocurrency regulation.

Cryptocurrency in Modern Money Laundering

In July 2019, the Ministry of Finance, Government of India, announced the submission of a report by an Inter-Ministerial Committee that recommended a complete ban on the possession or trading of cryptocurrencies, categorizing these activities as criminal offences. This article evaluates the alignment of such a ban with India's constitutional framework, positing that numerous crypto-asset activities are safeguarded by several fundamental rights outlined in the Constitution. After a thorough examination of the Committee's recommendation, the article determines that an outright ban would probably represent an unreasonable limitation on these rights, given its seemingly arbitrary and excessive nature. The article suggests adopting a more balanced approach, given that crypto-assets, similar to the Internet, function as neutral technologies (Makhija, Unregulated Cryptocurrency: Need for Legal Regulation in Digital Economy, 2024). The recommendation is for empirical research to be undertaken to evaluate the risks linked to crypto-assets, subsequently leading to the establishment of a regulatory framework to address those risks, instead of opting for prohibition. This approach would more effectively align with the principles of liberty, innovation, and consumer protection, promoting a balanced and progressive legal framework (Reddy, 2019). The emergence of cryptocurrency has initiated considerable regulatory discussions, primarily because its decentralized nature presents challenges for central banks globally. Cryptocurrencies are frequently viewed as substitutes for central banks, prompting questions regarding their possible effects on inflation and monetary policy (Mishra, 2023).

The Reserve Bank of India (RBI) has repeatedly issued warnings regarding virtual currencies (VCs) in India, highlighting concerns related to their high volatility, absence of regulatory frameworks, and potential risks associated with money laundering. In light of this, the rise in cryptocurrency's popularity has led to increased regulatory scrutiny. The RBI's 2018 circular, which restricted banks from engaging with entities involved in virtual currencies, emerged as a significant point of contention (Rajagopal, 2021). The Supreme Court case resulted in a ruling that affirmed the RBI's regulatory authority over virtual currencies, yet it concluded that a complete ban on banking access to VC exchanges was unconstitutional (R.Ananthesh, 2021). In light of the ruling, the Ministry of Finance subsequently put forth a proposal for the introduction of a central bank-backed digital currency, concurrently advocating for a ban on other virtual currencies. This indicates a broader pattern, as certain governments are investigating the implementation of state-controlled digital currencies to address the risks linked to decentralized cryptocurrencies.

Cryptocurrencies, although not recognized as legal tender in India, are classified as "goods" according to the Sale of Goods Act, 1930, and consequently fall under the purview of taxation. Nonetheless, the government exercises caution by differentiating between Distributed Ledger Technologies (DLTs) and virtual currencies (VCs). Distributed Ledger Technologies, including blockchain, are under examination for their possible advantages in areas such as finance and governance, with organizations like SEBI and RBI investigating their uses. On a global scale, the cryptocurrency sector has encountered a rise in regulatory challenges, especially in China. China, recognized as a center for cryptocurrency mining, has implemented measures to restrict its use, driven by apprehensions regarding energy consumption, environmental consequences, and the potential for capital flight. Countries such as Turkey have encountered comparable regulatory challenges, leading to a ban on cryptocurrencies attributed to insufficient oversight by central banks. One possible alternative is state-issued digital currencies, exemplified by China's digital yuan, which provides the government with enhanced control over monetary policy and addresses issues such as tax evasion. The idea of Multi-Central Bank Digital Currencies (mCBDCs) is increasingly being recognized as a viable approach for facilitating cross-border transactions, with the objective of optimizing international money transfers and minimizing associated frictions (Ranaweera, 2024).

CONCEPTUALISING MONEY LAUNDERING AND CRYPTOCURRENCY

Concept and Overview of Money Laundering

Money laundering involves the methodical transformation of illegally acquired funds to create an illusion of legitimacy, effectively obscuring their criminal origins. This represents a significant financial offence that functions covertly within the global economy, profoundly impacting the political and economic stability of countries (Pillai & Julian). Pillai & Julian asserts that money laundering is fundamentally a cross-border activity that often involves multiple jurisdictions, aiming to conceal the origins of illicit funds. Criminals frequently take advantage of jurisdictions with weak anti-money laundering (AML) laws, resulting in a complicated network of financial transactions that complicates the efforts of law enforcement agencies to track the origins of the funds. In response to international resolutions, particularly those advocated by the United Nations, India implemented the Prevention of Money Laundering Act (PMLA) in 2002 as a measure to address this issue (Poddar & Shalini). Nonetheless, the act has frequently encountered criticism regarding its implementation, indicating significant potential for enhancement. Money laundering fundamentally involves the process of legitimizing "dirty" money acquired through unlawful activities, including extortion, drug trafficking, arms smuggling, and organized crime, among various other means. The objective is to incorporate these illicit funds into the financial system in a way that renders them seemingly legitimate (Shah, 2013). The process frequently occurs via a legitimate business or through the transfer of funds to jurisdictions with minimal regulatory scrutiny, thereby complicating the identification of the original illicit source.

The Mechanism of Money Laundering

Money laundering generally occurs in three separate phases:

i. Placement: This involves the introduction of illicit proceeds into the legitimate financial system during this initial stage. This process typically involves depositing funds into banking institutions, acquiring valuable assets, or reallocating resources into a front company or shell corporation. The objective is to transfer the illicit funds from their origin to minimize the likelihood of detection.
ii. Layering: This involves a series of intricate transactions that take place after the money has entered the financial system, aimed at concealing its origins. The process may entail the movement of funds through several bank accounts, frequently spanning different nations, transforming them into a range of financial

instruments such as bonds or stocks, or directly acquiring high-value goods and assets. The purpose of layering is to establish a sophisticated series of transactions that obscures the money's illicit origins, rendering it nearly untraceable.

iii. Integration: In the concluding phase, the "cleaned" money is systematically reintroduced into the economy. Currently, the funds seem to be legitimate, allowing the individual to utilize them without attracting any suspicion. The funds can now be allocated to legitimate enterprises, real estate, or high-value assets, creating an appearance of a lawful income stream for the individual involved in criminal activities.

Effects of Money Laundering

The implications of money laundering reach far beyond the confines of the financial sector. The implications for the political and economic stability of nations are profound and extensive. The primary effects encompass:

i. Economic Instability: The presence of laundered money interferes with the typical operations of the economy, leading to distortions in market dynamics. It frequently contributes to inflation, creates an artificial increase in asset values, and disrupts equitable competition. Furthermore, it undermines financial institutions by subjecting them to elevated levels of risk, given that criminals frequently take advantage of regulatory loopholes. The reinvestment of laundered money into criminal activities plays a crucial role in sustaining and amplifying the ongoing cycle of crime. This action not only disrupts law and order but also contributes to the expansion of organized crime syndicates.

ii. Political Corruption: The introduction of illicit funds into the political arena via bribery and unlawful financing undermines governance frameworks, complicating the operational efficacy of law enforcement and judicial entities. This undermines the rule of law and diminishes public confidence in institutions.

Essential Elements Influencing Money Laundering

A variety of elements play a role in the prevalence and effectiveness of money laundering, such as:

Criminals frequently aim to channel their laundered funds into illegal ventures, thereby perpetuating a continuous cycle of crime and money laundering. The phenomenon of money laundering enables criminals to minimize the total transaction costs associated with their illegal activities, thereby facilitating the continuation of their operations.

Criminals require access to “clean” money to support their illicit activities. The integration of laundered money into the formal economy creates liquidity, which helps to keep these activities concealed.
The anticipated returns from illicit activities frequently exceed those of legitimate enterprises, creating compelling financial motivations for individuals to participate in money laundering.
The substantial amount of illegal revenues necessitates intricate and extensive laundering operations.

The Prevention of Money Laundering Act (PMLA), 2002, in India was established to address the issue of money laundering through the implementation of rigorous protocols for the detection, investigation, and penalization of individuals involved in money laundering activities. The Act facilitates the attachment and confiscation of assets obtained through money laundering, thereby preventing offenders from reaping rewards from their unlawful activities. It establishes penalties for those who facilitate or engage in money laundering activities (Nimma, 2022). Despite these efforts, the implementation of the PMLA has faced criticism for insufficient enforcement, leading to a disconnect between the law’s intent and its practical application. Money laundering represents a complex criminal activity that has extensive implications for the economy and society as a whole. It contributes to the proliferation of organized crime, diminishes the stability of financial institutions, and erodes the integrity of political systems (Girme & Ray). India has made notable progress in addressing this issue through the implementation of the PMLA; however, there is a clear necessity for enhanced enforcement mechanisms to effectively address the existing gaps in its execution. A comprehensive global strategy, (Gururaj, 2005) along with targeted national efforts, is crucial to address the sophisticated methods utilized by money launderers. Coordinated efforts among nations and robust regulatory frameworks will be essential in addressing this escalating threat (Schneider, 2008).

Cryptocurrency Meaning

The swift advancement of cryptocurrencies in the digital era has significantly transformed the worldwide financial environment. The COVID-19 pandemic significantly influenced both traditional and novice investors to explore alternative investment avenues, with cryptocurrencies rising as a notably unconventional and increasingly favored option during this time (Jabotinsky & Sarel, 2021). Cryptocurrencies, including Bitcoin and Ethereum, represent digital or virtual currencies that employ cryptographic techniques for security and function on a decentralized framework referred to as blockchain (Richards, 2024). Blockchain is a distributed ledger technology that enables transactions to be recorded in a manner that is both permanent and resistant to alteration. This approach fosters transparency while simultaneously providing exceptional levels of anonymity via pseudonymous addresses. Criminals take advantage of this anonymity through a method known as "layering," which entails dividing illicit funds into smaller sums and transferring them across various digital wallets. This practice significantly complicates the ability of regulators to trace the original source of the funds. Additionally, they utilize services that involve combining multiple transactions into a single pool before redistributing them to users, effectively obscuring the origin and destination of funds.Blockchain guarantees that transactions remain unchanged, are visible to all, and are protected, providing cryptocurrencies with the advantages of both security and user anonymity. The following represent the usage of Blockchain technology across the globe by all economies Contributions represented by a graph:

Cryptocurrencies exhibit distinct characteristics that set them apart from conventional currencies. In contrast to fiat currency, which is managed and regulated by a central authority, cryptocurrencies function within a decentralized framework, indicating the absence of a singular governing entity or bank overseeing their operations. This decentralization grants users increased control over their assets; however, it simultaneously presents considerable risks. The cryptographic mechanisms that underpin cryptocurrency transactions ensure their security and resistance to tampering (Allcot, 2021). However, this very characteristic also facilitates illicit activities, including the acquisition of illegal goods or services, money laundering, and tax evasion, due to the challenges associated with tracing transactions.

While cryptocurrencies possess built-in security features, they face two major risks that contribute to their increased volatility relative to traditional banking systems: (i) market volatility and (ii) the lack of regulatory oversight and federal insurance. The valuation of cryptocurrencies exhibits significant speculation, characterized by abrupt and unpredictable variations, thereby rendering investments inherently risky (Adrian, He, Ismail, & Moretti, 2023). The absence of governmental regulation or protection, exemplified by the insurance offered by entities like the Federal Deposit Insurance Corporation (FDIC) in conventional banking frameworks, renders cryptocurrency investors more susceptible to financial loss.

In the year 2021, the global cryptocurrency market has exceeded a valuation of $1 trillion (Subramanian, 2021). Estimates indicate that investments in cryptocurrencies in India have approached around $1.4 billion (ITP, 2021). Additionally, PwC's 2020 Time for Trust report estimated that blockchain technology, which underpins cryptocurrencies, has the potential to contribute as much as $1.76 trillion (approximately 1.4%) to the global Gross Domestic Product (GDP) by the year 2030 (Helms, 2020). This emerging industry is drawing significant interest from affluent individuals, as evidenced by a global survey revealing that 73% of millionaires intended to invest in cryptocurrencies like Bitcoin and Ethereum by the conclusion of 2022 (PwC, 2020). Cryptocurrencies have emerged as a significant factor in the global economy, presenting a complex interplay of opportunities and risks. Although they offer users increased autonomy and security, they simultaneously present new challenges concerning market volatility, regulatory oversight, and financial crime. The regulatory environment in India is characterized by uncertainty, as the government seeks to balance the promotion of blockchain innovation with the management of risks linked to private cryptocurrencies.

The ongoing discussion regarding cryptocurrency regulation necessitates a careful examination of a balanced strategy that promotes technological advancement while ensuring the integrity of the financial system and safeguarding consumer interests (Department of Economic Affairs, 2019). The integration of cryptocurrencies within the PMLA framework represents a potential advancement in achieving a balanced approach, facilitating the secure and responsible use of digital currencies in India's dynamic financial landscape. The future of cryptocurrency in India hinges on the government's capacity to develop well-considered and impactful regulations that tackle the distinct challenges presented by this emerging digital asset.

THE ROLE OF CRYPTOCURRENCY IN MONEY LAUNDERING

Cryptocurrencies like Monero, Zcash, DASH, Verge, and Horizen are engineered to offer users enhanced privacy, rendering it exceedingly difficult to trace the individuals participating in transactions (Seth, 2024). The anonymity feature, although appealing to numerous users, also fosters an environment conducive to illicit activities. In contrast to Bitcoin, which maintains a publicly accessible ledger of all transactions, privacy-focused cryptocurrencies allow individuals to obscure the sources of their funds (Biswas, Kumar, Jajoo, & Sehgal, 2023). Despite the transparency of Bitcoin, it is estimated that criminals laundered US $2.8 billion through Bitcoin exchanges in 2019, an increase from US $1 billion in 2018. This increase underscores the potential of cryptocurrencies to serve as instruments for money laundering, characterized by minimal oversight or regulatory control. Cryptocurrencies function through peer-to-peer (P2P) mechanisms, offering a notable advantage to those engaged in money laundering activities. The utilization of these digital assets enables individuals engaged in criminal activities to convert their illicit earnings at a significantly reduced cost—frequently under 15% of the total proceeds—when contrasted with conventional laundering techniques, which may entail expenses reaching up to 50%. The main factor contributing to this reduced cost is the anonymous characteristic of cryptocurrency transactions, which significantly complicates the tracing of fund sources. The anonymity associated with cryptocurrencies presents a considerable challenge for authorities, as they currently operate beyond the reach of numerous existing anti-money laundering (AML) regulations, including the Prevention of Money Laundering Act, 2002 (PMLA), which requires financial institutions and intermediaries to maintain transaction records.

The absence of transparency in cryptocurrency transactions presents significant challenges for agencies such as the Enforcement Directorate (ED) in their efforts to track or freeze digital wallets that are suspected of containing illicit funds. The Indian government has acknowledged this issue and proposed a Draft Bill that seeks to ban cryptocurrencies. This legislation also aims to classify activities such as mining, generating, holding, and using cryptocurrencies as *"scheduled offences"* under the PMLA (Kepli & Zulhuda, 2019). This initiative aimed to tackle the issue of anonymity and reduce the utilization of cryptocurrencies in money laundering activities. Additionally, prominent cryptocurrency exchanges in India, such as WazirX, CoinDCX, and CoinSwitch Kuber, have partnered with the Internet and Mobile Association of India to form an advisory board and introduce a code of conduct for the sector. Regulatory challenges continue to be a significant concern, despite these efforts. Recently, WazirX received a notice from the ED for purportedly breaching the Foreign Exchange Management Act (FEMA) concerning transactions amounting to 2,790.74 crore. While India has not yet enacted comprehensive cryptocurrency legislation, specific transactions involving cryptocurrencies are currently under examination and may incur penalties. The Supreme Court of India, in the case of *Internet and Mobile Association of India (IMAI) v. Reserve Bank of India*, noted that virtual currencies are not broadly recognized as methods of payment and therefore cannot be considered a definitive settlement of debt. The legal status of cryptocurrencies in India is increasingly complex, as the government navigates the decision to either embrace or impose restrictions on these digital assets. Money laundering continues to be a major issue on a global scale. The United Nations estimates that 2% to 5% of global GDP, which amounts to $800 billion to $2 trillion, is laundered each year. As the global community strives to achieve sustainable development objectives, cryptocurrency mining introduces an additional challenge. Bitcoin mining consumes approximately 110 terawatt hours of electricity annually, accounting for roughly 0.55% of global electricity production. This figure has initiated discussions regarding the justification of energy consumption in cryptocurrency mining, especially in the context of global efforts to decrease carbon emissions.

Numerous nations have implemented regulations to mitigate the risks associated with cryptocurrencies (Gowda & Chakravorty, 2021). In Canada, digital currencies do not hold the status of legal tender; however, they are regulated under the Proceeds of Crime (Money Laundering) and Terrorist Financing Act, 2000. In Singapore, the Payment Services Act of 2019 mandates that cryptocurrency businesses secure licenses and adhere to anti-money laundering regulations. The United Kingdom requires cryptocurrency-related businesses to register with the Financial Conduct

Authority and comply with the Money Laundering, Terrorist Financing and Transfer of Funds (Information on the Payer) Regulations, 2017. Due to these stringent regulations, numerous cryptocurrency companies in the UK may be compelled to cease operations after not meeting AML requirements. In the United States, while there is no comprehensive federal regulation for cryptocurrencies, the Financial Crimes Enforcement Network (FinCEN) oversees money services businesses (MSBs) in accordance with the Bank Secrecy Act of 1970. MSBs are required to perform a thorough risk assessment and establish a compliance program for anti-money laundering measures. Individuals engaged in cryptocurrency-related offences have encountered significant repercussions. The proprietor of a Bitcoin exchange was found guilty for his involvement in a transnational fraud scheme and received a sentence of 121 months in prison. In a similar case, another individual was sentenced to 121 months in prison for conspiring to distribute methamphetamine, with transactions conducted via cryptocurrency.

These cases highlight the increasing risks associated with unregulated and anonymous cryptocurrency transactions. In the absence of rigorous oversight and regulation, cryptocurrencies may pose a significant risk as a refuge for money laundering and various unlawful activities.

REGULATORY FRAMEWORK PERTAINING TO THE CRYPTOCURRENCY AND ANTI MONEY LAUNDERING MEASURES

Categories of Cryptocurrencies

Cryptocurrencies represent digital assets that enable secure transactions through decentralized networks of users, operating in a manner akin to digital currency. In addition to the widely recognized Bitcoin and Ethereum (Dejan, Dijana, & Sinisa, 2018), there exists a variety of other digital currencies referred to as "altcoins" or "value tokens." The currencies utilized for diverse functions in specialized applications constitute a fundamental component of the cryptocurrency ecosystem. Here are several of the most notable categories of cryptocurrencies:

The legal framework regarding cryptocurrency in India is undergoing a gradual transformation, influenced by various policy considerations, economic factors, and the imperative for technological advancement (Lakshmikumaran Sridharan Attorneys, 2018). The Indian government has taken a measured approach to cryptocurrency, carefully weighing the risks associated with decentralized digital currencies against the possible advantages of blockchain technology.

Preliminary Efforts to Prohibit Cryptocurrency

In 2019, the Indian government put forward a proposal to prohibit the buying and selling of cryptocurrencies, as outlined in a bill approved by a committee established by the government (Mehrotra, 2021). The reasoning for this ban originated from apprehensions regarding price fluctuations, cybersecurity vulnerabilities, energy usage, and the possibility of cryptocurrency enabling illicit activities like money laundering and terrorism. The Supreme Court of India invalidated the effort to prohibit digital assets in the significant case of *Internet and Mobile Association of India v. Reserve Bank of India* in March 2020. The court determined that the total prohibition on cryptocurrencies violated the essential right to engage in trade and profession, as safeguarded by Article 19(1)(g) of the Indian Constitution (India, 1950). The Supreme Court's ruling highlighted the decentralized characteristics of cryptocurrencies, indicating their operation without reliance on any central authority, including governmental entities. The Court expressed the view that cryptocurrencies ought to be classified as commodities or goods, permitting their free trade unless there are specific regulations or prohibitions in place. The ruling has created an opportunity for the legal trading of digital assets in India, though it remains within a regulatory grey area.

The Proposed Cryptocurrency and Regulation of Official Digital Currency Bill, 2021

The Indian government responded to the Supreme Court's decision by aiming to regulate the emerging sector with the introduction of the Cryptocurrency and Regulation of Official Digital Currency Bill, 2021 (PRS, 2019). The proposed legislation outlines the establishment of a state-supported Central Bank Digital Currency (CBDC), which would be issued and overseen by the Reserve Bank of India (RBI). Additionally, it seeks to prohibit the utilization of private cryptocurrencies, including Bitcoin and Ethereum, for transactional purposes. The draft bill aims to allow specific exceptions to facilitate the advancement of blockchain technology, acknowledging its capacity to revolutionize various sectors (Reif, 2024). The primary emphasis continues to be on prohibiting the utilization of private cryptocurrencies for financial transactions within the nation, due to their decentralized nature and absence of governmental regulation.

Taxation of cryptocurrency and virtual digital assets (VDAs)

The Indian government has established a definitive tax framework for transactions related to digital assets, even amidst the prevailing regulatory ambiguity surrounding cryptocurrencies. The Finance Bill, 2022 introduced modifications to the Income Tax Act, 1961, aiming to establish a 30% tax on income generated from the transfer of virtual digital assets (VDAs), encompassing cryptocurrencies and non-fungible tokens (NFTs). The implementation of this tax rate indicates the government's objective to impose taxes on virtual currencies while simultaneously developing comprehensive regulations for the future. The Income Tax Act of 1961, specifically Section 2(47A), provides a definition for VDAs, identifying them as digital assets created through cryptographic methods, which are capable of being transferred, stored, or traded in an electronic format. The assets in question, while offering a digital representation of value, differ from conventional currency. Furthermore, the government retains the authority to announce additional digital assets that may fall under the VDA definition. The tax treatment indicates the government's effort to oversee financial activities associated with digital currencies while refraining from recognizing them as legal tender.

Regulatory frameworks include the Foreign Exchange Management Act (FEMA) and the Securities Contracts Regulation Act (SCRA)

A significant aspect of legal discourse involves the classification of cryptocurrencies and their alignment with financial instruments as defined by Indian regulations, including FEMA and the Securities Contracts Regulation Act (SCRA), 1956. FEMA specifies that "currency" refers to currency notes or comparable financial instruments that possess legal tender status, explicitly excluding cryptocurrencies from this classification due to their lack of recognition by the RBI. The SCRA provides definitions for "goods" and "securities" within a centralized framework, which stands in contrast to the inherently decentralized characteristics of cryptocurrencies. The lack of explicit inclusion in these acts indicates that the government is relying on future regulations or judicial interpretations to define the treatment of cryptocurrencies within the larger framework of financial regulation. At present, cryptocurrencies are not classified as either currency or securities, resulting in their placement within a distinct legal category that is subject to ongoing examination.

The Emergence of Central Bank Digital Currency (CBDC)

The Reserve Bank of India has proposed the introduction of the Digital Rupee, a central bank digital currency (CBDC), as a government-regulated alternative to cryptocurrencies. In the 2022 Union Budget, the RBI revealed intentions to initiate a pilot program for the e-Rupee, designed to function as a digital equivalent of traditional paper currency. The Digital Rupee, in contrast to cryptocurrencies, will be issued and regulated by the RBI, establishing it as a legal tender in India. This development is consistent with international patterns, as numerous other countries are investigating CBDCs to leverage the advantages of digital currencies while mitigating the risks associated with private cryptocurrencies.

The Fall of Cryptocurrency

The decline of cryptocurrency can be analyzed through the interplay of regulatory actions, fluctuations in the market, and a decrease in investor trust. The primary reason stems from insufficient regulation, which has facilitated the use of cryptocurrencies in illicit activities like money laundering and fraud. This has prompted governments globally to implement stricter controls or consider outright bans (Cibin). The combination of regulatory ambiguity and significant price volatility has rendered cryptocurrencies a precarious and unreliable investment option. The departure of numerous investors from the market has played a significant role in the overall decline of digital currencies (Lang, Howcroft, & Wilson, 2023).

LEGAL ISSUES AND CHALLENGES OF CRYPTOCURRENCY IN INDIA

The regulation of cryptocurrency in India presents a multifaceted challenge, necessitating a careful equilibrium between fostering innovation and ensuring adequate financial and legal oversight. In 2018, the Reserve Bank of India (RBI) released a circular that prohibited banks and financial institutions from providing services associated with cryptocurrency transactions. The RBI highlighted apprehensions regarding financial instability, possible legal implications, and the potential for cryptocurrencies to be exploited in unlawful activities such as money laundering, fraud, and the funding of illegal operations. The central bank has consistently highlighted concerns regarding the risks linked to cryptocurrencies since 2013, a time when the adoption of digital currencies was just beginning in India.

The Ministry of Finance established an Inter-Ministerial Committee in light of the increasing prominence of digital assets, which produced a comprehensive report on virtual currencies in 2019. This report emphasizes significant concerns including consumer protection, the stability of the financial system, and the risks of criminal exploitation associated with cryptocurrency. The Committee's report led to the formulation of the Banning of Cryptocurrency and Regulation of Official Digital Currency Bill, 2019, which proposed a total prohibition on private cryptocurrencies in India. Section 8(1) of the Draft Bill outlines significant penalties for individuals engaged in the mining, generation, holding, or trading of cryptocurrency, including imprisonment terms that may extend to 10 years. The harshness of these penalties corresponds with the strict regulations outlined in the Prevention of Money Laundering Act (PMLA), indicating the government's serious perspective on cryptocurrency transactions as possible risks to the economy and public safety.

In a significant ruling issued in 2020, the Supreme Court of India, in the case *of Internet and Mobile Association of India v. RBI (IMAI),* annulled the RBI's 2018 circular. The Court determined that the ban was excessive and infringed upon the constitutional right to engage in trade or business, as outlined in Article 19(1)(g) of the Indian Constitution. This decision was interpreted as a significant advancement for the cryptocurrency community, as it reinstated opportunities for cryptocurrency exchanges and investors in India. The ruling highlighted that although the RBI possesses the authority to oversee financial institutions, implementing a complete ban on cryptocurrency usage, in the absence of compelling evidence demonstrating harm, constitutes an overly stringent and limiting action. Following the Supreme Court ruling, the Indian government introduced the Cryptocurrency and Regulation of Official Digital Currency Bill, 2021. This legislation sought to ban private cryptocurrencies and investigate the potential implementation of a Central Bank Digital Currency (CBDC). The government's measured strategy indicates apprehensions regarding the possible transition from the Indian rupee to private cryptocurrencies, which may undermine the nation's regulatory and taxation systems. The government aims to foster innovation through the adoption of blockchain technology while simultaneously rejecting the use of private cryptocurrencies, thereby maintaining oversight of its financial systems (Singh & Chawla, 2019).

In light of recent developments, the Indian cryptocurrency market continues to exist in a state of uncertainty, given the absence of a definitive regulatory framework. The government has expressed its intention to obtain expert legal opinions and conduct comprehensive consultations prior to reaching any conclusive decisions regarding cryptocurrency regulation. The ambiguity regarding the future of cryptocurrencies in India has placed investors and businesses in a challenging situation, as many seek more definitive information on the legal standing of their assets and transactions.

The Immediate Requirement for Cryptocurrency Regulation under the PMLA

The decentralized and peer-to-peer (P2P) characteristics of cryptocurrencies introduce distinct challenges for regulators globally, with India being no exception. The potential of cryptocurrency to enable money laundering, tax evasion, and various illicit activities stands out as a major concern. The anonymity inherent in cryptocurrency transactions, coupled with the lack of a central authority, presents significant challenges for law enforcement agencies attempting to track and trace these transactions. This complexity renders cryptocurrency an appealing option for individuals involved in criminal activities (Parthasarathy & R, 2023). One potential solution to address these concerns is the regulation of cryptocurrencies under the Prevention of Money Laundering Act (PMLA). The PMLA, enacted to address money laundering in India, establishes rigorous reporting and compliance requirements for financial institutions. These obligations necessitate the maintenance of comprehensive transaction records and the reporting of any suspicious activities to the relevant authorities. The inclusion of cryptocurrency exchanges and digital asset platforms within the framework of the PMLA would necessitate that these entities adhere to comparable compliance protocols (Tax Guru, 2024). This entails the implementation of obligatory Know Your Customer (KYC) protocols, ongoing transaction monitoring, and consistent reporting of suspicious activities, thereby reducing the risks linked to money laundering and terrorist financing.

Implementing PMLA regulations for cryptocurrencies presents considerable enforcement difficulties. The decentralized characteristics inherent in many cryptocurrencies contribute to their resilience against conventional regulatory scrutiny. Transactions take place on a worldwide level, frequently spanning various jurisdictions, which adds complexity to enforcement initiatives. Furthermore, numerous cryptocurrency platforms function without a tangible presence, complicating the ability of national authorities to implement sanctions or ensure compliance. However, a carefully designed regulatory framework, potentially inspired by effective international models like Japan's Financial Services Agency (FSA) or Switzerland's FINMA, could assist in addressing these challenges. A framework of this nature could effectively reconcile the necessity for oversight with the promotion of innovation within blockchain technology. In this context, it is essential for India to implement a detailed strategy that emphasizes consumer protection, financial stability, and the deterrence of illicit activities, while also fostering the development of the digital asset ecosystem. The expansion of the cryptocurrency market in India highlights the pressing necessity for well-defined and effective regulations. Integrating cryptocurrencies into the current legal framework through regulations such as the PMLA allows India to protect its financial system while also harnessing the advantages of this transformative technology.

COMPARATIVE ANALYSIS OF CRYPTOCURRENCY REGULATIONS IN OTHER COUNTRIES

Cryptocurrencies are subject to varying regulations across different jurisdictions, with certain countries imposing bans while others have established regulatory frameworks. This document provides a summary of the responses from important jurisdictions.

United States of America

In the United States, regulatory oversight of cryptocurrencies is conducted by both federal and state authorities. The Commodity Futures Trading Commission (CFTC) classifies virtual currencies (VCs) as commodities in accordance with the U.S. Commodity Exchange Act of 1936. A federal court ruling has affirmed this decision, permitting VCs to serve as the underlying assets in futures contracts (Jafari, Vo-Huu, Jabiyev, Mera, & farkhani, 2018). The Securities and Exchange Commission (SEC) regulates cryptocurrencies, especially in instances of fraud and public offerings. In the case of *SEC v. Trendon Shavers*, the court acknowledged that bitcoins qualify as securities due to their capacity to be exchanged in a manner similar to currency (SECURITIES AND EXCHANGE COMMISSION v. TRENDON T. SHAVERS and BITCOIN SAVINGS AND TRUST, 2014). Furthermore, the Internal Revenue Service (IRS) classifies cryptocurrencies as property, which are subject to taxation according to their fair market value. Furthermore, the Financial Crimes Enforcement Network (FinCEN) mandates that cryptocurrency exchanges register as money transmitters in accordance with the Bank Secrecy Act (Bloomberg, 2021).

United Kingdom

The United Kingdom lacks a dedicated regulatory framework for cryptocurrency; however, the Financial Conduct Authority (FCA) assesses regulation according to the specifics of each transaction. Cryptocurrencies fall under the classification of "exchange tokens" and do not qualify as legal tender. The FCA oversees "security tokens" that offer rights akin to traditional securities, as well as "e-money tokens" (Hillman, 2020). The United Kingdom typically classifies cryptocurrencies as property, adhering to the regulations set forth by Her Majesty's Revenue and Customs (HMRC) for taxation purposes. This classification may entail income or capital gains taxes, contingent upon the specifics of the holding.

China

China has implemented a strict policy, prohibiting financial institutions from offering services to VC platforms since 2013. In 2017, a collective statement from multiple regulatory authorities highlighted that virtual currencies such as bitcoin and ethereum are not to be treated as currency, resulting in the suspension of all token issuance and associated financing activities. China is in the process of developing its own sovereign digital currency, with the People's Bank of China (PBC) planning to issue a state-backed digital yuan.

Russia

Russia permits the use of cryptocurrencies for the exchange of goods and services; however, there is currently no specific legislation regulating their application. The *Russian Civil Code* has undergone amendments to enhance the protection of digital rights and financial assets. A draft law currently under consideration in the State Duma aims to regulate digital financial assets (DFAs) and mining, while prohibiting the use of cryptocurrencies as a payment method. The Russian central bank has expressed its opposition to the legalization of cryptocurrencies, promoting the implementation of stricter regulations instead.

Australia

Australia has officially recognized cryptocurrencies as property, thereby subjecting them to capital gains tax regulations. The Australian Securities and Investments Commission (ASIC) initially did not categorize digital currencies as financial products; however, it subsequently revised its position. If a cryptocurrency operates as a financial product, such as being included in a managed investment scheme, it is subject to the financial regulations. Furthermore, AUSTRAC mandates that cryptocurrency exchanges adhere to anti-money laundering (AML) and counter-terrorism financing (CTF) regulations, necessitating registration and compliance with rigorous reporting requirements.

Japan

Japan possesses one of the largest cryptocurrency markets in the world, having authorized cryptocurrency transactions on licensed exchanges in 2017. The Payment Services Act (PSA) and the Financial Instruments and Exchange Act (FIEA) govern cryptocurrency transactions. According to Article 2(5) of the PSA, virtual currency is characterized as property value that is stored electronically and can be utilized for payment or exchanged with other parties. Japan’s regulatory framework is regarded as one of the most accommodating for cryptocurrency globally.

The diverse regulatory approaches observed globally illustrate the dynamic evolution of cryptocurrency, as nations strive to balance innovation with the imperative of financial stability and security considerations.

Recommendations by the Inter-Ministerial Committee

Given the increasing apprehensions regarding cryptocurrencies and their possible effects on financial stability, legal liabilities, and unlawful activities, the subsequent recommendations are put forth for the regulation and oversight of virtual currencies (VCs) in India:

i. Compliance Rather than implementing a total prohibition: The Inter-Ministerial Committee (IMC), established on November 2, 2017, initially expressed concerns that prohibiting virtual currencies could push operators into the shadows, thereby heightening the risk of their involvement in illicit activities. The IMC put forward the Crypto Token and Crypto Asset (Banning, Control, and Regulation) Bill, 2018, as a response. This draft bill proposes the regulation of cryptocurrency exchanges and brokers involved in the buying and selling of virtual currencies. It also recommended the maintenance of a register for all holdings and transactions via recognized depositories to ensure transparency.
ii. Addressing Gaps in the Regulatory Framework: The Crypto Token Regulation Bill, 2018 emphasized the necessity of preventing individuals engaged in crypto tokens from misrepresenting them as securities or investment schemes. Regulatory frameworks must be established to ensure that operators do not take advantage of existing gaps, especially concerning financial instruments. It is essential to enforce clear definitions and classifications of tokens as securities, commodities, or other financial products to guarantee appropriate oversight and safeguard consumer interests.
iii. Total Ban on Private Cryptocurrencies: The IMC's initial proposal for regulation evolved through subsequent discussions, resulting in a consensus that supports a comprehensive ban on private cryptocurrencies. On February 28, 2019, the IMC put forth a recommendation for the implementation of the Banning of Cryptocurrency and Regulation of Official Digital Currency Bill, 2019 (BCRODC Bill). This legislation proposes a complete prohibition on all private cryptocurrencies in India, alongside the introduction of an official digital currency.
iv. Criminalization of Activities Related to Cryptocurrency: The BCRODC Bill establishes stringent penalties for actions related to cryptocurrencies. Prohibited activities encompass mining, purchasing, selling, or engaging in transactions involving cryptocurrency, in addition to utilizing cryptocurrencies as a medium of exchange, store of value, or unit of account. Individuals found in violation may incur fines or face imprisonment for a duration of up to 10 years, contingent upon the severity of the offence. The bill also prohibits the issuance of financial products related to cryptocurrency, trading in cryptocurrencies, and utilizing

cryptocurrencies as a means for raising funds or credit. The purpose of these measures is to safeguard against the misuse of digital currencies and to serve as a deterrent to unlawful activities.

v. Promoting Innovation through Structured Experimentation: The BCRODC Bill suggests a prohibition on cryptocurrency transactions; however, it allows for the utilization of foundational technologies, such as blockchain, for experimentation, research, and educational initiatives. This exemption creates avenues for innovation, contingent upon the absence of cryptocurrency in actual transactions. Establishing controlled environments for research and development in blockchain technology will enable India to maintain its leadership in technological advancements while ensuring adherence to the regulatory framework.

vi. Amendments to the Prevention of Money Laundering Act (PMLA): The BCRODC Bill proposes modifications to the Prevention of Money Laundering Act, 2002 (PMLA), which would categorize cryptocurrency-related offences as subject to penalties under the PMLA. This step is essential in tackling issues associated with money laundering, tax evasion, and the possible utilization of cryptocurrencies in funding terrorism. The amendment aims to guarantee that digital currency exchanges and users adhere to rigorous anti-money laundering (AML) and counter-terrorism financing (CTF) regulations.

vii. Introduction of a Digital Rupee: The central government, in collaboration with the Reserve Bank of India (RBI), may endorse the establishment of a "digital rupee" as an official digital currency. The Reserve Bank of India will issue this digital currency, which will possess legal tender status within the country. The bill also allows for the recognition of foreign digital currencies, enabling the RBI to designate certain official foreign digital currencies as legal tender in India. This proposal is in accordance with international trends, as numerous countries are investigating or advancing the development of central bank digital currencies (CBDCs) to retain oversight of their monetary systems in the digital era.

viii. Penalties for Non-Compliance and Provisions for Transition: The BCRODC Bill establishes stringent penalties for violations, including fines that may reach up to three times the profit gained or the loss incurred, whichever amount is greater. Violators may incur fines between 25 lakh and 50 crore, contingent upon the nature of the infraction. The bill also specifies a transitional period of 90 days following its enactment, during which individuals in possession of cryptocurrencies are required to declare and liquidate their assets. The objective of this transition phase is to allow sufficient time for compliance, while facilitating the gradual discontinuation of private cryptocurrencies.

ix. Authority of Exemption and Immunity: The central government possesses the power to exempt specific activities from the prohibition list when it considers such exemptions essential for the public interest. Additionally, the government has the authority to grant immunity to individuals from prosecution, provided they offer a complete and honest account of their participation in cryptocurrency-related activities. The provisions facilitate adaptability in law enforcement while promoting voluntary adherence.

In conclusion, the regulatory framework for cryptocurrencies in India needs to achieve a careful equilibrium between promoting innovation and safeguarding the financial system. The recommendations presented above, which encompass the regulation of crypto assets, modifications to anti-money laundering legislation, and the introduction of a digital rupee, are designed to tackle the challenges associated with cryptocurrencies while ensuring that India continues to be a center for technological progress in a secure and regulated framework.

Future Directions

The future trajectory of cryptocurrency laws is expected to be influenced by a combination of technological advancements, evolving regulatory frameworks, and shifting public perception. Governments and regulatory bodies globally are anticipated to prioritize the establishment of clearer and more comprehensive legal frameworks for cryptocurrencies. This may include determining the legal classification of different digital assets, specifying regulatory obligations for exchanges, and tackling issues pertaining to investor protection and financial stability. Considering the worldwide scope of cryptocurrencies, there is likely to be heightened initiatives aimed at international collaboration in regulatory strategies. Entities such as the Financial Action Task Force (FATF) have the potential to significantly influence the establishment of international standards designed to combat money laundering and terrorist financing, thereby impacting the regulatory frameworks of individual nations (Nica, Piotrowska, & Schenk-Hoppé, 2017). As cryptocurrencies increasingly achieve mainstream acceptance, it is likely that regulators will focus on their integration into current financial systems. This integration may encompass the development of frameworks for central bank digital currencies (CBDCs) and the exploration of methods to align traditional financial regulations with the advancements of decentralized technologies like blockchain (Dialani, 2021). Regulators are expected to focus on safeguarding consumer interests, preventing fraud, and ensuring the security of user funds. Striking a balance between promoting innovation and protecting users will be essential for facilitating sustainable cryptocurrency adoption. Additionally, regulatory responses must evolve in accordance with technological advancements, such as innovations in blockchain technology, smart contracts, and decentralized finance (DeFi). Regulators must consistently evaluate and revise their frameworks to stay aligned with this swiftly changing environment. The increasing involvement of institutional investors and traditional financial institutions in the cryptocurrency sector is expected to impact regulatory strategies. Policymakers may aim to create regulations that consider the distinct features of cryptocurrencies while also addressing the needs of institutional stakeholders. It is essential to acknowledge that the future of cryptocurrency regulations will differ across jurisdictions, showcasing the varied strategies adopted by different nations. As the cryptocurrency industry evolves, achieving the appropriate equilibrium between fostering innovation and maintaining regulatory compliance will be essential for the sustained growth and stability of the sector.

India's strategy for regulating cryptocurrency is still evolving. The Ministry of Finance, during the 2021 Winter Session, highlighted the importance of global collaboration in the regulation of cryptocurrencies, given their inherently borderless characteristics. The ministry emphasized the risks associated with regulatory arbitrage, highlighting the necessity for a cohesive global strategy to tackle the challenges presented by digital currencies. The Indian government has not enacted a total ban on cryptocurrencies; however, it is diligently assessing the associated risks and benefits. The taxation of Virtual Digital Assets (VDAs) and the expected introduction of the Digital Rupee demonstrate India's careful yet forward-thinking strategy in addressing the emergence of digital currencies. The trajectory of cryptocurrency regulation in India is expected to hinge on forthcoming judicial rulings, policy decisions, and international regulatory advancements. In conclusion, India's evolving legal framework demonstrates a thoughtful balance between fostering innovation in blockchain technology and mitigating the financial, security, and social risks associated with cryptocurrencies (Manikandan & Mittal, 2021). As the sector evolves, it is anticipated that more detailed regulations will be introduced, offering enhanced clarity and protection for both consumers and the economy.

CONCLUSION

Despite the initiatives undertaken by regulatory bodies globally, law enforcement agencies still encounter considerable challenges in tackling the misuse of cryptocurrency for money laundering. A significant challenge lies in the global nature of cryptocurrency transactions, which frequently traverse jurisdictions, thereby complicating enforcement and investigative efforts. Criminals take advantage of these cross-border complexities, hindering the ability of any single jurisdiction to address the issue effectively. This research contends that the absence of global coordination and standardized regulatory practices will result in fragmented and ineffective efforts to address cryptocurrency-based financial crime.

Cryptocurrency requires regulation; however, existing legal frameworks, including the Prevention of Money Laundering Act (PMLA), fall short in addressing the increasing threat of money laundering associated with cryptocurrencies. To tackle this gap, two primary strategies may be evaluated. Initially, it is essential to amend the PMLA, specifically Section 2(s)(sa), to clearly incorporate cryptocurrency businesspersons into the definition *of "person carrying on designated business or profession."* Cryptocurrency exchange providers would be classified as "reporting entities" under Section 2(w)(wa) of the Act. This classification would necessitate the implementation of "client due diligence" and KYC (Know Your Customer) requirements for these businesses, as outlined in Rule 9 of the Prevention of Money Laundering (Maintenance of Records) Rules, 2005. Secondly, India has the potential to implement a standalone legislative framework aimed at regulating cryptocurrencies, overseen by an independent regulatory authority that guarantees the secure use of these digital assets. India should carefully evaluate the potential risks associated with decentralized and unregulated cryptocurrencies. In the absence of adequate regulation, there is a risk that the Reserve Bank of India's authority over the financial system may be compromised, potentially leading to economic destabilization and the promotion of unlawful activities, including money laundering, circumvention of capital controls, and unauthorized purchases. India's regulatory approach has been predominantly reactionary and fragmented, resulting in an environment of uncertainty for cryptocurrency users and law enforcement agencies alike. The absence of a thorough regulatory framework presents significant challenges for Indian authorities in tracing illegal funds and effectively prosecuting offenders. The Reserve Bank of India (RBI) has adopted a cautious stance regarding cryptocurrencies by implementing restrictions on banking services for crypto-related businesses; however, these measures are inadequate to effectively curb illicit activities. The Supreme Court's ruling in the *IMAI case* deemed the ban on cryptocurrencies unconstitutional and a breach of the fundamental right to trade (Internet And Mobile Association of India Versus Reserve Bank of India, 2018). However, this decision warrants reconsideration as the associated risks of cryptocurrencies become increasingly apparent. A legislative prohibition may be enacted should cryptocurrencies be determined to present a considerable risk to national security and financial stability.

The cryptocurrency market has experienced significant growth, both on a global scale and within India, accompanied by considerable financial investments involved. The future of these investments remains ambiguous, as it is contingent upon the developments in cryptocurrency regulation. Despite the legal complexities associated with cryptocurrencies, investors remain undeterred and are actively seeking opportunities to leverage the Indian cryptocurrency market. The Central Government is set to introduce the Cryptocurrency and Regulation of Official Digital Currency Bill, 2021, while the Reserve Bank of India is preparing to launch its own official digital currency. This development indicates that the regulatory landscape is currently at a pivotal point. The categorization of cryptocurrencies presents an interesting challenge—will they be classified as currency, security, or commodity? Leaders of specific cryptocurrency exchanges have approached the Central Government, advocating for the regulation of cryptocurrencies by the Securities and Exchange Board of India (SEBI). They contend that cryptocurrencies are traded primarily as commodities rather than as currencies. The author believes that the Indian government ought to collaborate with industry stakeholders to comprehensively grasp the complex aspects of cryptocurrencies prior to formulating any legislation. This approach is essential, given that the regulatory framework established will significantly impact the market landscape. Cryptocurrencies present a dual nature of advantages and disadvantages; they create novel opportunities for enterprises, yet simultaneously pose significant challenges for regulatory bodies and consumers. The challenges encompass cybersecurity risks, tax evasion, the promotion of illegal activities, and the potential for providing financial support for terrorism.

Authorities have undertaken initiatives to modify current legislation in order to address or mitigate the potential misuse of cryptocurrencies. Nonetheless, achieving a balance between safety and efficiency continues to present challenges. Contemporary legal frameworks continue to face challenges in establishing effective regulations for this emerging and swiftly advancing technology. Creating legislation without thoroughly examining all facets of the issue may result in regulations that are ineffective or potentially detrimental. Consequently, it is essential for lawmakers to invest in research regarding different aspects of virtual currencies to develop more reliable and comprehensive legislation. Projects such as the BITCRIME initiative and the Crypto Valley Association have been created to investigate these matters and aid in the development of more informed legislative measures. The introduction of cryptocurrency has had a considerable impact on various sectors, garnering attention only recently, even though it has been in existence for a significant period. The landscape of cryptocurrency law and economics is in a state of constant evolution, characterized by a multifaceted relationship among regulation, decentralization, taxation, and technological innovation. Some countries have adopted cryptocurrencies, whereas others exercise caution by enacting regulations aimed at reducing risks associated with fraud, security, and money laundering. Cryptocurrencies have posed significant challenges to conventional financial models, presenting potential advantages like enhanced financial inclusion and expedited, borderless transactions. Nonetheless, factors like volatility, regulatory ambiguity, and environmental issues persist in influencing the trajectory of cryptocurrency law and economics.

In summary, as cryptocurrency solidifies its position within the global economy, the necessity for strong and thorough regulatory frameworks becomes more evident. Achieving equilibrium between promoting innovation and maintaining financial and legal stability is essential for the sustainable development of the cryptocurrency ecosystem. India, similar to numerous other nations, finds itself at a pivotal juncture, and its decisions regarding cryptocurrency regulation will significantly influence its financial system while also establishing benchmarks for international regulatory practices in this swiftly evolving domain.

REFERENCES

Adrian, T., He, D., Ismail, A., & Moretti, M. (2023, July 18). *Crypto Needs Comprehensive Policies to Protect Economies and Investors*. IMF Blog. https://www.imf.org/en/Blogs/Articles/2023/07/18/crypto-needs-comprehensive-policies-to-protect-economies-and-investors

Allcot, D. (2021, May 2). *How Does Cryptocurrency Work - And Is It Safe?* Yahoo Finance. Retrieved from https://finance.yahoo.com/news/does-cryptocurrency-safe-150059419.html?guccounter=1

Anand, N., Agrawala, P., & Das, D. (2024). *Blockchain & Cryptocurrency Laws and Regulations 2024*. Global Legal Insights. https://www.globallegalinsights.com/practice-areas/blockchain-laws-and-regulations/india/

Ananthesh, R. N. K. (2021, June 17). Cryptocurrency in India- Regulatory Challenges and the way forward. *Manupatra*. https://articles.manupatra.com/article-details/Cryptocurrency-in-India-Regulatory-Challenges-and-the-way-forward

Aslam, M. R. (2023, July 26). *3 legal and regulatory challenges surrounding the use of cryptocurrencies*. The Economic Times. https://economictimes.indiatimes.com/markets/cryptocurrency/3-legal-and-regulatory-challenges-surrounding-the-use-of-cryptocurrencies/articleshow/102137752.cms?from=mdr

Baydakova, A. (2023, June 27). *Wyoming: Regulatory Clarity and Crypto-Friendly Banks Fuel Blockchain Revolution*. Retrieved October 20, 2024, from CoinDesk: https://www.coindesk.com/consensus-magazine/2023/06/27/wyoming-regulatory-clarity-and-crypto-friendly-banks-fuel-blockchain-revolution/

Biswas, A., Kumar, A., Jajoo, A., & Sehgal, A. (2023, October 30). *Cryptocurrency trading Subject to Anti-Money Laundering Laws*. Retrieved October 20, 2024, from Lexology: https://www.lexology.com/library/detail.aspx?g=0e6e9a42-fb65-4a69-9b09-38c405a3bda0

Bloomberg. (2021, June 01). *Can a cryptocurrency break the buck?* Retrieved October 20, 2024, from Mint: https://www.livemint.com/opinion/online-views/can-a-cryptocurrency-break-the-buck-11622504970042.html

Cibin, K. (n.d.). Regulation of cryptocurrency in India tackling money laundering and cross-border terrorism: a comparative analysis with the EU mica act. *Indian Journal of Law and Legal Research, 6*(2), 2955-2968. Retrieved October 20, 2024, from https://3fdef50c-add3-4615-a675-a91741bcb5c0.usrfiles.com/ugd/3fdef5_58ee16f8c66b4fb6807b29691bd402db.pdf

Dejan, D., & Sinisa. (2018). Blockchain technology, bitcoin, and Ethereum: A brief overview. *17th International Symposium INFOTEH-JAHORINA (INFOTEH)*. DOI: 10.1109/INFOTEH.2018.8345547

Department of Economic Affairs. M. o. (2019). *Report of the Committee to propose specific actions to be taken in relation to virtual currencies.* Economic Affairs. New Delhi: Ministry of Finance. https://dea.gov.in/sites/default/files/Approved%20and%20Signed%20Report%20and%20Bill%20of%20IMC%20on%20VCs%2028%20Feb%202019.pdf

Dialani, P. (2021, June 04). *Future of Cryptocurrency? Will it Grow or Stoop Low?* Analytics Insight. https://www.analyticsinsight.net/cryptocurrency-analytics-insight/future-of-cryptocurrency-will-it-grow-or-stoop-low

Ganguly, S. (2022, October 24). *Cryptocurrency Regime in India: The Journey So Far.* Mondaq. https://www.mondaq.com/india/fin-tech/1234600/cryptocurrency-regime-in-india-the-journey-so-far

Girme, D. A., & Ray, A. (n.d.). The Anatomy of Money Laundering. *Indian Journal of Law and Legal Research, V*(2), 1-13. Retrieved October 2024, 2024, from https://3fdef50c-add3-4615-a675-a91741bcb5c0.usrfiles.com/ugd/3fdef5_6b61d9108b234a549f87b5a99226a17c.pdf

Gowda, N., & Chakravorty, C. (2021, August). Comparative Study on Cryptocurrency Transaction and Banking Transaction. *Global Transitions Proceedings*, *2*(2), 530–534. Advance online publication. DOI: 10.1016/j.gltp.2021.08.064

Guru, T. (2024, July 02). *Using crypto-currencies for money laundering*. Retrieved October 20, 2024, from Tax Guru: https://taxguru.in/finance/crypto-currencies-money-laundering.html

Gururaj, B. (2005). Commentaries on FEMA. Money Laundering Act and COFEPOSA., Retrieved October 19, 2024, from.

Helms, K. (2020, November 19). *Millionaires FOMO: 73% Will Own Bitcoin by 2022, Survey*. Retrieved from Bitcoin.com News: https://news.bitcoin.com/millionaires-fomo-73-own-bitcoin/

Hillman, H. D. (2020). Money laundering through cryptocurrencies: analysing the responses of the United States and Australia and providing recommendations for the UK to address the money laundering risks posed by cryptocurrencies. *University of West of England, Bristol.* Retrieved October 20, 2024, from https://uwe-repository.worktribe.com/preview/7003847/Amended%20Thesis%20-%20H%20Hillman%20-%20Money%20Laundering%20through%20Cryptocurrencies.pdf

India, C. o. (1950). Article 19(1)(g). India. Retrieved October 20, 2024, from https://cdnbbsr.s3waas.gov.in/s380537a945c7aaa788ccfcdf1b99b5d8f/uploads/2024/07/20240716890312078.pdf

Internet And Mobile Association of India Versus Reserve Bank of India. (2018). *Writ Petition (Civil) No.528 of 2018*. Supreme Court of India.

ITP. (2021, April 20). *Crypto investors get a shock as India drafts bill to ban digital currency*. Retrieved from Arabian Business: https://www.arabianbusiness.com/money/wealth/alternative-assets/462324-crypto-investors-get-shock-as-india-circulates-draft-bill-to-ban-the-digital-currency

Jabotinsky, H. Y., & Sarel, R. (2021, March 26). *How the Covid -19 Pandemic Affected Cryptocurrency Market?* CLS Bluesky Blog. https://clsbluesky.law.columbia.edu/2021/03/26/how-the-covid-19-pandemic-affected-the-cryptocurrency-market/

Jafari, S., Vo-Huu, T., Jabiyev, B., Mera, A., & farkhani, R. M. (2018, May 02). Cryptocurrency: A Challenge to Legal System. *SSRN*, 1-21. DOI: 10.2139/ssrn.3172489

Joseph, V., Ray, D., & Agarwal, S. (2020, June 01). *Cryptocurrencies in India - Past, Present & Future*. Retrieved October 19, 2024, from Mondaq: https://www.mondaq.com/india/fin-tech/944312/cryptocurrencies-in-india--past-present-future

Kepli, M. Y., & Zulhuda, S. (2019, August 26). Cryptocurrencies and Anti-money Laundering Laws: The Need for an Integrated Approach. *Emerland Insight*, pp. 247-263. DOI: 10.1108/978-1-78973-545-120191020

Kumar, V. A. (2012). Money Laundering: Concept, Significance and its Impact. *European Journal of Business and Management*, •••, 113–119.

Lakshmikumaran Sridharan Attorneys. (2018, April 03). *Trading in Virtual Currencies: An analysis under foreign exchange laws of India*. Retrieved October 20, 2024, from LKS: https://www.lakshmisri.com/insights/articles/trading-in-virtual-currencies-an-analysis-under-foreign-exchange-laws-of-india/#

Lang, H., Howcroft, E., & Wilson, T. (2023, November 03). *The crypto market bears the scars of FTX's Collapse*. Retrieved October 20, 2024, from Reuters: https://www.reuters.com/technology/crypto-market-still-bears-scars-ftxs-collapse-2023-10-03/

Law, F. (n.d.). *Legal Issues Surrounding Cryptocurrency*. Retrieved October 20, 2024, from Freeman Law: https://freemanlaw.com/legal-issues-surrounding-cryptocurrency/

Makhija, R. (2024). Unregulated Cryptocurrency: Need for Legal Regulation in Digital Economy. *Trinity Law Review*, *4*(1), 18–24. DOI: 10.48165/tlr.2024.4.1.4

Malhotra, S. (1900, January 01). Prevention Of Money Laundering and Terrorism: An Indian Perspective. *Manupatra.*

Manikandan, A., & Mittal, A. (2021, June 03). *India's cryptocurrency industry draws up 'legitimacy plan'.* The Economic Times. https://economictimes.indiatimes.com/tech/technology/indias-cryptocurrency-industry-draws-up-legitimacy-plan/articleshow/83188685.cms

Mataković, I. C. (2022). Crypto-Assets Illicit Activities: Theoretical Approach with. *International E-Journal of Criminal Sciences*, 1-30.

Mehrotra, U. (2021, November 03). *Cryptocurrency: A Regulatory Conundrum.* SCC Online. https://www.scconline.com/blog/post/2021/11/03/cryptocurrency-a-regulatory-conundrum/

Mishra, U. (2023, July 25). Regulatory Evolution of Cryptocurrency In India. *Mondaq*. Retrieved October 20, 2024, from https://www.mondaq.com/india/fin-tech/1346578/regulatory-evolution-of-cryptocurrency-in-india

Nica, O., Piotrowska, K., & Schenk-Hoppé, K. R. (2017, October 27). Cryptocurrencies: Economic Benefits and Risks. SSRN. Retrieved October 20, 2024, from https://papers.ssrn.com/sol3/papers.cfm?abstract_id=3059856 DOI: 10.2139/ssrn.3059856

Nimma, D. S. (2022, March 22). Curbing the Menance of Money Laundering International Initiatives. *International Journal for Legal Research and Analysis*, *2*(6), 4–23. Retrieved October 19, 2024, from https://www.ijlra.com/productImage/Dr.Sudarshan%20Nimma.pdf

Ogbeide, H., Thomson, M. E., Gonul, M. S., Pollock, A. C., Bhowmick, S., & Bello, A. U. (2023). The anti-money laundering risk assessment: A probabilistic approach. *Journal of Business Research*, *162*, 162. DOI: 10.1016/j.jbusres.2023.113820

Parthasarathy, S., & R, A. (2023, March 15). PMLA   Crypto Currency: When Prevention is Better than Cure. *SCC Online*. Retrieved October 20, 2024, from https://www.scconline.com/blog/post/2023/03/15/pmla-crypto-currency-when-prevention-is-better-than-cure/

Pillai, D. K., & Julian, A. F. (n.d.). Prevention of Monet Laundering: Legal and Financial Issues. *Indian Law Institute Law Review*, 1-9. Retrieved October 19, 2024

Poddar, B., & Shalini. (n.d.). Prevention of Money Laundering Act, 2002 - An Overview. *Manupatra*. Retrieved October 18, 2024, from https://www.manupatra.com/roundup/314/Articles/Prevention%20of%20Money%20Laundering.pdf

PRS. (2019). *Virtual Currencies in India.* New Delhi: PRS Legislative Reseacrh ndia. Retrieved October 20, 2024, from https://prsindia.org/files/bills_acts/bills_parliament/1970/PRS%20Committee%20Report%20and%20Bill%20Summary%20on%20Virtual%20Currencies.pdf

PwC. (2020, October 13). *Blockchain technologies could boost the global economy US$1.76 trillion by 2030 through raising levels of tracking, tracing and trust.* Retrieved October 20, 2024, from PwC: https://www.pwc.com/gx/en/news-room/press-releases/2020/blockchain-boost-global-economy-track-trace-trust.html

PwC. (2020). *Time for Trust.* PwC. Retrieved October 19, 2024, from https://image.uk.info.pwc.com/lib/fe31117075640475701c74/m/2/434c46d2-a889-4fed-a030-c52964c71a64.pdf

Rajagopal, K. (2021, December 03). *Supreme Court sets aside RBI ban on cryptocurrency transactions.* Retrieved October 2024, 2024, from The Hindu: https://www.thehindu.com/news/national/supreme-court-sets-aside-rbi-ban-on-cryptocurrency-transactions/article61967124.ece

Ranaweera, N. (2024, May 27). The role of cryptocurrencies in money laundering: challenges and regulatory responses. *Innovare Journal of Social Sciences*, *12*(4), 10–13. Retrieved October 18, 2024, from. DOI: 10.22159/ijss.2024v12i4.51219

Reddy, J. (2019). The Case for Regulating Crypto Assets. *Indian Journal of Law and Technology*, *15*(2), 380–423. DOI: 10.55496/GIGZ6133

Reif, N. (2024, August 30). *What Does It Mean to Burn Crypto? Practical Applications.* Retrieved October 20, 2024, from Investopedia: https://www.investopedia.com/tech/cryptocurrency-burning-can-it-manage-inflation/

Richards, K. (2024, March). *TechTarget.* Retrieved from What is Cryptography?: https://www.techtarget.com/searchsecurity/definition/cryptography

Schneider, F. G. (2008, February). Money Laundering and Financial Means of Organised Crime: Some Preliminary Empirical Findings. *Research Gate*, pp. 309-330. DOI: 10.1504/GBER.2008.019986

Securities And Exchange Commission v. Trendon T. Shavers and Bitcoin Savings and Trust, 4:13-CV-416 (United States District Court Eastern District of Texas Sherman Division September 18, 2014). Retrieved October 20, 2024, from https://casetext.com/case/sec-exch-commn-v-shavers

Seth, S. (2024, May 05). *The 5 Most Private Cryptocurrencies.* Investopedia. https://www.investopedia.com/tech/five-most-private-cryptocurrencies/

Shah, T. V. (2013). *Comments on Prevention of Money Laundering Act, 2002*. Retrieved October 19, 2024

Singh, A., & Chawla, S. (2019). Cryptocurrency Regulation: Legal Issues and Challenges. *International Journal of Reviews and Research in Social Sciences, VII*(2), 365–375. DOI: 10.5958/2454-2687.2019.00028.5

Subramanian, S. (2021, January 12). *Crypto is now the world's fifth-most circulated currency by value*. Quartz. https://qz.com/1954555/all-the-worlds-crypto-is-now-worth-more-than-1-trillion

Tambe, N. (2024, August 17). *All You Need to Know About India's Crypto Bill*. Retrieved October 20, 2024, from Forbes Advisor: https://www.forbes.com/advisor/in/investing/cryptocurrency/crypto-bill/#:~:text=Cryptocurrency%20is%20used%20anonymously%20to,support%20the%20use

United Nations. (n.d.). *Money Laundering*. Retrieved October 20, 2024, from UNODC Romena: https://www.unodc.org/romena/en/money-laundering.html

Yadav, R. (n.d.). Legal aspects of cryptocurrency law: cryptocurrency bill in India. *Indian Journal of Law and Legal Research, 4*(6), 1-15. Retrieved October 20, 2024, from https://3fdef50c-add3-4615-a675-a91741bcb5c0.usrfiles.com/ugd/3fdef5_e332b9076c25451d8eb902ead0cc778b.pdf

Chapter 13
Smart Tourism as a Strategic Driver for Sustainable Digital Transformation in the Rural Himalayas:
Global Lessons and Local Insights

Runa Das
http://orcid.org/0000-0001-6409-8420
Lovely Professional University, India

Amrik Singh
http://orcid.org/0000-0003-3598-8787
Lovely Professional University, India

Kankan Roy
http://orcid.org/0009-0007-8186-4116
Siliguri College, Darjeeling, India

Senjuti Sen
http://orcid.org/0009-0008-4177-4447
Symbiosis Institute of Geoinformatics, India

ABSTRACT

This research explores how emerging technologies such as Artificial Intelligence (AI), the Internet of Things (IoT), Geographic Information Systems (GIS), and Virtual Reality (VR) have the potential to enable Sustainable Digital Transformation

DOI: 10.4018/979-8-3373-5052-3.ch013

as a strategic driver for tourism in the Rural Himalayas. The goal is to promote sustainable digital transformation through emerging technologies and inclusive growth in tourism within the rural Himalayas of West Bengal, India. It utilises a thematic literature review from a global platform and case studies from areas in the rural Himalayas. Results indicate that local stakeholders are increasingly eager to adopt digital tools to enhance destination marketing, improve visitor experiences. Nonetheless, challenges such as digital exclusion, inadequate infrastructure, and lack of policy coordination hinder wider adoption. Furthermore, it provides actionable policy suggestions and outlines future research avenues, positioning the rural Himalayas of West Bengal.

1. INTRODUCTION

Incorporating emerging technology into the tourism industry is helping to advance sustainable development and is a strategic driver in destination management and visitor experience. In areas like the rural Himalayas of India, which have a rich ecological and cultural heritage, this sustainable digital transformation has been significant. Incorporating smart tourism technologies, such as information and communication technologies (ICTs), artificial intelligence (AI), the Internet of Things (IoT), and renewable energy solutions, offers the potential to balance growth with social equity, environmental stewardship, and economic resilience as the state embraces tourism as a pillar of economic development (Chadha et al., 2024).

Globally, tourism is undergoing a notable transformation driven by digital innovation. Smart tourism systems are being incorporated to boost operational efficiency, increase visitor satisfaction, and reduce ecological footprints. In line with the Sustainable Development Goals (SDGs), particularly SDG 12 (Responsible Consumption and Production) and SDG 13 (Climate Action), these technologies enable real-time data monitoring, predictive analytics, and eco-friendly infrastructure design (Usman et al., 2023; Razzaq et al., 2021). For instance, IoT-enabled sensors support waste management and energy monitoring, while AI algorithms support personalised travel experiences and demand forecasting. Furthermore, blockchain technologies are being investigated for transparent, decentralised booking and payment systems, enhancing accountability and trust within the tourism value chain (Gretzel et al., 2015).

In the context of the rural Himalayas in West Bengal, tourism presents a crucial development opportunity for both urban centres and rural landscapes. Areas such as Darjeeling and Dooars are progressively integrating digital solutions to enhance tourism infrastructure and service delivery. These regions are increasingly leveraging information and communication technologies (ICTs) to strengthen stakeholder communication, promote local crafts and cultural heritage, and support community-based microenterprises. Such transformations align with the broader paradigm of smart tourism, where digital tools facilitate sustainable destination management and inclusive growth (Sen, 2019; Buhalis & Amaranggana, 2015). In the Indian context, the adoption of ICT in tourism has been found to improve market access for rural entrepreneurs and enhance visitor engagement, particularly in the Indian context, where digital infrastructure, governance quality, and institutional support significantly influence tourism demand and destination competitiveness (Sharma et al., 2025). The Darjeeling tea tourism initiative exemplifies ICT-enabled tourism, fostering local entrepreneurship, with tourists accessing digital platforms to explore plantation stays, book guided experiences, and learn about sustainable tea cultivation practices (Sen, 2019; Buhalis & Amaranggana, 2015; Rai et al., 2024).

Similarly, in Santiniketan, a renowned cultural heritage site, digital technologies are now being used to enhance visitor engagement. Interactive mobile applications, augmented reality experiences, and GPS-based guides offer immersive storytelling that aligns with the ethos of Rabindranath Tagore's legacy while also supporting conservation efforts (Ganguly, 2018). In the Dooars region, known for its biodiversity and tribal communities, ecotourism initiatives are being enhanced by GIS and remote sensing technologies to map eco-sensitive zones and optimise eco-lodge locations (Islam et al., 2022). Geospatial mapping has helped identify tourism potential, infrastructure shortages, strategic planning, and climate-resilient tourism in disaster risk zones, coastal, and tribal areas like Purba Medinipur and Bankura. (Samaddar et al., 2024; Samanta & Baitalik, 2015).

Despite advancements in emerging technologies, significant challenges persist in rural regions. The digital transformation divide, manifested through limited internet access, inadequate infrastructure, and low levels of digital literacy, continues to hinder the equitable adoption of smart tourism technologies in rural and tribal areas of India. Furthermore, the lack of a cohesive policy framework that integrates technology with sustainable tourism objectives limits the scalability and coordination of these initiatives. While several case studies report local successes, there is no presence of a state-wide strategic vision that aligns technological innovations with the socio-cultural and environmental contexts of differing regions (Rajam et al., 2021; Shruthi et al., 2021).

Another critical concern is the environmental cost associated with emerging technologies. Although ICTs and digital platforms offer significant sustainability benefits, their implementation often entails increased energy consumption, e-waste generation, and lifecycle sustainability trade-offs. Studies have shown that the deployment of 5G networks, cloud computing, and data centres can contribute substantially to carbon emissions if not powered by renewable sources (Fettweis & Zimmermann, 2008; Schluep et al., 2013). Thus, the integration of green ICT practices, including the use of solar-powered infrastructure and circular economy principles, is essential to ensure that the technological externalities do not outweigh the ecological advantages of smart tourism. (Antonioli & Mazzanti, 2017)

The global literature emphasises the potential of technology to enhance sustainability in tourism, yet it often focuses on developed, urbanised settings. Research by Buhalis and Amaranggana (2015) highlights how smart cities utilise real-time data to manage tourist flows, reduce congestion, and personalise services. However, a significant knowledge gap remains regarding the applicability of such models in rural and resource-constrained regions. In this context, West Bengal presents a compelling case for investigating how digital innovation can be localised to foster inclusive and regenerative tourism systems.

However, the social dimensions of technology adoption, such as cultural acceptance, gender equity, and community participation, are often overlooked. Studies have demonstrated that without culturally sensitive approaches, even the most advanced technological interventions may encounter resistance or fail to achieve the intended outcomes (Venkatesh et al., 2003). Therefore, participatory planning and co-design of digital tools with local stakeholders are vital for ensuring relevance, ownership, and long-term impact.

1.2 The Objectives of this Study are Twofold

First, to investigate the transformative role of emerging technologies in enhancing sustainable tourism from global studies; and second, to synthesise regional innovations in the Himalayan region of West Bengal with global best practices to outline a pathway for inclusive, tech-enabled tourism development.

By drawing on regional case studies and international frameworks, this research aims to provide a holistic understanding of how digital technologies can be utilised to enhance resource efficiency, promote community empowerment, and contribute to climate resilience and socio-economic equity in the tourism sector.

This study fills a critical gap in the existing literature by offering a comparative and integrative perspective that connects isolated regional successes with broader global narratives. Unlike prior research that focuses on specific technologies or singular destinations, this work adopts a systems-oriented approach to examine the synergies between digital transformation and sustainable tourism across multiple dimensions, technological, environmental, economic, and social. By doing so, it aims to inform policy, guide strategic planning, and support the development of context-sensitive digital tourism frameworks tailored to the diverse landscapes of the rural Himalayas in West Bengal.

The tourism sector struggles with the dual challenges of post-pandemic recovery and environmental sustainability, and emerging technologies offer both opportunities and risks. The rural Himalayas, with their mosaic of ecological treasures and cultural richness, stand at a pivotal moment to harness the power of digital innovation for sustainable and inclusive tourism. Through a comprehensive analysis of regional applications and global benchmarks, this study aspires to contribute to a resilient, equitable, and future-ready tourism ecosystem.

2. LITERATURE REVIEW

2.1 A Thematic Literature Review on Smart Tourism as a Strategic Driver for Sustainable Digital Transformation

The integration of digital technologies into tourism has emerged as a pivotal driver of sustainable transformation, reshaping how destinations manage resources, engage visitors, and promote environmental conservation. Recent literature emphasises that smart tourism extends beyond technological adoption to represent a strategic framework that aligns digital innovation with sustainability objectives. Technologies such as artificial intelligence (AI), the Internet of Things (IoT), mobile applications, big data analytics, and immersive platforms are increasingly recognised for their capacity to enhance tourist experiences, optimise operational efficiency, and support long-term environmental stewardship.

Smart tourism destinations (STDs) are characterised by the systematic use of digital infrastructure to support real-time decision-making, personalised service delivery, and sustainable destination management. Community involvement plays a central role in ensuring that smart tourism initiatives contribute to local empowerment rather than technological exclusion. Kusumastuti et al. (2024) demonstrate that integrating local knowledge with smart technologies enables communities to personalise tourism resources while preserving cultural identity and strengthening destination resilience. Such participatory approaches ensure that technology-driven tourism development remains socially embedded and culturally sensitive. Innovation and technological adaptation are particularly crucial in developing-country contexts, where tourism competitiveness must be balanced with sustainability concerns. Davronov (2024) highlights how emerging technologies, including IoT and data analytics, enhance tourism attractiveness by improving resource efficiency and reducing environmental pressure. These findings underline the importance of adaptive innovation strategies that respond to infrastructural and socio-economic realities rather than replicating models from technologically advanced destinations.

Emerging technologies such as AI, IoT, blockchain, and ICTs are increasingly recognised for their capacity to enhance efficiency, personalisation, and sustainability in tourism systems. Smart tourism frameworks facilitate real-time data collection and visitor management, though existing studies predominantly focus on urban or technologically advanced destinations (Buhalis, 2020; Gretzel et al., 2015). This bias highlights the need for context-sensitive research in rural and developing regions. Within West Bengal, ICT-based initiatives support regional tourism promotion and local entrepreneurship. Mobile platforms in Darjeeling's tea tourism sector facilitate sustainable travel planning and cultural interaction, while augmented reality applications in Santiniketan enhance heritage storytelling (Islam et al., 2022; Ganguly, 2018; Samaddar et al., 2024; Samanta & Baitalik, 2015). These examples illustrate local adaptations of global smart tourism practices.

Tourist perceptions of sustainability are increasingly shaped by digital engagement, particularly among younger cohorts. Generation Z tourists exhibit strong preferences for technology-enabled travel experiences that align with environmental responsibility. Sfodera et al. (2024) identify a positive relationship between technological integration and perceived sustainability, noting that mobile applications, digital platforms, and augmented reality (AR) significantly influence eco-conscious travel choices. This demographic's familiarity with digital tools positions technology as a key mediator between sustainability awareness and behavioural intention. The operational role of smart technologies in enhancing sustainability is further reinforced through IoT-based systems that improve efficiency and reduce tourism's environmental footprint. Khalid (2024) illustrates how smart destination technologies support energy optimisation and waste reduction, while Singh and Kaunert (2024) highlight the role of AI and IoT in shaping sustainable urban tourism within smart city frameworks. Together, these studies demonstrate that technological engagement influences both tourist behaviour and destination sustainability outcomes.

Emerging technologies are increasingly central to sustainable tourism governance and resilience building. Insights from the *Information and Communication Technologies in Tourism 2024* conference proceedings underscore the transformative role of digital services and smart tourism systems in enhancing destination adaptability. Mihalic (2024) argues that digital technologies support sustainability by improving operational efficiency while enabling environmental responsibility across tourism operations. The evolution of tourism from traditional models to e-tourism further reflects the growing centrality of technology. Pilelienė et al. (2024), through a bibliometric analysis, trace this transformation and position digital innovation as a cornerstone of contemporary tourism development. The application of AI in sustainable tourism management enhances planning accuracy and service optimisation (Patrichi, 2024), while digital platforms increasingly facilitate cultural heritage promotion and interpretation (Suryani, 2024), reinforcing the role of technology in safeguarding intangible assets.

Digital technologies contribute significantly to SDG 12 and SDG 13 by enabling predictive analytics, resource monitoring, and waste reduction (Usman et al., 2023;

Razzaq et al., 2021). IoT-based systems support sustainable infrastructure management, particularly in ecologically sensitive areas such as the Dooars (Chadha et al., 2024). GIS and remote sensing tools further assist eco-tourism planning and risk mitigation in regions like Purba Medinipur and Bankura (Samaddar & Mondal et al., 2024; Samanta & Baitalik, 2015).

Information and Communication Technology (ICT) has been widely acknowledged as a catalyst for sustainable tourism practices. ICT applications support efficient resource management, environmental awareness, and eco-friendly service delivery (Charfeddine & Umlai, 2023; Hilty & Aebischer, 2015). For example, ICT-enabled monitoring systems allow hospitality enterprises to track energy consumption in real time, reducing waste and operational inefficiencies (Lange et al., 2020).ICT tools also contribute to managing tourist flows, thereby preventing overcrowding in ecologically sensitive destinations and minimising environmental degradation (Xin et al, 2022).

However, the environmental implications of digitalisation cannot be overlooked. The production, use, and disposal of electronic devices contribute to carbon emissions and e-waste generation (Schluep et al., 2013; Fettweis & Zimmermann, 2008). To address these challenges, policy interventions promoting energy-efficient technologies and sustainable e-waste management have been advocated (European Commission, 2021).

The integration of renewable energy systems within tourism operations represents a critical dimension of sustainable smart destinations. Gössling et al. (2019) document how tourism enterprises adopt solar, wind, and geothermal energy solutions to reduce dependence on fossil fuels and appeal to environmentally conscious travellers. Digital technologies further strengthen these initiatives by enabling smart energy management and performance monitoring. Blockchain technology has emerged as a complementary tool that enhances transparency in carbon offset mechanisms and sustainability certification. Smart tourism destinations further demonstrate how digital infrastructure enables intelligent service systems and supports sustainability-oriented innovation (Buhalis & Amaranggana, 2015). Additionally, virtual reality (VR) platforms provide immersive experiences that reduce the need for physical travel, thereby lowering environmental pressure on fragile destinations.

AI and big data analytics are transforming sustainable tourism by enabling real-time monitoring, predictive planning, and adaptive resource allocation. Gretzel et al. (2020) demonstrate how AI-driven systems optimise visitor experiences while reducing environmental impacts through data-informed decision-making. Digital branding and social media strategies further strengthen sustainable tourism engagement by boosting the destination's green image and encouraging tourists to participate in eco-friendly activities (Singh & Das, 2025). Bibliometric evidence shows a rapid growth of AI applications in sustainable tourism research. Del Vasto and Castro (2024) reveal that AI enhances operational efficiency and workflow optimisation across tourism services. Likewise, Khan et al. (2024) emphasise AI's role in supporting responsible travel by analysing behavioural data to improve conservation efforts and visitor satisfaction.

Virtual and augmented reality technologies offer innovative solutions to sustainability challenges by providing digital access to heritage sites and ecologically fragile areas. By reducing physical visitation pressures, VR and AR contribute to cultural preservation and environmental protection. These technologies also support experiential learning and responsible tourist behaviour when integrated into interpretive and educational tourism experiences (Huang & Leung, 2025).

Communication technologies play a critical role in fostering local engagement and inclusive tourism development. Social media platforms and internet-based tools enable community-led tourism initiatives and strengthen local visibility (Rattanamanee, 2024). In the post-pandemic context, technology has also facilitated the reconstruction of greener tourism supply chains and enhanced destination resilience (Chiwaridzo & Masengu, 2025).

Regenerative tourism represents a shift from impact mitigation to ecosystem and community restoration. Alhitmi, Rahman, and Bayram (2024) conceptualise regenerative tourism as a framework that actively enhances social and ecological systems. Critiquing conventional sustainability approaches, Niewiadomski and Brouder (2024) advocate for socio-technical transitions that integrate energy systems, social justice, and multi-actor collaboration to achieve systemic change.

The interaction between tourism and industrialisation has implications for sustainable economic development. Song et al. (2024) demonstrate that coordinated tourism–industrial development contributes positively to economic growth while supporting SDGs 8 and 9. Their findings highlight the importance of integrating tourism innovation with broader industrial and environmental policies. Digital tourism platforms facilitate local empowerment by supporting microenterprises, expanding market access, and preserving cultural heritage through digital storytelling (Rai et al., 2024). However, digital exclusion and infrastructural gaps constrain equitable participation. Community capacity building and digital literacy initiatives are essential to prevent marginalisation (Rajam & Banerjee, 2021).

The literature highlights fragmented governance and the absence of an integrated digital tourism policy framework in West Bengal. Effective smart tourism development requires multi-level coordination that aligns technological innovation with socio-cultural contexts and sustainability goals (Gretzel et al., 2015; Samaddar & Mondal, 2024). Despite extensive global literature, research on smart tourism in rural and resource-constrained settings remains limited. West Bengal's diverse socio-ecological landscape offers a valuable context for developing place-based smart tourism models. As noted by Buhalis and Michopoulou (2013), technological systems must be locally grounded to ensure effectiveness and sustainability.

2.2 Discussion: Case-Based Evidence on Smart Tourism from Global and West Bengal Contexts

Across the destinations in the European Union, several case-based studies explicitly situate smart and digital tourism practices within clear geographical contexts, illustrating how sustainability outcomes are shaped by local conditions. Research on smart tourism development in Europe demonstrates how integrated digital ecosystems support sustainable destination management. These cases show that real-time data exchange, interoperability platforms, and smart governance frameworks help European destinations manage visitor flows, reduce energy consumption, and enhance service personalisation while maintaining environmental standards (Gretzel et al., 2015).

Evidence from mountain regions in Southern Europe, especially Italy, highlights how digital technologies are applied in environmentally fragile landscapes. Case studies from Italian mountain areas illustrate the use of digital platforms and smart monitoring tools to support sustainable mobility, energy efficiency, and rural economic resilience. These interventions enable destinations to preserve natural resources while enhancing tourism competitiveness, demonstrating the relevance of technology-enabled sustainability in peripheral and alpine contexts (Sgroi & Modica, 2024).

Across Spain and other European destinations, smart tourism infrastructure contributes to SDG 11 and SDG 12 through efficient visitor management, energy optimisation, and intelligent waste systems. Real-time data and interoperability platforms enable destinations to reduce resource intensity while improving service personalisation and visitor satisfaction. These outcomes reflect how technologically advanced destinations can integrate sustainability principles into urban and regional tourism governance frameworks (Buhalis & Law, 2008).

The Zimbabwean case of green tourism supply chain recovery after COVID-19 directly supports SDG 8 (Decent Work and Economic Growth) and SDG 12 (Responsible Consumption and Production). ICT adoption and social media branding facilitated the revival of tourism enterprises, protected employment, and promoted environmentally responsible supply chain practices. By strengthening market access and encouraging greener production and consumption patterns, digital tools played a crucial role in fostering sustainable economic recovery in a developing economy context (Chiwaridzo & Masengu, 2025).

Studies examining smart destination initiatives in Southeast Asia, with a focus on Thailand, further underline the geographical specificity of digital sustainability practices. In these destinations, the integration of AI and IoT technologies supports real-time environmental monitoring, intelligent waste management, and personalised tourist services. Such cases reveal how emerging economies can leverage advanced digital tools to balance tourism growth with environmental protection and governance efficiency in rapidly developing tourism regions (Suanpang & Pothipassa, 2024).

In Indonesia, the post-smart tourism village model aligns closely with SDG 5 (Gender Equality) and SDG 11 (Sustainable Cities and Communities) by integrating digital tourism practices into local value systems and participatory governance. Community-based digital tools create inclusive spaces for women's involvement in tourism decision-making and entrepreneurial activities, while reinforcing social cohesion and cultural integrity at the village level. This approach illustrates how smart tourism can advance empowerment and community sustainability when grounded in local socio-cultural contexts (Kusumawardhani et al., 2024).

In Purba Medinipur and Bankura districts of West Bengal, India, ICT-enabled eco-tourism planning aligns with SDG 11 and SDG 12 by supporting environmentally responsible land-use planning and risk-informed destination development. The application of GIS and remote sensing strengthens conservation efforts, promotes sustainable tourism zoning, and mitigates environmental hazards, thereby enhancing long-term community resilience in ecologically sensitive regions (Samaddar & Mondal, 2024).

Ultimately, the Darjeeling tea tourism of West Bengal, India, contributes to achieving SDG 5, SDG 8, and SDG 12 by linking digital engagement with cultural preservation and sustainable livelihoods(Das et al., 2026). ICT platforms enhance women's participation in tourism-related enterprises, support decent work through local value chains, and encourage responsible tourism consumption rooted in heritage and place-based identity. This Himalayan case underscores how digital tourism tools can simultaneously advance gender empowerment, economic sustainability, and responsible production practices in rural tourism settings (Sgroi & Modica, 2024).

3. METHODOLOGY

The study adopts a mixed-methods research design, integrating both quantitative and qualitative approaches. Secondary data are utilised to examine emerging trends in smart tourism, the application of digital technologies in the tourism sector, and to identify existing research gaps. Primary data collection is undertaken to assess the current status, adoption, and practical implementation of smart tourism initiatives in remote tourist villages of West Bengal. This approach enables a comprehensive understanding of both macro-level trends and ground-level realities.

3.1 Study Area

The study area comprises two Himalayan districts of West Bengal, Darjeeling and Kalimpong. These districts are widely recognised for their panoramic views of the Kanchenjunga range and the historical and global significance of Darjeeling tea. Presently, the region has faced multiple challenges, including the impacts of mass tourism, climate change–induced threate on the tea industry, and recurring political disturbances. These factors have contributed to a gradual decline in conventional tourism, encouraging a transition toward rural and alternative tourism models.

The study identifies remote rural destinations located within wildlife sanctuaries, farm-based tourism villages, and tea tourism areas across the selected districts. Additionally, two villages that have recently adopted renewable energy initiatives within tourism activities are selected for detailed analysis. The spatial distribution and accessibility of these locations are mapped using ArcGIS Pro software.

3.2 Data Collection Methods and Discussion

Primary data were collected through a series of semi-structured interviews and focus group discussions (FGDs) with 60 stakeholders between February and May 2025. A flexible checklist guided the interviews to allow respondents to elaborate on context-specific issues. FGDs facilitated community-level insights into shared experiences and collective aspirations for a technology-enabled tourism model. In addition, participant observation was conducted during field visits to homestays, local tourism hubs, and training centres.

The discussions were conducted in two phases. The first phase focused on understanding the significance of the study area from the perspectives of key stakeholders, including established tour operators and welfare organisations. The second phase analysed insights from interviews with the 60 stakeholders to identify their expectations, perceived benefits, and challenges related to the adoption of new technologies in the evolving tourism landscape.

4. CASE STUDY AND EMPIRICAL FINDINGS

4.1 About Study Areas

Figure 1. Represent the study area

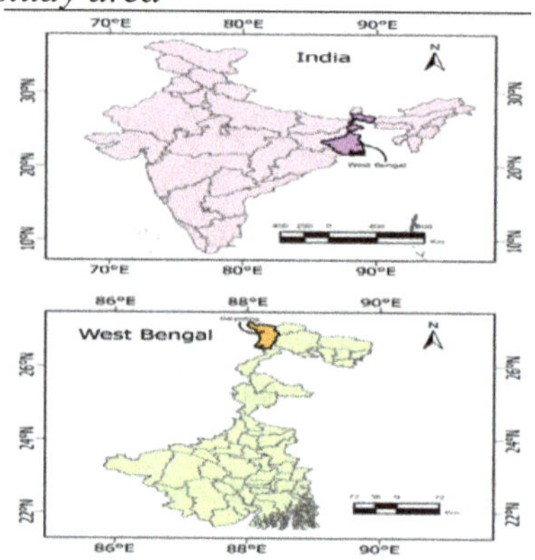

Source: Author (ArcGIS Pro Software)

The Himalayan region of West Bengal (Figure 1) is widely recognised for its tea industry, tourism potential, scenic landscapes, adventure activities, and rich cultural heritage. Despite these attributes, scholarly investigation into the integration of emerging technologies in rural areas of this region remains limited and insufficiently developed. Figures 2, 3, and 4 illustrate the survey locations selected for this study. Nestled along the eastern Himalayan slopes near the majestic Kanchenjunga mountain range, a cluster of rural and forested villages, including Lepchajagat, Lamahatta, Tinchuley, Chatakpur, Takdah, and Lava, offers a distinctive eco-tourism experience deeply rooted in nature and traditional rural life. These villages are characterised by serene landscapes, dense forests, and panoramic mountain vistas, making them ideal destinations for travellers seeking tranquillity, authenticity, and a close connection with the natural environment.

The local communities in these areas are predominantly agrarian, relying on small-scale farming, horticulture, and forest-based livelihoods. Daily life revolves around seasonal agriculture, organic vegetable cultivation, and the sustainable use of natural resources. This strong dependence on the land has fostered a harmonious relationship between people and nature, reflected in the preservation of rich bio-diversity. The surrounding forests are home to a diverse array of flora and fauna, including rhododendrons, orchids, medicinal plants, birds, and small wildlife species, thereby enhancing the ecological value of these eco-tourism destinations.

One of the most compelling attractions of these villages is their breathtaking views of Kanchenjunga, often visible at sunrise, when the snow-clad peaks glow in shades of gold and pink. This dramatic natural spectacle, combined with mist-covered valleys and forest trails, creates a powerful sensory experience for visitors. Beyond scenic beauty, these villages maintain strong cultural ties with Darjeeling's heritage, particularly through tea cultivation, which remains an integral part of the region's identity. Tea gardens and tea tourism destinations such as Glenburn, Sitong, Tumsong, Happy Valley, Chamong, Gopaldhara, Ambootia, Makaibari, Selim Hill, and Rohini (Figure 3) reflect the historical, economic, and cultural significance of tea in shaping local livelihoods and landscapes.

With increasing interest among urban tourists in nature-oriented and sustainable holidays, eco-tourism in these rural areas has gradually embraced renewable energy solutions. Visitors are increasingly drawn to destinations that combine environmental responsibility with authentic rural experiences. In response, villages such as Lepchajagat and Tinchuley (Figure 4) have adopted renewable energy systems, particularly solar power, in tourism-related establishments, including homestays and eco-resorts. Although challenges persist due to infrastructural limitations and economic constraints, the integration of renewable energy presents significant opportunities to enhance livelihoods, reduce environmental pressure, and promote sustainable rural development.

Together, the ecological richness, cultural depth, scenic beauty, and emerging sustainable practices of these villages create a distinctive eco-tourism landscape. This study explores local requirements, challenges, expectations, and the adoption of emerging technologies, such as AI, GPS, GIS, and renewable energy, to support sustainable tourism, gender equality, economic sustainability, and capacity enhancement. It also examines infrastructure gaps and draws lessons from the COVID-19 period to inform the development of resilient and inclusive rural tourism in the Himalayan region of West Bengal.

Figure 2.

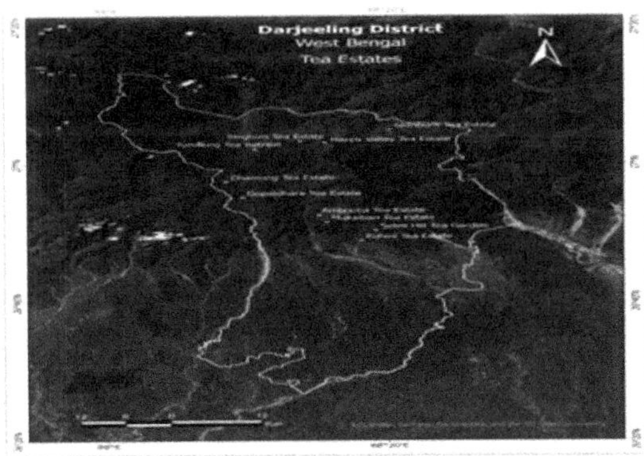

Figure 3.

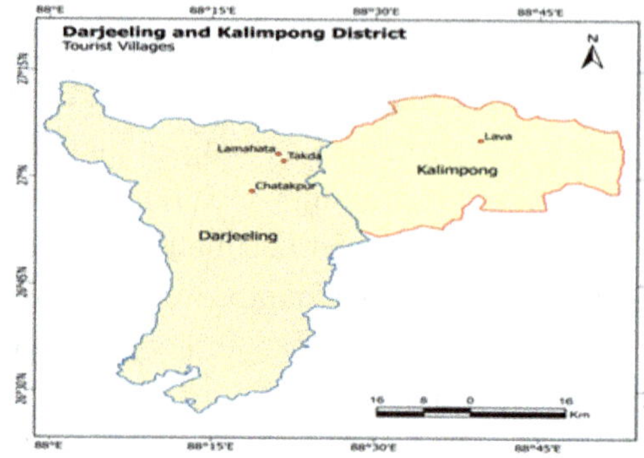

Figure 4.

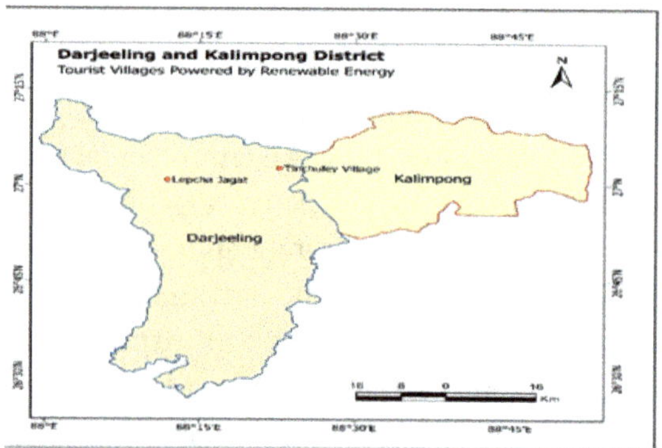

Source: Author (ArcGIS Pro Software)

4.2 Socio-Demographic Profile of Respondents

Table 1.

Characteristic	Choices	%
Age	20-25	5.6
	25-30	14.3
	35-40	33.8
	40-45	38.1
	45 above	8.2
Educational Qualification	Secondary	37.2
	Higher Secondary	36.8
	Graduate	12.6
	More than it	1.7
	Vocational trained	0.9
	Less than secondary	10.8
Present occupation	Farming & Homestay	47.6
	Homestay	9.5
	Homestay& shopkeeping	10.8
	Homestay & Travels	3.9
	Homestay & Restaurant	7.4
	Farming & Roade side shop	14.3
	Homestay &Dairy	1.3
	Service	1.3
	Homestay & service	3.9
Primary occupation of the family	Farming	44.2
	business	0.0
	Service	5.2
	Dairy	.9
	Tourism	49.8
Secondary Occupation	Tourism	53.2
	Farming	19.9
	Business	24.7
	service	2.2

continued on following page

Table 1. Continued

Characteristic	Choices	%
Monthly Income (in Rs)	20000-30000	7.8
	30000-40000	17.7
	40000-50000	21.2
	Above 50000	53.2

The demographic profile (Table 1) indicates that the respondents are predominantly middle-aged, with the largest proportion belonging to the 40–45 years (38.1%) and 35–40 years (33.8%) age groups, suggesting mature and experienced participation in tourism-related activities. Educational attainment is largely secondary (37.2%) and higher secondary (36.8%), while a smaller proportion has graduate-level education, reflecting moderate formal education with practical skill orientation. In terms of occupation, farming combined with homestay activities (47.6%) emerges as the dominant livelihood, highlighting the integration of agriculture and rural tourism. Tourism plays a crucial role in household livelihoods, with 49.8% of families primarily dependent on tourism and 53.2% engaged in tourism as a secondary occupation. Income levels indicate relatively strong economic returns, as over 53% of respondents earn above 50,000 per month, demonstrating the economic significance of tourism-based diversification in rural households.

4.3 Expectations and Challenges for Local Stakeholders in the Technology Era

Inclusive Virtual Reality in Adventure and Eco-Tourism

Stakeholders in the adventure tourism sector showed a keen interest in embracing VR technologies to create immersive experiences for physically limited tourists, senior citizens, and retired adventure sports buffs. These technologies can simulate activities such as trekking, rafting, or mountaineering, enabling sensitive tourists to experience the excitement without the need for physical effort or danger. Similarly, eco-tourism operators observed that VR could enhance the off-season tourist experience and attract environmentally conscious individuals who are unable to physically visit due to health or mobility issues. By gradually integrating VR with natural storytelling and environmental education, rural eco-tourism can provide both enjoyment and awareness without disrupting the ecosystem. Environmental enthusiasts and rural stakeholders emphasised the growing role of AI in promoting sustainable tourism practices. AI-powered systems can monitor visitor flows, predict environmental impact, and optimise resource use, all of which align with the goals of responsible tourism.

However, there is a general lack of modern internet infrastructure, which limits the adoption of these smart solutions. Stakeholders highlighted the urgent need for digital infrastructure investment and training to make sustainable AI-based tourism a reality.

Willingness to Adapt GPS and GIS

In extremely remote locations, homestay operators often face severe visibility and accessibility constraints, as reflected in the observation of one owner who noted that they are "too offbeat to be traced by tourists." In such contexts, access to reliable internet connectivity can play a transformative role by enabling GPS tracking and GIS-based location mapping. These spatial tools enhance the digital visibility of homestays and eco-resorts on online platforms, improving navigability and marketing reach for tourists seeking offbeat and nature-based experiences.

This is particularly relevant in forest-fringe destinations of the Darjeeling–Kalimpong region, such as Chatakpur and Latpanjar, where farm tourism and homestay activities have been permitted by the Forest Department as a livelihood compensation mechanism for local communities affected by wildlife incursions and crop or livestock losses. In these areas, tourism is not merely recreational but functions as a risk-mitigation and livelihood diversification strategy for forest-dependent households. Recognising these dynamics, Divisional Forest Officers (DFOs) are increasingly advocating the use of GIS-based planning frameworks to regulate tourism growth. GIS is being considered as a tool to spatially control visitor flows, demarcate permissible tourism zones, and prevent the emergence of mass tourism that could threaten fragile ecosystems. By supporting controlled accessibility, monitoring carrying capacity, and aligning tourism development with conservation objectives, GIS can facilitate sustainable community development while safeguarding forest landscapes and local livelihoods.

Gendered Perspectives for Smart Tourism

Aged women stakeholders in the region highlighted the need for household-level technological tools to reduce domestic labour burdens. They expressed a strong willingness to adopt renewable energy solutions to ease their workload and improve their ability to focus on professional activities, particularly tourism-related entrepreneurship. Access to smart devices, clean energy appliances, and mobile-based business applications was viewed as essential for balancing domestic responsibilities with income-generating and entrepreneurial roles. Regional economic organisations dependent on tourism emphasised the necessity for training in digital payment systems, social media marketing, and basic tech literacy. Because certain stakeholders are still uncertain due to a lack of understanding, though they consider technology essential for resilience in a post-COVID world and for future competitiveness.

However, unlike parts of rural Himachal Pradesh that managed to continue tourism during COVID-19 through digital platforms, stakeholders in rural Himalayan Bengal pointed out their inability to do the same due to weak infrastructure. The shift to remote work during the pandemic boosted interest in eco-resorts and homestays, but without high-speed internet and AI-backed support systems, these businesses missed out on a major opportunity.

4.4 Result Discussion

This study demonstrates that smart tourism has the potential to act as a powerful strategic driver for sustainable digital transformation in the rural Himalayan regions of West Bengal, particularly in the districts of Darjeeling and Kalimpong. By integrating global theoretical insights with ground-level empirical evidence, the research highlights how emerging technologies can address long-standing structural, environmental, and socio-economic challenges faced by remote mountain destinations. The findings clearly indicate that smart tourism is not merely a technological upgrade but a holistic development paradigm that aligns digital innovation with sustainability principles, community participation, and destination resilience.

Globally, tourism scholarship has shown a clear transition from traditional notions of sustainable tourism toward digitally enabled, system-oriented, and transition-focused approaches that emphasise innovation, data-driven governance, and long-term resilience (Agarwal et al., 2024; Niewiadomski & Brouder, 2024). The experiences of rural Himalayan West Bengal resonate strongly with this shift. The region's geographical remoteness, fragile ecosystems, climate vulnerability, and infrastructural limitations make it particularly suitable for smart tourism interventions that prioritise efficiency, conservation, and inclusivity. As conceptualised in global literature, smart tourism destinations function as interconnected ecosystems where ICTs, governance frameworks, local communities, and tourists interact to co-create value and optimise resource use (Boes et al., 2016; Ionescu & Sârbu, 2024). The study's findings confirm that such an ecosystem approach is both relevant and necessary for rural Himalayan contexts.

The empirical evidence highlights strong stakeholder interest in adopting technologies such as GIS, GPS, AI, VR, mobile applications, and renewable energy systems. These technologies are perceived as tools to overcome accessibility constraints, enhance digital visibility of offbeat destinations, manage environmental risks, and improve visitor experiences. In particular, GIS-based mapping emerged as a critical instrument for spatial planning, disaster risk management, and regulating tourism growth in forest-fringe and wildlife-sensitive areas. This aligns with global research that emphasises the role of ICT adoption in supporting environmental monitoring, operational efficiency, and sustainable destination management (Khatri, 2019; Law & Chen, 2024; Chien et al., 2021). For Himalayan regions prone to landslides, climate-induced disruptions, and biodiversity loss, such data-driven tools are indispensable.

The study further reveals that experiential technologies, especially Virtual Reality and immersive digital storytelling, hold considerable promise for rural eco-tourism and adventure tourism. VR-based simulations can reduce physical pressure on fragile landscapes while enabling inclusive tourism experiences for elderly, physically limited, or environmentally conscious tourists. These findings reflect global evidence that immersive technologies can enhance engagement while supporting conservation objectives by decreasing direct physical intrusion into sensitive environments (Guttentag, 2010; Tussyadiah et al., 2018). In the Himalayan context, VR also offers opportunities for off-season engagement and international outreach, thereby stabilising tourism incomes and reducing seasonal vulnerability.

Environmental sustainability emerges as a key justification for smart tourism incorporation in the study area. Stakeholders consistently integrate renewable energy, particularly solar power, with both ecological responsibility and livelihood enhancement. This reflects broader empirical findings that connect tourism activity, energy consumption, and environmental quality, and highlight the role of green technologies and smart systems in mitigating carbon emissions (Irfan et al., 2023; Lu, 2018). The adoption of renewable energy in homestays and eco-resorts not only reduces dependence on unreliable grid infrastructure but also empowers local women and youth through training, entrepreneurship, and reduced domestic labour burdens. Such outcomes reinforce the argument that smart tourism can contribute simultaneously to environmental sustainability, gender equity, and economic resilience.

Importantly, the study underscores that smart tourism transformation must be socially inclusive and context-sensitive. Gendered perspectives revealed that women view smart technologies and clean energy as enablers of economic participation and work–life balance, particularly in tourism-related entrepreneurship. However, the digital divide, especially affecting elderly residents and indigenous communities, remains a critical concern. This finding aligns with global scholarship cautioning that technological adoption without parallel investment in sustainability literacy, digital skills, and capacity building can exacerbate existing inequalities (Stewart & Gorman, 2024). Therefore, inclusive digital training programmes tailored to local socio-cultural contexts are essential for ensuring that smart tourism benefits are equitably distributed.

At the same time, the study identifies persistent structural barriers, including weak digital infrastructure, limited internet connectivity, digital illiteracy, and inadequate institutional coordination. These challenges reinforce global lessons that effective governance capacity, policy support, and stakeholder collaboration are prerequisites for successful smart tourism implementation (Rafi & Novriana, 2024; Kapoor & Jain, 2024). The COVID-19 experience further illustrates the cost of digital exclusion and the urgent need for resilient, technology-enabled tourism systems (Le et al., 2020). The COVID-19 pandemic serves as a crucial reference point in understanding the urgency of digital resilience. Global studies show that the crisis accelerated digital transformation and forced a rethinking of tourism models toward smarter, safer, and more adaptive systems (Gretzel et al.,2015). While some rural regions elsewhere managed to sustain tourism through digital platforms during the pandemic, stakeholders in rural Himalayan West Bengal highlighted their inability to do so due to weak internet connectivity and inadequate digital infrastructure. This missed opportunity underscores the cost of technological exclusion and reinforces global lessons that smart tourism is essential for crisis preparedness, continuity, and recovery (Le et al., 2020; Srivastava & Shandilya, 2024).

Another key conclusion of the study is the central role of governance and institutional readiness. Stakeholders repeatedly emphasised the need for coordinated policy support, public–private partnerships, and strategic investment to move beyond fragmented and pilot-level technological adoption. Global research similarly stresses that effective local government capacity, supportive regulatory frameworks, and multi-stakeholder collaboration are prerequisites for sustainable tourism development (Rafi & Novriana, 2024). Experiences from ASEAN and other Asian destinations further demonstrate that smart tourism can be successfully adapted to rural and developing contexts when aligned with broader development goals and local governance structures (Leong et al., 2024; Kapoor & Jain, 2024).

Lastly, the study emphasises how crucial it is to approach digital change with care and ethics. Long-term environmental and social effects must be taken into account when integrating smart systems, data platforms, and intelligent infrastructure, especially when it comes to resource usage, waste management, and data governance (Wu et al., 2021). Uncontrolled technological development could pose new threats to delicate Himalayan ecosystems if it is not directed by sustainability principles and local involvement.

5. CONCLUSION

The findings from the stakeholder consultations across Kalimpong, Darjeeling, and neighbouring rural areas reveal a growing consensus on the transformative potential of emerging technologies in overcoming the structural barriers faced by the region's tourism sector. Despite infrastructural challenges, such as limited internet connectivity, poor transportation networks, and unreliable energy supply, local stakeholders demonstrate a proactive interest in embracing tools like Virtual Reality (VR), Artificial Intelligence (AI), Geographic Information Systems (GIS), and renewable energy systems.

One of the most significant themes to emerge is the potential for GIS mapping to enhance environmental management and tourist navigation in ecologically sensitive areas. Stakeholders noted that interactive maps can assist not only in promoting lesser-known trails and heritage sites but also in disaster risk reduction by identifying landslide-prone regions and emergency response routes, which are crucial for terrain vulnerable to monsoon-induced disruptions.

Virtual Reality (VR) is particularly favoured by homestay owners and eco-tourism operators as a pre-visit engagement tool. VR can simulate the Himalayan experience for potential tourists, thereby enhancing visibility and interest in offbeat rural destinations. This is especially beneficial for attracting international or urban visitors during the off-season or amid travel restrictions.

Stakeholders involved in adventure tourism and nature-based experiences suggested the use of AI-powered chatbots and mobile applications for real-time weather updates, trail safety information, and personalised itineraries. These digital tools could significantly enhance visitor satisfaction while alleviating pressure on local operators and natural resources.

Another recurring theme was the integration of renewable energy technologies, particularly solar power, to tackle the region's energy deficit. Stakeholders emphasised the dual role of clean energy systems: enhancing the sustainability of tourism operations and empowering local women and youth through training, employment, and entrepreneurship in energy-based services.

Nevertheless, the discussions revealed significant constraints. Numerous stakeholders pointed out the digital divide, especially affecting older residents and indigenous communities, which raised concerns regarding the inclusiveness of technology-oriented tourism strategies. They promoted capacity-building programmes and digital literacy initiatives designed to fit the local socio-cultural context.

Additionally, the necessity for policy backing and cooperation between the public and private sectors was repeatedly emphasised. Participants contended that, in the absence of strategic investments and institutional support, the integration of emerging technologies would remain fragmented and disconnected from broader regional development objectives.

Overall, feedback from stakeholders reveals a robust eagerness to embrace new technologies for sustainable tourism in rural Himalayan West Bengal. Nevertheless, effective implementation requires tackling infrastructural shortcomings, promoting inclusive digital capacity-building, and enhancing institutional collaboration. Closing the divide between technological advancements and the realities of rural life is crucial for nurturing a resilient and inclusive tourism economy in this ecologically and culturally vibrant region.

In conclusion, this research affirms that smart tourism offers a strategic and contextually appropriate pathway for sustainable digital transformation in the rural Himalayas of West Bengal. By bridging global best practices with local knowledge, addressing infrastructural and capacity gaps, and prioritising inclusivity and environmental stewardship, smart tourism can foster a resilient, competitive, and socially just tourism economy. The study contributes to both theory and practice by demonstrating how emerging technologies, when thoughtfully integrated, can support conservation, empower communities, enhance visitor experiences, and build long-term resilience in one of India's most ecologically and culturally significant mountain regions.

5.1 Importance of the Study

This study holds significant academic, practical, and policy relevance by examining smart tourism as a strategic driver for sustainable digital transformation in the rural Himalayan regions of West Bengal, specifically Darjeeling and Kalimpong. While global tourism literature increasingly recognises the role of digital technologies in promoting sustainability and destination resilience, empirical research focusing on remote, rural, and ecologically fragile mountain regions, particularly in Eastern Himalaya, remains limited. By addressing this gap, the study contributes context-specific insights that extend smart tourism discourse beyond urban and technologically advanced destinations.

From an academic perspective, the study enriches the existing body of knowledge by integrating smart tourism, sustainable tourism transitions, rural tourism, renewable energy adoption, and gendered empowerment within a single analytical framework. Much of the existing smart tourism literature is dominated by studies from developed economies or metropolitan destinations. This research is important because it demonstrates how smart tourism principles can be adapted to rural Himalayan contexts characterised by limited infrastructure, forest-based livelihoods, and strong community–nature interdependencies. The findings thus demonstrate a nuanced understanding of how global smart tourism models interact with local socio-ecological realities, thereby contributing to constructing theory for sustainable and rural tourism studies.

The study is also practically significant for local communities and tourism stakeholders. Rural Himalayan villages rely heavily on tourism as a supplementary livelihood, yet they face challenges including seasonal demand, poor accessibility, environmental vulnerability, and limited market visibility. By documenting stakeholder expectations, challenges, and readiness for technologies such as GIS, AI, VR, mobile applications, and renewable energy systems, the study provides actionable insights into how digital tools can enhance destination visibility, improve visitor management, reduce environmental pressures, and diversify income opportunities. The focus on renewable energy and household-level technologies further highlights pathways to reduce domestic labour burdens, particularly for women, thereby strengthening gender equity and entrepreneurship in rural tourism.

The study has significant policy and planning implications for tourist development initiatives at the state and regional levels. The results highlight the necessity of coordinated governance, investments in digital infrastructure, and inclusive capacity-building initiatives to guarantee that the adoption of smart tourism does not worsen already-existing disparities. The study offers information to assist policy decisions aimed at striking a balance between conservation goals and livelihood creation by emphasising the relevance of GIS-based planning in forest-fringe and wildlife-sensitive areas. This is especially crucial in areas where tourism serves as a risk-reduction tactic for populations impacted by diminishing agricultural returns, wildlife conflict, and climate change.

The study also gains importance in the post-COVID-19 context, where digital resilience has become a critical determinant of tourism recovery and competitiveness. By reflecting on missed opportunities during the pandemic due to weak digital infrastructure, the research underscores the urgency of transitioning toward smarter, more adaptive tourism systems capable of withstanding future shocks. In doing so, it aligns tourism development with broader goals of sustainable development, climate action, and inclusive growth.

Overall, the importance of this study lies in its ability to bridge global smart tourism scholarship with local Himalayan realities, offering evidence-based insights for researchers, policymakers, planners, and practitioners. It positions smart tourism not merely as a technological solution, but as a comprehensive development strategy that can support environmental sustainability, community empowerment, gender equity, and long-term resilience in rural Himalayan tourism destinations.

This study highlights how cutting-edge technology like VR, AI, GIS, and clean energy can promote inclusive, sustainable tourism in West Bengal's rural Himalayas. Future projects should prioritise gender equity, climate resilience, and local participation, according to a study on smart tourism as a strategic driver for grassroots needs and sustainable digital transformation in the Rural Himalayas.

5.2 Future Scope of the Study

Although the current study offers insightful information on how smart tourism and new technology might promote sustainable tourist development in West Bengal's rural Himalayan regions, there are still a number of areas that could use more investigation.

First, to experimentally test the connections between smart tourism technology, environmental sustainability, visitor enjoyment, and socioeconomic empowerment, future research may use a quantitative or mixed-methods approach. Large-scale surveys involving visitors, homestay hosts, female businesses, and local organisations could improve the findings' generalisability and allow for statistical confirmation of results generated by technology.

Second, there is scope for longitudinal research to examine the long-term impacts of smart tourism interventions. Tracking changes over time would help assess whether technologies such as GIS-based planning, AI-driven services, and renewable energy adoption lead to sustained improvements in destination resilience, income stability, environmental conservation, and community well-being.

Third, future research could place a stronger focus on gender-specific and intersectional perspectives, particularly examining how smart tourism and clean energy adoption reshape women's roles, decision-making power, and entrepreneurial opportunities in rural Himalayan households. Comparative studies between women-led and male-led tourism enterprises could further illuminate the differential impacts of digital transformation.

Fourth, comparative and cross-regional studies may be undertaken by contrasting rural Himalayan West Bengal with other mountain or peripheral destinations in India (e.g., Uttarakhand, Himachal Pradesh, Sikkim) or in developing countries. For the development of smart tourism in fragile ecosystems, such comparisons would aid in identifying transferable best practices, contextual constraints, and region-specific policy lessons.

Fifth, future studies may explore the policy and governance dimensions of smart tourism in greater depth. This includes evaluating the effectiveness of public–private partnerships, local governance capacity, institutional readiness, and regulatory frameworks in enabling inclusive digital transformation. Scenario-based policy analysis could support evidence-based planning at the district and state levels.

Sixth, as digitalisation progresses, there is more opportunity to look into the ethical, social, and environmental dangers related to smart tourism, such as data privacy, surveillance issues, technological dependency, e-waste generation, and unequal access to digital resources. Research in this direction would contribute to responsible innovation and sustainability-oriented technology governance.

Finally, future research could examine the role of education, training, and digital literacy programmes in reducing the digital divide among indigenous communities, elderly residents, and marginalised groups. Evaluating the design and outcomes of community-based capacity-building initiatives would provide practical guidance for ensuring that smart tourism remains inclusive and culturally sensitive.

Overall, expanding research along these dimensions will deepen theoretical understanding and strengthen practical applications of smart tourism as a catalyst for sustainable, inclusive, and resilient development in rural Himalayan regions and other ecologically sensitive destinations.

Declaration of Artificial Intelligence (AI) Assistance

The authors used an AI language model (Grammarly, GPT-5.1) to assist with language editing. All research design, literature review, data collection, data interpretation of results, and conclusions are the sole responsibility of the authors, who carefully constructed and approved the final text.

REFERENCES

Agarwal, R., Mehrotra, A., Mishra, A., Rana, N. P., Nunkoo, R., & Cho, M. (2024). Four decades of sustainable tourism research: Trends and future research directions. *International Journal of Tourism Research, 26*(2), e2643. Advance online publication. DOI: 10.1002/jtr.2643

Alhitmi, H. K., Rahman, E. Z., & Bayram, G. E. (2024). Regenerative tourism–The concept of moving beyond responsible and sustainable tourism. In *The Role of Artificial Intelligence in Regenerative Tourism and Green Destinations*. Emerald Publishing., DOI: 10.1108/978-1-83753-746-420241003

Antonioli, D., & Mazzanti, M. (2017). Towards a green economy through innovations: The role of trade union involvement. *Ecological Economics, 131*, 286–299. DOI: 10.1016/j.ecolecon.2016.09.003

Boes, K., Buhalis, D., & Inversini, A. (2016). Smart tourism destinations: Ecosystems for tourism destination competitiveness. *International Journal of Tourism Cities, 2*(2), 108–124. DOI: 10.1108/IJTC-12-2015-0032

Buhalis, D. (2020). Technology in tourism: From information communication technologies to eTourism and smart tourism towards ambient intelligence tourism: A perspective article. *Tourism Review, 75*(1), 267–272. DOI: 10.1108/TR-06-2019-0258

Buhalis, D., & Amaranggana, A. (2015). Smart tourism destinations: Enhancing tourism experience through personalisation of services. In Tussyadiah, I., & Inversini, A. (Eds.), *Information and communication technologies in tourism 2015* (pp. 377–389). Springer., DOI: 10.1007/978-3-319-14343-9_28

Buhalis, D., & Law, R. (2008). Progress in information technology and tourism management: 20 years on and 10 years after the Internet—The state of eTourism research. *Tourism Management, 29*(4), 609–623. DOI: 10.1016/j.tourman.2008.01.005

Buhalis, D., & Michopoulou, E. (2013). Accessibility: A key objective for the tourism industry. *Information and Communication Technologies in Tourism, 2013*, 317–327. DOI: 10.1007/978-3-642-36309-2_27

Chadha, P., Gera, R., Awasthi, S., Yadav, A., Kansal, L., Kumar, A. V., Saxena, A. K., & Parashar, K. (2024). Unlocking sustainable tourism: A holistic examination of mobile applications' impact and evolution in travel experiences (2013-2023). *E3S Web of Conferences, 511*, 01029. https://doi.org/DOI: 10.1051/e3sconf/202451101029

Charfeddine, L., & Umlai, M. (2023). ICT sector, digitization and environmental sustainability: A systematic review of the literature from 2000 to 2022. *Renewable & Sustainable Energy Reviews*, *184*, 113482. DOI: 10.1016/j.rser.2023.113482

Chien, F., Anwar, A., Hsu, C.-C., Sharif, A., Razzaq, A., & Sinha, A. (2021). The role of information and communication technology in encountering environmental degradation: Proposing an SDG framework for the BRICS countries. *Technology in Society*, *65*, 101587. DOI: 10.1016/j.techsoc.2021.101587

Chiwaridzo, O. T., & Masengu, R. (2025). Rebuilding sustainable green tourism supply chain through technology adoption and social media branding in Zimbabwe post-COVID-19. *Environment, Development and Sustainability*, *27*(8), 18105–18128. DOI: 10.1007/s10668-024-04718-y

Das, R., Singh, A., Kaur, H., Suhag, N., & Roy, K. (2026). Exploring the mediating role of women's participation in the relationship between rural tourism and the commercialisation and preservation of rural culture and natural beauty. *International Research Journal of Multidisciplinary Scope*, *7*(1), 1463–1477. DOI: 10.47857/irjms.2026.v07i01.08828

Davronov, A. (2024). Emerging technologies and trends in tourism management for developing countries. *Academic research in modern science*. Retrieved from https://econferences.ru

del Vasto, P. M. H., & Castro, M. L. A. (2024). Artificial Intelligence (AI) in sustainable tourism: Bibliometric analysis. *Cuadernos de Turismo*, *53*(53), 157–185. DOI: 10.6018/turismo.616431

European Commission. (2021). *Waste electrical and electronic equipment (WEEE)*. European Commission.https://environment.ec.europa.eu/topics/waste-and-recycling/waste-electrical-and-electronic-equipment-weee_en

Fettweis, G., & Zimmermann, E. (2008). ICT energy consumption—Trends and challenges. In *Proceedings of the 11th International Symposium on Wireless Personal Multimedia Communications (WPMC 2008)* (pp. 6–10). Dresden, Germany.

Ganguly, P. (2018). Role of information and communication technologies (ICTs) in sustainable tourism development in Santiniketan, West Bengal, India. *International Journal of Management Studies*, *5*(Special Issue 2), 54–59. https://doi.org/DOI: 10.18843/ijms/v5iS2/07

Gössling, S., Hall, C. M., & Scott, D. (2019). The decarbonisation impasse: Global tourism leaders' views on climate change mitigation. *Journal of Sustainable Tourism*, *27*(6), 899–908.

Gretzel, U., Sigala, M., Xiang, Z., & Koo, C. (2015). Smart tourism: Foundations and developments. *Electronic Markets*, *25*(3), 179–188. DOI: 10.1007/s12525-015-0196-8

Guttentag, D. A. (2010). Virtual reality: Applications and implications for tourism. *Tourism Management*, *31*(5), 637–651. DOI: 10.1016/j.tourman.2009.07.003

Hilty, L. M., & Aebischer, B. (2015). ICT for sustainability: An emerging research field. In Hilty, L. M., & Aebischer, B. (Eds.), *ICT innovations for sustainability* (pp. 3–36). Springer International Publishing., DOI: 10.1007/978-3-319-09228-7_1

Huang, H., & Leung, X. Y. (2025). Experimental design for sustainable tourism: A horizon 2050 paper. *Tourism Review*, *80*(1), 286–298. DOI: 10.1108/TR-12-2023-0867

Ionescu, A. M., & Sârbu, F. A. (2024). Exploring the impact of smart technologies on the tourism industry. *Sustainability (Basel)*, *16*(2), 789–805. DOI: 10.3390/su16083318

Irfan, M., Ullah, S., Razzaq, A., Cai, J., & Adebayo, T. S. (2023). Unleashing the dynamic impact of tourism industry on energy consumption, economic output, and environmental quality in China: A way forward towards environmental sustainability. *Journal of Cleaner Production*, *387*, 135778. DOI: 10.1016/j.jclepro.2022.135778

Islam, N., Sarkar, B., Basak, A., Das, P., Paul, I., Debnath, M., & Roy, R. (2022). A novel GIS-based MCDM approach to identify the potential eco-tourism sites in the Eastern Dooars region (Himalayan foothill) of West Bengal, India. *Geocarto International*, *37*(3), 1–30. DOI: 10.1080/10106049.2022.2076917

Kapoor, D., & Jain, A. (2024). Sustainable tourism and its future research directions: A bibliometric analysis of twenty-five years of research. *Tourism Review*. Advance online publication. DOI: 10.1108/TR-03-2022-0110

Khalid, M. S. (2024). Sustainable tourism's tomorrow: Navigating the future with technological innovations. In *Achieving Sustainable Transformation in Tourism and Hospitality* (pp. 123–145). IGI Global., DOI: 10.4018/979-8-3693-3390-7.ch008

Khan, N., Khan, W., Humayun, M., & Naz, A. (2024). Unlocking the potential: Artificial intelligence applications in sustainable tourism. In *Advances in Regenerative Tourism and Hospitality*. Emerald Publishing. DOI: 10.1108/978-1-83753-746-420241020

Khatri, I. (2019). Information technology in tourism & hospitality industry: A review of ten years' publications. *Journal of Tourism & Hospitality Education*, *9*, 74–87. DOI: 10.3126/jthe.v9i0.23682

Kusumastuti, H., Pranita, D., Viendyasari, M., Rasul, M. S., & Sarjana, S. (2024). Leveraging local value in a post-smart tourism village to encourage sustainable tourism. *Sustainability (Basel), 16*(2), 873. DOI: 10.3390/su16020873

Kusumawardhani, Y., Hilmiana, H., Widianto, S., & Azis, Y. (2024). Smart tourism practice in the scope of sustainable tourism in emerging markets: A systematic literature review. *Cogent Social Sciences, 10*(1), 2384193. DOI: 10.1080/23311886.2024.2384193

Lange, S., Pohl, J., & Santarius, T. (2020). Digitalization and energy consumption: Does ICT reduce energy demand? *Ecological Economics, 176*, 106760. DOI: 10.1016/j.ecolecon.2020.106760

Law, R., & Chen, S. (2024). Developments and implications of tourism information technology: A horizon 2050 paper. *Tourism Review*. Advance online publication. DOI: 10.1108/TR-03-2024-0123

Leong, W. Y., Leong, Y. Z., & Leong, W. S. (2024). Smart tourism in ASEAN: Leveraging technology for sustainable development and enhanced visitor experiences. *The International Journal of Social Sciences (Islamabad)*. Advance online publication. DOI: 10.1080/23311886.2024.2384193

Lu, W.-C. (2018). The impacts of information and communication technology, energy consumption, financial development, and economic growth on carbon dioxide emissions in 12 Asian countries. *Mitigation and Adaptation Strategies for Global Change, 23*(8), 1351–1365. DOI: 10.1007/s11027-018-9787-y

Mihalic, T. (2024). Metaversal sustainability: Conceptualisation within the sustainable tourism paradigm. *Tourism Review*. Advance online publication. DOI: 10.1108/TR-05-2024-0214

Niewiadomski, P., & Brouder, P. (2024). From 'sustainable tourism' to 'sustainability transitions in tourism'? *Tourism Geographies, 26*(2), 141–150. DOI: 10.1080/14616688.2023.2299832

Patrichi, I. C. (2024). Ai solutions for sustainable tourism management: A comprehensive review. *Journal of Information Systems & Operations Management, 18*(1), 172–185.

Pilelienė, L., Grigaliūnaitė, V., & Bogoyavlenska, Y. (2024). A bibliometric review of innovations in sustainable tourism research: Current trends and future research agenda. *Sustainability (Basel), 16*(16), 7124. DOI: 10.3390/su16167124

Rafi, M., & Novriana, R. (2024). Local government capability in sustainable tourism development. *Jurnal Kebijakan Publik, 15*(1), 55–70. DOI: 10.31292/jkp.v15i1.2024

Rai, P., & Bera, S. (2024). Machine learning-based empirical investigation of user's perception of digitalisation in pandemic immunisation programs. *Journal of Decision Systems*, 1–27. Advance online publication. DOI: 10.1080/12460125.2024.2365492

Rajam, V., Reddy, A. B., & Banerjee, S. (2021). Explaining caste-based digital divide in India. *Telematics and Informatics*, *65*, 101719. DOI: 10.1016/j.tele.2021.101719

Rattanamanee, K. (2024). Future perspectives on communication management for promoting tourism in Chachoengsao Province (2024–2027). *International Journal of Professional Business Review*, *9*(1), e04307. DOI: 10.26668/businessreview/2024.v9i1.4307

Razzaq, A., Sharif, A., Ahmad, P., & Jermsittiparsert, K. (2021). Asymmetric role of tourism development and technology innovation on carbon dioxide emission reduction in the Chinese economy: Fresh insights from QARDL approach. *Sustainable Development (Bradford)*, *29*(1), 176–193. DOI: 10.1002/sd.2139

Samaddar, K., & Mondal, S. (2024). AR and VR-based travel: A responsible practice towards sustainable tourism. *International Journal of Tourism Cities*. Advanced online publication. https://doi.org/DOI: 10.1108/IJTC-03-2024-0015

Samanta, S., & Baitalik, A. (2015). Potential site selection for eco-tourism: A case study of four blocks in Bankura district using remote sensing and GIS technology, West Bengal. *International Journal of Advanced Research*, *3*(4), 978–989.

Schluep, M., Müller, E., Hilty, L. M., Ott, D., Widmer, R., & Böni, H. (2013). Insights from a decade of development cooperation in e-waste management. In L. M. Hilty, B. Aebischer, G. Andersson, & W. Lohmann (Eds.), *ICT innovations for sustainability* (pp. 223–230). ETH E-Collection. http://e-collection.library.ethz.ch/view/eth:6558

Sen, D. (2019). What makes Darjeeling tea authentic? Colonial heritage and contemporary sustainability practice in Darjeeling, India. *Südasien-Chronik – South Asia Chronicle, 9*, 177–203.

Sfodera, F., Cain, L. N., & Di Leo, A. (2024). Is technology everywhere? Exploring Generation Z's perceptions of sustainable tourism in developing countries. *International Hospitality Review, 38*(1), 45-47. https://www.emerald.com/insight/2516-8142

Sgroi, F., & Modica, F. (2024). Digital technologies for the development of sustainable tourism in mountain areas. *Smart Agricultural Technology*, *8*, 100475. DOI: 10.1016/j.atech.2024.100475

Sharma, M., Mohapatra, G., & Giri, A. K. (2025). Assessing the role of ICT, governance, and infrastructure on inbound tourism demand in India. *Journal of Economic and Administrative Sciences*, *41*(1), 320–335. DOI: 10.1108/JEAS-03-2022-0064

Shruthi, K. A., Ihita, G. V., & Chaudhari, S. (2021). *A survey on rural internet connectivity in India*. arXiv. https://arxiv.org/abs/2111.10219

Singh, A., & Das, R. (2025). Exploring tourism opportunities in the metaverse and technology era: Insights from scholarly literature. In *Metaverse and sustainable business models in SMEs* (p. 12). IGI Global., DOI: 10.4018/979-8-3693-9005-4.ch007

Singh, B., & Kaunert, C. (2024). Transforming smart city and smart sustainable tourism projecting artificial intelligence and IoT: Immersive potential for revolutionizing urban living and enhancing travel experience. In *Technological and Managerial Approaches to Fostering Sustainable Travel* (pp. 26–50). IGI Global., DOI: 10.4018/979-8-3693-8115-1.ch003

Song, C., Zhang, Q., Yang, J., & Li, X. (2024). *Tourism, industrialization, and sustainable economic growth. Smart Tourism, 5(2), 3044.* Asia Pacific Academy of Science Pte. Ltd., DOI: 10.54517/st3044

Srivastava, P., & Shandilya, G. (2024). Unveiling the impact of perceived smart tourism technology on tourist satisfaction. In Singh, M. K., & Jain, P. K. (Eds.), *Multidisciplinary Applications of Artificial Intelligence in Regenerative Tourism* (pp. 112–130). IGI Global., DOI: 10.4018/979-8-3693-2432-5.ch008

Stewart, J., & Gorman, C. (2024). Authentic assessment and embedding sustainable literacy and technology skills in tourism education. *Irish Journal of Academic Practice*. https://doi.org/DOI: 10.21427/abcd-efgh

Suanpang, P., & Pothipassa, P. (2024). Integrating generative AI and IoT for sustainable smart tourism destinations. *Sustainability (Basel)*, *16*(17), 7435. DOI: 10.3390/su16177435

Suryani, W. (2024). Cultural and heritage tourism trends for sustainable tourism. In *Special interest trends for sustainable tourism*. IGI Global., DOI: 10.4018/979-8-3693-5903-7.ch001

Tussyadiah, I. P., Jung, T. H., & tom Dieck, M. C. (2018). Embodiment of wearable augmented reality technology in tourism experiences. *Journal of Travel Research*, *57*(5), 597–611. DOI: 10.1177/0047287517709090

Usman, K., Younas, A., Kumar, S., Akbar, A., & Poulova, P. (2023). The progression of sustainable development goals in tourism: A systematic literature review of past achievements and future promises. *Journal of Innovation & Knowledge*, *8*(4), 1–12. DOI: 10.1016/j.jik.2023.100442

Venkatesh, V., Morris, M. G., Davis, G. B., & Davis, F. D. (2003). User acceptance of information technology: Toward a unified view. *Management Information Systems Quarterly*, *27*(3), 425–478. DOI: 10.2307/30036540

Wu, H., Xue, Y., Hao, Y., & Ren, S. (2021). How does internet development affect energy-saving and emission reduction? Evidence from China. *Energy Economics*, *103*, 105577. DOI: 10.1016/j.eneco.2021.105577

Xin, L., Ahmad, M., & Khattak, S. I. (2022). Impact of innovation in marine energy generation, distribution, or transmission-related technologies on carbon dioxide emissions in the United States. *Renewable & Sustainable Energy Reviews*, *167*, 112225. DOI: 10.1016/j.rser.2022.112225

Chapter 14
A Review of Research on Digital Equity in Healthcare:
Critical Realist (CR)-Critical Discourse Analysis (CDA) Insights for a Sustainable Digital Eco

Darijana Antonić
http://orcid.org/0000-0002-6656-1885

Centre for Health System Development and International Cooperation, Public Health Institute of the Republic of Srpska, Bosnia and Herzegovina

Imran Aslan
http://orcid.org/0000-0001-5307-4474

Faculty of Health Sciences, Health Management Department, Bingöl University, Turkey

Slobodan Stanić
http://orcid.org/0009-0007-7118-6833

Centre for Health System Development and International Cooperation, Public Health Institute of the Republic of Srpska, Bosnia and Herzegovina

ABSTRACT

The accelerating digital transformation of healthcare systems highlights the growing importance of digital equity within a sustainable digital health economy. This chapter examines access, digital literacy, infrastructure, policy inclusion, and socio-economic disparities shaping the use of digital health tools. Using interdisciplinary literature

DOI: 10.4018/979-8-3373-5052-3.ch014

and critical discourse analysis from a critical realist perspective, it explores key enablers and barriers across patients, providers, and policymakers, and identifies practical directions for equitable and sustainable digital health strategies.

1. BACKGROUND

The rapid digitalization of healthcare is reshaping how health systems deliver services, manage resources, and interact with patients. Digital innovations promise greater efficiency, accessibility, and improved health outcomes, yet they also raise complex questions about equity. Unequal access to digital tools, differences in digital literacy, and persistent socio-economic disparities threaten to widen existing health inequalities. As a result, digital equity has emerged as a critical determinant not only of fair health outcomes but also of the long-term sustainability of digital health systems and the broader digital economy.

Positioning digital equity at the intersection of healthcare delivery and economic sustainability enables a comprehensive understanding of its systemic impact. Ensuring that all stakeholders—patients, providers, and policymakers—benefit equitably from digital transformation strengthens health system resilience and contributes to a more inclusive digital economy. To analyze how equity is conceptualized in existing literature, this study employs critical discourse analysis (CDA) informed by a critical realist (CR) perspective (Imafuku, Saiki, & Woodward-Kron, 2022; Mullet, 2018). Within this framework, the *real* refers to structures and their causal powers, the *actual* to the events and processes enacted in reality, and the *empirical* to how actors experience these events. Discourse therefore provides a lens for exploring how equality and inequality in digital health are constructed globally. CDA investigates how discourse legitimizes or challenges inequities, influences decision-making, and frames digital health practices and policies (Fairclough, 1992, 2001; van Dijk, 1993). CR clarifies that these discourses do not exist in isolation; they are rooted in real social structures—such as economic systems, technological infrastructures, and institutional norms—which may not be directly observable but nonetheless shape what is said, how it is said, and whose voices are heard (Bhaskar, 1975, 1998; Sayer, 2000). Together, CR–CDA enables researchers to analyse both visible discursive patterns and the deeper causal mechanisms that generate them, offering a more comprehensive understanding of digital equity, power dynamics, and socio-technical change (Archer, 1995; Fairclough, Jessop, & Sayer, 2002).

1.1 Empirical Evidence on Digital Inequities

A substantial and growing body of empirical research demonstrates that digital health inequities arise from multiple intersecting factors. Global connectivity assessments by the International Telecommunication Union (2023) show that significant portions of the world's population remain offline, with access gaps most pronounced in low-income and rural areas. Even among individuals technically "connected," inconsistent bandwidth, limited device availability, and affordability barriers reduce engagement with digital health services.

Digital literacy further shapes the extent to which individuals can benefit from digital innovation. Studies indicate that older adults, individuals with lower educational attainment, and minority language speakers face substantial barriers in using online health information, navigating patient portals, or engaging in telemedicine (Henson et al., 2021; Organisation for Economic Co-operation and Development, 2020a). During the COVID-19 pandemic, these disparities became even more visible. While telehealth expanded rapidly, adoption was highest among digitally literate and socioeconomically advantaged groups, whereas low-income and rural populations demonstrated far lower levels of use (Campos-Castillo & Anthony, 2021).

Socioeconomic and demographic characteristics remain strong predictors of digital health engagement. Lower-income households report reduced utilization of online health resources, limited access to private digital devices, and greater difficulty sustaining reliable internet connections (Robinson et al., 2015). People with disabilities often encounter accessibility barriers, including non-adaptive interfaces and incompatible platforms, while marginalized racial and ethnic communities may face linguistic mismatches or cultural inappropriateness in digital health tools (Sieck et al., 2021). Structural inequities across health systems further compound these challenges; facilities serving disadvantaged populations are less likely to have robust digital infrastructure or integrated digital care pathways (World Health Organization, 2021). The COVID-19 pandemic made these inequities particularly visible. Although digital health platforms were widely deployed, the benefits were unequally distributed. High-income, urban, and digitally skilled users saw substantial improvements in telehealth access, while underserved communities experienced minimal gains (Donaghy et al., 2019; Nouri et al., 2020). These patterns demonstrate how digital transformation, without targeted equity measures, can unintentionally reinforce or exacerbate existing disparities.

1.2 Conceptualizing Digital Equity: A Multidimensional Framework

A growing body of empirical research demonstrates that digital inequities remain pervasive and structurally embedded across populations and health systems. Global assessments by the International Telecommunication Union (ITU) and the World Health Organization (WHO) consistently show substantial gaps in access, digital literacy, infrastructure, affordability, and algorithmic fairness of digital health tools (See Figure 1). These disparities directly affect individuals' ability to access telehealth, use patient portals, engage with remote monitoring technologies, and benefit from emerging digital innovations (the International Telecommunication Union, 2023; Kuhn et al., 2023; World Health Organization, 2021).

Figure 1. A multidimensional framework (Source: Own Made)

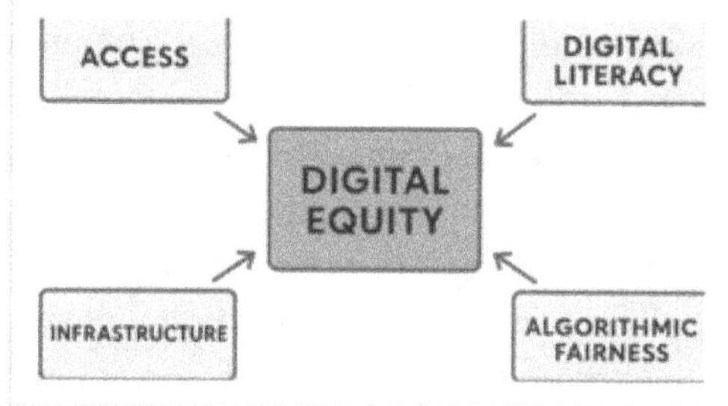

Access is the foundational dimension and involves stable connectivity, device availability, and accessible platforms for individuals with disabilities. Despite rapid global progress in digital infrastructure, meaningful internet access remains uneven. ITU estimates indicate that billions of people worldwide remain offline, with the highest concentrations in low-income countries and rural regions. Even among those technically "connected," bandwidth limitations, unstable networks, and shared device use undermine reliable participation in digital health services. These access gaps are strongly correlated with income, geography, and education, demonstrating that digital transformation disproportionately benefits socioeconomically advantaged groups (the International Telecommunication Union, 2023).

Digital literacy encompasses the skills required to navigate digital environments, evaluate online health information, and communicate effectively in digital settings. Empirical studies consistently show that literacy gaps are among the strongest barriers to meaningful digital health engagement. Empirical studies across OECD and non-OECD countries show that limited digital literacy significantly reduces the adoption and effective use of digital health tools. Research on patient portal and telemedicine use during and after the COVID-19 pandemic indicates that users with higher literacy, better access to support, and greater prior digital experience are far more likely to engage with digital health platforms (OECD, 2020b).

Infrastructure reflects health system capacity, including digital readiness, interoperability, workforce training, and integration of digital tools into routine care. When infrastructure varies widely between regions or institutions, structural inequities emerge. Socioeconomic status remains one of the strongest predictors of digital health use. Studies conducted in North America, Europe, and Asia report lower telehealth utilization among low-income populations, even when services are available, due to factors such as lack of private devices, limited data plans, and competing resource demands. Facilities serving rural or low-income communities are more likely to report insufficient digital infrastructure, fewer trained staff, and limited integration of digital health into routine care pathways. These institutional differences create uneven digital health ecosystems, where the quality and availability of digital services depend heavily on local resources rather than population need.Additionally, people with disabilities often face technological and accessibility barriers, while ethnic minorities may encounter linguistic and cultural mismatches in digital platforms. These inequities compound existing health disparities, particularly for marginalized and vulnerable groups (Tong et al., 2022).

Affordability refers to the economic capacity to engage with digital health. The costs of devices, data plans, and digital services disproportionately burden low-income users, creating indirect barriers even when digital tools are available.

Algorithmic fairness introduces an ethical and technological dimension. As AI-driven systems and data analytics expand in healthcare, concerns about biased data, unequal model performance, and opaque decision-making become central to discussions of digital equity. These issues highlight that equitable access alone is insufficient if the technologies themselves reproduce or deepen disparities (Chen et al., 2023).

These dimensions are interdependent. Improving one in isolation rarely produces equitable outcomes. For example, expanding broadband access does little for populations without sufficient literacy or ability to afford devices; likewise, even well-designed digital systems can generate inequities if underlying algorithms are biased. Digital equity thus requires a holistic, systems-oriented approach involving coordinated investments across all dimensions as shown in Figure 1.

1.3 Synthesis and Rationale for the Present Study

Integrating empirical evidence with this conceptual framework demonstrates that digital health inequity is a complex and layered phenomenon shaped by technological, socioeconomic, structural, and ethical forces. However, while many studies document these inequities, far less attention has been paid to the discourses through which digital equity is defined, justified, and operationalized in the literature. Because discourse shapes policy priorities, resource allocation, and institutional practices, examining the narratives surrounding digital health inequity is critical.

Through CDA, this study examines the values, assumptions, and normative positions embedded in digital health discourse, revealing how certain ways of thinking about equity are constrained or enabled within the literature. Our analysis highlights the conceptual dualism of equity in digital healthcare—shaped by variations in health system organization, differences between highly developed and low-resource settings, and disparities across specific population groups, including marginalized and vulnerable communities. Consequently, the concept of digital health equity remains as complex and context-dependent as other equity-related constructs within healthcare. In addition to mapping this conceptual dualism, our discourse analysis investigates how digital health is interpreted with respect to contextual (institutional, economic, infrastructural) and individual (socio-demographic, literacy-related) characteristics. Examining these discourses is essential, particularly as digital health continues to be promoted as a mechanism for enhancing communication, improving outcomes, and reducing healthcare costs.

This study adopts a combined Critical Realist (CR) and Critical Discourse Analysis (CDA) framework to examine the multilevel digital divide in health. CR provides an ontological foundation for identifying the structures, mechanisms, and contextual conditions that generate inequitable digital health outcomes (Bhaskar, 1975; Archer, 1995; Sayer, 2000). From this perspective, disparities in digital access, literacy, and health-system integration are not merely surface-level events but manifestations of deeper causal powers embedded in socioeconomic structures, institutional capacities, and infrastructural arrangements. CR and CDA are epistemologically compatible: both reject positivist explanations of social phenomena and emphasize the interplay between observable events, underlying structures, and discursive constructions. CR highlights *why* inequities persist through generative mechanisms such as infrastructural deficiencies, economic constraints, and institutional fragmentation, while CDA examines *how* discourse shapes public understanding, policy responses, and assumptions about digital inclusion and technological inevitability.

Problem Statement

Despite rapid advancements in digital health technologies, significant disparities persist in access, digital literacy, affordability, and usability. These inequities disproportionately affect vulnerable populations—such as rural communities, low-income groups, older adults, and individuals with disabilities—limiting their ability to benefit from digital healthcare innovations. As digital health becomes increasingly embedded in modern health systems, these disparities risk reinforcing broader socio-economic inequalities and undermining the transition toward an inclusive and sustainable digital economy.

Research Aim

The aim of this study is to critically examine how digital equity within the healthcare sector shapes, enables, or constrains the development of a sustainable digital economy. Through a combined CR and CDA aprroach, the study seeks to uncover both observable barriers and the underlying structural mechanisms that influence equitable digital health access and outcomes.

Rationale of the Study

Digital health is now a core driver of economic modernization, efficiency, and innovation. However, without equitable access and participation, digital transformation can produce uneven benefits and deepen socio-economic divides. Understanding digital equity in healthcare is therefore essential not only for improving health outcomes but also for ensuring that digital economic growth is socially inclusive, ethically grounded, and sustainable. By analysing systemic inequities, discourses, and structural determinants, this study offers a foundation for developing policies and strategies that promote fair digital participation and strengthen the long-term sustainability of digital health ecosystems.

This chapter positions digital equity as both an ethical imperative and a structural requirement for building sustainable and just digital health ecosystems. It builds upon existing scholarship by focusing specifically on how digital health inequity is constructed within academic and policy discourse. The research sample includes studies addressing digital health inequities from the perspective of end-users—patients and citizens—as well as research examining structural and systemic drivers of inequity from the standpoint of health professionals and policymakers. Despite rapid advances, inequities in access, literacy, and infrastructure continue to undermine health outcomes and threaten the sustainability of the digital health economy. Addressing these gaps is therefore essential to ensure that digital transformation fosters resilience and fairness rather than reinforcing existing disparities.

2. RESEARCH METHODOLOGY

This study employed a qualitative literature-based research design informed by CR and CDA to examine how digital equity in the healthcare sector shapes, and is shaped by, the sustainable digital economy. A structured literature search was conducted across Scopus, Web of Science, Google Scholar, and major policy repositories (WHO, OECD, EU Commission). Search terms encompassed digital equity, digital health, digital literacy, telemedicine, remote care, and digital economic sustainability. Inclusion criteria focused on English-language sources, covering empirical, conceptual, and policy-oriented discussions. Data were examined using a combined CR–CDA framework, enabling analysis at both structural and discursive levels. Critical Realism guided identification of underlying mechanisms—including infrastructure inequities, socio-economic constraints, digital literacy gaps, and institutional incentives—that influence digital health outcomes. This integrated methodology strengthened analytical rigor by linking observable inequalities, deep structural conditions, and discursive framings. It enabled a holistic evaluation of how digital health initiatives can both enable and constrain equity, particularly for marginalized populations, and how these dynamics intersect with broader digital economic transformations. The approach provides a transparent, replicable framework for future studies examining equity challenges in digitally transforming health systems.

3. INTERSECTIONS OF DIGITAL EQUITY, DIGITAL ECONOMY, AND DIGITAL HEALTH: A SYNTHESIZED LITERATURE REVIEW

According to the The World Health Organization (WHO), digital health is the field of knowledge and practice associated with developing and using digital technologies to improve health (World Health Organisation, 2021). Digital transformation is reshaping health systems worldwide and enabling individuals to participate more actively in their care (Iyawa et al., 2016; Stoumpos et al., 2023). Active inclusion in digital health promotes social and economic justice and helps individuals thrive in a technology-driven society. WHO believes that digital health has the potential to reach more people and make health services more accessible to them (Peterson, Hamilton, & Hasvold, 2016). Yet health remains among the least digitally mature sectors compared to finance or media, highlighting persistent structural gaps (Stoumpos et al., 2023). These gaps underscore the importance of digital equity, a concept increasingly recognized as central to public health, social sustainability, and the digital economy. As digital health becomes embedded in routine care, understanding how inequity is conceptualized in the literature is essential for addressing structural disadvantages and ensuring that digital innovations do not widen existing health disparities.

3.1 Digital Equity: Concepts and Determinants

Digital equity is broadly defined as fair and inclusive access to digital resources, literacy, infrastructure, affordability, and algorithmic fairness (Grybauskas et al., 2022). Empirical research consistently demonstrates that inequities cluster around PROGRESS-PLUS dimensions, an acronym for Place of Residence, Race/Ethnicity/Culture/Language, Occupation, Gender, Religion, Education, Socioeconomic Status and Social Capital (Eriksen et al., 2023). Digital health has revolutionary potential, but if principles of equity or digital equity do not guide it, marginalized communities may be left behind, exacerbating existing inequities and hindering social progress. Measured health inequalities should be viewed in light of the distribution of these inequalities across the population and whether such a distribution is socially acceptable (fair). Health system biases further fuel the spread of social injustice (Sieck et al., 2021).

The advancement of digital health and its integration into health systems has made it essential to ensure that technologies are accessible and equitable for all users, resulting in a greater interest in health inequalities. Health organizations, governments and health professionals increasingly consider digital health technologies to be key components in advancing medicine and health in general (Robinson et al., 2015). Socioeconomic status is among the strongest predictors of digital health utilisation, with low-income groups less likely to use telehealth even when services are available, due to limited devices, unstable connectivity, or competing resource demands (Litchfield et al., 2021; Rich et al., 2019). Rural and remote communities continue to face structural barriers related to broadband availability and service reliability (Benda et al., 2020). Age-related gaps such as the "grey digital divide" further restrict the use of digital health among older adults (Chen et al., 2020). These patterns show that digital inequity is not incidental but deeply embedded in broader social and structural conditions.

3.2. Digital Equity and the Digital Economy in Health

The economic growth brought about by the digital economy is irreversible. Technological innovation, technological integration, and the continuous emergence of information elements continue to drive the share of production value associated with the digital economy in the economies of all countries, further promoting sustainable economic growth (Mottaeva, Khussainova, & Gordeyeva, 2023). Digital technology creatively enables economic development, not only through demographic dividend, market dividend, wage levels, and foreign investment, but also by providing knowledge and data for economic growth and industrial modernization. At the same time, the digital age of massive growth of digital information becomes a new production factor, undermines traditional factors of production patterns, elements in significant changes of position, integrates new elements, accelerates the spread of knowledge and technology and the transformation of achievements, optimizes the distribution of resources, accelerates the development of a green, clean, intelligent industrial chain, reshapes the global value chain of industry. Digital equity is foundational to a sustainable digital economy. Participating in a digitally driven labour market requires reliable connectivity, digital skills, and access to digital platforms (Su et al., 2022).

Digital equity and the digital economy in health are fundamentally shaped by the development of digital infrastructure, which encompasses the hardware, software, and network systems that enable information and communication activities. As a core pillar of new infrastructure, this digital foundation is a prerequisite for meaningful participation in digital health services (OECD, 2020). Populations excluded from digital infrastructures and services face reduced employment opportunities, limited access to e-government and financial services, and weakened capacity to benefit from digital innovation (Mottaeva et al., 2023). The digital economy is driven largely by the Internet and sustained by continuous advancements in mobile devices and network technologies, which together accelerate the expansion of digitalization across sectors (International Telecommunication Union (ITU), 2021). In this ecosystem, the digital environment provides the spatial and technological conditions that allow digital health applications to emerge, while digital output materializes through the ongoing process of digital upgrading—where enterprises deliver digital services and society actively adopts digital tools and platforms for transactions and service use. Such societal uptake is crucial, as it reflects the real-world diffusion and impact of digital health innovations (Su et al., 2022; World Health Organization, 2023). Importantly, the transformative economic and health benefits of digitalization do not appear instantaneously; rather, they become evident only after reaching a certain level of maturity within the broader digital economy (UN Department of Economic and Social Affairs (UNDESA), 2022). As digital services, products, and platforms scale—integrating with sectors such as retail, education, hospitality, and health—they create new opportunities for inclusive growth, expand service accessibility, and support emerging models such as platform-based care, shared digital resources, and personalized, user-centered ("tailor-made") digital health solutions (OECD, 2021; WHO, 2022).

Digital equity and the digital economy in health are fundamentally shaped by the development of digital infrastructure, which includes the hardware, software, and network systems required to support widespread information and communication activities. As a pillar of new infrastructure, this digital foundation is essential not only for general economic participation but also for meaningful engagement with digital health services (OECD, 2020). Investment in digital innovation—encompassing digital data, digital talent, and advanced technologies—further accelerates this transformation. Such investment functions as a sustained driving force that enhances the vitality of the digital economy and enables it to reach unprecedented levels of productivity and societal impact (Su et al., 2022). Continuous advancements in mobile technology, broadband networks, and cloud-based platforms provide the technological environment where both digital health and broader digital economic activities can flourish (ITU, 2021). Within this environment, digital output becomes visible through the processes of digital upgrading, in which enterprises provide digital services and society increasingly adopts digital tools and platforms for transactions, service delivery, and daily functioning (WHO, 2023).

Because digital health systems rely on the same infrastructures that underpin the digital economy, inequity in digital health cannot be separated from inequity in digital participation. Regions lacking adequate connectivity, technological literacy, or affordable digital access experience slower technological diffusion, reduced productivity growth, and weaker resilience to economic and public health shocks (OECD, 2021). These disparities translate directly into unequal access to telehealth, digital diagnostics, electronic health records, and AI-driven health tools. Consequently, digital health inequity becomes not only a health system challenge but also a barrier to inclusive and sustainable economic development (UNDESA, 2022). As digital services, platforms, and innovations scale across sectors—integrating with education, commerce, public services, and healthcare—they create new opportunities for inclusive growth while also amplifying the risks of exclusion for populations not equipped to participate fully. Ensuring digital equity therefore becomes foundational to realizing the economic and health benefits of digital transformation and to preventing the deepening of existing social and structural inequalities.

3.3 Digital Literacy and Its Role in Equity in Health

From a CR perspective, digital literacy functions as a *causal mechanism* shaping the distribution of digital health opportunities. It is embedded within broader structural conditions—including education systems, socioeconomic inequalities, linguistic access, and institutional design—that determine individuals' real ability to benefit from digital health innovations (WHO, 2021; OECD, 2021). Digital health literacy is therefore understood not merely as a personal skillset but as a *multidimensional capability* dependent on technical, cognitive, and critical competences necessary to navigate digital environments effectively (De la Hoz et al., 2021). This includes the ability to search, evaluate, interpret, and apply digital health information to address health problems, as well as the capacity to recognize risks, biases, and reliability issues in online health sources (Norman & Skinner, 2006; WHO, 2022).

However, CDA highlights that discourses surrounding digitalization often frame digital literacy as an individual responsibility—focusing on "training," "skills," or "user competence"—while obscuring the structural inequities (e.g., inadequate infrastructure, language accessibility, platform design) that shape who can realistically achieve high digital health literacy. Such discursive repertoires can individualize blame, positioning low-literacy users as "non-adopters," rather than revealing the systemic barriers that constrain their choices (van Dijk, 2020). These narratives influence policy priorities by emphasizing personal deficits rather than structural determinants, reinforcing inequities in digital participation.

Empirical studies reveal that poor digital literacy significantly limits engagement with telehealth, patient portals, electronic health records, and digital triage tools (Abdulai et al., 2021; European Commission, 2020). Importantly, individuals frequently overestimate their digital abilities, and self-reported digital skill does not reliably reflect performance in real tasks (Arias López et al., 2023). Moreover, high general literacy does not guarantee effective digital health literacy, especially when navigating complex information ecosystems such as COVID-19 health communication (Abdulai et al., 2021). These findings illustrate the CR principle that observable behaviors (e.g., difficulty using digital health tools) stem from unobserved deeper mechanisms, such as educational inequities, inaccessible design interfaces, and the cognitive demands of digital environments.

Digital literacy also operates at the collective level. Communities with low digital capacity experience cumulative disadvantage due to fewer digitally skilled residents, reduced peer support networks, and limited community digital infrastructure (Nickel et al., 2023; UNDESA, 2022). From a CDA lens, this produces community-level discourses of disempowerment (e.g., "we don't use those technologies here"), which in turn shape expectations around digital health adoption and reinforce structural marginalization. Thus, digital literacy is both a discursive resource—constructed through language, framing, and policy narratives—and a structural resource—embedded in material conditions and institutional arrangements. Ensuring digital equity in health requires addressing these dual dimensions: dismantling deficit-based narratives around low-literacy populations while simultaneously transforming the structural mechanisms that constrain digital capacity. When viewed through CDA and CR together, digital literacy becomes central to understanding how digital health inequities are produced, reproduced, and potentially transformed.

3.4 Digital Technology, Sustainability, and Systemic Inequities

From a CR perspective, sustainability in digital health extends far beyond the continued operation of technological tools; it concerns the endurance and interaction of underlying structures, generative mechanisms, and relational capacities that shape health-system performance over time (Bhaskar, 1975; Archer, 1995; Sayer, 2000). CR highlights that digital technologies are embedded in stratified social systems, meaning their outcomes depend on interactions between material infrastructures, institutional arrangements, economic conditions, cultural norms, and unequal power relations. Sustainability, therefore, is inseparable from successful implementation because digital health interventions only produce intended benefits when the mechanisms that enable them—such as institutional readiness, funding stability, digital literacy, and supportive governance—are activated within specific contexts (Elder-Vass, 2010). These multi-layered dependencies challenge the idea that technological innovation alone can drive health-system improvement, underscoring the structural conditions that reproduce inequity.

CDA complements this ontological depth by examining how digital health is discursively constructed in policy, academic, and global health narratives. Dominant discourses routinely portray digital technology as inherently progressive, efficiency-enhancing, and morally desirable (Fairclough, 1995; Chouliaraki & Fairclough, 1999). In global health policy documents, digital tools are increasingly framed as neutral determinants of health, comparable to socioeconomic or demographic factors (van Kessel et al., 2022), while the WHO defines digital health primarily as the use of digital technologies to improve health outcomes (Das et al., 2025). CDA reveals how such framings naturalize optimistic narratives and obscure ideological assumptions—particularly the technocratic belief that digital transformation is universally beneficial and that inequities derive from individual rather than structural limitations. These discursive constructions depoliticize digital health by masking structural constraints and legitimizing interventions that may be misaligned with local realities.

While digital technologies can indeed enhance access, productivity, and coordination, especially in remote or resource-constrained settings (Davis et al., 2020; Nickel et al., 2023), CR cautions that these potential benefits are emergent properties dependent on underlying contextual mechanisms. The global diffusion of digital health tools, including rapid expansion across low- and middle-income countries, offers opportunities to reduce inequities (Kaboré et al., 2022). Yet CDA highlights how policy discourses around "digital inclusion" often reduce inequity to issues of access, overlooking deeper socio-structural determinants of digital capability and agency (Jessop, 2008; Badr et al., 2024). Empirical evidence shows that digital health interventions disproportionately advantage those with higher digital literacy, socioeconomic stability, and social capital, thereby reproducing or intensifying existing power asymmetries (Craig et al., 2022).

Persistent structural barriers, including limited broadband coverage, unreliable electricity, high hardware costs, and fragmented donor-driven digital health pilots continue to undermine sustainable integration, particularly in low- and middle-income countries (Kaboré et al., 2022). From a CR standpoint, these barriers reflect enduring generative mechanisms such as economic dependency, infrastructural deficits, and institutional fragmentation (Sayer, 2000; Archer, 1995). CDA shows how innovation-oriented policy narratives frequently downplay these constraints, foregrounding technological optimism and sidelining concerns about system capacity, workforce burden, and long-term governance. Health workers themselves are often excluded from digital design and procurement decisions, reinforcing hierarchical decision-making structures that limit meaningful adoption (Yeung et al., 2023). The misalignment between discursive promises and structural realities contributes to low system uptake, limited interoperability, and unsustained benefits.

The digital divide illustrates the layered and relational nature of digital inequity. First-level divides concern physical access to devices and connectivity; second-level divides relate to digital skills and literacy; and third-level divides reflect broader socio-structural differences in social networks, institutional supports, and the capacity to convert digital access into meaningful outcomes (Chen et al., 2020). For older adults, a "grey digital divide" further exacerbates exclusion, affecting autonomy, participation, and health. Although digital inclusion initiatives attempt to bridge these gaps, CDA uncovers how they often rely on universalistic assumptions that all individuals aspire to digital engagement, thereby overlooking diverse user contexts, preferences, and constraints.

In many low-income settings, the proliferation of digital pilot projects rarely translates into sustained national adoption, illustrating the persistent influence of structural mechanisms that CR identifies as shaping implementation outcomes (Swartz et al., 2021; Akeju et al., 2022). Sustainable digital health defined as the ongoing generation of value for patients, professionals, and health systems requires confronting the infrastructural, economic, and institutional conditions that reproduce exclusion across contexts. Because digital inclusion exists along a continuum rather than as a simple binary (Abdelaal & Andrey, 2022), addressing inequity necessitates attention to both material circumstances and the discursive framings that normalize uneven access. Ultimately, the assumption that digital technologies inherently democratize health is unfounded: persistent differences in connectivity, affordability, literacy, institutional capacity, and political-economic environments mean that benefits accrue unevenly to those best positioned to use digital tools (Litchfield et al., 2021). Integrating CDA and CR therefore illuminates not only observable disparities in digital health but also the deeper structures, power relations, and discursive formations that shape sustainability and systemic inequity across global health systems.

3.5 The Digital Divide: A Multilevel Phenomenon in Health Equity

From a CR perspective, the digital divide is a stratified and multi-layered social phenomenon rooted in deeper generative mechanisms that condition access to, capabilities with, and benefits from digital health technologies (Bhaskar, 1975; Sayer, 2000). CR conceptualizes inequity not as a surface-level disparity in digital access but as the outcome of interacting structural, cultural, and agential forces that operate across different levels of reality (Archer, 1995; Elder-Vass, 2010). Material infrastructures such as broadband availability, device affordability, and electrical stability—constitute only one layer of constraint. Beneath these lie institutional mechanisms (e.g., governance quality, financing models, workforce capacity), economic structures (e.g., income inequality, dependency on donor-funded pilots), and sociocultural processes (e.g., literacy norms, gender relations, age-based exclusions) that shape individuals' and communities' ability to participate meaningfully in digital health systems.

CDA adds a complementary dimension by exposing how dominant narratives surrounding digital innovation frame these inequities. Policy and global health discourses often construct digital health as inherently transformative, neutral, and universally empowering (Fairclough, 1995; van Kessel et al., 2022), while minimizing the structural barriers that limit participation. CDA reveals how terms such as "digital transformation," "empowerment," and "inclusion" can naturalize technocratic assumptions and obscure underlying power relations, marginalizing voices who lack the resources or capabilities assumed by these narratives (Chouliaraki & Fairclough, 1999; Jessop, 2008). In this way, discourse does not merely describe the digital divide, it actively shapes policy priorities, legitimizes specific forms of intervention, and determines which inequities become visible or invisible.

Together, CR and CDA illuminate the digital divide as a multi-level phenomenon composed of at least three interrelated dimensions. First-level divides concern disparities in physical access to devices, connectivity, and infrastructure (Chen et al., 2020). Second-level divides involve differences in digital literacy, skills, and confidence, shaped by education, socioeconomic status, and cultural norms. Third-level divides reflect inequalities in the ability to convert digital access into meaningful health benefits, mediated by social capital, institutional trust, and broader political-economic structures. For older adults, this is compounded by a "grey digital divide" that intersects with ageism and health vulnerability (Kaboré et al., 2022; Swartz et al., 2021). By integrating CR and CDA, it becomes clear that digital equity cannot be achieved through technological provision alone. Addressing the digital divide requires transforming the structural mechanisms that limit participation such as inequitable funding models, inadequate infrastructure, and exclusionary governance, while simultaneously challenging the discursive framings that present digital health as universally beneficial and politically neutral. This combined lens demonstrates that digital inequity is not a failure of adoption but a systemic outcome of how social structures, material resources, and dominant discourses interact to shape health opportunities across populations(See Table 1).

Table 1. Integration of Critical Realism (CR) and Critical Discourse Analysis (CDA) in Understanding the Digital Divide in Health

Analytical Focus	Critical Realism (CR): Structures & Mechanisms	Critical Discourse Analysis (CDA): Discourses & Ideologies	Integrated Insight for Digital Health Equity
Ontology of the Digital Divide	Generative mechanisms rooted in infrastructure, institutions, and socioeconomic structures (Bhaskar, 1975; Sayer, 2000; Archer, 1995).	Discourses normalize technology as neutral and progressive (Fairclough, 1995; Chouliaraki & Fairclough, 1999).	Inequity is both materially produced and discursively reinforced.
Access (1st-Level Digital Divide)	Broadband, electricity, and affordability constraints (Chen et al., 2020; Kaboré et al., 2022).	Policy frames equate access with equity (Jessop, 2008).	Access discourse masks persistent structural deficits.
Digital Literacy (2nd-Level Divide)	Skills constrained by education, income, and community resources (Arias López et al., 2023; Abdulai et al., 2021).	Users framed as individually responsible for "catching up" (Fairclough, 2001).	Literacy is structural, not simply personal.
Meaningful Use (3rd-Level Divide)	Outcomes shaped by trust, economic stability, and social capital (Elder-Vass, 2010; Nickel et al., 2023).	Adoption metrics obscure distributional inequities (Badr et al., 2024).	Must assess who benefits, not just who uses.
Power & Agency	Agency conditioned by structural constraints (Archer, 1995).	Discourses emphasize empowerment while obscuring power asymmetries (Fairclough, 2010).	Interventions require structural and discursive change.
Low- and middle-income countries Structural Constraints	Resource scarcity, donor dependency, institutional fragmentation (Kaboré et al., 2022; Swartz et al., 2021).	Innovation discourses obscure contextual inequities (Chouliaraki, 2006).	Universalist digital narratives must be contextualized.
Sustainability	Depends on capacity, financing, infrastructure (Akeju et al., 2022; Yeung et al., 2023).	Sustainability framed as technologically inherent (Blandford et al., 2020).	Sustainable equity requires structural investment + discursive reframing.

3.6 Digital Health Opportunities, Risks, and Ethical Considerations Through a CR–CDA and Equity Lens

Within this study, CR and CDA provide complementary lenses for analysing digital health as both a material system of infrastructures, technologies, and institutions, and a discursive field shaped by narratives of innovation, efficiency, and modernity. From a CR perspective, the opportunities of digital health, expanded access, improved provider-patient communication, better information management, enhanced follow-up and decision-making, and the potential to reach underserved populations emerge only when the underlying generative mechanisms (infrastructure, affordability, digital literacy, institutional capacity, regulatory frameworks, and sociocultural acceptance) are activated within specific contexts (Bhaskar, 1975; Sayer, 2000; Elder-Vass, 2010; Kaboré et al., 2022). Digital health systems therefore depend not simply on the availability of technologies, but on multi-layered structural conditions that determine whether such tools can produce equitable, sustainable benefits.

CDA extends this analysis by interrogating how digital health is framed in policy, industry, and global health discourse. Many influential narratives depict digital technologies as inherently progressive, transformative, and universal solutions, framing them as "must-have" components of modern health systems (Fairclough, 1995; Chouliaraki & Fairclough, 1999). While these discourses highlight values such as transparency, interoperability, privacy, and scalability (Figueirêdo et al., 2025), they often obscure the ideological assumptions underpinning digital health and mask persistent inequalities in digital participation, connectivity, and capability. CDA therefore reveals how dominant narratives normalize technology-driven solutions while minimizing systemic constraints such as infrastructural deficits, economic inequalities, fragmented governance, and commercial power asymmetries in data ownership (Jessop, 2008; Yeung et al., 2023).

Bringing CR and CDA together foregrounds the digital divide as a stratified, multi-level phenomenon. CR identifies disparities in access, skills, and digital capability, particularly among rural populations, older adults, minorities, and people with disabilities as outcomes of enduring structural mechanisms such as poverty, exclusion, and uneven resource distribution (Archer, 1995; Chen et al., 2020). CDA clarifies how policy discourses around "digital inclusion" can be narrowly focused on access while ignoring deeper capability gaps and the social relations that shape meaningful digital engagement (Craig et al., 2022; Badr et al., 2024). Through this combined lens, the digital divide is understood not simply as a technological problem but as the product of intersecting structural, social, and discursive mechanisms that shape health-system equity.

A CR–CDA synthesis also strengthens the ethical analysis of digital transformation. Ethical risks including low digital literacy, high costs, lack of usability, privacy and security concerns, and uncertainties around data ownership reflect deeper structural and institutional mechanisms rather than isolated implementation failures (Swartz et al., 2021; Yeung et al., 2023). At the same time, CDA reveals how "innovation-first" discourse can legitimize corporate control over health data while downplaying the distributional and structural harms of digitalization. Rawlsian theories of justice further underscore the need for digital health to benefit the least advantaged; however, without explicit attention to equity, digital interventions risk reinforcing "permanent disadvantage" among the very populations they intend to support (Winters et al., 2021). Finally, integrating CR and CDA aligns digital health with broader commitments to equitable, people-centred systems. Rather than treating digitalization as an unquestioned progression, CR emphasizes examining the structural conditions and causal mechanisms necessary for digital health to be sustainable and effective. CDA reminds us that digital innovation should be viewed not as an end in itself, but as a discursively constructed means to health-system improvement that requires careful scrutiny of whose interests are represented and whose needs remain marginalized. This integrated theoretical framework therefore supports a deeper, equity-oriented understanding of digital transformation and informs the study's analytic approach to digital health sustainability, participation, and justice.

4. DIGITAL EMPOWERMENT, DECISION-MAKING, AND REMOTE CARE: A CRITICAL REALIST AND CRITICAL DISCOURSE ANALYSIS OF EQUITY IN DIGITAL HEALTH EMPOWERMENT IN DIGITAL HEALTH

4. 1 Empowerment in Digital Health for Equity

Across global health systems, the movement toward patient-centered digital care positions individuals as "healthcare consumers" who increasingly seek autonomy, personalization, immediacy, and convenience in managing their health (Stoumpos et al., 2023). Digital Technologies from mobile health platforms to wearable sensors and AI-enabled tools are framed as drivers of empowerment that promise to improve self-management, expand access, and enhance patient–provider collaboration (Gjellebæk et al., 2020). From the perspective of CR, however, genuine empowerment depends not on the mere availability of digital tools but on whether the underlying generative mechanisms including digital literacy, socioeconomic resources, institutional capacity, and sociocultural norms enable individuals to convert digital opportunities into real capabilities (Bhaskar, 1975; Sayer, 2000; Archer, 1995). Empowerment is thus a relational and context-dependent process, shaped by structural inequalities that condition who can meaningfully engage with digital health systems.

CDA extends this analysis by interrogating how global health discourses construct digital empowerment. Dominant narratives frequently depict digital health as an inherently democratizing force that enables patients to become active managers of their own care (Lupton, 2016; Fairclough, 1995). These discourses often naturalize a neoliberal logic of individual responsibility, implying that empowered patients should self-monitor, self-educate, and self-regulate through technological means (Greenhalgh et al., 2019). CDA reveals how such discourses mask structural constraints ; limited connectivity, affordability issues, low digital skills, disability, or cultural barriers that restrict individuals' capacity to participate fully in digital health environments (Chouliaraki & Fairclough, 1999; Jessop, 2008). Thus, empowerment rhetoric may obscure the inequities embedded in the unequal distribution of digital resources.

Digital empowerment holds transformative potential: it can expand access to information, support informed decision-making, and strengthen relational dynamics between patients and healthcare professionals (Aujoulat et al., 2007; Nickel et al., 2023). However, CR reminds us that empowerment requires the activation of specific mechanisms: trust, usability, accessibility, institutional support, and literacy without which empowerment becomes merely symbolic (Elder-Vass, 2010). Indeed, the populations most frequently celebrated as beneficiaries: rural residents, individuals with disability, older adults, and minorities are also those most susceptible to digital exclusion. Emotional reluctance, low confidence, and unfamiliarity with digital systems constitute real barriers to engagement that cannot be solved by technology alone (Nickel et al., 2023; Vassli & Farshchian, 2018).

Debates surrounding empowerment in digital health further illustrate tensions between utilitarian health-policy logics and equity-oriented ethical frameworks. Large-scale digital interventions are often justified using utilitarian principles, maximizing outcomes for the greatest number (Winters et al., 2020). However, this orientation risks sidelining the needs of disadvantaged populations whose inclusion requires more intensive support and investment. Prioritization frameworks inspired by Rawlsian ethics emphasize that inequalities are justified only if they benefit the least advantaged (Rawls, 2001; Zarif, 2022). For empowerment to be ethically meaningful in digital health, tools must therefore be designed and deployed in ways that explicitly prioritize those who are structurally marginalized.

Empowerment strategies manifest in both direct forms such as personalized apps, reminders, and digital coaching and indirect forms, such as reallocating institutional resources or modifying service delivery models. Yet these strategies face significant technical, social, and ethical challenges, especially when digital interventions are assumed to replace or reduce traditional care pathways (Kreitmair, 2024). Telemedicine, for instance, is frequently promoted as a cost-saving strategy, but evidence shows that such savings are not uniformly realized and may not benefit patients directly (Greenhalgh et al., 2019). Moreover, as seen throughout the history of medical Technologies even the stethoscope adoption is rarely smooth or universal, reflecting broader cultural and institutional contingencies (Zarif, 2022).

CR encourages deeper attention to the structural and causal conditions that shape empowerment—including broadband availability, affordability, interoperability, regulation, clinical workflow alignment, and data governance. CDA, meanwhile, highlights how empowerment is discursively mobilized to legitimize digital transformation while downplaying concerns about data ownership, corporate power, surveillance, and privacy (Yeung et al., 2023; Andrejevic, 2022; Couldry & Mejias, 2019). A critical equity lens recognizes that data-driven technologies can produce new forms of dependency and asymmetrical power relations, particularly when commercial actors control platforms, analytics, and health data infrastructures.

Ultimately, empowerment in digital health must be conceptualized not as a technological outcome but as a structurally conditioned capability that depends on equitable access, meaningful literacy support, culturally responsive design, and inclusive governance. Integrating CR and CDA reveals that empowerment is simultaneously shaped by structural inequalities, sociotechnical affordances, and discursive constructions that determine who benefits from digital transformation and who is left behind. For digital health to advance equity, policies and interventions must explicitly recognize these multi-layered conditions rather than assuming that digital tools automatically confer empowerment.

4.2 Decision Making in Digital Health for Equity

Decision-making in healthcare is widely recognized as a collaborative and relational practice in which patients and professionals jointly establish the most appropriate course of care. Within digital health contexts, this collaboration increasingly depends on digital infrastructures, platforms, and data flows. However, a CR lens reveals that this ostensibly collaborative process is shaped by underlying structural mechanisms, such as unequal access to digital tools, institutional norms, and material resource distribution (Bhaskar, 1978, 1998; Archer, 1995). These structural conditions generate "unequal enablements and constraints," which means that the potential of digital technologies for shared decision-making remains stratified across socioeconomic groups. A CDA perspective further emphasizes that these inequities are also reproduced discursively through professional narratives that frame digital technologies as either burdensome, optional, or risky for certain patient groups (Fairclough, 1992, 2001; van Dijk, 2015). Thus, disparities in digital engagement are not merely technical gaps but manifestations of broader social and discursive power relations.

Digital health technologies increasingly enable patients to self-manage their conditions, redistributing responsibilities traditionally associated with clinicians. CR conceptualizes this as a mechanism of decentralization, in which tasks, knowledge, and accountability shift from institutional actors to patients, often without adequately addressing their differential capacities to assume these responsibilities (Sayer, 2000; Elder-Vass, 2010). Such redistribution, while framed in policy discourse as "empowerment," can unintentionally reproduce inequity when material and cultural resources are unevenly distributed (Nickel et al., 2023). CDA helps illuminate how empowerment discourse can obscure the moral and practical consequences of this displacement by recasting structural shortcomings as individual failures to adopt or adapt to technology (Fairclough, 2013).

As Zarif (2022) notes, technologies reshape not only practices but also our normative orientations, influencing what is considered "good care" or "responsible patienthood." Within a patient-centered paradigm, this raises ethical concerns about the routinization of digital tools that may devalue the relational aspects of care, particularly for those with lower digital literacy or reduced access. Health professionals, therefore, increasingly function as consultants or guides, but this role shift assumes that patients possess the capacity and social conditions to participate actively in decision-making.

Decision-making is further shaped by push and pull mechanisms (Nickel et al., 2023). Push factors involve the authority of healthcare professionals and institutions to determine which technologies are available or reimbursed. Pull factors reflect individuals' motivation, literacy, and material ability to access devices and services, including privately funded digital tools. CR identifies these as structural and agential causal powers, which interact in contingent ways to produce or inhibit equitable outcomes. CDA extends this by examining how push-pull dynamics are framed in policy and professional discourse, often positioning technologically reluctant or disadvantaged groups as "hard-to-reach" rather than structurally excluded.

A major equity concern is that patients are rarely engaged as co-designers or co-decision-makers in digital health technologies. Instead, they remain positioned as passive recipients, a discursive pattern documented widely in health policy analyses (Shaw et al., 2017; Lupton, 2016). A CR framework shows that excluding patients from design processes removes an important feedback mechanism necessary for ensuring that digital interventions align with diverse needs, particularly those of marginalized groups. CDA similarly critiques how technocratic discourse legitimates expert-driven design, thereby delegitimizing lay knowledge and reinforcing asymmetrical power relations (Fairclough, 2001).

Furthermore, exclusionary practices intersect with structural injustices, including clinician bias, discriminatory algorithms, and institutional mistrust among marginalized communities (Benjamin, 2019; Dyer, 2022). These can act as demi-regularities persistent but not universal patterns within CR ontology, producing predictable inequitable outcomes. CDA reveals how such injustices are discursively masked through narratives of neutrality, efficiency, and objectivity in digital health innovation.

Ultimately, the barriers to equitable digital decision-making extend far beyond technology. They include historical mistrust, unequal digital access, emotional reluctance, and broader sociopolitical determinants of engagement, all of which require interventions at structural, institutional, discursive, and relational levels. Digital transformation must therefore move from rhetorical commitments to empowerment toward genuine patient participation, addressing both the structural conditions and the discursive constructions that currently limit equitable involvement in decision-making.

4.3 Remote Care in Digital Health for Equity

Implementing digital health in remote-care contexts requires a dynamic, adaptive, and multi-layered approach, as the interactions among technologies, end-users, healthcare teams, and environmental conditions are constantly evolving (Krahe et al., 2024). From a CR perspective, remote digital care is shaped by the interaction of deep generative mechanisms including structural inequalities, infrastructural access, institutional norms, and user competences that condition both the potential and the limitations of digital health (Bhaskar, 1978, 1998; Archer, 1995). These structures exert enabling and constraining causal powers, which means that remote-care technologies cannot be assumed to benefit all patients equally, even when their design claims universality.

Digital health technologies hold significant potential to reduce geographical inequalities by delivering care remotely. Yet achieving equitable scalability requires not only technological deployment but also patient readiness, motivation, literacy, digital confidence, and structural access (Yeung et al., 2023). CR highlights this as a case of stratified access, where material and social resources mediate whether individuals can benefit from remote digital care. A CDA lens reveals how the discourse of "digital readiness" often individualizes responsibility, subtly shifting the burden of access away from institutions and onto patients themselves (Fairclough, 2001, 2013; van Dijk, 2015).

Remote care also raises new equity issues for older adults, people with limited digital literacy, and communities in socioeconomically disadvantaged or geographically isolated areas. The most immediate barrier is the inability to use or access digital tools, often intensified among older adults and low-literacy groups (Yeung et al., 2023). Poor app design, insufficient training, inaccessible interfaces, and a lack of culturally responsive features further impede adoption. CR frames these barriers as contextual contingencies, features of the social and material environment that condition outcomes in non-linear ways (Sayer, 2000; Elder-Vass, 2010). CDA contributes by identifying how discourses that frame older adults as "non-digital" or "resistant" reproduce stereotypes and invisibilize structural exclusions embedded in design and policy (Lupton, 2016; van Dijk, 2015).

Even when remote technologies exist, inadequate reimbursement policies limit their availability in low-resource settings. Because many telehealth interventions are not covered by insurance, they remain effectively inaccessible to the communities most likely to benefit. CR conceptualizes this as institutional causal mechanisms that shape who is structurally included or excluded from remote digital care (Archer, 1995). CDA further reveals how policy discourse portrays remote care as inherently cost-saving, masking the ways such policies reinforce existing inequities (Fairclough, 2013; Shaw et al., 2017).

Poor rural telecommunications infrastructure exacerbates these inequities by constraining the real-world feasibility of remote care. Lack of broadband, intermittent connectivity, and unstable networks restrict digital engagement, widen regional development gaps, and ultimately reinforce national competitiveness disparities (Esteban-Navarro et al., 2020). Yet, as CDA scholars emphasize, digital inequality is often represented as a technical failure rather than a reproduction of pre-existing social inequalities, including youth outmigration, economic isolation, and cultural marginalization (van Dijk, 2015). Access does not equate to participation; merely possessing connectivity does not guarantee engagement (Esteban-Navarro et al., 2020). CR conceptualizes this as a case of non-linear causation, where enabling conditions do not automatically produce intended outcomes.

The adoption of remote technologies is further shaped by the Technology Acceptance Model, which emphasizes perceived ease of use and usefulness as determinants of intention and adoption (Zarif, 2022). Yet this model insufficiently captures the structural injustices, institutional incentives, professional workloads, and hidden expectations that shape adoption in real contexts. For example, healthcare providers may resist telehealth when reimbursement structures reward in-person visits. CR interprets this as a misalignment of structural and agential interests, while CDA highlights how professional discourse frames workload, risk, and responsibility in ways that shape technology uptake (Fairclough, 2001).

Further challenges arise from mismatches between the assumptions of developers, policymakers, and end-users. Remote technologies assume that patients can self-manage chronic conditions, yet many cannot physically, cognitively, or socially. Without a philosophical and ethical framework that prioritizes equity, these mismatches risk intensifying disparities (Fritz & Cox, 2020). CDA shows that "efficiency" discourses often legitimize these technologies despite limited evidence of patient benefit, reinforcing the dominance of technocratic narratives.

Scaling remote digital care in resource-constrained contexts often exposes institutional dysfunction—including resistance to change, insufficient training, unclear roles, and conflicting priorities. These are not merely operational challenges; they are manifestations of deeper realist causal mechanisms, including organizational cultures, political pressures, and fragmented governance structures (Archer, 1995; Sayer, 2000). Finally, acceptability plays a crucial role in remote digital care. Acceptability encompasses affective attitudes, intentions, engagement frequency, and satisfaction before, during, and after use (Nadal et al., 2020; Perski & Short, 2021). CR frames acceptability as an emergent property of interactions among structural conditions, user characteristics, and technological affordances. CDA reveals how acceptability is shaped by narratives that position remote care as modern, efficient, and inevitable, influencing how patients understand their digital participation.

5. DISCUSSION

Digital health continues to be framed in global health discourse as an inherently progressive, innovative, and democratizing force capable of transforming service delivery, improving efficiency, and expanding access. However, a CDA perspective reveals that such narratives reproduce a dominant techno-solutionist ideology, one in which digital technologies are portrayed as neutral tools capable of overcoming longstanding structural disparities. This discourse obscures the enduring social, cultural, political, and economic inequalities that shape how digital health is implemented, accessed, and experienced. By unmasking the ideological assumptions embedded in global digital health narratives, CDA highlights how concepts such as empowerment, inclusion, and efficiency often mask structural neglect and the uneven distribution of digital capabilities.

CR complements this discursive lens by illuminating the underlying causal mechanisms that generate inequities in digital health systems. While digital technologies may appear to extend access and autonomy at the empirical level, their impact is conditioned by deeper structural determinants such as inadequate infrastructure, limited digital literacy, policy fragmentation, commercial interests, and socio-economic precarity. These generative mechanisms operate independently of the observable outcomes of digital interventions and explain why similar technologies produce vastly different effects across contexts. For instance, mobile health applications may empower urban, educated users while simultaneously excluding rural communities with insufficient network coverage or older adults with low digital literacy.

By integrating CR and CDA, this chapter demonstrates that digital inequity is not merely a consequence of individual-level barriers (e.g., fear of technology, privacy concerns, low skills) but is embedded in systemic relations of power, historical marginalization, and discursive constructions that privilege certain users while rendering others invisible. Rural communities, socioeconomically disadvantaged populations, racialized or minority groups, individuals with disabilities, and older adults consistently face pronounced barriers not simply because they lack devices, but because health systems, digital markets, and public policy have not been designed with their needs at the center.

Digital healthcare is therefore not a universal or neutral solution but a socially structured and politically produced system whose benefits and burdens are unevenly distributed. While remote care, telemedicine, and mobile health can reduce travel burdens, strengthen continuity of care, and provide new forms of patient engagement, these benefits are contingent upon equitable access to digital infrastructures, supportive policies, and culturally and linguistically appropriate tools. Without intervention, digitalization can deepen what CR terms the stratified social reality of healthcare, reinforcing existing socio-economic and geographic inequalities.

At the discursive level, CDA exposes how policy rhetoric frames digital participation as an individual responsibility placing expectations on patients to be "digitally engaged" without appropriately addressing the structural conditions that limit access. Such narratives risk pathologizing those who cannot engage digitally, portraying them as resistant or lacking motivation, rather than acknowledging systemic exclusion. The combined CR-CDA perspective therefore urges a shift from individualistic framings to structural and relational understandings of digital equity. Together, these insights call for deliberate and justice-oriented digital health policy, design, and implementation strategies. Digital literacy programs, affordable access to devices and connectivity, participatory and inclusive design approaches, and strong regulatory frameworks for privacy, accessibility, and data rights are essential prerequisites for equitable digital health ecosystems. Digital health cannot be sustainably advanced without addressing both the discourses that shape its meaning and the structures that condition its effects.

6. CONCLUSION

This chapter argues that achieving digital equity is not a peripheral concern, it is central to the ethical legitimacy, sustainability, and economic resilience of digital health systems and the broader digital economy. From a CR perspective, inequities in digital health are produced by stratified social structures that shape access, capability, and opportunity. From a CDA perspective, these inequities are reinforced and legitimized through dominant narratives that frame digitalization as universally beneficial while obscuring exclusionary mechanisms and structural disadvantages.

The combined CR–CDA inquiry reveals that digital health transformation is a double-edged process:

- It can empower patients, strengthen provider–patient collaboration, and expand access through remote care.
- Yet it can also entrench inequality when digital literacy gaps, affordability barriers, infrastructural deficits, and biased discourses go unaddressed.

Digital health initiatives must therefore be carefully designed to support, but not replacing existing health systems, and must include meaningful participation from marginalized communities. Ensuring equitable digital access and capability is not only a matter of justice but a foundational requirement for sustaining a digital economy that benefits all. Investments in broadband infrastructure, inclusive platform design, culturally responsive technologies, and robust data governance are essential components of equitable digital transformation. Ultimately, the sustainability of digital health depends on acknowledging and addressing both visible barriers (e.g., connectivity, devices, cost) and invisible mechanisms (e.g., policy priorities, market incentives, power asymmetries, discursive biases) that shape digital participation. Only by integrating structural analysis with critical examination of discourse can policymakers and practitioners design interventions that avoid reproducing structural inequities and instead build fair, inclusive, and resilient digital health ecosystems. Digital equity is therefore not an outcome of technological adoption but the result of deliberate social, political, and ethical choices. A CR–CDA informed approach provides a robust foundation for guiding these choices toward a sustainable and just digital future.

REFERENCES

Abdelaal, N., & Andrey, S. (2022). *Towards a Digital Equity Policy For the City of Toronto*. Retrieved from https://www.ryersonleadlab.com/toronto-digital-equity

Abdulai, A. F., Tiffere, A. H., Adam, F., & Kabanunye, M. M. (2021). COVID-19 information-related digital literacy among online health consumers in a low-income country. *International Journal of Medical Informatics*, *145*, 104322. Advance online publication. DOI: 10.1016/j.ijmedinf.2020.104322 PMID: 33157342

Akeju, D., Okusanya, B., Okunade, K., Ajepe, A., Allsop, M. J., & Ebenso, B. (2022). Sustainability of the Effects and Impacts of Using Digital Technology to Extend Maternal Health Services to Rural and Hard-to-Reach Populations: Experience From Southwest Nigeria. *Frontiers in Global Women's Health*, *3*, 696529. Advance online publication. DOI: 10.3389/fgwh.2022.696529 PMID: 35211694

Andrejevic, M. (2022). Meta-surveillance in the digital enclosure. *Surveillance & Society*, *20*(4), 390–396. DOI: 10.24908/ss.v20i4.16008

Archer, M. (1995). Realist Social Theory: The Morphogenetic Approach. Cambridge University Press. , ISBN-13.DOI: 10.1017/CBO9780511557675

Aujoulat, I., d'Hoore, W., & Deccache, A. (2007). Patient empowerment in theory and practice: Polysemy or cacophony? *Patient Education and Counseling*, *66*(1), 13–20. DOI: 10.1016/j.pec.2006.09.008 PMID: 17084059

Badr, J., Motulsky, A., & Denis, J. L. (2024). Digital health technologies and inequalities: A scoping review of potential impacts and policy recommendations. *Health Policy (Amsterdam)*, *146*, 105122. Advance online publication. DOI: 10.1016/j.healthpol.2024.105122 PMID: 38986333

Benda, N. C., Veinot, T. C., Sieck, C. J., & Ancker, J. S. (2020). Broadband Internet Access Is a Social Determinant of Health! *American Journal of Public Health*, *110*(8), 1123–1125. DOI: 10.2105/AJPH.2020.305784 PMID: 32639914

Benjamin, R. (2019). *Race after technology: Abolitionist tools for the New Jim Code*. Polity. https://www.politybooks.com/bookdetail?book_slug=race-after-technology-abolitionist-tools-for-the-new-jim-code--9781509526390

Bhaskar, R. (1975). *A realist theory of science*. Leeds Books. DOI: 10.4324/9780203090732

Bhaskar, R. (1998). *The possibility of naturalism: A philosophical critique of the contemporary human sciences* (3rd ed.). Routledge. https://books.google.com.tr/books/about/The_Possibility_of_Naturalism.html?id=6OqXjiouAZYC&redir_esc=y

Blandford, A., Wesson, J., Amalberti, R., AlHazme, R., & Allwihan, R. (2020). Opportunities and challenges for telehealth within, and beyond, a pandemic. *The Lancet. Global Health*, *8*(11), e1364–e1365. DOI: 10.1016/S2214-109X(20)30362-4 PMID: 32791119

Campos-Castillo, C., & Anthony, D. L. (2021). Racial and ethnic differences in telehealth use during the COVID-19 pandemic: A cross-sectional analysis of a large U.S. health system. *Journal of the American Medical Informatics Association : JAMIA*, *28*(1), 119–123. DOI: 10.1093/jamia/ocaa221 PMID: 32894772

Chen, R. J., Wang, J. J., Williamson, D. F., Chen, T. Y., Lipkova, J., Lu, M. Y., Sahai, S., & Mahmood, F. (2023). Algorithmic fairness in artificial intelligence for medicine and healthcare. *Nature Biomedical Engineering*, *7*(6), 719–742. DOI: 10.1038/s41551-023-01056-8 PMID: 37380750

Chen, X., Östlund, B., & Frennert, S. (2020). Digital Inclusion or Digital Divide for Older Immigrants? A Scoping Review. *Lecture Notes in Computer Science (Including Subseries Lecture Notes in Artificial Intelligence and Lecture Notes in Bioinformatics), 12209 LNCS*, 176–190. DOI: 10.1007/978-3-030-50232-4_13

Chouliaraki, L., & Fairclough, N. (1999). *Discourse in late modernity*. Edinburgh University Press. https://edinburghuniversitypress.com/book-discourse-in-late-modernity.html

Couldry, N., & Mejias, U. A. (2019). The costs of connection: How data is colonizing human life and appropriating it for capitalism. In *The costs of connection*. Stanford University Press.

Craig, S., McPeak, K. E., Madu, C., & Dalembert, G. (2022). Health information technology and equity: Applying history's lessons to tomorrow's innovations. *Current Problems in Pediatric and Adolescent Health Care*, *52*(1), 101110. Advance online publication. DOI: 10.1016/j.cppeds.2021.101110 PMID: 34974991

Das, S., Ahmed, N., Al Rahbi, I., Al-Jubori, Y., Al Busaidi, R., Al Harbi, A., Al Tobi, M., & Albalushi, H. (2025). Medical and Biomedical Students' Perspective on Digital Health and Its Integration in Medical Curricula: Recent and Future Views. *International Journal of Environmental Research and Public Health*, *22*(8), 1193. DOI: 10.3390/ijerph22081193 PMID: 40869779

Davis, T. C., Hoover, K. W., Keller, S., & Replogle, W. H. (2020). Mississippi Diabetes Telehealth Network: A Collaborative Approach to Chronic Care Management. *Telemedicine Journal and e-Health : The Official Journal of the American Telemedicine Association, 26*(2), 184–189. DOI: 10.1089/tmj.2018.0334 PMID: 30822265

De la Hoz, A., Cubero, J., Melo, L., Durán-Vinagre, M. A., & Sánchez, S. (2021). Analysis of Digital Literacy in Health through Active University Teaching. *International Journal of Environmental Research and Public Health 2021, Vol. 18, Page 6674, 18*(12), 6674. DOI: 10.3390/ijerph18126674

del Pilar Arias López, M., Ong, B. A., Frigola, X. B., Fernández, A. L., Hicklent, R. S., Obeles, A. J. T., & Celi, L. A. (2023). Digital literacy as a new determinant of health: A scoping review. *PLOS Digital Health, 2*(10), e0000279. Advance online publication. DOI: 10.1371/journal.pdig.0000279 PMID: 37824584

Donaghy, E., Atherton, H., Hammersley, V., McNeilly, H., Bikker, A., Robbins, L., Campbell, J., & McKinstry, B. (2019). Acceptability, benefits, and challenges of video consulting: A qualitative study in primary care. *The British Journal of General Practice, 69*(686), e586–e594. DOI: 10.3399/bjgp19X704141 PMID: 31160368

Dyer, Z. (2022). The Structural Racism Effect Index: A Multi-Dimensional Tool to Measure Neighborhood-Level Structural Racism. https://hdl.handle.net/20.500.14038/51835

Elder-Vass, D. (2010). *The causal power of social structures*. Cambridge University Press. DOI: 10.1017/CBO9780511761720

Eriksen, J., Ebbesen, M., Eriksen, K. T., Hjermitslev, C., Knudsen, C., Bertelsen, P., . . . Weber, D. (2023). Equity in digital healthcare – the case of Denmark. *Frontiers in Public Health, 11*, 1225222. DOI: 10.3389/FPUBH.2023.1225222/BIBTEX

European Commission. (2020). *Digital Economy and Society Index (DESI) 2020: Human capital.* Publications Office of the European Union. https://digital-strategy.ec.europa.eu/en/library/digital-economy-and-society-index-desi-2020

Esteban-Navarro, M.-Á., García-Madurga, M.-Á., Morte-Nadal, T., & Nogales-Bocio, A.-I. (2020). The rural digital divide in the face of the COVID-19 pandemic in Europe—recommendations from a scoping review. *Mdpi.Com*. DOI: 10.3390/informatics7040054

Fairclough, N. (1992). *Discourse and social change*. Polity Press. DOI: 10.1017/S0047404500017309

Fairclough, N. (1995). *Critical discourse analysis: The critical study of language*. Longman.

Fairclough, N. (2001). *Language and power* (2nd ed.). Routledge.

Fairclough, N. (2013). *Critical discourse analysis: The critical study of language*. Routledge. DOI: 10.4324/9781315834368

Fairclough, N., Jessop, B., & Sayer, A. (2002). Critical realism and semiosis. *Alethia*, *5*(1), 2–10. DOI: 10.1558/aleth.v5i1.2

Figueirêdo, R. C. de, Silva, Í. de S., Xavier, P. B., Araújo, A. J. de, Silva, A. J. B. da, Silva, C. R. D. V., … Uchôa, S. A. da C. (2025). Digital Health and Primary Health Care Quality: A Survey Case Study. *International Journal of Environmental Research and Public Health 2025, Vol. 22, Page 1015, 22*(7), 1015. DOI: 10.3390/ijerph22071015

Fritz, Z., & Cox, C. L. (2020). Integrating philosophy, policy and practice to create a just and fair health service. *Journal of Medical Ethics*, *46*(12), 797–802. DOI: 10.1136/medethics-2020-106853 PMID: 33028624

Gjellebæk, C., Svensson, A., Bjørkquist, C., Fladeby, N., & Grundén, K. (2020). Management challenges for future digitalization of healthcare services. *Futures*, *124*, 102636. Advance online publication. DOI: 10.1016/j.futures.2020.102636

Greenhalgh, T., Hinton, L., Finlay, T., Macfarlane, A., Fahy, N., Clyde, B., & Chant, A. (2019). Frameworks for supporting patient and public involvement in research: Systematic review and co-design pilot. *Health Expectations : An International Journal of Public Participation in Health Care and Health Policy*, *22*(4), 785–801. DOI: 10.1111/hex.12888 PMID: 31012259

Grybauskas, A., Stefanini, A., & Ghobakhloo, M. (2022). Social sustainability in the age of digitalization: A systematic literature Review on the social implications of industry 4.0. *Technology in Society*, *70*, 101997. DOI: 10.1016/j.techsoc.2022.101997

Henson, P., Sappenfield, O. W., Zhai, Y., & Torous, J. (2021). Digital literacy and engagement with health technology in older adults. *Frontiers in Psychiatry*, *12*, 734112.

Imafuku, R., Saiki, T., & Woodward-Kron, R. (2022). Revisiting discourse analysis in medical education research. *International Journal of Medical Education*, *13*, 138–142. DOI: 10.5116/ijme.6278.c1b7 PMID: 35640066

International Telecommunication Union (ITU). (2021). *Measuring digital development: Facts and figures 2021*. ITU.

Iyawa, G. E., Herselman, M., & Botha, A. (2016). Digital Health Innovation Ecosystems: From Systematic Literature Review to Conceptual Framework. *Procedia Computer Science, 100*, 244–252. DOI: 10.1016/j.procs.2016.09.149

Jessop, B. (2008). *State power: A strategic-relational approach.* Polity Press. https://www.politybooks.com/bookdetail?book_slug=state-power--9780745633206

Kaboré, S. S., Ngangue, P., Soubeiga, D., Barro, A., Pilabré, A. H., Bationo, N., Pafadnam, Y., Drabo, K. M., Hien, H., & Savadogo, G. B. L. (2022). Barriers and facilitators for the sustainability of digital health interventions in low and middle-income countries: A systematic review. *Frontiers in Digital Health*, *4*, 1014375. DOI: 10.3389/fdgth.2022.1014375 PMID: 36518563

Krahe, M. A., Baker, S., Woods, L., & Larkins, S. L. (2024). Factors that influence the implementation of digital health in rural, regional, and remote Australia: Protocol for an overview of reviews. *MedRxiv*, 2024.11.13.24317285. DOI: 10.1101/2024.11.13.24317285

Kreitmair, K. V., & Karola Kreitmair, C. V. (2024). Mobile health technology and empowerment. *Bioethics*, *38*(6), 481–490. DOI: 10.1111/bioe.13157 PMID: 36950727

Kuhn, C., Khoo, S.-M., Czerniewicz, L., Lilley, W., Bute, S., Crean, A., Abegglen, S., Burns, T., Sinfield, S., Jandrić, P., Knox, J., & MacKenzie, A. (2023). Understanding digital inequality: A theoretical kaleidoscope. *Postdigital Science and Education*, *5*(3), 894–932. DOI: 10.1007/s42438-023-00395-8 PMID: 40479087

Litchfield, I., Shukla, D., & Greenfield, S. (2021). Impact of COVID-19 on the digital divide: A rapid review. *BMJ Open*, *11*(10), e053440. Advance online publication. DOI: 10.1136/bmjopen-2021-053440 PMID: 34642200

Lupton, D. (2016). *The quantified self.* John Wiley & Sons.

Mottaeva, A., Khussainova, Z., & Gordeyeva, Y. (2023). Impact of the digital economy on the development of economic systems. *E3S Web of Conferences, 381*. DOI: 10.1051/e3sconf/202338102011

Mullet, D. R. (2018). A General Critical Discourse Analysis Framework for Educational Research. *Journal of Advanced Academics*, *29*(2), 116–142. DOI: 10.1177/1932202X18758260

Nadal, C., Sas, C., & Doherty, G. (2020). Technology Acceptance in Mobile Health: Scoping Review of Definitions, Models, and Measurement. *J Med Internet Res 22(7):E17256* Https://Www.Jmir.Org/2020/7/E17256, DOI: 10.2196/17256

Nickel, P. J., Loosman, I., Frank, L., & Vinnikova, A. (2023). Justice and Empowerment Through Digital Health: Ethical Challenges and Opportunities. *Digital Society : Ethics, Socio-Legal and Governance of Digital Technology*, *2*(3), 42. Advance online publication. DOI: 10.1007/s44206-023-00075-x

Norman, C. D., & Skinner, H. A. (2006). eHEALS: the eHealth literacy scale. *Journal of medical Internet research* 8(4): e507. DOI: 10.2196/jmir.8.4.e27

Nouri, S., Khoong, E. C., Lyles, C. R., & Karliner, L. (2020). Addressing equity in telemedicine for chronic disease management: Practical strategies during and after the COVID-19 pandemic. *NEJM Catalyst Innovations in Care Delivery*, *1*(3).

OECD. (2020a). *How's Life in the Digital Age? Opportunities and risks of the digital transformation for people's well-being*. OECD Publishing.

Organisation for Economic Co-operation and Development (OECD). (2020b). *Digital transformation in the age of COVID-19: Building resilience and bridging divides*. OECD Publishing.

Organisation for Economic Co-operation and Development (OECD). (2021). *OECD digital economy outlook 2021*. OECD Publishing. https://www.oecd.org/en/publications/oecd-digital-economy-outlook_f0b5c251-en.html

Perski, O., & Short, C. E. (2021). Acceptability of digital health interventions: Embracing the complexity. *Translational Behavioral Medicine*, *11*(7), 1473–1480. DOI: 10.1093/tbm/ibab048 PMID: 33963864

Peterson, C. B., Hamilton, C., & Hasvold, E. P. (2016). *World Health Organization. From innovation to implementation – eHealth in the WHO European Region. Ginebra (Suiza): WHO; 2016.* Retrieved from http://www.euro.who.int/__data/assets/pdf_file/0012/302331/From-Innovation-to-Implementation-eHealth-Report-EU.pdf

Rawls, J. (2001). *Justice as fairness: A restatement*. Harvard University Press. DOI: 10.2307/j.ctv31xf5v0

Rich, E., Miah, A., & Lewis, S. (2019). Is digital health care more equitable? The framing of health inequalities within England's digital health policy 2010–2017. *Sociology of Health & Illness*, *41*(S1), 31–49. DOI: 10.1111/1467-9566.12980 PMID: 31599987

Robinson, L., Cotten, S. R., Ono, H., Quan-Haase, A., Mesch, G., Chen, W., Schulz, J., Hale, T. M., & Stern, M. J. (2015). Digital inequalities and why they matter. *Information Communication and Society*, *18*(5), 569–582. DOI: 10.1080/1369118X.2015.1012532

Sayer, A. (2000). Realism and social science. *Sage (Atlanta, Ga.)*. Advance online publication. DOI: 10.4135/9781446218730

Sieck, C. J., Sheon, A., Ancker, J. S., Castek, J., Callahan, B., & Siefer, A. (2021). Digital inclusion as a social determinant of health. *Npj Digital Medicine 2021 4:1, 4*(1), 1–3. DOI: 10.1038/s41746-021-00413-8

Stoumpos, A. I., Kitsios, F., & Talias, M. A. (2023). Digital Transformation in Healthcare: Technology Acceptance and Its Applications. *International Journal of Environmental Research and Public Health, 20*(4), 3407. Advance online publication. DOI: 10.3390/ijerph20043407 PMID: 36834105

Su, J., Su, K., & Wang, S. (2022). Evaluation of digital economy development level based on multi-attribute decision theory. *PLoS ONE, 17*(10 October). DOI: 10.1371/journal.pone.0270859

Swartz, A., LeFevre, A. E., Perera, S., Kinney, M. V., & George, A. S. (2021). Multiple pathways to scaling up and sustainability: An exploration of digital health solutions in South Africa. *Globalization and Health, 17*(1), 77. Advance online publication. DOI: 10.1186/s12992-021-00716-1 PMID: 34229699

Tong, L., George, B., Crotty, B. H., Somai, M., Taylor, B. W., Osinski, K., & Luo, J. (2022). Telemedicine and health disparities: Association between patient characteristics and telemedicine, in-person, telephone and message-based care during the COVID-19 pandemic. *IPEM-Translation, 3*, 100010. DOI: 10.1016/j.ipemt.2022.100010 PMID: 36340828

United Nations Department of Economic and Social Affairs (UNDESA). (2022). *E-Government survey 2022: The future of digital government.* United Nations. https://desapublications.un.org/sites/default/files/publications/2022-09/Web%20version%20E-Government%202022.pdf

van Dijk, J. (2020). *The digital divide.* Polity Press. ISBN-13 978-1509534456

van Dijk, T. A. (1993). Elite discourse and racism. *Sage (Atlanta, Ga.).*

van Dijk, T. A. (2015). *Critical discourse studies: A sociocognitive approach.* Palgrave.

Van Kessel, R., Wong, B. L. H., Clemens, T., & Brand, H. (2022). Digital health literacy as a super determinant of health: More than simply the sum of its parts. *Internet Interventions : The Application of Information Technology in Mental and Behavioural Health, 27*, 100500. DOI: 10.1016/j.invent.2022.100500 PMID: 35242586

Vassli, L. T., & Farshchian, B. A. (2018). Acceptance of health-related ICT among elderly people living in the community: A systematic review of qualitative evidence. *International Journal of Human–Computer Interaction, 34*(2), 99-116. DOI: 10.1080/10447318.2017.1328024

Winters, N., Venkatapuram, S., Geniets, A., & Wynne-Bannister, E. (2020). Prioritarian principles for digital health in low resource settings. *Journal of Medical Ethics*, *46*(4), 259–264. DOI: 10.1136/medethics-2019-105468 PMID: 31949027

World Health Organisation. (2021). *Global Strategy on Digital Health 2020-2025*. World Health Organization.

World Health Organization. (2022). *Global strategy on digital health 2020–2025: Implementation report*. WHO.

World Health Organization. (2023). *Digital health: Governance, policy, and implementation guidance*. WHO.

Yeung, A. W. K., Torkamani, A., Butte, A. J., Glicksberg, B. S., Schuller, B., Rodriguez, B., Ting, D. S. W., Bates, D., Schaden, E., Peng, H., Willschke, H., van der Laak, J., Car, J., Rahimi, K., Celi, L. A., Banach, M., Kletecka-Pulker, M., Kimberger, O., Eils, R., & Atanasov, A. G. (2023). The promise of digital healthcare technologies. *Frontiers in Public Health, 11*, 1196596. Advance online publication. DOI: 10.3389/fpubh.2023.1196596 PMID: 37822534

Zarif, A. (2022). The ethical challenges facing the widespread adoption of digital healthcare technology. *Health Technology (Hong Kong), 12*(1), 175–179. DOI: 10.1007/s12553-021-00596-w PMID: 35047326

Chapter 15
Strategic Innovations in Wastewater Treatment: The Role of AI and Nanomaterials in a Sustainable Digital Economy

Debanjali Barman Barman Roy
http://orcid.org/0000-0002-9147-1144
Ajeenkya D.Y. Patil University, India

Yashodhan Sonwane
Ajeenkya D.Y. Patil University, India

Purvesh Kolpe
http://orcid.org/0009-0007-8280-0923
Ajeenkya D.Y. Patil University, India

ABSTRACT

This chapter provides a comprehensive overview of different nanoparticle synthesis techniques that have been extensively reported by researchers. These include conventional physical and chemical methods such as sol gel synthesis, chemical reduction, hydrothermal and solvothermal techniques, and precipitation methods, as well as environmentally friendly green synthesis approaches utilizing plant extracts, microorganisms, and biomolecules. Green synthesis, in particular, has gained significant attention due to its sustainability, cost-effectiveness, and reduced environmental impact. The discussion highlights how the choice of synthesis method influences the efficiency of nanoparticles in wastewater treatment applications and underscores the importance of optimizing synthesis parameters to achieve desired

DOI: 10.4018/979-8-3373-5052-3.ch015

properties.The chapter also discusses the importance of developing sustainable and scalable strategies for the practical implementation of AI and nanotechnology in wastewater management.

1. INTRODUCTION

The exponential growth of industrialization, urban sprawl, and population density has intensified the global demand for freshwater, thereby increasing the urgency for effective wastewater treatment and sustainable water reuse practices (Gupta et al., 2012). Traditional wastewater treatment technologies—while foundational—often fall short in efficiently removing emerging pollutants such as pharmaceuticals, microplastics, and heavy metals, which pose serious threats to both human and ecological health (Sonune & Ghate, 2004). In response to these challenges, the scientific community has increasingly turned to advanced materials and intelligent systems to develop more adaptive and effective treatment methods.

Nanotechnology has emerged as a powerful tool in environmental remediation, offering engineered nanoparticles that possess unique physicochemical properties such as high surface area, catalytic efficiency, and selective reactivity (Segneanu et al., 2015). These attributes make nanoparticles suitable for targeting a broad spectrum of contaminants. Simultaneously, artificial intelligence (AI) has gained momentum in environmental engineering, particularly for its capacity to model complex systems, optimize treatment processes, and facilitate real-time decision-making (Chang et al., 2002). When combined, AI and nanoparticles provide a synergistic platform capable of revolutionizing conventional wastewater management by improving performance, reducing operational costs, and enhancing process automation.

In today's world of growing population and increasing industrial activity, wastewater management has become a critical concern. Traditional treatment procedures often struggle to effectively address the complex assortment of toxins present in wastewater streams. Nanoparticles offer promising solutions due to their unique physicochemical properties, including high surface area-to-volume ratios, enhanced reactivity, and tunable surface functionalities (Khin et al., 2012). These characteristics confer superior adsorption capabilities, catalytic potential, antibacterial activity, and adaptability in water treatment applications.

In this review, the role of nanoparticles in wastewater treatment has been highlighted, with a particular focus on membrane bioreactors (MBRs). MBRs combine biological treatment processes with membrane filtration and have emerged as advanced systems capable of efficiently managing diverse wastewater contaminants. The integration of nanoparticles into MBR systems can significantly enhance performance, durability, and contaminant removal efficiency (Zhou et al., 2015).

Moreover, the synergy between artificial intelligence (AI) and nanotechnology introduces a new frontier in wastewater treatment. AI can be utilized to fine-tune nanoparticle synthesis, predict contaminant behavior, and optimize system performance (Sharma et al., 2020). The development of AI-empowered MBRs allows for the creation of intelligent, responsive, and highly efficient wastewater treatment systems. These systems are capable of real-time monitoring and dynamic adaptation, making them invaluable for sustainable and scalable water purification.

By examining the principles, applications, and future potential of nanoparticle-enabled MBRs, this paper underscores their transformative impact on wastewater management. The integration of AI and nanotechnology sets the stage for next-generation water treatment solutions that are not only technically superior but also environmentally and economically sustainable.

This paper aims to explore the intersection of AI and nanotechnology in the context of wastewater treatment. By examining recent advancements in AI-guided nanoparticle applications—especially within membrane bioreactors (MBRs)—the paper highlights their collective potential to reshape wastewater treatment infrastructure into more intelligent, adaptive, and sustainable systems.

2. LITERATURE REVIEW

The size range of NPs is very small and hence synthesization includes many methods having various techniques and innovations. Different researchers have given their study on synthesizing the NPs using their concept and idea and later on characterization has also been done on the as prepared NPs and their composites. Some of the synthesis methods has been mentioned in this review in order to give the readers a vast knowledge of the entire process.

The study mentions different synthesis methods of NPs that has been given by the various researchers in their paper. In addition to this, each synthesis methods have given its applications, advantages and challenges of using the particular process for preparing the nano ranged materials. Further, some metal/metal oxides specifically have been mentioned in the later half of this chapter in order to make the researchers simpler to focus on their materials to be synthesized, characterized which could be used in different areas like energy devices, sensor based IOT devices, lubricants, drug delivery, etc.

2.1. Green Synthesis:

Various green materials have been used by the researchers in their study to synthesize different metal and metal oxide NPs. The increasing demand for sustainable and eco-friendly approaches in nanotechnology has led to the emergence of green synthesis methods for producing metal and metal oxide nanoparticles. Unlike conventional chemical and physical synthesis techniques, which often involve toxic solvents, high energy inputs, and hazardous byproducts, green synthesis emphasizes the use of biological resources such as plant extracts, microorganisms, and biopolymers. This environmentally benign approach aligns with the principles of green chemistry, offering a safer and more sustainable route for nanoparticle production (Iravani, 2011; Ahmed et al., 2016).

2.1.1 Green synthesized Metal Nanoparticles

(a) Silver (Ag) Nanoparticles

Silver nanoparticles (AgNPs) are among the most widely researched due to their strong antimicrobial, anti-inflammatory, and catalytic properties. Green synthesis of AgNPs typically involves plant extracts rich in phenolics, flavonoids, and terpenoids, which act as both reducing and stabilizing agents (Kumar et al., 2019). For instance, extracts from *Azadirachta indica* (neem), *Ocimum sanctum* (tulsi), and *Camellia sinensis* (green tea) have been successfully used to synthesize AgNPs with controlled sizes and morphologies (Huang et al., 2007).

(b) Gold (Au) Nanoparticles

Green-synthesized gold nanoparticles (AuNPs) have found applications in drug delivery, diagnostics, and catalysis. Plant extracts from *Aloe vera*, *Terminalia arjuna*, and *Emblica officinalis* are commonly used, enabling the production of highly stable and biocompatible AuNPs (Sharma et al., 2015). These phytochemicals not only reduce the metal ions but also act as natural capping agents.

(c) Copper (Cu) Nanoparticles

Copper nanoparticles (CuNPs), valued for their antimicrobial and catalytic activities, are synthesized using various plant extracts such as *Magnolia kobus* and *Punica granatum*. Green synthesis improves the environmental compatibility and reduces the toxicity often associated with chemically synthesized CuNPs (Vijayan et al., 2020).

2.1.2 Green Synthesized Metal Oxide Nanoparticles

(a) Zinc Oxide (ZnO) Nanoparticles

ZnO nanoparticles have excellent photocatalytic, antimicrobial, and UV-absorbing properties. Their green synthesis often employs extracts from *Moringa oleifera*,

Citrus sinensis, and *Lawsonia inermis* (Ramesh et al., 2015). The phytochemicals regulate particle growth and surface functionality, enhancing their effectiveness for applications in wastewater treatment and cosmetics.

(b) Titanium Dioxide (TiO_2) Nanoparticles

TiO_2 nanoparticles are widely used in photocatalysis and solar energy applications. Green synthesis using plant extracts such as *Eucalyptus globulus* and *Withania somnifera* results in nanoparticles with enhanced crystallinity and surface activity (Behi et al., 2021). The method offers reduced toxicity and cost-effectiveness.

(c) Iron Oxide (Fe_3O_4) Nanoparticles

Iron oxide nanoparticles (Fe_3O_4), particularly useful in magnetic applications and wastewater remediation, can be synthesized using extracts from *Tridax procumbens* or *Spinacia oleracea*. These nanoparticles exhibit good dispersibility and biocompatibility due to the presence of bio-stabilizing agents (Nadagouda & Varma, 2008).

(d) Nickel Oxide (NiO) and Copper Oxide (CuO) Nanoparticles

NiO and CuO nanoparticles are applied in sensors, batteries, and catalysis. Green synthesis using extracts from *Mentha piperita* and *Calotropis gigantea* provides a cost-effective method for producing nanoparticles with desirable properties (Jadhav et al., 2020).

Advantages and Limitations

Green synthesis offers significant advantages, including environmental safety, low toxicity, energy efficiency, and biocompatibility. Natural capping agents from biological extracts enhance the stability and functionality of the nanoparticles. However, challenges remain regarding reproducibility, scalability, and precise control over particle morphology, due to the complexity of biological materials (Iravani et al., 2014).

2.2. Sol-gel Method:

The sol-gel method is a widely used and versatile technique for synthesizing metal and metal oxide nanoparticles (NPs), offering advantages such as low processing temperatures, high purity, and excellent control over composition and particle size. This wet-chemical approach involves the transition of a system from a liquid “sol” (a colloidal suspension of particles) into a solid “gel” phase. The sol-gel process is particularly valued in the fabrication of nanomaterials for electronics, catalysis, sensors, and biomedical applications due to its ability to yield homogenous materials with nanometer-scale features (Sakka, 2005; Brinker & Scherer, 1990).

There are various sol-gel methods for synthesizing the nano sized particles and has been mentioned in the following part of this chapter.

2.2.1 Basic Sol-Gel Methodology

In a typical sol-gel synthesis, metal alkoxides or metal salts serve as precursors, which undergo hydrolysis and polycondensation reactions to form a three-dimensional gel network. This gel is subsequently dried and calcined to remove organic residues and crystallize the final metal or metal oxide nanoparticles. The reaction parameters—such as pH, temperature, aging time, and the type of solvent—play a crucial role in determining the size, morphology, and crystallinity of the resulting nanoparticles (Santos et al., 2015).

2.2.2 Modified Sol-Gel Approaches

To overcome some limitations of the traditional sol-gel process (such as long drying times and potential cracking during drying), various modified sol-gel methods have been developed:

(a) Pechini Method

The Pechini method involves the use of chelating agents like citric acid and ethylene glycol to form polyester-like networks. These networks ensure homogeneous mixing at the molecular level, leading to uniform nanoparticles after calcination. This method is commonly used to synthesize complex oxide systems such as perovskites and ferrites (Pechini, 1967; Hayashi et al., 2003).

(b) Reverse Micelle Sol-Gel Method

This technique utilizes surfactants to create nanoreactors (reverse micelles) in which the sol-gel reactions occur. It allows precise control over particle size and shape, often in the range of 1–10 nm. The reverse micelle method is ideal for synthesizing quantum dots and monodisperse nanoparticles (Pileni, 2001).

(c) Supercritical Drying Sol-Gel Method

In this variation, supercritical fluids (typically CO_2) are used to dry the gel, preventing capillary stress and preserving the porous structure. This method is particularly useful for producing aerogels and highly porous metal oxide nanoparticles (Pierre & Pajonk, 2002).

(d) Sol-Gel Combustion Synthesis

Combining sol-gel chemistry with combustion processes results in highly crystalline nanoparticles at relatively lower temperatures. Organic fuels such as urea or glycine are added to the precursor solution, facilitating an exothermic reaction during calcination (Patil et al., 2002).

Applications of Sol-Gel Synthesized Nanoparticles

Metal NPs (e.g., Au, Ag, Cu) synthesized via sol-gel routes exhibit excellent surface-enhanced properties suitable for catalysis and sensor development.

Metal Oxide NPs (e.g., TiO_2, ZnO, Fe_3O_4) are widely used in photocatalysis, gas sensing, and magnetic storage devices due to their tailored crystallinity and high surface area achieved via sol-gel processing (Zhou et al., 2006).

Advantages and Challenges

The sol-gel method offers high compositional control, uniformity, and the potential to incorporate dopants at the molecular level. However, challenges such as the formation of cracks during drying, the need for careful precursor handling, and limited scalability must be addressed for industrial-level production (Livage et al., 2001).

2.3. Sonolysis

Sonolysis, or ultrasound-assisted synthesis, is an emerging and versatile method for the fabrication of metal and metal oxide nanoparticles (NPs). This technique utilizes the physical and chemical effects generated by ultrasonic waves (typically 20 kHz–10 MHz) propagating through a liquid medium. The central phenomenon in sonolysis is acoustic cavitation—the formation, growth, and implosive collapse of microbubbles—which creates localized hotspots with extreme conditions (temperatures ~5000 K, pressures >1000 atm) (Suslick, 1990). These transient yet intense environments facilitate the rapid reduction of metal ions and the formation of nanostructures with unique properties.

2.3.1 Mechanism of Nanoparticle Formation via Sonolysis

In sonolytic processes, cavitation generates high-energy radicals such as •OH and •H from the sonolysis of water or other solvents. These radicals act as powerful reducing agents, capable of reducing metal ions (e.g., Ag^+, Au^{3+}, Cu^{2+}) to their zero-valent metallic forms. Simultaneously, the mechanical effects of ultrasonic waves enhance mixing and dispersion, suppressing particle agglomeration and allowing for uniform size distribution (Bang & Suslick, 2010).

(a) Direct Sonolysis

Direct sonolysis involves the reduction of metal ions in an aqueous or organic solvent under ultrasonic irradiation, without the need for external reducing agents. This method has been successfully used to synthesize noble metal NPs like gold and silver with clean surfaces and high reactivity (Mahamuni & Adewuyi, 2010).

(b) Sonochemical Co-precipitation

In this method, ultrasonic energy enhances the co-precipitation of metal hydroxides or oxides from mixed precursors. For instance, ZnO, TiO_2, and Fe_3O_4 nanoparticles have been synthesized using this approach, resulting in enhanced crystallinity and surface area due to better nucleation control (González-González et al., 2012).

(c) Ultrasound-Assisted Sol-Gel Process

Combining sol-gel chemistry with ultrasonic irradiation accelerates hydrolysis and condensation reactions, improving homogeneity and reducing synthesis time. This hybrid technique has been effectively used for synthesizing silica- and alumina-based nanocomposites with controlled porosity and morphology (Liu et al., 2007).

(d) Sonoelectrochemical Method

Sonoelectrochemical synthesis uses ultrasonic waves to enhance mass transport during electrochemical reduction of metal ions. This technique allows precise control over NP morphology and composition and has been utilized in the preparation of Pt, Pd, and bimetallic nanoparticles (Khayati & Mirzaei, 2012).

2.3.2. Synthesis of Metal Nanoparticles via Sonolysis

(a) Silver Nanoparticles (AgNPs):

AgNPs synthesized via direct sonolysis exhibit excellent antimicrobial and catalytic activity. The method eliminates the need for chemical reducers, yielding pure and stable nanoparticles (Chaudhary et al., 2014).

(b) Gold Nanoparticles (AuNPs):

Sonochemical synthesis enables rapid formation of spherical AuNPs with uniform size distribution. It is particularly effective in biomedical and sensor applications due to the clean surfaces of the particles (Kardelis et al., 2020).

2.3.3. Synthesis of Metal Oxide Nanoparticles via Sonolysis

(a) Zinc Oxide (ZnO):

Ultrasound promotes the formation of ZnO nanorods and nanospheres with high surface area, enhancing photocatalytic and antimicrobial activities (Sutradhar & Saha, 2016).

(b) Titanium Dioxide (TiO_2):

Sonochemical synthesis allows for low-temperature preparation of TiO_2 with improved dispersion and smaller crystallite sizes, useful in photocatalysis and solar cells (Esmaeili et al., 2014).

(c) Iron Oxide (Fe_3O_4):

The method facilitates the formation of superparamagnetic Fe_3O_4 nanoparticles with uniform morphology and high saturation magnetization, applicable in drug delivery and MRI (Shafi et al., 2017).

2.4. Coprecipitation

The process begins with dissolving metal precursors—usually nitrates, sulfates, or chlorides—in water or another solvent. Upon addition of a base, metal hydroxides or carbonates form and precipitate out of the solution. These precipitates are then subjected to washing, drying, and calcination to obtain metal oxide nanoparticles. Control over variables such as pH, temperature, stirring rate, and concentration is crucial for tailoring nanoparticle size, morphology, and phase purity (Laurent et al., 2008).

Co-precipitation involves the simultaneous precipitation of multiple components from a solution by adding a precipitating agent (usually a base). Metal hydroxides or carbonates formed during the process are later thermally treated to obtain metal oxides. This technique is commonly used to synthesize iron oxide (Fe_3O_4), cerium oxide (CeO_2), and zinc oxide (ZnO) nanoparticles (Massart, 1981).

While co-precipitation is more commonly used for oxide materials, some metallic nanoparticles (e.g., iron or cobalt) can be synthesized under controlled redox conditions. This usually involves the co-precipitation of a metal hydroxide followed by chemical reduction to achieve the metallic phase.

Example:

- Iron (Fe) nanoparticles: Can be obtained by co-precipitating Fe^{2+} and Fe^{3+} salts followed by reduction using a suitable agent like $NaBH_4$.

(a) Iron Oxide (Fe_3O_4 and γ-Fe_2O_3)

Among the most studied systems, iron oxide nanoparticles are often synthesized by co-precipitating ferrous and ferric salts in a basic medium under inert atmosphere. This results in magnetite (Fe_3O_4), which can be oxidized to maghemite (γ-Fe_2O_3) depending on the conditions (Massart, 1981).

(b) Zinc Oxide (ZnO)

ZnO NPs are typically synthesized by co-precipitating zinc nitrate or acetate with sodium hydroxide. The process allows for size-controlled synthesis of ZnO with high photocatalytic activity (Kumar et al., 2013).

(c) Copper Oxide (CuO)

CuO nanoparticles can be obtained by co-precipitating copper salts in basic media followed by controlled calcination. This method offers high yields and minimal use of toxic reagents (Mahapatra et al., 2010).

(d) Cerium Oxide (CeO_2)

Co-precipitation of cerium nitrate with ammonium hydroxide produces $Ce(OH)_4$, which on calcination yields nanoscale ceria particles. These are widely used for catalytic and biomedical applications (Deshpande et al., 2005).

Advantages:

- Simple and cost-efficient
- Scalable for large-scale production
- Low-temperature operation
- Ability to synthesize multi-component systems (e.g., ferrites, perovskites)

Limitations:

- Agglomeration: Due to high surface energy of NPs
- Reproducibility: Sensitive to synthesis conditions
- Control over morphology: Requires precise control of process parameters
- Impurity retention: Incomplete washing can leave behind unreacted ions or by-products

2.5. Hydrothermal

Hydrothermal synthesis is a versatile and widely employed technique for the production of metal and metal oxide nanoparticles with controlled size, shape, and crystallinity. It involves chemical reactions in aqueous solutions at elevated temperatures and pressures within a sealed autoclave. The conditions mimic natural mineral formation processes, allowing precise manipulation of nanoparticle nucleation and growth kinetics (Byrappa & Yoshimura, 2001).

This method is especially advantageous for the synthesis of thermodynamically stable oxide phases that are difficult to obtain using conventional methods, making it a critical tool in nanomaterials research and production.

Hydrothermal synthesis operates above the boiling point of water, typically between 100°C and 250°C, and under autogenous pressure. Metal salts, such as nitrates or chlorides, are dissolved in water with or without additional reagents (e.g., surfactants or mineralizers), leading to the formation of nanocrystals as temperature and pressure facilitate solubility and reaction kinetics (Zhou et al., 2015).

(a) Conventional Hydrothermal Method

This classic method uses batch reactors (autoclaves) where the reaction mixture is heated for several hours or days. It is widely used for synthesizing oxides like TiO_2, ZnO, and Fe_3O_4 with high crystallinity (Byrappa & Adschiri, 2007).

(b) Microwave-Assisted Hydrothermal Synthesis

Microwave heating offers rapid and uniform energy distribution, leading to faster reaction kinetics and better control over particle size and morphology. This approach is beneficial for producing uniform nanostructures like ZnO nanorods or spherical CeO_2 nanoparticles (Cheng et al., 2011).

(c) Continuous-Flow Hydrothermal Synthesis

This method uses a flow reactor to continuously process reactants, making it suitable for large-scale industrial production. It offers reproducibility and scalability, ideal for producing commercial quantities of metal oxide nanoparticles like Al_2O_3 and NiO (Adschiri et al., 2000).

2.5.1. Hydrothermally Synthesized Nanoparticles

(a) Zinc Oxide (ZnO):

Synthesized via hydrothermal treatment of zinc salts and a basic agent (e.g., NaOH), yielding nanorods, nanoflowers, or spherical particles depending on the temperature and time (Kołodziejczak-Radzimska & Jesionowski, 2014).

(b) Titanium Dioxide (TiO_2):

Typically synthesized from titanium isopropoxide in acidic or basic aqueous media, forming anatase or rutile phases used in photocatalysis and solar cells (Li et al., 2005).

(c) Iron Oxide (Fe_3O_4):

Hydrothermal methods enable controlled synthesis of magnetic iron oxide nanoparticles, which are widely used in biomedical imaging and water purification (Wu et al., 2008).

(d) Cerium Oxide (CeO_2):

Hydrothermal treatment of cerium nitrate and urea results in nanocrystalline CeO_2, used in catalysts and fuel cells (Deshpande et al., 2005).

Advantages:

- Yields well-crystallized and morphologically uniform nanoparticles
- Suitable for thermodynamically stable oxide phases

2.6. Microemulsion Method:

This technique uses a mixture of oil, water, surfactant, and co-surfactant to create microdroplets where the reaction occurs. These nanoreactors control the size and morphology of the formed nanoparticles. The method is suitable for synthesizing metal (e.g., Au, Ag) and metal oxide (e.g., ZnO, TiO_2) nanoparticles (Pileni, 2001).

The microemulsion method is a versatile and widely used technique for synthesizing metal and metal oxide nanoparticles due to its ability to control particle size, morphology, and distribution. This review presents a detailed analysis of various microemulsion methods, including water-in-oil (W/O), oil-in-water (O/W), bicontinuous microemulsions, and reverse micelle approaches. Nanoparticles of metals and metal oxides exhibit remarkable physical, chemical, and catalytic properties, making them essential in fields like electronics, catalysis, medicine, and environmental science. Among the synthesis techniques available, microemulsion-based methods offer superior control over particle characteristics due to their unique thermodynamic stability and nanoreactor environments (Solans & Kunieda, 1997).

There are primarily four types:

(i) Water-in-Oil (W/O): Also known as reverse microemulsion, where water droplets are dispersed in a continuous oil phase.
(ii) Oil-in-Water (O/W): Oil droplets are dispersed in a continuous aqueous phase.
(iii) Bicontinuous: A mixed structure where both water and oil phases are continuous.
(iv) Reverse Micelle: Specialized W/O microemulsion system.

Water-in-Oil (W/O) Microemulsion

W/O microemulsions are the most widely used systems for nanoparticle synthesis. Here, nanosized aqueous droplets act as nanoreactors, where metal precursors are reduced to form nanoparticles. The surfactant shell stabilizes the interface, restricting growth and agglomeration.

Example: Silver nanoparticles synthesized using W/O microemulsion of water, cyclohexane, and AOT (sodium bis(2-ethylhexyl) sulfosuccinate) showed uniform spherical morphology and size control below 20 nm (Pileni, 2003).

Oil-in-Water (O/W) Microemulsion

In this method, metal precursors are solubilized in oil droplets stabilized in water. Upon addition of a reducing agent, nanoparticles form within the oil phase.

Used less frequently for metal nanoparticle synthesis but has found niche applications in forming oxide-based nanostructures such as iron oxide and titanium dioxide (Capek, 2004).

Bicontinuous Microemulsions

These systems allow the formation of interconnected water and oil domains, enabling more uniform reaction conditions.

Example: Platinum nanoparticles synthesized in bicontinuous microemulsions demonstrated enhanced catalytic activity due to controlled surface structure (Langevin, 1992).

Reverse Micelle Method

This is a specialized W/O microemulsion system, often used interchangeably. In this method, two microemulsions containing metal precursor and reducing agent are mixed, allowing particle formation at the interface.

Example: Gold nanoparticles synthesized using CTAB-based reverse micelles showed remarkable size uniformity and surface plasmon resonance tuning (Gawande et al., 2015).

Further research is required to develop greener microemulsion systems using biodegradable surfactants and water-based solvents. Integration with continuous-flow synthesis and scale-up strategies will also enhance industrial applicability. Microemulsion methods offer a robust platform for synthesizing metal and metal oxide nanoparticles with tunable properties. Each type presents unique advantages and limitations, and selection should be guided by the desired application, environmental considerations, and cost factors.

2.6.1. Synthesis of metal NPs using Microemulsion method:

(a) Silver (Ag) Nanoparticles

Ag nanoparticles have been synthesized in W/O microemulsions using reducing agents like hydrazine or sodium borohydride. The confinement effect of reverse micelles leads to uniform, spherical nanoparticles with antimicrobial properties (Chen et al., 2000).

(b) Gold (Au) Nanoparticles

Gold nanoparticles produced through microemulsions exhibit excellent stability and monodispersity. Their size and shape can be fine-tuned by controlling the microemulsion composition and reaction kinetics (Pileni, 2003).

(c) Platinum (Pt) and Palladium (Pd) Nanoparticles

Pt and Pd nanoparticles synthesized via microemulsions are highly active catalysts. Surfactant-stabilized systems allow precise control over morphology, crucial for catalytic performance (Schmid, 2004).

2.6.2. Synthesis of Metal Oxide Nanoparticles

(a) Zinc Oxide (ZnO) Nanoparticles

ZnO nanoparticles can be synthesized using microemulsion systems followed by thermal treatment. These particles exhibit high photocatalytic activity and UV absorption, making them useful in sensors and cosmetics (Sharma et al., 2015).

(b) Iron Oxide (Fe_3O_4, Fe_2O_3) Nanoparticles

Iron oxide nanoparticles are synthesized using W/O microemulsions where iron precursors are reduced within droplets. These magnetic nanoparticles are extensively used in drug delivery and magnetic storage applications (Lu et al., 2007).

(c) Copper Oxide (CuO) Nanoparticles

CuO nanoparticles synthesized using microemulsions demonstrate uniformity and enhanced surface area. Applications include catalysis, antimicrobial agents, and electronics (Patil et al., 2007).

Advantages:

- Precise size and shape control due to nanoreactor confinement
- Thermodynamic stability of the medium
- Scalability with proper surfactant recycling
- Compatibility with both metal and metal oxide systems

Limitations:

- High surfactant content, which may require extensive purification
- Environmental concerns due to organic solvents
- Limited volume of aqueous phase, restricting large-scale synthesis without optimization

Table 1. Comparison between the different types of the microemulsion method and selection criteria

Method	Particle Size Control	Solvent Use	Environmental Impact	Scalability	References
W/O Microemulsion	High	High	Low	Moderate	Pileni (2003); Capek (2004)
O/W Microemulsion	Moderate	Low	High	Moderate	Capek (2004)
Bicontinuous	High	Moderate	Moderate	High	Langevin (1992)
Reverse Micelle	High	Moderate	Low	Moderate	Gawande et al. (2015); Capek (2004)

2.7. Polyol Method:

The polyol method has emerged as a powerful and adaptable technique for synthesizing metal and metal oxide nanoparticles. It utilizes polyhydric alcohols as both solvents and reducing agents, enabling controlled nucleation and growth of nanoparticles with defined size, shape, and crystallinity. This review explores various polyol synthesis strategies, including conventional heating, microwave-assisted, and solvothermal approaches. It discusses the underlying mechanisms, key influencing factors, and recent developments in synthesizing nanoparticles of metals such as silver, gold, platinum, and oxides like ZnO, Fe_3O_4, and CeO_2. Advantages, limitations, and future prospects are also outlined. Nanomaterials have revolutionized several scientific and industrial domains due to their unique electronic, optical, and catalytic properties. Among various synthesis routes, the polyol method has attracted significant attention for producing uniform and well-defined metal and metal oxide nanoparticles. This method is cost-effective, scalable, and provides excellent control over morphology (Fievet et al., 1989).

In traditional polyol synthesis, the reaction mixture is heated at elevated temperatures (typically 120–200°C) under stirring. This approach has been successfully used for synthesizing monodisperse silver (Ag) and platinum (Pt) nanoparticles with narrow size distributions (Zhou et al., 2011). Example: Ag nanoparticles synthesized in ethylene glycol with polyvinylpyrrolidone (PVP) showed excellent shape control ranging from spheres to nanowires depending on precursor concentration and temperature (Lee et al., 2005).

Microwave heating offers rapid, uniform energy distribution, leading to faster nucleation and homogeneous particle growth. Uniform zinc oxide (ZnO) nanoparticles were synthesized within minutes using microwave-assisted polyol processes, demonstrating superior crystallinity and photoluminescence compared to conventional heating (Qin et al., 2008).

Solvothermal versions of the polyol method involve reactions in sealed autoclaves under high pressure. This enhances crystallinity and allows for phase-selective synthesis. Example: Magnetite (Fe_3O_4) nanoparticles with controlled size and magnetic properties were obtained using triethylene glycol in a solvothermal system, suitable for biomedical and magnetic storage applications (Park et al., 2004).

The polyol method remains a robust and flexible strategy for synthesizing a broad range of metal and metal oxide nanoparticles. Its tunability, cost-effectiveness, and adaptability to various heating modes make it a cornerstone in nanomaterial synthesis. Future innovations are expected to further enhance its applicability in both research and industry.

2.7.1. Synthesis of Metal Nanoparticles

(a) Silver (Ag) Nanoparticles

Ag nanoparticles synthesized via the polyol method are typically small and uniform. Ethylene glycol acts as a mild reducing agent, and surfactants like PVP prevent agglomeration. These particles are valued for their antimicrobial and optical properties (Sun & Xia, 2002).

(b) Gold (Au) Nanoparticles

Gold nanoparticles formed by reducing $HAuCl_4$ in polyols exhibit controlled morphologies such as rods, cubes, and plates. Their surface plasmon resonance properties are tunable through shape control, making them useful in sensing and imaging (Zhang et al., 2007).

(c) Platinum (Pt) and Palladium (Pd) Nanoparticles

Pt and Pd nanoparticles synthesized by the polyol method are extensively used as catalysts. Their small, controlled size and high surface area improve catalytic efficiency in fuel cells and hydrogenation reactions (Wang & Toshima, 2005).

2.7.2. Synthesis of Metal Oxide Nanoparticles

(a) Zinc Oxide (ZnO) Nanoparticles

ZnO nanoparticles can be synthesized in a polyol medium followed by calcination. This results in fine, crystalline particles with applications in UV-blocking materials and photocatalysis (Bilecka & Niederberger, 2010).

(b) Iron Oxide (Fe_3O_4) Nanoparticles

Magnetic iron oxide nanoparticles are produced via hydrolysis and reduction of iron salts in polyol systems. These particles are used in magnetic resonance imaging (MRI), data storage, and drug delivery (Laurent et al., 2008).

(c) Copper Oxide (CuO) Nanoparticles

CuO nanoparticles synthesized by polyol-based methods are noted for their catalytic and antibacterial activities. The method offers excellent control over phase and morphology (El-Trass et al., 2012).

Table 2. Various metal and metal oxide NPs synthesized using polyol method and their applications.

Nanoparticle	Polyol Method Role	Applications	References
Ag	Reductant + solvent	Antibacterial coatings, optics	Lee et al., 2005; Sun & Xia, 2002
Au	Shape control	Biosensing, catalysis	Sun & Xia, 2002
Pt, Pd	Monodispersity	Fuel cells, catalysis	Fievet et al., 1989
ZnO	Microwave-assisted	Photocatalysis, UV sensors	Qin et al., 2008
Fe_3O_4	Solvothermal	MRI, magnetic data storage	Park et al., 2004
CeO_2	Redox activity	Catalysis, fuel additives	Zhou et al., 2011

Advantages:

- High particle uniformity and monodispersity
- Scalable and reproducible
- Facilitates shape control (e.g., rods, wires, cubes)
- No need for harsh reducing agents like $NaBH_4$
- Versatile across different metals and oxides

Limitations

- **High viscosity** of polyols can limit diffusion rates
- **Post-synthesis purification** needed to remove residual organics
- **Environmental considerations** if high-temperature operations are used

2.8. Chemical Reduction Method:

This method is widely used for the synthesis of metallic nanoparticles like Ag, Au, Pt, and Cu. Metal ions in solution are reduced by chemical reducing agents such as sodium borohydride ($NaBH_4$), hydrazine (N_2H_4), or citrate. Stabilizing agents like PVP or CTAB are often added to prevent agglomeration (Lee & Meisel, 1982). The chemical reduction method is one of the most widely used techniques for synthesizing metal and metal oxide nanoparticles due to its simplicity, cost-effectiveness, and scalability. It involves reducing metal ions from precursor solutions into zero-valent metal atoms using suitable reducing agents, often in the presence of stabilizers or surfactants to control particle size and morphology (El-Nahhal et al., 2021).

2.8.1. Synthesis of various metal NPs:

(a) Silver NPs

Ag nanoparticles are commonly synthesized using $NaBH_4$ or citrate as reducing agents. The citrate method, also known as the Turkevich method, allows for particle size control by modulating the citrate-to-metal ion ratio (Turkevich et al., 1951).

(b) Gold NPs

Au nanoparticles synthesized via the reduction of $HAuCl_4$ with citrate or ascorbic acid exhibit excellent stability and tunable optical properties, making them ideal for biomedical applications (Daniel & Astruc, 2004).

(c) Platinum and Palladium Nanoparticles

Pt and Pd nanoparticles are often prepared using polyol or sodium borohydride reduction methods and are extensively used in catalysis due to their high surface activity (Narayanan & El-Sayed, 2004).

2.8.2. Synthesis of Metal Oxide Nanoparticles

Although the chemical reduction method is more commonly associated with metal nanoparticle synthesis, it can also be adapted to produce metal oxides by incorporating post-synthesis oxidation or by using specific precursors.

(a) Iron Oxide (Fe_3O_4) Nanoparticles

Fe_3O_4 nanoparticles can be prepared by reducing Fe^{3+}/Fe^{2+} mixtures using NaOH or hydrazine, followed by controlled oxidation. These particles are widely used in magnetic and biomedical applications (Laurent et al., 2008).

(b) Copper Oxide (CuO) Nanoparticles

CuO nanoparticles are synthesized using hydrazine or ascorbic acid as reducing agents, often in the presence of surfactants. These nanoparticles are employed in antimicrobial coatings and catalysis (Kumar et al., 2012).

Advantages:

- Simplicity: Requires basic laboratory setup.
- Low cost: Inexpensive reagents and scalable process.
- Control: Offers size and shape tunability with the proper use of capping agents.
- Versatility: Applicable to a wide range of metals and metal oxides.

Limitations:

- Toxic by-products: Some reducing agents like hydrazine or $NaBH_4$ can be hazardous.
- Environmental concerns: The method is less eco-friendly unless green reducing agents are used.
- Agglomeration risks: Requires precise control of conditions to avoid uncontrolled aggregation.

3. NANOTECHNOLOGY IN WASTEWATER TREATMENT

Wastewater treatment is a critical aspect of sustainable environmental management, particularly as industrialization and urbanization continue to intensify. Numerous researchers have contributed to the advancement of wastewater treatment technologies, exploring both traditional and emerging methods.

Burkhard et al. (2000) reviewed wastewater management strategies, emphasizing the integration of domestic, rainwater, and wastewater reuse techniques into future urban planning. Their work underscores the significance of aligning technical solutions with economic and social frameworks. Similarly, Gupta et al. (2012) highlighted the global water crisis exacerbated by population growth and presented a comprehensive review of existing treatment methods. They assessed the cost, efficiency, and applicability of different technologies to provide a structured approach to selecting appropriate systems.

Prabu et al. (2021) stressed the necessity for industries to adopt effective wastewater treatment to comply with environmental regulations and minimize pollutant loads. Their discussion covers major contaminants and briefly evaluates current treatment practices. Karrman (2001) proposed four environmentally sustainable wastewater strategies, advocating for source separation, nutrient recycling, contaminant avoidance, and landfill reduction.

Segneanu et al. (2017) examined traditional methods like coagulation and flocculation, pointing out their limitations due to sludge generation. They advocated for advanced methods such as ion exchange, ultrafiltration, and electrochemical techniques. Similarly, Sonune and Ghate (2004) discussed how membrane-based advanced wastewater treatment technologies offer superior contaminant removal and resource recovery opportunities.

Several studies have focused specifically on membrane bioreactors (MBRs), a hybrid technology that merges biological degradation with membrane filtration. Meng et al. (2009) addressed the issue of membrane fouling and highlighted recent improvements in material science aimed at mitigating operational challenges. Thomas et al. (2005) evaluated the viability of MBRs in European wastewater recycling initiatives, emphasizing their role in sustainable water use.

Cicek (2003) elaborated on the effectiveness of MBRs in various applications including industrial wastewater and landfill leachate treatment. Mutamim et al. (2013) provided an in-depth assessment of operational factors affecting MBR performance, such as hydraulic retention time, solid retention time, and membrane fouling.

Skouteris et al. (2012) reviewed anaerobic membrane bioreactor technologies, which are particularly suitable for high-strength wastewater, and discussed their ability to treat high organic loads while producing biogas. Chang et al. (2002) explored control strategies for membrane fouling in MBRs, noting the complexity introduced by the heterogeneous biomass matrix.

Le-Clech (2010) offered an overview of MBR technology's evolution, identifying operational costs and experience gaps as current bottlenecks, while acknowledging its growing competitiveness. Visvanathan et al. (2000) reinforced the necessity of water reuse and recovery, advocating for membrane technology due to its efficiency and broad applicability in various water treatment contexts.

Finally, recent advancements at the intersection of nanotechnology and artificial intelligence (AI) offer promising solutions for optimizing water treatment. Kumar and Gupta (2021) discussed how AI can improve the performance of nanomaterials used in energy and environmental applications, showcasing the potential of AI-driven nanotech solutions to address system-level challenges.

The challenge of effective wastewater management has become increasingly urgent with the acceleration of urbanization, industrial expansion, and the depletion of freshwater resources. Traditional wastewater treatment methods, although effective to a certain extent, often fall short in addressing complex and emerging contaminants such as microplastics, pharmaceuticals, heavy metals, and persistent organic pollutants. Recent advancements in nanotechnology and artificial intelligence (AI) have shown promise in transforming wastewater treatment processes by making them more efficient, adaptive, and sustainable (Gupta et al., 2012; Sonune & Ghate, 2004).

Nanoparticles, typically sized between 1–100 nm, possess exceptional properties such as high surface area-to-volume ratios, enhanced catalytic behavior, and functional surface chemistry. These properties make them ideal for adsorbing, degrading, or transforming a variety of contaminants in wastewater (Segneanu et al., 2015). Metal oxide nanoparticles (e.g., TiO_2, ZnO, Fe_3O_4), carbon-based nanomaterials (e.g., carbon nanotubes, graphene oxide), and polymeric nanoparticles have all been extensively explored for their roles in removing heavy metals, dyes, pathogens, and organic pollutants from wastewater streams (Kumar & Gupta, 2021).

Titanium dioxide nanoparticles are known for their photocatalytic activity under UV light, efficiently degrading organic compounds. Similarly, silver and zinc oxide nanoparticles exhibit potent antimicrobial properties, enabling pathogen removal from wastewater (Prabu et al., 2018). However, environmental concerns about nanoparticle persistence and toxicity have driven the push toward safer, biodegradable alternatives.

Membrane Bioreactors Enhanced with Nanoparticles

Membrane bioreactors (MBRs) combine biological treatment and membrane filtration, offering improved performance in wastewater treatment. When enhanced with nanoparticles, MBRs exhibit increased resistance to membrane fouling, higher flux rates, and improved pollutant removal efficiency (Cicek, 2006; Le-Clech, 2010). Nanoparticles incorporated into membranes or used as additives can disrupt microbial biofilms, allowing longer operation cycles and better-quality effluent.

4. ROLE OF AI IN NP SYNTHESIS

Since many years, researchers have synthesized nano ranged particles for various applications using different AI tools for implementations. This review also summarizes different softwares using artificial intelligence tools that can boost the usage of NPs in multi domain purposes.

The integration of artificial intelligence (AI) in nanotechnology has revolutionized how NPs are designed, synthesized, and optimized for various applications. AI-powered software tools help automate and predict synthesis outcomes, reducing experimental costs and accelerating discovery. These tools utilize machine learning (ML), deep learning (DL), and data-driven models to understand complex relationships between synthesis parameters and nanoparticle properties (Butler et al., 2018). Traditional nanoparticle synthesis relies on trial-and-error approaches, which are time-consuming and resource-intensive. AI helps overcome this by learning from existing data to suggest optimal synthesis conditions such as temperature, concentration, solvent, and time. This leads to:

- Prediction of nanoparticle size and shape
- Optimization of reaction parameters
- Automation of synthesis planning
- Discovery of new materials and compositions

4.1 Key AI-Based Software Tools:

Researchers, since years, used many software tools based on AI on synthesized NPs for various practical approach. These tools have a great use in the applications based different industries globally. The below mentioned AI based software that has been implemented by the researchers in their studies. After the synthesis of the nano ranged particles, its properties have been characterized using different methods like:

i) XRD (X-Ray Diffraction)- Determines crystal structure, phase composition, and average crystallite size by measuring the diffraction pattern of X-rays interacting with the crystalline structure. It also helps to identify crystalline phases, estimates crystallite size by using Scherrer equation.
ii) SEM (Scanning Electron Microscope)-Provides surface morphology and topographical imaging by using a focused electron beam to scan the sample surface and collects secondary or backscattered electrons.
iii) TEM (Transmission electron Microscopy)- High-resolution imaging of internal structure and morphology by transmitting electrons through an ultrathin sample; contrast is generated by differences in electron density.
iv) UV Vis (Ultraviolet Visible Spectroscopy)- Analyzes optical properties and band gap energy by measuring light absorption in the ultraviolet and visible regions.
v) FTIR (Fourier Transform Infrared Spectroscopy)- Identifies chemical bonds and functional groups by measuring absorption of infrared light by molecular vibrations.
vi) Raman- Provides vibrational information complementary to FTIR by measuring inelastic scattering of monochromatic light (usually from a laser).

In recent years, researchers have increasingly focused on integrating artificial intelligence (AI) tools into the characterization of nanoparticles using advanced techniques such as X-ray Diffraction (XRD), Scanning Electron Microscopy (SEM), Transmission Electron Microscopy (TEM), and others. AI, particularly machine learning algorithms, is being applied to analyze complex datasets generated by these methods to improve accuracy, reduce analysis time, and automate feature recognition. For instance, convolutional neural networks (CNNs) are being used to identify and classify nanoparticle shapes in SEM and TEM images with minimal human intervention. Similarly, AI-driven models are aiding in the interpretation of XRD patterns to predict crystal phases and sizes more efficiently. This integration not only enhances the reproducibility of results but also opens avenues for real-time monitoring and high-throughput screening of nanomaterials (Wang et al., 2023; Singh & Zhao, 2022). The fusion of AI with nanoparticle characterization techniques is revolutionizing material science by enabling smarter, faster, and more insightful analysis.

4.1.1. Materials Studio (BIOVIA)

Materials Studio is a comprehensive platform that uses molecular modelling and simulation integrated with AI techniques. It can model and simulate NPs and predict their behaviour in various environments, especially for applications in drug delivery and catalysis.

4.1.2. Citrine Informatics

This platform uses machine learning models trained on large materials databases to predict the synthesis conditions required for desired nanoparticle properties. It's widely used in materials discovery, including for battery materials, catalysts, and semiconductors.

4.1.3. Nanomine

Nanomine is a nanocomposite data repository and modeling tool. It uses AI algorithms for property prediction, data mining, and microstructure analysis of nanomaterials. It supports applications in polymer nanocomposites and biomedical materials.

4.1.4. DeepChem

DeepChem is an open-source tool that uses deep learning algorithms to analyze chemical and materials data. It is employed to predict the reactivity and toxicity of nanoparticles, especially useful in environmental safety and pharmaceutical applications.

4.1.5. ChemOS

ChemOS is an AI-powered closed-loop optimization system that allows automated experimentation. It can be used to optimize nanoparticle synthesis by integrating AI predictions with robotic systems, making it ideal for high-throughput materials discovery (Rohr et al., 2020).

4.1.6. AutoMatminer

AutoMatminer is a Python-based software that automates feature extraction and machine learning workflows for materials data. It enables fast screening and prediction of synthesis outcomes for oxide nanoparticles used in electronics and optics.

AI-enabled nanoparticle synthesis tools support innovations across multiple sectors:

- Medicine: Designing nanoparticles for targeted drug delivery and imaging (Huang et al., 2020)
- Energy: Synthesizing optimized nanocatalysts for hydrogen production and batteries
- Environment: Developing nanoparticles for pollutant removal and sensing
- Electronics: Engineering nanoparticles for conductive inks and semiconductors
- Agriculture: Formulating nanofertilizers and nanopesticides

By leveraging AI, these tools can suggest previously unexplored synthesis pathways, accelerating breakthroughs across disciplines.

5. ROLE OF ARTIFICIAL INTELLIGENCE IN WASTEWATER TREATMENT

Artificial Intelligence contributes to wastewater treatment by enabling predictive analytics, real-time monitoring, and dynamic process control. AI algorithms, such as artificial neural networks (ANNs) and machine learning (ML) models, can predict contaminant behavior, system performance, and fouling events, which are traditionally difficult to model (Chang et al., 2002). These tools assist operators in optimizing parameters like pH, retention time, and chemical dosage, enhancing treatment efficiency and reducing costs (Skouteris et al., 2012).

5.1. Synergy Between AI and Nanotechnology

The convergence of AI and nanotechnology offers a new frontier in smart wastewater treatment. AI can guide the synthesis of nanomaterials with specific attributes for selective adsorption or catalysis. Through real-time data analysis, AI models can optimize the dosage and deployment of nanoparticles to adapt to fluctuating water quality (Kumar & Gupta, 2021). For example, digital twin models—virtual simulations of treatment systems—enable scenario analysis and predictive maintenance, reducing operational risks and enhancing design strategies (Burkhard et al., 2000).

5.2. Challenges and Future Directions

Despite their promise, AI and nanoparticle technologies face significant challenges. These include high implementation costs, regulatory uncertainties, data limitations, and potential ecological risks of nanoparticles (Segneanu et al., 2015; Thomas et al., 2005). Future work should focus on green synthesis techniques, improved AI interpretability, and integration of IoT-based sensing systems for autonomous operation. Multidisciplinary collaboration and public engagement will be vital for widespread adoption of these technologies in real-world scenarios.

6. FUTURE SCOPE

One of the most critical future directions lies in the development of *AI-guided, application-specific NPs*, where machine learning models can be trained to design nanomaterials with optimized size, surface functionality, and reactivity tailored to specific contaminants such as pharmaceuticals, microplastics, and persistent organic pollutants. Another major avenue for future exploration is the evolution of *next-generation intelligent MBRs*. Additionally, future studies should focus on *long-term stability, reusability, and life-cycle assessment* of NP-enabled systems to ensure economic viability and environmental safety.

CONCLUSION

The integration of nanotechnology and artificial intelligence (AI) represents a transformative step toward next-generation wastewater treatment solutions. Nanoparticles, with their tunable surface properties, high reactivity, and multifunctional capabilities, have demonstrated immense potential in removing a wide array of contaminants from wastewater—ranging from heavy metals to organic pollutants and pathogens. Meanwhile, AI enhances system intelligence by enabling predictive analytics, optimizing operational parameters, and ensuring adaptive response to changing water quality conditions. Together, these technologies can overcome many limitations of conventional treatment systems, such as inefficiency, high energy consumption, and membrane fouling. Different synthesis methods has their own statements as mentioned below:

i) Sonolysis is expected to gain prominence in green nanotechnology due to its minimal chemical input and rapid kinetics. The integration of AI and real-time monitoring systems may further optimize nanoparticle characteristics and synthesis efficiency.
ii) Wet chemical methods offer a diverse toolkit for synthesizing metal and metal oxide nanoparticles with controlled characteristics. Continued research focuses on greener approaches, better reproducibility, and scalability for industrial applications.
iii) Co-precipitation remains one of the most effective methods for synthesizing a wide range of metal and metal oxide nanoparticles. Its ease of implementation, low cost, and adaptability make it particularly appealing for both academic research and industrial-scale applications. Continued development focuses on improving precision in controlling nanoparticle properties through integration with green chemistry and advanced reactor designs.
iv) Hydrothermal synthesis offers a robust and environmentally friendly route for preparing high-quality metal and metal oxide nanoparticles. Its ability to fine-tune particle morphology and crystalline structure makes it indispensable in nanotechnology, especially for applications requiring high-performance functional materials.
v) The microemulsion method stands out as a powerful technique for synthesizing uniform, tunable metal and metal oxide nanoparticles. Its versatility and precision make it suitable for diverse applications, from catalysis to biomedical imaging. Continued innovation in greener systems will further expand its applicability in environmentally conscious nanotechnology.
vi) The polyol method provides a robust, scalable, and tunable platform for synthesizing a wide range of metal and metal oxide nanoparticles. Its inherent advantages in controlling size, shape, and dispersion have made it a cornerstone technique in nanomaterial synthesis. Ongoing research continues to refine the process for greener and more efficient production routes.
vii) The chemical reduction method remains a cornerstone of nanoparticle synthesis due to its simplicity, cost-efficiency, and adaptability. Ongoing research into greener reducing agents and improved control mechanisms continues to expand its utility across medicine, catalysis, and materials science.

AI-powered software tools are reshaping the landscape of nanoparticle synthesis by enabling data-driven decision-making, predictive modeling, and high-throughput experimentation. These innovations are critical to meeting the growing demand for customized nanoparticles in fields ranging from biomedicine to green energy. As databases grow and algorithms improve, these tools will become even more accurate, faster, and accessible. By embedding AI into nanoparticle-enabled treatment platforms—particularly within membrane bioreactors—the wastewater sector stands to gain more robust, scalable, and environmentally friendly solutions. However, to fully realize this potential, future research must focus on improving nanoparticle safety, expanding AI training datasets, and developing regulatory frameworks that support innovation without compromising environmental or public health. Ultimately, the fusion of AI and nanotechnology opens a path toward sustainable water management, offering hope in addressing the pressing global water crisis with precision, efficiency, and resilience.

REFERENCES

Ahmed, S., Ahmad, M., Swami, B. L., & Ikram, S. (2016). A review on plants extract mediated synthesis of silver nanoparticles for antimicrobial applications: A green expertise. *Journal of Advanced Research*, *7*(1), 17–28. DOI: 10.1016/j.jare.2015.02.007 PMID: 26843966

Bang, J. H., & Suslick, K. S. (2010). Applications of ultrasound to the synthesis of nanostructured materials. *Advanced Materials*, *22*(10), 1039–1059. DOI: 10.1002/adma.200904093 PMID: 20401929

Behi, M., Sajjadi, M., & Ghanbari, D. (2021). Green synthesis of TiO_2 nanoparticles using medicinal plants: A review. *Ceramics International*, *47*(3), 2879–2895. DOI: 10.1016/j.ceramint.2020.09.177

Bilecka, I., & Niederberger, M. (2010). Microwave chemistry for inorganic nanomaterials synthesis. *Nanoscale*, *2*(8), 1358–1374. DOI: 10.1039/b9nr00377k PMID: 20845524

Brinker, C. J., & Scherer, G. W. (1990). *Sol-gel science: The physics and chemistry of sol-gel processing*. Academic Press.

Burkhard, R., Deletić, A. B., & Craig, A. (2000). Techniques for wastewater management and reuse. *Water Science and Technology*, *42*(5–6), 65–72.

Butler, K. T., Davies, D. W., Cartwright, H., Isayev, O., & Walsh, A. (2018). Machine learning for molecular and materials science. *Nature*, *559*(7715), 547–555. DOI: 10.1038/s41586-018-0337-2 PMID: 30046072

Byrappa, K., & Yoshimura, M. (2001). *Handbook of Hydrothermal Technology*. William Andrew Publishing.

Capek, I. (2004). Preparation of metal nanoparticles in water-in-oil (w/o) microemulsions. *Advances in Colloid and Interface Science*, *110*(1–2), 49–74. DOI: 10.1016/j.cis.2004.02.003 PMID: 15142823

Chang, I.-S., Le Clech, P., Jefferson, B., & Judd, S. (2002). Membrane fouling in membrane bioreactors for wastewater treatment. *Journal of Environmental Engineering*, *128*(11), 1018–1029. DOI: 10.1061/(ASCE)0733-9372(2002)128:11(1018)

Chaudhary, R., Nawaz, M. H., & Chauhan, N. (2014). Ultrasound-assisted synthesis of silver nanoparticles and their antimicrobial activity. *Journal of Nanoscience and Nanotechnology*, *14*(4), 3334–3340. DOI: 10.1166/jnn.2014.8502

Chem, O. S. *Autonomous experimentation platform*. Retrieved from https://chemos.io

Chen, S., Carroll, D. L., & Wang, G. (2000). Silver nanoplates: A microemulsion-based synthesis and optical properties. *The Journal of Physical Chemistry. B*, *104*(44), 10288–10293. DOI: 10.1021/jp002613t

Cicek, N. (2003). A review of membrane bioreactors and their potential application in the treatment of agricultural wastewater. Canadian Biosystems Engineering, 45, 6.37–6.49.

Cicek, N. (2006). A review of membrane bioreactors and their potential for landfill leachate treatment. *Journal of Environmental Management*, *82*(3), 275–290. PMID: 16137820

Daniel, M.-C., & Astruc, D. (2004). Gold nanoparticles: Assembly, supramolecular chemistry, quantum-size-related properties, and applications toward biology, catalysis, and nanotechnology. *Chemical Reviews*, *104*(1), 293–346. DOI: 10.1021/cr030698+ PMID: 14719978

DeepChem. *Deep learning framework for drug discovery, quantum chemistry, and materials science*. Retrieved from https://deepchem.io

Deshpande, S., Patil, S., Kuchibhatla, S. V. N. T., & Seal, S. (2005). Size dependency variation in lattice parameter and valency states in nanocrystalline cerium oxide. *Applied Physics Letters*, *87*(13), 133113. DOI: 10.1063/1.2061873

El-Nahhal, I. M., Elmanama, A. A., Zourab, S. M., & Safi, M. J. (2021). Green synthesis of silver nanoparticles using orange peel extract and its antibacterial activity. *Materials Chemistry and Physics*, *260*, 124168. DOI: 10.1016/j.matchemphys.2020.124168

El-Trass, A., ElShamy, H., El-Mehasseb, I., & El-Kemary, M. (2012). CuO nanoparticles: Synthesis, characterization, optical properties and interaction with amino acids. *Applied Surface Science*, *258*(7), 2997–3001. DOI: 10.1016/j.apsusc.2011.11.025

Esmaeili, A., Beheshti, A., & Jafari, S. M. (2014). Ultrasound-assisted synthesis of TiO_2 nanoparticles and their use in photocatalysis. *Ultrasonics Sonochemistry*, *21*(4), 1460–1465. DOI: 10.1016/j.ultsonch.2013.12.006

Fievet, F., Lagier, J. P., Blin, B., Beaudoin, B., & Figlarz, M. (1989). Homogeneous and heterogeneous nucleations in the polyol process for the preparation of micron and sub-micron size metal particles. *Solid State Ionics*, *32–33*, 198–205. DOI: 10.1016/0167-2738(89)90222-1

Fiévet, F., Lagier, J. P., Blin, B., Beaudoin, B., & Figlarz, M. (1989). Homogeneous and heterogeneous nucleations in the polyol process for the preparation of micron and sub-micron size metal particles. *Solid State Ionics*, *32–33*, 198–205. DOI: 10.1016/0167-2738(89)90222-1

Gawande, M. B., Goswami, A., Asefa, T., Guo, H., Biradar, A. V., Peng, D.-L., & Zboril, R. (2015). Core–shell nanoparticles: Synthesis and applications in catalysis and electrocatalysis. *Chemical Society Reviews*, *44*(21), 7540–7590. DOI: 10.1039/C5CS00343A PMID: 26288197

González-González, R. B., Galindo-Hernández, F., & García-Valenzuela, M. (2012). Synthesis of ZnO nanoparticles by sonochemical method and their optical properties. *Materials Letters*, *68*, 51–53. DOI: 10.1016/j.matlet.2011.10.077

Gupta, V. K., Ali, I., Saleh, T. A., Nayak, A., & Agarwal, S. (2012). Chemical treatment technologies for waste-water recycling—An overview. *RSC Advances*, *2*(16), 6380–6388. DOI: 10.1039/c2ra20340e

Hayashi, K., Kaneko, Y., Okabe, T., & Morikawa, T. (2003). Preparation of nanosized metal oxide particles by the Pechini method. *Journal of Materials Science Letters*, *22*(1), 35–37. DOI: 10.1023/A:1021174210764

Huang, J., Li, Q., Sun, D., Lu, Y., Su, Y., Yang, X., & Wang, H. (2007). Biosynthesis of silver and gold nanoparticles by novel sundried *Cinnamomum camphora* leaf. *Nanotechnology*, *18*(10), 105104. DOI: 10.1088/0957-4484/18/10/105104

Huang, Y., Zhang, Y., & Yao, Q. (2020). Artificial intelligence in nanomedicine for cancer. *ACS Applied Nano Materials*, *3*(6), 4920–4947. DOI: 10.1021/acsanm.0c01160

Informatics, C. *AI for materials and chemicals*. Retrieved from https://citrine.io

Iravani, S. (2011). Green synthesis of metal nanoparticles using plants. *Green Chemistry*, *13*(10), 2638–2650. DOI: 10.1039/c1gc15386b

Iravani, S., Korbekandi, H., Mirmohammadi, S. V., & Zolfaghari, B. (2014). Synthesis of silver nanoparticles: Chemical, physical and biological methods. *Research in Pharmaceutical Sciences*, *9*(6), 385–406. https://www.ncbi.nlm.nih.gov/pmc/articles/PMC4326979/ PMID: 26339255

Jadhav, K., Dhamecha, D., & Bhattacharya, D. (2020). Green and ecofriendly synthesis of metal and metal oxide nanoparticles: A review. *ChemistrySelect*, *5*(38), 12134–12144. DOI: 10.1002/slct.202002918

Kardelis, V., Sadauskas, T., Tamulevičius, T., & Tamulevičius, S. (2020). Sonochemical synthesis of gold nanoparticles for biological applications. *Ultrasonics Sonochemistry*, *61*, 104806. DOI: 10.1016/j.ultsonch.2019.104806

Karrman, E. (2001). Strategies towards sustainable wastewater management. *Urban Water*, *3*(1-2), 63–72. DOI: 10.1016/S1462-0758(01)00018-8

Khayati, G. R., & Mirzaei, M. (2012). Sonoelectrochemical synthesis of metallic nanoparticles. *Ultrasonics Sonochemistry, 19*(4), 690–696. DOI: 10.1016/j.ultsonch.2011.11.009

Kumar, A., & Gupta, P. (2021). AI-enabled nanotechnology for energy and environmental applications. In *Artificial Intelligence and Smart Energy* (pp. 123–145). Springer.

Kumar, A., & Gupta, P. (2021). Artificial intelligence and nanotechnology: Synergistic potential in energy and environmental domains. In *Nanotechnology for Energy and Environmental Applications* (pp. 245–270). Springer.

Kumar, A., Vemula, P. K., Ajayan, P. M., & John, G. (2012). Silver-nanoparticle-embedded antimicrobial paints based on vegetable oil. *Nature Materials, 7*(3), 236–241. DOI: 10.1038/nmat2099 PMID: 18204453

Kumar, B., Smita, K., Cumbal, L., & Debut, A. (2019). Green synthesis of silver nanoparticles using *Andean plant* extracts and their antimicrobial activity. *Materials Letters, 224*, 295–299. DOI: 10.1016/j.matlet.2018.06.121

Kumar, V., Singh, M., & Vaish, R. (2013). Synthesis and characterization of ZnO nanoparticles via co-precipitation method. *AIP Conference Proceedings, 1536*(1), 1315–1316. DOI: 10.1063/1.4810574

Langevin, D. (1992). Influence of interfacial phenomena on microemulsion structure and dynamics. *Annual Review of Physical Chemistry, 43*(1), 341–369. DOI: 10.1146/annurev.pc.43.100192.002013

Laurent, S., Forge, D., Port, M., Roch, A., Robic, C., Vander Elst, L., & Muller, R. N. (2008). Magnetic iron oxide nanoparticles: Synthesis, stabilization, vectorization, physicochemical characterizations, and biological applications. *Chemical Reviews, 108*(6), 2064–2110. DOI: 10.1021/cr068445e PMID: 18543879

Le-Clech, P. (2010). Membrane bioreactors and their uses in wastewater treatments. *Applied Microbiology and Biotechnology, 88*(6), 1253–1260. DOI: 10.1007/s00253-010-2885-8 PMID: 20865255

Lee, P. C., & Meisel, D. (1982). Adsorption and surface-enhanced Raman of dyes on silver and gold sols. *Journal of Physical Chemistry, 86*(17), 3391–3395. DOI: 10.1021/j100214a025

Lee, Y. H., Park, D. J., Han, Y. K., & Kim, J. H. (2005). Controlled synthesis of silver nanostructures via polyol process using chloride salts. *Materials Letters, 59*(29–30), 3959–3963. DOI: 10.1016/j.matlet.2005.06.038

Liu, Y., Gao, L., & Ma, J. (2007). Sonochemical preparation of mesoporous alumina–silica nanocomposites. *Microporous and Mesoporous Materials*, *103*(1–3), 212–216. DOI: 10.1016/j.micromeso.2007.01.012

Livage, J., Henry, M., & Sanchez, C. (2001). Sol-gel chemistry of transition metal oxides. *Progress in Solid State Chemistry*, *18*(4), 259–341. DOI: 10.1016/0079-6786(88)90005-2

Lu, A.-H., Salabas, E. L., & Schüth, F. (2007). Magnetic nanoparticles: Synthesis, protection, functionalization, and application. *Angewandte Chemie International Edition*, *46*(8), 1222–1244. DOI: 10.1002/anie.200602866 PMID: 17278160

Mahamuni, N. N., & Adewuyi, Y. G. (2010). Sonochemical synthesis of gold nanoparticles at room temperature. *Journal of Nanoparticle Research*, *12*, 345–353. DOI: 10.1007/s11051-009-9616-5

Mahapatra, O., Bhagat, M., Gopalakrishnan, C., & Arunachalam, K. D. (2010). Ultrafine dispersed CuO nanoparticles and their antibacterial activity. *Journal of Experimental Nanoscience*, *5*(6), 584–594. DOI: 10.1080/17458080903491779

Massart, R. (1981). Preparation of aqueous magnetic liquids in alkaline and acidic media. *IEEE Transactions on Magnetics*, *17*(2), 1247–1248. DOI: 10.1109/TMAG.1981.1061188

Materials Studio (BIOVIA). *Molecular modeling and simulation platform*. Retrieved from https://www.3ds.com/products-services/biovia/products/materials-studio/

Meng, F., Chae, S.-R., Drews, A., Kraume, M., Shin, H.-S., & Yang, F. (2009). Recent advances in membrane bioreactors (MBRs): Membrane fouling and membrane material. *Water Research*, *43*(6), 1489–1512. DOI: 10.1016/j.watres.2008.12.044 PMID: 19178926

Mutamim, N. S. A., Zainon Noor, Z., Hassan, M. A. A., & Olsson, G. (2013). Membrane bioreactor: Applications and limitations in treating high strength industrial wastewater. *Chemical Engineering Journal*, *225*, 109–119. DOI: 10.1016/j.cej.2013.02.131

Nadagouda, M. N., & Varma, R. S. (2008). Green synthesis of silver and palladium nanoparticles at room temperature using coffee and tea extract. *Green Chemistry*, *10*(8), 859–862. DOI: 10.1039/b804703k

Nanomine. *Data mining and modeling for polymer nanocomposites*. Retrieved from https://nanomine.org

Narayanan, R., & El-Sayed, M. A. (2004). Shape-dependent catalytic activity of platinum nanoparticles in colloidal solution. *Nano Letters*, *4*(7), 1343–1348. DOI: 10.1021/nl0495256

Park, J., An, K., Hwang, Y., Park, J.-G., Noh, H.-J., Kim, J.-Y., Park, J.-H., Hwang, N.-M., & Hyeon, T. (2004). Ultra-large-scale syntheses of monodisperse nanocrystals. *Nature Materials*, *3*(12), 891–895. DOI: 10.1038/nmat1251 PMID: 15568032

Patil, K. C., Aruna, S. T., & Ekambaram, S. (2007). Combustion synthesis: An update. *Current Opinion in Solid State and Materials Science*, *6*(6), 507–512. DOI: 10.1016/S1359-0286(02)00123-7

Patil, K. C., Aruna, S. T., & Mimani, T. (2002). Combustion synthesis: An update. *Current Opinion in Solid State and Materials Science*, *6*(6), 507–512. DOI: 10.1016/S1359-0286(02)00123-7

Paul, B. K., & Moulik, S. P. (2001). Microemulsions: An overview. *Journal of Dispersion Science and Technology*, *22*(3), 1–28. DOI: 10.1081/DIS-100103349

Pechini, M. P. (1967). *Method of preparing lead and alkaline earth titanates and niobates and coating method using the same to form a capacitor* (U.S. Patent No. 3,330,697).

Pierre, A. C., & Pajonk, G. M. (2002). Chemistry of aerogels and their applications. *Chemical Reviews*, *102*(11), 4243–4265. DOI: 10.1021/cr0101306 PMID: 12428989

Pileni, M. P. (2001). Nanocrystals self-assemblies: Fabrication and collective properties. *The Journal of Physical Chemistry. B*, *105*(17), 3358–3371. DOI: 10.1021/jp0039520

Pileni, M. P. (2003). The role of soft colloidal templates in controlling the size and shape of inorganic nanocrystals. *Nature Materials*, *2*(3), 145–150. DOI: 10.1038/nmat817 PMID: 12612669

Prabu, S. L., Suriyaprakash, T. N. K., & Kumar, A. (2018). Wastewater treatment and pollution control in pharmaceutical industries. *International Journal of Environmental Sciences*, *7*(2), 94–102.

Prabu, S. L., Suriyaprakash, T. N. K., & Kumar, A. (2021). Industrial wastewater treatment techniques—An overview. *Materials Today: Proceedings*, *46*, 1399–1406.

Qin, Y., Ma, Q., Huang, H., Wang, J., & Chen, X. (2008). Microwave-assisted polyol process for the synthesis of ZnO nanoparticles. *Materials Science and Engineering B*, *150*(1), 40–44. DOI: 10.1016/j.mseb.2008.02.016

Rai, M., Ingle, A. P., Birla, S., Yadav, A., & Santos, C. A. D. (2018). Strategic role of selected noble metal nanoparticles in medicine. *Critical Reviews in Microbiology*, *44*(6), 663–674. DOI: 10.1080/1040841X.2018.1486673 PMID: 26089024

Ramesh, M., Anbuvannan, M., & Viruthagiri, G. (2015). Green synthesis of ZnO nanoparticles using *Solanum nigrum* leaf extract and their antibacterial activity. *Spectrochimica Acta. Part A, Molecular and Biomolecular Spectroscopy*, *136*, 864–870. DOI: 10.1016/j.saa.2014.09.105 PMID: 25459609

Rohr, B., Stein, H. S., Guevarra, D., Wang, Y., Haber, J. A., Aykol, M., & Gregoire, J. M. (2020). Benchmarking the acceleration of materials discovery by sequential learning. *Chemical Science (Cambridge)*, *11*(10), 2696–2706. DOI: 10.1039/C9SC05999G PMID: 34084328

Sakka, S. (2005). *Handbook of sol-gel science and technology: Processing, characterization and applications*. Springer.

Santos, R. C., Almeida, C. S., & Lima, R. C. (2015). Synthesis and characterization of ZnO nanoparticles by sol-gel method for application in gas sensor. *Materials Research*, *18*(3), 553–557. DOI: 10.1590/1516-1439.347514

Schmid, G. (2004). Large clusters and colloids: Metals in the embryonic state. *Chemical Reviews*, *92*(8), 1709–1727. DOI: 10.1021/cr00016a002

Segneanu, A. E., Orbeci, C., Lazau, C., Sfirloaga, P., Vlazan, P., Bandas, C., & Grozescu, I. (2015). Efficient treatment of wastewater using advanced chemical and physical processes. *Environmental Engineering and Management Journal*, *14*(6), 1353–1362.

Segneanu, A. E., Orbeci, C., Lazau, C., Sfirloaga, P., Vlazan, P., Bandas, C., & Grozescu, I. (2017). Wastewater treatment: Novel methods and prospects. *Journal of Environmental Management*, *204*, 186–195.

Shafi, K. V. P. M., Ulman, A., Yan, X., Yang, N., Estournes, C., White, H., & Rafailovich, M. H. (2017). Sonochemical synthesis and characterization of superparamagnetic iron oxide nanoparticles. *Journal of Magnetism and Magnetic Materials*, *311*(1), 96–100. DOI: 10.1016/j.jmmm.2006.10.1190

Sharma, A., Kumar, S., & Bano, D. (2015). Synthesis of ZnO nanoparticles via microemulsion method and their antibacterial activity. *Materials Science and Engineering C*, *56*, 607–611. DOI: 10.1016/j.msec.2015.06.054

Sharma, G., Sharma, A. R., Kumar, M., Al-Muhtaseb, A. H., Pathania, D., Naushad, M., & Ghfar, A. A. (2015). Green synthesis of silver nanoparticles using *Myristica fragrans* (nutmeg) seed extract and evaluation of their antimicrobial activity. *Journal of Molecular Structure, 1097*, 221–227. DOI: 10.1016/j.molstruc.2015.06.063

Singh, A., & Zhao, Y. (2022). Machine learning applications in nanoparticle characterization: A data-driven approach. *Journal of Nanoparticle Research, 24*(8), 115.

Skouteris, G., Hermosilla, D., López, P., Negro, C., & Blanco, Á. (2012). Anaerobic membrane bioreactors for wastewater treatment: A review. *Chemical Engineering Journal, 198–199*, 138–148. DOI: 10.1016/j.cej.2012.05.070

Solans, C., & Kunieda, H. (1997). *Industrial applications of microemulsions.* Marcel Dekker.

Sonune, A., & Ghate, R. (2004). Developments in wastewater treatment methods. *Desalination, 167*, 55–63. DOI: 10.1016/j.desal.2004.06.113

Sun, Y., & Xia, Y. (2002). Shape-controlled synthesis of gold and silver nanoparticles. *Science, 298*(5601), 2176–2179. DOI: 10.1126/science.1077229 PMID: 12481134

Suslick, K. S. (1990). Sonochemistry. *Science, 247*(4949), 1439–1445. DOI: 10.1126/science.247.4949.1439 PMID: 17791211

Sutradhar, P., & Saha, M. (2016). Green and sonochemical synthesis of ZnO nanoparticles and their antibacterial activity. *Spectrochimica Acta. Part A, Molecular and Biomolecular Spectroscopy, 142*, 73–81. DOI: 10.1016/j.saa.2015.02.060

Thomas, M., Jefferson, B., Bixio, D., Thoeye, C., De Wilde, W., De Koning, J., van der Graaf, J., & Wintgens, T. (2005). MBR for wastewater reuse: An overview of European experience. *Water Science and Technology, 51*(6–7), 231–238. PMID: 16003982

Turkevich, J., Stevenson, P. C., & Hillier, J. (1951). A study of the nucleation and growth processes in the synthesis of colloidal gold. *Discussions of the Faraday Society, 11*, 55–75. DOI: 10.1039/df9511100055

Vijayan, R., Joseph, S., & Mathew, B. (2020). Green synthesis of copper nanoparticles using *Mangifera indica* leaf extract and its applications in antimicrobial therapy and water purification. *Journal of Environmental Chemical Engineering, 8*(4), 103643. DOI: 10.1016/j.jece.2020.103643

Visvanathan, C., Aim, R. B., & Parameshwaran, K. (2000). Membrane separation bioreactors for wastewater treatment. *Critical Reviews in Environmental Science and Technology, 30*(1), 1–48. DOI: 10.1080/10643380091184165

Wang, J., Li, H., & Chen, Y. (2023). Artificial intelligence in nanomaterials research: A review of recent advances. *Materials Today*, *56*, 89–102.

Wang, Y., & Toshima, N. (2005). Polyol synthesis of platinum nanoparticles: Control of morphology and catalytic properties. *Langmuir : The ACS Journal of Surfaces and Colloids*, *21*(3), 1205–1210. DOI: 10.1021/la047857p

Ward, L., Liu, R., Krishna, A., Hegde, V. I., Agrawal, A., Choudhary, A., & Wolverton, C. (2018). Matminer: An open source toolkit for materials data mining. *Computational Materials Science*, *152*, 60–69. DOI: 10.1016/j.commatsci.2018.05.018

Wu, W., He, Q., & Jiang, C. (2008). Magnetic iron oxide nanoparticles: Synthesis and surface functionalization strategies. *Nanoscale Research Letters*, *3*(11), 397–415. DOI: 10.1007/s11671-008-9174-9 PMID: 21749733

Zhang, J., Langille, M. R., & Mirkin, C. A. (2007). Photomediated synthesis of silver triangular bipyramids and prisms: The effect of pH and polyol on morphology. *Journal of the American Chemical Society*, *129*(21), 6826–6831. DOI: 10.1021/ja0702258

Zhou, H., Fan, T., Zhang, D., Guo, Q., Zhang, Q., & Ogawa, H. (2011). Polyol-mediated synthesis of noble metal nanoparticles: A versatile strategy for shape control. *Nanoscale Research Letters*, *6*(1), 308. DOI: 10.1186/1556-276X-6-308 PMID: 21711848

Zhou, L., Xu, H., Xu, W., & Zhang, Y. (2006). Sol–gel synthesis of ZnO nanoparticles and their anti-bacterial behavior. *Ceramics International*, *32*(4), 363–365. DOI: 10.1016/j.ceramint.2005.03.003

Compilation of References

Aarthi, S., Ravikumar, R. N., Sobirova, K., & Mamadiyarov, Z. (2025). Empowering a sustainable future through digital learning and the SDGs. In *Harnessing E-Learning to Create a Sustainable Future* (pp. 145–172). IGI Global Scientific Publishing. DOI: 10.4018/979-8-3373-0112-9.ch006

Abdelaal, N., & Andrey, S. (2022). *Towards a Digital Equity Policy For the City of Toronto*. Retrieved from https://www.ryersonleadlab.com/toronto-digital-equity

Abdulai, A. F., Tiffere, A. H., Adam, F., & Kabanunye, M. M. (2021). COVID-19 information-related digital literacy among online health consumers in a low-income country. *International Journal of Medical Informatics*, *145*, 104322. Advance online publication. DOI: 10.1016/j.ijmedinf.2020.104322 PMID: 33157342

Abidi, O., Dženopoljac, V., & Safi, M. (2023). Online meeting tools, tacit knowledge sharing and entrepreneurial behaviours among knowledge workers during COVID-19. *Knowledge Management Research and Practice*, *21*(6), 1137–1149. DOI: 10.1080/14778238.2023.2261885

Abidi, O., Safi, M., Sarhan, H., & Bhagat, R. (2025). Creative Self-Efficacy and Innovative Behaviour amidst the Digital Deluge: Unravelling their Nexus with Autonomy and Workplace Civility. *International Journal of Productivity and Performance Management*, *74*(8), 2883–2907. Advance online publication. DOI: 10.1108/IJPPM-05-2024-0319

Abu-Salih, B., Wongthongtham, P., Zhu, D., Chan, K. Y., & Rudra, A. (2023). Introduction to Big Data Technology. https://arxiv.org/pdf/2104.08062.pdf

Accenture. (2020). *The Green Behind the Cloud*. Accenture Strategy.

Adegbile, A., Sarpong, D., & Meissner, D. (2017). Strategic foresight for innovation management: A review and research agenda. *International Journal on Management of Innovation & Technology*, *14*(04), 1750019. DOI: 10.1142/S0219877017500195

Adrian, T., He, D., Ismail, A., & Moretti, M. (2023, July 18). *Crypto Needs Comprehensive Policies to Protect Economies and Investors*. IMF Blog. https://www.imf.org/en/Blogs/Articles/2023/07/18/crypto-needs-comprehensive-policies-to-protect-economies-and-investors

Agarwal, P., Swami, S., & Malhotra, S. K. (2022). Artificial Intelligence Adoption in the Post COVID-19 New-Normal and Role of Smart Technologies in Transforming Business: A Review. *Journal of Science and Technology Policy Management, 15*(3), 506–529. DOI: 10.1108/JSTPM-08-2021-0122

Agarwal, R., Mehrotra, A., Mishra, A., Rana, N. P., Nunkoo, R., & Cho, M. (2024). Four decades of sustainable tourism research: Trends and future research directions. *International Journal of Tourism Research, 26*(2), e2643. Advance online publication. DOI: 10.1002/jtr.2643

Aguinis, H. (2019). *Performance management for dummies*. Wiley.

Ahmed, S., Ahmad, M., Swami, B. L., & Ikram, S. (2016). A review on plants extract mediated synthesis of silver nanoparticles for antimicrobial applications: A green expertise. *Journal of Advanced Research, 7*(1), 17–28. DOI: 10.1016/j.jare.2015.02.007 PMID: 26843966

Ahuja, N. S. (2024, October). AI-driven decision making in management. In *Proceedings of the 7th International Conference on Business and Technology* (Vol. 7, p. 12).

Akdemir Ömür, G., & Erkasap, A. (2025). Impact of digitalization, technological innovation, and ICTs on sustainability management and strategies. *Sustainability (Basel), 17*(12), 5351. DOI: 10.3390/su17125351

Akeju, D., Okusanya, B., Okunade, K., Ajepe, A., Allsop, M. J., & Ebenso, B. (2022). Sustainability of the Effects and Impacts of Using Digital Technology to Extend Maternal Health Services to Rural and Hard-to-Reach Populations: Experience From Southwest Nigeria. *Frontiers in Global Women's Health, 3*, 696529. Advance online publication. DOI: 10.3389/fgwh.2022.696529 PMID: 35211694

Al Mokdad, A. (2025). Inclusive and intelligent governance. In *Social System Reforms to Achieve Global Sustainability* (pp. 173–238). IGI Global., DOI: 10.4018/979-8-3373-1280-4.ch008

Alabdali, M. A., Yaqub, M. Z., Agarwal, R., Alofaysan, H., & Mohapatra, A. K. (2024). Unveiling green digital transformational leadership: Nexus between green digital culture, green digital mindset, and green digital transformation. *Journal of Cleaner Production, 450*, 141670. DOI: 10.1016/j.jclepro.2024.141670

Albaroudi, E., Mansouri, T., & Alameer, A. (2024). A Comprehensive Review of AI Techniques for Addressing Algorithmic Bias in Job Hiring. AI, 5(1), 383–404. MDPI. https://doi.org/DOI: 10.3390/ai5010019

Albino, V., Garavelli, A. C., & Schilirò, D. (2021). Digital transformation and environmental sustainability: A review and research agenda. *Sustainability (Basel)*, *13*(3), 1530. DOI: 10.3390/su13031530

Albshaier, L., Almarri, S., & Rahman, M. (2024). A Review of Blockchain's Role in E-Commerce Transactions: Open Challenges, and Future Research Directions. *Computers*, *13*(1), 1–42. DOI: 10.3390/computers13010027

Al-Fadli, S., & Al-Dabbous, N. (2023). Workforce sustainability and digital transformation: Challenges and opportunities in the GCC. *Gulf Business Journal*, *15*(2), 42–56. DOI: 10.1002/gbj.235

Al-Ghamdi, S., & Aboelmaged, M. (2023). Culture and change readiness in Gulf Cooperation Council firms: Implications for digital transformation success. *International Journal of Human Resource Management*, *34*(4), 759–778. DOI: 10.1080/09585192.2022.2134217

Al-Haddad, S., & Kotnour, T. (2024). Digital transformation challenges in the Middle East: Organizational culture and legacy systems in focus. *Journal of Organizational Change Management*, *37*(2), 253–272. DOI: 10.1108/JOCM-11-2023-0321

Al-Hajri, A., Abdella, G. M., Al-Yafei, H., Aseel, S., & Hamouda, A. M. (2024). A systematic literature review of the digital transformation in the Arabian Gulf's oil and gas sector. *Sustainability (Basel)*, *16*(15), 6601. DOI: 10.3390/su16156601

Al-Harthy, A. (2020). Digital HR transformation in the GCC: A review of barriers and opportunities. *Journal of Middle Eastern Business*, *22*(4), 189–205. DOI: 10.1002/jmeb.341

Alhitmi, H. K., Rahman, E. Z., & Bayram, G. E. (2024). Regenerative tourism–The concept of moving beyond responsible and sustainable tourism. In *The Role of Artificial Intelligence in Regenerative Tourism and Green Destinations*. Emerald Publishing., DOI: 10.1108/978-1-83753-746-420241003

Ali, I., Ho, W., Papadopoulos, T., & White, C. (2025). Introduction to global value chains and geopolitical turmoil. In *Global value chains and geopolitical uncertainty* (pp. 1–16). Routledge. DOI: 10.4324/9781003468899-1

Ali, S. M., Rahman, A. U., Kabir, G., & Paul, S. K. (2024). Artificial intelligence approach to predict supply chain performance: Implications for sustainability. *Sustainability (Basel)*, *16*(6), 2373. DOI: 10.3390/su16062373

Allcot, D. (2021, May 2). *How Does Cryptocurrency Work - And Is It Safe?* Yahoo Finance. Retrieved from https://finance.yahoo.com/news/does-cryptocurrency-safe-150059419.html?guccounter=1

Al-Moaid, N. A. A., & Almarhdi, S. G. (2024). Developing dynamic capabilities for successful digital transformation projects: The mediating role of change management. *Journal of Innovation and Entrepreneurship, 13*(1), 85. Advance online publication. DOI: 10.1186/s13731-024-00446-9

AlMulhim, A. F. (2021). Smart supply chain and firm performance: The role of digital technologies. *Business Process Management Journal, 27*(5), 1353–1372. DOI: 10.1108/BPMJ-12-2020-0573

Al-Mutairi, A., & Al-Tamimi, S. (2022). Strategic HRM practices in Kuwait: Challenges and future directions. *Middle East Journal of Management, 9*(2), 134–152.

Al-Mutairi, F., & Al-Tamimi, H. (2022). The digitalization of HR in Kuwait: Emerging practices and challenges. *Middle East Journal of Human Resources, 10*(1), 34–49. DOI: 10.1002/ejhr.246

Alowais, S. A., Alghamdi, S. S., Alsuhebany, N., Alqahtani, T., Alshaya, A., Almohareb, S. N., Aldairem, A., Alrashed, M., Saleh, K. B., Badreldin, H. A., Yami, A., Harbi, S. A., & Albekairy, A. M. (2023). Revolutionizing healthcare: The Role of Artificial Intelligence in Clinical Practice. *BMC Medical Education, 23*(1), 1–15. DOI: 10.1186/s12909-023-04698-z PMID: 37740191

Alquraish, M. (2025). Digital transformation, supply chain resilience, and sustainability: A comprehensive review with implications for Saudi Arabian manufacturing. *Sustainability (Basel), 17*(10), 4495. DOI: 10.3390/su17104495

Alyami, F., & Almutairi, S. (2021). Implementing Integrity Assurance System for Big Data. In F. Alyami & S. Almutairi, Wireless Personal Communications (Vol. 122, Issue 3, p. 2585). Springer Science+Business Media. DOI: 10.21203/rs.3.rs-485987/v1

Amazon Türkiye. (2024). Amazon global selling Türkiye raporu 2024. Amazon.com.tr. https://www.amazon.com.tr

Ambrosini, V., Bowman, C., & Collier, N. (2009). Dynamic capabilities: An exploration of how firms renew their resource base. *British Journal of Management, 20*(s1), S9–S24. DOI: 10.1111/j.1467-8551.2008.00610.x

Anand, N., Agrawala, P., & Das, D. (2024). *Blockchain & Cryptocurrency Laws and Regulations 2024*. Global Legal Insights. https://www.globallegalinsights.com/practice-areas/blockchain-laws-and-regulations/india/

Ananthesh, R. N. K. (2021, June 17). Cryptocurrency in India- Regulatory Challenges and the way forward. *Manupatra*. https://articles.manupatra.com/article-details/Cryptocurrency-in-India-Regulatory-Challenges-and-the-way-forward

Andersen, E. (2023). *Digital technology on financial performance.* BI Norwegian Business School, Master Thesis.

Andrejevic, M. (2022). Meta-surveillance in the digital enclosure. *Surveillance & Society*, *20*(4), 390–396. DOI: 10.24908/ss.v20i4.16008

Antonio De Almeida, M., Barbosa, C., Moreira, J., Souza, D., & Schneider, D. (n.d.). AI and Digital Nomads: Glimpsing the Future Human-Computer Interaction AI and Digital Nomads: Glimpsing the Future Human-Computer Interaction.

Antonioli, D., & Mazzanti, M. (2017). Towards a green economy through innovations: The role of trade union involvement. *Ecological Economics*, *131*, 286–299. DOI: 10.1016/j.ecolecon.2016.09.003

Archer, M. (1995). Realist Social Theory: The Morphogenetic Approach. Cambridge University Press. , ISBN-13.DOI: 10.1017/CBO9780511557675

Arellano, M. (2003). *Panel data econometrics*. Oxford University Press. DOI: 10.1093/0199245282.001.0001

Arellano, M., & Bond, S. (1991). Some tests of specification for panel data: Monte Carlo evidence and an application to employment equations. *The Review of Economic Studies*, *58*(2), 277–297. DOI: 10.2307/2297968

Armstrong, M. (2020). *Armstrong's handbook of performance management: An evidence-based guide to delivering high performance* (6th ed.). Kogan Page.

Arokodare, & Asikhia. (2020). Strategic agility: Achieving superior organizational performance through strategic foresight. Global Journal of Management and Business Research, 7–16. DOI: 10.34257/GJMBRAVOL20IS3PG7

Aroles, J., Bonneau, C., & Bhankaraully, S. (2022). Conceptualising "Meta-Work" in the Context of Continuous, Global Mobility: The Case of Digital Nomadism. *Work, Employment and Society*, *37*(5), 1261–1278. DOI: 10.1177/09500170211069797

Arshad, A., Ghaffar, A., Siddqiue, M. U., & Rehman, A. (2024). The Role of IT Infrastructure in Enabling Remote Work: Productivity and Employee Satisfaction. *Journal of Excellence in Social Sciences*, *3*(1). Advance online publication. DOI: 10.69565/jess.v3i1.194

Asbeetah, Z., Alzubi, A., Khadem, A., & Iyiola, K. (2025). Harnessing Digital Transformation for Sustainable Performance: Exploring the Mediating Roles of Green Knowledge Acquisition and Innovation Performance Under Digital Transformational Leadership. *Sustainability (Basel), 17*(5), 2285. DOI: 10.3390/su17052285

Asian Development Bank (ADB), & World Trade Organization (WTO). (2021). Global value chain development report 2021: Beyond production. Asian Development Bank & WTO. https://www.adb.org/publications/global-value-chain-development-report-2021

Aslam, M. R. (2023, July 26). *3 legal and regulatory challenges surrounding the use of cryptocurrencies*. The Economic Times. https://economictimes.indiatimes.com/markets/cryptocurrency/3-legal-and-regulatory-challenges-surrounding-the-use-of-cryptocurrencies/articleshow/102137752.cms?from=mdr

Association of Certified Fraud Examiners. (2022). *Occupational Fraud 2022: A Report to the Nations*. ACFE.

Aston, M., McCombie, S., Reardon, B., & Watters, P. (2009, July). A preliminary profiling of Internet money mules: An Australian perspective. In Symposia and Workshops on Ubiquitous, Autonomic and Trusted Computing (UIC-ATC '09) (pp. 482–487). IEEE. DOI: 10.1109/UIC-ATC.2009.63

Auer, C., Dolfi, M., de Carvalho, A. C. P. L. F., Ramis, C. B., & Staar, P. (2022). *Delivering Document Conversion as a Cloud Service with High Throughput and Responsiveness*., DOI: 10.1109/CLOUD55607.2022.00060

Aujoulat, I., d'Hoore, W., & Deccache, A. (2007). Patient empowerment in theory and practice: Polysemy or cacophony? *Patient Education and Counseling, 66*(1), 13–20. DOI: 10.1016/j.pec.2006.09.008 PMID: 17084059

Azeroual, O. (2020). Data Wrangling in Database Systems: Purging of Dirty Data. In O. Azeroual, Data (Vol. 5, Issue 2, p. 50). Multidisciplinary Digital Publishing Institute. DOI: 10.3390/data5020050

Badr, J., Motulsky, A., & Denis, J. L. (2024). Digital health technologies and inequalities: A scoping review of potential impacts and policy recommendations. *Health Policy (Amsterdam), 146*, 105122. Advance online publication. DOI: 10.1016/j.healthpol.2024.105122 PMID: 38986333

Bag, S., Gupta, S., & Kumar, S. (2021). Industry 4.0 adoption and 10R advance manufacturing capabilities for sustainable development. *International Journal of Production Economics, 231*, 107844. DOI: 10.1016/j.ijpe.2020.107844

Baldwin, R. (2016). *The great convergence: Information technology and the new globalization*. Harvard University Press. DOI: 10.2307/j.ctv24w655w

Bang, J. H., & Suslick, K. S. (2010). Applications of ultrasound to the synthesis of nanostructured materials. *Advanced Materials, 22*(10), 1039–1059. DOI: 10.1002/adma.200904093 PMID: 20401929

Bank Negara Malaysia. (2024). Annual Report 2023. https://www.bnm.gov.my/ar2023

Bansal, P., Kim, A., & Wood, M. O. (2018). Hidden in plain sight: The importance of scale in organizations' attention to issues. *Academy of Management Review, 43*(2), 217–241. DOI: 10.5465/amr.2014.0238

Baral, G., & Arachchilage, N. A. G. (2018). Building Confidence not to be Phished through a Gamified Approach: Conceptualising User's Self-Efficacy in Phishing Threat Avoidance Behaviour. arXiv

Barja-Martinez, S., Aragüés-Peñalba, M., Munné-Collado, Í., Lloret-Gallego, P., Bullich-Massagué, E., & Villafafila-Robles, R. (2021). Artificial intelligence techniques for enabling Big Data services in distribution networks: A review. *Renewable & Sustainable Energy Reviews, 150*, 111459–111459. DOI: 10.1016/j.rser.2021.111459

Barney, J. (1991). Firm resources and sustained competitive advantage. *Journal of Management, 17*(1), 99–120. DOI: 10.1177/014920639101700108

Barrientos, S., Gereffi, G., & Rossi, A. (2011). Economic and social upgrading in global production networks: A new paradigm for a changing world. *International Labour Review, 150*(3–4), 319–340. DOI: 10.1111/j.1564-913X.2011.00119.x

Batool, A., Zowghi, D., & Bano, M. (2025). AI governance: A systematic literature review. *AI and Ethics, 5*(1), 3265–3279. DOI: 10.1007/s43681-024-00653-w

Batool, H. (2024). Influence of distributed leadership on employee innovative behaviour: The mediating role of psychological empowerment. *Journal of Innovation and Entrepreneurship, 13*(1), 82. DOI: 10.1186/s13731-024-00448-7

Baydakova, A. (2023, June 27). *Wyoming: Regulatory Clarity and Crypto-Friendly Banks Fuel Blockchain Revolution*. Retrieved October 20, 2024, from CoinDesk: https://www.coindesk.com/consensus-magazine/2023/06/27/wyoming-regulatory-clarity-and-crypto-friendly-banks-fuel-blockchain-revolution/

Behi, M., Sajjadi, M., & Ghanbari, D. (2021). Green synthesis of TiO_2 nanoparticles using medicinal plants: A review. *Ceramics International, 47*(3), 2879–2895. DOI: 10.1016/j.ceramint.2020.09.177

Belenguer, L. (2022). AI bias: Exploring discriminatory algorithmic decision-making models and the application of possible machine-centric solutions adapted from the pharmaceutical industry. *AI and Ethics*, *2*(4), 771–787. DOI: 10.1007/s43681-022-00138-8 PMID: 35194591

Belhadi, A., Venkatesh, M., Kamble, S., & Abedin, M. Z. (2024). Data-driven digital transformation for supply chain carbon neutrality: Insights from cross-sector supply chain. *International Journal of Production Economics*, *270*, 109178. DOI: 10.1016/j.ijpe.2024.109178

Benda, N. C., Veinot, T. C., Sieck, C. J., & Ancker, J. S. (2020). Broadband Internet Access Is a Social Determinant of Health! *American Journal of Public Health*, *110*(8), 1123–1125. DOI: 10.2105/AJPH.2020.305784 PMID: 32639914

Ben-Daya, M., Hassini, E., & Bahroun, Z. (2019). Internet of Things and supply chain management: A literature review. *International Journal of Production Research*, *57*(15–16), 4719–4742. DOI: 10.1080/00207543.2017.1402140

Benjamin, R. (2019). *Race after technology: Abolitionist tools for the New Jim Code*. Polity. https://www.politybooks.com/bookdetail?book_slug=race-after-technology-abolitionist-tools-for-the-new-jim-code--9781509526390

Bersin, J. (2020). Employee experience: The definitive guide. Josh Bersin Academy. https://joshbersin.com

Bhaskar, R. (1975). *A realist theory of science*. Leeds Books. DOI: 10.4324/9780203090732

Bhaskar, R. (1998). *The possibility of naturalism: A philosophical critique of the contemporary human sciences* (3rd ed.). Routledge. https://books.google.com.tr/books/about/The_Possibility_of_Naturalism.html?id=6OqXjiouAZYC&redir_esc=y

Bhattacharya, C. B., Sen, S., Edinger-Schons, L. M., & Neureiter, M. (2023). Corporate purpose and employee sustainability behaviors. *Journal of Business Ethics*, *183*(4), 963–981. DOI: 10.1007/s10551-022-05090-5

Bibri, S. E. (2021). The core academic and scientific disciplines underlying data-driven smart sustainable urbanism: An interdisciplinary and transdisciplinary framework. *Computational Urban Science*, *1*(1), 1–32. DOI: 10.1007/s43762-021-00001-2

Bican, P. M., & Brem, A. (2020). Digital Business Model, Digital Transformation, Digital Entrepreneurship: Is There a Sustainable "Digital"? *Sustainability (Basel)*, *12*(13), 5239. DOI: 10.3390/su12135239

Bilecka, I., & Niederberger, M. (2010). Microwave chemistry for inorganic nanomaterials synthesis. *Nanoscale*, *2*(8), 1358–1374. DOI: 10.1039/b9nr00377k PMID: 20845524

Birkel, H., & Müller, J. M. (2021). Potentials of Industry 4.0 for supply chain management within the triple bottom line of sustainability: A systematic literature review. *Journal of Cleaner Production*, *289*, 125612. DOI: 10.1016/j.jclepro.2020.125612

Bisarya, S. B., Shukla, A., & Kumar, S. (2023). Data Preparation in Context of Social Sciences Research. In S. S. B. -, A. S. -, & S. K. -, International Journal For Multidisciplinary Research (Vol. 5, Issue 3). DOI: 10.36948/ijfmr.2023.v05i03.3937

Biswas, A., Kumar, A., Jajoo, A., & Sehgal, A. (2023, October 30). *Cryptocurrency trading Subject to Anti-Money Laundering Laws*. Retrieved October 20, 2024, from Lexology: https://www.lexology.com/library/detail.aspx?g=0e6e9a42-fb65-4a69-9b09-38c405a3bda0

Blandford, A., Wesson, J., Amalberti, R., AlHazme, R., & Allwihan, R. (2020). Opportunities and challenges for telehealth within, and beyond, a pandemic. *The Lancet. Global Health*, *8*(11), e1364–e1365. DOI: 10.1016/S2214-109X(20)30362-4 PMID: 32791119

Blessinger, P. (2024, October 13). Human creativity as a renewable resource. Dr. Patrick Blessinger. https://www.patrickblessinger.com/human-creativity-as-a-renewable-resource/

Bloomberg. (2021, June 01). *Can a cryptocurrency break the buck?* Retrieved October 20, 2024, from Mint: https://www.livemint.com/opinion/online-views/can-a-cryptocurrency-break-the-buck-11622504970042.html

Blundell, R., & Bond, S. (1998). Initial conditions and moment restrictions in dynamic panel data models. *Journal of Econometrics*, *87*(1), 115–143. DOI: 10.1016/S0304-4076(98)00009-8

Boaks, J. (2025). Ethics in management: Business and the professions. Emerald Publishing. https://www.emerald.com/books/edited-volume/17354/Ethics-in-Management-Business-and-the-Professions?redirectedFrom=PDF

Boes, K., Buhalis, D., & Inversini, A. (2016). Smart tourism destinations: Ecosystems for tourism destination competitiveness. *International Journal of Tourism Cities*, *2*(2), 108–124. DOI: 10.1108/IJTC-12-2015-0032

Boldosova, V., & Luoto, S. (2019). Storytelling, business analytics and big data interpretation. In V. Boldosova & S. Luoto, Management Research Review (Vol. 43, Issue 2, p. 204). Emerald Publishing Limited. DOI: 10.1108/MRR-03-2019-0106

Boman, M., & Heger, T. (2019). Circles of impression: External foresight in global enterprises. In *Futures Thinking and Organizational Policy* (pp. 179–199). Springer International Publishing., DOI: 10.1007/978-3-319-94923-9_9

Borgatti, S. P., & Li, X. (2009). On social network analysis in a supply chain context. *The Journal of Supply Chain Management, 45*(2), 5–22. DOI: 10.1111/j.1745-493X.2009.03166.x

Boudreau, J. W., & Jesuthasan, R. (2020). Reimagining talent management for the digital age. *MIT Sloan Management Review.* https://sloanreview.mit.edu/article/reimagining-talent-management-for-the-digital-age/

Boudreau, J. W., & Jesuthasan, R. (2020). *Lead the work: Navigating a world beyond employment.* Wiley.

Bourdieu, P. (1984). *Distinction: A Social Critique of the Judgement of Taste.* Harvard University Press.

Bouwman, H., Nikou, S., Molina-Castillo, F. J., & de Reuver, M. (2018). The impact of digitalization on business models. *Digital Policy. Regulation & Governance, 20*(2), 105–124.

Brinch, M., Gunasekaran, A., & Wamba, S. F. (2021). Firm-level capabilities towards big data value creation. *Journal of Business Research, 131*, 539–548. DOI: 10.1016/j.jbusres.2020.07.036

Brinker, C. J., & Scherer, G. W. (1990). *Sol-gel science: The physics and chemistry of sol-gel processing.* Academic Press.

Brock, J. M., & von Wangenheim, F. (2021). Demystifying AI: What digital transformation leaders can teach you about realistic AI adoption. *Business Horizons, 64*(6), 709–720. DOI: 10.1177/1536504219865226

Brown, T. (2008). Design thinking. *Harvard Business Review, 86*(6), 84. PMID: 18605031

Bucher, A. (2023). The Patient Experience of the Future is Personalized: Using Technology to Scale an N of 1 Approach. In A. Bucher, Journal of Patient Experience (Vol. 10, p. 237437352311679). SAGE Publishing. DOI: 10.1177/23743735231167975

Bughin, J., & van Zeebroeck, N. (2017). The best response to digital disruption. *MIT Sloan Management Review.* https://sloanreview.mit.edu/article/the–right–response–to–digital–disruption/

Buhalis, D. (2020). Technology in tourism: From information communication technologies to eTourism and smart tourism towards ambient intelligence tourism: A perspective article. *Tourism Review*, *75*(1), 267–272. DOI: 10.1108/TR-06-2019-0258

Buhalis, D., & Amaranggana, A. (2015). Smart tourism destinations: Enhancing tourism experience through personalisation of services. In Tussyadiah, I., & Inversini, A. (Eds.), *Information and communication technologies in tourism 2015* (pp. 377–389). Springer., DOI: 10.1007/978-3-319-14343-9_28

Buhalis, D., & Law, R. (2008). Progress in information technology and tourism management: 20 years on and 10 years after the Internet—The state of eTourism research. *Tourism Management*, *29*(4), 609–623. DOI: 10.1016/j.tourman.2008.01.005

Buhalis, D., & Michopoulou, E. (2013). Accessibility: A key objective for the tourism industry. *Information and Communication Technologies in Tourism*, *2013*, 317–327. DOI: 10.1007/978-3-642-36309-2_27

Burkhard, R., Deletić, A. B., & Craig, A. (2000). Techniques for wastewater management and reuse. *Water Science and Technology*, *42*(5–6), 65–72.

Butler, K. T., Davies, D. W., Cartwright, H., Isayev, O., & Walsh, A. (2018). Machine learning for molecular and materials science. *Nature*, *559*(7715), 547–555. DOI: 10.1038/s41586-018-0337-2 PMID: 30046072

Byrappa, K., & Yoshimura, M. (2001). *Handbook of Hydrothermal Technology*. William Andrew Publishing.

Cai, H., Wang, Z., Ji, Y., & Xu, L. (2024). Digitalization and innovation: How does the digital economy drive technology transfer in China? *Economic Modelling*, *136*, 106758. Advance online publication. DOI: 10.1016/j.econmod.2024.106758

Campos-Castillo, C., & Anthony, D. L. (2021). Racial and ethnic differences in telehealth use during the COVID-19 pandemic: A cross-sectional analysis of a large U.S. health system. *Journal of the American Medical Informatics Association : JAMIA*, *28*(1), 119–123. DOI: 10.1093/jamia/ocaa221 PMID: 32894772

Cancinoa, C., Amirbagheri, K., Merigo, J., & Dessouky, Y. (2019). A bibliometric analysis of supply chain analytical techniques published in Computers & Industrial Engineering. *Computers & Industrial Engineering*, *137*, 106015. DOI: 10.1016/j.cie.2019.106015

Cao, S., Zeng, Y., Yang, S., & Cao, S. (2021). Research on Python Data Visualization Technology. In S. Cao, Y. Zeng, S. Yang, & S. Cao, Journal of Physics Conference Series (Vol. 1757, Issue 1, p. 12122). IOP Publishing. DOI: 10.1088/1742-6596/1757/1/012122

Cao, Z. (2024a). Challenges and opportunities of the digital economy for sustainable development. Advances in Economics. *Management and Political Sciences*, *76*(1), 1–7. DOI: 10.54254/2754-1169/76/20241869

Capek, I. (2004). Preparation of metal nanoparticles in water-in-oil (w/o) microemulsions. *Advances in Colloid and Interface Science*, *110*(1–2), 49–74. DOI: 10.1016/j.cis.2004.02.003 PMID: 15142823

CEPR. (2023). Global value chain transformation to 2030: Overall direction and policy implications. Centre for Economic Policy Research. https://cepr.org

Chadha, P., Gera, R., Awasthi, S., Yadav, A., Kansal, L., Kumar, A. V., Saxena, A. K., & Parashar, K. (2024). Unlocking sustainable tourism: A holistic examination of mobile applications' impact and evolution in travel experiences (2013-2023). *E3S Web of Conferences, 511*, 01029. https://doi.org/DOI: 10.1051/e3sconf/202451101029

Chang, I.-S., Le Clech, P., Jefferson, B., & Judd, S. (2002). Membrane fouling in membrane bioreactors for wastewater treatment. *Journal of Environmental Engineering, 128*(11), 1018–1029. DOI: 10.1061/(ASCE)0733-9372(2002)128:11(1018)

Charfeddine, L., & Umlai, M. (2023). ICT sector, digitization and environmental sustainability: A systematic review of the literature from 2000 to 2022. *Renewable & Sustainable Energy Reviews, 184*, 113482. DOI: 10.1016/j.rser.2023.113482

Chartered Institute of Personnel and Development (CIPD). (2021). *People profession 2021: Insights into HR practices in the digital age.* https://www.cipd.org/uk/knowledge/reports/people-profession-2021/

Chartered Institute of Personnel and Development (CIPD). (2022). *People profession 2022: International insights on people practice.* https://www.cipd.org/uk/knowledge/reports/people-profession-international-insights/

Chatzimparmpas, A., Kucher, K., & Kerren, A. (2024). Visualization for Trust in Machine Learning Revisited: The State of the Field in 2023. In A. Chatzimparmpas, K. Kucher, & A. Kerren, IEEE Computer Graphics and Applications (Vol. 44, Issue 3, p. 99). Institute of Electrical and Electronics Engineers. DOI: 10.1109/MCG.2024.3360881

Chaudhary, R., Nawaz, M. H., & Chauhan, N. (2014). Ultrasound-assisted synthesis of silver nanoparticles and their antimicrobial activity. *Journal of Nanoscience and Nanotechnology*, *14*(4), 3334–3340. DOI: 10.1166/jnn.2014.8502

Checkland, P. B. (1988). Information systems and systems thinking: Time to unite? *International Journal of Information Management*, *8*(4), 239–248. DOI: 10.1016/0268-4012(88)90031-X

Chem, O. S. *Autonomous experimentation platform*. Retrieved from https://chemos.io

Chen, X., Östlund, B., & Frennert, S. (2020). Digital Inclusion or Digital Divide for Older Immigrants? A Scoping Review. *Lecture Notes in Computer Science (Including Subseries Lecture Notes in Artificial Intelligence and Lecture Notes in Bioinformatics), 12209 LNCS*, 176–190. DOI: 10.1007/978-3-030-50232-4_13

Chen, C. T., Khan, A., & Chen, S. C. (2024). Modeling the impact of big data analytics–artificial intelligence (BDA–AI) on sustainable innovation ambidexterity and environmental performance. *Journal of Big Data*, *11*(1), 124. DOI: 10.1186/s40537-024-00995-6

Cheng, C.-Y. (2023). A novel approach of information visualization for machine operation states in industrial 4.0. https://www.sciencedirect.com/science/article/pii/S0360835218302316

Chen, L., & Tan, J. (2024). Does the COVID-19 pandemic exacerbate the disincentive effect of trade tariffs on global value chains (GVCs) embeddedness? *Economic Analysis and Policy*, *83*, 404–420. DOI: 10.1016/j.eap.2024.04.033

Chen, R. J., Wang, J. J., Williamson, D. F., Chen, T. Y., Lipkova, J., Lu, M. Y., Sahai, S., & Mahmood, F. (2023). Algorithmic fairness in artificial intelligence for medicine and healthcare. *Nature Biomedical Engineering*, *7*(6), 719–742. DOI: 10.1038/s41551-023-01056-8 PMID: 37380750

Chen, S., Carroll, D. L., & Wang, G. (2000). Silver nanoplates: A microemulsion-based synthesis and optical properties. *The Journal of Physical Chemistry. B*, *104*(44), 10288–10293. DOI: 10.1021/jp002613t

Cherkasova, V. A., & Slepushenko, G. A. (2021). The impact of digitalization on the financial performance of Russian companies. *Finance: Theory and Practice*, *25*(2), 128–142.

Chien, F., Anwar, A., Hsu, C.-C., Sharif, A., Razzaq, A., & Sinha, A. (2021). The role of information and communication technology in encountering environmental degradation: Proposing an SDG framework for the BRICS countries. *Technology in Society*, *65*, 101587. DOI: 10.1016/j.techsoc.2021.101587

Chin, H.-S., Marasini, D. P., & Lee, D.-H. (2023). Digital transformation trends in service industries. *Service Business*, *17*(1), 11–36. DOI: 10.1007/s11628-022-00516-6

Chiwaridzo, O. T., & Masengu, R. (2025). Rebuilding sustainable green tourism supply chain through technology adoption and social media branding in Zimbabwe post-COVID-19. *Environment, Development and Sustainability*, *27*(8), 18105–18128. DOI: 10.1007/s10668-024-04718-y

Choi, T. M., Wallace, S. W., & Wang, Y. (2020). Big data analytics in operations management. *Production and Operations Management, 29*(5), 1024–1031. DOI: 10.1111/poms.13122

Choo, Y. B., Yoke, S. K., & Ismail, N. H. (2022). A Systematic Literature Review on the Use of Digital Media among Malaysian Teachers and Students During the COVID-19 Pandemic. *International Journal of Academic Research in Progressive Education and Development, 11*(2). Advance online publication. DOI: 10.6007/IJARPED/v11-i2/14130

Chouliaraki, L., & Fairclough, N. (1999). *Discourse in late modernity*. Edinburgh University Press. https://edinburghuniversitypress.com/book-discourse-in-late-modernity.html

Christopher, M. L. (1992). *Logistics and supply chain management.* Pitman Publishing.

Christozov, D., & Rasheva-Yordanova, K. (2023). Data Literacy: Developing Skills on Exploring Big Data Applications. https://www.igi-global.com/gateway/article/191259

Chui, M., Manyika, J., & Miremadi, M. (2018). Notes from the AI frontier: Applications and value of deep learning. McKinsey Global Institute. Retrieved on November 10,2025. https://www.mckinsey.com

Cibin, K. (n.d.). Regulation of cryptocurrency in India tackling money laundering and cross-border terrorism: a comparative analysis with the EU mica act. *Indian Journal of Law and Legal Research, 6*(2), 2955-2968. Retrieved October 20, 2024, from https://3fdef50c-add3-4615-a675-a91741bcb5c0.usrfiles.com/ugd/3fdef5_58ee16f8c66b4fb6807b29691bd402db.pdf

Cicek, N. (2003). A review of membrane bioreactors and their potential application in the treatment of agricultural wastewater. Canadian Biosystems Engineering, 45, 6.37–6.49.

Cicek, N. (2006). A review of membrane bioreactors and their potential for landfill leachate treatment. *Journal of Environmental Management, 82*(3), 275–290. PMID: 16137820

Cisco. (2023). *Designing energy-efficient products.* In The Plan for Possible — ESG report. https://blogs.cisco.com/our-corporate-purpose/designing-energy-efficient-products

Closs, D. J., Speier, C., & Meacham, N. (2011). Sustainability to support end-to-end value chains: The role of supply chain management. *Journal of the Academy of Marketing Science, 39*(1), 101–116. DOI: 10.1007/s11747-010-0207-4

Cohen, D., Lindvall, M., & Costa, P. (2004). An introduction to agile methods. *Advances in Computers*, *62*(3), 1–66.

Colquitt, J. A., Lepine, J. A., & Wesson, M. J. (2013). *Organizational behavior: Improving performance and commitment in the workplace* (3rd ed.). McGraw-Hill.

Cosa, M., & Torelli, R. (2024). Digital transformation and flexible performance management: A systematic literature review of the evolution of performance measurement systems. *Global Journal of Flexible Systems Managment*, *25*(3), 445–466. DOI: 10.1007/s40171-024-00409-9

Coşkun, A. G. (2004). Elektronik ticaretin gelişiminde temel dinamikler ve gelişimi önündeki engeller. *Çukurova Üniversitesi Sosyal Bilimler Enstitüsü Dergisi*, 243-258.

Costa, P., & Rodrigues, H. (2024). The ever-changing business of e-commerce-net benefits while designing a new platform for small companies. *Review of Managerial Science*, *18*(9), 2507–2545. DOI: 10.1007/s11846-023-00681-6

Côté, P.-O., Nikanjam, A., Ahmed, N., Humeniuk, D., & Khomh, F. (2024). Data cleaning and machine learning: a systematic literature review. In P.-O. Côté, A. Nikanjam, N. Ahmed, D. Humeniuk, & F. Khomh, Automated Software Engineering (Vol. 31, Issue 2). Springer Science+Business Media. DOI: 10.1007/s10515-024-00453-w

Couldry, N., & Mejias, U. A. (2019). The costs of connection: How data is colonizing human life and appropriating it for capitalism. In *The costs of connection*. Stanford University Press.

Couldry, N., & Mejias, U. A. (2019). *The Costs of Connection: How Data Is Colonizing Human Life and Appropriating It for Capitalism*. Stanford University Press.

Craig, S., McPeak, K. E., Madu, C., & Dalembert, G. (2022). Health information technology and equity: Applying history's lessons to tomorrow's innovations. *Current Problems in Pediatric and Adolescent Health Care*, *52*(1), 101110. Advance online publication. DOI: 10.1016/j.cppeds.2021.101110 PMID: 34974991

Criveanu, M. M. (2023). Investigating digital intensity and E-commerce as drivers for sustainability and economic growth in the EU countries. *Electronics (Basel)*, *12*(10), 2318. DOI: 10.3390/electronics12102318

Cubric, M. (2020). Drivers, barriers and social considerations for AI adoption in business and management: A tertiary study. *Technology in Society*, *62*, 101257. DOI: 10.1016/j.techsoc.2020.101257

Curtis, S. K., & Mont, O. (2020). Sharing economy business models for sustainability. *Journal of Cleaner Production, 266*(121519), 121519. DOI: 10.1016/j.jclepro.2020.121519 PMID: 32884181

Curzon, J., Kosa, T. A., Akalu, R., & El-Khatib, K. (2021). Privacy and Artificial Intelligence. *IEEE Transactions on Artificial Intelligence, 2*(2), 96–108. DOI: 10.1109/TAI.2021.3088084

Dahlman, C., Mealy, S., & Wermelinger, M. (2016). *Harnessing the digital economy for developing countries.* OECD Development Centre Working Paper, 334. DOI: DOI: 10.1787/18151949

Daniel, M.-C., & Astruc, D. (2004). Gold nanoparticles: Assembly, supramolecular chemistry, quantum-size-related properties, and applications toward biology, catalysis, and nanotechnology. *Chemical Reviews, 104*(1), 293–346. DOI: 10.1021/cr030698+ PMID: 14719978

Das, R., Singh, A., Kaur, H., Suhag, N., & Roy, K. (2026). Exploring the mediating role of women's participation in the relationship between rural tourism and the commercialisation and preservation of rural culture and natural beauty. *International Research Journal of Multidisciplinary Scope, 7*(1), 1463–1477. DOI: 10.47857/irjms.2026.v07i01.08828

Das, S., Ahmed, N., Al Rahbi, I., Al-Jubori, Y., Al Busaidi, R., Al Harbi, A., Al Tobi, M., & Albalushi, H. (2025). Medical and Biomedical Students' Perspective on Digital Health and Its Integration in Medical Curricula: Recent and Future Views. *International Journal of Environmental Research and Public Health, 22*(8), 1193. DOI: 10.3390/ijerph22081193 PMID: 40869779

Davis, F. D. (1989). Perceived usefulness, perceived ease of use, and user acceptance of information technology. *Management Information Systems Quarterly, 13*(3), 319–340. DOI: 10.2307/249008

Davis, T. C., Hoover, K. W., Keller, S., & Replogle, W. H. (2020). Mississippi Diabetes Telehealth Network: A Collaborative Approach to Chronic Care Management. *Telemedicine Journal and e-Health : The Official Journal of the American Telemedicine Association, 26*(2), 184–189. DOI: 10.1089/tmj.2018.0334 PMID: 30822265

Davronov, A. (2024). Emerging technologies and trends in tourism management for developing countries. *Academic research in modern science.* Retrieved from https://econferences.ru

De la Hoz, A., Cubero, J., Melo, L., Durán-Vinagre, M. A., & Sánchez, S. (2021). Analysis of Digital Literacy in Health through Active University Teaching. *International Journal of Environmental Research and Public Health 2021, Vol. 18, Page 6674, 18*(12), 6674. DOI: 10.3390/ijerph18126674

De Sousa Jabbour, A. B. L., Laguir, I., Stekelorum, R., & Gupta, S. (2025). The nexus of artificial intelligence and sustainability performance: Unveiling the impact of supply chain transparency and customer pressure on ethical conduct. *Journal of Environmental Management, 379*, 124847. DOI: 10.1016/j.jenvman.2025.124847 PMID: 40054355

DeepChem. *Deep learning framework for drug discovery, quantum chemistry, and materials science.* Retrieved from https://deepchem.io

Dejan, D., & Sinisa. (2018). Blockchain technology, bitcoin, and Ethereum: A brief overview. *17th International Symposium INFOTEH-JAHORINA (INFOTEH).* DOI: 10.1109/INFOTEH.2018.8345547

Del Giudice, M., Scuotto, V., Papa, A., Tarba, S. Y., Bresciani, S., & Warkentin, M. (2021). A self-tuning model for smart manufacturing SMEs: Effects on digital innovation. *Journal of Product Innovation Management, 38*(1), 68–89. DOI: 10.1111/jpim.12560

del Pilar Arias López, M., Ong, B. A., Frigola, X. B., Fernández, A. L., Hicklent, R. S., Obeles, A. J. T., & Celi, L. A. (2023). Digital literacy as a new determinant of health: A scoping review. *PLOS Digital Health, 2*(10), e0000279. Advance online publication. DOI: 10.1371/journal.pdig.0000279 PMID: 37824584

del Vasto, P. M. H., & Castro, M. L. A. (2024). Artificial Intelligence (AI) in sustainable tourism: Bibliometric analysis. *Cuadernos de Turismo, 53*(53), 157–185. DOI: 10.6018/turismo.616431

Deloitte. (2021). *2021 Global human capital trends: The social enterprise in a world disrupted.* Deloitte Insights. https://www2.deloitte.com/global/en/pages/human-capital/articles/global-human-capital-trends.html

Deloitte. (2023). *Uncovering the connection between digital maturity and financial performance.* https://www2.deloitte.com/content/dam/insights/us/articles/6561_digital-transformation/DI_Digital-transformation.pdf

DeNisi, A. S., & Murphy, K. R. (2017). Performance appraisal and performance management: 100 years of progress? *The Journal of Applied Psychology, 102*(3), 421–433. DOI: 10.1037/apl0000085 PMID: 28125265

Denning, S. (2018). *The age of agile: How smart companies are transforming the way work gets done.* AMACOM.

Department of Economic Affairs. M. o. (2019). *Report of the Committee to propose specific actions to be taken in relation to virtual currencies.* Economic Affairs. New Delhi: Ministry of Finance. https://dea.gov.in/sites/default/files/Approved%20and%20Signed%20Report%20and%20Bill%20of%20IMC%20on%20VCs%2028%20Feb%202019.pdf

Deshpande, S., Patil, S., Kuchibhatla, S. V. N. T., & Seal, S. (2005). Size dependency variation in lattice parameter and valency states in nanocrystalline cerium oxide. *Applied Physics Letters, 87*(13), 133113. DOI: 10.1063/1.2061873

Dessart, L., & Standaert, W. (2023). Strategic storytelling in the age of sustainability. *Business Horizons, 66*(3), 371–385. DOI: 10.1016/j.bushor.2023.01.005

Devineni, S. (2024). Cite this Article: Siva Karthik Devineni, AI in Data Privacy and Security. [IJAIML]. *International Journal of Artificial Intelligence and Machine Learning, 3*(1), 35–49. DOI: 10.17605/OSF.IO/WCN8A

Dhuheir, M., Erbad, A., & Sabeeh, S. (2023). LLHR: Low Latency and High Reliability CNN Distributed Inference for Resource-Constrained UAV Swarms. In M. Dhuheir, A. Erbad, & S. Sabeeh, 2022 IEEE Wireless Communications and Networking Conference (WCNC). DOI: 10.1109/WCNC55385.2023.10118908

Dialani, P. (2021, June 04). *Future of Cryptocurrency? Will it Grow or Stoop Low?* Analytics Insight. https://www.analyticsinsight.net/cryptocurrency-analytics-insight/future-of-cryptocurrency-will-it-grow-or-stoop-low

DiMaggio, P. J., & Powell, W. W. (1983). The iron cage revisited: Institutional isomorphism and collective rationality in organizational fields. *American Sociological Review, 48*(2), 147–160. DOI: 10.2307/2095101

Dingsøyr, T., Nerur, S., Balijepally, V., & Moe, N. B. (2012). A decade of agile methodologies: Towards explaining agile software development. *Journal of Systems and Software, 85*(6), 1213–1221. DOI: 10.1016/j.jss.2012.02.033

Dobbs, R., Koller, T., Ramaswamy, S., Woetzel, J., Manyika, J., Krishnan, R., & Andreula, N. (2015). *Playing to win: The new global competition for corporate profits.* McKinsey Global Institute.

Donaghy, E., Atherton, H., Hammersley, V., McNeilly, H., Bikker, A., Robbins, L., Campbell, J., & McKinstry, B. (2019). Acceptability, benefits, and challenges of video consulting: A qualitative study in primary care. *The British Journal of General Practice, 69*(686), e586–e594. DOI: 10.3399/bjgp19X704141 PMID: 31160368

Dong, K., Yang, S., & Wang, J. (2023). How digital economy lead to low-carbon development in China? The case of e-commerce city pilot reform. *Journal of Cleaner Production, 391*, 136177. Advance online publication. DOI: 10.1016/j.jclepro.2023.136177

Donthu, N., Kumar, S., Mukherjee, D., Pandey, N., & Lim, W. (2021). How to conduct a bibliometric analysis: An overview and guidelines. *Journal of Business Research, 133*, 285–296. DOI: 10.1016/j.jbusres.2021.04.070

Dreisbach, C., Koleck, T. A., Bourne, P. E., & Bakken, S. (2019). A systematic review of natural language processing and text mining of symptoms from electronic patient-authored text data. *International Journal of Medical Informatics, 125*, 37–46. DOI: 10.1016/j.ijmedinf.2019.02.008 PMID: 30914179

Drucker, P. F. (1999). *Management challenges for the 21st century*. HarperBusiness.

Dubey, R., Gunasekaran, A., Childe, S. J., Blome, C., & Papadopoulos, T. (2019). Big data and predictive analytics and manufacturing performance: Integrating institutional theory, resource-based view and big data culture. *British Journal of Management, 30*(2), 341–361. DOI: 10.1111/1467-8551.12355

Dunning, J. H. (1993). *Multinational enterprises and the global economy*. Addison-Wesley.

Dutta, A., Lee, H., & Yasai-Ardekani, M. (2014). Digital systems and competitive responsiveness: The dynamics of IT business value. *Information & Management, 51*(6), 762–773. DOI: 10.1016/j.im.2014.05.005

Dyer, Z. (2022). The Structural Racism Effect Index: A Multi-Dimensional Tool to Measure Neighborhood-Level Structural Racism. https://hdl.handle.net/20.500.14038/51835

Dyer, J. H., & Singh, H. (1998). The relational view: Cooperative strategy and sources of interorganizational competitive advantage. *Academy of Management Review, 23*(4), 660–679. DOI: 10.2307/259056

Eccles, R. G., & Klimenko, S. (2019). The investor revolution. *Harvard Business Review, 97*(3), 106–116.

Elder-Vass, D. (2010). *The causal power of social structures*. Cambridge University Press. DOI: 10.1017/CBO9780511761720

Elkington, J. (1997). *Cannibals with forks: The triple bottom line of 21st century business*. Capstone Publishing.

El-Nahhal, I. M., Elmanama, A. A., Zourab, S. M., & Safi, M. J. (2021). Green synthesis of silver nanoparticles using orange peel extract and its antibacterial activity. *Materials Chemistry and Physics, 260*, 124168. DOI: 10.1016/j.matchemphys.2020.124168

El-Trass, A., ElShamy, H., El-Mehasseb, I., & El-Kemary, M. (2012). CuO nanoparticles: Synthesis, characterization, optical properties and interaction with amino acids. *Applied Surface Science, 258*(7), 2997–3001. DOI: 10.1016/j.apsusc.2011.11.025

ENISA. (2023). ENISA Threat Landscape 2023. European Union Agency for Cybersecurity. https://www.enisa.europa.eu/publications/enisa-threat-landscape-2023

Eriksen, J., Ebbesen, M., Eriksen, K. T., Hjermitslev, C., Knudsen, C., Bertelsen, P., . . . Weber, D. (2023). Equity in digital healthcare – the case of Denmark. *Frontiers in Public Health, 11*, 1225222. DOI: 10.3389/FPUBH.2023.1225222/BIBTEX

Erturk, A., Colbran, S. E., Coşkun, E., Theofanidis, F., & Abidi, O. (Eds.). (2024). *Convergence of digitalization, innovation, and sustainable development in business.* IGI Global. DOI: 10.4018/979-8-3693-0798-4

Esmaeili, A., Beheshti, A., & Jafari, S. M. (2014). Ultrasound-assisted synthesis of TiO_2 nanoparticles and their use in photocatalysis. *Ultrasonics Sonochemistry, 21*(4), 1460–1465. DOI: 10.1016/j.ultsonch.2013.12.006

Esteban-Navarro, M.-Á., García-Madurga, M.-Á., Morte-Nadal, T., & Nogales-Bocio, A.-I. (2020). The rural digital divide in the face of the COVID-19 pandemic in Europe—recommendations from a scoping review. *Mdpi.Com.* DOI: 10.3390/informatics7040054

European Commission. (2020). *A new Circular Economy Action Plan: For a cleaner and more competitive Europe* (COM(2020) 98 final). https://eur-lex.europa.eu/legal-content/EN/TXT/?uri=CELEX%3A52020DC0098

European Commission. (2020). *Digital Economy and Society Index (DESI) 2020: Human capital.* Publications Office of the European Union. https://digital-strategy.ec.europa.eu/en/library/digital-economy-and-society-index-desi-2020

European Commission. (2021). *European green deal: Striving to be the first climate-neutral continent* (Publication No. NA-02-21-151-EN-N). https://op.europa.eu/publication/manifestation_identifier/PUB_NA0221151ENC

European Commission. (2021). *Proposal for a regulation laying down harmonised rules on artificial intelligence (Artificial Intelligence Act), COM(2021) 206 final.* https://eur-lex.europa.eu/legal-content/EN/TXT/?uri=CELEX:52021PC0206

European Commission. (2021). *Waste electrical and electronic equipment (WEEE)*. European Commission.https://environment.ec.europa.eu/topics/waste-and-recycling/waste-electrical-and-electronic-equipment-weee_en

European Commission. (2022a). Directive (EU) 2022/2464 of the European Parliament and of the Council on corporate sustainability reporting. *Official Journal of the European Union, L, 322*, 15–80.

European Commission. (2022b). *Proposal for a Regulation of the European Parliament and of the Council establishing a framework for setting ecodesign requirements for sustainable products and repealing Directive 2009/125/EC*. COM (2022) 142 final.

European Commission. (2024). *The digitalisation of the energy system: A green, efficient and affordable energy system fit for the future*. Publications Office of the European Union.

European Parliament & Council of the European Union. (2022). *Directive (EU) 2022/2464 on corporate sustainability reporting (Corporate Sustainability Reporting Directive, CSRD)*. OJ L 322, 16 December 2022.

EUROPOL-Public Awareness and Prevention Guides. (2019). *Public Awareness and Prevention Guides*. EUROPOL.

Fairclough, N. (1992). *Discourse and social change*. Polity Press. DOI: 10.1017/S0047404500017309

Fairclough, N. (1995). *Critical discourse analysis: The critical study of language*. Longman.

Fairclough, N. (2001). *Language and power* (2nd ed.). Routledge.

Fairclough, N., Jessop, B., & Sayer, A. (2002). Critical realism and semiosis. *Alethia, 5*(1), 2–10. DOI: 10.1558/aleth.v5i1.2

Fairphone. (2022). *Impact Report 2022*. Fairphone. Retrieved from https://www.fairphone.com/wp-content/uploads/2023/04/Impact-Report-2022.pdf

Fan, X., Wang, Y., & Lu, X. (2022). Digital transformation drives sustainable innovation capability improvement in manufacturing enterprises: Based on FsQCA and NCA approaches. *Sustainability (Basel), 15*(1), 542. DOI: 10.3390/su15010542

Fareed, N., Swoboda, C. M., Chen, S., Potter, E., Wu, D. T. Y., & Sieck, C. J. (2023). U.S. COVID-19 State Government Public Dashboards: An Expert Review. https://www.thieme-connect.de/products/ejournals/abstract/10.1055/s-0041-1723989

Farfán Chilicaus, G. C., Licapa-Redolfo, G. S., Arbulú Ballesteros, M. A., Corrales Otazú, C. D., Apaza Miranda, S. J., Flores Castillo, M. M., Castro Ijiri, G. L., Guzmán Valle, M. D. Á., & Arbulú Castillo, J. C. (2025). Digital transformation and sustainability in post-pandemic supply chains: A global bibliometric analysis of technological evolution and research patterns (2020–2024). *Sustainability (Basel), 17*(7), 3009. DOI: 10.3390/su17073009

Fernandez-Portillo, A., Almodovar-Gonzalez, M., Sanchez-Escobedo, M. C., & Coca-Perez, J. L. (2022). The role of innovation in the relationship between digitalisation and economic and financial performance. A company-level research. *European Research on Management and Business Economics, 28*(3), 100190. DOI: 10.1016/j.iedeen.2021.100190

Fernández-Rovira, C., Valdés, J. Á., Molleví, G., & Nicolas-Sans, R. (2021). The digital transformation of business. Towards the datafication of the relationship with customers. *Technological Forecasting and Social Change, 162*, 120339. DOI: 10.1016/j.techfore.2020.120339

Ferrer-Gomila, J.-L., Hinarejos, M., & Isern-Deyà, A.-P. (2019). A fair contract signing protocol with blockchain support. *Electronic Commerce Research and Applications, 36*, 1567–4223. DOI: 10.1016/j.elerap.2019.100869

Fettweis, G., & Zimmermann, E. (2008). ICT energy consumption—Trends and challenges. In *Proceedings of the 11th International Symposium on Wireless Personal Multimedia Communications (WPMC 2008)* (pp. 6–10). Dresden, Germany.

Fievet, F., Lagier, J. P., Blin, B., Beaudoin, B., & Figlarz, M. (1989). Homogeneous and heterogeneous nucleations in the polyol process for the preparation of micron and sub-micron size metal particles. *Solid State Ionics, 32–33*, 198–205. DOI: 10.1016/0167-2738(89)90222-1

Figueirêdo, R. C. de, Silva, Í. de S., Xavier, P. B., Araújo, A. J. de, Silva, A. J. B. da, Silva, C. R. D. V., … Uchôa, S. A. da C. (2025). Digital Health and Primary Health Care Quality: A Survey Case Study. *International Journal of Environmental Research and Public Health 2025, Vol. 22, Page 1015, 22*(7), 1015. DOI: 10.3390/ijerph22071015

Floridi, L. (2020). The Fight for Digital Sovereignty: What It Is, and Why It Matters, Especially for the EU. *Philosophy & Technology, 33*(3), 369–378. DOI: 10.1007/s13347-020-00423-6 PMID: 35194548

Floridi, L., & Cowls, J. (2019). A unified framework of five principles for AI in society. *Harvard Data Science Review, 1*(1). Advance online publication. DOI: 10.1162/99608f92.8cd550d1

Forti, V., Baldé, C. P., Kuehr, R., & Bel, G. (2020). *The Global E-waste Monitor 2020: Quantities, flows and the circular economy potential.* United Nations University / UNITAR; International Telecommunication Union (ITU); International Solid Waste Association (ISWA).

Freeman, R. E., & Phillips, R. A. (2002). Stakeholder theory: A libertarian defense. *Business Ethics Quarterly*, *12*(3), 331–349. DOI: 10.2307/3858020

Fritz, Z., & Cox, C. L. (2020). Integrating philosophy, policy and practice to create a just and fair health service. *Journal of Medical Ethics*, *46*(12), 797–802. DOI: 10.1136/medethics-2020-106853 PMID: 33028624

Fu, T., & Li, J. (2023). An empirical analysis of the impact of ESG on financial performance: The moderating role of digital transformation. *Frontiers in Environmental Science*, *11*, 1256052. DOI: 10.3389/fenvs.2023.1256052

Gallup. (2021). *State of the global workplace: 2021 report.* Gallup, Inc. https://www.gallup.com/workplace

Ganguly, P. (2018). Role of information and communication technologies (ICTs) in sustainable tourism development in Santiniketan, West Bengal, India. *International Journal of Management Studies, 5*(Special Issue 2), 54–59. https://doi.org/DOI: 10.18843/ijms/v5iS2/07

Ganguly, S. (2022, October 24). *Cryptocurrency Regime in India: The Journey So Far*. Mondaq. https://www.mondaq.com/india/fin-tech/1234600/cryptocurrency-regime-in-india-the-journey-so-far

Gawande, M. B., Goswami, A., Asefa, T., Guo, H., Biradar, A. V., Peng, D.-L., & Zboril, R. (2015). Core–shell nanoparticles: Synthesis and applications in catalysis and electrocatalysis. *Chemical Society Reviews*, *44*(21), 7540–7590. DOI: 10.1039/C5CS00343A PMID: 26288197

GCC HR Summit Report. (2022). *Human capital transformation in the GCC: Trends, tools, and strategies.* [Publisher information missing].

Gebauer, H., Fleisch, E., Lamprecht, C., & Wortmann, F. (2020). Growth paths for overcoming the digitalization paradox. *Business Horizons*, *63*(3), 313–323. DOI: 10.1016/j.bushor.2020.01.005

Gebauer, H., Paiola, M., Saccani, N., & Rapaccini, M. (2021). Digital servitization: Crossing the perspectives of digitization and servitization. *Industrial Marketing Management*, *93*, 382–388. DOI: 10.1016/j.indmarman.2020.05.011

Gedik, Y. (2021). E-Ticaret: Teorik Bir Çerçeve. *Ankara Üniversitesi Sosyal Bilimler Dergisi, 12*(1), 184–198. DOI: 10.33537/sobild.2021.12.1.16

General Secretariat of the Supreme Council for Planning and Development. (2019). *Kuwait Vision 2035: New Kuwait.* Government of Kuwait. https://www.newkuwait.gov.kw

General Secretariat of the Supreme Council for Planning and Development. (2020). *Kuwait Vision 2035: New Kuwait.* Government of Kuwait. https://www.newkuwait.gov.kw

George, A. S. (2024). The metamorphosis of work: How technology is transforming the employee experience from industrial to digital. *Partners Universal Innovative Research Publication, 2*(1), 93–112.

George, G., Merrill, R. K., & Schillebeeckx, S. J. D. (2021). Digital sustainability and entrepreneurship: How digital innovations are helping tackle climate change and sustainable development. *Entrepreneurship Theory and Practice, 45*(5), 999–1027. DOI: 10.1177/1042258719899425

Gereffi, G. (1999). International trade and industrial upgrading in the apparel commodity chain. *Journal of International Economics, 48*(1), 37–70. DOI: 10.1016/S0022-1996(98)00075-0

Gereffi, G., & Fernandez-Stark, K. (2018). Global value chain analysis: A primer. In Gereffi, G. (Ed.), *Global value chains and development: Redefining the contours of 21st century capitalism* (2nd ed., pp. 305–342). Cambridge University Press.

Ghobakhloo, M. (2020). Industry 4.0, digitization, and opportunities for sustainability. *Journal of Cleaner Production, 252*, 119869. DOI: 10.1016/j.jclepro.2019.119869

Girme, D. A., & Ray, A. (n.d.). The Anatomy of Money Laundering. *Indian Journal of Law and Legal Research, V*(2), 1-13. Retrieved October 2024, 2024, from https://3fdef50c-add3-4615-a675-a91741bcb5c0.usrfiles.com/ugd/3fdef5_6b61d9108b234a549f87b5a99226a17c.pdf

Gjellebæk, C., Svensson, A., Bjørkquist, C., Fladeby, N., & Grundén, K. (2020). Management challenges for future digitalization of healthcare services. *Futures, 124*, 102636. Advance online publication. DOI: 10.1016/j.futures.2020.102636

Goetschalckx, M. (2011). *Supply chain engineering.* Springer.

González-González, R. B., Galindo-Hernández, F., & García-Valenzuela, M. (2012). Synthesis of ZnO nanoparticles by sonochemical method and their optical properties. *Materials Letters, 68*, 51–53. DOI: 10.1016/j.matlet.2011.10.077

Google. (2020). Our data centers now work harder when the sun shines and wind blows. *Google Blog*. https://blog.google/inside-google/infrastructure/data-centers-work-harder-sun-shines-wind-blows

Gössling, S., Hall, C. M., & Scott, D. (2019). The decarbonisation impasse: Global tourism leaders' views on climate change mitigation. *Journal of Sustainable Tourism, 27*(6), 899–908.

Goswami, P., & Sharma, A. (2023). Realtime analysis and visualization of data for instant decisions: A futuristic requirement of the digital world. https://www.sciencedirect.com/science/article/pii/S221478532101275X

Government of Kuwait. (2023). *Kuwait digital transformation strategy 2023–2035*. Ministry of Communications and Information Technology.

Gowda, N., & Chakravorty, C. (2021, August). Comparative Study on Cryptocurrency Transaction and Banking Transaction. *Global Transitions Proceedings, 2*(2), 530–534. Advance online publication. DOI: 10.1016/j.gltp.2021.08.064

Grand View Research. (2025). Retrieved from E-commerce Market (2024 - 2030): https://www.grandviewresearch.com/industry-analysis/e-commerce-market

Greenhalgh, T., Hinton, L., Finlay, T., Macfarlane, A., Fahy, N., Clyde, B., & Chant, A. (2019). Frameworks for supporting patient and public involvement in research: Systematic review and co-design pilot. *Health Expectations : An International Journal of Public Participation in Health Care and Health Policy, 22*(4), 785–801. DOI: 10.1111/hex.12888 PMID: 31012259

Green, P. (2020). Disruptions of self, place and mobility: Digital nomads in Chiang Mai, Thailand. *Mobilities, 15*(3), 431–445. DOI: 10.1080/17450101.2020.1723253

Gretzel, U., Sigala, M., Xiang, Z., & Koo, C. (2015). Smart tourism: Foundations and developments. *Electronic Markets, 25*(3), 179–188. DOI: 10.1007/s12525 015-0196-8

Grybauskas, A., Stefanini, A., & Ghobakhloo, M. (2022). Social sustainability in the age of digitalization: A systematic literature Review on the social implications of industry 4.0. *Technology in Society, 70*, 101997. DOI: 10.1016/j.techsoc.2022.101997

Guandalini, I. (2022). Sustainability through digital transformation: A systematic literature review for research guidance. *Journal of Business Research, 148*, 456–471. DOI: 10.1016/j.jbusres.2022.05.003

Guo, L., & Xu, L. (2021). The effects of digital transformation on firm performance: Evidence from China's manufacturing sector. *Sustainability (Basel), 13*(22), 12844. DOI: 10.3390/su132212844

Gupta, S., Jaiswal, R., & Gupta, S. K. (2024). Digital nomads: A systematic literature review and future research agenda. *Tourism Review*. Advance online publication. DOI: 10.1108/TR-12-2023-0869

Gupta, V. K., Ali, I., Saleh, T. A., Nayak, A., & Agarwal, S. (2012). Chemical treatment technologies for waste-water recycling—An overview. *RSC Advances, 2*(16), 6380–6388. DOI: 10.1039/c2ra20340e

Gurbaxani, V., & Dunkle, D. (2019). Gearing up for successful digital transformation. *MIS Quarterly Executive*, *18*(3), 6. DOI: 10.17705/2msqe.00017

Guru, T. (2024, July 02). *Using crypto-currencies for money laundering*. Retrieved October 20, 2024, from Tax Guru: https://taxguru.in/finance/crypto-currencies-money-laundering.html

Gururaj, B. (2005). Commentaries on FEMA. Money Laundering Act and COFEPOSA., Retrieved October 19, 2024, from.

Guttentag, D. A. (2010). Virtual reality: Applications and implications for tourism. *Tourism Management, 31*(5), 637–651. DOI: 10.1016/j.tourman.2009.07.003

Ha, S., & Kim, S. (2023). Developing a digital platform literacy framework. Econstor. https://www.econstor.eu/bitstream/10419/277969/1/Ha-Kim.pdf

Haans, R. F., Pieters, C., & He, Z. L. (2016). Thinking about U: Theorizing and testing U-and inverted U-shaped relationships in strategy research. *Strategic Management Journal, 37*(7), 1177–1195. DOI: 10.1002/smj.2399

Haefner, N., Parida, V., Gassmann, O., & Wincent, J. (2023). Implementing and scaling artificial intelligence: A review, framework, and research agenda. *Technological Forecasting and Social Change*, *197*, 122878–122878. DOI: 10.1016/j.techfore.2023.122878

Hamroqulovna, H. S.Associate Professor Finnish Pedagogical Institute of Uzbekistan PhD Uzbekistan. (2025). Competencies developed in students through foresight methods. *European International Journal of Pedagogics*, *5*(8), 35–37. DOI: 10.55640/eijp-05-08-08

Han, S., & Kwak, I. (2023). Mastering data visualization with Python: practical tips for researchers. In S. Han & I. Kwak, Daehan nae'si'gyeong bog'gang'gyeong oe'gwa haghoeji/Journal of minimally invasive surgery (Vol. 26, Issue 4, p. 167). DOI: 10.7602/jmis.2023.26.4.167

Hanelt, A., Bohnsack, R., Marz, D., & Antunes Marante, C. (2021). A systematic review of the literature on digital transformation: Insights and implications for strategy and organizational change. *Journal of Management Studies*, *58*(5), 1159–1197. DOI: 10.1111/joms.12639

Han, G., & Li, F. (2025). Digital economy of trading partner countries, outward investment, and cross-border E-commerce exports. *Finance Research Letters*, *85*, 108034. Advance online publication. DOI: 10.1016/j.frl.2025.108034

Hansen, L. P. (1982). Large sample properties of generalized method of moments estimators. *Econometrica*, *50*(4), 1029–1054. DOI: 10.2307/1912775

Hargaden, H., & Sills, C. (2014). *Transactional analysis: A relational perspective.* Routledge. DOI: 10.4324/9781315820279

Hashim, R., & Abdul Rahman, A. (2020). Peranan mule account dalam pengubahan wang haram di malaysia: Satu perbincangan melalui kajian kes. *International Journal of Social Science Research*, *2*(4), 108–145. http://myjms.mohe.gov.my/index.php/ijssr/article/view/1159/

Hayashi, K., Kaneko, Y., Okabe, T., & Morikawa, T. (2003). Preparation of nanosized metal oxide particles by the Pechini method. *Journal of Materials Science Letters*, *22*(1), 35–37. DOI: 10.1023/A:1021174210764

Hayes, E., & Partlow, M. (2020). Tutorial: Georeferencing and Displaying Historical Maps using Map Warper and StoryMapJS. https://doi.org/DOI: 10.17605/osf.io/7qd56

He, F., & Liu, H. (2019). Assessment of the performance enhancemen effect of digital change in real enterprises from the perspective of digital economy. *Reformation*, *04*, 137–148.

Heiets, I., La, J., Zhou, W., Xu, S., Wang, X., & Xu, Y. (2022). Digital transformation of airline industry. *Research in Transportation Economics*, *92*, 101186. DOI: 10.1016/j.retrec.2022.101186

Heilig, T., & Scheer, I. (2023). *Decision intelligence: Transform your team and organization with AI-driven decision-making*. John Wiley & Sons.

Heinz, D., Hu, M., Benz, C., & Satzger, G. (2025). Digital service innovation for sustainable development: A systematic literature review. In *Transforming the digitally sustainable enterprise* (pp. 167–185). Springer. DOI: 10.1007/978-3-031-80125-9_10

Helms, K. (2020, November 19). *Millionaires FOMO: 73% Will Own Bitcoin by 2022, Survey*. Retrieved from Bitcoin.com News: https://news.bitcoin.com/millionaires-fomo-73-own-bitcoin/

Hendricks, S., & Mwapwele, S. D. (2024). A systematic literature review on the factors influencing e-commerce adoption in developing countries. *Data and Information Management, 8*(1), 100045. Advance online publication. DOI: 10.1016/j.dim.2023.100045

Henson, P., Sappenfield, O. W., Zhai, Y., & Torous, J. (2021). Digital literacy and engagement with health technology in older adults. *Frontiers in Psychiatry, 12*, 734112.

Hepsiburada. (2024). Hepsiburada annual report 2024. Hepsiburada Group. https://corporate.hepsiburada.com

Herari, N. (2024). Piramida Kebutuhan dan Passion Economy: Pemenuhan Kebutuhan Diri melalui Media Digital di Indonesia. In Transformasi Komunikasi digital Menuju Indonesia Berkelanjutan: Komunikasi digital Dan Inovasi Bagi Masyarakat. Elex Media Komputindo. https://www.researchgate.net/publication/390760825_Piramida_Kebutuhan_dan_Passion_Economy_Pemenuhan_Kebutuhan_Diri_melalui_Media_Digital_di_Indonesia

Herari, N., & Marlina, M. (2024). Digital Marketing Transformation of Local MSME Through Instagram Account of Community: A Case Study of Paguyuban UMKM Kecamatan Bekasi Timur. In Albakri, M. (Ed.), *Digital transformation and innovation in emerging markets*. IGI Global Scientific Publishing., DOI: 10.4018/979-8-3373-0086-3.ch002

Herari, N., Waluyo, W., & Rubiyanto, R. (2025). Leading Alone, Leading Forward: Solopreneurs and the Quiet Power of the Passion Economy. In Paradiso-Testa, M. (Ed.), *The purpose of passion in leadership* (pp. 333–358). IGI Global Scientific Publishing., DOI: 10.4018/979-8-3373-2404-3.ch012

Hermann, I., & Paris, C. M. (2020). Digital Nomadism: The nexus of remote working and travel mobility. *Information Technology & Tourism, 22*(3), 329–334. DOI: 10.1007/s40558-020-00188-w

Hess, T., Matt, C., Benlian, A., & Wiesböck, F. (2016). Options for formulating a digital transformation strategy. *MIS Quarterly Executive, 15*(2), 123–139.

Hillman, H. D. (2020). Money laundering through cryptocurrencies: analysing the responses of the United States and Australia and providing recommendations for the UK to address the money laundering risks posed by cryptocurrencies. *University of West of England, Bristol*. Retrieved October 20, 2024, from https://uwe-repository.worktribe.com/preview/7003847/Amended%20Thesis%20-%20H%20Hillman%20-%20Money%20Laundering%20through%20Cryptocurrencies.pdf

Hilmy Rizqullah Ramadhan, M., Ramadhani, K., Isrok, M., Anggraeny, I., & Prasetyo, R. (2024). Legal Protection of Personal Data in Artificial Intelligence for Legal Protection Viewed From Legal Certainty Aspect. *KnE Social Sciences, 9(1), 125–13, 9*(1). DOI: 10.18502/kss.v8i21.14710

Hilty, L. M., & Aebischer, B. (2015). ICT for sustainability: An emerging research field. In Hilty, L. M., & Aebischer, B. (Eds.), *ICT innovations for sustainability* (pp. 3–36). Springer International Publishing., DOI: 10.1007/978-3-319-09228-7_1

Hinings, B., Gegenhuber, T., & Greenwood, R. (2018). Digital innovation and transformation: An institutional perspective. *Information and Organization, 28*(1), 52–61. DOI: 10.1016/j.infoandorg.2018.02.004

Holzinger, A., Zatloukal, K., & Müller, H. (2024). Is human oversight to AI systems still possible? *New Biotechnology, 85*, 59–62. DOI: 10.1016/j.nbt.2024.12.003 PMID: 39675423

Holzmann, V., Zitter, D., & Peshkess, S. (2022). The Expectations of Project Managers from Artificial Intelligence: A Delphi Study. Project Management Journal, 53(5). Sagepub. https://doi.org/DOI: 10.1177/87569728211061779

Hossain, S., Fernando, M., & Akter, S. (2025). The influence of artificial intelligence-driven capabilities on responsible leadership: A future research agenda. *Journal of Management & Organization, 31*(5), 2360–2384. DOI: 10.1017/jmo.2025.10010

Huang, C., Du, A. M., & Lin, B. (2025). How does the digital economy affect the green transition: The role of industrial intelligence and E-commerce. *Research in International Business and Finance, 73*, 102541. Advance online publication. DOI: 10.1016/j.ribaf.2024.102541

Huang, C., Wang, H. T., & Huang, T.-Y. (2020). Initial evidence on the impact of big data implementation on firm performance. *Information Systems Frontiers, 22*(2), 475–487. DOI: 10.1007/s10796-018-9872-5

Huang, H., & Leung, X. Y. (2025). Experimental design for sustainable tourism: A horizon 2050 paper. *Tourism Review, 80*(1), 286–298. DOI: 10.1108/TR-12-2023-0867

Huang, J., Li, Q., Sun, D., Lu, Y., Su, Y., Yang, X., & Wang, H. (2007). Biosynthesis of silver and gold nanoparticles by novel sundried *Cinnamomum camphora* leaf. *Nanotechnology, 18*(10), 105104. DOI: 10.1088/0957-4484/18/10/105104

Huang, Y., Zhang, Y., & Yao, Q. (2020). Artificial intelligence in nanomedicine for cancer. *ACS Applied Nano Materials, 3*(6), 4920–4947. DOI: 10.1021/acsanm.0c01160

Humphery, C., & Hugh-Jones, S. (1992). *Barter, Exchange and Value: An Anthropological Approach.* Cambridge University Press. DOI: 10.1017/CBO9780511607677

Hund, E. (2023). *The Influencer Industry: Constructing And Commodifying Authenticity On Social Media.* Publicly Accessible Penn Dissertations., DOI: 10.1353/book.110091

Hüsnüoğlu, N., & Öztürk, L. (2017). Dijital Bölünme: Nedenleri Ve Türleri. *Giresun Üniversitesi İktisadi ve İdari Bilimler Dergisi, 3*(5), 6–21.

Huyett, B., & Viguerie, S. P. (2005). Extreme competition. *The McKinsey Quarterly*, (1), 47–57.

Hwa Baek, C. (2021). A study on the change in service quality in the era of the 4th industrial revolution compared to the existing service quality evaluation. 2021 21st ACIS International Winter Conference on Software Engineering, Artificial Intelligence, Networking and Parallel/Distributed Computing (SNPD-Winter), 156–158. https://doi.org/DOI: 10.1109/SNPDWinter52325.2021.00041

IBM. (2023). *IBM furthers commitment to climate action through free training in green and technology skills for vulnerable communities.* IBM Newsroom.

Iivari, N. (2020). Empowering children to make and shape our digital futures – from adults creating technologies to children transforming cultures. *The International Journal of Information and Learning Technology, 37*(5), 279–293. DOI: 10.1108/IJILT-03-2020-0023

IKEA. (2024). *IKEA Sustainability Report FY23.* Inter IKEA Group. https://www.ikea.com/global/en/images/IKEA_SUSTAINABILITY_Report_FY_23_20240125_1b190c008f.pdf

Imafuku, R., Saiki, T., & Woodward-Kron, R. (2022). Revisiting discourse analysis in medical education research. *International Journal of Medical Education, 13*, 138–142. DOI: 10.5116/ijme.6278.c1b7 PMID: 35640066

Immonen, M., & Sintonen, S. (2015). Evolution of technology perceptions over time. *Information Technology & People, 28*(3), 589–606. DOI: 10.1108/ITP-12-2013-0219

India, C. o. (1950). Article 19(1)(g). India. Retrieved October 20, 2024, from https://cdnbbsr.s3waas.gov.in/s380537a945c7aaa788ccfcdf1b99b5d8f/uploads/2024/07/20240716890312078.pdf

Informatics, C. *AI for materials and chemicals*. Retrieved from https://citrine.io

International Energy Agency. (2023). *Energy Technology Perspectives 2023*. IEA., DOI: 10.1787/7c6b23db-

International Telecommunication Union (ITU). (2021). *Measuring digital development: Facts and figures 2021*. ITU.

Internet And Mobile Association of India Versus Reserve Bank of India. (2018). *Writ Petition (Civil) No.528 of 2018*. Supreme Court of India.

Ionescu, A. M., & Sârbu, F. A. (2024). Exploring the impact of smart technologies on the tourism industry. *Sustainability (Basel)*, *16*(2), 789–805. DOI: 10.3390/su16083318

Iravani, S. (2011). Green synthesis of metal nanoparticles using plants. *Green Chemistry*, *13*(10), 2638–2650. DOI: 10.1039/c1gc15386b

Iravani, S., Korbekandi, H., Mirmohammadi, S. V., & Zolfaghari, B. (2014). Synthesis of silver nanoparticles: Chemical, physical and biological methods. *Research in Pharmaceutical Sciences*, *9*(6), 385–406. https://www.ncbi.nlm.nih.gov/pmc/articles/PMC4326979/ PMID: 26339255

Irfan, M., Ullah, S., Razzaq, A., Cai, J., & Adebayo, T. S. (2023). Unleashing the dynamic impact of tourism industry on energy consumption, economic output, and environmental quality in China: A way forward towards environmental sustainability. *Journal of Cleaner Production*, *387*, 135778. DOI: 10.1016/j.jclepro.2022.135778

Islam, N., Sarkar, B., Basak, A., Das, P., Paul, I., Debnath, M., & Roy, R. (2022). A novel GIS-based MCDM approach to identify the potential eco-tourism sites in the Eastern Dooars region (Himalayan foothill) of West Bengal, India. *Geocarto International*, *37*(3), 1–30. DOI: 10.1080/10106049.2022.2076917

ITP. (2021, April 20). *Crypto investors get a shock as India drafts bill to ban digital currency*. Retrieved from Arabian Business: https://www.arabianbusiness.com/money/wealth/alternative-assets/462324-crypto-investors-get-shock-as-india-circulates-draft-bill-to-ban-the-digital-currency

Ivanova, V. N., Poltarykhin, A. L., Szromnik, A., & Anichkina, O. (2019). Economic policy for country's digitalization: A case study. *Journal of Entrepreneurship and Sustainability Issues*, *7*(1), 649–661. DOI: 10.9770/jesi.2019.7.1(46)

Iyawa, G. E., Herselman, M., & Botha, A. (2016). Digital Health Innovation Ecosystems: From Systematic Literature Review to Conceptual Framework. *Procedia Computer Science*, *100*, 244–252. DOI: 10.1016/j.procs.2016.09.149

Jabotinsky, H. Y., & Sarel, R. (2021, March 26). *How the Covid -19 Pandemic Affected Cryptocurrency Market?* CLS Bluesky Blog. https://clsbluesky.law.columbia.edu/2021/03/26/how-the-covid-19-pandemic-affected-the-cryptocurrency-market/

Jadhav, K., Dhamecha, D., & Bhattacharya, D. (2020). Green and ecofriendly synthesis of metal and metal oxide nanoparticles: A review. *ChemistrySelect*, *5*(38), 12134–12144. DOI: 10.1002/slct.202002918

Jafari, S., Vo-Huu, T., Jabiyev, B., Mera, A., & farkhani, R. M. (2018, May 02). Cryptocurrency: A Challenge to Legal System. *SSRN*, 1-21. DOI: 10.2139/ssrn.3172489

Jaiswal, R., Gupta, S., & Gupta, S. K. (2024). The impending disruption of digital nomadism: Opportunities, challenges, and research agenda. *World Leisure Journal*, *67*(1), 74–104. DOI: 10.1080/16078055.2024.2346091

James, B. D., Boyle, P. A., Yu, L., Han, S. D., & Bennett, D. A. (2020). Older and wiser: Age differences in susceptibility to investment fraud: The protective role of emotional intelligence. *Aging & Mental Health*, *24*(5), 691–696. DOI: 10.1080/13607863.2018.1544211

Jardak, M. K., & Ben Hamad, S. (2022). The effect of digital transformation on firm performance: Evidence from Swedish listed companies. *The Journal of Risk Finance*, *23*(4), 329–348. DOI: 10.1108/JRF-12-2021-0199

Jessop, B. (2008). *State power: A strategic-relational approach*. Polity Press. https://www.politybooks.com/bookdetail?book_slug=state-power--9780745633206

Jin, C., Xu, A., Zhu, Y., & Li, J. (2023). Technology growth in the digital age: Evidence from China. *Technological Forecasting and Social Change*, *187*, 122221. Advance online publication. DOI: 10.1016/j.techfore.2022.122221

Josella, T. (2025). Eksistensi dalam Klik: Fenomena “Apapun demi Konten” dalam Perspektif homo digitalis Budi Hardiman. Aradha: Journal of Divinity. *Peace and Conflict Studies*, *5*(1), 57–74. DOI: 10.21460/aradha.2025.51.1419

Joseph, V., Ray, D., & Agarwal, S. (2020, June 01). *Cryptocurrencies in India - Past, Present & Future*. Retrieved October 19, 2024, from Mondaq: https://www.mondaq.com/india/fin-tech/944312/cryptocurrencies-in-india--past-present-future

Joshi, A. P., & Patel, B. V. (2021). Data Preprocessing: The Techniques for Preparing Clean and Quality Data for Data Analytics Process. In A. P. Joshi & B. V. Patel, Oriental journal of computer science and technology (Vol. 13, Issue 203, p. 78). DOI: 10.13005/ojcst13.0203.03

Kaboré, S. S., Ngangue, P., Soubeiga, D., Barro, A., Pilabré, A. H., Bationo, N., Pafadnam, Y., Drabo, K. M., Hien, H., & Savadogo, G. B. L. (2022). Barriers and facilitators for the sustainability of digital health interventions in low and middle-income countries: A systematic review. *Frontiers in Digital Health*, *4*, 1014375. DOI: 10.3389/fdgth.2022.1014375 PMID: 36518563

Kalinin, A. A., Palanimalai, S., Zhu, J., Wu, W., Devraj, N., Ye, C., Ponarul, N., Husain, S. S., & Dinov, I. D. (2022). SOCRAT: A Dynamic Web Toolbox for Interactive Data Processing, Analysis and Visualization. In A. A. Kalinin, S. Palanimalai, J. Zhu, W. Wu, N. Devraj, C. Ye, N. Ponarul, S. S. Husain, & I. D. Dinov, Information (Vol. 13, Issue 11, p. 547). Multidisciplinary Digital Publishing Institute. DOI: 10.3390/info13110547

Kane, G. C., Palmer, D., Phillips, A. N., Kiron, D., & Buckley, N. (2019). Accelerating digital innovation inside and out: Agile teams, ecosystems, and ethics. *MIT Sloan Management Review and Deloitte Insights.* https://sloanreview.mit.edu/projects/accelerating-digital-innovation-inside-and-out

Kane, G. C., Palmer, D., Phillips, A. N., Kiron, D., & Buckley, N. (2015). Strategy, not technology, drives digital transformation. *MIT Sloan Management Review.*

Kano, L. (2018). Global value chain governance: A relational perspective. *Journal of International Business Studies*, *49*(6), 684–705. DOI: 10.1057/s41267-017-0086-8

Kapoor, D., & Jain, A. (2024). Sustainable tourism and its future research directions: A bibliometric analysis of twenty-five years of research. *Tourism Review*. Advance online publication. DOI: 10.1108/TR-03-2022-0110

Karakus, F. (2021). A retrospective view from traditional to boundaryless career and career success. International Journal of Research in Business and Social Science (2147- 4478), 10(3), 65–81. https://doi.org/DOI: 10.20525/ijrbs.v10i3.1131

Kardelis, V., Sadauskas, T., Tamulevičius, T., & Tamulevičius, S. (2020). Sonochemical synthesis of gold nanoparticles for biological applications. *Ultrasonics Sonochemistry*, *61*, 104806. DOI: 10.1016/j.ultsonch.2019.104806

Karrman, E. (2001). Strategies towards sustainable wastewater management. *Urban Water*, *3*(1-2), 63–72. DOI: 10.1016/S1462-0758(01)00018-8

Kawamura, S., & Yoshino, T. (2023). Technonationalism and global value chains: Implications for supply chain resilience. *Journal of Asian Economics*, *84*, 101567. DOI: 10.1016/j.asieco.2023.101567

Kaya, Y. (2023). Agile leadership from the perspective of dynamic capabilities and creating value. *Sustainability (Basel)*, *15*(21), 15253. DOI: 10.3390/su152115253

Kc, H., & Triandafyllidou, A., (2025). Digital Nomadism and the Emergence of Digital Nomad Visas: What Policy Objectives Do States Aim to Achieve? *The International Migration Review*, *60*(1), 71–92. Advance online publication. DOI: 10.1177/01979183241306367

Kepli, M. Y., & Zulhuda, S. (2019, August 26). Cryptocurrencies and Anti-money Laundering Laws: The Need for an Integrated Approach. *Emerland Insight*, pp. 247-263. DOI: 10.1108/978-1-78973-545-120191020

Kero, C. A., & Bogale, A. T. (2023). A systematic review of resource-based view and dynamic capabilities of firms and future research avenues. *International Journal of Sustainable Development and Planning*, *18*(10), 3137–3154. DOI: 10.18280/ijsdp.181016

Khajeh Naeeni, S., & Nouhi, N. (2023). The environmental impacts of AI and digital technologies. *AI and Tech in Behavioral and Social Sciences*, *1*(4), 11–18. DOI: 10.61838/kman.aitech.1.4.3

Khalid, M. S. (2024). Sustainable tourism's tomorrow: Navigating the future with technological innovations. In *Achieving Sustainable Transformation in Tourism and Hospitality* (pp. 123–145). IGI Global., DOI: 10.4018/979-8-3693-3390-7.ch008

Khalife, D., Subrahmanyam, S., & Farah, A. (2024). A sustainable circular business model to improve the performance of small and medium-sized enterprises using blockchain technology. *Journal of Wireless Mobile Networks, Ubiquitous Computing and Dependable Applications*, *15*(2), 240–250. DOI: 10.58346/JOWUA.2024.I2.016

Khallaf, A., Abdallah, A.-N., Zoubi, T., & Alnesafi, A. (2024). Blockchain-Driven Carbon Accountability in Supply Chains. *Sustainability (Basel)*, *16*(24), 10872. DOI: 10.3390/su162410872

Khan, M. A., Syamil, A., Rana, J. A. S., Subekti, R., & Amin, N. (2025). Digital Nomadism: Remote Work Practices and Emerging Forms of Entrepreneurship. *Gadjah Mada International Journal of Business*, *28*(1), 25–46. DOI: 10.22146/gamaijb.v28i1.17133

Khan, M. H., & Al-Kuwari, M. (2021). Adapting digital HR practices in GCC countries: A roadmap for future success. *Journal of Gulf Economic Studies*, *14*(3), 76–91. DOI: 10.1108/jges.2021.32456

Khan, N., Khan, W., Humayun, M., & Naz, A. (2024). Unlocking the potential: Artificial intelligence applications in sustainable tourism. In *Advances in Regenerative Tourism and Hospitality*. Emerald Publishing. DOI: 10.1108/978-1-83753-746-420241020

Khatri, I. (2019). Information technology in tourism & hospitality industry: A review of ten years' publications. *Journal of Tourism & Hospitality Education*, *9*, 74–87. DOI: 10.3126/jthe.v9i0.23682

Khayati, G. R., & Mirzaei, M. (2012). Sonoelectrochemical synthesis of metallic nanoparticles. *Ultrasonics Sonochemistry*, *19*(4), 690–696. DOI: 10.1016/j.ultsonch.2011.11.009

Khedr, A. M., & Sheeja, R. S. (2024). Enhancing Supply Chain Management with Deep Learning and Machine Learning Techniques: A Review. Journal of Open Innovation Technology Market and Complexity, 10(4), 100379–100379. Sciencedirect. https://www.sciencedirect.com/science/article/pii/S2199853124001732

Klein, C. (2023). Understanding the relevance of digital media in higher education. [IJTES]. *International Journal of Technology in Education and Science*, *7*(1), 71–82. DOI: 10.46328/ijtes.451

Kohtam¨aki, M., Parida, V., Patel, P. C., & Gebauer, H. (2020). The relationship between digitalization and servitization: The role of servitization in capturing the financial potential of digitalization. *Technological Forecasting and Social Change*, *151*(6), 119804. DOI: 10.1016/j.techfore.2019.119804

Kong, J., Goh, M., & Cao, Y. (2024). Can digital economy development facilitate corporate ESG performance? *Sustainability (Basel)*, *16*(10), 3956. DOI: 10.3390/su16103956

Koskela, K., & Beckers, P. (2024). Typologizing Digital Nomad Visas: Comparing Policy Rationales from Tourism to Wealth Accumulation to Immigration. *Journal of Comparative Policy Analysis*, *26*(5), 407–425. DOI: 10.1080/13876988.2024.2343696

Kotter, J. P. (2012). *Leading change*. Harvard Business Review Press.

Kouki, R., Poulin, D., & Pellerin, R. (2006). *ERP assimilation challenge: An integrative framework for a better post-implementation assimilation*. CIRRELT.

Kovalerchuk, B., Andonie, R., Datia, N., Nazemi, K., & Banissi, E. (2022). Visual Knowledge Discovery with Artificial Intelligence: Challenges and Future Directions. In B. Kovalerchuk, R. Andonie, N. Datia, K. Nazemi, & E. Banissi, arXiv (Cornell University). Cornell University. https://doi.org//arxiv.2205.01296DOI: 10.48550

KPMG. (2023). *Future of HR: Navigating digital transformation in the Middle East.* KPMG International. https://home.kpmg/xx/en/home/insights/2023/01/future-of-hr.html

Kraaijenbrink, J., Spender, J. C., & Groen, A. J. (2010). The resource-based view: A review and assessment of its critiques. *Journal of Management*, *36*(1), 349–372. DOI: 10.1177/0149206309350775

Krahe, M. A., Baker, S., Woods, L., & Larkins, S. L. (2024). Factors that influence the implementation of digital health in rural, regional, and remote Australia: Protocol for an overview of reviews. *MedRxiv*, 2024.11.13.24317285. DOI: 10.1101/2024.11.13.24317285

Krajčík, M., Schmidt, D. A., & Baráth, M. (2023). Hybrid Work Model: An Approach to Work–Life Flexibility in a Changing Environment. *Administrative Sciences*, *13*(6), 150. DOI: 10.3390/admsci13060150

Krasota, T., Bazhenov, R., Abdyldaeva, U., Bedrina, S., & Mironova, I. (2020). Development of the digital economy in the context of sustainable competitive advantage. E3S Web of Conferences, 208, 03042. DOI: 10.1051/e3sconf/202020803042

Kraus, S., Jones, P., Kailer, N., Weinmann, A., Chaparro-Banegas, N., & Roig-Tierno, N. (2021). Digital transformation: An overview of the current state of the art of research. *SAGE Open*, *11*(3), 21582440211047576. Advance online publication. DOI: 10.1177/21582440211047576

Kreitmair, K. V., & Karola Kreitmair, C. V. (2024). Mobile health technology and empowerment. *Bioethics*, *38*(6), 481–490. DOI: 10.1111/bioe.13157 PMID: 36950727

Kruglov, A., Succi, G., & Kholmatova, Z. (2023). *Metrics of sustainability and energy efficiency of software products and process.* In *Developing Sustainable and Energy-Efficient Software Systems* (SpringerBriefs in Computer Science, pp.?). Springer. https://doi.org/DOI: 10.1007/978-3-031-11658-2_2

Kuang, Y., Fan, M., Fan, Y., Jiang, Y., & Bin, J. (2023). Digitalization, financing constraints and firm performance. *Frontiers in Environmental Science*, *11*, 1090537. DOI: 10.3389/fenvs.2023.1090537

Kuhn, C., Khoo, S.-M., Czerniewicz, L., Lilley, W., Bute, S., Crean, A., Abegglen, S., Burns, T., Sinfield, S., Jandrić, P., Knox, J., & MacKenzie, A. (2023). Understanding digital inequality: A theoretical kaleidoscope. *Postdigital Science and Education*, *5*(3), 894–932. DOI: 10.1007/s42438-023-00395-8 PMID: 40479087

Kukreja, M., & Rashmi, R. (2022). Consumer's Behaviour while Purchasing Apparels in Sale Period. In M. Kukreja & R. Rashmi, Deleted Journal (Vol. 16, Issue 1, p. 1). DOI: 10.57198/2583-4932.1072

Kumar, A., & Gupta, P. (2021). AI-enabled nanotechnology for energy and environmental applications. In *Artificial Intelligence and Smart Energy* (pp. 123–145). Springer.

Kumar, A., & Gupta, P. (2021). Artificial intelligence and nanotechnology: Synergistic potential in energy and environmental domains. In *Nanotechnology for Energy and Environmental Applications* (pp. 245–270). Springer.

Kumar, A., Vemula, P. K., Ajayan, P. M., & John, G. (2012). Silver-nanoparticle-embedded antimicrobial paints based on vegetable oil. *Nature Materials*, *7*(3), 236–241. DOI: 10.1038/nmat2099 PMID: 18204453

Kumar, B., Smita, K., Cumbal, L., & Debut, A. (2019). Green synthesis of silver nanoparticles using *Andean plant* extracts and their antimicrobial activity. *Materials Letters*, *224*, 295–299. DOI: 10.1016/j.matlet.2018.06.121

Kumar, V. A. (2012). Money Laundering: Concept, Significance and its Impact. *European Journal of Business and Management*, •••, 113–119.

Kumar, V., & Sandhu, A. (2018). From bricks to mobile: The evolution of the retail shop and the role of technology. *Journal of the Academy of Marketing Science*, *46*(4), 537–556.

Kumar, V., Singh, A., & Gupta, R. (2024). How does artificial intelligence affect the environmental performance of organizations? The role of green innovation and green culture. *Information & Management*, *61*(2), 103924. DOI: 10.1016/j.im.2024.103924

Kumar, V., Singh, M., & Vaish, R. (2013). Synthesis and characterization of ZnO nanoparticles via co-precipitation method. *AIP Conference Proceedings*, *1536*(1), 1315–1316. DOI: 10.1063/1.4810574

Kusumastuti, H., Pranita, D., Viendyasari, M., Rasul, M. S., & Sarjana, S. (2024). Leveraging local value in a post-smart tourism village to encourage sustainable tourism. *Sustainability (Basel)*, *16*(2), 873. DOI: 10.3390/su16020873

Kusumawardhani, Y., Hilmiana, H., Widianto, S., & Azis, Y. (2024). Smart tourism practice in the scope of sustainable tourism in emerging markets: A systematic literature review. *Cogent Social Sciences*, *10*(1), 2384193. DOI: 10.1080/23311886.2024.2384193

Kwilinski, A., Lyulyov, O., & Pimonenko, T. (2023). Unlocking Sustainable Value through Digital Transformation: An Examination of ESG Performance. *Information (Basel)*, *14*(8), 444. Advance online publication. DOI: 10.3390/info14080444

La Londe, B. J., & Masters, J. M. (1994). Emerging logistics strategies: Blueprints for the next century. *International Journal of Physical Distribution & Logistics Management*, *24*(7), 35–47. DOI: 10.1108/09600039410070975

Lacárcel, F. J. S. (2025). Digital technologies, sustainable lifestyle, and tourism: How digital nomads navigate global mobility? *Sustainable Technology and Entrepreneurship*, *4*(2), 100096. DOI: 10.1016/j.stae.2025.100096

Laengle, S., Lobos, V., Merigo, J., Herrera-Viedma, E., Cobo, M., & De Baets, B. (2021). Forty years of Fuzzy Sets and Systems: A bibliometric analysis. *Fuzzy Sets and Systems*, *402*, 155–183. DOI: 10.1016/j.fss.2020.03.012

Laine, J., Minkkinen, M., & Mäntymäki, M. (2024). Ethics-based AI auditing: A systematic literature review on conceptualizations of ethical principles and knowledge contributions to stakeholders. *Information & Management*, *61*(5), 103969–103969. DOI: 10.1016/j.im.2024.103969

Lakshmikumaran Sridharan Attorneys. (2018, April 03). *Trading in Virtual Currencies: An analysis under foreign exchange laws of India*. Retrieved October 20, 2024, from LKS: https://www.lakshmisri.com/insights/articles/trading-in-virtual-currencies-an-analysis-under-foreign-exchange-laws-of-india/#

Lambert, D. M., Stock, J. R., & Ellram, L. M. (1998). *Fundamentals of logistics management*. McGraw-Hill/Irwin.

Lang, H., Howcroft, E., & Wilson, T. (2023, November 03). *The crypto market bears the scars of FTX's Collapse*. Retrieved October 20, 2024, from Reuters: https://www.reuters.com/technology/crypto-market-still-bears-scars-ftxs-collapse-2023-10-03/

Lange, S., Pohl, J., & Santarius, T. (2020). Digitalization and energy consumption: Does ICT reduce energy demand? *Ecological Economics*, *176*, 106760. DOI: 10.1016/j.ecolecon.2020.106760

Langevin, D. (1992). Influence of interfacial phenomena on microemulsion structure and dynamics. *Annual Review of Physical Chemistry*, *43*(1), 341–369. DOI: 10.1146/annurev.pc.43.100192.002013

Langroodi, F. (2021). ARTICLE INFO. *Journal of Insurance and Financial Management*, *4*, 65–81.

Laurent, S., Forge, D., Port, M., Roch, A., Robic, C., Vander Elst, L., & Muller, R. N. (2008). Magnetic iron oxide nanoparticles: Synthesis, stabilization, vectorization, physicochemical characterizations, and biological applications. *Chemical Reviews*, *108*(6), 2064–2110. DOI: 10.1021/cr068445e PMID: 18543879

Law, F. (n.d.). *Legal Issues Surrounding Cryptocurrency*. Retrieved October 20, 2024, from Freeman Law: https://freemanlaw.com/legal-issues-surrounding-cryptocurrency/

Law, R., & Chen, S. (2024). Developments and implications of tourism information technology: A horizon 2050 paper. *Tourism Review*. Advance online publication. DOI: 10.1108/TR-03-2024-0123

Leathwood, C., & Read, B. (2013). Research policy and academic performativity: Compliance, contestation and complicity. *Studies in Higher Education*, *38*(8), 1162–1174. DOI: 10.1080/03075079.2013.833025

Le-Clech, P. (2010). Membrane bioreactors and their uses in wastewater treatments. *Applied Microbiology and Biotechnology*, *88*(6), 1253–1260. DOI: 10.1007/s00253-010-2885-8 PMID: 20865255

Lee, J., Suh, T., Roy, D., & Baucus, M. (2019). Emerging Technology and Business Model Innovation: The Case of Artificial Intelligence. *Journal of Open Innovation*, *5*(3), 44. DOI: 10.3390/joitmc5030044

Lee, P. C., & Meisel, D. (1982). Adsorption and surface-enhanced Raman of dyes on silver and gold sols. *Journal of Physical Chemistry*, *86*(17), 3391–3395. DOI: 10.1021/j100214a025

Lee, S., & Lim, S. (2018). *Living innovation: from value creation to the greater good*. Emerald Publishing Limited. DOI: 10.1108/9781787567139

Lee, W., Jang, S. S., & Kim, H. S. (2024). The effect of digital transformation: Boosting productivity in the restaurant industry. *International Journal of Hospitality Management*, *123*, 103896. DOI: 10.1016/j.ijhm.2024.103896

Lee, Y. H., Park, D. J., Han, Y. K., & Kim, J. H. (2005). Controlled synthesis of silver nanostructures via polyol process using chloride salts. *Materials Letters*, *59*(29–30), 3959–3963. DOI: 10.1016/j.matlet.2005.06.038

Lei, L., Yang, S., & Chen, N. (2022). The impact of digital transformation on enterprise investment efficiency. *Soft Science*, *36*(11), 23–29.

Levitt, T. (1983). The globalization of markets. *Harvard Business Review*, *61*(3), 92–102.

Lewin, K. (1951). *Field theory in social science: Selected theoretical papers*. Harper & Row.

Li, H., & Xu, H. (2024). The impact of digital transformation on ESG performance. *International Review of Economics & Finance, 96*(Part B), 103686. https://doi.org/ DOI: 10.1016/j.iref.2024.103686

Li, H., Wu, M., Wang, Y., & Zeng, A. (2022). Bibliographic coupling networks reveal the advantage of diversification in scientific projects. *16*. DOI: 10.1016/j.joi.2022.101321

Li, K., Dan, K. J., Lang, K. R., Kauffman, R. J., & Naldi, M. (2020). How should we understand the digital economy in Asia? Critical assessment and research agenda. *44*. DOI: 10.1016/j.elerap.2020.101004

Liang, M., & Chen, H. (2025). Digital economy development, regional openness, and high-quality foreign trade. *Finance Research Letters*, *81*, 107469. Advance online publication. DOI: 10.1016/j.frl.2025.107469

Liao, J. (2024). Enabling a Sustainable Digital Transformation. *Journal of Latin American Sciences and Culture*, *6*(9), 33–43. DOI: 10.52428/27888991.v6i9.1192

Libert, B., Beck, M., & Wind, Y. (2016). Questions to ask before your next digital transformation. *Harvard Business Review*, *60*(12), 11–13.

Lichtenthaler, U. (2019). An intelligence-based view of firm performance: Profiting from artificial intelligence. *Journal of Innovation Management*, *7*(1), 7–20. DOI: 10.24840/2183-0606_007.001_0002

Li, M. (2025). Digital transformation and supply chain resilience in SMEs: Empirical evidence from the manufacturing sector in the Yangtze River Delta. *Journal of Economic and Managerial Dynamics*, *1*(1), 1–7.

Lim, W., Kumar, S., & Donthu, N. (2024). How to combine and clean bibliometric data and use bibliometric tools synergistically: Guidelines using metaverse research. *Journal of Business Research*, *182*, 114760. DOI: 10.1016/j.jbusres.2024.114760

Lind, J. T., & Mehlum, H. (2010). With or Without U? – The appropriate test for a U-shaped relationship. *Oxford Bulletin of Economics and Statistics*, *72*(1), 109–118. DOI: 10.1111/j.1468-0084.2009.00569.x

Lin, J., & Mao, M. (2024). How does digital transformation affect sustainable innovation performance? The pivotal roles of digital technology-business alignment and environmental uncertainty. *Sustainable Development (Bradford), 32*(4), 3163–3181. DOI: 10.1002/sd.2830

Linkov, I., Trump, B., Poinsatte-Jones, K., & Florin, M.-V. (2018). Governance strategies for a sustainable digital world. *Sustainability (Basel), 10*(2), 440. DOI: 10.3390/su10020440

Litchfield, I., Shukla, D., & Greenfield, S. (2021). Impact of COVID-19 on the digital divide: A rapid review. *BMJ Open, 11*(10), e053440. Advance online publication. DOI: 10.1136/bmjopen-2021-053440 PMID: 34642200

Liu, X., Ahmad, S., Sayed, F., Fayaz, A., Anser, M., & Ke, J. (2022). Cyber security threats: A never-ending challenge for e-commerce. *Frontiers in Psychology, 13*, 927398. Advance online publication. DOI: 10.3389/fpsyg.2022.927398 PMID: 36337532

Liu, Y., Gao, L., & Ma, J. (2007). Sonochemical preparation of mesoporous alumina–silica nanocomposites. *Microporous and Mesoporous Materials, 103*(1–3), 212–216. DOI: 10.1016/j.micromeso.2007.01.012

Livage, J., Henry, M., & Sanchez, C. (2001). Sol-gel chemistry of transition metal oxides. *Progress in Solid State Chemistry, 18*(4), 259–341. DOI: 10.1016/0079-6786(88)90005-2

Li, Z., Li, H., & Wang, S. (2022). How multidimensional digital empowerment affects technology innovation performance: The moderating effect of adaptability to technology embedding. *Sustainability (Basel), 14*(23), 15916. DOI: 10.3390/su142315916

Lopez-Gonzalez, J. (2017). *Mapping the participation of SMEs in global value chains. OECD Trade Policy Papers, 211*. OECD Publishing., DOI: 10.1787/8bbebdb9-

Lozić, J., & Čiković, K. F. (2021). The impact of digital transformation on the business efficiency of the New York Times. *UTMS Journal of Economics, 12*(2), 225-239.

Lu, A.-H., Salabas, E. L., & Schüth, F. (2007). Magnetic nanoparticles: Synthesis, protection, functionalization, and application. *Angewandte Chemie International Edition, 46*(8), 1222–1244. DOI: 10.1002/anie.200602866 PMID: 17278160

Lupton, D. (2016). *The quantified self.* John Wiley & Sons.

Lu, S. (2024). Examining green innovation and digital transformation as essential factors of sustainable performance. Highlights in Business. *Economics and Management, 39*, 625–630. DOI: 10.54097/d8c3yk70

Lu, W.-C. (2018). The impacts of information and communication technology, energy consumption, financial development, and economic growth on carbon dioxide emissions in 12 Asian countries. *Mitigation and Adaptation Strategies for Global Change, 23*(8), 1351–1365. DOI: 10.1007/s11027-018-9787-y

Ma, R., Sun, E., & Zou, J. (2023). A spectral method for assessing and combining multiple data visualizations. In R. Ma, E. Sun, & J. Zou, Nature Communications (Vol. 14, Issue 1). Nature Portfolio. DOI: 10.1038/s41467-023-36492-2

Maalouf, E. (2024). Achieving corporate environmental responsibility through emerging sustainability laws. *Asia Pacific Journal of Environmental Law, 27*(1), 64–99. DOI: 10.4337/apjel.2024.01.03

Macher, J. T., & Richman, B. D. (2008). Transaction cost economics: An assessment of empirical research in the social sciences. *Business and Politics, 10*(1), 1–63. DOI: 10.2202/1469-3569.1210

Mahamuni, N. N., & Adewuyi, Y. G. (2010). Sonochemical synthesis of gold nanoparticles at room temperature. *Journal of Nanoparticle Research, 12*, 345–353. DOI: 10.1007/s11051-009-9616-5

Mahapatra, O., Bhagat, M., Gopalakrishnan, C., & Arunachalam, K. D. (2010). Ultrafine dispersed CuO nanoparticles and their antibacterial activity. *Journal of Experimental Nanoscience, 5*(6), 584–594. DOI: 10.1080/17458080903491779

Majeed, M. T., & Khan, M. A. (2024). Green supply chain management based on artificial intelligence of everything. *Journal of Economics and Management, 46*(1), 171–188. DOI: 10.22367/jem.2024.46.07

Makhija, R. (2024). Unregulated Cryptocurrency: Need for Legal Regulation in Digital Economy. *Trinity Law Review, 4*(1), 18–24. DOI: 10.48165/tlr.2024.4.1.4

Malhotra, S. (1900, January 01). Prevention Of Money Laundering and Terrorism: An Indian Perspective. *Manupatra*.

Manikandan, A., & Mittal, A. (2021, June 03). *India's cryptocurrency industry draws up 'legitimacy plan'*. The Economic Times. https://economictimes.indiatimes.com/tech/technology/indias-cryptocurrency-industry-draws-up-legitimacy-plan/articleshow/83188685.cms

Manning, L., Brewer, S., Craigon, P. J., Frey, J., Gutierrez, A., Jacobs, N., Kanza, S., Munday, S., Sacks, J., & Pearson, S. (2022). Artificial intelligence and ethics within the food sector: Developing a common language for technology adoption across the supply chain. *Trends in Food Science & Technology, 125*, 33–42. DOI: 10.1016/j.tifs.2022.04.025

Marjaei, S., Yazdi, F. A., & Chandrashekara, M. (2019). MAXQDA and its application to LIS research. *Library Philosophy and Practice,* 1-9. Retrieved from https://www.proquest.com/scholarly-journals/maxqda-application-lis-research/docview/2236131089/se-2

Maroufkhani, P., Wagner, R., Ismail, W. K. W., Baroto, M. B., & Nourani, M. (2019). Big Data Analytics and Firm Performance: A Systematic Review [Review of Big Data Analytics and Firm Performance: A Systematic Review]. Information, 10(7), 226. Multidisciplinary Digital Publishing Institute. DOI: 10.3390/info10070226

Martín-Peña, M.-L., Sánchez-López, J.-M., & Díaz-Garrido, E. (2019). Servitization and digitalization in manufacturing: The influence on firm performance. *Journal of Business and Industrial Marketing*, *35*(3), 564–574. DOI: 10.1108/JBIM-12-2018-0400

Marwick, A. E., & boyd, . (2014). Networked privacy: How teenagers negotiate context in social media. *New Media & Society*, *16*(7), 1051–1067. DOI: 10.1177/1461444814543995

Masoud, R., & Basahel, S. (2023). The effects of digital transformation on firm performance: The role of customer experience and IT innovation. *Digital*, *3*(2), 109–126. DOI: 10.3390/digital3020008

Massart, R. (1981). Preparation of aqueous magnetic liquids in alkaline and acidic media. *IEEE Transactions on Magnetics*, *17*(2), 1247–1248. DOI: 10.1109/TMAG.1981.1061188

Mataković, I. C. (2022). Crypto-Assets Illicit Activities: Theoretical Approach with. *International E-Journal of Criminal Sciences*, 1-30.

Materials Studio (BIOVIA). *Molecular modeling and simulation platform*. Retrieved from https://www.3ds.com/products-services/biovia/products/materials-studio/

Maurya, S., Shavkidinova, D., Shrivastava, V., & Subrahmanyam, S. (2025). Effects of Green Supply Chain Management Practices on Environmental and Firm Sustainability Performance. *ACTA INNOVATIONS*, 55, 13–22. https://www.actainnovations.com/index.php/pub/article/view/401

Ma, X., & Gu, X. (2024). New marketing strategy model of E-commerce enterprises in the era of digital economy. *Heliyon, 10*(8), e29038. Advance online publication. DOI: 10.1016/j.heliyon.2024.e29038 PMID: 38628774

Ma, Z., Santos, A. Q., Shaker, H. R., Yussof, S., Eriksen, P. M., Hornum, J., & Jørgensen, B. N. (2022). CELSIUS: An international project providing integrated, systematic, cost-effective large-scale IoT solutions for improving energy efficiency of medium- and large-sized buildings. *Energy Informatics*, *5*(S4, Suppl 4), 41. DOI: 10.1186/s42162-022-00221-8

McGowan, L. D., Peng, R. D., & Hicks, S. C. (2022). Design Principles for Data Analysis. In L. D. McGowan, R. D. Peng, & S. C. Hicks, Journal of Computational and Graphical Statistics (Vol. 32, Issue 2, p. 754). Taylor & Francis. DOI: 10.1080/10618600.2022.2104290

McKinsey & Company. (2022). *A digital path to sustainability*. McKinsey & Company. https://www.mckinsey.com/capabilities/operations/our-insights/a-digital-path-to-sustainability

Mehrabi, N., Morstatter, F., Saxena, N., Lerman, K., & Galstyan, A. (2021). A survey on bias and fairness in machine learning. *ACM Computing Surveys, 54*(6). *ACM Computing Surveys*, *115*(6), 1–35. DOI: 10.1145/3457607

Mehrotra, U. (2021, November 03). *Cryptocurrency: A Regulatory Conundrum*. SCC Online. https://www.scconline.com/blog/post/2021/11/03/cryptocurrency-a-regulatory-conundrum/

Meira, S. (2025). Everything platforms. *SSRN*. https://doi.org/DOI: 10.2139/ssrn.5160171

Meltzer, J. (2024). The Impact of Foundational AI on International Trade, Services and Supply Chains in Asia. *Asian Economic Policy Review*, *19*(1), 129–147. DOI: 10.1111/aepr.12451

Mendling, J., Weber, I., van der Aalst, W., Vom Brocke, J., Cabanillas, C., Daniel, F., & Zhang, L. (2018). Blockchains for business process management: Challenges and opportunities. *ACM Transactions on Management Information Systems*, *9*(1), 1–16. DOI: 10.1145/3183367

Meng, F., Chae, S.-R., Drews, A., Kraume, M., Shin, H.-S., & Yang, F. (2009). Recent advances in membrane bioreactors (MBRs): Membrane fouling and membrane material. *Water Research*, *43*(6), 1489–1512. DOI: 10.1016/j.watres.2008.12.044 PMID: 19178926

Menon, V., Sigurdsson, V., Larsen, M., Fagerstrøm, A., Sørensen, H., Marteinsdottir, H. G., & Foxall, G. R. (2019). How to grow brand post engagement on Facebook and twitter for airlines? An empirical investigation of design and content factors. *Journal of Air Transport Management*, *79*, 90–95. DOI: 10.1016/j.jairtraman.2019.05.002

Mentzer, J. T., DeWitt, W., Keebler, J. S., Min, S., Nix, N. W., Smith, C. D., & Zacharia, Z. G. (2001). Defining supply chain management. *Journal of Business Logistics*, *22*(2), 1–25. DOI: 10.1002/j.2158-1592.2001.tb00001.x

Metwally, A. B. M., Ali, H. A. A., Aly, S. A. S., & Ali, M. A. S. (2024). The interplay between digital technologies, supply chain resilience, robustness, and sustainable environmental performance: Does supply chain complexity matter? *Sustainability (Basel)*, *16*(14), 6175. DOI: 10.3390/su16146175

Microsoft. (2020). *Microsoft will be carbon negative by 2030*. Microsoft Official Blog. https://blogs.microsoft.com/blog/2020/01/16/microsoft-will-be-carbon-negative-by-2030/

Microsoft. (2023). *2022 Environmental Sustainability Report*. Microsoft. https://www.microsoft.com/en-us/corporate-responsibility/reports-hub

Microsoft. (2025). *Our sustainability journey*. Microsoft. https://www.microsoft.com/en-us/corporate-responsibility/sustainability-journey

Mihalic, T. (2024). Metaversal sustainability: Conceptualisation within the sustainable tourism paradigm. *Tourism Review*. Advance online publication. DOI: 10.1108/TR-05-2024-0214

Mikalef, P., Boura, M., Lekakos, G., & Krogstie, J. (2019). Big data analytics and firm performance: Findings from a mixed-method approach. *Journal of Business Research*, *98*, 261–276. DOI: 10.1016/j.jbusres.2019.01.044

Mikalef, P., Boura, M., Lekakos, G., & Krogstie, J. (2020). The role of information governance in big data analytics-driven innovation. *Information & Management*, *57*(7), 103361. Advance online publication. DOI: 10.1016/j.im.2020.103361

Mishra, U. (2023, July 25). Regulatory Evolution of Cryptocurrency In India. *Mondaq*. Retrieved October 20, 2024, from https://www.mondaq.com/india/fin-tech/1346578/regulatory-evolution-of-cryptocurrency-in-india

Mitchell, S., & Clark, M. (2020). Telling a different story: How nonprofit organizations reveal strategic purpose through storytelling. In S. Mitchell & M. Clark, Psychology and Marketing (Vol. 38, Issue 1, p. 142). Wiley. DOI: 10.1002/mar.21429

Mithas, S., Tafti, A., Bardhan, I. R., & Goh, J. M. (2012). Information technology and firm profitability: Mechanisms and empirical evidence. *Management Information Systems Quarterly*, *36*(1), 205–224. DOI: 10.2307/41410414

Modic, D., Anderson, R., & Palomäki, J. (2018). We will make you like our research: The use of persuasion in scam emails. PLOS ONE, 13(9), e0204129. OECD / EUIPO. (2022). Dangerous Fakes: Trade in Counterfeit Goods that Pose Health, Safety and Environmental Risks. OECD Publishing, Paris. https://doi.org/DOI: 10.1371/journal.pone.0204129

Mohamed, A., Ismail, I., & AlDaraawi, M. (2025). IoT-Driven Intelligent Energy Management: Leveraging Smart Monitoring Applications and Artificial Neural Networks (ANN) for Sustainable Practices. *Computers*, *14*(7), 269. DOI: 10.3390/computers14070269

Mohamed, M., Helmy, O., & Ibrahiem, D. (2025). Digitalization and Carbon Footprint: Does ICT Reduce Carbon Footprint? *Digital Technologies Research and Applications*, *4*(3), 136–158. DOI: 10.54963/dtra.v4i3.1306

Mohammad, R. A., Alahmari, A. M. O., Faqih, R. H. A., Alshehri, A. I. A., & Al-Kahtani, S. M. (2024). Linking strategic intelligence, strategic leadership, strategic planning, and strategic thinking and business performance: The moderating effect of strategic flexibility. *Discover Sustainability*, *5*(1), 434. DOI: 10.1007/s43621-024-00670-z

Mone, E. M., & London, M. (2018). *Employee engagement through effective performance management: A practical guide for managers*. Routledge., DOI: 10.4324/9781315626529

Mo, R., & Wang, S. (2025). E-commerce Research in the Past Decade: A Bibliometric Analysis. *SAGE Open*, *15*(3), 21582440251381152. Advance online publication. DOI: 10.1177/21582440251381152

Mottaeva, A., Khussainova, Z., & Gordeyeva, Y. (2023). Impact of the digital economy on the development of economic systems. *E3S Web of Conferences, 381*. DOI: 10.1051/e3sconf/202338102011

Mullet, D. R. (2018). A General Critical Discourse Analysis Framework for Educational Research. *Journal of Advanced Academics*, *29*(2), 116–142. DOI: 10.1177/1932202X18758260

Mun, S. G., & Jang, S. S. (2018). Restaurant operating expenses and their effects on profitability enhancement. *International Journal of Hospitality Management*, *71*, 68–76. DOI: 10.1016/j.ijhm.2017.12.002

Murthy, K., Kalsie, A., & Shankar, R. (2021). Digital economy in a global perspective: Is there a digital divide? *Transnational Corporations Review*, *13*(1), 1–15. DOI: 10.1080/19186444.2020.1871257

Murthy, K., Ram, K. R., Al Farsi, R. I., Sharma, R. V., & Al Habsi, L. S. (2024). Navigating leadership development in college-based higher education. In *Advances in Higher Education and Professional Development* (pp. 61–88). IGI Global., DOI: 10.4018/979-8-3693-0467-9.ch004

Muse, B. A., Nafi, K. W., Khomh, F., & Antoniol, G. (2024). Data-access performance anti-patterns in data-intensive systems. In B. A. Muse, K. W. Nafi, F. Khomh, & G. Antoniol, Empirical Software Engineering (Vol. 29, Issue 6). Springer Science+Business Media. DOI: 10.1007/s10664-024-10535-8

Mutamim, N. S. A., Zainon Noor, Z., Hassan, M. A. A., & Olsson, G. (2013). Membrane bioreactor: Applications and limitations in treating high strength industrial wastewater. *Chemical Engineering Journal*, *225*, 109–119. DOI: 10.1016/j.cej.2013.02.131

Mwencha, P. (2019). Taxation Of Electronic Commerce-A Commentary. *Finance & Development*, *1*(1), 70–79.

Nadagouda, M. N., & Varma, R. S. (2008). Green synthesis of silver and palladium nanoparticles at room temperature using coffee and tea extract. *Green Chemistry*, *10*(8), 859–862. DOI: 10.1039/b804703k

Nadal, C., Sas, C., & Doherty, G. (2020). Technology Acceptance in Mobile Health: Scoping Review of Definitions, Models, and Measurement. *J Med Internet Res 22(7):E17256* Https://Www.Jmir.Org/2020/7/E17256, DOI: 10.2196/17256

Naneva, V., & Stefanova, K. (2021). Optimization techniques for business intelligence reports. In Naneva, V., & Stefanova, K. (Eds.), *American Institute of Physics*. AIP conference proceedings, DOI: 10.1063/5.0042199

Nanomine. *Data mining and modeling for polymer nanocomposites*. Retrieved from https://nanomine.org

Narayanan, R., & El-Sayed, M. A. (2004). Shape-dependent catalytic activity of platinum nanoparticles in colloidal solution. *Nano Letters*, *4*(7), 1343–1348. DOI: 10.1021/nl0495256

Nasiri, M., Saunila, M., Rantala, T., & Ukko, J. (2022). Sustainable innovation among small businesses: The role of digital orientation, the external environment, and company characteristics. *Sustainable Development (Bradford)*, *30*(4), 703–712. DOI: 10.1002/sd.2267

Nasiri, M., Ukko, J., Saunila, M., Rantala, T., & Rantanen, H. (2020). Digital-related capabilities and financial performance: The mediating effect of performance measurement systems. *Technology Analysis and Strategic Management, 31*(12), 1393–1406. DOI: 10.1080/09537325.2020.1772966

Nayyar, G., Hallward-Driemeier, M., & Davies, E. (2021). *At Your Service: the Promise of Services-Led Development*. World Bank Publications., DOI: 10.1596/978-1-4648-1671-0

Ndubuisi, G., Owusu, S., Asiama, R., & Avenyo, E. K. (2023). Drivers of services sector growth acceleration in developing countries. World Institute for Development Economics Research (WIDER). *Working Paper, 2023*(87).

Nguyen, T. H., Doan, X. H., & Tran, P. (2025). Human–artificial intelligence collaboration in supply chain outcomes: The mediating role of responsible artificial intelligence. *Annals of Operations Research, 354*(1), 35–69. Advance online publication. DOI: 10.1007/s10479-025-06534-7

Nica, O., Piotrowska, K., & Schenk-Hoppé, K. R. (2017, October 27). Cryptocurrencies: Economic Benefits and Risks. SSRN. Retrieved October 20, 2024, from https://papers.ssrn.com/sol3/papers.cfm?abstract_id=3059856 DOI: 10.2139/ssrn.3059856

Nickel, P. J., Loosman, I., Frank, L., & Vinnikova, A. (2023). Justice and Empowerment Through Digital Health: Ethical Challenges and Opportunities. *Digital Society : Ethics, Socio-Legal and Governance of Digital Technology, 2*(3), 42. Advance online publication. DOI: 10.1007/s44206-023-00075-x

Nie, C., Kushinsky, D., & Ren, T. (2025). Digital transformation, CEO compensation, and ESG performance: Evidence from Chinese listed companies. *Sustainability (Basel), 17*(9), 4033. DOI: 10.3390/su17094033

Niewiadomski, P., & Brouder, P. (2024). From 'sustainable tourism' to 'sustainability transitions in tourism'? *Tourism Geographies, 26*(2), 141–150. DOI: 10.1080/14616688.2023.2299832

Niguse, T., Borji, B., & Kant, S. (2025). Effect of Strategic alignment and strategic foresight on competitive advantage with mediating role of human capital a case of medium and large firms in Ethiopia. *Future Business Journal, 11*(1), 161. Advance online publication. DOI: 10.1186/s43093-025-00574-y

Nimma, D. S. (2022, March 22). Curbing the Menance of Money Laundering International Initiatives. *International Journal for Legal Research and Analysis, 2*(6), 4–23. Retrieved October 19, 2024, from https://www.ijlra.com/productImage/Dr.Sudarshan%20Nimma.pdf

Niu, F. (2021). The role of the digital economy in rebuilding and maintaining social governance mechanisms. *Frontiers in Public Health, 9*, 819727. DOI: 10.3389/fpubh.2021.819727 PMID: 35096761

Norman, C. D., & Skinner, H. A. (2006). eHEALS: the eHealth literacy scale. *Journal of medical Internet research* 8(4): e507. DOI: 10.2196/jmir.8.4.e27

Nosratabadi, S., Atobishi, T., & Hegedűs, S. (2023). Social sustainability of digital transformation: Empirical evidence from. *Administrative Sciences, 13*(5), 126. DOI: 10.3390/admsci13050126

Nouri, S., Khoong, E. C., Lyles, C. R., & Karliner, L. (2020). Addressing equity in telemedicine for chronic disease management: Practical strategies during and after the COVID-19 pandemic. *NEJM Catalyst Innovations in Care Delivery, 1*(3).

Nyathani, R. (2023). AI in performance management: Redefining performance appraisals in the digital age. *Journal of Artificial Intelligence & Cloud Computing, SRC/JAICC-146*, 134, 2–5.

O'Neill, M., Morgan, J., & Burke, K. (2021). Process Visualization of Manufacturing Execution System (MES). *Data*, 659–664. Advance online publication. DOI: 10.1109/SWC50871.2021.00098

OECD. (2020). *OECD Digital Economy Outlook 2020*. OECD Publishing., DOI: 10.1787/bb167041-

OECD. (2020a). *How's Life in the Digital Age? Opportunities and risks of the digital transformation for people's well-being*. OECD Publishing.

OECD. (2021). *OECD Publishing*. doi:http://dx.doi.org/.DOI: 10.1787/10.1787/9789264113-41-en

OECD. (2024). *Harnessing Public Procurement for the Green Transition: Good Practices in OECD Countries*. OECD Publishing. https://www.oecd.org/en/publications/harnessing-public-procurement-for-the-green-transition_e551f448-en.html

Office of the United States Trade Representative (USTR). (2022). 2022 national trade estimate report on foreign trade barriers. USTR. https://ustr.gov

Ofosu-Ampong, K., & Acheampong, B. (2022). Adoption of contactless technologies for remote work in Ghana post-Covid-19: Insights from technology-organisation-environment framework. *Digital Business, 2*(2), 100023. DOI: 10.1016/j.digbus.2022.100023

Ogbeide, H., Thomson, M. E., Gonul, M. S., Pollock, A. C., Bhowmick, S., & Bello, A. U. (2023). The anti-money laundering risk assessment: A probabilistic approach. *Journal of Business Research, 162*, 162. DOI: 10.1016/j.jbusres.2023.113820

Olivetti, E. A., & Cullen, J. M. (2018). Toward a sustainable materials system. *Science, 360*(6396), 1396–1398. DOI: 10.1126/science.aat6821 PMID: 29954965

Olusanya, M. O., & Isinkaye, F. (2025). A Review and Bibliometric Study on the Trends and E-Commerce Recommenders. [IJKM]. *International Journal of Knowledge Management, 21*(1), 1–26. DOI: 10.4018/IJKM.367729

Omisola, J. O., Bihani, D., Daraojimba, A. I., Osho, G. O., Ubamadu, B. C., & Etukudoh, E. A. (2023). Blockchain in supply chain transparency: A conceptual framework for real-time data tracking and reporting using blockchain and AI. *International Journal of Multidisciplinary Research and Growth Evaluation, 4*(1), 1238–1253. DOI: 10.54660/.IJMRGE.2023.4.1.1238-1253

Onukwulu, E. C., Agho, M. O., & Eyo-Udo, N. L.Ekene Cynthia OnukwuluMercy Odochi AghoNsisong Louis Eyo-Udo. (2021). Framework for sustainable supply chain practices to reduce carbon footprint in energy. *Open Access Research Journal of Science and Technology, 1*(2), 12–34. DOI: 10.53022/oarjst.2021.1.2.0032

Ooi, G. L. (2008). Cities and sustainability: Southeast Asian and European perspectives. *Asia Europe Journal, 6*(2), 193–204. DOI: 10.1007/s10308-008-0176-0

Opoku Agyemang, K., & Irannezhad, E. (2025). The impact of the COVID-19 pandemic on global freight movement and logistics. *Transportation Research Procedia, 82*, 3604–3627. DOI: 10.1016/j.trpro.2024.12.073

Organisation for Economic Co-operation and Development (OECD). (2020b). *Digital transformation in the age of COVID-19: Building resilience and bridging divides.* OECD Publishing.

Organisation for Economic Co-operation and Development (OECD). (2021). *OECD digital economy outlook 2021.* OECD Publishing. https://www.oecd.org/en/publications/oecd-digital-economy-outlook_f0b5c251-en.html

Organisation for Economic Co-operation and Development. (2021). *State of implementation of the OECD AI Principles: Insights from national AI policies.* OECD Digital Economy Papers, No. 311. OECD Publishing. https://doi.org/DOI: 10.1787/20716826

Organization for Economic Co-operation and Development (OECD). (2021). SMEs in a digitized and globalized economy: Trends and policy challenges. OECD. https://www.oecd.org/industry/smes-in-a-digitised-and-globalised-economy.htm

Ørsted. (2021). Ørsted. *Sustainability Report*, •••, 2021.

Otter, V., & Robinson, D. (2024). Transparency and changing stakeholder roles in the digital age of sustainable agri-food supply chain networks. *Frontiers in Sustainable Food Systems*, *8*, 1449684. DOI: 10.3389/fsufs.2024.1449684

Paiola, M., & Gebauer, H. (2020). Internet of things technologies, digital servitization and business model innovation in BtoB manufacturing firms. *Industrial Marketing Management*, *89*, 245–264. DOI: 10.1016/j.indmarman.2020.03.009

Panjaitan, W. J., Sholihah, E., Koerniawan, I., & Andriana, M. (2022). Maintaining organizational sustaincapability towards management innovation using strategic foresight. *Journal of Management and Informatics*, *1*(1), 12–20. DOI: 10.51903/jmi.v1i1.145

Pan, L., Chen, Y., Zhang, Z., & Liu, J. (2023). Rethinking globalization: The impact of geopolitics and digital technologies on global value chain reconfiguration. *Journal of International Business Policy*, *6*(2), 215–234. DOI: 10.1016/j.jibp.2023.05.002

Papastamoulou, P., & Antonopoulos, N. (2025). Artificial Intelligence in E-Commerce: A Comparative Analysis of Best Practices Across Leading Platforms. *Systems*, *13*(746), 746. Advance online publication. DOI: 10.3390/systems13090746

Parida, V., Sjödin, D., & Reim, W. (2019). Reviewing literature on digitalization, business model innovation, and sustainable industry: Past achievements and future promises. *Sustainability (Basel)*, *11*(2), 1102391. DOI: 10.3390/su11020391

Park, J., An, K., Hwang, Y., Park, J.-G., Noh, H.-J., Kim, J.-Y., Park, J.-H., Hwang, N.-M., & Hyeon, T. (2004). Ultra-large-scale syntheses of monodisperse nanocrystals. *Nature Materials*, *3*(12), 891–895. DOI: 10.1038/nmat1251 PMID: 15568032

Park, S. R., & Jang, J. Y. (2021). The impact of ESG management on investment decision: Institutional investors' perceptions of country-specific ESG criteria. *International Journal of Financial Studies*, *9*(3), 48. DOI: 10.3390/ijfs9030048

Parmar, B. L., Freeman, R. E., Harrison, J. S., Wicks, A. C., Purnell, L., & De Colle, S. (2010). Stakeholder theory: The state of the art. *The Academy of Management Annals*, *4*(1), 403–445. DOI: 10.5465/19416520.2010.495581

Parry, E., & Battista, V. (2019). The impact of emerging technologies on work: A review of the evidence and implications for the human resource function. *Emerging Markets Journal*, *9*(1), 1–19. DOI: 10.5195/emaj.2019.184

Parthasarathy, S., & R, A. (2023, March 15). PMLA – Crypto Currency: When Prevention is Better than Cure. *SCC Online*. Retrieved October 20, 2024, from https://www.scconline.com/blog/post/2023/03/15/pmla-crypto-currency-when-prevention-is-better-than-cure/

Partners, M. B. O. (2023). Digital Nomads - The 2021 Workforce Trend. MBO Partners. https://www.mbopartners.com/state-of-independence/digital-nomads/

Patil, K. C., Aruna, S. T., & Ekambaram, S. (2007). Combustion synthesis: An update. *Current Opinion in Solid State and Materials Science*, *6*(6), 507–512. DOI: 10.1016/S1359-0286(02)00123-7

Patrichi, I. C. (2024). Ai solutions for sustainable tourism management: A comprehensive review. *Journal of Information Systems & Operations Management*, *18*(1), 172–185.

Paul, B. K., & Moulik, S. P. (2001). Microemulsions: An overview. *Journal of Dispersion Science and Technology*, *22*(3), 1–28. DOI: 10.1081/DIS-100103349

Pechini, M. P. (1967). *Method of preparing lead and alkaline earth titanates and niobates and coating method using the same to form a capacitor* (U.S. Patent No. 3,330,697).

Peres, R., Jia, X., Lee, J., Sun, K., Colombo, A., & Barata, J. (2020). Industrial artificial intelligence in industry 4.0 - systematic review, challenges and outlook. https://doi.org/DOI: 10.1109/ACCESS.2020.3042874

Perski, O., & Short, C. E. (2021). Acceptability of digital health interventions: Embracing the complexity. *Translational Behavioral Medicine*, *11*(7), 1473–1480. DOI: 10.1093/tbm/ibab048 PMID: 33963864

Peterson, C. B., Hamilton, C., & Hasvold, E. P. (2016). *World Health Organization. From innovation to implementation – eHealth in the WHO European Region. Ginebra (Suiza): WHO; 2016.* Retrieved from http://www.euro.who.int/__data/assets/pdf_file/0012/302331/From-Innovation-to-Implementation-eHealth-Report-EU.pdf

Petry, T. (2018). Digital leadership. In North, K., Maier, R., & Haas, O. (Eds.), *Knowledge management in digital change: New findings and practical cases* (pp. 209–218). Springer Cham., https://ideas.repec.org/h/spr/prochp/978-3-319-73546-7_12.html DOI: 10.1007/978-3-319-73546-7_12

Phang, D., Wang, K., Wang, Q., Kauffman, R., & Naldi, M. (2019). How to derive causal insights for digital commerce in China? A research commentary on computational social science methods. *Electronic Commerce Research and Applications*, *35*, 100837. Advance online publication. DOI: 10.1016/j.elerap.2019.100837

Pierre, A. C., & Pajonk, G. M. (2002). Chemistry of aerogels and their applications. *Chemical Reviews*, *102*(11), 4243–4265. DOI: 10.1021/cr0101306 PMID: 12428989

Pilelienė, L., Grigaliūnaitė, V., & Bogoyavlenska, Y. (2024). A bibliometric review of innovations in sustainable tourism research: Current trends and future research agenda. *Sustainability (Basel)*, *16*(16), 7124. DOI: 10.3390/su16167124

Pileni, M. P. (2001). Nanocrystals self-assemblies: Fabrication and collective properties. *The Journal of Physical Chemistry. B*, *105*(17), 3358–3371. DOI: 10.1021/jp0039520

Pileni, M. P. (2003). The role of soft colloidal templates in controlling the size and shape of inorganic nanocrystals. *Nature Materials*, *2*(3), 145–150. DOI: 10.1038/nmat817 PMID: 12612669

Pillai, D. K., & Julian, A. F. (n.d.). Prevention of Monet Laundering: Legal and Financial Issues. *Indian Law Institute Law Review*, 1-9. Retrieved October 19, 2024

Pinto, M. M. A., Kovaleski, J. L., Mick, R. L., & Chiroli, D. M. G. (2024). Developing a sustainable digital transformation roadmap for SMEs: Integrating digital maturity and strategic alignment. *Sustainability (Basel)*, *16*(20), 8745. DOI: 10.3390/su16208745

Poddar, B., & Shalini. (n.d.). Prevention of Money Laundering Act, 2002 - An Overview. *Manupatra*. Retrieved October 18, 2024, from https://www.manupatra.com/roundup/314/Articles/Prevention%20of%20Money%20Laundering.pdf

Polyakov, M., & Kovshun, N. (2021). Diffusion of Innovations as a Key Driver of the Digital Economy Development. *Baltic Journal of Economic Studies*, *7*(1), 84–92. DOI: 10.30525/2256-0742/2021-7-1-84-92

Poperwi, L., Hondoma, T., & Mataba, A. (2025). Futures focus-A systematic review of Scenario Planning, Strategic Foresight and Dynamic Capabilities. Futures: The Zimbabwe Ezekiel Guti University Journal of Leadership, Governance and Development, 301–322. DOI: 10.71458/721nkq04

Porter, M. E. (1985). *Competitive advantage: Creating and sustaining superior performance*. Free Press.

Postma, A., & Yeoman, I. S. (2021). A systems perspective as a tool to understand disruption in travel and tourism. *Journal of Tourism Futures*, *7*(1), 67–77. DOI: 10.1108/JTF-04-2020-0052

Prabu, S. L., Suriyaprakash, T. N. K., & Kumar, A. (2018). Wastewater treatment and pollution control in pharmaceutical industries. *International Journal of Environmental Sciences*, *7*(2), 94–102.

Prabu, S. L., Suriyaprakash, T. N. K., & Kumar, A. (2021). Industrial wastewater treatment techniques—An overview. *Materials Today: Proceedings*, *46*, 1399–1406.

Procter & Gamble. (2022). *2022 Citizenship Report.* Procter & Gamble. https://us.pg.com/2022_Citizenship_Report.pdf

PRS. (2019). *Virtual Currencies in India.* New Delhi: PRS Legislative Reseacrh ndia. Retrieved October 20, 2024, from https://prsindia.org/files/bills_acts/bills_parliament/1970/PRS%20Committee%20Report%20and%20Bill%20Summary%20on%20Virtual%20Currencies.pdf

Pulakos, E. D., Mueller-Hanson, R. A., & O'Leary, R. S. (2015). Performance management in the United States. In Wilkinson, A., Bacon, N., Lepak, D., & Snell, S. (Eds.), *The Sage handbook of human resource management* (pp. 224–241). Sage.

PWC. (2018). The potential impact of Artificial Intelligence in the Middle East - PwC Middle East. PwC. https://www.pwc.com/m1/en/publications/potential-impact-artificial-intelligence-middle-east.html

PwC. (2020). *Time for Trust.* PwC. Retrieved October 19, 2024, from https://image.uk.info.pwc.com/lib/fe31117075640475701c74/m/2/434c46d2-a889-4fed-a030-c52964c71a64.pdf

PwC. (2020, October 13). *Blockchain technologies could boost the global economy US$1.76 trillion by 2030 through raising levels of tracking, tracing and trust.* Retrieved October 20, 2024, from PwC: https://www.pwc.com/gx/en/news-room/press-releases/2020/blockchain-boost-global-economy-track-trace-trust.html

Qawasmeh, E., Qawasmeh, F., & Daoud, M. K. (2024). Digital transformation in HRM: Leveraging AI and big data for employee engagement and retention. *Journal of Ecohumanism*, *3*(3), 3479. DOI: 10.62754/joe.v3i3.3479

Qin, Y., Ma, Q., Huang, H., Wang, J., & Chen, X. (2008). Microwave-assisted polyol process for the synthesis of ZnO nanoparticles. *Materials Science and Engineering B*, *150*(1), 40–44. DOI: 10.1016/j.mseb.2008.02.016

Radovanović, A., Koningstein, R., Schneider, I., Chen, B., Duarte, A., Roy, B., Xiao, D., Haridasan, M., Hung, P., Care, N., Talukdar, S., Mullen, E., Smith, K., Cottman, M. E., & Cirne, W. (2023). Carbon-Aware Computing for Datacenters. *IEEE Transactions on Power Systems*, *38*(2), 1270–1280. DOI: 10.1109/TPWRS.2022.3173250

Rafi, M., & Novriana, R. (2024). Local government capability in sustainable tourism development. *Jurnal Kebijakan Publik, 15*(1), 55–70. DOI: 10.31292/jkp.v15i1.2024

Rai, M., Ingle, A. P., Birla, S., Yadav, A., & Santos, C. A. D. (2018). Strategic role of selected noble metal nanoparticles in medicine. *Critical Reviews in Microbiology, 44*(6), 663–674. DOI: 10.1080/1040841X.2018.1486673 PMID: 26089024

Raina, K., Sharma, G. D., Taheri, B., Dev, D., & Chavriya, S. (2025). Artificial intelligence-driven management: Bridging innovation, knowledge creation, and sustainable business practices. *Journal of Innovation & Knowledge, 11*, 100860. DOI: 10.1016/j.jik.2025.100860

Rai, P., & Bera, S. (2024). Machine learning-based empirical investigation of user's perception of digitalisation in pandemic immunisation programs. *Journal of Decision Systems*, 1–27. Advance online publication. DOI: 10.1080/12460125.2024.2365492

Raisch, S., & Krakowski, S. (n.d.). Artificial intelligence and management.

Raja Santhi, A., & Muthuswamy, P. (2023). Industry 5.0 or industry 4.0S? Introduction to industry 4.0 and a peek into the prospective industry 5.0 technologies. [IJIDeM]. *International Journal on Interactive Design and Manufacturing, 17*(2), 947–979. DOI: 10.1007/s12008-023-01217-8 PMID: 40478102

Rajagopal, K. (2021, December 03). *Supreme Court sets aside RBI ban on cryptocurrency transactions*. Retrieved October 2024, 2024, from The Hindu: https://www.thehindu.com/news/national/supreme-court-sets-aside-rbi-ban-on-cryptocurrency-transactions/article61967124.ece

Rajam, V., Reddy, A. B., & Banerjee, S. (2021). Explaining caste-based digital divide in India. *Telematics and Informatics, 65*, 101719. DOI: 10.1016/j.tele.2021.101719

Ramesh, M., Anbuvannan, M., & Viruthagiri, G. (2015). Green synthesis of ZnO nanoparticles using *Solanum nigrum* leaf extract and their antibacterial activity. *Spectrochimica Acta. Part A, Molecular and Biomolecular Spectroscopy, 136*, 864–870. DOI: 10.1016/j.saa.2014.09.105 PMID: 25459609

Ranaweera, N. (2024, May 27). The role of cryptocurrencies in money laundering: challenges and regulatory responses. *Innovare Journal of Social Sciences, 12*(4), 10–13. Retrieved October 18, 2024, from. DOI: 10.22159/ijss.2024v12i4.51219

Ransbotham, S., Kiron, D., Gerbert, P., & Reeves, M. (2017). *Reshaping business with artificial intelligence: Closing the gap between ambition and action*. MIT Sloan Management Review & Boston Consulting Group.

Rashid, A. B., & Kausik, A. K. (2024). AI Revolutionizing Industries Worldwide: A Comprehensive Overview of Its Diverse Applications. *Hybrid Advances*, *7*(100277), 100277–100277. DOI: 10.1016/j.hybadv.2024.100277

Rattanamanee, K. (2024). Future perspectives on communication management for promoting tourism in Chachoengsao Province (2024–2027). *International Journal of Professional Business Review*, *9*(1), e04307. DOI: 10.26668/businessreview/2024.v9i1.4307

Ravikumar, A. S., Kalandarov, A., Djumaniyazova, M., & Habib, M. (2025). A roadmap to a sustainable future. In Advances in Computational Intelligence and Robotics (pp. 267–302). IGI Global Scientific Publishing. DOI: 10.4018/979-8-3373-3017-4.ch010

Ravikumar, R. N., & Aarthi, S. (2025). Digital Twin-driven green energy systems. In *The Future of Green Energy* (pp. 1–28). IGI Global Scientific Publishing., DOI: 10.4018/979-8-3373-3226-0.ch001

Rawashdeh, A., Abdallah, A. B., Alfawaeer, M., Al Dweiri, M., & Al-Jaghbeer, F. (2024). The impact of strategic agility on environmental sustainability: The mediating role of digital transformation. *Sustainability (Basel)*, *16*(3), 1338. DOI: 10.3390/su16031338

Rawls, J. (2001). *Justice as fairness: A restatement*. Harvard University Press. DOI: 10.2307/j.ctv31xf5v0

Raworth, K. (2023). Kate Raworth on creating regenerative and distributive economies by design. In Alexander, A., Pascucci, S., & Charnley, F. (Eds.), *Handbook of the Circular Economy: Transitions and Transformation* (pp. 45–52). De Gruyter., DOI: 10.1515/9783110723373-005

Raza, M. S., Zhan, Q., & Rubab, S. (2020). Role of money mules in money laundering and financial crimes: A discussion through case studies. *Journal of Financial Crime*, *27*(3), 911–993. DOI: 10.1108/JFC-02-2020-0028

Razzaq, A., Sharif, A., Ahmad, P., & Jermsittiparsert, K. (2021). Asymmetric role of tourism development and technology innovation on carbon dioxide emission reduction in the Chinese economy: Fresh insights from QARDL approach. *Sustainable Development (Bradford)*, *29*(1), 176–193. DOI: 10.1002/sd.2139

Razzouk, R., & Shute, V. (2012). What is design thinking and why is it important? *Review of Educational Research*, *82*(3), 330–348. DOI: 10.3102/0034654312457429

Reddy, J. (2019). The Case for Regulating Crypto Assets. *Indian Journal of Law and Technology*, *15*(2), 380–423. DOI: 10.55496/GIGZ6133

Rehman, N. U., & Nunziante, G. (2023). The effect of the digital economy on total factor productivity in European regions. *Telecommunications Policy*, *47*(10), 102650. Advance online publication. DOI: 10.1016/j.telpol.2023.102650

Reif, N. (2024, August 30). *What Does It Mean to Burn Crypto? Practical Applications*. Retrieved October 20, 2024, from Investopedia: https://www.investopedia .com/tech/cryptocurrency-burning-can-it-manage-inflation/

Ren, S. (2022). Optimization of Enterprise Financial Management and Decision-Making Systems Based on Big Data. In S. Ren, Journal of Mathematics (Vol. 2022, Issue 1). Hindawi Publishing Corporation. DOI: 10.1155/2022/1708506

Ribeiro-Navarrete, S., Botella-Carrubi, D., Palacios-Marqués, D., & Orero-Blat, M. (2021). The effect of digitalization on business performance: An applied study of KIBS. *Journal of Business Research*, *126*, 319–326. DOI: 10.1016/j.jbusres.2020.12.065

Richards, K. (2024, March). *TechTarget*. Retrieved from What is Cryptography?: https://www.techtarget.com/searchsecurity/definition/cryptography

Rich, E., Miah, A., & Lewis, S. (2019). Is digital health care more equitable? The framing of health inequalities within England's digital health policy 2010–2017. *Sociology of Health & Illness*, *41*(S1), 31–49. DOI: 10.1111/1467-9566.12980 PMID: 31599987

Richer, G., Pister, A., Abdelaal, M., Fekete, J.-D., Sedlmair, M., & Weiskopf, D. (2023). Scalability in Visualization. https://arxiv.org/pdf/2210.06562.pdf

Rindfleisch, A., & Heide, J. B. (1997). Transaction cost analysis: Past, present, and future applications. *Journal of Marketing*, *61*(4), 30–54. DOI: 10.1177/002224299706100403

Riswanto, A., Zafar, T. S., P, M. A., Sunijati, E., Harto, B., Boari, Y., Astaman, P., Dassir, M., & Hikmah, A. N. (2023). Ekonomi KREATIF: Inovasi, Peluang, Dan Tantangan Ekonomi Kreatif Di Indonesia. PT. Sonpedia Publishing Indonesia.

Rivard, S., Raymond, L., & Verreault, D. (2006). Resource-based view and competitive strategy: An integrated model of the contribution of information technology to firm performance. *The Journal of Strategic Information Systems*, *15*(1), 29–50. DOI: 10.1016/j.jsis.2005.06.003

Roberts, S. (2003). Supply chain specific: Understanding the patchy success of ethical sourcing initiatives. *Journal of Business Ethics*, *44*(2), 159–170. DOI: 10.1023/A:1023395631811

Robinson, L., Cotten, S. R., Ono, H., Quan-Haase, A., Mesch, G., Chen, W., Schulz, J., Hale, T. M., & Stern, M. J. (2015). Digital inequalities and why they matter. *Information Communication and Society*, *18*(5), 569–582. DOI: 10.1080/1369118X.2015.1012532

Rodriguez, J. L., & Rodriguez, R. M. G. (2005). Technology and export behaviour: A resource-based view approach. *International Business Review*, *14*(5), 539–557. DOI: 10.1016/j.ibusrev.2005.07.002

Rogers, E. M. (2003). *Diffusion of innovations* (5th ed.). Free Press.

Rohr, B., Stein, H. S., Guevarra, D., Wang, Y., Haber, J. A., Aykol, M., & Gregoire, J. M. (2020). Benchmarking the acceleration of materials discovery by sequential learning. *Chemical Science (Cambridge)*, *11*(10), 2696–2706. DOI: 10.1039/C9SC05999G PMID: 34084328

Romagnoli, S., Tarabusi, C., Maleki Vishkaei, B., & De Giovanni, P. (2023). The impact of digital technologies and sustainable practices on circular supply chain management. *Logistics (Basel)*, *7*(1), 1. DOI: 10.3390/logistics7010001

Rong, K. (2022). Research agenda for the digital economy. *Journal of Digital Economy*, *1*(1), 20–31. Advance online publication. DOI: 10.1016/j.jdec.2022.08.004

Rosário, A. T., & Dias, J. C. (2023). The new digital economy and sustainability: Challenges and opportunities. *Sustainability (Basel)*, *15*(14), 10902. DOI: 10.3390/su151410902

Roy, S. K., Balaji, M., Sadeque, S., Nguyen, B., & Melewar, T. (2017). Constituents and consequences of smart customer experience in retailing. *Technological Forecasting and Social Change*, *124*, 257–270. DOI: 10.1016/j.techfore.2016.09.022

Roy, S. K., Tehrani, A. N., Pandit, A., Apostolidis, C., & Ray, S. (2025). Ai-capable relationship marketing: Shaping the future of customer relationships. *Journal of Business Research*, *192*, 115309–115309. DOI: 10.1016/j.jbusres.2025.115309

Rupeika-Apoga, R., & Petrovska, K. (2022). Barriers to sustainable digital transformation in micro-, small-, and medium-sized enterprises. *Sustainability (Basel)*, *14*(20), 13558. DOI: 10.3390/su142013558

Rybchak, Z., & Basystiuk, O. (2017). Analysis of methods and means of text mining. *ECONTECHMOD: An International Quarterly Journal on Economics of Technology and Modelling Processes*, *6*(2), 73–78.

Saberi, R., & Sadegh, S. (2022). The Future of Global E-Commerce Regulation: LegEnsuring Fair Competition, Consumer Rights, and Data Protection. *Legal Studies in Digital Age*, *1*(1), 39–52.

Saberi, S., Kouhizadeh, M., Sarkis, J., & Shen, L. (2019). Blockchain technology and its relationships to sustainable supply chain management. *International Journal of Production Research, 57*(7), 2117–2135. DOI: 10.1080/00207543.2018.1533261

Sahut, J. M., & Lissillour, R. (2023). The adoption of remote work platforms after the Covid-19 lockdown: New approach, new evidence. *Journal of Business Research, 154*, 113345. DOI: 10.1016/j.jbusres.2022.113345 PMID: 36193197

Sakka, S. (2005). *Handbook of sol-gel science and technology: Processing, characterization and applications*. Springer.

Samaddar, K., & Mondal, S. (2024). AR and VR-based travel: A responsible practice towards sustainable tourism. ***International Journal of Tourism Cities***. Advanced online publication. https://doi.org/DOI: 10.1108/IJTC-03-2024-0015

Samanta, S., & Baitalik, A. (2015). Potential site selection for eco-tourism: A case study of four blocks in Bankura district using remote sensing and GIS technology, West Bengal. *International Journal of Advanced Research, 3*(4), 978–989.

Samimi, M., Cortés, A. F., Anderson, M. H., & Herrmann, P. (2022). What is strategic leadership? Developing a framework for future research. *The Leadership Quarterly, 33*(3), 101353. Advance online publication. DOI: 10.1016/j.leaqua.2019.101353

Sampat, B., Raj, S., Behl, A., & Schöbel, S. (2022). An empirical analysis of facilitators and barriers to the hybrid work model: A cross-cultural and multi-theoretical approach. *Personnel Review, 51*(8), 1990–2020. DOI: 10.1108/PR-02-2022-0176

Samuel, P. (1939). The Gains from International Trade. *The Canadian Journal of Economics and Political Science, 5*(2), 195-205. . JSTOR 137133.DOI: 10.2307/137133

Santos, R. C., Almeida, C. S., & Lima, R. C. (2015). Synthesis and characterization of ZnO nanoparticles by sol-gel method for application in gas sensor. *Materials Research, 18*(3), 553–557. DOI: 10.1590/1516-1439.347514

SAP SE. (2021). SAP's Climate 21 initiative: Integrating climate action end to end. *SAP News*. https://news.sap.com/2021/10/integrating-climate-action-end-to-end/

Saqib, N. A., Salam, A. A., Rahman, A.-U.-, & Dash, S. (2023). Reviewing risks and vulnerabilities in web 2.0 for matching security considerations in web 3.0. https://www.tandfonline.com/doi/full/10.1080/09720529.2020.1857903

Sargan, J. D. (1958). The estimation of economic relationships using instrumental variables. *Econometrica, 26*(3), 393–415. DOI: 10.2307/1907619

Sayer, A. (2000). Realism and social science. *Sage (Atlanta, Ga.)*. Advance online publication. DOI: 10.4135/9781446218730

Schluep, M., Müller, E., Hilty, L. M., Ott, D., Widmer, R., & Böni, H. (2013). Insights from a decade of development cooperation in e-waste management. In L. M. Hilty, B. Aebischer, G. Andersson, & W. Lohmann (Eds.), *ICT innovations for sustainability* (pp. 223–230). ETH E-Collection. http://e-collection.library.ethz.ch/view/eth:6558

Schmid, G. (2004). Large clusters and colloids: Metals in the embryonic state. *Chemical Reviews*, *92*(8), 1709–1727. DOI: 10.1021/cr00016a002

Schneider Electric. (2021). *Edge computing solutions: sustainability at the edge*. Schneider Electric. https://www.se.com/ww/en/work/solutions/edge-computing/sustainability-at-the-edge.jsp

Schneider Electric. (2021). Smart factories triple-bottom-line success! *Schneider Electric Blog*. https://blog.se.com/sustainability/2021/06/03/smart-factories-triple-bottom-line-success/

Schneider Electric. (2022). *2022 Sustainability Report*. Schneider Electric. https://www.se.com/ww/en/about-us/sustainability/sustainability-reports/

Schneider, F. G. (2008, February). Money Laundering and Financial Means of Organised Crime: Some Preliminary Empirical Findings. *Research Gate*, pp. 309-330. DOI: 10.1504/GBER.2008.019986

Schot, J., & Steinmueller, W. E. (2018). Three frames for innovation policy: R&D, systems of innovation and transformative change. *Research Policy*, *47*(9), 1554–1567. DOI: 10.1016/j.respol.2018.08.011

Schwartz, R., Dodge, J., Smith, N. A., & Etzioni, O. (2020). Green AI. *Communications of the ACM*, *63*(12), 54–63. DOI: 10.1145/3381831

Scott, W. R. (2014). *Institutions and organizations: Ideas, interests, and identities* (4th ed.). Sage Publications.

Securities And Exchange Commission v. Trendon T. Shavers and Bitcoin Savings and Trust, 4:13-CV-416 (United States District Court Eastern District of Texas Sherman Division September 18, 2014). Retrieved October 20, 2024, from https://casetext.com/case/sec-exch-commn-v-shavers

Segneanu, A. E., Orbeci, C., Lazau, C., Sfirloaga, P., Vlazan, P., Bandas, C., & Grozescu, I. (2015). Efficient treatment of wastewater using advanced chemical and physical processes. *Environmental Engineering and Management Journal*, *14*(6), 1353–1362.

Segneanu, A. E., Orbeci, C., Lazau, C., Sfirloaga, P., Vlazan, P., Bandas, C., & Grozescu, I. (2017). Wastewater treatment: Novel methods and prospects. *Journal of Environmental Management, 204*, 186–195.

Sen, D. (2019). What makes Darjeeling tea authentic? Colonial heritage and contemporary sustainability practice in Darjeeling, India. *Südasien-Chronik – South Asia Chronicle, 9*, 177–203.

Seth, S. (2024, May 05). *The 5 Most Private Cryptocurrencies*. Investopedia. https://www.investopedia.com/tech/five-most-private-cryptocurrencies/

Sfodera, F., Cain, L. N., & Di Leo, A. (2024). Is technology everywhere? Exploring Generation Z's perceptions of sustainable tourism in developing countries. *International Hospitality Review, 38*(1), 45-47. https://www.emerald.com/insight/2516-8142

Sgroi, F., & Modica, F. (2024). Digital technologies for the development of sustainable tourism in mountain areas. *Smart Agricultural Technology, 8*, 100475. DOI: 10.1016/j.atech.2024.100475

Shaalan, D., & Jusoh, S. (2020). Visualization in Medical System Interfaces: UX Guidelines. In D. Shaalan & S. Jusoh, 2022 14th International Conference on Electronics, Computers and Artificial Intelligence (ECAI). DOI: 10.1109/ECAI50035.2020.9223236

Shafi, K. V. P. M., Ulman, A., Yan, X., Yang, N., Estournes, C., White, H., & Rafailovich, M. H. (2017). Sonochemical synthesis and characterization of superparamagnetic iron oxide nanoparticles. *Journal of Magnetism and Magnetic Materials, 311*(1), 96–100. DOI: 10.1016/j.jmmm.2006.10.1190

Shah, T. V. (2013). *Comments on Prevention of Money Laundering Act, 2002*. Retrieved October 19, 2024

Shao, B., & Wang, H. (2025). Digital economy, industrial structure advancement and human capital accumulation. *Finance Research Letters, 83*, 107727. Advance online publication. DOI: 10.1016/j.frl.2025.107727

Sharma, P., Bhattacharya, S., & Bhattacharya, S. (2025). HR analytics and AI adoption in IT sector: Reflections from practitioners. *Journal of Work-Applied Management, ahead-of-print*(ahead-of-print). https://doi.org/DOI: 10.1108/JWAM-12-2024-0179

Sharma, A., Kumar, S., & Bano, D. (2015). Synthesis of ZnO nanoparticles via microemulsion method and their antibacterial activity. *Materials Science and Engineering C, 56*, 607–611. DOI: 10.1016/j.msec.2015.06.054

Sharma, G., Sharma, A. R., Kumar, M., Al-Muhtaseb, A. H., Pathania, D., Naushad, M., & Ghfar, A. A. (2015). Green synthesis of silver nanoparticles using *Myristica fragrans* (nutmeg) seed extract and evaluation of their antimicrobial activity. *Journal of Molecular Structure*, *1097*, 221–227. DOI: 10.1016/j.molstruc.2015.06.063

Sharma, M., Mohapatra, G., & Giri, A. K. (2025). Assessing the role of ICT, governance, and infrastructure on inbound tourism demand in India. *Journal of Economic and Administrative Sciences*, *41*(1), 320–335. DOI: 10.1108/JEAS-03-2022-0064

Sheng, J., Amankwah-Amoah, J., & Wang, X. (2019). Technology in the 21st century: New challenges and opportunities. *Technological Forecasting and Social Change*, *143*, 321–335. DOI: 10.1016/j.techfore.2018.06.009

Sherson, J., Rabecq, B., Dellermann, D., & Rafner, J. (2023). A multi-dimensional development and deployment framework for Hybrid Intelligence. In *Frontiers in Artificial Intelligence and Applications*. IOS Press., DOI: 10.3233/FAIA230119

Shi, W., Cao, J., Zhang, Q., Li, Y., & Xu, L. (2016). Edge computing: Vision and challenges. *IEEE Internet of Things Journal*, *3*(5), 637–646. DOI: 10.1109/JIOT.2016.2579198

Shruthi, K. A., Ihita, G. V., & Chaudhari, S. (2021). *A survey on rural internet connectivity in India*. arXiv. https://arxiv.org/abs/2111.10219

Sieck, C. J., Sheon, A., Ancker, J. S., Castek, J., Callahan, B., & Siefer, A. (2021). Digital inclusion as a social determinant of health. *Npj Digital Medicine 2021 4:1*, *4*(1), 1–3. DOI: 10.1038/s41746-021-00413-8

Siemens. (2022). Siemens shows new digital solutions for the transition to sustainable infrastructure. Press release. https://press.siemens.com/global/en/pressrelease/siemens-shows-new-digital-solutions-transition-sustainable-infrastructure

Siguaw, J., Simpson, P., & Enz, C. (2006). Conceptualizing Innovation Orientation: A Framework for Study and Integration of Innovation Research. *Journal of Product Innovation Management*, *23*(6), 556–574. DOI: 10.1111/j.1540-5885.2006.00224.x

Simeli, I., Christou, E., & Chatzigeorgiou, C. (2025). Digital Nomads as Unintentional Influencers in Destination Branding: A Multi-Method Study of Ambient Influence. *Journal of Theoretical and Applied Electronic Commerce Research*, *20*(4), 340. DOI: 10.3390/jtaer20040340

Sinaga, A. R., & Pranata, G. D. (2023). Clustering Data Penjualan Produk pada Toko Yudha dngan Algoritma K-Means. In A. R. Sinaga & G. D. Pranata, SisInfo Jurnal Sistem Informasi dan Informatika (Vol. 3, Issue 2, p. 135). DOI: 10.37278/sisinfo.v3i2.638

Singh, A., & Chawla, S. (2019). Cryptocurrency Regulation: Legal Issues and Challenges. *International Journal of Reviews and Research in Social Sciences, VII*(2), 365–375. DOI: 10.5958/2454-2687.2019.00028.5

Singh, A., & Das, R. (2025). Exploring tourism opportunities in the metaverse and technology era: Insights from scholarly literature. In *Metaverse and sustainable business models in SMEs* (p. 12). IGI Global., DOI: 10.4018/979-8-3693-9005-4.ch007

Singh, A., & Zhao, Y. (2022). Machine learning applications in nanoparticle characterization: A data-driven approach. *Journal of Nanoparticle Research, 24*(8), 115.

Singh, B., & Kaunert, C. (2024). Transforming smart city and smart sustainable tourism projecting artificial intelligence and IoT: Immersive potential for revolutionizing urban living and enhancing travel experience. In *Technological and Managerial Approaches to Fostering Sustainable Travel* (pp. 26–50). IGI Global., DOI: 10.4018/979-8-3693-8115-1.ch003

Singh, R. K., Gunasekaran, A., & Kumar, P. (2024). Artificial intelligence in logistics optimization with sustainable criteria: A review. *Sustainability (Basel), 16*(21), 9145. DOI: 10.3390/su16219145

Si, S., Hall, J., Suddaby, R., Ahlstrom, D., & Wei, J. (2023). Technology, entrepreneurship, innovation and social change in digital economics. *Technovation, 119*, 102484. Advance online publication. DOI: 10.1016/j.technovation.2022.102484

Sisak, A. (2013). *How to Combat the Money Mule Phenomenon*. European Police Science & Research.

Sjödin, D., Parida, V., & Kohtamäki, M. (2023). Artificial intelligence enabling circular business model innovation in digital servitization: Conceptualizing dynamic capabilities, AI capacities, business models and effects. *Technological Forecasting and Social Change, 197*, 122903. DOI: 10.1016/j.techfore.2023.122903

Skillspark The Finishing School. (2026, January 20). Skillspark. https://skillspark.training/impact-of-automation-and-ai-on-accounting-jobs

Skorupinska, A., & Torrent-Sellens, J. (2017). ICT, innovation and productivity: Evidence based on eastern European manufacturing companies. *Journal of the Knowledge Economy, 8*(2), 768–788. DOI: 10.1007/s13132-016-0441-1

Skouteris, G., Hermosilla, D., López, P., Negro, C., & Blanco, Á. (2012). Anaerobic membrane bioreactors for wastewater treatment: A review. *Chemical Engineering Journal, 198–199*, 138–148. DOI: 10.1016/j.cej.2012.05.070

Sodhi, M., & Tang, C. (2021). Research opportunities in supply chain transparency. *Production and Operations Management, 30*(3), 675–688. DOI: 10.1111/poms.13351

Solans, C., & Kunieda, H. (1997). *Industrial applications of microemulsions*. Marcel Dekker.

Song, C., Zhang, Q., Yang, J., & Li, X. (2024). *Tourism, industrialization, and sustainable economic growth. Smart Tourism, 5(2), 3044*. Asia Pacific Academy of Science Pte. Ltd., DOI: 10.54517/st3044

Song, L., & Jo, S. J. (2023). How job crafting behaviors influence the innovative behavior of knowledge workers in the gig economy: Based on the organismic integration theory. *Frontiers in Psychology, 14*, 1228881. Advance online publication. DOI: 10.3389/fpsyg.2023.1228881 PMID: 37731880

Sonune, A., & Ghate, R. (2004). Developments in wastewater treatment methods. *Desalination, 167*, 55–63. DOI: 10.1016/j.desal.2004.06.113

Srinivasa, R. C., Arun, S., James, L., & Zhu, Y. (2021). Visualization — a vital decision driving tool for enterprises. In R. C. Srinivasa, S. Arun, L. James, & Y. Zhu, arXiv (Cornell University). Cornell University. https://doi.org/DOI: 10.48550/arXiv.2105

Srivastava, P., & Shandilya, G. (2024). Unveiling the impact of perceived smart tourism technology on tourist satisfaction. In Singh, M. K., & Jain, P. K. (Eds.), *Multidisciplinary Applications of Artificial Intelligence in Regenerative Tourism* (pp. 112–130). IGI Global., DOI: 10.4018/979-8-3693-2432-5.ch008

Steen, J., Klein, G., & Potts, J. (2022). 21st-Century General-Purpose Technologies and the Future of Project Management. *Project Management Journal, 53*(5), 435–437. DOI: 10.1177/87569728221125095

Stewart, J., & Gorman, C. (2024). Authentic assessment and embedding sustainable literacy and technology skills in tourism education. *Irish Journal of Academic Practice*. https://doi.org/DOI: 10.21427/abcd-efgh

Stock, J. R., & Boyer, S. L. (2009). Developing a consensus definition of supply chain management: A qualitative study. *International Journal of Physical Distribution & Logistics Management, 39*(8), 690–711. DOI: 10.1108/09600030910996323

Stoumpos, A. I., Kitsios, F., & Talias, M. A. (2023). Digital Transformation in Healthcare: Technology Acceptance and Its Applications. *International Journal of Environmental Research and Public Health, 20*(4), 3407. Advance online publication. DOI: 10.3390/ijerph20043407 PMID: 36834105

Stroumpoulis, A., Kopanaki, E., & Chountalas, P. T. (2024). Enhancing sustainable supply chain management through digital transformation: A comparative case study analysis. *Sustainability (Basel), 16*(16), 6778. DOI: 10.3390/su16166778

Strubell, E., Ganesh, A., & McCallum, A. (2020). Energy and policy considerations for modern deep learning research. *Proceedings of the AAAI Conference on Artificial Intelligence, 34*(09), 13693–13696. DOI: 10.1609/aaai.v34i09.7123

Su, J., Su, K., & Wang, S. (2022). Evaluation of digital economy development level based on multi-attribute decision theory. *PLoS ONE, 17*(10 October). DOI: 10.1371/journal.pone.0270859

Suanpang, P., & Pothipassa, P. (2024). Integrating generative AI and IoT for sustainable smart tourism destinations. *Sustainability (Basel), 16*(17), 7435. DOI: 10.3390/su16177435

Subermaniam, L., Kuppusamy, M., Isakulova, N., Ghate, A. D., Subrahmanyam, S., & John, B. (2025). A Systematic Review of Sustainability Management in Small and Medium Enterprises to Improve Sustainable Development Goals. *ACTA INNOVATIONS*, 55, 38–48. https://www.actainnovations.com/index.php/pub/article/view/403

Subrahmanyam, S. (2024). Leadership and cultural change management for technology adoption in operations. In Martínez-Falcó, J., Sánchez-García, E., Marco-Lajara, B., & Visser, G. (Eds.), *Convergence of technology and operations management in modern businesses* (pp. 175–202). IGI Global Scientific Publishing., DOI: 10.4018/979-8-3693-6200-6.ch005

Subrahmanyam, S. (2025). AI-Driven Leadership in the Modern Era for Revolutionizing Next-Generation Strategies: Organizational Impacts and Future Development. In Agnihotri, A., & Balusamy, B. (Eds.), *Leadership Paradigms and the Impact of Technology* (pp. 61–86). IGI Global Scientific Publishing., DOI: 10.4018/979-8-3693-7175-6.ch003

Subrahmanyam, S. (2025). Building a Digital-First Organizational Culture. In Pawirosumarto, S. (Ed.), *Innovative Approaches for International Competitiveness Through Human Resource Management* (pp. 101–124). IGI Global Scientific Publishing., DOI: 10.4018/979-8-3373-1005-3.ch004

Subrahmanyam, S. (2025). Corporate Sustainability Leadership in a Technology-Driven Educational Environment. In Dall'Acqua, L., & Gironacci, I. (Eds.), *Navigating Complexity, AI, and Legal Challenges in Organizations* (pp. 177–208). IGI Global Scientific Publishing., DOI: 10.4018/979-8-3373-2419-7.ch008

Subrahmanyam, S. (2025). Leveraging AI and ML for Enhanced Efficiency and Innovation in Manufacturing. In Vyas, V., Bi, X., Pandey, D., Xu, Z., & Pandey, B. (Eds.), *AI's Role in Enhanced Automotive Safety* (pp. 319–344). IGI Global Scientific Publishing., DOI: 10.4018/979-8-3373-0442-7.ch021

Subrahmanyam, S. (2025). Shaping Tomorrow's Talent Strategies with Predictive Workforce Intelligence. In Badouch, M., & Boutaounte, M. (Eds.), *Emerging Technologies for Recruitment Strategy and Practice* (pp. 211–236). IGI Global Scientific Publishing., DOI: 10.4018/979-8-3373-6516-9.ch008

Subrahmanyam, S. (2025). Strategic Collaboration and Partnerships in R&D for Innovation. In Martínez-Falcó, J., Sánchez-García, E., & Marco-Lajara, B. (Eds.), *Research and Development Practices in Innovation* (pp. 283–314). IGI Global Scientific Publishing., DOI: 10.4018/979-8-3373-0812-8.ch010

Subrahmanyam, S. (2025). Sustainability and AI. In Younas, A., & Kassim, A. (Eds.), *Transforming Business Through Digital Sustainability Models* (pp. 363–392). IGI Global Scientific Publishing., DOI: 10.4018/979-8-3373-0608-7.ch016

Subrahmanyam, S. (2025). Using AI-Driven Analysis for Training and Leadership Growth. In Mrabet, J., Boudagga, S., Sharma, R., & Bansal, R. (Eds.), *Harnessing Emotion AI for Customer Support and Employee Wellbeing* (pp. 321–352). IGI Global Scientific Publishing., DOI: 10.4018/979-8-3373-3658-9.ch013

Subrahmanyam, S., & El Samra, H. (2025). Startups and AI: Fostering Entrepreneurship in the MENA Region. In Azoury, N., & Yahchouchi, G. (Eds.), *AI in the Middle East for Growth and Business* (pp. 77–92). Palgrave Macmillan., DOI: 10.1007/978-3-031-75589-7_6

Subramanian, S. (2021, January 12). *Crypto is now the world's fifth-most circulated currency by value*. Quartz. https://qz.com/1954555/all-the-worlds-crypto-is-now-worth-more-than-1-trillion

Sui, D. Z., & Rejeski, D. W. (2002). Environmental Impacts of the Emerging Digital Economy: The E-for-Environment E-Commerce? *Environmental Management*, *29*(2), 155–163. DOI: 10.1007/s00267-001-0027-X PMID: 11815820

Sun, X., Feng, W., Liu, S., Xie, Y., Bhatia, S., Hooi, B., Wang, W., & Cheng, X. (2023). MonLAD: Money Laundering Agents Detection in Transaction Streams. https://arxiv.org/pdf/2201.10051.pdf

Sun, Y., & Xia, Y. (2002). Shape-controlled synthesis of gold and silver nanoparticles. *Science*, *298*(5601), 2176–2179. DOI: 10.1126/science.1077229 PMID: 12481134

Supriadi, A., & Mulyani, A. S. (2024). Digital transformation in operational management: A systematic review of current trends and practices. [PRODUCTIVITY]. *Management Studies and Business Journal, 1*(3), 496–506. DOI: 10.62207/07xvt585

Suryani, W. (2024). Cultural and heritage tourism trends for sustainable tourism. In *Special interest trends for sustainable tourism*. IGI Global., DOI: 10.4018/979-8-3693-5903-7.ch001

Suslick, K. S. (1990). Sonochemistry. *Science, 247*(4949), 1439–1445. DOI: 10.1126/science.247.4949.1439 PMID: 17791211

Sutradhar, P., & Saha, M. (2016). Green and sonochemical synthesis of ZnO nanoparticles and their antibacterial activity. *Spectrochimica Acta. Part A, Molecular and Biomolecular Spectroscopy, 142*, 73–81. DOI: 10.1016/j.saa.2015.02.060

Swartz, A., LeFevre, A. E., Perera, S., Kinney, M. V., & George, A. S. (2021). Multiple pathways to scaling up and sustainability: An exploration of digital health solutions in South Africa. *Globalization and Health, 17*(1), 77. Advance online publication. DOI: 10.1186/s12992-021-00716-1 PMID: 34229699

Szerszynski, B. (1999). Risk and trust: The performative dimension. *Environmental Values, 8*(2), 239–252. DOI: 10.3197/096327199129341815

Taeihagh, A. (2021). Governance of artificial intelligence. *Policy and Society, 40*(2), 137–157. DOI: 10.1080/14494035.2021.1928377

Taglioni, D., & Winkler, D. (2016). *Making global value chains work for development*. World Bank Publications. DOI: 10.1596/978-1-4648-0157-0

Tambe, N. (2024, August 17). *All You Need to Know About India's Crypto Bill*. Retrieved October 20, 2024, from Forbes Advisor: https://www.forbes.com/advisor/in/investing/cryptocurrency/crypto-bill/#:~:text=Cryptocurrency%20is%20used%20anonymously%20to,support%20the%20use

Tams, S., Grover, V., & Thatcher, J. (2014). Modern information technology in an old workforce: Toward a strategic research agenda. *The Journal of Strategic Information Systems, 23*(4), 284–304. DOI: 10.1016/j.jsis.2014.10.001

Tan, L., Yang, Z., Irfan, M., Ding, C. J., Hu, M., & Hu, J. (2024). Toward low-carbon sustainable development: Exploring the impact of digital economy development and industrial restructuring. *Business Strategy and the Environment, 33*(3), 2159–2172. DOI: 10.1002/bse.3584

Tapscott, D. (1996). *The digital economy: Promise and peril in the age of networked intelligence*. McGraw-Hill.

Tariq, M. U. (2025). Developing a model for sustainable entrepreneurship competencies. In *Building a Green Future Through Essential Decision-Making Competencies* (pp. 137–158). IGI Global., DOI: 10.4018/979-8-3373-0189-1.ch006

Tathavadekar, V. P., & Mahankale, N. (2023). Digital leadership for sustainability: An integrated framework for organizational learning, resilience, and social value creation. *Journal of Cross-Disciplinary Sustainability Innovations*. https://doi.org/ DOI: 10.64229/tbqr6714

Teece, D. (2007). Explicating dynamic capabilities: The nature and microfoundations of (sustainable) enterprise performance. *Strategic Management Journal*, *28*(13), 1319–1350. DOI: 10.1002/smj.640

Teece, D. J., Peteraf, M., & Leih, S. (2016). Dynamic capabilities and organizational agility: Risk, uncertainty, and strategy in the innovation economy. *California Management Review*, *58*(4), 13–35. DOI: 10.1525/cmr.2016.58.4.13

Teece, D. J., Pisano, G., & Shuen, A. (1997). Dynamic capabilities and strategic management. *Strategic Management Journal*, *18*(7), 509–533. DOI: 10.1002/(SICI)1097-0266(199708)18:7<509::AID-SMJ882>3.0.CO;2-Z

Theofanidis, F., Abidi, O., Erturk, A., Colbran, S., & Coskun, E. (Eds.). (2024). *Digital transformation and sustainable development in cities and organizations*. IGI Global. DOI: 10.4018/979-8-3693-3567-3

Theofanidis, F., Tsianaka, E., & Livas, C. (2025). *Towards systemic leadership resilience: Proposing the hybrid artificial intelligent leader in response to economic crises*. Canadian Journal of Administrative Sciences / Revue Canadienne des Sciences de l'Administration., DOI: 10.1002/cjas.70000

Thibaud, E. (2022). What's wrong with the passion economy? Daily Philosophy. https://daily-philosophy.com/ezechiel-thibaud-davidson-passion-economy/

Thomas, M., Jefferson, B., Bixio, D., Thoeye, C., De Wilde, W., De Koning, J., van der Graaf, J., & Wintgens, T. (2005). MBR for wastewater reuse: An overview of European experience. *Water Science and Technology*, *51*(6–7), 231–238. PMID: 16003982

Tiwari, S., & Yadav, M. (2025). Circular economy in manufacturing: Current trends and future directions. In *Rethinking resources: Strategies, policies, and partnerships for a circular future* (pp. 395–416). Springer Nature Singapore. DOI: 10.1007/978-981-96-9055-8_23

Tong, L., George, B., Crotty, B. H., Somai, M., Taylor, B. W., Osinski, K., & Luo, J. (2022). Telemedicine and health disparities: Association between patient characteristics and telemedicine, in-person, telephone and message-based care during the COVID-19 pandemic. *IPEM-Translation*, *3*, 100010. DOI: 10.1016/j.ipemt.2022.100010 PMID: 36340828

Too Good To Go. (2023). *2023 Impact Report*. Retrieved from https://www.toogoodtogo.com/impact-report

Topal, R., & Shargh, F. (2023). Teaching students how to find and identify reliable online sources: A series of exercises. *Journal of Political Science Education*, *19*(3), 475–484.

Treiblmaier, H., & Sillaber, C. (2021). The impact of blockchain on e-commerce: A framework for salient research topics. *Electronic Commerce Research and Applications*, *48*, 101054. Advance online publication. DOI: 10.1016/j.elerap.2021.101054

Trendyol. (2024). Trendyol 2024 yıl sonu faaliyet raporu. Trendyol Group. https://www.trendyol.com

Trist, E. L. (1981). *The evolution of socio-technical systems* (Vol. 2). Ontario Quality of Working Life Centre.

Truant, E., Broccardo, L., & Dana, L. (2021). Digitalisation boosts company performance: An overview of Italian listed companies. *Technological Forecasting and Social Change*, *173*, 121173. DOI: 10.1016/j.techfore.2021.121173

Tumpa, R. J., & Naeni, L. (2025). Improving decision-making and stakeholder engagement at project governance using digital technology for sustainable infrastructure projects. *Smart and Sustainable Built Environment*, *14*(4), 1292–1329. DOI: 10.1108/SASBE-10-2024-0451

Turkevich, J., Stevenson, P. C., & Hillier, J. (1951). A study of the nucleation and growth processes in the synthesis of colloidal gold. *Discussions of the Faraday Society*, *11*, 55–75. DOI: 10.1039/df9511100055

Turki, H. (2025). AI-powered personalization in e-commerce: Governance, consumer behavior, and exploratory insights from big data analytics. *Technology in Society*, *83*, 103033. Advance online publication. DOI: 10.1016/j.techsoc.2025.103033

Türkkan, H. (2021). The significance of typography in data visualization. In H. Türkkan, Global Journal of Computer Sciences Theory and Research (Vol. 11, Issue 1, p. 12). DOI: 10.18844/gjcs.v11i1.5030

Tussyadiah, I. P., Jung, T. H., & tom Dieck, M. C. (2018). Embodiment of wearable augmented reality technology in tourism experiences. *Journal of Travel Research, 57*(5), 597–611. DOI: 10.1177/0047287517709090

U.S. Securities and Exchange Commission. (2022). *The enhancement and standardization of climate-related disclosures for investors (Proposed rule).* https://www.sec.gov/news/press-release/2022-46

Uddin, J., & Chanda, K. (2025). The impact of Artificial Intelligence on the modern economy. *International Journal of Information Technology and Management, 20*(1), 167–178. DOI: 10.29070/npwgsz38

Uddin, M. Z., Uddin Jamal, M. Z., Umair, M., Khader, M. A., & Kumar, D. M. U. (2024). AI-Powered financial modeling and valuation analysis: Unleashing data-driven insights. *International Journal of Multidisciplinary Research and Growth Evaluation, 5*(2), 626–629. DOI: 10.54660/.IJMRGE.2024.5.2.626-629

Ulrich, D., Brockbank, W., Johnson, D., Sandholtz, K., & Younger, J. (2017). *HR competencies: Mastery at the intersection of people and business.* Society for Human Resource Management.

Ulrich, D., Younger, J., & Brockbank, W. (2019). *HR transformation: Building human resources from the inside out.* McGraw-Hill Education.

Umboh, B. Y. (2023). Work Transformation in The Digital Era Changing the Public Values in Indonesia. https://www.researchgate.net/publication/374813686_WORK_TRANSFORMATION_IN_THE_DIGITAL_ERA_CHANGING_THE_PUBLIC_VALUES_IN_INDONESIA#:~:text=Digital%20transformation%20has%20a,access%20services%20from%20government%20and

UNCTAD. (2024, October 4). Creative economy booms, with services leading the growth. UN Trade and Development (UNCTAD). https://unctad.org/news/creative-economy-booms-services-leading-growth

United Nations Conference on Trade and Development. (2024). *Environmental implications of digitalization and green transformation. In Digital Economy Report 2024.* UNCTAD Publishing.

United Nations Department of Economic and Social Affairs (UNDESA). (2022). *E-Government survey 2022: The future of digital government.* United Nations. https://desapublications.un.org/sites/default/files/publications/2022-09/Web%20version%20E-Government%202022.pdf

United Nations Department of Economic and Social Affairs. (2022). *United Nations E-Government Survey 2022: The future of digital government.* United Nations.

United Nations. (n.d.). *Money Laundering*. Retrieved October 20, 2024, from UNODC Romena: https://www.unodc.org/romena/en/money-laundering.html

Usman, K., Younas, A., Kumar, S., Akbar, A., & Poulova, P. (2023). The progression of sustainable development goals in tourism: A systematic literature review of past achievements and future promises. *Journal of Innovation & Knowledge*, *8*(4), 1–12. DOI: 10.1016/j.jik.2023.100442

Valaskova, K., Nagy, M., & Juracka, D. (2025). Digital transformation and financial performance: An empirical analysis of strategic alignment in the digital age. *Journal of Enterprising Communities: People and Places in the Global Economy*, *19*(5), 1178–1205. DOI: 10.1108/JEC-11-2024-0241

Vallance, D. (2021, April 13). (Manuscript submitted for publication). The passion economy is the hustle culture antidote we all need. [| Dropbox Blog. https://blog.dropbox.com/topics/work-culture/the-passion-economy-is-the-hustle-culture-antidote]. *Work : A Journal of Prevention, Assessment, and Rehabilitation*.

van der Haar, S., & Zeinstra, G. G. (2019). *The impact of Too Good To Go on food waste reduction at the consumer household level: An explorative study*. Wageningen Food & Biobased Research. https://agris.fao.org/search/en/providers/122575/records/66d9bbfb5fdc8021c2c500be

van Dijk, J. (2020). *The digital divide*. Polity Press. ISBN-13 978-1509534456

van Dijk, T. A. (1993). Elite discourse and racism. *Sage (Atlanta, Ga.)*.

van Dijk, T. A. (2015). *Critical discourse studies: A sociocognitive approach*. Palgrave.

Van Kessel, R., Wong, B. L. H., Clemens, T., & Brand, H. (2022). Digital health literacy as a super determinant of health: More than simply the sum of its parts. *Internet Interventions : The Application of Information Technology in Mental and Behavioural Health*, *27*, 100500. DOI: 10.1016/j.invent.2022.100500 PMID: 35242586

Van Rooy, D. (2024). Human–machine collaboration for enhanced decision-making in governance. *Data & Policy*, *6*(e60), e60. Advance online publication. DOI: 10.1017/dap.2024.72

Vassli, L. T., & Farshchian, B. A. (2018). Acceptance of health-related ICT among elderly people living in the community: A systematic review of qualitative evidence. *International Journal of Human–Computer Interaction, 34*(2), 99-116. DOI: 10.1080/10447318.2017.1328024

Venkatesh, V., Morris, M. G., Davis, G. B., & Davis, F. D. (2003). User acceptance of information technology: Toward a unified view. *Management Information Systems Quarterly*, *27*(3), 425–478. DOI: 10.2307/30036540

Verhoef, P. C., Broekhuizen, T., Bart, Y., Bhattacharya, A., Dong, J. Q., Fabian, N., & Haenlein, M. (2019). Digital transformation: A multidisciplinary reflection and research agenda. *Journal of Business Research*, *122*(1), 889–901.

Vial, G. (2019). Understanding digital transformation: A review and a research agenda. *The Journal of Strategic Information Systems*, *28*(2), 118–144. DOI: 10.1016/j.jsis.2019.01.003

Vijayan, R., Joseph, S., & Mathew, B. (2020). Green synthesis of copper nanoparticles using *Mangifera indica* leaf extract and its applications in antimicrobial therapy and water purification. *Journal of Environmental Chemical Engineering*, *8*(4), 103643. DOI: 10.1016/j.jece.2020.103643

Vinuesa, R., Azizpour, H., Leite, I., Balaam, M., Dignum, V., Domisch, S., Felländer, A., Langhans, S. D., Tegmark, M., & Fuso Nerini, F. (2020). The role of artificial intelligence in achieving the Sustainable Development Goals. *Nature Communications*, *11*(1), 233. DOI: 10.1038/s41467-019-14108-y PMID: 31932590

Visvanathan, C., Aim, R. B., & Parameshwaran, K. (2000). Membrane separation bioreactors for wastewater treatment. *Critical Reviews in Environmental Science and Technology*, *30*(1), 1–48. DOI: 10.1080/10643380091184165

Vitari, C., & Raguseo, E. (2016). Digital data, dynamic capability and financial performance: An empirical investigation in the era of big data. *Systemes d'Information Management*, *21*(3), 63–92. DOI: 10.3917/sim.163.0063

Vohra, V., Banishetty, S., Dutta, T., & Joshi, A. (2024). Work, wander and repeat: Modeling the enablers of digital nomadic lifestyle. *Journal of Global Mobility*, *13*(1), 77–106. DOI: 10.1108/JGM-05-2024-0044

Vu, K. M. (2011). ICT as a source of economic growth in the information age: Empirical evidence from the 1996-2005 period. *Telecommunications Policy*, *35*(4), 357–372. DOI: 10.1016/j.telpol.2011.02.008

Vu, K., Lu, Y., & Shiba, S. (2025). The evolution of the digital economy: Comparative insights from. *Telecommunications Policy*, *49*(10), 103075. Advance online publication. DOI: 10.1016/j.telpol.2025.103075

Walmart. (2018). *Walmart and Sam's Club to require real-time, end-to-end food traceability with blockchain.* https://corporate.walmart.com/news/2018/09/24/in-wake-of-romaine-e-coli-scare-walmart-deploys-blockchain-to-track-leafy-greens

Wamba, S. F., Gunasekaran, A., Akter, S., Ren, S. J. F., Dubey, R., & Childe, S. J. (2017). Big data analytics and firm performance: Effects of dynamic capabilities. *Journal of Business Research, 70*, 356–365. DOI: 10.1016/j.jbusres.2016.08.009

Wang, D., Wu, L., Zhang, D., Zhou, J., Sun, L., & Fu, Y. (2023). Human-Instructed Deep Hierarchical Generative Learning for Automated Urban Planning. In D. Wang, L. Wu, D. Zhang, J. Zhou, L. Sun, & Y. Fu, Proceedings of the AAAI Conference on Artificial Intelligence (Vol. 37, Issue 4, p. 4660). Association for the Advancement of Artificial Intelligence. DOI: 10.1609/aaai.v37i4.25589

Wang, B., Tao, F., Fang, X., Liu, C., Liu, Y., & Freiheit, T. (2020). Smart Manufacturing and Intelligent Manufacturing: A Comparative Review. *Engineering (Beijing), 7*(6), 738–757. DOI: 10.1016/j.eng.2020.07.017

Wang, J., Li, H., & Chen, Y. (2023). Artificial intelligence in nanomaterials research: A review of recent advances. *Materials Today, 56*, 89–102.

Wang, Y., Liu, C., Wang, H., & Javaid, M. (2024). Digital economy empowers enterprises to decrease financialization: Evidence from e-commerce demonstration cities. *Finance Research Letters, 67*, 105801. Advance online publication. DOI: 10.1016/j.frl.2024.105801

Wang, Y., & Toshima, N. (2005). Polyol synthesis of platinum nanoparticles: Control of morphology and catalytic properties. *Langmuir : The ACS Journal of Surfaces and Colloids, 21*(3), 1205–1210. DOI: 10.1021/la047857p

Ward, L., Liu, R., Krishna, A., Hegde, V. I., Agrawal, A., Choudhary, A., & Wolverton, C. (2018). Matminer: An open source toolkit for materials data mining. *Computational Materials Science, 152*, 60–69. DOI: 10.1016/j.commatsci.2018.05.018

Wernerfelt, B. (1984). A resource-based view of the firm. *Strategic Management Journal, 5*(2), 171–180. DOI: 10.1002/smj.4250050207

Westerman, G., Bonnet, D., & McAfee, A. (2011). The Digital Capabilities Your Company Needs. *MIT Center for digital business and capgemini consulting*.

Westerman, G., Bonnet, D., & McAfee, A. (2014). *Leading digital: Turning technology into business transformation*. Harvard Business Review Press.

Williamson, O. E. (1989). Transaction cost economics. In Schmalensee, R., & Willig, R. D. (Eds.), *Handbook of industrial organization* (Vol. 1, pp. 135–182). Elsevier.

Williamson, O. E. (1998). Transaction cost economics: How it works; where it is headed. *De Economist, 146*(1), 23–58. DOI: 10.1023/A:1003263908567

Willie, M. (2025). Leveraging digital resources: A resource-based view perspective. *Golden Ratio of Human Resource Management*, *5*(1), 1–14. DOI: 10.52970/grhrm.v5i1.415

Windmann, A., Wittenberg, P., Schieseck, M., & Niggemann, O. (2017). *Artificial Intelligence in Industry 4.0: A Review of Integration Challenges for Industrial Systems*. IEEE., DOI: 10.1109/IN-

Windmeijer, F. (2005). A finite sample correction for the variance of linear efficient two-step GMM estimators. *Journal of Econometrics*, *126*(1), 25–51. DOI: 10.1016/j.jeconom.2004.02.005

Winkelmann, S., Fischer, M., & Schmidt, T. (2024). Back to a resilient future: Digital technologies for a sustainable supply chain. *Information Systems and e-Business Management*, *22*(2), 315–350. DOI: 10.1007/s10257-024-00677-z

Winters, N., Venkatapuram, S., Geniets, A., & Wynne-Bannister, E. (2020). Prioritarian principles for digital health in low resource settings. *Journal of Medical Ethics*, *46*(4), 259–264. DOI: 10.1136/medethics-2019-105468 PMID: 31949027

Wintoki, M. B., Linck, J. S., & Netter, J. M. (2012). Endogeneity and the dynamics of internal corporate governance. *Journal of Financial Economics*, *105*(3), 581–606. DOI: 10.1016/j.jfineco.2012.03.005

Wooldridge, J. M. (2010). *Econometric analysis of cross section and panel data*. The MIT Press.

World Bank. (2017). Measuring the determinants of backward participation in global value chains. World Bank Policy Research Working Paper.

World Bank. (2020). *Kuwait country economic update: Toward a sustainable economy*. World Bank Publications. https://www.worldbank.org/en/country/kuwait

World Bank. (2023). *The future of work and digital transformation in the MENA region*. World Bank Group. https://www.worldbank.org/en/news/feature/2023/03/02/future-of-work-mena

World Economic Forum. (2024). The digital economy. https://intelligence.weforum.org/topics/a1Gb0000001SH21EAG

World Health Organisation. (2021). *Global Strategy on Digital Health 2020-2025*. World Health Organization.

World Health Organization. (2022). *Global strategy on digital health 2020–2025: Implementation report*. WHO.

World Health Organization. (2023). *Digital health: Governance, policy, and implementation guidance*. WHO.

World Trade Organization (WTO). (2021). World trade report 2021: Economic resilience and trade. WTO. https://www.wto.org/english/res_e/publications_e/wtr21_e.htm

World Trade Organization. (2013). World Trade Organization. Retrieved from E-commerce in Developing Countries: Opportunities and Challenges for Small and Medium-sized Enterprises.

Worldbank. (2024). World Development Indicators: Structure of value. https://wdi.worldbank.org/table/4.2

Wroblewski, J. B. (2018). *Digitalization and firm performance: Are digitally mature firms outperforming their peers?* Lund University School of Economics and Management, Master Thesis.

Wu, F., Hu, H. Z., Lin, H. Y., & Ren, X. Y. (2021). Digital transformation of enterprises and capital market performance: Empirical evidence from stock liquidity. *Journal of Management World*, *37*(07), 130–144.

Wu, H., Xue, Y., Hao, Y., & Ren, S. (2021). How does internet development affect energy-saving and emission reduction? Evidence from China. *Energy Economics*, *103*, 105577. DOI: 10.1016/j.eneco.2021.105577

Wu, J. (2025). Green supply chains: The dual challenges of achieving sustainable development. In *Global trends in manufacturing supply chains* (pp. 297–323). Springer Nature Singapore. DOI: 10.1007/978-981-96-3228-2_12

Wu, W., He, Q., & Jiang, C. (2008). Magnetic iron oxide nanoparticles: Synthesis and surface functionalization strategies. *Nanoscale Research Letters*, *3*(11), 397–415. DOI: 10.1007/s11671-008-9174-9 PMID: 21749733

Xia, L., Baghaie, S., & Sajadi, S. M. (2024). The digital economy: Challenges and opportunities in the new era of technology and electronic communications. *Ain Shams Engineering Journal*, *15*(2), 102411. Advance online publication. DOI: 10.1016/j.asej.2023.102411

Xianbin, T., & Qiong, W. (2021). Sustainable digital economy through good governance: Mediating roles of social reforms and economic policies. *Frontiers in Psychology*, *12*, 773022. DOI: 10.3389/fpsyg.2021.773022 PMID: 34899522

Xiao, L., Guo, F., Guo, F., Yu, F., & Liu, S. (2019). The Effects of Online Shopping Context Cues on Consumers' Purchase Intention for Cross-Border E-Commerce Sustainability. *Sustainability (Basel), 11*(10), 2777. Advance online publication. DOI: 10.3390/su11102777

Xin, L., Ahmad, M., & Khattak, S. I. (2022). Impact of innovation in marine energy generation, distribution, or transmission-related technologies on carbon dioxide emissions in the United States. *Renewable & Sustainable Energy Reviews, 167*, 112225. DOI: 10.1016/j.rser.2022.112225

Yadav, R. (n.d.). Legal aspects of cryptocurrency law: cryptocurrency bill in India. *Indian Journal of Law and Legal Research, 4*(6), 1-15. Retrieved October 20, 2024, from https://3fdef50c-add3-4615-a675-a91741bcb5c0.usrfiles.com/ugd/3fdef5_e332b9076c25451d8eb902ead0cc778b.pdf

Yang, A. (2024). Sustainable finance exploration: Analyzing the impact of environmental, social, governance (ESG) information disclosure in the supply chain. *Supply Chain and Sustainability Research, 15*–31. https://doi.org/DOI: 10.14456/scsr.2024.9

Yang, G., Yang, G., & Wanping, Y. (2025). The impact of AI on enterprise energy management: From the perspective of carbon emissions. [STET]. *Science and Technology for Energy Transition, 80*, 8. Advance online publication. DOI: 10.2516/stet/2024096

Yang, J., Wu, R., & Yang, H. (2023). Digital transformation and enterprise sustainability: The moderating role of regional virtual agglomeration. *Sustainability (Basel), 15*(9), 7597. DOI: 10.3390/su15097597

Yee, L., Chui, M., Roberts, R., & Smit, S. (2025, July 22). McKinsey Technology Trends Outlook 2025. McKinsey & Company. https://www.mckinsey.com/capabilities/tech-and-ai/our-insights/the-top-trends-in-tech

Yeung, A. W. K., Torkamani, A., Butte, A. J., Glicksberg, B. S., Schuller, B., Rodriguez, B., Ting, D. S. W., Bates, D., Schaden, E., Peng, H., Willschke, H., van der Laak, J., Car, J., Rahimi, K., Celi, L. A., Banach, M., Kletecka-Pulker, M., Kimberger, O., Eils, R., & Atanasov, A. G. (2023). The promise of digital healthcare technologies. *Frontiers in Public Health, 11*, 1196596. Advance online publication. DOI: 10.3389/fpubh.2023.1196596 PMID: 37822534

Yilmaz, M.K., Hacioglu, U., Tatoglu, E., Aksoy, M., & Duran, S. (2023). Measuring the impact of board gender and cultural diversity on corporate governance and social performance: evidence from emerging markets. *Economic Research-Ekonomska Istraživanja, 36(*2).

Yonghong, L., Jie, S., Ge, Z., & Ru, Z. (2023). The impact of enterprise digital transformation on financial performance-Evidence from Mainland China manufacturing firms. *MDE. Managerial and Decision Economics, 44*(4), 2110–2124. DOI: 10.1002/mde.3805

Yukl, G. (2013). *Leadership in organizations* (8th ed.). Pearson.

Yu, L., Mottola, G., Barnes, L. L., Valdes, E. G., Wilson, R. S., & Bennett, D. A. (2022). Financial fragility and scam susceptibility in community-dwelling older adults. *Frontiers in Psychology, 13*, 863870. DOI: 10.3389/fpsyg.2022.863870 PMID: 35484831

Yuliansyah, H., Othman, Z. A., & Bakar, A. A. (2025). Co-authorship prediction method based on degree of gravity and article keywords similarity. *Physica A, 665*, 130511. Advance online publication. DOI: 10.1016/j.physa.2025.130511

Yumuşak, İ. (2001). *Elektronik ticaretin gelişmekte olan ülkelere etkileri ve Türkiye üzerine bir değerlendirme.* 2025 tarihinde https://econwpa.ub.uni-muenchen.de/econ-wp/mac/papers/0404/0404032.pdf adresinden alındı

Yusuf, S. O., Durodola, R. L., Ocran, G., Abubakar, J. E., Echere, A. Z., & Paul-Adeleye, A. H. (2024). Challenges and opportunities in AI and digital transformation for SMEs: A cross-continental perspective. *World Journal of Advanced Research and Reviews, 23*(3), 668–678. DOI: 10.30574/wjarr.2024.23.3.2511

Zaghmout, B., & Harrison, C. (2025). Distributed leadership: A systematic literature review. *Strategy and Leadership, 53*(3), 299–320. Advance online publication. DOI: 10.1108/SL-10-2024-0119

Zaida, M., Farooqi, R., & Azmi, S. N. (2025). Driving sustainable supply chain performance through digital transformation: The role of information exchange and responsiveness. *Cogent Business & Management, 12*(1), 2443047. DOI: 10.1080/23311975.2024.2443047

Zarif, A. (2022). The ethical challenges facing the widespread adoption of digital healthcare technology. *Health Technology (Hong Kong), 12*(1), 175–179. DOI: 10.1007/s12553-021-00596-w PMID: 35047326

Zeng, H., Ran, H., Zhou, Q., Jin, Y., & Cheng, X. (2022). The financial effect of firm digitalization: Evidence from China. *Technological Forecasting and Social Change, 183*, 121951. DOI: 10.1016/j.techfore.2022.121951

Zervas, I., & Stiakakis, E. (2024). Economic sustainable development through digital skills acquisition: The role of human resource leadership. *Sustainability (Basel), 16*(17), 7664. DOI: 10.3390/su16177664

Zhang, S., Heck, P. R., Meyer, M. N., Chabris, C. F., Goldstein, D. G., & Hofman, J. M. (2023). An illusion of predictability in scientific results: Even experts confuse inferential uncertainty and outcome variability. In S. Zhang, P. R. Heck, M. N. Meyer, C. F. Chabris, D. G. Goldstein, & J. M. Hofman, Proceedings of the National Academy of Sciences (Vol. 120, Issue 33). National Academy of Sciences. DOI: 10.1073/pnas.2302491120

Zhang, J., Langille, M. R., & Mirkin, C. A. (2007). Photomediated synthesis of silver triangular bipyramids and prisms: The effect of pH and polyol on morphology. *Journal of the American Chemical Society*, *129*(21), 6826–6831. DOI: 10.1021/ja0702258

Zhang, J., Liu, Y., & Chen, Z. (2024). Digitalisation driving sustainable corporate performance: The mediation of green innovation and green supply chain management. *Journal of Cleaner Production*, *446*, 141290. DOI: 10.1016/j.jclepro.2024.141290

Zhang, Q., & Liang, H. (2022). Greening the cloud: Carbon-aware data center management. *Energy Policy*, *162*, 112–129.

Zhang, Y., & Jin, S. (2023). How does digital transformation increase corporate sustainability? The moderating role of top management teams. *Systems*, *11*(7), 355. DOI: 10.3390/systems11070355

Zhang, Z., Fu, W. K., & Ma, L. (2022). The impact of digital economy on green development in China. *Frontiers in Environmental Science*, *10*, 991278. Advance online publication. DOI: 10.3389/fenvs.2022.991278

Zhao, X., Li, X., Li, Y., & Wang, Z. (2024). The impact of digital transformation on firm performance. *Industrial Management & Data Systems*, *124*(8), 2567–2587. DOI: 10.1108/IMDS-09-2023-0661

Zhou, H., Fan, T., Zhang, D., Guo, Q., Zhang, Q., & Ogawa, H. (2011). Polyol-mediated synthesis of noble metal nanoparticles: A versatile strategy for shape control. *Nanoscale Research Letters*, *6*(1), 308. DOI: 10.1186/1556-276X-6-308 PMID: 21711848

Zhou, J., Lan, H., Zhao, C., & Zhou, J. (2021). Haze Pollution Levels, Spatial Spillover Influence, and Impacts of the Digital Economy: Empirical Evidence from China. *Sustainability (Basel)*, *13*(16), 9076. Advance online publication. DOI: 10.3390/su13169076

Zhou, L., Xu, H., Xu, W., & Zhang, Y. (2006). Sol–gel synthesis of ZnO nanoparticles and their anti-bacterial behavior. *Ceramics International*, *32*(4), 363–365. DOI: 10.1016/j.ceramint.2005.03.003

Zhou, Y., Ock, Y.-S., Alnafrah, I., & Dagestani, A. A. (2023). What aspects explain the relationship between digital transformation and financial performance of firms? *Journal of Risk and Financial Management*, *16*(11), 110479. DOI: 10.3390/jrfm16110479

Zhu, W. (2021). A Study of Big-Data-Driven Data Visualization and Visual Communication Design Patterns. In W. Zhu, Scientific Programming (Vol. 2021, p. 1). Hindawi Publishing Corporation. DOI: 10.1155/2021/6704937

Zizic, M. C., Mladineo, M., Gjeldum, N., & Celent, L. (2022). From Industry 4.0 towards Industry 5.0: A Review and Analysis of Paradigm Shift for the People, Organization and Technology. *Energies*, *15*(14), 5221. DOI: 10.3390/en15145221

About the Contributors

Mehtap Özşahin received her BA degree from Bogaziçi University, Faculty of Economics and Administrative Sciences in 2001. She had her masters and Ph.D. degrees in the field of Management from Gebze Institute of Technology, in 2005 and 2011 respectively. She has worked as a research assistant between the years of 2002-2013 at Gebze Institute of Technology and as an assistant professor between the years of 2014-2019 at Yalova University. She was promoted to associate professor position in 2020 and since has been working as an associate professor at Gebze Technical University. She has taught courses and conducted research in the fields of strategic management, leadership, digital transformation, business ethics, international business and organizational behavior.

Vladimir Simović is the Head of Digital Economics Department at the Institute of Economic Sciences (IES) in Belgrade, Serbia and Associate Professor at the Australian University, Kuwait (AU). The areas of his professional interests are digital marketing, digital entrepreneurship, digital competencies, and information systems in business. He is a project manager of the European ESF+ project on digital marketing competencies and the participant of European COST Action on Artificial intelligence in business with 15+ years of experience in research and teaching. He is the founder of several digital start ups in Serbia as well as a think tank dedicated to innovative learning practices.

Alper Erturk obtained his B.Sc. in Industrial Engineering from Turkish Naval Academy, received his M.Sc. in Information Technology Management (with distinction) from Naval Postgraduate School, CA, USA in 2000. He got his Ph.D. in Management Science from Gebze Technical University, Turkey in 2003. Very recently, he obtained his Post Graduate Diploma in Data Science and Business Analytics from Texas University McCombs Business School, USA in 2023. Prof. Erturk has been an active academician and researcher in Business Management & Analytics field for more than 20 years of experience in Turkey, the U.S., Belgium,

Germany, Morocco, and Kuwait. Throughout his academic studies, he published 8 books, more than 30 articles, more than 10 book chapters and presented more than 40 papers in international academic conferences. He is an internationally recognized researcher with an h-index of 23 and i-index of 40. During his career, Prof.Ertürk achieved to receive many awards including "Most Cited Researcher of the year", "Outstanding Teaching Award", "Best Paper Award", as well as he was also a recipient of Fulbright Scholarship in 2019 and studied at Portland State University, OR, USA. Prof.Ertürk is currently working as a Full Professor and Chair of Management Department at Australian University – Kuwait since February 2022.

***

Mine Aksoy is a Professor of Finance at Yalova University, Yalova. She received her BSc in Computer Sciences Engineering from Yildiz Technical University in 1992, her MSc in Management of Information Technologies from Sunderland University in 1995 and her PhD in Finance and Banking from Kadir Has University in 2008. She worked as an IT project manager at Istanbul Settlement and Custody Bank Inc. (Takasbank) from 2000 to 2010. She has an over 15 years of IT experience in finance sector. Her current research interests are in corporate finance, investment, corporate sustainability, and digitalization.

Abdusamatov Alisher is affiliated with the Department of Preschool and Primary Education at Termez University of Economics and Service, Termez, Uzbekistan. His academic and research interests focus on early childhood education, primary education pedagogy, curriculum development, and innovative teaching methodologies for young learners. He is actively engaged in promoting modern educational practices that enhance the cognitive, social, and emotional development of children at the preschool and primary levels. His work emphasizes the integration of learner-centered teaching strategies, digital learning tools, and inclusive education approaches to improve the quality of foundational education. Abdusamatov Alisher also contributes to academic discussions on teacher training, educational policy, and the development of effective instructional frameworks for early education systems. Through his research and academic involvement, he aims to support the advancement of early childhood education and strengthen pedagogical practices that foster holistic learning environments for young students.

Darijana Antonić has been working in the Public Health Institute of the Republic of Srpska since 2001. She works in the Centre of Healthcare System Development and International Cooperation in the position of Coordinator of Activities. She is an Associate Professor and works part-time at the Paneuropean

University "Apeiron" in Banja Luka, on the Faculty of Health Science, teaching the subjects Healthcare Management, Organisation of Healthcare, and Health Insurance.

Imran Aslan is a lecturer at Bingöl University, Türkiye, with research focusing on Industry 4.0 and occupational health and safety. He trained as an Emergency Medical Technician (1996–2000) and holds a degree in Industrial Engineering from Marmara University (2005). He completed his master's at FHOOW, Germany, on supply chain management and his PhD at Atatürk University (2009–2014) on the impact of IT in Turkish healthcare systems. Prof. Aslan has attended courses at MIT-Zaragoza Logistics Center and participated in Erasmus exchanges in Lithuania, Poland, and Germany, also serving as a guest lecturer at Jönköping University, Sweden. He has authored 54 international articles, 5 books, 19 book chapters, and presented at over 30 conferences.

Devendra Gajanan Bhave is a distinguished academician and an accomplished researcher in the field of commerce, with a career spanning over two decades marked by scholarly excellence, innovative pedagogy, and committed academic leadership. He currently serves as the Head of the Department of Commerce at Sanskar Mandir Arts and Commerce College, Warje-Malwadi, Pune, where he has been instrumental in enhancing the academic culture and research ecosystem of the institution. Dr. Bhave holds a doctorate in Commerce and has consistently contributed to the advancement of knowledge through his prolific research in areas such as financial management, corporate governance, taxation, and higher education reforms. His work is widely recognized in academic circles, with several research papers published in reputed national and international journals, conference presentations, and invited lectures.

Dilnoza Butanova is affiliated with the Department of Accounting at Mamun University, Khiva, Uzbekistan. Her academic interests focus on accounting systems, financial reporting, auditing, and business finance. She is engaged in teaching and academic activities that support the development of strong accounting knowledge and analytical skills among students. Her work emphasizes the importance of accurate financial documentation, transparent reporting practices, and the application of modern accounting standards in business environments. Dilnoza Butanova also shows interest in integrating digital technologies and contemporary financial tools into accounting education to enhance efficiency and decision-making in organizations. Through her academic involvement and professional engagement, she aims to contribute to the advancement of accounting education and the preparation of competent professionals capable of addressing modern financial and organizational challenges.

Saurabh Chandra is an accomplished legal scholar and currently serves as an Associate Professor & Assistant Dean at the School of Law, Bennett University, India. With a robust academic foundation, he earned his Bachelor of Arts and Bachelor of Laws (B.A. LL.B.) from the prestigious Aligarh Muslim University (A.M.U.). He further specialized in Business Laws, completing his Master of Laws (LL.M.) at the renowned National Law School of India University (NLSIU), Bangalore. Dr. Chandra's academic journey culminated in a Doctorate in Law (Ph.D.) from the esteemed National Law University (NLU) Delhi. In addition to his impressive legal education from some of India's most prestigious institutions, Dr. Chandra also holds a master's degree in management with specialization in Human Resources in Management and another in Journalism and Mass Communication. With almost two decades of teaching experience, he has numerous publications to his credit. His expertise is complemented by a robust portfolio of scholarly publications.

Supriya Dutta is a dedicated student of B.Com in Financial Analytics at CHRIST University, known for her keen interest in the intersection of finance and data-driven decision-making. She has developed strong analytical skills through coursework in financial modelling, investment analysis, and data visualization using tools such as Excel, Python, and Power BI. Supriya has actively participated in academic projects and co-curricular activities that sharpen her understanding of real-world financial scenarios. Passionate about sustainability and ethical finance, she aspires to build a career in financial analytics, with a focus on responsible investing and data-backed strategic planning.

Christo George is associated with the Department of Civil Engineering at the Dayananda Sagar College of Engineering, Bengaluru, India. His academic and research interests primarily focus on civil engineering technologies, sustainable infrastructure, and innovative engineering practices that contribute to modern urban development. Dr. George is actively involved in teaching, research, and mentoring students in various areas of civil engineering, while also contributing to scholarly publications and academic collaborations. His work emphasizes the integration of engineering principles with emerging technologies to address real-world challenges in construction, structural design, and infrastructure management.

Noprita Herari, M.I.Kom is a lecturer and researcher in Communication Studies with a strong focus on digital empowerment, the passion economy, and human-centered digital communication. She is affiliated with State University of Jakarta (Universitas Negeri Jakarta) and has an active publication record in international journals and edited books indexed in platforms such as Scopus, Web of Science, and IGI Global. Her interdisciplinary work bridges communication science, digital platforms, education, and creative economies, with particular attention to ethical digital practices, portfolio-based learning, and youth empowerment. Beyond academia, she is also engaged in creative and entrepreneurial initiatives, allowing her research to remain closely connected to real-world digital ecosystems and societal challenges.

Rituraj Jain is currently working in the Department of Information Technology, Marwadi University, Rajkot, Gujarat, India. He has published many papers in International Journals and Conferences. He has published 4 books. He is an Oracle Database SQL Certified Expert. He is also associated with professional bodies like the Indian Society of Technical Education (ISTE), Computer Science Teachers Association (CSTA), Academy & Industry Research Collaboration Center (AIRCC), International Association of Computer Science and Information Technology (IACSIT), International Association of Engineers (IAENG). His research interests include Cloud Computing, Machine Learning, Deep Learning, Fuzzy Logic, IoT, Genetic Algorithms, Big Data and Software Engineering.

Blesson James, Head of Academic and Industry Extension at CHRIST (Deemed to be University) Pune Lavasa, specializes in Accounting, Investments, Finance, and Taxation. With a decade of teaching experience and UGC NET qualification, he has served as adjunct faculty at prestigious institutions. His academic journey includes B.Com and M.Com from Savitribai Phule Pune University, and he has contributed to research with publications in esteemed national and international journals.

Jeanne Kaspard is an Assistant Professor of Finance at the Business School, Holy Spirit University of Kaslik (USEK), Lebanon. Her research focuses on sustainable finance, energy economics, information systems, and the role of digital and organizational capabilities in firm performance, with particular attention to SMEs and emerging economies. She has co-authored several articles published in peer-reviewed, Scopus-indexed journals and contributes to interdisciplinary research at the intersection of finance, sustainability, and technology.

Purvesh Kolpe is a third-year B.Tech student in Computer Science and Engineering (Cybersecurity) at Ajeenkya D. Y. Patil University, Pune. He presented at the G-Cared 2025 Conference on AI-based outbreak detection and is actively pursuing research in reinforcement learning, swarm robotics, mobile networks, nanobiotechnology, digital health, and AI ethics. He holds a granted patent for a Hyperloop Transportation Pod and has filed patents for a YOLOv8-based Urban Heat Zone Detection System and a Mechanised Cattle Dung Cleaner. He has authored and co-authored book chapters in Green Environmental Technologies and HYPERLOOP: Next Generation Frictionless Transportation. His key innovations include Precautia, an ML-powered health app; a Resume & Interview Prep AI Platform; a Smart Cool Pavement Monitoring System; and IoT-based solutions such as the Smart Blind Stick. Proficient in YOLOv8, TensorFlow, GNSS (NavIC), and embedded microcontrollers, his current focus is on hybrid AI frameworks for APT detection in critical infrastructure. He is grateful for the mentorship and guidance of Dr. Debanjali Barman Roy, whose constant support has shaped his research journey. ORCID: 0009-0007-8280-0923

Pradeep Kulshrestha, Professor & Dean, School of Law, Bennett University

Pawan Kumar, PhD, is a prominent academic and researcher with over 20 years of expertise in business studies. A professor at Graphic Era Deemed to be University, Dehradun, India, he has supervised six PhD scholars and published over 60 research papers, including 51 in SCOPUS/ 06 in Web of Science, and 14 books, including eight indexed in Scopus. His works, featured by prominent publishers like Emerald, IGI Global, Nova Science, and Cambridge Scholars, have gained recognition. Dr. Kumar earned his PhD in Commerce from Kurukshetra University in 2007 and holds an M.Phil. and M.Com. Degrees. Specializing in finance, banking, and securities markets, he has authored books on green finance, AI, and fintech. His innovative research includes five patents and has served as a guest editor for Scopus-indexed journals. In 2022, he received the prestigious Researcher Award from Chandigarh University. Dr. Kumar's impactful work on sustainable finance, blockchain, and fintech is globally recognized. His active participation in high-impact conferences and faculty development programs reflects his commitment to advancing research, teaching, and innovation in commerce and management.

Suparna Kundu is pursuing Ph.D (Law) from Amity Law School, Amity University, Kolkata, India . She has completed Master in Laws from Symbiosis Law School Noida, Symbiosis International (Deemed University). She has completed Bachelor in Law from KIIT School of Law - KSOL | KIIT Deemed to be University.

Xolmirzayev Furqatbek Muxtarjonovich is a Senior Teacher in the Department of Finance at Alfraganus University, Tashkent, Uzbekistan. His academic interests focus on financial management, banking systems, investment analysis, and contemporary financial practices. He is actively involved in teaching undergraduate and postgraduate students, contributing to the development of strong financial and analytical skills necessary for modern economic and business environments. His work emphasizes practical financial knowledge, effective financial decision-making, and the application of modern financial tools and methodologies. Xolmirzayev Furqatbek Muxtarjonovich also participates in academic discussions and research related to financial policy, corporate finance, and economic development. Through his teaching and scholarly engagement, he aims to enhance financial education and support the preparation of skilled professionals capable of addressing current financial and economic challenges.

Mega Ayu Permatasari, M.Si have focused research on gender, digital channel and sustainability. She holds bachelor's degree in communication from UPN "V" Yogyakarta and magister degree in communication from University of Indonesia. Her thesis about "Symbolic Violence from Heterosexual toward Homosexual in the Workplace" serves as a milestone for her academic writing. She currently serves in Communication Science Program at Jakarta State University. Her other works can be seen in Sinta ID: 6826249 and she can be reached at mega.ap@unj.ac.id

Ravikumar R. Natarajan is an experienced academician with over 12+ years of teaching and research expertise across institutions in India, the UAE, and the Maldives. He currently serves as an Assistant Professor at Marwadi University, Rajkot, specializing in Machine Learning, Recommender Systems, and AI-driven applications in healthcare and security. He holds a Ph.D. in Machine Learning and Recommender Systems from Amity University, Jaipur, a Master of Engineering in CSE from VMRF University, Salem, and a Bachelor of Engineering in CSE from Anna University. He also has a MiniMBA from the Swiss eLearning Institute. Dr. Ravikumar has authored more than 8+ multiple SCIE/Scopus-indexed journal articles, 25+ IEEE/Springer conference papers, and co-authored a book on Artificial Intelligence. He has also published 9 patents and contributed 10+ book chapters in emerging domains such as Federated Learning, Blockchain, and Digital Twins for IGI Global, Wiley and Springer publisher. He actively mentors students through initiatives like the Research Activities Club (RAC) and Student Research Internship Training (SRIT), promoting innovation and research culture.

Debanjali Barman Roy has completed her PhD from ICFAI University, Dehradun on 2022. Her research interest includes fabrication and characterization of various nanoparticles and their applications in multidisciplinary fields. She has done more than 20 publications in various journals, conference proceedings and in book chapters of repute. She has also done two design patents and 5 are on process. In addition, she has edited four books and few are in que.

Aarthi S is a dedicated Assistant Professor in Computer Science with over six years of teaching experience. She is currently pursuing her Ph.D. at Marwadi University, Gujarat, and holds an M.Phil. and MCA from Bharathiar University, Tamil Nadu. Throughout her academic career, Aarthi has specialized in programming languages such as C++, Java, and C, and contributed to research in recommender systems and AI-related data privacy. She has published journal articles, contributed to book chapters, and actively participated in technical workshops. Known for her student mentorship and engagement in academic events, Aarthi remains committed to fostering innovation and excellence in computer science education.

Senjuti Sen is currently a Master's student in the Department of Geoinformatics at Symbiosis International University, India. She holds a Bachelor's degree in Geography from University of North Bengal and P.G. Diploma in Applied Geoinformatics from Jadavpur University. Her research interests include Remote Sensing and GIS Applications, GIS-based Spatial Analysis and Urban Planning. She has contributed to various GIS-based Master Plan Projects under AMRUT scheme.

Amrik Singh is working as Professor in the School of Hotel Management and Tourism at Lovely Professional University, Punjab, India. He obtained his Ph.D. degree in Hotel Management from Kurukshetra University, Kurukshetra. He started his academic career at Lovely Professional University, Punjab, India in the year 2007. He has published more than 40 research papers in UGC and peer-reviewed and Scopus/Web of Science) journals. He has published 12 patents and 01 patent has been granted in the inter-disciplinary domain. Dr. Amrik Singh participated and acted as a resource person in various national and international conferences, seminars, research workshops, and industry talks. His area of research interest is accommodation management, ergonomics, green practices, human resource management in hospitality, waste management, AR VR in hospitality, etc. He is currently guiding 8Ph.D. scholars and 2 Ph.D. scholars have been awarded Ph.D.

Yashodhan Sonwane is currently working as an Assistant Professor, Mechanical Department. He has done 2 design patents. He is an expert CAD designs and mentoring the students as an advisor in one of the university technical club. He has done his masters from SRM, Chennai in 2022.

Slobodan Stanić has been working in the Public Health Institute of the Republic of Srpska since 2008. She works in the Centre of Healthcare System Development and International Cooperation in the position of Coordinator of Activities. She is an Associate Professor and works part-time at the University of Travnik in Travnik, on the Faculty of Health and Pharmacy, teaching the subjects Social Medicine, Ethics in Healthcare and Surgery.

Satya Subrahmanyam is a distinguished academic leader, researcher, and institutional strategist with over 28 years of experience in higher education, business research, leadership and management. He holds two PhDs and a Postdoctoral qualification from the Polytechnic Institute of Leiria, Portugal. Currently serving as Professor and Dean (Research) at Holy Spirit University of Kaslik (USEK), Lebanon, he spearheads research initiatives that enhance academic excellence and institutional reputation. He played a pivotal role in the development of the Catholic University in Erbil, Kurdistan, where he established new departments, led research programs, and collaborated on international educational projects. As a founding member and Managing Partner of Vignan Institute of Technology and Management, India, he contributed to its transformation into a premier institution. With expertise in AI-driven business strategies, HR analytics, and leadership in technology adoption, he has published extensively, guided PhD research, and led training programs in corporate and academic settings.

Faidon Theofanidis is an Associate Professor of Marketing at Australian University – Kuwait, College of Business. He holds a PhD in Advertising from the University of Piraeus, an MBA in Marketing from Cardiff University and a BSc in Business Administration from University of Piraeus. His extensive teaching career (2000-2025) includes appointments at various prestigious institutions, such as the University of Piraeus, the University of Patras, the Greek Open University, the Technological Scientific Institute of Athens (University of West Attica), Alpine Centre - The Swiss Business School for Hotel and Tourism Studies, Business College of Athens (BCA), and the Australian University – Kuwait (formerly Australian College of Kuwait - ACK). Through these roles, he has delivered both undergraduate and postgraduate courses. From 2003-2010 he represented the Research Center of Piraeus University at the Board of Directors of the European Network for Social and Economic Research (ENSR), implementing over 30 European research projects. His research interests include: Marketing Research, Advertising Research, Consumer Behavior, Digital Marketing, Artificial Intelligence and European Social and Economic Policies. His publication record includes 3 books, 2 book chapters, 14 peer-reviewed journal articles (published in reputable journals such as the Journal of Cleaner Production, the Canadian Journal of Administrative Sciences, the International Journal of Inclusive Education, etc.), 27 international conference papers (presented at EMAC, ICORIA, Global Marketing Conference, International Conference of the Arab Academy of Sciences etc.), and 2 honorary volume contributions.

Index

A

B

C

D

E

F

G

I

L

M

N

O

P

R

S

T

U

V

www.ingramcontent.com/pod-product-compliance
Lightning Source LLC
LaVergne TN
LVHW081319300926
849161LV00008B/1817